Early Praise for *Effective Haskell*

As the author of the "State of the Haskell Ecosystem," I've understood for some time that the Haskell ecosystem is missing a well-written book. But no longer. That well-written book is here.

➤ **Gabriella Gonzalez**
Staff Engineer, Mercury Technologies

The code written is readable, elegant, and pragmatic. It would be a must-have on my shelf or for anyone who cares about the craftsmanship of functional programming and reasoning. I can see myself coming back to this book again and again; it's honestly the best Haskell book I've ever read.

➤ **Krystal Maughan**
PhD student researcher and habitual Haskell enthusiast, University of Vermont

As a professional Haskell programmer, it was always difficult to recommend a single up-to-date learning resource for new team members. This book fills that niche perfectly, providing both a gentle introduction to the language and a deeper hands-on dive into the practical side of software engineering in Haskell.

➤ **Tikhon Jelvis**
Chair, Haskell.org Committee

Even if you never use Haskell again, this book will teach you how to use strong typing and functional programming concepts to solve real-world problems in ways that are safe and elegant.

➤ **Artem Chernyak**
Senior Software Developer, Horizon Investments

Effective Haskell

Solving Real-World Problems with Strongly Typed Functional Programming

Rebecca Skinner

The Pragmatic Bookshelf
Raleigh, North Carolina

For our complete catalog of hands-on, practical, and Pragmatic content for software developers, please visit *https://pragprog.com*.

The team that produced this book includes:

CEO: Dave Rankin
COO: Janet Furlow
Managing Editor: Tammy Coron
Development Editor: Michael Swaine
Copy Editor: Karen Galle
Indexing: Potomac Indexing, LLC
Layout: Gilson Graphics
Founders: Andy Hunt and Dave Thomas

For sales, volume licensing, and support, please contact *support@pragprog.com*.

For international rights, please contact *rights@pragprog.com*.

ISBN-13: 978-1-68050-934-2
Book version: P1.0—July 2023

Contents

Acknowledgments

Writing this book has been a monumental effort, and I wouldn't have finished it without the incredible and generous help of the many people who contributed their own time, knowledge, energy, and support. First and foremost, I would like to express my gratitude to the technical reviewers of this book. Tikhon Jelvis, who lent an incredible amount of technical knowledge and experience teaching in his reviews. Krystal Maughan, whose relentless positivity and encouragement made me believe in the book even when I was in dispair over the difficulty in writing. Artem Chernyak, whose attentiveness and careful attention to detail helped me eliminate circular dependencies and improve the organization of the content. Ryan Jones, one of the first people I taught Haskell, who helped to find many bugs in the examples. Janet Riley, who helped me focus on the perspective of readers without Haskell experience. I would also like to thank Gabriella Gonzalez. Not only have I learned a great deal from her over the years, I deeply appreciate that she has taken time away from her own book to read and write a foreword for Effective Haskell.

Next I would like to thank my editor, Michael Swaine, who offered guidance, acted as a sounding board, and spent several patient years tolerating my promises that "I only have three chapters left to write." I would also like to thank Brian MacDonald, who gave me the inspiration and confidence to begin working on this book and everyone at The Pragmatic Programmers who have helped me to go from an idea to a truly amazing book.

This book would also have not been possible without the support of my spouse, Ren Wilding, who was my frequent reader, sounding board, grammar consultant, and writers block remover. Without their knowledge of the process of writing, I would have been hopelessly mired in writers block or stuck searching for ways to reword awkward sentences. My parrot, George, has also been instrumental as both comic relief and inspiration for many of the examples in this book.

Finally, I want to thank the Haskell community and all of the many people who have worked on the Haskell language, its compilers, libraries, tools, and ecosystem. The world is a richer, grander place thanks to all of you and the work you have done.

Foreword

When Rebecca asked me to write a foreword to her book I didn't have to think twice about endorsing it.

Our paths had crossed numerous times before. I've been a professional Haskell programmer for almost a decade now and I've been teaching and evangelizing Haskell for even longer. If you've used Haskell you've probably used one of my packages or read one of my blog posts.

Rebecca immediately made an impression on me when we met at the Haskell Love conference. I was struck by her extremely sensible and pragmatic approach to Haskell. Now I know Rebecca as a colleague as well as an active member of the Haskell community. She's an engineering manager for a Haskell team, a Haskell.org committee member, and has presented and hosted workshops at numerous Haskell conferences. Rebecca knows Haskell.

As the author of the "State of the Haskell Ecosystem," I've understood for some time that the Haskell ecosystem is missing a well-written book. But no longer. That well-written book is here.

Yes, Rebecca writes well, but I think the secret ingredient in Rebecca's teaching style is patience. I don't just mean that she's a patient teacher; she instills patience in her students, too. Haskell is a language that rewards patience by paying amazing dividends in the long run. But "in the long run" means that the payoff doesn't come until you get beyond the beginner level. Rebecca truly understands how to mold beginners into intermediate Haskell programmers.

You might be one of the many Haskell beginners looking for some way to graduate to that intermediate Haskell programmer where you really leverage the strengths of Haskell. If that's you, then look no further: *Effective Haskell* is the book for you. You'll find that this book is patient but not tedious; you might even say it's *effective*. You'll derive value from the book early on because Rebecca expertly interleaves foundational concepts with opportunities to get your hands dirty with useful applications.

If that sounds like what you're looking for, then read on. With *Effective Haskell* you're well on your way to pursuing a long and rewarding journey with a remarkably powerful language.

Gabriella Gonzalez

Introduction

Software development is harder than it's ever been, and the unfortunate reality is that every year things continue to get harder. Much of this difficulty is due to the complexity inherent in modern systems. Today, software needs to do more things, it needs to do them at a larger scale, and the consequences for failure are higher. To be effective in the market today, we have to use every tool at our disposal to rein in the complexity of our systems. I believe that Haskell is one of the greatest tools that we have at our disposal today to help us craft systems that are both more reliable and less complex.

Haskell isn't a new language. In fact, the first version of Haskell was published in 1990, a year before Python and five years before Java. In many ways Haskell has always been a remarkably successful language. It's been used widely in both industry and academia for the research and development of programming languages, and the design of Haskell has been incredibly influential in shaping other languages that are in wide use today.

Although it's been wildly successful as a research tool and programming language "influencer," industrial adoption of Haskell has lagged behind. Today, there are more Haskell jobs than ever, and more companies are choosing Haskell to build their products and key parts of their infrastructure. Right now, Haskell remains more of a secret weapon than a mainstream tool, but the clear benefits of Haskell for the kinds of systems that people are building today means that an inflection point in the popularity of the language is inevitable. If Haskell doesn't become the next big thing, then the next big thing will certainly end up looking even more like Haskell than any of the other myriad of languages that have been influenced by it.

Why Choose Haskell?

The reason that Haskell is such a good choice for modern software is that it gives us everything we need to build reliable, predictable, and maintainable systems that run efficiently and can be easily scaled horizontally. This is thanks to Haskell's design as a lazy pure functional language with an exceptionally powerful and expressive static type system.

When you think of functional programming, the first thing that likely comes to mind are the sorts of functional programming features that are recently being added to mainstream object-oriented languages. These include things like:

- Support for closures or lambda functions
- Using functions like `map` and `reduce` instead of traditional loops
- Immutable data structures that copy their results rather than mutating their inputs

Haskell is different. The benefits we get from Haskell go far beyond being able to pass around functions and have immutable data structures. Thanks to its purity, Haskell can offer us strict guarantees about immutability across our entire program. This means that we never have to worry about unintended changes to shared or global state causing our program to crash, or think about how to coordinate access to mutable data.

One of the reasons that Haskell can give us strong guarantees about what our program does where other languages can't is thanks to the power of its type system. Haskell's type system is more expressive than the type system of any other mainstream programming language in use these days. Thanks to the type system, a Haskell program can keep track of information about what kind of data a variable holds, where it came from, what can be done with it, and even whether the function that calculates that value could possibly fail.

Of course, this type information doesn't just help us write better programs once. Every time we make changes to our program, the type checker does its job to ensure that we haven't introduced any new problems, and helps us track down things that might need to change. As applications grow and teams get larger, the power of the type system to help us refactor becomes even more important. Types become a way that we can communicate with our peers, to provide guard rails for how they use our code, and to make sure we are using the code they wrote as it was intended. In this way, Haskell doesn't just solve for the problems of complexity with the software we're writing, it also helps with the complexity inherent in building that software with a large team.

Why This Book

Haskell can offer enormous benefits to individuals and developers who want to write high quality software, but as the saying goes, "if it were easy, everyone would do it." The benefits of Haskell come at the cost of a steep learning curve. Haskell is hard to learn, but this book will help.

Learning Haskell can be hard in part because it's so different from other languages you've probably used. This ends up being a particularly hard problem because many of the most unusual concepts that you need to learn often show up all at the same time, leading to circular dependencies in your learning plan. This book has been carefully designed, especially in the first half, to provide an on-ramp to the language that avoids the need to get into circular knowledge references.

Rather than teach you how to translate your programs from other languages, in this book you'll develop an intuition for how to think about programs in Haskell from the ground up. This will make it easier for you to read other developers' code, make you more effective at writing code, and help you with troubleshooting.

Most of the chapters in this book build on concepts from previous chapters, and no content in any chapter relies on concepts that have not yet been introduced. You'll never be forced to use something that hasn't yet been fully explained. In the last half of this book, once you have worked through the fundamental materials, you may be able to approach some material out of order if there are particular areas that you are interested in.

Some features of Haskell can seem unnecessarily complex the first time you encounter them. Some people, when they are faced with a feature that makes no sense, will assume the feature was a bad idea and give up on learning it altogether. Other people will put the concept on a pedestal and assign it disproportionate significance. In either case, the lack of motivation for the things Haskell does differently can be a barrier to learning. To help with that, each time a new concept is introduced in this book, we'll dedicate a significant amount of time to establishing a motivation for that concept to help you better internalize the reason for the design decisions Haskell makes. Understanding the motivation will ensure you're better positioned to make informed choices about how to design your applications, and when and how to use features of the language.

Since you'll be learning to think about programming in an entirely new way, we'll approach the material quite slowly in the beginning, carefully outlining all of the intermediate steps that go into executing some code and walking through multiple examples. As you approach the middle of the book, the pace will pick up, and by the last few chapters you should be learning new concepts at the pace of a native Haskell developer.

What to Expect as You Read

This book focuses on teaching through the demos and hands-on example code. Most of the chapters in this book will start with a motivating example followed by several interactive demonstrations of a concept that you can reproduce using the interactive Haskell development environment `ghci`. Most chapters will also include some projects you can build as you are working through material. The chapters will include all of the code you need to build a functioning minimal example, but you are encouraged to make modifications and experiment with the code as you are working through the book. At the end of each chapter you'll also have some exercises that build on the examples you wrote. These examples will help you learn how to navigate Haskell's documentation and work within its ecosystem to self teach, so you are better equipped to continue learning after you've finished the book.

Compared to other programming language communities, parts of the Haskell community can tend to be a little "math jargon" heavy. It's not uncommon to see terms from theoretical computer science and math make their way into blog posts, articles, and even library documentation. This book aims to teach Haskell without requiring either a strong background in mathematics or familiarity with mathematical jargon. Since knowing the jargon and getting comfortable using it will ultimately help make you a more effective Haskell developer, common jargon terms will be introduced, defined, and then used consistently throughout the book. If you are skipping ahead and see some intimidating sounding language, turn back a few pages and you're likely to find a definition and several examples to help you make sense of the words before they start being used regularly.

How to Read This Book

This book has been designed to be read cover-to-cover as a tutorial and workbook, or to be used in a classroom or reading group setting. Starting with Chapter 1, each new chapter will continue a theme or build on some knowledge that you picked up in the previous chapter. If you have some prior experience with Haskell, it's worthwhile to start reading from the beginning so that you can follow along with the subsequent references to earlier material.

For more experienced Haskell developers, this book can also serve as a useful resource to help you learn some practical ways to apply more advanced techniques. If you've used Haskell in school or written a few small programs and are looking to move into building larger production applications, you may find it helpful to skim the first half of this book and then start reading the second half more thoroughly.

As you are working through the book, you'll encounter several different kinds of example code. You should always be able to tell what type of environment you should be working in based on the formatting of the examples:

- Code that starts with a λ character should be typed into ghci.
- Lines that start with user@host$ should be typed into a shell like bash or zsh.
- Other code can be written in Haskell files using your text editor, or written directly into ghci at your discretion.

Until you have finished Chapter 5, create a new directory for each chapter. Inside of the directory you create for each chapter, create a file named after the current chapter, for example, Chapter1.hs. You can use this for keeping track of example code and experiments you want to run. You'll also create several files named Main.hs as you are working through the examples. You can put each of these in a subdirectory, for example, one subdirectory per chapter, or you can rename your old Main.hs files when you are no longer actively working through them. Whatever organizational scheme you prefer, ensure you keep around all your examples and experiments since you'll want to refer to them frequently as you are learning.

Once you've worked through the chapter on Cabal on page 155 you'll be better equipped to create fully stand-alone projects that you can build. You'll also learn how to re-use code that you've written. From that point onward, you can create a new project for each chapter or each major example.

Following Along with Example Code

As you read this book, you'll work through examples iteratively, making changes to earlier code and adding new features. Once you've learned about how to import code from other modules, we'll begin introducing new features iteratively that require adding additional imports. Similarly, once you've learned how to work with language extensions, we'll add them as we work through examples. The rest of this section will discuss how we'll approach introducing new imports and extensions in example code. Don't worry too much about the syntax yet. As you work through the book, you'll learn about imports and language extensions before they are required for any examples. For now, skim this section and feel free to come back to it later if you need to.

Most of the chapters in this book will focus on building up a few small example programs. In some cases, we'll explicitly define a new module when we're starting a new example. In this case, these new modules may start out including a few language extensions or imports.

```
{-# LANGUAGE TypeApplications #-}
{-# LANGUAGE DerivingStrategies #-}
module Main Where

import Data.Text (Text)

main :: IO ()
main = print helloWorld
```

As we iterate through the example, we'll add new features that might require additional language extensions or add-ons. When we're getting ready to use a new module or extension, we'll add them to the top of an example:

```
{-# LANGUAGE OverloadedStrings #-}
import Data.ByteString (ByteString)

helloWorld :: ByteString
helloWorld = "Hello, World"
```

In your own code, you should add these to the relevant parts of your module. Here's an example of what your own code should look like as you follow along with the examples:

```
{-# LANGUAGE TypeApplications #-}
{-# LANGUAGE DerivingStrategies #-}
{-# LANGUAGE OverloadedStrings #-}
module Main Where

import Data.ByteString (ByteString)
import Data.Text (Text)

helloWorld :: ByteString
helloWorld = "Hello, World"

main :: IO ()
main = print helloWorld
```

Not all of the examples that you work through will start with a module and a set of imports or extensions. In these cases, you can start with your own empty module, or you can work though the examples in `ghci`.

Compiler Versions, Language Standards, and Extensions

Although there have been several different implementations of Haskell over the years, the Glasgow Haskell Compiler (GHC) is the de facto standard Haskell compiler. In this book we'll focus on Haskell as implemented by GHC 9.4, which is the newest stable release at the time of this writing. All of the examples have also been tested with GHC 8.10.

Compiler Version Differences

A few examples in this book will use newer features of GHC not available in version 8.10. Look out for an aside, like this one, to learn about newer features and how to write code without those features when you need to support older compilers.

As Haskell evolves, new features are typically added through *extensions*. Language extensions allow you to enable and disable specific language features. The Haskell2010 language standard is the default language version that's used by GHC 8.10, and it includes a number of extensions that are enabled by default. In GHC 9.4, the GHC2021 language version is used by default. GHC2021 isn't an officially published Haskell standard; instead it represents a number of commonly accepted GHC specific nonstandard extensions to Haskell2010 that are enabled by default.

In this book, we'll target Haskell2010 Any language extensions that aren't included in Haskell2010 will be introduced and discussed. Complete example programs will always include all extensions that would be required when using Haskell2010. Shorter examples may omit language extensions for the sake of readability.

GHC2021 Extensions

We'll target Haskell2010 as a baseline when choosing which language extensions to highlight in this book. If you're using GHC2021, look for an aside like this to tell you when an extension is included by default and doesn't need to be enabled explicitly.

Extension	Enabled
AllowAmbiguousTypes	Manually
BangPatterns	GHC2021
ConstraintKinds	GHC2021
DataKinds	Manually
DefaultSignatures	Manually
DeriveAnyClass	Manually
DerivingStrategies	Manually
DerivingVia	Manually
ExistentialQuantification	GHC2021
ExplicitForAll	GHC2021
FlexibleContexts	GHC2021
FlexibleInstances	GHC2021
FunctionalDependencies	Manually
GADTs	Manually
GeneralizedNewtypeDeriving	GHC2021
KindSignatures	GHC2021
MultiParamTypeClasses	GHC2021
OverloadedStrings	Manually
PolyKinds	GHC2021

Extension	Enabled
QuantifiedConstraints	Manually
RankNTypes	GHC2021
RecordWildCards	Manually
ScopedTypeVariables	GHC2021
TupleSections	GHC2021
TypeApplications	GHC2021
TypeFamilies	Manually
TypeOperators	GHC2021
UndecidableInstances	Manually
NoStarIsType	Manually
PolyKinds	GHC2021
StandaloneDeriving	GHC2021

Libraries and Library Versions

The examples in this book stick to the standard library, base, as much as possible. For features that aren't available in base, we'll stick to a small selection of popular libraries. This should ensure maximum compatibility, at the cost of not showing off some very interesting libraries that are worth learning. The following table includes the exact versions of each package that were used for the examples. In any cases where there are incompatible changes between library versions, we'll use the most recent version of the library.

Package	Version (GHC 9.4)	Version (GHC 8.10)
base	4.17.0.0	4.14.3.0
bytestring	0.11.3.1	0.10.12.0
base64-bytestring	1.2.1.0	1.2.1.0
text	2.0.1	1.2.4.1
containers	0.6.6	0.6.5.1
vector	0.12.3.1	0.12.3.1
time	1.12.2	1.9.3
unix	2.7.3	2.7.2.2
mtl	2.2.2	2.2.2
transformers	0.5.6.2	0.5.6.2
process	1.6.15.0	1.6.13.2

CHAPTER 1

Getting Started with Haskell

Haskell lives at the intersection between practical applied languages and research languages created to push the boundaries of what's possible to do in a programming language. The expressiveness and flexibility that makes Haskell useful for computer science research turns out to also be incredibly useful for the working engineer who wants to build reliable and maintainable systems. That's why you'll find it used in everything from web applications to data pipelines to compilers and configuration management tools.

The Haskell motto *avoid success at all costs* is a reminder that programming in Haskell sometimes means trading away immediate familiarity or comfort for power, flexibility, and correctness. Avoiding short-term success and doing what's right is the Haskell path to long-term success. This trade-off means that things that you might take for granted in other languages work a little bit differently in Haskell. Haskell is no harder to learn than any other language, but for experienced developers, the challenge is in unlearning old practices and preconceptions.

One of the ways Haskell is different is that it's a *pure* functional language. Haskell developers like to throw the words *pure* and *purity* around frequently, but you won't always find an exact definition of what it means. For our purposes, we can think of purity like this: in a Haskell program, all values are immutable, and all functions have to be free of any side effects. That means we can't ever modify in place or change the value of variables, we can't modify any global state, and we can't *arbitrarily* do things like read from files on disk, access the network, or print something to the screen. At first, this might seem like an onerous set of restrictions, but as you'll see starting in Chapter 7 on page 263, Haskell gives you a rich set of tools and alternative patterns so that you can write the same sorts of programs that you would write in an *impure* language.

Another way that Haskell differs from many other popular languages is in the power and expressiveness of its type system. You'll start to learn more about how to make use of Haskell's type system starting in Chapter 4 on page 89. In the mean time, we'll take advantage of Haskell's sophisticated *type inference* which will allow us to start getting familiar with the language without worrying too much about types.

Finally, Haskell is a *lazy* language. That means Haskell has the powerful ability to avoid running parts of our program until it's sure that we will need the results. This can let us write programs in ways that feel more natural but might have significant negative performance costs in a strict language. You'll have an opportunity to start learning about laziness starting in the next chapter on page 47.

For now, we'll focus on getting familiar with the basic syntax of Haskell. In this chapter you'll start learning Haskell from the ground up by getting a handle on foundational concepts like defining variables, creating and calling functions, and working with lists. A lot of this will feel familiar, but working through it carefully will ensure that you don't get tripped up by subtle but fundamental features of Haskell as we get deeper into the language in later chapters.

Exploring Haskell Interactively

We'll start our Haskell journey by diving into ghci to run some commands interactively. ghci is Haskell's REPL, an interactive environment that lets you run commands, call functions, and even debug your programs. Most Haskell developers rely on ghci extensively as they develop their programs, and it's a natural starting point for you to start familiarizing yourself with the basic syntax of the language. For instructions on getting ghci and the rest of your Haskell environment installed and configured, you can consult the instructions online at haskell.org.[1]

When you start up ghci you'll see a default prompt:

```
$ ghci
GHCi, version 9.4.2: https://www.haskell.org/ghc/  :? for help
Prelude>
```

The first thing you'll see is some information about the current version of GHC that you have installed. It's okay if you are using a newer, or slightly older, version of ghci.

1. https://www.haskell.org

The next line is the ghci prompt. The prompt shows you a list of all of the current modules that you have imported; in this case it's just Prelude, which is the name given to all of the built-in things that are available by default from Haskell's standard library.

For the sake of readability, in this book we'll use a slightly different prompt. First, we'll omit the list of imported modules. Second, we'll change our prompt character to the lowercase Greek letter lambda: λ. You can use any letter or symbol you like, but λ is both a nod to the origins of functional programming and a nice visually distinctive way to help you quickly see when we're working in an interactive session.

```
$ ghci
GHCi, version 9.4.2: https://www.haskell.org/ghc/  :? for help
λ
```

Configuring Your ghci Prompt

If you'd like to make your prompt look like the one in the examples, you can type: :set prompt "λ" when you first start ghci. You can also add it to your ghci configuration file, at ${HOME}/.ghci.

Now try typing in a few simple arithmetic expressions to see how you can use ghci as a simple calculator:

```
λ 1 + 2
3
λ 3 + 4 + 5
12
λ 12 * (1 + 2 - 2) / 6
2.0
```

Try experimenting with basic arithmetic using parentheses and the –,-,*,/ operators to get comfortable working with ghci and entering different expressions.

Working with Lists

Now that you're comfortable using ghci as a calculator, try creating some lists:

```
λ [1,2,3]
[1,2,3]
λ ["one", "two", "three"]
["one","two","three"]
```

When you are working with numbers, you can also create a list using the range syntax. You create a range by creating a list with a starting and ending number separated with two dots (..):

```
λ [1..10]
[1,2,3,4,5,6,7,8,9,10]
λ [2..5]
[2,3,4,5]
```

As you can see, the range syntax gives us a list of numbers starting at the first number and going up, one at a time, to the final value. If the starting and ending values are the same, we'll just get a single element list:

```
λ [10..10]
[10]
```

If the starting value is *larger* than the ending value, then you'll get back an empty list.

```
λ [10..1]
[]
```

If you start your range with two numbers instead of a single number, then the range will increment, or decrement, by the difference between the two starting numbers. Here's how you'd get a list of the even numbers up to ten:

```
λ [2,4..10]
[2,4,6,8,10]
```

Or the first one hundred numbers in increments of 23:

```
λ [0,23..100]
[0,23,46,69,92]
```

In this example, you'll notice that our list stops at 92 since that's the last multiple of 23 that is less than the end of our range.

You can use the same technique to generate a range that counts down. For example, if you want to get a range that counts down from 10, you just need to provide the first two numbers:

```
λ [10,9..0]
[10,9,8,7,6,5,4,3,2,1,0]
```

You can embed arithmetic expressions inside of lists too. Look at this example. Do you see what the output will be when you run it?

```
λ [10 + 2, 10 * 2, 10 - 2, 10 / 2]
```

When you're playing around with longer lists, reading the code in ghci can start to become difficult, especially if you have lines of code longer than the width of your terminal. You can break up a long expression across multiple lines by typing :{ on its own line, entering as many lines as you like, and finishing with :}, also on its own line:

```
λ :{
Prelude| [ 1
Prelude| , 2
Prelude| ]
Prelude| :}
[1,2]
```

This feature isn't limited to lists; you can also use it for any other type of expression when you find that it helps readability while working in ghci.

Creating Lists with More Than One Type

You might have noticed that all of our examples are of lists that only contain a single type of value, for example, a list of all strings, or a list of all numbers. In Haskell, a list can only contain one type of value at a time. If you try to create a list that has two different types of values, like a number and a string in the example, you'll get an error message:

```
λ [1, "two"]

<interactive>:6:1: error:
    • Ambiguous type variable ‘a0’ arising from a use of ‘print’
      prevents the constraint ‘(Show a0)’ from being solved.
      Probable fix: use a type annotation to specify what ‘a0’ should be.
      These potential instances exist:
        instance Show Ordering -- Defined in ‘GHC.Show’
        instance Show Integer -- Defined in ‘GHC.Show’
        instance Show a => Show (Maybe a) -- Defined in ‘GHC.Show’
        ...plus 22 others
        ...plus 15 instances involving out-of-scope types
        (use -fprint-potential-instances to see them all)
    • In a stmt of an interactive GHCi command: print it
```

This error message should look pretty confusing right now, and that's okay. As you are getting started with Haskell you'll run into many situations where unexpected things might cause you to see some errors. Some errors, like this one about ambiguous type errors, will be particular common early on. Don't worry about these too much yet. As you progress through this text you'll learn more about what causes these errors, and how to fix them. You'll be able to understand more about this error in particular once you learn more about lists and Haskell's type system. You'll learn much more about how to construct lists and use them effectively in the next chapter on page 47. Later, when you start to learn more about Haskell's type system on page 89, you'll learn how to read and better interpret error messages like this.

Creating Pairs

Tuples in Haskell let you store pairs, or more than pairs, of values. A list can hold any number of values, but they all have to be the same type. A tuple can hold different types of values, but size is fixed. You can't add or remove items from a tuple. Tuples are defined with parentheses:

```
λ tuple = (2, "two-pule")
λ thruple = (3, "triple", "thruple")
λ quadruple = (4, "quadruple", 4.0, False)
```

Two-element tuples are the most common kind of tuple, and so there are functions to help you get the first and second elements out of them easily. The functions are called fst and snd:

```
λ fst (2, "tuple")
2
λ snd (2, "tuple")
"tuple"
```

You can nest tuples and lists with other tuples and lists however you like:

```
λ ([1,2,3],["one","two","three"])
([1,2,3],["one","two","three"])
λ [(1,2),(3,4)]
[(1,2),(3,4)]
```

Although the fields of a tuple can be different types, when you have a list of tuples they have to all have the same number of elements, and the types have to all be the same at each position in the tuple. For example, we can have a list of tuples that contain numbers and strings:

```
λ [("haskell", 7), ("is", 2), ("fun", 3)]
[("haskell",7),("is",2),("fun",3)]
```

However, we'll get an error if we try to swap the order of fields in some of the tuples:

```
λ [("haskell",7),(2,"is"),("fun",3)]

<interactive>:3:1: error:
    • Ambiguous type variable ‘a0’ arising from a use of ‘print’
      prevents the constraint ‘(Show a0)’ from being solved.
      Probable fix: use a type annotation to specify what ‘a0’ should be.
      These potential instances exist:
        instance (Show a, Show b) => Show (Either a b)
          -- Defined in ‘Data.Either’
        instance Show Ordering -- Defined in ‘GHC.Show’
        instance Show a => Show (Maybe a) -- Defined in ‘GHC.Show’
        ...plus 24 others
```

```
    ...plus 47 instances involving out-of-scope types
    (use -fprint-potential-instances to see them all)
• In a stmt of an interactive GHCi command: print it
```

We'll also get an error if one of the tuples has a different number of elements, even if the elements are all of the same type:

```
λ [(1,2), (4,5), (5,6,7)]

<interactive>:5:16: error:
    • Couldn't match expected type: (a, b)
                  with actual type: (a0, b0, c0)
    • In the expression: (5, 6, 7)
      In the expression: [(1, 2), (4, 5), (5, 6, 7)]
      In an equation for 'it': it = [(1, 2), (4, 5), (5, 6, 7)]
    • Relevant bindings include
        it :: [(a, b)] (bound at <interactive>:5:1)
```

As with the other error messages you'll see in this chapter, you don't need to worry about understanding the details of what went wrong just yet. You'll learn how to read these sorts of error messages later on in the book.

Printing Things to the Screen

Although ghci automatically prints the value of an expression to the screen, when you're writing full programs you'll want to control when you print things out to the screen. The putStrLn function will print a string to the screen with a newline (you can use putStr if you don't want the extra newline). You can print values in ghci as well.

Try it out yourself by typing putStrLn "Hello, World!" into ghci. Notice that in Haskell calling a function doesn't require any parentheses. Calling a function (or as we often say in Haskell, applying a function to some arguments) is as simple as functionName arg1 arg2 arg3.

If you try to use putStrLn to print a number to the screen you'll get another type error, since it only works with strings. Pick your favorite number and try passing it to putStrLn to see an example of this.

You can convert most types, like numbers and lists, into strings using the show function, as in the following examples. Try running these yourself to get a feel for how it works:

```
putStrLn (show 12)
putStrLn (show [1..10])
putStrLn (show "Hello, World!")
```

Calling show manually can add a lot of unnecessary boilerplate to your code. The print function combines show and putStrLn into a single function. Try it yourself by using print with your favorite number to print it onto the screen.

Spend as much time as you'd like trying out different expressions in ghci. When you're ready to move onto the next section, you'll write your first real Haskell program. Throughout the rest of this chapter you'll learn more about the basics of Haskell's syntax and semantics and be able to write more useful expressions in ghci.

Writing Your First Haskell Program

Now that you have some experience evaluating expressions, it's time to write your first complete Haskell program. We'll start with an obligatory "Hello World" program by creating a new empty file named Main.hs in your Chapter1 directory.

Open Main.hs and copy this example:

```
module Main where
main = print "Hello, World!"
```

You'll learn what each of these lines is doing as you work your way through the chapter, but for now let's build the application and run your program.

From your command line you can compile your program by typing ghc Main. After the program is built you'll have a new executable, Main, that you can run to see your message:

```
user@host$ ghc Main
[1 of 1] Compiling Main             ( Main.hs, Main.o )
Linking Main ...
user@host$ ./Main
"Hello, World!"
```

Compiling your program upfront makes sense if you're going to run your program several times, but if you just want to run it once or twice while you are developing it, then you can skip the separate compilation step and just run your module by calling runhaskell Main.hs:

```
user@host$ runhaskell Main.hs
"Hello, World!"
```

As an alternative to runhaskell you can also load your module directly into ghci using the :load command. Loading your module into ghci not only lets you run your main function, like in the following example, but also gives you access to all of the other functions and variables that are in scope. Loading modules for interactive testing while you are actively developing code is a great way to design better APIs and get a feel for how your code is working. Just keep in mind that code running in ghci won't be as performant as code compiled ahead of time.

Open ghci from the Chapter1 directory where you saved Main.hs and load your module and run Main.hs:

```
λ :load Main.hs
λ main
"Hello, World!"
```

Congratulations! You've written and executed your very first Haskell program. To write something more sophisticated, you'll need to learn some more syntax.

Formatting Haskell Code

Haskell is a whitespace sensitive language, meaning that statements are grouped together based on their level of indentation, like Python, instead of using braces as in JavaScript. Individual lines are terminated with a newline, and don't require any punctuation.

The amount of indentation you use is up to you, as long as you are consistent within a given block of code. All the examples in this book will use two spaces, which is common practice in Haskell.

Creating New Variables

Haskell variables must start with a lowercase letter and can contain letters, numbers, underscores, and the single quote character ('). You can use Unicode letters in Haskell variable names, but we'll stick to ASCII in this book. By convention, Haskell variables use camelCase. Here are some examples:

```
helloWorld = "Hello, World"
number5 = 5
snake_case_variable = True
number5' = 6
```

As you might expect, we can also assign a variable to another variable:

```
five = 5
number = five
```

In ghci you can enter the name of a variable to see its value:

```
λ helloGeorge = "Hello, George"
λ helloGeorge
"Hello, George"
λ five = 2 + 3
λ five
5
```

You can also re-use a variable name in ghci. For example, let's create a new greeting, and then change it:

```
λ greeting = "Good Morning"
λ greeting
"Good Morning"
λ greeting = "Good Afternoon"
λ greeting
"Good Afternoon"
```

In this example, we are *re-using* the variable name greeting, but we are not *changing* the value of the variable. This can be a subtle distinction, so let's look at an example to help make it more clear. We'll start by creating two new variables, one and two:

```
λ one = 1
λ one
1
λ two = one + one
λ two
2
```

If we re-use the variable name one, and this time set it to five, we can see that the value of two doesn't change:

```
λ one = 5
λ one
5
λ two
2
```

From the time that we re-use the name one, anytime we type one we will be referring to the new variable, but any code that was written before we re-used the variable name will continue referring to the original variable.

In languages where we can change the value of a variable, it's common to set the new value of a variable based on the old value. If we try to do that in ghci, the result might be surprising. Let's try setting two to one, and then incrementing it:

```
λ two = 1
λ two = two + 1
```

So far, so good. Unfortunately, if we try to print out the value of two you'll see that ghci will seem to get stuck. Press control+c to regain control of ghci:

```
λ two
^CInterrupted.
```

So what happened? This is a common bug that causes problems for people first learning Haskell, and occasionally even catches experienced Haskellers off guard. The problem is, since all of our variables in Haskell are immutable, we can't actually modify two to increment it. Instead, when we say two = two + 1 we're creating a brand new variable named two, and its definition is *recursive*. The two on the right hand side of the expression is referring to the brand new two that we just defined. We have essentially just asked ghci to count forever. Since Haskell is a *lazy* language, it doesn't actually try to run this infinitely recursive code until we ask it to print out the value of two. You'll learn more about recursion, and how to apply it usefully, later on in this chapter, and you'll learn more about laziness in the next chapter on page 47.

For now, we can fix our infinite recursion bug by choosing a different name for our variable. The problem of wanting a variable that represents a slightly modified version of an earlier variable comes up frequently in Haskell, so there's a common pattern: using *prime* variables. Let's look at an example:

```
λ two = 1
λ two' = two + 1
λ two'
2
```

In this example, you can see that instead of re-using the variable name two directly, we have added a single quote (') to the end of the variable name. Haskellers sometimes pronounce this "prime" as in "two prime." You might also see the symbol pronounced "tick" when it's used in this context. There's no special meaning to the character, it's simply another letter that you're allowed to use anywhere, except as the first character, when you are naming variables. You can add as many as you like:

```
λ two' = two + 1
λ two'' = two' + two
λ two''' = two'' + two'
λ two'''
5
```

In practice, variables with a single tick are common. Double prime variable names, like two'', are rare but occasionally useful. If you're using three or more primes then it's probably time to refactor your code.

Now that you've worked with variables in ghci, let's get a feel for how they work in normal applications by building a full program that defines some variables and then prints them out. We'll start by creating a new Main.hs. Next, we'll define a pair of strings named salutation and person. Finally, we'll make a third variable named greeting that joins the two strings. We can join strings in Haskell using the (<>) operator: "like" <> " " <> "this!". In some code bases, especially older ones, you might also see the (++) operator being used to join strings: "like" ++ " " ++ "this!". The (++) operator is a less general way to join things, and it only works for lists and plain Haskell strings. Since (<>) is more general and more commonly used, we'll stick to it throughout this book.

```
module Main where

salutation = "Hello"
person = "George"
greeting =
  salutation <> " " <> person

main = print greeting
```

You'll notice that all of the variables we created in this example are defined at the top level, outside of main. We'll stick with this approach for now, and you'll also learn how to define variables inside of functions later in this chapter.

Working with variables inside of a Haskell program is generally the same as working with them in ghci, with one exception. As a concession to practical usability, ghci allows us to redefine variable names. Outside of ghci we would rather not risk bugs caused by having an ambiguous value for a variable, so re-using names inside of the same scope isn't allowed. If we try to add two variables named message into the top level of Main.hs we'll get an error. Let's try it to see what happens:

```
module Main where

message = "Hello, George"
message = "Hiya, Porter"

main = print message
```

If you try to run this program, you'll get an error:

```
Main.hs:4:1: error:
    Multiple declarations of ‘message’
    Declared at: Main.hs:3:1
                 Main.hs:4:1
  |
4 | message = "Hiya, Porter"
  | ^^^^^^^
```

You can see in this example that the compiler has helpfully pointed us to the exact location of the error, and told us what's wrong. From here we could either remove the duplicate definition, or we can choose a different name. In the next section, you'll learn about writing your own functions, and later on in this chapter you'll learn about creating new local variables using let and `where`. It's useful to keep in mind as you learn about these things that you can always re-use variable names in a new scope.

Writing Functions

Defining functions in Haskell may look strange, because of how lightweight the syntax is compared to other languages. In fact, the syntax for defining functions and variables in Haskell looks almost identical.

To define a new named function, give the function a name along with names for each of the parameters that you want to accept. To look at a concrete example, let's rewrite our greeting program from earlier so that we can take a variable greeting and person to greet.

We'll start by creating a new function, `makeGreeting`, that takes two arguments, `salutation` and `person`. We'll use the `<>` operator to concatenate the two strings and add a space between them. The return value of the function is the concatenated string. Create a new `Main.hs` and copy the following example to get started.

```
module Main where

makeGreeting salutation person =
  salutation <> " " <> person

main = print "no salutation to show yet"
```

Now load up `ghci` and test out your new function by calling `makeGreeting "Hello" "George"`.

You might notice that we're not doing anything special to return a value from our function. Later in this book you'll learn how to be explicit about the return value of your function. For now though, you can rely on knowing that the value of the expression in your function is the return value of the function.

You can also create anonymous functions using a backslash (`\`) followed by the parameters for the function, and then an arrow (`->`) followed by the body. For example, you could create an anonymous version of the `makeGreeting` function with:

```
\salutation person -> salutation <> " " <> person
```

In addition to the term "anonymous function," you'll sometimes see these unnamed functions referred to as "lambda functions," "lambda abstractions," or simply "lambdas." All of these names refer to the same concept. In this book we'll use "anonymous function" consistently.

Functions close over the values that are in scope when they are defined, meaning that the variables that were in scope when you defined the function are also in scope inside of the function. That means you can also nest anonymous functions. All of the functions in the next example will behave the same way:

```
makeThruple a b c = (a,b,c)
lambdaThruple a b = \c -> (a,b,c)
lambdaThruple' = \a -> \b -> \c -> (a,b,c)
```

In fact, in Haskell all functions only take a single argument. Functions that appear to take multiple arguments, like makeThruple and lambdaThruple are really just shorthand for a function like lambdaThruple' that creates a new function for each parameter. The process of converting a function that takes multiple arguments into a series of single-argument functions is called *currying*. Although many languages support some form of currying, Haskell is somewhat unusual in the fact that all functions are curried by default. As you'll see later in this section, and throughout this chapter, automatic currying makes some common Haskell idioms much easier to use.

You've already called functions several times as you've worked through this chapter, from functions like print to main. So far, every time you've called a function you've given it all the arguments that it expects. When a function is called with all of its arguments and can return a value that isn't a function, we call it *fully saturated*. It's also possible, and common, to call a function with only some of its arguments. We say these functions are *partially applied*.

makeGreeting:

```
greetPerson = makeGreeting "Hello"
λ greetPerson "George"
"Hello George"
λ greetPerson "Jane"
"Hello Jane"
```

In this example, you created a new function called greetPerson by giving makeGreeting its first argument, but not the second. This pattern of partial application also works when you're defining new functions. Say you wanted to make a new function that makes greetings more enthusiastic by adding an exclamation point to the salutation, but otherwise you wanted to re-use the logic from makeGreeting. You can do that by writing a function that partially applies a modified salutation to makeGreeting. Let's see an example:

```
enthusiasticGreeting salutation =
  makeGreeting (salutation <> "!")
```

You could also add an extra parameter to enthusiasticGreeting just to pass it along to makeGreeting:

```
enthusiasticGreeting salutation name =
  makeGreeting (salutation <> "!") name
```

In fact, the process of adding or removing those extra parameters has a name that you'll sometimes see used in Haskell. Removing the extra parameter, as in the first example, is called *eta reduction* or *η-reduction*. Adding a parameter and passing it along is called *eta expansion*. It's useful to know these terms because you'll run into them occasionally in the Haskell community, and may see them used in the output of some tools like code linters. For now it's enough to know that η-reduction is generally idiomatic in Haskell.

Operators, like (*) and (<>), are just functions that are infix by default. You can partially apply them like any other function, except that you need to put parentheses around the expression. In fact, you can partially apply the left or right-hand operand independently. Try running these examples in ghci to get a feel for how you can use partial application:

```
λ half = (/2)
λ twoOver = (2/)
λ half 10
λ half 20
λ twoOver 2
λ twoOver 8
```

You can also turn regular functions into infix functions by surrounding the function name with backticks. This can sometimes help make code more readable in general, and is especially handy when you want to partially apply the second argument of a function. Here are some examples. Try typing them into ghci.

```
λ greetGeorge = (`makeGreeting` "George")
λ greetGeorge "Hello"
λ greetGeorge "Good Evening"
```

The flip function is another handy way to apply only the second argument of a function. You could write flip yourself easily:

```
flip someFunction arg1 arg2 = someFunction arg2 arg1
```

You can use flip in the same place that you'd backticks:

```
λ greetGeorge = flip makeGreeting "George"
λ greetGeorge "Good Afternoon"
"Good Afternoon George"
```

You might notice that when you write flip makeGreeting "George" that makeGreeting is applied to flip first, and then "George" is passed in to the resulting function. That is because of the *precedence* of function application. In Haskell, function application has a high precedence, and it associates left to right, so flip makeGreeting "George" is the same as writing (flip makeGreeting) "George". Sometimes the precedence of function application will require you to use parentheses. For example, imagine a function that combines three strings:

```
λ sayThree a b c = a <> " " <> b <> " " <> c
```

If you call flip on this, as you've done in the earlier examples, you'll flip the first and second arguments:

```
λ flip sayThree "Good" "Afternoon" "George"
"Afternoon Good George"
```

If you want to flip the second and final arguments, you need to use parentheses to partially apply the first argument to the function first:

```
λ flip (sayThree "Good") "Afternoon" "George"
"Good George Afternoon"
```

Composing Functions

Now that you understand more about creating and calling functions in Haskell, it's time to learn about function composition. Fundamentally, function composition is about building functions that bring together two or more smaller functions into a single larger function. In this general sense, using function composition to build abstractions is what all programming is about.

Let's look at an example of some code we might write without function composition. We'll start by defining a few new functions that will do some basic arithmetic on a number. You can write these in ghci or follow along with the example by creating Chapter1.hs and adding them there.

```
module Chapter1 where

addOne num = num + 1
timesTwo num = num * 2
squared num = num * num
minusFive num = num - 5
```

Now that we've defined some functions that we want to use, let's load them into ghci and use them to generate a final value:

```
λ :load Chapter1.hs
[1 of 1] Compiling Chapter1         ( Chapter1.hs, interpreted )
Ok, one module loaded.
λ result1 = addOne 1
λ result2 = timesTwo result1
λ result3 = squared result2
λ minusFive result3
11
```

In this example, we're composing all of our functions by creating intermediate values and passing them around. This works, but it's tedious and error prone since we might accidentally pass in the wrong intermediate variable, and if we want to edit code like this later we could end up having to rename several intermediate variables. Instead, we can use parentheses to call one function directly with the output of another function. This makes it much easier for us to re-use a particular collection of functions that are being called in a certain way. For example, let's add a findResult function to Chapter1.hs that will compose the functions this way:

```
module Chapter1 where

addOne num = num + 1
timesTwo num = num * 2
squared num = num * num
minusFive num = num - 5

findResult num = minusFive (squared (timesTwo (addOne num)))
```

Let's see this in action by loading the file up in ghci again. If you haven't closed your ghci session already, you can use the :reload command to load the newest version of Chapter1.hs. For a single file, this won't make much difference, but :reload can be substantially faster when you are editing large projects.

```
λ :reload
[1 of 1] Compiling Chapter1         ( Chapter1.hs, interpreted )
Ok, one module loaded.
λ findResult 1
11
λ findResult 7
251
```

As you can see, our new version of the function is not only easier to read, it's also easier to call with different values.

Since composition is something we do so frequently in Haskell programs, there are a couple of tools we have at our disposal to make this even easier: two functions named ($) and (.). The *function application operator*, ($), helps us avoid having too many parentheses when we write code. The *function composition operator*, (.), helps us quickly build new functions by combining existing ones.

Let's start by looking at an example of how we can use ($) to help us write easier-to-read code. As you've seen, Haskell's normal function application syntax is extremely lightweight. We just add the names of arguments right after the name of the function.

```
λ addOne 1
```

As you work through this book, you'll learn about several advantages to this syntax, but it has a significant drawback: if we want to use the output of a function call as the input of a second call, the obvious way to write that would have some ambiguity. Look at this example:

```
λ addOne timesTwo 1

<interactive>:36:1: error:
    • Non type-variable argument in the constraint: Num (a -> a)
      (Use FlexibleContexts to permit this)
    • When checking the inferred type
        it :: forall {a}. (Num a, Num (a -> a)) => a
```

As the authors of this code, we might know that our intent is to pass the result of timesTwo 1 into addOne, but Haskell will interpret this as though we are trying to pass two arguments to addOne, the first argument being the function timesTwo and the second argument the number 1. Haskell is a functional programming language that makes heavy use of passing around first class functions, so this is an entirely sensible thing we might want to do sometimes, but for now it just means we'll get an error message. Don't worry about the specific meaning of the error text here. You'll learn more about how to read error messages later, when you start to learn more about working with types on page 89.

One way that we can fix this error is by adding parentheses:

```
λ addOne (timesTwo 1)
```

In small examples like this, parentheses are a helpful way to ensure that the code is evaluated the way you intend. In other cases, parentheses may not be very readable, and in those situations you can use the function application operator ($), which applies the function on the left-hand side to the value on the right-hand side. The trick is that this operator has very low precedence, so the right-hand side will be evaluated before the function is applied to it. This has the same effect as wrapping everything after the ($) in parentheses. So you could rewrite the earlier example this way:

```
λ addOne $ timesTwo 1
```

The choice of when to use ($) is largely stylistic. We'll use it in this book when it enhances readability, and skip it when it makes the code less readable.

Next, let's look at the function composition operator, (.). This operator is a *higher-order function*, a term you'll hear used from time to time to describe functions that accept another function as an argument, or return a function. The (.) operator does both. It combines two functions and gives you a new function that accepts an argument to the right-hand function, and passes that function's output on as input to the left-hand function. It's a simple function that you could easily write yourself:

```
(.) func1 func2 = \arg -> func1 (func2 arg)
```

You use (.) like any other operator, except its operands are functions. Let's see an example:

```
λ timesTwoPlusOne = timesTwo . addOne
```

The timesTwoPlusOne function returns a new function that will double a value after incrementing it. Notice that although timesTwoPlusOne is a function, you don't have to specify any parameters for it directly. When you combine timesTwo and addOne with (.), the result is a new function that takes a parameter. You can also chain multiple functions with (.):

```
λ timesEight = timesTwo . timesTwo . timesTwo
λ timesEight 3
24
```

Let's look at a few more examples:

```
λ doubleIncremented = addOne . addOne
λ doubleIncremented 4
6

λ (timesTwo . addOne . squared . minusFive) 128
30260
```

It's common to want to use (.) without making a named function. If you try to call a function that you've composed you might run into the same problem that you saw earlier when trying to manually compose functions:

```
λ timesTwo . timesTwo 3

<interactive>:34:1: error:
    • Non type-variable argument in the constraint: Num (a -> c)
      (Use FlexibleContexts to permit this)
    • When checking the inferred type
        it :: forall {c} {a}. (Num c, Num (a -> c)) => a -> c
```

You can ignore the specifc text of the error message for now. The reason that you are getting the error is that calling timesTwo 3 is higher precedence than composing timesTwo . timesTwo. To create a composed function you need to use parentheses, or you can use the function application operator you learned about earlier in this section:

```
λ (timesTwo . timesTwo . timesTwo) 3
24
λ timesTwo . timesTwo . timesTwo $ 2
16
```

Using function composition to build more complex functions from smaller functions is one of the most common things that you'll do while writing Haskell programs.

Writing Functions with No Named Parameters

Pointfree programming, sometimes called *tacit programming*, takes the ideas of η-reduction and function composition to their logical conclusion by writing functions that take no named parameters at all. For example, consider our original makeGreeting function:

```
makeGreeting salutation person = salutation <> " " <> person
```

We can apply η-reduction once to remove the final named parameter quite easily:

```
λ makeGreeting' salutation = ((salutation <> " ") <>)
```

To take it a step further and write a pointfree version of the function requires that we rethink the structure of our function definition a little bit. Let's re-write makeGreeting' while retaining salutation first:

```
λ makeGreeting' salutation = (<>) (salutation <> " ")
```

This version of the function makes the second call to (<>) into a prefix function. Its first argument is the first half of our string, which combines salutation with a trailing whitespace. The second argument to the function, which we aren't binding to a variable name here, is the string that will become the last half of the combined greeting.

As a next step, let's replace the named salutation parameter with an anonymous function defined where we are using it:

```
λ makeGreeting' = (<>) . (\salutation -> salutation <> " ")
λ makeGreeting' "hello" "george"
"hello george"
```

This is getting closer to a completely pointfree program: we're no longer binding any variables in our top level function declaration, but you might already see that we can easily drop the explicitly bound variable name inside of our anonymous function as well. We know that we could refactor this inner expression. For example, imagine if we broke this up into two separate functions:

```
λ firstPart salutation = salutation <> " "
λ makeGreeting' = (<>) . firstPart
λ makeGreeting' "hello" "george"
"hello george"
```

You could refactor firstPart to be pointfree by rewriting it:

```
λ firstPart = (<> " ")
λ makeGreeting' = (<>) . firstPart
λ makeGreeting' "hello" "george"
"hello george"
```

Now you can substitute the definition of firstPart back into the definition of makeGreeting', leaving you with a fully pointfree definition:

```
λ makeGreeting' = (<>) . (<> " ")
λ makeGreeting' "hello" "george"
"hello george"
```

Pointfree functions in Haskell can sometimes make code much cleaner and easier to read, and can offer a more principled way of writing functions, or they can also greatly reduce the readability and maintainability of code. The threshold for whether to make a function pointfree or not is a matter of debate in the Haskell community. In this book we will use a mixture of pointfree and pointful functions. Try writing functions in both styles and figure out which approach you prefer.

Precedence, Operators, and Fixity

Pointfree style is a great example of the flexibility that Haskell's syntax can afford you in writing code that's short and to the point. Since Haskell's grammar requires very little in the way of additional punctuation to separate out different parts of an expression, pointfree style feels like a natural evolution of Haskell's already generally minimalist style. The downside of both pointfree style specifically, and Haskell's lightweight syntax in general, is that it relies on implicit rules about how things are parsed, rather than explicit punctuation where characters and symbols are used to tell both the compiler and the reader how to parse the code.

Thankfully, although these parsing rules are implicit and not written directly into the code you read or write, there are only a few of them. In this section we'll start by looking at some concrete examples of how Haskell parses things in different circumstances, and the rules behind the choices it makes. Next, you'll learn how to define your own custom operators. This will give you the opportunity to learn about two other important factors in how Haskell code gets parsed: binding precedence and associativity.

Let's start with a simple example of something that does what we would expect:

```
λ "the first number is " <> show 1
"the first number is 1"
```

We've written code like this before, and at the time we didn't remark on it, but this is a good example of one of the implicit rules that helps Haskell avoid too many parentheses: passing an argument to a function always has higher precedence than passing that argument to an operator. In formal Haskell speak, we'd say that function application has a higher *binding precedence* than operator application. Without this rule, our example wouldn't work because the (<>) operator would get passed to the function show instead of the string we get back when we say show 1. This same rule also lets us call functions in the middle of a longer string of calls to operators:

```
λ "the sum of " <> show 1 <> " and " <> show 2 <> " is " <> show 3
"the sum of 1 and 2 is 3"
```

The higher binding precedence of functions means we can omit the parentheses in this example, but there are other cases where it means we have to add some parentheses. For example, if we try show the sum of two numbers without parentheses, we'll get an error:

```
λ show 1 + 2

<interactive>:119:8: error:
    • No instance for (Num String) arising from a use of '+'
    • In the expression: show 1 + 2
      In an equation for 'it': it = show 1 + 2
```

The problem here is the binding precedence of functions means show is called with 1 first, giving us the string "1". Next, we try to add the string "1" to the numeric literal 2. Haskell won't let us add a number and a string together, so we get an error instead. We can introduce parentheses to solve this problem:

```
λ show (1 + 2)
"3"
```

Parentheses override all other precedence and let us explicitly set the order in which things should be evaluated. Within the parentheses, all of the normal rules about precedence and binding still apply, but from the outside the entire parenthetical expression is treated as a single thing. In the case of our example, that means that even though function application has the highest precedence, the thing that's being applied is the result of evaluating the entire parenthetical expression.

Function application having higher precedence than operator application is a helpful rule for resolving ambiguity in code like show 1 + 2, but what happens if we try to pass the result of one function call into another function and introduce some ambiguity. As an example, let's write a function that adds two numbers:

```
λ add a b = a + b
```

We could try to add the result of two other additions together by writing something like:

```
λ add add 1 2 add 3 4
```

As you can probably guess, this doesn't work. If you try this you should get an error like this:

```
<interactive>:123:1: error:
    • Non type-variable argument in the constraint: Num (a -> a -> a)
      (Use FlexibleContexts to permit this)
    • When checking the inferred type
        it :: forall {a}.
              (Num a, Num (a -> a -> a),
               Num ((a -> a -> a) -> (a -> a -> a) -> a -> a -> a)) =>
              a
```

We can add parentheses to fix our error:

```
λ add (add 1 2) (add 3 4)
10
```

Although this might be intuitive, there's no particular reason parsing has to work this way. When faced with some ambiguity around what to parse, for example, because two things have the same precedence, the compiler needs to pick an order. We can visualize this by adding parentheses to help develop an intuition for the order that things get evaluated in.

Our original statement:

```
add add 1 2 add 3 4
```

Becomes:

```
((((((add add) 1) 2) add) 3) 4)
```

In this approach, each time that there's a function being called, we need to figure out how to prioritize what to evaluate first, so we start with the left and work our way "out" or to the right. Alternatively, we could have worked right-to-left. It's hard to visualize exactly what this would look like, especially if you are accustomed to working in left-to-right languages. The fact that we write functions to the left of their arguments in Haskell means that parsing function application right-to-left would look strange indeed. We can imagine it would be something like this:

```
(add ((add 1 2) (add 3 4)))
```

The choice of whether to parse things left-to-right or right-to-left is known as its *associativity*. We would say that our first example is *left associative* and the second example is *right associative*. Normal function application in Haskell is *left associative*. Infix functions and operators have a bit more flexibility.

We can't control the binding precedence or associativity of normal function application in Haskell, but we can configure these for infix functions. This combination of properties is called its *fixity*, and we declare it using a *fixity declaration*. You're most likely to see fixity declarations when creating custom operators.

Creating Custom Operators

Haskell allows you to define your own operators, and as you'll see later on in chapter 6 on page 209, allows you to provide your own implementation of some commonly used operators. Used sparingly, custom operators can improve the experience of using a library, but be careful—overuse of operators can lead to unreadable and unmaintainable code.

Another benefit to creating your own operators, and the one we'll focus on in this section, is that they can give you a useful insight into some of the parsing rules you've just learned about. In this section, we'll implement a few different operators to get a feel for how they work, with a special focus on what we can learn about Haskell's syntax as we're creating them.

First things first, what is an operator? You've already seen that operators work a lot like regular Haskell functions, but there are a few important differences:

1. Operators are *infix* by default, and can be made to work like regular functions when surrounded by parentheses. Regular functions need to be surrounded in backticks to be used infix.

2. Functions have a higher *binding precedence* than operators, so when it's ambiguous whether an argument belongs to a function or an operator, the function will always be chosen.

3. A function can have any number of arguments, but a custom operator must always have exactly two arguments. We call these *binary operators*.

4. Functions can be named using any letters. Operators must be named using symbols.

5. A function whose name starts with an uppercase letter is a *type constructor*, which you'll learn about when you start creating your own types on page 117. Similarly, operators that start with the colon symbol, :, are reserved for type constructors.

Haskell operators can be named using nearly any combination of ASCII and Unicode symbols, but they can't contain letters or spaces. For the purposes of operator naming, the underscore character, _, is considered a letter, so you can't use it in your operator names. You also can't use parentheses, (), or square brackets, [], in your operator names. Angle brackets <> are allowed, and are popular when naming operators.

Let's start by defining our own addition operator, which we'll call (+++). There are two ways that we can define an operator. First, we can write the definition as though we were writing the function in prefix form, with parentheses:

```
module OperatorExample where

(+++) a b = a + b
```

Alternatively, we can write it as though we were using it in infix form:

```
module OperatorExample where

a +++ b = a + b
```

The difference here is entirely stylistic. You can still use the operator as a normal infix operator even if you define it using the prefix form; you can also still use parentheses to call the operator in prefix form even if you've defined it using the infix style. We'll use infix form for the examples in this section, but you can choose whichever you like better.

If you load this example up in ghci you can see that it does work as an operator and lets you add numbers. You can also still do all of the normal operator things you'd do, like use it in prefix form, or partially apply it:

```
λ :load OperatorExample.hs
[1 of 1] Compiling OperatorExample  ( OperatorExample.hs, interpreted )
Ok, one module loaded.
λ 1 +++ 1
2
λ (+++) 1 2
3
λ increment = (+++ 1)
λ increment 8
9
λ anotherIncrementer = (1 +++)
λ anotherIncrementer 0
1
```

This is looking pretty good, but if we try to use our new operator as part of a longer expression, we'll see that our operator is giving us different results compared to the standard addition operator:

```
λ 1 +++ 2 * 3
9
λ 1 + 2 * 3
7
```

The problem is that our new operator has higher precedence than multiplication, so in our first example we're calculating (1 +++ 2) * 3. In normal arithmetic, multiplication has a higher precedence than addition, and in Haskell (*) has a higher precedence than (+) operator. That means that in our second example we're calculating 1 + (2* 3). We can fix this by adding a *fixity declaration*.

A fixity declaration has three parts. First, you declare the operator's associativity:

- infixl for left associativity
- infixr for right associativity
- infix if the operator is not associative

Next, you set the operators binding precedence. The binding precedence is a number from 0 (the lowest precedence) to 9 (the highest precedence). The last part of the fixity declaration is the name of the operator, or infix function, that you are declaring the fixity for.

Normal addition in Haskell is left associative and has a precedence of 6. You can find this out from the online documentation, or by looking at the info in ghci using the :info command:

```
λ :info (+)
type Num :: * -> Constraint
class Num a where
  (+) :: a -> a -> a
  ...
        -- Defined in 'GHC.Num'
infixl 6 +
```

There's a lot of extra information in this output that you won't understand until chapter 3, when you learn more about types on page 91. What's important for us is the last line of output:

```
infixl 6 +
```

This is the fixity declaration for addition. If we use the same fixity declaration for (+++) then we should see the same behavior in our example. Let's give it a try:

```
module OperatorExample where

infixl 6 +++
a +++ b = a + b
```

```
λ :load OperatorExample
[1 of 1] Compiling OperatorExample  ( OperatorExample.hs, interpreted )
Ok, one module loaded.
λ 1 +++ 2 * 3
7
```

Now that we've lowered the binding precedence from the default of 9 to 6, our new addition operator behaves like we would expect.

Copying the fixity declaration from (+) helped us get working code, but we don't always have some existing work we can reference. Let's look at some different fixity definitions and how they would have changed the behavior.

Since we're going to be experimenting with several different versions of the same function, with different fixity declarations, it may be easier for you to work in ghci rather than making the changes in your file and re-loading it. As a matter of convenience you can enter the definition of your operator and its fixity declaration on the same line in ghci separated by a semicolon:

```
λ a +++ b = a + b; infixl 6 +++
```

You can use the up-arrow key to scroll backwards through history and re-edit this line to save yourself some typing. You can also type Control-r to search backwards through history to get back to this line if you've been running several different experiments. This can be a fast way to iteratively test different minor changes to a piece of code.

The first change we'll try is changing the binding precedence from 6 to 7. The fixity of (*) is infixl 7 *, so in this example both operators will have the same precedence:

```
λ a +++ b = a + b; infixl 7 +++
```

If we run our first example, we'll see that we're once again adding before we multiply:

```
λ 1 +++ 2 * 3
9
```

However, if we re-order our example and have the multiplication on the left-hand side of the expression, when both operators have the same precedence, then we'll multiply first:

```
λ 3 * 2 +++ 1
7
```

If the precedence of (+++) is higher or lower than (*), then the output will be consistent regardless of the order in which we type the expression:

```
λ a +++ b = a + b; infixl 6 +++
λ 3 * 2 +++ 1
7
λ 1 +++ 2 * 3
7
λ a +++ b = a + b; infixl 8 +++
λ 3 * 2 +++ 1
9
λ 1 +++ 2 * 3
9
```

This example tells us that when the binding precedence for two left-associative operators is the same, then they are evaluated left-to-right. If we had two right-associative operators of the same precedence, then the evaluation will apply right-to-left. We can see an example of this if we define a right-associative version of (*), (***) and re-run some of our examples using it:

```
λ a +++ b = a + b; infixr 7 +++
λ a *** b = a * b; infixr 7 ***
λ 1 +++ 2 *** 3
7
λ 3 *** 2 +++ 1
9
```

```
λ a *** b = a * b; infixl 7 ***
λ a +++ b = a + b; infixl 7 +++
λ 1 +++ 2 *** 3
9
λ 3 *** 2 +++ 1
7
```

What if we have two operators with different associativity? As long as they have a different binding precedence, everything will work as we'd expect. For example, if we keep (***) left associative, and make (+++) right associative, you'll see that the behavior remains the same when they have different precedence:

```
λ a *** b = a * b; infixl 7 ***
λ a +++ b = a + b; infixr 6 +++
λ 1 +++ 2 *** 3
7
λ 3 *** 2 +++ 1
7
λ a +++ b = a + b; infixr 8 +++
λ 1 +++ 2 *** 3
9
λ 3 *** 2 +++ 1
9
```

If the binding precedence is the same though, we'll get an error. The statement is ambiguous and the parser doesn't have any way to resolve the situation:

```
λ a +++ b = a + b; infixr 7 +++
λ a *** b = a * b; infixl 7 ***
λ 1 +++ 2 *** 3

<interactive>:289:1: error:
  Precedence parsing error
    cannot mix '+++' [infixr 7] and '***' [infixl 7]
      in the same infix expression
```

When the precedence of the operations is the same and they have different associativity, there are no rules that will tell the compiler how to evaluate the expression, so it gives up. We can still evaluate this if we use parentheses:

```
λ (1 +++ 2) *** 3
9
λ 1 +++ (2 *** 3)
7
```

Another case where we have to use parentheses is when an operator doesn't define associativity at all. The equals operator, (==) is an example of a commonly used operator without associativity. Its fixity declaration is:

```
infix 4 ==
```

We can see this in action from ghci:

```
λ True == True == False

<interactive>:294:1: error:
  Precedence parsing error
    cannot mix '==' [infix 4] and '==' [infix 4]
      in the same infix expression
```

Just like when we have operators with different associativity, you have to use parentheses if you want to write an expression that uses multiple operators that are not associative:

```
λ True == (True == True)
True
λ (True == True) == True
True
```

All of the examples of fixity declarations that we've looked at so far have focused on operators. You can also write a fixity declation for a standard function that is being used as an infix operator. For example, let's write a division function that does the same thing as normal numeric division:

```
module OperatorExample where

divide = (/)
```

Since we haven't given a specific fixity declaration to divide, when we use it as an infix operator it will have the usual operator fixity: a binding precedence of 9 and left associativity. The (/) operator is also left associative, but has a precedence of 7, the same as multiplication. That means that repeated calls to divide should give us the same result as repeated calls to (/):

```
λ :load OperatorExample.hs
[1 of 1] Compiling OperatorExample  ( OperatorExample.hs, interpreted )
Ok, one module loaded.
λ 1 / 2 / 3 / 4
4.1666666666666664e-2
λ 1 `divide` 2 `divide` 3 `divide` 4
4.1666666666666664e-2
```

We can give divide a fixity declaration, just like we'd do with an operator. For example, if we change divide to be right associative, then we can see that repeated calls will start giving us a very different answer:

```
λ divide = (/); infixr 9 `divide`
λ 1 `divide` 2 `divide` 3 `divide` 4
0.375
```

You'll notice in this example that when we write a fixity declaration for a regular function, we need to put it in backticks. The fixity declaration doesn't change anything about how the function will behave if it's not being called infix. As an example, let's set the precedence of divide to 0, and then call it a few times infix as well as calling it as a normal function. You'll see that when it's called infix it will have low precedence, but when it's called as a normal function it will continue to have a higher precedence than any other operator:

```
λ divide = (/); infixr 0 `divide`
λ divide 1 2 * 10
5.0
λ 1 `divide` 2 * 10
5.0e-2
```

As you can see, the fixity rules for operators, and for functions that are being used in infix form, have a big impact on how your code is evaluated. Although you might only create custom operators occasionally, the rules for binding and associativity are important to keep in mind because they impact if, and when, you need to use parentheses or the ($) operator when you are writing programs. Throughout this book we will occasionally add parentheses or use the ($) when the binding and precedence rules mean that they aren't strictly needed. This isn't typical in most Haskell code. The common style in Haskell is to omit these things whenever you can. They are included in some examples in this book to add clarity. If you are looking at some example code later on in this book and find it confusing, the parsing rules around fixity are a common culprit. Consider returning to this section and reviewing the material to see if it makes the syntax of the example easier to follow.

Creating Local Variables Using Let Bindings

Now that you've learned how to create new top-level variables and functions, it's time to look at how to build more complex functions. In this section, you'll learn how to build larger and more complex functions by building up intermediate computations using *let bindings*.

Let bindings allow you to give a name to some particular expression in your program. Let's start with an example. We'll rewrite our makeGreeting function from before to use an intermediate value. If you still have access to your previous file where you defined makeGreeting, feel free to re-use it. Otherwise, create a new Main.hs with a function named makeGreeting with the following definition:

```
module Main where

makeGreeting salutation person =
  salutation <> " " <> person

main = print $ makeGreeting "Hello" "George"
```

Next, update your makeGreeting method to create an intermediate value using a let binding. A let binding consists of the keyword let followed by some variable definitions, and then the keyword in followed by an expression. In short: let vars in expr.

Let's see how to we can add a let binding to makeGreeting:

```
makeGreeting salutation person =
  let messageWithTrailingSpace = salutation <> " "
  in messageWithTrailingSpace <> person
```

You aren't limited to a single variable inside of a let binding; you can create as many different local variables as you want. We can write an extended greeting function that demonstrates how we can create multiple local variables in a single let binding:

```
extendedGreeting person =
  let hello = makeGreeting "Hello" person
      goodDay = makeGreeting "I hope you have a nice afternoon" person
      goodBye = makeGreeting "See you later" person
  in hello <> "\n" <> goodDay <> "\n" <> goodBye
```

As with top-level bindings, you are free to reference bindings that you define later in the same let expression. For example, we could have rewritten extendedGreeting by saying:

```
extendedGreeting person =
  let hello = makeGreeting helloStr person
      goodDay = makeGreeting "I hope you have a nice afternoon" person
      goodBye = makeGreeting "See you later" person
      helloStr = "Hello"
  in hello <> "\n" <> goodDay <> "\n" <> goodBye
```

In this example, hello references the helloStr variable that we don't define until later in the same let binding.

When you create a let binding, the expression you are binding a name to doesn't need to be a constant, like a string or a number. You can also use let bindings to define new functions. The syntax is the same as defining a top-level function:

```
extendedGreeting person =
  let joinWithNewlines a b = a <> "\n" <> b
      hello = makeGreeting "Hello" person
      goodbye = makeGreeting "Goodbye" person
  in joinWithNewlines hello goodbye
```

Haskell supports *recursive let bindings*, which means that the items inside of our let bindings can refer to one another. The order doesn't matter; you can refer to items that you define further down in the let binding like in this example:

```
exntededGreeting person =
  let joinWithNewlines a b = a <> "\n" <> b
      joined = joinWithNewlines hello goodbye
      hello = makeGreeting "Hello" person
      goodbye = makeGreeting "Goodbye" person
  in joined
```

Let bindings can also be nested. For example, if you are defining a new function inside of a let expression, and you want to define some variables inside of that function, you can use nested let expressions.

Now that you understand a little bit more about let bindings, follow along with the next example to create an extendedGreeting function that uses let bindings to define intermediate values and functions:

```
extendedGreeting person =
  let joinWithNewlines a b = a <> "\n" <> b
      helloAndGoodbye hello goodbye =
        let hello' = makeGreeting hello person
```

```
          goodbye' = makeGreeting goodbye person
      in joinWithNewlines hello' goodbye'
  in helloAndGoodbye "Hello" "Goodbye"
```

There's one final type of binding called a *where binding*. A where binding follows all the same rules as a let binding, except it comes at the end of a function instead of the beginning, and uses the where keyword instead of let .. in. Any parameters that you've bound to a variable name in your function will be available to your where binding, but not anything you've defined in a let binding. Conversely, anything you define inside of a where binding will be available to use in let bindings:

```
letWhereGreeting name place =
  let
    salutation = "Hello " <> name
    meetingInfo = location "Tuesday"
  in salutation <> " " <> meetingInfo
  where
    location day = "we met at " <> place <> " on a " <> day
```

You can see in this example that the location function in our where clause can access the place parameter to the function, but we have to explicitly pass in day as a parameter, since location does not have access to variables defined in the let binding.

Try rewriting your extendedGreeting function to use a where binding instead of a let binding:

```
extendedGreeting person =
  helloAndGoodbye "Hello" "Goodbye"
  where
    helloAndGoodbye hello goodbye =
      joinWithNewlines hello' goodbye'
      where
        hello' = makeGreeting hello person
        goodbye' = makeGreeting goodbye person
    joinWithNewlines a b = a <> "\n" <> b
```

The choice of whether to use let or where bindings is a matter of personal style and what seems to be the most readable as you are writing the code. In this book we'll use a mixture of both, and it's common to see them both used in real applications. As a general rule of thumb, we'll use let bindings for intermediate values and where bindings for ancillary and helper functions, but this is an arbitrary choice and we might deviate from the pattern from time to time if doing so will help make the code more readable. As you work through the examples in this book, consider experimenting with both styles of bindings to get a feel for your own personal style.

Running Code Conditionally Using Branches

Haskell supports quite a few ways to take different branches in your code. Some, like the venerable if expression will look familiar. Others, like *guard clauses* might not. In this section, you'll learn the basics of branching in your program. Later, on page 66, you'll learn about *pattern matching*, a powerful technique you can combine with branches to make your code incredibly expressive.

The branching structure that you're probably most familiar with from other languages is the if expression. Like most other languages, if expressions in Haskell allow you to return one value if some predicate is true, and a different value if the predicate is false. In Haskell, if structures are *expressions*, meaning that you can assign a variable to the result of an if expression, and also that you must have both a true and false branch for every expression. This makes the behavior of Haskell if expressions similar to the ternary ?: operator in languages like C and JavaScript.

Let's look at a basic example to start with, by writing a program that will print a number if it's smaller than 10, or otherwise print an error. Let's start by opening up an empty Main.hs file and copying the following example:

```
module Main where

printSmallNumber num =
  if num < 10
  then print num
  else print "the number is too big!"

main = printSmallNumber 3
```

Once you've copied the example, test to make sure it runs:

```
user@host$ runhaskell Main.hs
3
```

You might next want to refactor your program to take advantage of the fact that if expressions always return a value. If you try to run the updated version in the example, you'll quickly notice that the obvious solution introduces a new bug.

```
printSmallNumber num =
  let msg = if num < 10
        then num
        else "the number is too big!"
  in print msg
```

When you ran this snippet you should have gotten an error that looks like this one:

```
[1 of 1] Compiling MaybeTooBig      ( MaybeTooBig.hs, interpreted )

MaybeTooBig.hs:4:22: error:
    • No instance for (Num [Char]) arising from the literal '10'
    • In the second argument of '(<)', namely '10'
      In the expression: num < 10
      In the expression:
        if num < 10 then num else "the number is too big!"
  |
4 |   let msg = if num < 10
  |                      ^^
Failed, no modules loaded.
```

The reason you got this error is, since if expressions return a value, and values in Haskell have types, you have to make sure that both the then and else clauses of the branch return the *same* type. Otherwise the compiler doesn't know what type the return value should be and it has to raise an error.

You can resolve the bug in your program by making sure both branches return a string and then try running your program again with ghci. You can use the show function from earlier in this chapter to convert your number to a string:

```
printSmallNumber num =
  let msg = if num < 10
        then show num
        else "the number is too big!"
  in print msg
```

Sometimes a single branch isn't enough to express what we want. Although Haskell doesn't have any special syntax for chaining together multiple if expressions, you can nest them as much as you want. Consider a function that gives a size approximation for a number:

```
sizeNumber num =
  if num < 3
  then "that's a small number"
  else
    if num < 10
    then "that's a medium sized number"
    else "that's a big number"
```

This can get tedious and difficult to read as you add more branches. Enter guard clauses. Let's look at an example:

```
guardSize num
  | num < 3 = "that's a small number"
  | num < 10 = "that's  a medium number"
  | num < 100 = "that's a pretty big number"
  | num < 1000 = "wow, that's a giant number"
  | otherwise = "that's an unfathomably big number"
```

As you can see from the example, this is the general syntax for using a function with guards:

```
functionName argument1 argument2 -- as many arguments as you want
  | predicate1 = body1
  | predicate2 = body2
  -- as many predicates as you want
  | otherwise = body3
```

In short, each guard clause starts with a vertical bar, followed by a predicate, then an equals sign and the body of the function. You'll notice in these examples that we've ended our guard clauses with otherwise. This is an ordinary value that's defined for us by the standard library to make guard clauses more readable. Its value is always True.

Predicates are evaluated from top to bottom. If we added another clause to our function that checks to see if a number is greater than zero, we could end up always hitting the first branch:

```
guardSize num
  | num > 0 = "that's a positive number"
  | num < 3 = "that's a small number"
  | num < 10 = "that's  a medium number"
  | num < 100 = "that's a pretty big number"
  | num < 1000 = "wow, that's a giant number"
  | otherwise = "that's an unfathomalbly big number"
```

In this version of the function, we'll get back "that's a positive number" for any positive number, and we'll never end up hitting our other cases.

You can use let expressions and where clauses with guards just like with other functions. Anything that you define in a let expression will only be in scope for the particular branch where it's defined. On the other hand, variables defined inside of a where clause will be in scope for all of the branches of your function:

```
guardSize num
  | num > 0 =
      let size = "positive"
      in exclaim size
  | num < 3 = exclaim "small"
  | num < 100 = exclaim "medium"
  | otherwise = exclaim "large"
  where
    exclaim message = "that's a " <> message <> " number!"
```

In this example, the size variable is only defined inside of the first branch. We'd get an error if we tried to refer to it from any of our other branches. The exclaim function on the other hand is defined inside of a where clause, so it's available in all of the branches of our function.

A common syntax error that you might run into, especially if you are refactoring your code to add guard clauses, comes from accidentally having an extra = symbol between the last argument to your function and before the first predicate. Let's look at an example:

```
invalidFunction n =
  | n > 5 = "bigger than five"
  | otherwise = "smaller than five"
```

If you write a function like this into a file and try to load it into ghci you'll see a syntax error like this:

```
Main.hs:9:3: error: parse error on input '|'
  |
9 |     | n > 5 = "bigger than five"
  |     ^
Failed, no modules loaded.
```

When you see an error like this around a function with a guard clause, it's a good sign that you might have accidentally left a stray = symbol around at the end of the list of arguments.

Guard clauses and if expressions are only two ways to branch in Haskell. You'll learn about a third type of branching, *case expressions*, later on in this book.

Looping

If you've been programming for very long, you might've heard of the "fizzbuzz" problem. It was once a common interview question that was asked to see whether candidates could write a simple program, and it's still used these days as a common example when teaching new programmers. There are a few minor variations of the problem, but let's consider this version of it:

Given a number, fizzBuzzCount, return a string that contains all of the numbers from one, up to and including fizzBuzzCount, except:

1. If the number is evenly divisible by 3, but not evenly divisible by 5, replace it with the word "fizz".
2. If the number is evenly divisible by 5, but not evenly divisible by 3, replace it with the word "buzz".
3. If the number is evenly divisible by both 3 and 5, replace it with the word "fizzbuzz".

For any given individual number, we can use what we've already learned in this chapter to write a function that will return the right output. Let's start there by writing a new function, fizzBuzzFor, that will calculate the "fizzbuzz string" for any given number:

```
module FizzBuzz where

fizzBuzzFor number
  | 0 == number `rem` 15 = "fizzbuzz"
  | 0 == number `rem` 5  = "buzz"
  | 0 == number `rem` 3  = "fizz"
  | otherwise = show number
```

The rem function that we're calling here returns the remainder after dividing two numbers. By checking to see if the remainder is zero, we can tell if one number is evenly divisible by another. You might also notice that our first case tests to see if our number is evenly divisible by 15. This is a shortcut that will tell us if the number is divisible by both 3 and 5.

This solves the problem for a particular number, but how can we go about calling this function repeatedly for each of the numbers up to our fizzBuzzCount? Most idiomatic Haskell solutions to this particular problem would use lists and list functions that you'll learn about in the next chapter on page 47. For now though, we'll focus on the fundamentals.

In procedural and object-oriented languages, the common approach to solving a problem like this would be to use a *loop*, for example, a while or for loop. Let's look at an example of how we might write this in a procedural way. This example will use JavaScript, but don't worry if you aren't familiar with JavaScript. We're only using this example so that we have something concrete to reference when discussing the differences between procedural style looping and writing loops in Haskell.

```
function rem(a,b) {
  return a % b;
}

function fizzBuzzFor(number) {
    if (0 == rem(number, 15)) {
      return "fizzbuzz";
    } else if (0 == rem(number, 5)) {
      return "buzz";
    } else if (0 == rem(number, 3)) {
      return "fizz";
    } else {
      return number.toString();
    }
}
```

```
function fizzbuzz(fizzBuzzCount) {
  var fizzBuzzString = "";
  for (var curNum = 1; curNum <= fizzBuzzCount; curNum = curNum + 1) {
    fizzBuzzString = fizzBuzzString + " " + fizzBuzzFor(curNum);
  }
  return fizzBuzzString;
}
```

We'll ignore the definition of rem here, which is included to keep our function names consistent with the Haskell code we've already written. We'll also skip past fizzBuzFor, which is more or less identical to our earlier Haskell implementation, except for the obvious differences in syntax. Instead, let's jump right to our definition of fizzbuzz.

The first thing we do in our fizzbuzz implementation is to declare some new *mutable variable* named fizzBuzzString. We initialize this variable to the empty string, and we *accumulate* the results of our loop into it. Our loop starts out by creating another mutable variable named curNum. At each iteration of the loop we first test to see if the current value of our mutable curNum counter is still within the bounds of our fizzBuzzCount. If it is, then we we modify our mutable fizzBuzzString value to append the current fizzbuzz value, and then we increment the counter. Eventually, when the counter is past the bounds of fizzBuzzCount the loop will exit and we'll return the final value of fizzBuzzString.

Some of the words we just used to describe our procedural algorithm, like *mutable* and *update*, are clues that we might not be able to directly translate this looping approach to Haskell. After all, Haskell variables aren't mutable, and in a pure function we have nothing to update. It's true that we don't want to directly translate the use of mutable values and state into Haskell, but an idiomatic Haskell implementation is still quite similar to this procedural one. Let's look at a couple of ways that we can approach this sort of problem in Haskell.

The first thing we want to do when we're thinking about writing a looping function in Haskell is to ask ourselves *"what's changing?"* In our procedural implementation, we have three important pieces of *state*:

1. fizzBuzzCount is immutable and tells us when to stop looping.
2. fizzBuzzString is mutable, and accumulates the output of the function.
3. curNum is the current number we're fizzbuzzing. It's also mutable and changes once per loop iteration.

Our pure functional fizzbuzz implementation will need the same state that the procedural one did. The key difference is that the state in our pure functional version will be immutable. When we had mutable state we needed to start our function by initializing the state, and we had to finish our function be extracting the final return value from our state. In the pure functional version, we'll accept immutable state as input, so there's nothing to initialize. That means our Haskell function will be equivalent to the body of our procedural loop—we don't need to worry about the initial setup of the function, nor how to extract a final return value.

Let's start our pure functional implementation by creating a new function. We'll start with the most straightforward translation of our procedural algorithm, and refactor based on what we learn, so let's call this first implementation naiveFizzBuzz:

```
module FizzBuzz where

naiveFizzBuzz fizzBuzzCount curNum fizzBuzzString
```

The first thing the body of our for loop did was check to see if our mutable curNum value was greater than the target fizzBuzzCount. If so, we would exit the loop and return the final string. Comparing two values and returning another value doesn't require any mutation, so we can translate that step directly:

```
module FizzBuzz where

naiveFizzBuzz fizzBuzzCount curNum fizzBuzzString =
  if curNum > fizzBuzzCount
  then fizzBuzzString
  else
    -- fill this in next
```

In this expanded example, we're looking to see if we've finished our loop, and if so we return fizzBuzzString. Just like in the procedural example, we're making an assumption here that when we get to the end of our loop, the *state* of fizzBuzzString should be right, and we can return it. But how do we get the state there without changing it? In the body of our procedural loop, if we weren't finished looping then we would change the state of the string by appending the next fizzbuzz number to it. Let's add that to our Haskell example:

```
module FizzBuzz where

naiveFizzBuzz fizzBuzzCount curNum fizzBuzzString =
  if curNum > fizzBuzzCount
  then fizzBuzzString
  else
    let nextFizzBuzzString = fizzBuzzString <> fizzBuzzFor curNum <> " "
    -- fill this in next
```

Instead of modifying the string in place, our pure implementation will generate a new string. In this example, we're calling that new string nextFizzBuzzString.

The next thing our procedural loop did was update the curNum counter by incrementing it. Just like with nextFizzBuzzString we're going to create a new counter instead of modifying the one we have:

```
module FizzBuzz where

naiveFizzBuzz fizzBuzzCount curNum fizzBuzzString =
  if curNum > fizzBuzzCount
  then fizzBuzzString
  else
    let nextFizzBuzzString = fizzBuzzString <> fizzBuzzFor curNum <> " "
        nextNumber = curNum + 1
    in -- fill this in next
```

The last thing that our procedural loop did was to, well, *loop*. After updating the mutable state, we would re-execute the same code in the body of the loop, and do the same things, but of course on the next run all of the values have been updated. The state of fizzBuzzString would have one more entry appended to it, and curNum would be one step closer to the end of our range of numbers.

In our pure functional version, we're going to do the same thing. We'll run the same code, but this time our curNum will be one step closer to the end, and fizzBuzzString will have one more entry added. How? By calling naiveFizzBuzz with the new values we've just calculated:

```
module FizzBuzz where

naiveFizzBuzz fizzBuzzCount curNum fizzBuzzString =
  if curNum > fizzBuzzCount
  then fizzBuzzString
  else
    let nextFizzBuzzString = fizzBuzzString <> fizzBuzzFor curNum <> " "
        nextNumber = curNum + 1
    in naiveFizzBuzz fizzBuzzCount nextNumber nextFizzBuzzString
```

If you haven't spent much time working with recursion, this can be a little bit confusing. Let's work through what's going on in this example to help make it a bit more clear. You can start by copying the code into a file and loading it into ghci so you can have an idea of what to expect:

```
λ :load FizzBuzz.hs
[1 of 1] Compiling FizzBuzz         ( FizzBuzz.hs, interpreted )
Ok, one module loaded.
λ naiveFizzBuzz 3 1 ""
"1 2 fizz "
```

When you need to understand what's happening in a particular Haskell function, or even an entire program, one incredibly useful feature of Haskell is *referential transparency*. This is a fancy sounding term, but it basically means since everything in a Haskell program is a pure value, we can always replace a variable with its value, and any function call with the value that it returns, and the program shouldn't behave any differently. Let's take advantage of this and replace the variables we're using to hold our state with their actual values in our function. This will represent the very first iteration of our loop:

```
naiveFizzBuzz 3 1 "" =
  if 1 > 3
  then ""
  else
    let nextFizzBuzzString = "" <> fizzBuzzFor 1 <> " "
        nextNumber = 1 + 1
    in naiveFizzBuzz 3 nextNumber nextFizzBuzzString
```

Now that we've replaced the inputs with their values, let's do some simplification. First, we can remove our if expression since we know that 1 > 3 will never be true. While we're at it, we can replace our call to fizzBuzzFor 1 with the actual value, and combine all of the string fragments. We can also simplify the addition that we're using to calculate nextNumber. When we do all that, we'll end up with:

```
naiveFizzBuzz 3 1 "" =
  let nextFizzBuzzString = "1 "
      nextNumber = 2
  in naiveFizzBuzz 3 nextNumber nextFizzBuzzString
```

Finally, let's make one more set of substitutions, and replace nextNumber and nextFizzBuzzString with their values:

```
naiveFizzBuzz 3 1 "" =
  naiveFizzBuzz 3 2 "1 "
```

Now that we've simplified out all of the intermediate steps, we can see that when we call naiveFizzBuzz with one state, it simply calls *itself* with the next state. This is analogous to how our procedural loop runs with a new state each time it evaluates the loop body.

Recursion can be tricky to follow, so let's take advantage of referential transparency and expand our call again. We can replace the call to naiveFizzBuzz with its definition, just like we replaced variables with their values:

```
naiveFizzBuzz 3 1 "" =
  if 2 > 3
  then "1 "
  else
    let nextFizzBuzzString = "1 " <> fizzBuzzFor 2 <> " "
        nextNumber = 2 + 1
    in naiveFizzBuzz 3 nextNumber nextFizzBuzzString
```

Again, let's simplify things by removing our if expression and simplifying our nextFizzBuzzString and nextNumber expressions:

```
naiveFizzBuzz 3 1 "" =
  let nextFizzBuzzString = "1 2 "
      nextNumber = 3
  in naiveFizzBuzz 3 nextNumber nextFizzBuzzString
```

After simplifying our expressions, we're again left with a recursive call, but this time our state is one step closer to our final goal. Expanding naiveFizzBuzz and simplifying once more, we'll have:

```
naiveFizzBuzz 3 1 "" =
  if 3 > 3
  then "1 2 "
  else
    let nextFizzBuzzString = "1 2 fizz "
        nextNumber = 4
    in naiveFizzBuzz 3 nextNumber nextFizzBuzzString
```

Again we can remove our conditional, since 3 > 3 will always be false, and replace our variables with their values in our call to naiveFizzBuzz to get a simple recursive call:

```
naiveFizzBuzz 3 1 "" =
  naiveFizzBuzz 3 4 "1 2 fizz "
```

This last call will be a little different. When we expand it this time the first branch in our if expression will be True:

```
naiveFizzBuzz 3 1 "" =
  if 4 > 3
  then "1 2 fizz "
  else
    let nextFizzBuzzString = "1 2 fizz " <> fizzBuzzFor 4 <> " "
        nextNumber = 4 + 1
    in naiveFizzBuzz 3 nextNumber nextFizzBuzzString
```

When we simplify this time, we'll drop the second part of our if expression, and we're left with:

```
naiveFizzBuzz 3 1 "" = "1 2 fizz "
```

We never evaluate the second branch of our conditional, so we do not make another recursive call. The branch we did evaluate simply returns the input string that we've been accumulating. When we're writing recursive functions, we call the condition that causes the recursion to end the *base case*.

If you haven't spent much time with recursion, it is worth reading this section a few times. Internalizing how to think about problems recursively can take a little bit of time and is often a matter of looking at many examples, so if you are still finding it hard to fully understand this example you can continue reading and you'll have several more opportunities to work through similar problems over the next few chapters. The important thing to note here is that while we never introduced any mutable state, by using recursion we were able to implement the same kind of logic, and solve the same kinds of problems that you might use `for` and `while` loops for in a procedural language.

Summary

In this chapter, you learned the basic syntax of Haskell and learned how to create new variables and functions. As you work through the rest of this book you'll continue to build on the fundamentals that you've learned. Feel free to refer back to this chapter if you find yourself facing some syntax that you don't remember or recognize.

You also learned several built-in functions provided by Prelude. In the next chapter, you'll learn about Haskell's type system and what a function does based on its type signature.

Exercises

Now that you've learned a bit about the basics of Haskell's syntax and how to write some applications, try working through these exercises. You should be able to complete all of the following exercises using the material from this chapter, but if you find yourself stuck on an exercise, try reading ahead to the next chapter and coming back to the exercise after you've gotten a bit more practice thinking about how to implement programs in Haskell.

Factorials

The factorial function is a simple function that you can define recursively. You can compute the factorial of a number, `n`, by multiplying all of the numbers up to `n`:

```
factorial 5 = 5 * 4 * 3 * 2 * 1 = 120
```

Try implementing your own `factorial` function. You can test your implementation in `ghci` and compare its output to the example:

```
λ factorial 1
1
λ factorial 3
6
```

```
λ factorial 5
120
λ factorial 10
3628800
λ factorial 25
15511210043330985984000000
```

The Fibonacci Sequence

The Fibonacci sequence is a sequence of numbers that can be defined recursively. The first 10 numbers of the Fibonacci sequences are: 0,1,1,2,3,5,8,13,21,34. You can calculate any given Fibonacci number, n, by adding up the two previous Fibonacci numbers.

Write a function that will compute the nth Fibonacci number for any given number, n. You can test your implementation in ghci and compare it to the example:

```
λ fibonacci 0
0
λ fibonacci 1
1
λ fibonacci 5
5
λ fibonacci 10
55
λ fibonacci 25
75025
```

Manual Currying

You've learned how Haskell functions work by taking a single argument. One way to write a function that takes multiple arguments is to pass in a tuple of arguments. For example, consider this addition function:

```
uncurriedAddition nums =
  let
    a = fst nums
    b = snd nums
  in a + b
```

Haskell's standard library includes two functions, curry and uncurry, that make it easy for you to convert between functions that take two arguments and functions that take a tuple. The curry function transforms a function like our uncurriedAddition function and turns it into one that takes two separate arguments:

```
λ addition = curry uncurriedAddition
λ addOne = addition 1
λ addTwo = addition 2
λ addOne 1
2
λ addOne 2
3
λ addOne 3
4
λ addTwo 1
3
λ addTwo 2
4
λ addTwo 3
5
```

Similarly, the uncurry function takes a regular function with two arguments and converts it into a function that accepts a tuple. For example, using uncurry we could have rewritten uncurredAddition like this:

```
uncurriedAddition = uncurry (+)
```

Using what you've learned in this chapter, try implementing your own version of curry and uncurry.

Since the standard library already has functions named curry and uncurry, you should select different names for your implementations. After you've written your versions, compare the behavior to the standard library implementations to ensure that your versions behave the same way.

CHAPTER 2

Working with Lists

Linked lists are a first class data structure that you will use frequently throughout this book and as you are writing programs in Haskell. In the last chapter, you were introduced to the basics of Haskell's syntax and learned how to create some simple lists. In this chapter, you'll learn more about how to work with lists using *higher-order functions* like map and foldr, how to write recursive functions over lists effectively using *pattern matching*, and finally, you'll learn about how to deal with streaming data, generators, and infinitely long lists by exploiting Haskell's laziness.

Writing Code Using Lists

As you saw in the last chapter, lists of values are enclosed in square brackets, and separated by commas. We can make lists of any type we want, but a list can only hold a single type. Here are some examples of different types of lists. Try creating them in ghci:

```
λ listOfNums = [1, 2, 3]
λ listOfFloats = [1.1, 2.2, 3.3]
λ listOfStrings = ["hello", "world"]
```

There's also a special type of list that you've already used extensively: strings! In Haskell, regular strings are simply lists of characters. When you create a string using double quotes, it's really just a nice way of writing a list of individual characters. We can see this for ourselves in ghci:

```
λ ['h','e','l','l','o'] == "hello"
True
```

You'll rarely, if ever, write strings using the normal list syntax. However, you will frequently use other list functions when working with strings. This also means that some of the functions you've already used, like the (<>) operator, are actually more general than you might have realized. For example, we can combine lists of other values just as well as strings:

```
λ [1,2,3] <> [4,5,6]
[1,2,3,4,5,6]
```

```
λ ['h', 'e'] <> "llo"
"hello"
```

```
λ [[1,2,3],[4,5,6]] <> [[7,8,9]]
[[1,2,3],[4,5,6],[7,8,9]]
```

You can get the nth element of a list using the (!!) operator. List indices start at 0:

```
λ words = ["foo", "bar", "baz", "fizz", "buzz"]
words !! 0
"foo"
λ words !! 4
"buzz"
```

You need to be careful to not accidentally try to take an index that's larger than the length of a list:

```
λ words !! 5
"*** Exception: Prelude.!!: index too large
```

We're not limited to just single values; you can also create lists of lists:

```
λ nums = [[1,3,5],[2,4],[0]]
λ strings = [["hello", "good morning"], ["so long", "farewell"]]
```

We can create empty lists with just an opening and closing bracket, like this: [].

A list can only hold a single type of value. Because of this, you can't have a list with lists of different types. This would be an error, for example:

```
λ badList = [[1,2,3],["one","two","three"]]
```

Lists, like all other Haskell values, are immutable. Although you can't change the value of a list, you can efficiently construct lists by prepending a new element to the start of an existing list. The process of adding a new element to the beginning of a list is called "cons-ing," and the operator we use to add an element to the front of a list, (:), is generally pronounced "cons" as in "construct." This style of prepending an element to the beginning of a list is so ubiquitous that when someone says that they are "adding an element to a list" you should assume they are prepending it unless they say otherwise.

Let's look at a couple of examples of constructing lists using (:). Try typing out these examples yourself to see what the generated lists look like, and to get more used to creating lists.

```
λ 1 : [2,3]
λ 1 : 2 : [3]
λ 1 : 2 : 3 : []
λ 'h' : "ello"
λ 'h' : 'e' : ['l','l','o']
λ [1,2,3] : []
λ [1] : [2] : [3] : []
```

Although you've seen that you can append elements to a list with (<>), it's far more common in Haskell to build our lists by prepending elements with (:). In fact, prepending elements is so common that it's not unusual to see functions where an entire list is built backwards only to be reversed at the end before being returned. The reason for this is that in an immutable language, prepending an element to a list is much more efficient than appending an element to the end.

Later, on page 89, you'll learn how to create list-like data structures yourself, which will help you better understand the details of why prepending is more efficient than appending to lists.

However you approach creating a list, in the end it comes down to putting one element in front of another. When you add an element to the front of a list, we call the part that you are adding the *head* of the list. In fact, a common alternative phrase *cons-ing* is to *push an element onto the head of a list*. The list that you are adding the element onto becomes the *tail*.

```
head : tail
```

The tail of a list is itself either any empty list, or a list with its own head and tail, so you can also look at a list as a series of heads preceding a final empty list:

```
head : tail = head : (head : (head : ... : []))
```

Head and tail aren't just the terms we use to talk about parts of a list. The head and tail functions let you deconstruct a list and get the first element and the rest of the elements back out of a list you've constructed. Let's look at some examples of using head and tail so you can get a feel for how they work:

```
λ head [1,2,3]
1
λ tail [1,2,3]
[2,3]
λ head (tail [1,2,3])
2
λ tail (tail [1,2,3])
[3]
λ tail [1]
[]
```

The head and tail functions are quite useful when you need to get at different parts of a list that you've built, but some caution is necessary with these functions. Both head and tail are *partial functions*. A *partial function* is a function that doesn't work for all of its possible inputs, and might raise a runtime exception or cause the program to crash. In the case of head and tail, these functions will cause a runtime exception if you use them on an empty list:

```
λ head []
*** Exception: Prelude.head: empty list
λ tail []
*** Exception: Prelude.tail: empty list
```

You'll learn another way to get the head and tail of a list on page 66 that doesn't risk raising these exceptions, and later in this book you'll learn how to handle runtime exceptions. In the meantime, take care to make sure you check first to see if a list is empty before using these functions. You can check for an empty list with equality:

```
listIsEmpty list =
  if list == []
  then putStrLn "this list is empty"
  else putStrLn ("the first element of this list is: " <> show (head list))
```

Alternatively, you can use the null function, which will return True if a list is empty, and False otherwise:

```
listIsEmpty' list =
  if null list
  then putStrLn "this list is empty"
  else putStrLn ("the first element of this list is: " <> show (head list))
```

Creating Lists Recursively

A common pattern in Haskell is to create lists by pushing a new value onto the head of a list that is created with a recursive function call. In the last chapter, you worked through a few examples of recursion and built some small recursive functions, but it's worthwhile to spend a little bit of extra time diving into recursive list construction. As you'll see later on in this chapter, there are some subtleties to the way that we construct lists recursively in Haskell that can substantially change the way your program runs.

When you're creating a list recursively in this way, your base case will be a list, often the empty list [], and you'll add elements at each step of the recursion. If you haven't used recursion in a while, remember that the *base case* is the *end of the recursion*. It's how you know that you're done, since the base case doesn't make a recursive call. In most cases, it's easiest to write recursive functions by figuring out the base case first. Let's look at a simple example of a function that creates a countdown from a starting number using this technique:

```
countdown n =
  if n <= 0 then []
  else n : countdown (n - 1)
```

Load your module in ghci and try running it with a few different numbers to get a feel for it:

```
λ countdown 10
[10,9,8,7,6,5,4,3,2,1]
```

In this example, you start with a base case where n is less than or equal to 0. In the base case, you return an empty list. If n is greater than zero, you construct a list by prepending the current element to a recursive call that decrements the variable. This is a bit different than some of the recursive examples that you saw in the last chapter, because you're building up a value rather than reducing one.

To improve your intuition, let's step through a small example by hand. We'll start by calling countdown 3. In the first step we prepend 3 to countdown (3 - 1):

```
countdown 3 =
  if 3 <= 0 -- false
  then []
  else 3 : countdown (3 - 1)
```

If you keep expanding the calls to countdown you'd end up with something like this, which isn't quite valid Haskell, but gives you a sense of what's happening:

```
countdown 3 =
  if 3 <= 0 -- false
  then []
  else 3 : (
    if 2 <= 0 -- false
    then []
    else 2 : (
      if 1 <= 0 -- false
      then []
      else 1 : (
        if 0 <= 0 -- true
        then []
        else undefined
        )))
```

Resolving all of the branches you'd end up with:

```
countdown 3 = 3 : 2 : 1 : []
```

This style of recursively constructed list can build very powerful functions. Let's look at another example using recursively constructed lists to find the prime factors of an integer. Take some time to study this function and work through it the same way that you worked through countdown to better understand how it works.

```
factors num =
  factors' num 2
  where
    factors' num fact
      | num == 1 = []
      | (num `rem` fact) == 0 = fact : factors' (num `div` fact) fact
      | otherwise = factors' num (fact + 1)
```

This recursive function follows a common pattern where our algorithm requires some initial seed value that we don't want to require the user to pass in. To make our code more ergonomic to use, it's common to implement most of the algorithm as a helper function in a let or where binding. The top level function will just call the helper function with the initial seed value.

In the case of factors we're calculating the potential factors of a number starting from 2 and working our way up, so our starting value is 2. The recursive part of our function is handled in our helper function, factors'.

The way our factoring algorithm works is that we start with a number we'd like to factor—in this case we're calling it num—and a potential factor, which we're calling fact. Our base case is when num is 1, which has no other factors, so we can stop trying to find any.

The recursive case of our factoring function has two branches. The first of our recursive cases happens if our candidate factor is indeed an actual factor of our current number. We can figure this out using the rem function, which gives us the remainder after dividing the current number by the candidate factor. If the remainder is 0 then we've found a factor. When we have found an actual factor, we need to do two things. First, we need to add our newly discovered factor to our list of found factors. Second, we need to recursively find the rest of our factors.

The way that we add the current number onto the list of factors might look a little surprising at first:

```
fact : factors' (num `div` fact) fact
```

Remember that factors' will always return a list, whether it's an empty list when we encounter the base case, or a list with some factors in it if we're in a recursive case. Since the return value of factors' is a list, we can add our new factor by prepending it to the front of the list returned by our recursive call.

As for the recursive call, rather than just decrementing our number by one, we can save a lot of time by dividing out the factor we've just found. We don't change the candidate factor in our recursive call, because some numbers might have the same candidate factor multiple times. For example, the factors of four are two and two.

That covers our recursive case when we've found a factor. In our last case, when we haven't found a factor, we increment our candidate factor by one and try again. Eventually this will terminate because even if we have a prime number we'll eventually count all the way up so that our candidate factor equals the number we're trying to factor. In that case, the number will be divisible by itself and we'll add it to our list of factors, and then immediately hit our base case.

Deconstructing Lists

Recursively deconstructing a list is another pattern, like recursively constructing one, that you'll use frequently when writing Haskell applications. In a typical application you'll have a base case where a list is empty and a recursive case that does some computation with the head of the list and passes an accumulated value to itself recursively. Let's look at a concrete example by building a function that checks to see if the parentheses in a string are balanced (that there are the same number of opening and closing parentheses). Keep a copy of this function open, you'll be refactoring it shortly:

```
isBalanced s =
  0 == isBalanced' 0 s
  where
    isBalanced' count s
      | null s = count
      | head s == '(' = isBalanced' (count + 1) (tail s)
      | head s == ')' = isBalanced' (count - 1) (tail s)
      | otherwise = isBalanced' count (tail s)
```

Just like the factors example, we start this function off by calling a helper function that takes an accumulator value; in this case, isBalanced' takes a counter. The first thing that isBalanced' does is use the null function, which returns True if a list is empty. In the case of an empty list we're done and can return our accumulator. In the next two cases, we are destructuring the list to look at the head element; if it's an opening or closing parenthesis we increment or decrement our count respectively. In all of the cases, we recursively call the function with the tail of the input string.

Traversing a list and accumulating a result, like we've done here, is a common enough problem that you might want to create an implementation of it that you can re-use. Let's write a generic reduce function that provides the structure of recursion and then use it to re-implement isBalanced:

```
reduce func carryValue lst =
  if null lst then carryValue
  else
    let intermediateValue = func carryValue (head lst)
    in reduce func intermediateValue (tail lst)
```

You'll notice when you look at this code that it looks almost like a minimum viable example of what a recursive function should look like. In the Haskell community, when we're talking about the essential behavior of a function or a datatype, without any extraneous business logic or implementation details, we sometimes refer to that as the *shape* of the function or data structure. In this case, we might say that this function has the shape of any general recursive function over a list. Try using reduce to re-implement your isBalanced, then compare your implementations to the example:

```
isBalanced str = 0 == reduce checkBalance 0 str
  where
  checkBalance count letter
    | letter == '(' = count + 1
    | letter == ')' = count - 1
    | otherwise = count
```

Our new isBalanced function is a little shorter and much easier to read thanks to the fact that we're able to focus on the logic at each step of recursion without having to manage the recursion itself. Factoring out recursion into its own function is a small payoff the first time we use it, but as you use the pattern repeatedly over a larger codebase you can start to benefit from the reduced effort of understanding recursion each and every time, and instead you can start thinking in terms of reduction.

The reduce function that you implemented is actually already available in Prelude, where it's called foldl. The general term in Haskell for these functions that accumulate a value while recursing through a structure are called *folds*. Let's look at another common fold function that's part of the Prelude: foldr.

The foldl and foldr function names stand for "fold left" and "fold right" respectively. You can intuitively think of foldl as folding from left to right, and foldr as folding from right to left.

To understand this better, let's look at an example of how to build foldr, alongside the previous reduce (now renamed foldl) function. Both the foldr and foldl functions that we're building are part of the standard set of functions that are in scope when you start a new Haskell program. This will confuse the compiler, which will want to know which instance of the function you're intending to use. Later, on page 155, you'll learn more about how to manage library functions, but for now you can hide the default versions of these functions to prevent a collision:

```
module FoldExamples where
import Prelude hiding (foldl, foldr)
```

With the two functions no longer imported from the standard library, you are free to create your own implementation as you work through the rest of this chapter.

```
foldl func carryValue lst =
  if null lst
  then carryValue
  else foldl func (func carryValue (head lst)) (tail lst)

foldr func carryValue lst =
  if null lst
  then carryValue
  else func (head lst) $ foldr func carryValue (tail lst)
```

Comparing the implementations of foldr with your earlier reduce (aka foldl) implementation, you'll notice that they are broadly similar. They both return the accumulator on an empty list, and otherwise perform some destructuring and recursion. In the case of foldl we call the function that's been passed in with the current carry value and the head of the list, and then pass that into a recursive call. In foldr, instead of passing our carry value directly into the function, we pass the result of our recursive call. It's also worth noting that the order of arguments in the function that's passed in reverses between the two functions.

For a more hands-on picture of what's happening, let's pretend to be the compiler and use some pseudo-Haskell to explore exactly what happens when we make a call to foldl. We'll start with foldl (+) 0 [1,2,3]:

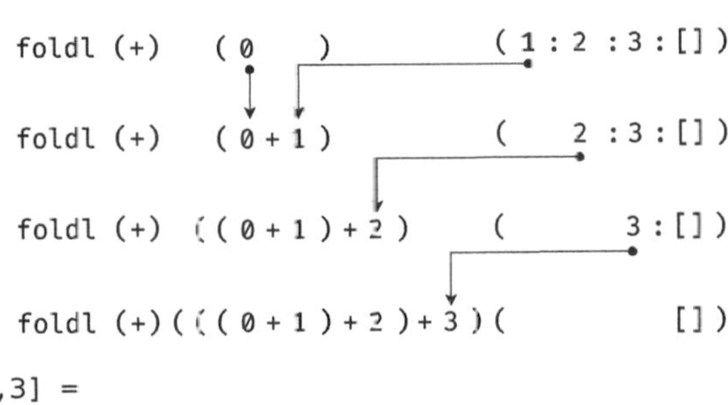


```
foldl (+) 0 [1,2,3] =
  if null [1,2,3] then 0
  else foldl (+) (0 + 1) [2,3]
```

```
foldl (+) (0 + 1) [2,3] =
  if null [2,3] then (0 + 1)
  else foldl (+) ((0 + 1) + 2) [3]

foldl (+) ((0 + 1) + 2) [3] =
  if null [3] then ((0 + 1) + 2)
  else foldl (+) (((0 + 1) + 2) +3) []

foldl (+) (((0 + 1) + 2) + 3) []
  if null [] then (((0 + 1) + 2) + 3)
  else undefined -- we'll never get here

(((0 + 1) + 2) + 3) = 0 + 1 + 2 + 3 = 6
```

Looking at the way parentheses grow when you expand the function calls, you can see that we end up working our way left-to-right through the list. You might recognize the way the operations have been grouped from the previous chapter when you learned about operators and fixity on page 21. The foldl function is a *left-associative* fold.

If foldl is left associative then you might guess based on the name that foldr is a *right-associative* fold. Let's step through an example of foldlr (+) 0 [1,2,3] to see if the guess is right:

```
              foldr (+) 0 (1 : 2 : 3 : [] )
            1 + foldr (+) 0 (    2 : 3 : [] )
        1 + 2 + foldr (+) 0 (        3 : [] )
    1 + 2 + 3 + foldr (+) 0 (            [] )
1 + 2 + 3 + 0
```

```
foldr (+) 0 [1,2,3] =
  if null [1,2,3] then 0
  else (1 + (foldr (+) 0 [2,3]))

foldr (+) 0 [2,3] =
  if null [1,2,3] then 0
  else (1 + (2 + (foldr (+) 0 [3])))

foldr (+) 0 [3] =
  if null [1,2,3] then 0
  else (1 + (2 + (3 + (foldr (+) 0 []))))

foldr (+) 0 [] =
  if null [1,2,3] then 0
  else undefined -- false

(1 + (2 + (3 + 0))) = 6
```

As you can see, based on the way that the operations have been grouped, foldr is indeed right associative.

Use Your Folds

As you are exploring the ideas in this chapter, you may have more success using your own definitions of foldl and foldr. The versions provided by default are more flexible, and they can work with data structures other than lists. This sometimes causes errors when the compiler doesn't know what kind of data structure it should be using. This is most likely to occur if you are writing code in a pointfree style. If you run into this problem, first try refactoring your code so that it isn't pointfree. If that doesn't help, you can use the implementations of foldl and foldr you just defined, or revisit this chapter after you've learned about type.

Let's look at another example that can help to highlight the difference in associativity between the two folds. You might recall in the last chapter we looked at left and right associativity of division on page 24 to better understand associativity of operators. Let's return to that example again, this time to explore the associativity of folds.

In that example, we learned that the normal division operator, (/) is left associative. We created a right-associative infix function, divide, and used that to see how left and right-associative operations gave us different results when doing repeated division:

```
λ divide = (/); infixr 9 `divide`

λ 1 / 2 / 3 / 4 / 5
8.333333333333333e-3

λ 1 `divide` 2 `divide` 3 `divide` 4 `divide` 5
1.875
```

When we're using folds, the operation that we're passing in is treated as a normal function, and its associativity doesn't impact the final result we get back. The associativity of the operation comes from the fold itself, rather than the function we pass in. You can see, for example, that we get the same result back from a call to foldl regardless of which division function we pass in:

```
λ foldl (/) 1 [1,2,3,4,5]
8.333333333333333e-3

λ foldl divide 1 [1,2,3,4,5]
8.333333333333333e-3
```

The same thing applies to foldr as well:

```
λ foldr (/) 1 [1,2,3,4,5]
1.875
```

```
λ foldr divide 1 [1,2,3,4,5]
1.875
```

Related to the associativity of the folds, another important difference between them is when in the call chain the initial element gets passed in. You can see this in practice with another small variation of our fold example. Let's look at another right fold using division, and compare it to the result we get back repeatedly applying the divide function by hand:

```
λ foldr divide 1 [2,3,4,5]
0.5333333333333333
```

```
λ 1 `divide` 2 `divide` 3 `divide` 4 `divide` 5
1.875
```

When you first see the difference between these two results, you might be somewhat surprised. If foldr is right associative and it's applying the divide repeatedly, we would expect to get the same value that we get when we call divide ourselves—but we seem to be getting something quite different!

If you look back at your implementation of foldr you might notice the problem: when we're dividing manually in this example, we have put our initial value at the beginning of the list of division, but in the implementation of foldr we apply the initial value last. Let's try to do manual division again, taking this into account:

```
λ 2 `divide` 3 `divide` 4 `divide` 5 `divide` 1
0.5333333333333333
```

With our starting value moved to the *right* place, we get the same result using manual repeated division as we do from the call to foldr. Now let's look at foldl. Since it's left associative, we'll compare it to (/):

```
λ foldl (/) 1 [2,3,4,5]
8.333333333333333e-3
```

```
λ 1 / 2 / 3 / 4 / 5
8.333333333333333e-3
```

This time we've put the initial value on the left, and again gotten the same result from manually doing repeated division.

It can be hard to keep the differences between foldl and foldr in your head when you are writing code, so it helps to remember these points:

1. The l in foldl stands for left associative.
2. In a left fold, the initial value is applied first, at the left-hand side of the unrolled expression.
3. In a left fold the accumulator value is the first (left) argument of the function you pass in.
4. The r in foldr stands for right associative.
5. In a right fold, the initial value is applied last, at the right-hand side of an unrolled expression.
6. In a right fold, the accumulator is the second (right) argument of the function that you pass in.

In the next chapter on page 89, you'll learn about how to look up the type of a function. Looking at the types is another easy way to remind yourself of the difference between the two folds.

Transforming List Elements

Folds are useful and extremely common in Haskell code, but sometimes instead of wanting to combine the elements of a list, you find yourself wanting to transform the elements of a list individually. Consider, for example, that you have a list of numbers and you want to double each of them. You could write this using manual recursion:

```
doubleElems :: [Int] -> [Int]
doubleElems nums =
  if null nums
  then []
  else
    let
      hd = head nums
      tl = tail nums
    in (2 * hd) : doubleElems tl
```

Like folding, applying a function to every element in a list is something quite common and so we may want to factor out the common code to apply a function to elements of a list from the specific logic of our function, in this case doubling the value of an element. In Haskell, we call applying a function to all the elements in a list "mapping," and the function we use is called map. The map function takes a function and applies it to every element in a list:

```
λ let incr x = x + 1 in map incr [1..3]
[2,3,4]
λ map (+2) [1..3]
[3,4,5]
```

```
λ map show [1..3]
["1","2","3"]
```

You can even use map to apply a value to a list of functions:

```
λ map ($ 10) [(+ 1), (* 3), (`div` 5)]
[11,30,2]
```

To get a better feel for how mapping works, we can also implement our own map function. We'll start by refactoring doubleElems to use a fold rather than manual recursion:

```
doubleElems = foldr doubleElem []
  where
    doubleElem num lst = (2 * num) : lst
```

In this refactored version of our code, we've created a helper function called doubleElem that multiplies each element by 2. Let's take another refactoring step and, instead of passing in a number to multiply by, we'll pass in a function that will do the multiplication:

```
doubleElems' elems = foldr (applyElem (*2)) [] elems
  where
    applyElem f elem accumulator = f elem : accumulator
```

In this version, our new applyElem function is quite general, but it's still only working on a single step of the fold. Let's take another refactoring step by making the foldr part of our new map' function:

```
map' f = foldr (applyElem f) []
  where
    applyElem f elem accumulator = (f elem) : accumulator

doubleWithMap elems = map' (*2) elems
```

We can take this one step further and manually expand out our call to foldr, giving us a more readable map function:

```
map'' f xs =
  if null xs then []
  else f (head xs) : map'' f (tail xs)
```

Filtering List Elements

Folding and mapping will both allow you to work with all the elements in a list, but it's common to find yourself only interested in a subset of items in the list. There are several functions in base that you'll be introduced to throughout this book that will help you select specific items out of a list. For now, we'll focus on one of the most general and useful of these, the filter function.

The filter function allows you to select elements from a list. To use it, provide a function that returns True for values that you want to keep, and False for values you want to discard. For example, if you wanted to find the sum of the first ten odd numbers you could use filter with the odd function, which returns True if a number is odd:

```
λ (foldr (+) 0 . filter odd) [0..10]
25
```

It's common to combine functions like map, fold, and filter into a data processing pipeline. Combining these building blocks can make it easy to write complex data transformations. Let's create an example by building a function, foodBudget, to help plan the food budget for a party.

We'll start by defining a function, checkGuestList, which will let us provide a list of people who will be attending the party. We'll make use of the built-in function elem that tells us if a value is an element of a list:

```
checkGuestList guestList name =
  name `elem` guestList
```

Next, we'll create a list of some friends and how much their favorite meal costs:

```
foodCosts =
  [("Ren", 10.00)
  ,("George", 4.00)
  ,("Porter", 27.50)]
```

Finally, we'll add a function to combine our guest list and our food cost list to find the budget we need for our party:

```
partyBudget isAttending =
  foldr (+) 0 . map snd . filter (isAttending . fst)
```

The partyBudget function might be a bit hard to read when you first look at it, since we are composing several different functions, so let's step through it for a simple dinner party and see what's happening:

```
λ partyBudget (checkGuestList ["Ren","Porter"]) foodCosts
37.5
```

We're passing in a guest list that contains two of our friends, *Ren* and *Porter*, along with a list that has food prices for all of our friends. If we expand all of our helper functions we'd end up with this:

```
partyBudget' =
  foldr (+) 0
  . map snd
  . filter (\name -> fst name `elem` ["Ren","Porter"])
  $ [("Ren", 10.00) ,("George", 4.00) ,("Porter", 27.50)]
```

When we're composing functions like this, we usually want to read right-to-left. In this case, we'll start with our call to filter. We'll call our filter function for each item in the list, keeping the items where it returned true:

```
λ fst ("Ren", 10.00) `elem` ["Ren","Porter"]
True
λ fst ("George", 4.00) `elem` ["Ren","Porter"]
False
λ fst ("Porter", 27.50) `elem` ["Ren","Porter"]
True
```

After filtering we're left with a smaller filtered list:

```
λ :{
> filteredNames =
>   filter (\name -> (fst name) `elem` ["Ren","Porter"]) $
>   [ ("Ren",10.00)
>   , ("George",4.00)
>   , ("Porter",27.50)]
> :}
λ filteredNames
[("Ren",10.0),("Porter",27.5)]
```

Next, we pass our new filteredNames list into our transform function, map snd. This will transform our tuples by looking at the second element:

```
map snd [("Ren",10.00),("Porter",27.5)]
  = [snd ("Ren",10.00), snd ("Porter",27.5)]
  = [10.00,27.5]
```

All that's left to do is add up the prices of our two guests' favorite meals:

```
λ foldr (+) 0 [10.0,27.5]
37.5
```

Pure functional data processing functions made by composing maps, filters, and folds can be extremely effective ways of quickly writing expressive and effective Haskell code. As you spend more time with the language and become more comfortable with function composition and Haskell idioms you will be able to quickly read and write functions like this without the need to manually break down each step of the processing pipeline.

Building Lists with Comprehensions

It's also possible to represent combinations of map and filter using *List Comprehensions*. List comprehensions provide an alternate syntax for building lists with maps and filters, and can sometimes make otherwise complex code much easier to read.

The basic syntax for a list comprehension looks like this:

```
double = [2 * number | number <- [0..10]]
```

A list comprehension is an expression inside of square brackets, like a list, but it uses a pipe to separate out an expression from some conditionals, like a piece-wise function. In the `double` example, you can see the expression `2 * number` on the left-hand side of the pipe. On the right-hand side of the pipe, we can select items from a list, like you would do with a `map`, and filter items out like you would do with a `filter`. If you wanted to double only odd numbers, for example, you could say:

```
doubleOdds = [2 * number | number <- [0..10], odd number]
```

In this example, you've added a new predicate that will limit the elements that get pulled out of the list.

Functions on one list and with just a single predicate can sometimes look nicer written as list comprehensions, but they are also easy to write in the data pipeline style that you've already seen:

```
doubleOdds = map (\number -> 2 * number) . filter odd $ [0..10]
```

Where list comprehensions start to really shine is when you have several lists that you want to work with, and many different filters. Let's start with an illustrative example by building a function that will take two lists of numbers and will return a list of pairs of elements in the first list that are also in the second list, paired with odd elements of the second list. We'll start by implementing this without using a list comprehension:

```
pairs as bs =
  let as' = filter (`elem` bs) as
      bs' = filter odd bs
      mkPairs a = map (\b -> (a,b)) bs'
  in concat $ map mkPairs as'
```

```
λ pairs [1..10] [2..5]
[(2,3),(2,5),(3,3),(3,5),(4,3),(4,5),(5,3),(5,5)]
```

Now let's look at the list comprehension version and compare it to the original version:

```
pairs as bs =
  [(a,b) | a <- as, b <- bs, a `elem` bs, odd b]
```

The list comprehension version is not only much shorter, but it also gives us much more declarative-looking code. Instead of having to use filters to create intermediate lists that we then map over, the list comprehension version lets us more clearly state what we want: "pairs of a and b, where a comes from the list of as, and b comes from the list of bs, where a is an element of bs, and b is odd".

To better see how we might make use of list comprehensions in practice, let's go back to our dinner party budgeting function and imagine we wanted to expand it to account for the fact that most guests may want to eat more than one dish. Instead of including a price for the guest's favorite meal, we'll instead get a list of a guest and the food they've requested. We'll also take two new functions. First, willEat will take a guest's name and a food, and will return true if the guest might want to eat that food. Second, foodCost will take a food and return its price.

To calculate our budget now, we want to go through the list of all the guests that are attending and, for each food that we'll be serving, add the cost for that food if the guest might eat it. Building this as a simple pipeline with map, filter, and fold could get quite complicated, but as you've just learned we can use list comprehensions to help simplify these types of functions.

Using a list comprehension we can tersely express our new party budget calculator:

```
partyBudget isAttending willEat foodCost guests =
  foldl (+) 0 $
  [ foodCost food
  | guest <- map fst guests
  , food  <- map snd guests
  , willEat guest food
  , isAttending guest
  ]
```

Take particular note of the fact that, unlike previous examples of list comprehensions, in this example, we're extracting a named element, guest, out of a list but not using it in the final list. Using list comprehensions can be a great way of expressing list processing code where you need to filter elements in one list based on a subset of elements from another list.

Using list comprehensions can be a handy way of expressing more complicated pipelines succinctly and without having to create many intermediate values. When you are writing list processing code it's useful to experiment with list comprehensions to see if they can help you simplify your code.

Folds and comprehensions make it easy for you to combine elements of a single list, but what should you do if you want to combine two different lists? Consider that you have a list of numbers and a list of roman numeral representations of the numbers. If you wanted to associate the number with its roman numeral representation you might first try to use a list comprehension, like the following example:

```
λ [(num,str) | num <- [1,2,3], str <- ["I","II","III"]]
[(1,"I"),(1,"II"),(1,"III")
,(2,"I"),(2,"II"),(2,"III")
,(3,"I"),(3,"II"),(3,"III")]
```

That won't work! List comprehensions are useful when we want all of the permutations of our lists, but we only want to match the first element. You can implement a function yourself to do this. Think about how you might write a function named combineLists that takes two lists and returns a list of tuples, like in this example:

```
λ combineLists [1..5] ["I","II","III","IV","V","VI","VII"]
[(1,"I"),(2,"II"),(3,"III"),(4,"IV"),(5,"V")]
```

One way you could implement a function like that is to use an explicit recursion, like in this example:

```
combineLists as bs =
  let
    a = head as
    b = head bs
    as' = tail as
    bs' = tail bs
  in if null as || null bs
     then []
     else (a,b) : combineLists as' bs'
```

Just like with map and the fold functions, there is already a standard library function that does exactly what combineLists does, and it's named zip. Try using your combineLists function with several contrived examples, and then use zip for the same examples to demonstrate to yourself that they are doing the same thing.

Combining lists into a tuple isn't generally very useful by itself, but zip can be combined with map and foldr to build much more sophisticated applications.

Imagine, for example, that you had two lists of numbers and you wanted to figure out the sum of each pair of elements from two lists. Try copying the next example:

```
pairwiseSum xs ys =
  let sumElems pairs =
        let a = fst pairs
            b = snd pairs
        in a + b
  in map sumElems $ zip xs ys
```

Alternatively, we could use the uncurry function, which makes it easy to apply a function of two elements to a tuple:

```
pairwiseSum xs ys = map (uncurry (+)) $ zip xs ys
```

Run your new function with several examples, like this one:

```
λ pairwiseSum [1..5] [6..10]
[7,9,11,13,15]
```

Destructuring Values with Pattern Matching

In the last section, as you worked with lists, you learned how the shape of a list was reflected in the way you worked with it using functions like (:), head and tail. The idea that the shape of a data structure can be reflected in how we write code to use that data structure is a powerful one, and it turns out to have much more broad-reaching applicability than just lists.

Using *pattern matching* lets you write powerful expressions that match parts of a value based on its shape. You'll learn several ways to use pattern matching in the remainder of this chapter. Let's start by looking at how you can use pattern matching with functions, case statements, and let bindings.

In its simplest form, a pattern lets you replace a variable with a specific value. The pattern will match if the variable is equal to that value. It's easier to understand with an example, so let's use pattern matching to build a program that will give a special greeting to George:

```
customGreeting "George" = "Oh, hey George!"
customGreeting name = "Hello, " <> name
```

Notice that we have two implementations of the customGreeting function. The first one will be used if the name matches "George", and otherwise we'll fall through to our more general function. The matches happen top-to-bottom so if you instead have:

```
customGreeting name = "Hello, " <> name
customGreeting "George" = "Oh, hey George!"
```

Then you'd never get the custom greeting, since you will always hit the general case before matching on the more specific "George" case.

Of course you're not limited to just pattern matching on strings. You can pattern match on most values, like numbers, booleans, even tuples and lists. Let's look at a few more examples:

```
matchNumber 0 = "zero"
matchNumber n = show n

matchList [1,2,3] = "one, two, three"
matchList list = show list

matchTuple ("hello", "world") = "greetings"
matchTuple tuple = show tuple

matchBool True = "yep"
matchBool bool = "this must be false"
```

Although all of these examples follow a general pattern where we match on a special case first, and otherwise fall back to a catch-all case, this isn't the only way that we can use pattern matching. We can match on several different cases. In the following example, we'll create several different patterns as we try to match different parts of a tuple.

```
matchTuple ("hello", "world") = "Hello there, you great big world"
matchTuple ("hello", name) = "Oh, hi there, " <> name
matchTuple (salutation, "George") = "Oh! " <> salutation <> " George!"
matchTuple n = show n
```

Notice that the final pattern in all of these examples is a variable that can match any remaining values that haven't already been matched. If we leave out the final function in the next example, we'll end up with a partial function. As you learned earlier in this chapter, a partial function is one that doesn't handle all of the possible input values it could get, and a *total function* is one that does handle all possible inputs. In this case, our partial function is caused by an incomplete pattern match. In other words, the compiler can't find a pattern that matches the input to our function. Try entering it yourself and running it for several different variations.

```
λ partialFunc 0 = "I only work for zero!"
λ partialFunc 0
"I only work for zero!"
λ partialFunc 1
"*** Exception: <interactive>:75:1-39: Non-exhaustive
patterns in function partialFunc
```

You don't need a wildcard value for a pattern if you've explicitly matched all the possible values a variable could have. For example, if we pattern match on a boolean value, we can provide cases for True and False to create a total function:

```
matchBool True = "True story!"
matchBool False = "Sorry, this is just not True"
```

At the end of this section, you'll learn some ways to ask the compiler to help you catch potential bugs caused by incomplete patterns.

Destructuring Lists

Throughout this chapter you've been learning about how to construct lists, but taking elements out of a list has been somewhat inconvenient. Up until now, if you wanted to write a function that used elements from a list, you would often end up writing the same boilerplate code that would

1. Check to see if the current list is empty (and if so return some base value),
2. Use the head function to get the first element of the list,
3. Use the tail function to get the rest of the list,
4. Possibly do some computation with the head of the list, and
5. Make a recursive call with the tail of the list.

With pattern matching, this becomes much easier. Let's look at an example:

```
addValues [] = 0
addValues (first:rest) = first + (addValues rest)
```

In this example, we're pattern matching over lists in two different ways. In the first case, we pattern match to quickly identify our base case where we have an empty list, and return 0. If we don't have an empty list, we use pattern matching to extract the head and tail of the list, which in this case we're calling first and rest.

You can also use pattern matching outside of the parameters of a function. One useful place to use pattern matching is in let bindings. Imagine that you have a function, fancyNumbers, which given some number, n, gives you back the nth Fibonacci number and the nth prime number:

```
λ fancyNumbers n = (zip fibs primes) !! n
λ fancyNumbers 27
(317811,103)
```

If you wanted to write a function that works with this data, you can use pattern matching on the tuple within a let expression to help make your code a bit easier to read. Let's look at an example:

```
printFancy n =
  let (fib, prime) = fancyNumbers n
      fib' = show fib
      prime' = show prime
  in "The fibonacci number is: " <> fib' <> " and the prime is: " <> prime'
```

In some cases you want to pattern match, but also get the original value that hasn't been deconstructed. You can do that by adding a variable before your pattern followed by an @ symbol. As an example, try copying in the following function that will accept a pair and replace the first or second elements if they match some special case, and otherwise will return the original pair:

```
modifyPair p@(a,b)
  | a == "Hello"  = "this is a salutation"
  | b == "George" = "this is a message for George"
  | otherwise = "I don't know what " <> show p <> " means"

λ modifyPair ("Hello", "George")
"this is a salutation"
λ modifyPair ("What's going on", "George")
"this is a message for George"
λ modifyPair ("this is", "a message")
"I don't know what (\"this is\",\"a message\") means"
```

Matching the entire element along with a pattern is particularly useful when you have a large number of items you are matching out of a complex data structure.

A special pattern that you can use is the wildcard pattern. A wildcard pattern will match any value, like a variable would, but without binding the value to a variable in your function. It's a useful way of saying, "a value should be here, but I don't care about it." One place this is useful is if you want to get specific elements out of a tuple. To use a wildcard pattern, use an underscore instead of a value or variable name. The fst and snd functions in Prelude give you the first and second elements of a two-element tuple. Let's use the wildcard pattern to implement versions of these functions that work for a triple:

```
module Tuples where
import Prelude hiding (fst, snd)

fst (x, _, _)  = x
snd (_, x, _)  = x
thrd (_, _, x) = x

λ map ($ (1,2,3)) [fst, snd, thrd]
[1,2,3]
```

In some cases, you might want to both ignore a particular value, as well as communicate to other developers working in your codebase what that value should be. In those cases, it's common to use a variable name that starts with an underscore prefix:

```
printHead [] = "empty!"
printHead lst@(hd:_tail) =
  "the head of " <> (show lst) <> " is " <> show hd
```

In this version of the function, we are using the name _tail to communicate to any future developer reading the code that the value is the tail of a list, and also that it's not a value we are going to be using.

You've seen that patterns allow you to branch at the function level: by using patterns for your function arguments you can create different implementations of your function for different inputs. Haskell offers another way to do this within a single function, using case statements. A case statement allows you to pattern match on a value inside of your function. You can combine pattern matching with guards to create expressive branching conditionals based on the values in your function.

In the simple case, a case statement looks much like a switch statement in other languages. Let's look at an example program that will tell us some of our friend's favorite foods using a case statement:

```
favoriteFood person =
  case person of
    "Ren"     -> "Tofu"
    "Rebecca" -> "Falafel"
    "George"  -> "Banana"
    name      -> "I Don't Know what " <> name <> " likes!"
```

You can also combine case statements with guards. To illustrate this, let's look at a different example. Copy the next example into a new file so you can try running it in ghci:

```
handleNums l =
  case l of
    [] -> "An empty list"
    [x] | x == 0 -> "a list called: [0]"
        | x == 1 -> "a singular list of [1]"
        | even x -> "a singleton list containing an even number"
        | otherwise -> "the list contains " <> (show x)
    _list -> "the list has more than 1 element"
```

Mixing case statements with guards can sometimes allow you to write terse code when you are dealing with complex business logic, but be careful to not use so many clauses in one place that it makes your code less readable.

Getting Warned About Incomplete Patterns

Before we move on from pattern matching, let's take a moment to look again at the problem of non-exhaustive patterns. Since we first introduced the idea of non-exhaustive patterns earlier in the section, we've been careful to avoid them in all of the examples. It's a good idea to avoid non-exhaustive patterns whenever you can, and it's rare for there to be a situation where you can't avoid them.

There are two situations where you might find yourself tempted to have an incomplete pattern: when you are confident that the patterns you are omitting won't happen, and when you are still actively working on some code and haven't yet had an opportunity to implement the missing code.

When you are confident that your incomplete pattern isn't really incomplete, it can be tempting to leave it in. Once you learn how to create your own types on page 117 and work with modules on page 155 you'll be better equipped to manage this situation. For now, an alternative is to use the error function. As you might guess, error causes your program to fail with a runtime error. Let's revisit our original partial function example and look at how we can use error:

```
module Main where

partialFunction 0 = "I only work for 0"
partialFunction impossibleValue = error $
  "I only work with 0 but I was called with " <> show impossibleValue

main = putStrLn $ partialFunction 3
```

If you compile and run this program, you'll see that it still crashes, but the output looks a bit different:

```
user@host$ ghc Main.hs
user@host$ ./Main
Main: I only work with 0 but I was called with 3
CallStack (from HasCallStack):
  error, called at Main.hs:5:3 in main:Main
```

In this example, we haven't prevented our program from crashing, but we have at least been explicit about the fact that we expect to crash, and we've gotten some useful information. The fact that your error can be explicit and carry an error message often makes error a better choice than an incomplete pattern for impossible cases.

Being explicit about intentionally incomplete patterns is one thing, but often times we have incomplete pattern matches on accident. This can be because we're actively working on the code and haven't written a match yet, or we overlooked a potential value. It's even possible that your code was complete when you originally wrote it, but someone else made some changes and introduced some additional values, and now, once-working code has some incomplete patterns lurking around waiting to cause trouble. These sorts of errors can lurk in code for a long time until they finally manifest themselves as a runtime error. Thankfully, the compiler can help us track them down before we ship errors to our users. All we need to do is enable the warnings.

In most projects, you'll enable or disable warnings at the project level. You'll learn how to customize the options that are used when building an entire project when you learn about cabal projects on page 155. For the kind of small projects you'll be building over the next few chapters, you can also enable and disable warnings directly from the command line when you build your programs with ghc or load them into ghci. To start, let's recreate the incomplete pattern we had earlier by removing the explicit error case from our partial function:

```
module Main where

partialFunction 0 = "I only work for 0"
main = putStrLn $ partialFunction 0
```

If we compile this without passing in any additional flags, we won't get a warning:

```
user@host$ ghc Main.hs
[1 of 1] Compiling Main             ( Main.hs, Main.o )
Linking Main ...
user@host$ ./Main
I only work for 0
```

One way that we can get warnings about non-exhaustive patterns is to ask for them explicitly by passing in the -Wincomplete-patterns option to ghc before the name of the file we're compiling:

```
user@host$ ghc -Wincomplete-patterns Main.hs
[1 of 1] Compiling Main             ( Main.hs, Main.o )

Main.hs:3:1: warning: [-Wincomplete-patterns]
    Pattern match(es) are non-exhaustive
    In an equation for ‘partialFunction’:
        Patterns not matched: p where p is not one of {0}
  |
3 | partialFunction 0 = "I only work for 0"
  | ^^^^^^^^^^^^^^^^^^^^^^^^^^^^^^^^^^^^^^^
Linking Main ...
user@host$ ./Main
I only work for 0
```

When we turn this flag on, the compiler helpfully points out exactly where we've used a non-exhaustive pattern. Warnings don't stop the program from compiling though, and you'll notice if you follow along with this example that you still end up with an application that you can run.

Next, let's try running our program in ghci. We'll start by launching ghci normally without any arguments:

```
user@host$ ghci
```

When we load our file, we don't get any warnings:

```
λ :load Main.hs
[1 of 1] Compiling Main             ( Main.hs, interpreted )
Ok, one module loaded.
```

One option that we have is to pass -Wincomplete-patterns to ghci on the command line when we start it:

```
ghci -Wincomplete-patterns
```

Now when we load our file in ghci we'll see the same warnings that we saw when we compiled the program:

```
λ :load Main.hs
[1 of 1] Compiling Main             ( Main.hs, interpreted )

Main.hs:3:1: warning: [-Wincomplete-patterns]
    Pattern match(es) are non-exhaustive
    In an equation for 'partialFunction':
        Patterns not matched: p where p is not one of {0}
  |
3 | partialFunction 0 = "I only work for 0"
  | ^^^^^^^^^^^^^^^^^^^^^^^^^^^^^^^^^^^^^^^
Ok, one module loaded.
```

If you like to keep a long-running ghci session going, you might want to toggle warnings on and off as you are developing without having to restart the program. You can do that with the :set command. For example, we can temporarily disable the warning by passing in -Wno-incomplete-patterns. If we do that, and reload the file, you'll see we stop getting warnings about the incomplete pattern:

```
λ :set -Wno-incomplete-patterns
λ :load Main.hs
[1 of 1] Compiling Main             ( Main.hs, interpreted )
Ok, one module loaded.
```

We can also turn them back on with :set:

```
λ :set -Wincomplete-patterns
λ :load Main.hs
[1 of 1] Compiling Main             ( Main.hs, interpreted )

Main.hs:3:1: warning: [-Wincomplete-patterns]
    Pattern match(es) are non-exhaustive
    In an equation for 'partialFunction':
        Patterns not matched: p where p is not one of {0}
  |
3 | partialFunction 0 = "I only work for 0"
  | ^^^^^^^^^^^^^^^^^^^^^^^^^^^^^^^^^^^^^^^
Ok, one module loaded.
```

GHC supports quite a lot of different warnings that can be individually enabled and disabled. The pattern we just used holds for all of them. You can enable a warning with -Wwarning-name and disable it with -Wno-warning-name. If you want to enable all warnings about things that might be problems with your program, you can also use -Wall. We won't cover -Wall for now, since it will warn us about some things that we haven't learned how to fix yet.

Understanding How Programs Are Evaluated

Throughout this chapter you've learned how to express computations with Haskell, and you've written several small working programs without thinking too much about how the computer will actually run the programs that you've written. If you have experience writing programs in other languages, you might have an intuition about how applications are executed, but Haskell's execution model is a bit different than what you might have run into in other languages, because it's a *lazy* language. More specifically, Haskell uses a form of laziness known as *call by need*. This means that when you define an expression in Haskell it won't be evaluated until the value is actually needed. The expressions that haven't been evaluated yet are called "thunks." When you're writing Haskell programs, you build up layers of thunks representing some work that might need to be evaluated at some point.

Laziness is particularly interesting when we're dealing with lists, because one of the consequences of the way that Haskell uses laziness is that it's easy for us to create and work with lists of elements that are very expensive to compute, or even infinitely long lists.

To understand how this works, let's take another look at Haskell lists, but this time we'll look a little bit more deeply at what the values actually look like. You'll learn much more about the inner workings of how Haskell stores values later on in this book on page 386, but for now we're going to keep the discussion somewhat abstract.

You know that a Haskell list is either an empty list, or a non-empty list, which is made up of a pair of values: the head of the list, and the tail. The head of a non-empty list is the value at the front of the list. The tail is another list (which may or may not be empty). Thunks add another dimension that we need to consider. The tail of a non-empty list might not be a list whose value has been computed. Most of the time, the tail of a list is actually a *thunk* that will be computed. The list that we get back when we compute that thunk may, in turn, be another non-empty list whose tail is yet another thunk. In fact, each time we evaluate a thunk to get a list, the result might be that we create a brand new thunk that represents incrementally more of the list that we're trying to create.

Let's take a look at this in practice with an example:

```
numbersStartingAt n =
  n : numbersStartingAt (n + 1)
```

This function generates a type of list called a *stream* or, occasionally, a *generator*. These functions work by taking advantage of lazy evaluation to make a list whose tail is a thunk. When we evaluate the thunk, it computes a new list whose head is the next step of the iteration, and whose tail is another thunk that will compute another step, and so on. We can visualize it in code:

```
numbersStartingAt 0 =
  0 : <thunk>
```

If we're only ever looking at the first element of a call to numbersStartingAt then the thunk will never be evaluated, and we are only carrying around the first number. If we do evaluate the thunk, then we'll end up computing one more step in the stream by calling numbersStartingAt again:

```
0 : numbersStartingAt 1
```

Which will give us:

```
0 : 1 : <thunk>
```

We can keep this pattern up forever. Every time we evaluate the thunk, we get one more element in the list, and the tail will always be a freshly generated thunk that will give us the next value when we need it.

This technique looks a lot like *recursion*, but it's not quite the same thing. Unlike recursive functions that we've written so far, streams don't count down to a base case. Instead, they start with a *seed value* and work their way up, potentially forever. The technical term for these kinds of functions is *co-recursive*, but more often than not, in a casual setting people will simply use the term "recursion" for this type of function. Since precisely defining the difference is outside of the scope of the book, we won't be overly rigorous and will also just use the term "recursion" here.

Generating infinite lists this way ends up having several useful applications. One example is it can help you avoid tricky modulo arithmetic. Instead of calculating the boundaries of an array, you can use the cycle function from Prelude to create an infinitely repeating list. Let's look at an example of this by writing a function to convert radians to degrees. Our function will always return a number of degrees between 0 and 359 (we'll only consider integer numbers of degrees), and instead of using modulo, we'll index into a repeating list:

```
radsToDegrees :: Float -> Int
radsToDegrees radians =
  let degrees = cycle [0..359]
      converted =  truncate $ (radians * 360) / (2 * pi)
  in  degrees !! converted
```

For practice, let's write our own version of cycle. Our version will be really cool, and we don't want it to conflict with the existing function already named cycle, so let's call ours epicCycle:

```
epicCycle inputList =
  cycleHelper inputList
  where
    cycleHelper [] = epicCycle inputList
    cycleHelper (x:xs) = x : cycleHelper xs
```

You'll notice that we're using a helper function in a where clause in this function. While you won't always need a helper function like this when you're creating streams, they are extremely common for this sort of problem. If you find yourself trying to create a stream and getting stuck on how to build it, think about whether you might need a auxiliary helper function.

Our helper function steps through each element of the input list, and adds it to the output list. The first trip through the elements of our list, our cyclic list will be the same as the list we started with. When we get to the end of the input, for a normal finite list we'd just return the empty list and exit. For our infinitely repeating stream, instead, we call epicCycle again, with the same list we just finished with.

Laziness in Haskell is pervasive. We don't have to go out of our way to manually construct lists like this to get an infinite list. We can use other normal list functions to construct and work with infinite lists as well. For example, we can write an even shorter and cooler version of our function, a moreEpicCycle, that uses (<>):

```
moreEpicCycle inputList =
  inputList <> moreEpicCycle inputList
```

This version of our function works just like the previous version. We create a new infinitely repeating list by taking the original list and appending a new infinitely repeating version of it.

Folds and Infinite Lists

One of the most surprising consequences of the way that lazy evaluation works in Haskell is that, in some cases, you can get a value back when you use a fold on an infinite list. That can seem very counterintuitive at first, so let's look at an example to prove to ourselves that it does, in fact, work. Then we'll look at how it works.

In this example, we'll write a function that will find the first element of a list that satisfies our predicate function and return it, even if the list is infinite. You'll learn how to deal with optional values in a couple of chapters on page 117, but for now we'll return our result in a list. If we found what we're looking for, we'll return it in a single item list. If we didn't find it, we'll return an empty list:

```
module InfiniteFind where

findFirst predicate =
  foldr findHelper []
  where
    findHelper listElement maybeFound
      | predicate listElement = [listElement]
      | otherwise = maybeFound
```

If you load this up into ghci you can see that we can find numbers in many different sorts of both finite and infinite lists:

```
λ findFirst (> 5) [1..100]
[6]

λ findFirst (> 10) [1..]
[11]

λ findFirst (> 50) (cycle [1..100])
[51]
```

Our function will also successfully return an empty list if we're looking for something that doesn't exist inside of a finite list:

```
λ findFirst (> 100) [1..10]
[]
```

Unfortunately, if we're looking for something that doesn't exist in an infinite list, the program will never stop looking. You can press Control-C to cancel something in ghci if you try this example:

```
λ findFirst (> 10) (cycle [1..5])
Interrupted.
```

It makes sense that if we're looking for a value in an infinite list, and the value isn't in the list, then we'll keep looking forever. Our program will simply keep looking at one element after another. What makes less sense is how we can successfully return a value if we do find one, when there's still an infinite amount of list left to go.

There are two important factors that let this work. First, this only works with foldr. We can't use foldl on an infinite list. Second, this only works if the function we're folding with is "sufficiently lazy." In other words, we need to be very careful about when we evaluate the thunk that is passed in as the second argument to our helper function. To understand why this works, let's pretend to be the compiler and walk through an example. We'll start our definition of foldr from earlier:

```
foldr func carryValue lst =
  if null lst
  then carryValue
  else func (head lst) $ foldr func carryValue (tail lst)
```

We'll start by putting this definition inline into findFirst:

```
findFirst predicate carryValue lst =
  if null lst
  then carryValue
  else findHelper (head lst) $ findFirst predicate carryValue (tail lst)
  where
    findHelper listElement maybeFound
      | predicate listElement = [listElement]
      | otherwise = maybeFound
```

We know that if we don't find what we're looking for, then we'll always return an empty list. We can use this knowledge to simplify our code a little bit by removing carryValue and replacing it with an empty list:

```
findFirst predicate lst =
  if null lst
  then []
  else findHelper (head lst) $ findFirst predicate (tail lst)
  where
    findHelper listElement maybeFound
      | predicate listElement = [listElement]
      | otherwise = maybeFound
```

Next, let's also move the definition of findHelper into the body of our function. We'll refactor it a little bit, using an if expression rather than guards, so that we can make the code syntactically valid:

```
findFirst predicate lst =
  if null lst
  then []
  else
    if predicate (head lst)
    then [head lst]
    else findFirst predicate (tail lst)
```

Finally, we're interested in understanding how we can fold over an infinite list, so we can entirely remove the test to see if we've reached the end of our list. We can also use pattern matching so that we don't have to keep typing head and tail. We wouldn't want to do this in real-world code, since it means our function would crash if we gave it an empty list, or even any finite list that doesn't have a matching element.

```
findFirst predicate (x:xs) =
  if predicate x
  then [x]
  else findFirst predicate xs
```

This simplified version of our function is a good starting place to see what happens when we call it with a real value. Let's try running through it manually, looking for the first number greater than two in our list. We could call it with an infinite list:

```
findFirst (> 2) [1..]
```

Let's replace this infinite list with something a little bit more explicit:

```
findFirst (> 2) (1 : <thunk>)
```

This won't compile or run, but it'll help us visualize what's happening. When we replace our variables in the body of our function we'll end up with this:

```
findFirst (> 2) (1 : <thunk>) =
  if (> 2) 1
  then [1]
  else findFirst (> 2) <thunk>
```

Our value is not greater than two, so the first branch of our expression doesn't get evaluated. Instead, we go to our second branch, where we call findFirst again, and this time we pass in our unevaluated thunk.

In the next step, we're pattern matching on our thunk. That means we need to actually evaluate it, so we'll compute the value. As you've seen from earlier examples, infinite lists like the one we're using tend to generate themselves one step at a time, so when we evaluate the thunk we'll get the next number at the head of our list, and the tail will be yet another unevaluated thunk:

```
findFirst (> 2) (1 : <thunk>) =
  if (> 2) 1
  then [1]
  else findFirst (> 2) (2 : <thunk>)
```

If we replace the recursive call with the body of our function again, we'll get this:

```
findFirst (> 2) (1 : <thunk>) =
  if (> 2) 1
  then [1]
  else
    if (> 2) 2
    then [2]
    else findFirst (>2) (3 : <thunk>)
```

The first branch of our if expression is still false (two is equal to, but not greater than, two), so we follow the second branch again. Let's expand the call one last time:

```
findFirst (> 2) (1 : <thunk>) =
  if (> 2) 1
  then [1]
  else
    if (> 2) 2
    then [2]
    else
      if (> 2) 3
      then [3]
      else findFirst (> 2) <thunk>
```

Finally, in this case, our predicate is true. Three is greater than two. That means we will return the value from our first branch, [3]. It also means we'll never evaluate the second branch, and never evaluate the thunk. Since we never evaluate any more of the thunk, we don't need to concern ourselves with the fact that we could keep evaluating it forever and not come to the end of it. As long as we're not trying to find the end, it doesn't matter that it might be infinite in theory.

Hands-On with Infinite Fibonacci Numbers

Thunks, Streams, Recursion, Co-Recursion! There's been a lot to learn in this chapter! Before we move on, let's take a look at one more example to help reinforce the concepts you've learned in this chapter. The Fibonacci series is a sequence of numbers that frequently makes an appearance in programming texts because it has the valuable property of having a simple recursive definition. In this section, you'll build an infinite stream of Fibonacci numbers, and then look at several different ways that you can refactor the code to be more efficient.

Let's start by defining the Fibonacci sequence. It's a sequence of integers starting with [0,1]. You can calculate each number in the series by adding up the two numbers that came before it. For example, the third Fibonacci number can be calculated by adding the first two: fibonacci 3 = fibonacci 2 + fibonacci 1 = 1 + 0 = 1.

You might already recognize that this definition looks a lot like a recursive program. Let's create a new module, Fibs, and add a new function, fib, that will take an index and return back that number in the Fibonacci sequence:

```
module Fibs where

fib n
  | n == 0 = 0
  | n == 1 = 1
  | otherwise = (fib $ n - 1) + (fib $ n - 2)
```

Load this program into ghci, and you can see that it works to give you a valid Fibonacci number. Trying numbers larger than around 20 to 30, depending on the speed of your particular computer, you will see that there's a noticeable delay to calculate the Fibonacci number. Later in this section you'll learn how to implement a more efficient algorithm, but for now this slowness is very useful because it will show you how laziness allows you to avoid calculating a value until you need it.

Now that you have a function that can find any given Fibonacci number, it's easy to create a function that will return a stream of Fibonacci numbers. Let's write a new function, fibs, that represents a list of all of the Fibonacci numbers:

```
fibs = map fib [0..]
```

This function creates a list of all of the Fibonacci numbers by mapping a function that finds the nth Fibonacci number of an infinite list of all natural numbers. Thanks to laziness, only the specific Fibonacci numbers that you request from the list will ever be calculated. As an example, let's write a program to get a list of all of the Fibonacci numbers that are less than 100. We can use the takeWhile function to help us. The takeWhile function will return elements of a list so long as the predicate we pass in is True. Since takeWhile stops as soon as it encounters a non-matching element, we can use it on infinite lists, like our infinite list of Fibonacci numbers.

```
module Fibs where

fib n
  | n == 0 = 0
  | n == 1 = 1
  | otherwise = (fib $ n - 1) + (fib $ n - 2)

fibs = map fib [0..]

smallFibs =
  takeWhile (< 100) fibs
```

As you can see, generating an infinite list of Fibonacci numbers this way works. Unfortunately, it's also extremely inefficient. We're doing a lot of re-work here, and our program will get much slower as we want to work with more and larger Fibonacci numbers. Thankfully, we can use laziness to our advantage and approach this problem in a different, and much more efficient way.

Creating Lazy Streams

You've already implemented a lazy stream of numbers that increment by one at each step. We can use the same general approach to create the Fibonacci series, but there's an additional challenge. We can't simply add one to each number, instead we need to calculate the next number using the *two* previous values.

When we created an infinite list of numbers, we had the user tell us what number we should start generating at. Let's continue with that approach for now, and ask the user to give us two numbers that start the sequence they want us to generate:

```
module Fibs where

fibs firstFib secondFib =
  let nextFib = firstFib + secondFib
  in firstFib : fibs secondFib nextFib
```

Let's walk through a couple of steps of generating this stream to get a feel for what's happening. We'll start at the beginning of the sequence, passing in the first two numbers, zero and one:

```
fibs 0 1 =
  let nextFib = 0 + 1
  in 0 : fibs 1 nextFib
```

Next, let's simplify the code and replace `nextFib` with the result of evaluating the arithmetic:

```
fibs 0 1 =
  0 : fibs 1 1
```

We can expand our call to fibs again to see the next step of the algorithm:

```
fibs 0 1 =
 0 : (let nextFib = 1 + 1
      in 1 : fibs 1 nextFib)
```

Once again, let's do the arithmetic and compute nextFib:

```
fibs 0 1 =
  0 : 1 : fibs 1 2
```

After a few steps through this program you might be getting a feel for the steps we're taking to calculate each new number, but there are some extra moving parts coming from the additional number we're tracking. Let's look at a picture to help us see what's going on:

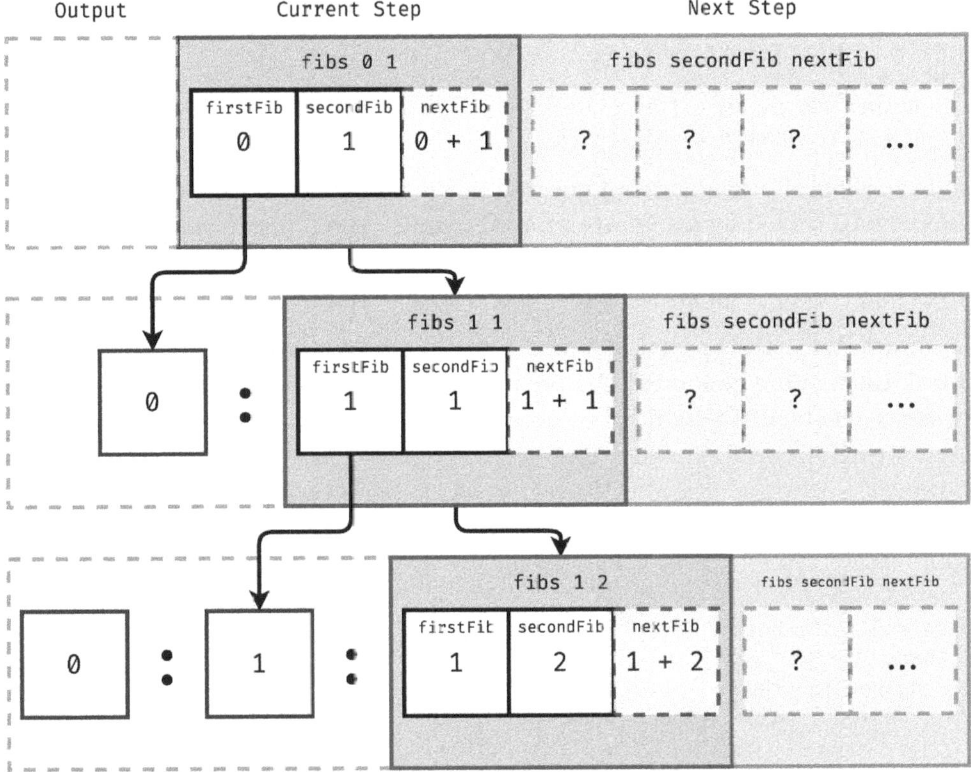

As you can see, our Fibonacci stream is following the pattern of the other streaming lists that you've created. At each step we're creating a new head with the next computed value, and the tail is a thunk that tells us how to compute the next list. Unfortunately, there are a couple of minor problems with the approach that we're taking. First, it's inconvenient to ask the user to pass in the first two numbers in the sequence. A user who wants to know what the first two numbers of the series are would be pretty irritated if they realized our API required them to tell us the first two numbers before we could return the list back to them. Second, our algorithm is requiring us to calculate a couple of steps ahead. Instead of looking at the two previous numbers in the list to generate the next one, we're effectively generating the list two numbers ahead. For the Fibonacci series, where this extra work only means that we're doing some extra addition, the consequences are pretty minor. If we were doing a more heavy-weight computation though, it could have a noticeable impact. In any case, we'd like to build this the right way and avoid doing unnecessary work.

We can address both of these concerns with one refactor. Let's take a look at the code, and then we'll step through this version to see how it compares to the previous implementation:

```
fibs = 0 : 1 : helper fibs (tail fibs)
  where
    helper (a:as) (b:bs) =
      a + b : helper as bs
```

This version of our algorithm goes all in on taking advantage of thunks and laziness to help us write a stream that avoids doing any rework, but at first the implementation might seem a little mind twisting. Let's step through a few iterations of it to get a better idea of what's happening.

We start out with fibs having two values that we're hard-coding, followed by a tail that's being generated thanks to a helper function. The implementation of helper by itself might not be too confusing now that you're familiar with generating streams. The fact that helper is being called with references to fibs, however, and understanding how that works, can be a challenge.

Let's start by replacing the references to fibs with their values in the first step of the program:

```
fibs = 0 : 1 : helper (0 : 1 : <thunk>) (tail $ 0 : 1 : <thunk>)
  where
    helper (a:<thunk>) (b:<thunk>) =
      a + b : helper <thunk> <thunk>
```

You can see right away that the two recursive references to fibs that we're passing into helper are benefiting from the fact that we've provided a couple of starting values. That means that we have two values to work with before we need to start doing any actual recursion. Luckily for us, two is exactly how many values we need in order to generate the next element of the list.

Let's simplify a bit by removing the explicit call to tail and replacing the values of a and b in helper with their actual values:

```
fibs = 0 : 1 : helper (0 : 1 : <thunk>) (1 : <thunk>)
  where
    helper (0 : 1 : <thunk>) (1 : <thunk>) =
      0 + 1 : helper (1 : <thunk>) <thunk>
```

When we replace the parameters we passed into helper with their actual values, we're able to generate a new list, its head is the new value we just calculated, and the tail is a thunk that will make another call to helper.

Next, let's substitute the value we just calculated for our call to helper back up into the body of fibs. You will notice that the parameters to helper are still the thunks, but we've consumed the first element from each of the lists. The second argument is now an entirely evaluated thunk:

```
fibs = 0 : 1 : 1 : helper (1 : <thunk>) <thunk>
```

So, we need to evaluate the thunk before we can move on. What value should it have? Let's rewind for a minute. The value we originally passed in was:

```
tail fibs
```

The value of fibs is a list with two hardcoded values, and a tail defined by our call to helper:

```
tail fibs = tail $ 0 : 1 : helper fibs (tail fibs)
          = 1 : helper fibs (tail fibs)
```

We've already taken one step through our program, so the value of our thunk is now whatever is returned by our call to helper:

```
helper fibs (tail fibs) = 1 : helper (1 : <thunk>) <thunk>
```

We don't need to evaluate the tail of the list yet, so we can simplify this a bit further:

```
helper fibs (tail fibs) = 1 : <thunk>
```

So, we've evaluated the thunk and gotten back a list whose tail is another thunk. Let's replace the unevaluated thunk in our call with this newly evaluated one. That will give us:

```
fibs = 0 : 1 : 1 : helper (1 : <thunk>) (1 : <thunk>)
  where
    helper (1 : <thunk>) (1 : <thunk>) =
      1 + 1 : helper <thunk> <thunk>
```

Now we have two unevaluated thunks. Let's replace our call to helper with the value we just calculated, and then we'll look at how to evaluate these two new thunks:

```
fibs = 0 : 1 : 1 : 2 : helper <thunk> <thunk>
```

Just like we did in the last step, we need to evaluate our thunks. Remember that the thunks here aren't referring to the original definition of fibs anymore. Instead, they are referring to the current lists that we've been stepping through. Those lists are actually two different points in the same list. The first argument is one step behind the second, which is itself always one step behind the next element that we're about to generate from our call to helper.

One way to think of this is our function has two head values that are "chasing" our helper. Each time we take a step forward, they all move one element further into the list. The first thunk, which was originally defined as fibs, is always one step behind the second thunk, which we defined with tail fibs.

An image can also help us visualize what's happening. Each time we evaluate the thunks that we're passing into helper they take one more step into the list that we're generating as we go. This means that the list and the two references are all moving in lockstep, with the thunks always one and two steps behind the next value that helper is returning as shown in the image on page 87.

If you're feeling a little bit overwhelmed after working through this section, it's okay! Take a deep breath! Understanding the way that lazy evaluation works, and especially how it interacts with techniques like recursive, co-recursive, and mutually recursive functions can be a lot to take in. You may need to revisit this section a few times, or even work ahead and come back to this section later to give it time to fully sink in.

Summary

In this chapter, you learned about lists, and along the way you had an opportunity to learn some of Haskell's more powerful and unique features, like pattern matching and lazy evaluation. As you learn more about Haskell you might find yourself using lists less frequently, because there are often better data structures for the specific problems at hand, but the techniques you've learned for working with lists will extend to these other data structures naturally and will form a foundational part of the knowledge you'll use to write Haskell effectively.

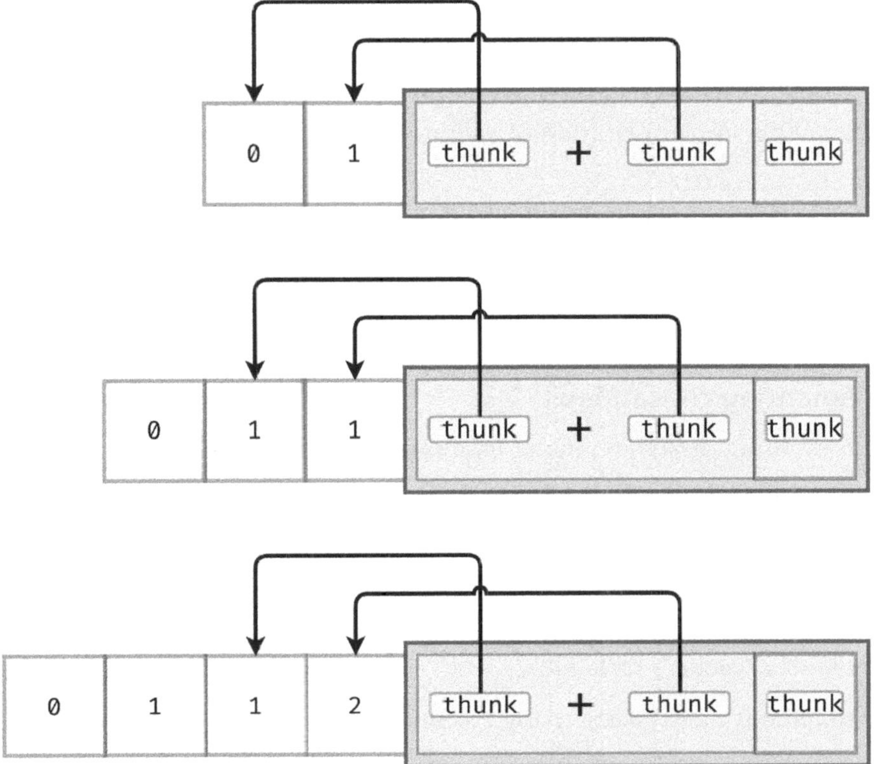

In the next chapter, you'll learn about Haskell's type system. Understanding the type system is one of the most important parts of learning how to use Haskell effectively. Combining the skills in recursion, pattern matching, and higher-order functions that you've gained from this chapter with the understanding of Haskell's type system that you'll gain in the next chapter will get you to a point where you can start to write even more useful programs.

Exercises

Reversing a List with Folds

It's possible to easily implement a `reverse` function using folds. Try to implement a function that will reverse a list using both `foldl` and `foldr`. Which one is simpler? why? Might one be more efficient than the other?

Zipping Lists

The zip function is a special case of a more general function available in Prelude called zipWith. The zipWith function combines two lists according to a function. Consider this implementation of zip in terms of zipWith:

```
λ let zip' = zipWith (,)
λ zip' [1..5] [5,4..1]
[(1,5),(2,4),(3,3),(4,2),(5,1)]
```

Implement the zipWith function with and without using list comprehensions. Can you implement zipWith using foldl?

Implementing concatMap

The concat function joins a list of lists into a single list:

```
concat [[1,2,3],[4,5,6]]
[1,2,3,4,5,6]
```

Prelude provides a function named concatMap that can be naively implemented by composing concat and map:

```
concatMap f = concat . map f
```

Try implementing concatMap using foldl and foldr. Which one is better? Why?

Thinking about Maps and Folds

Think about the following two lines of code that use map and foldr. When might they do the same thing? When might they differ? How might that change if you used foldl instead of foldr?

```
λ \f g -> foldr g 0 . map f
λ \f g -> foldr (g . f) 0
```

Folds and Infinite lists

You learned in this chapter that you can only use foldr on infinite lists, but not foldl. Try to work manually through calling foldl on an infinite list What happens? What does this tell you about why you can't use foldl on an infinite list? Are there any other benefits to foldr when dealing with large but finite lists?

CHAPTER 3

Getting Started with Types

Although a formal definition of types is outside of the scope of this book, informally you can think of a type as a way of identifying some collection of different values. For example, the Bool type is a way of naming the set of values True and False; similarly, the Integer type is a way of naming the set of all the whole numbers. To be precise, you can say the values True and False *inhabit* the type Bool, or they are its *inhabitants*, although informally throughout this book we'll simply say "True is a Bool."

Every value has a type, whether it's a number, some text, or a function. The way the value was created doesn't matter; a literal value of True defined at the top level of the program, returned by a function, or bound in a let expression will still have the type of Bool. Since there are many ways of creating a value with some type, it's common to say that, for example, an "expression has type Bool."

Later in this chapter, you'll learn about some of the commonly used types defined in the standard library, and after that you'll learn how to associate a value with a type.

Working with Basic Haskell Types

The names of types in Haskell always start with a capital letter, for example, Integer, not integer. You'll learn about several different built-in types throughout this chapter, but to get started let's take a look at a few of the most common types:

- Integer: A signed integer value. It's *unbounded*, meaning it can be arbitrarily large. Integer literals are written as numbers, as in 1234 or -1234.

- Int: A signed integer value. Its size (32-bit or 64-bit) depends on your platform. Int literals are written as numbers, as in 1234 or -1234.

- Word: An unsigned integer value. It's the same size as an Int. Word literals are written as numbers, as in 1234.
- Float: A single-precision IEEE floating-point value. Float literals may be written as numbers, with or without a fractional part, as in 1 or 1.2.
- Double: A double-precision IEEE floating-point value.
- Bool: A boolean value. It can be True or False.
- Char: A single character. A character literal is written with single-quotes, as in 'A'. Specifically, a Char is a Unicode code point.
- String: A string. A Haskell string is a list of characters. A string literal is written with double quotes, as in "string".
- [Int] : A list of Int values. List types are surrounded by square brackets.
- (Int, String) : A tuple of an Int and a String. Tuples are written as comma-separated lists of types surrounded by parentheses.
- ([Int],(String,String,String)) : A tuple whose first element is a list of Int and whose second element is a three-tuple of Strings

Annotating Values with Type Information

Type annotations, which are also sometimes called *type signatures*, are how Haskell lets you associate a type with an expression. Type annotations come after the name of a top-level function, a let or where binding, or after an expression. A type annotation starts with two colons (::) followed by the type name.

Adding a type annotation to a binding in a source file can be done in two separate lines. For example, open a new source file and copy in the following example to create a new top-level binding named pi and give it the Float type:

```
pi :: Float
pi = 3.14
```

If you have several bindings with the same type you can add them on multiple lines, or on a single line separated by commas:

```
one, two :: Int
one = 1
two = 2

three :: Int
three = 3

four :: Int
four = 4
```

You can use this same style to assign type bindings in ghci, but in order to do so you'll need to use :{ and :} to enter multiple lines. Note that you'll need to do this even if you've enabled multiline mode automatically in ghci, since the type annotation by itself isn't enough to tell ghci to start a multiline mode.

```
λ :{
> pi :: Float
> pi = 3.14
> :}
```

This is inconvenient, and so more often in ghci you'll want to provide a type to the expression in a single line. To do that, enter the type on the right hand side of an assignment, after the expression. Try it out as in the following example:

```
λ pi = 3.14 :: Float
```

You can also add type annotations to an expression without binding it to a name. Try out some of these examples to see it for yourself:

```
λ 1 :: Integer
1
λ [1,2] :: [Float]
[1.0,2.0]
λ "Hello" :: String
"Hello"
```

You aren't limited to just adding type annotations for top-level bindings and expressions in ghci. You can add type annotations to let and where bindings too. Try copying this example into a source file and testing it from ghci:

```
calculateTotalCost basePrice =
  let
    priceWithServiceFee :: Int
    priceWithServiceFee = basePrice + 1
    customaryTip = 7 :: Int
  in priceWithServiceFee + customaryTip
```

In this example, you can see both styles of type annotations being used inside of a let binding. In the case of priceWithServiceFee, you are adding an annotation to the variable, and in the case of customaryTip, you're assigning the variable a value that includes a type annotation. For now, we've skipped over adding a type for calculateTotalCost; in the next section, you'll learn how to write function types.

Looking Up Type Information

As you're writing Haskell and working with types, there are two ghci commands that will be immensely helpful to you. The :type command, which we often abbreviate :t, will give you the type of an arbitrary Haskell expression, and the :info command, which is often abbreviated :i, will give you a bit more information, but not for an arbitrary expression. :info will only work for functions that you've loaded in from a module or source file. Let's look at a few examples of using :type to get the type information from some expressions. You won't understand many of the types here yet, but as you work your way through the chapter, you'll get a chance to use all of the features individually, and by the end, you'll be able to fluidly read and understand these sorts of type signatures.

```
λ x = 1 :: Int
λ :type x
x :: Int
λ :type "Hello, World"
"Hello, World" :: [Char]
λ :type (True,False)
(True,False) :: (Bool, Bool)
λ :type (.)
(.) :: (b -> c) -> (a -> b) -> a -> c
λ :type (1 + )
(1 + ) :: Num a => a -> a
λ :type \f -> map (f . f)
\f -> map (f . f) :: (b -> b) -> [b] -> [b]
λ :type map (+ 5)
map (+ 5) :: Num b => [b] -> [b]
λ :type \f -> zipWith f [1..10] [10..1]
\f -> zipWith f [1..10] [10..1]
  :: (Num a, Num b, Enum a, Enum b) => (a -> b -> c) -> [c]
λ
```

Writing Type Annotations for Functions

Functions in Haskell have types just like non-function values do. The types of Haskell functions are written using an arrow (->). Let's look at an example of a function that takes an Int and adds 1 to it:

```
addOne :: Int -> Int
addOne n = n + 1
```

The type signature for this function says that it is going to accept an Int and will return an Int. From the type signature, you can also know that the variable n must be an Int. That's because n is the first parameter to the function, and we've said in the function's type that its parameter must be an Int.

It's also possible to have function types that have parameters even when you're not explicitly binding the parameter to a variable. For example, we can rewrite addOne to not use any intermediate variable, but the type will not change. Try this example yourself:

```
addOne :: Int -> Int
addOne = (+1)
```

What about functions that take multiple arguments? Let's take a look at an example first, and then pick apart why it works:

```
addThreeNumbers :: Int -> (Int -> (Int -> Int))
addThreeNumbers a b c = a + b + c
```

The function itself is pretty straightforward: we take in three numbers, add them together, and return the sum. Looking at the type signature though, you might notice that there are a lot of parentheses! Why do we need so many parentheses, and why are they grouped like that? Recall that functions in Haskell are *curried* automatically, so we could have written it like this:

```
addThreeNumbers = \a -> \b -> \c -> a + b + c
```

Let's use some let bindings with type annotations here to make sense of what's going on:

```
addThreeNumbers :: Int -> (Int -> (Int -> Int))
addThreeNumbers x y z =
  let
    f :: Int -> (Int -> (Int -> Int))
    f a =
      let
        g :: Int -> (Int -> Int)
        g b =
          let
            h :: Int -> Int
            h c = a + b + c
          in h
      in g
  in f x y z
```

In this example, we've rewritten our function to use explicit names instead of anonymous functions, and we've given each of the functions a type signature. Let's walk through this function's implementation and the type signatures for each of the functions we've defined to try to get a better feel for how the types and the implementation of the functions match up. Let's add a comment above our type annotation to help make it easier for us to see how the parameters and types line up:

```
--              :: x    -> (y    -> (z    -> Int))
addThreeNumbers :: Int -> (Int -> (Int -> Int))
addThreeNumbers x y z =
```

The next thing we do is create a `let` binding to define a new function, `f`. Our `f` function has the same type as `addThreeNumbers`, but we've only named a single one of its parameters, a. If you read through the definition of f, it becomes clear that the reason for this is that from f we're returning a new function named g that has the type (Int -> (Int -> Int)), so f really is taking one parameter and returning a function.

If we add a comment before the type annotation for f showing the parts of the annotation that match up with a and g we'd get:

```
--    a    -> (g)
f :: Int -> (Int -> (Int -> Int))
f a =
```

So f takes an Int and returns a function, and we've defined that function as another nested let binding that we've named g. Just like f, the g function takes a single parameter, in this case b, and returns a new function, which we've defined as h. Let's add comments to these functions as well:

```
--    b    -> (h)
g :: Int -> (Int -> Int)
g b =
  let
    --    c    -> (a + b + c)
    h :: Int -> Int
    h c = a + b + c
```

As a last step in our function, we call f with our three top level function parameters:

```
in f x y z
```

If this call to f with three parameters looks a little confusing, you can try re-writing it with parentheses to get a better idea of what's going on:

```
in ((f x) y) z
```

These parentheses are optional because function application in Haskell is left-to-right associative, so saying (f x) y is the same as saying f x y.

Just like function application at the value level, we can usually drop the extra parentheses when we're writing types for Haskell functions. Unlike function application, function types are right associative, so instead of Int -> (Int -> Int) we can write Int -> Int -> Int. In the case of addThreeNumbers, we can drop all of our parentheses and simply write:

```
addThreeNumbers :: Int -> Int -> Int -> Int
addThreeNumbers a b c = a + b + c
```

When you're passing a function as an argument to another function, you will need to use parentheses to capture the type of the function that's being passed in as an argument:

```
incrementAndShow :: Int -> (Int -> String) -> String
incrementAndShow num formatter = formatter (num + 1)
```

In this function, the formatter argument is a function with the type Int -> String. In the type annotation for the function we need to use parentheses to show the type of the second argument is a function type. If we omitted the parentheses here, we'd be telling the compiler that our function takes three non-function arguments.

As you might expect, you can also nest parentheses in types if you are passing higher-order functions to other higher order functions. To see an example of how this works, let's make a function that we can pass incrementAndShow into:

```
incrementAndShow' :: Int -> (Int -> (Int -> String) -> String) -> String
incrementAndShow' num f = f (num + 1) show
```

From the example you can see how we've taken the original type for incrementAndShow, put parentheses around it, and made it the second argument of our new incrementAndShow' function.

Considering Readability of η-Reduced and Pointfree Functions

So far we've looked at examples of type annotations for functions that bind names to all of their arguments, but one area where function type annotations particularly improve readability is in functions that have been η-reduced or are written in pointfree style. Let's look at how type annotations can make functions like this easier to read. We'll start with a function named pointful that calculates the sum of a list of numbers and then multiplies that sum by some constant:

```
pointful :: [Int] -> Int -> Int
pointful xs n = foldr (+) 0 xs * n
```

The type annotation here looks like you'd expect, with two named function arguments in the function definition associated with the two arguments shown in the type annotation. We can η-reduce this function to remove the binding for n, giving us this new implementation of the function:

```
etaReduced xs = (*) (foldr (+) 0 xs)
```

What should the type for this function look like? Our refactored function now takes a single named argument, xs, which holds the list of numbers we'll sum. We're partially applying the result of our sum to (*), and returning a function that will take the second argument to (*) and return an Int, so the type of our function should be:

```
etaReduced :: [Int] -> (Int -> Int)
```

As you've already seen, because arrows in function types are left-to-right associative, we can drop the parentheses:

```
etaReduced :: [Int] -> Int -> Int
```

The type of the η-reduced function is the same as our original function! In fact, the type signature will again be unchanged if we create a completely pointfree definition of our function. We can write a pointfree version by once again performing η-reduction to remove the binding for xs and instead using function composition:

```
pointfree :: [Int] -> Int -> Int
pointfree = (*) . foldr (+) 0
```

The type annotation of the pointfree version of the function in this case can significantly improve the ease of understanding the function by giving you a good starting point for thinking through the function composition.

Reading Type Errors

One of the most beneficial aspects of Haskell's type system is in its ability to generate *type errors*. Errors might sound like a bad thing, but Haskell's type errors help you refactor your code more quickly and find problems with your program early on in the development cycle before your code gets to users. In this section, you'll see some simple type errors and learn how to read the compiler's output and use it to fix errors in your program. Haskell type errors can grow quite long and become complex to read as you introduce more features of the type system into your program. For now, we'll start out with some minimal examples, and throughout this book we'll return to type errors that might come up as you're using new features of the language, so your understanding of these messages can grow along with your comfort in the language.

To start, let's bring up ghci and look at some simple examples of type errors we could introduce in a program and see how the compiler will tell us about them. Type out each of these examples and read the error messages yourself, and try to get comfortable with the format and spot the common elements of the messages. Afterwards, we'll review each of these errors one by one:

```
λ "one" :: Int
λ (True, False) :: (Bool, Int)
λ let f = (+) :: Int -> Int -> Int in f 1 (2 :: Float)
```

Now that you've gotten the error messages yourself, let's look at them individually, starting with the first of our erroneous expressions:

```
λ "one" :: Int

<interactive>:1:1: error:
    • No instance for (Data.String.IsString Int)
        arising from the literal ‘"one"’
    • In the expression: "one" :: Int
      In an equation for ‘it’: it = "one" :: Int
```

We're getting this error because we've added a type annotation saying that we expect our expression to have type Int, but the value we're supplying is actually a [Char] (plain Haskell strings are stored as a list of characters). Everything that we need to diagnose the problem is in the error message, so let's go line by line:

```
<interactive>:1:1: error:
```

The very first part of our error message is telling us what happened (an error), and where. The <interactive> marker is telling us that this error occurred in an interactive session through ghci. If your error message was in a file, then it would have the full path to the file containing the error. The next two numbers are the line number of the error and the column of text where the expression containing the error started. In this case, the error occurred starting with the first character, on the first line of our ghci session. If you ran this command in an existing ghci session, or typed the example into a file instead of the REPL, then you might have had a different location in your error message.

```
• Couldn't match expected type ‘Int’ with actual type ‘[Char]’
```

The next line of the error message tells exactly what went wrong. The compiler expected an Int, because we told it that's what it should expect with our type annotation, but the actual value of the expression was [Char]. The way the compiler phrases this error message gives you a hint into how it detects errors. A lot of error messages that the compiler will find for you happen because you have a value that the compiler has inferred a type for, and you're trying to use it in an expression that has some other type, and the compiler can't figure out how the two types can match up.

```
• In the expression: "one" :: Int
```

The next line of the error message tells you what expression contained the error. In this case, the entire line only contained a single expression. When you have errors in longer programs, this section of the error message can become quite long, and it can take some practice to get a better understanding of how to read it effectively.

```
In an equation for 'it': it = "one" :: Int
```

The final line of the error message is providing some additional context to the error. In this case, it's telling you that the expression was being assigned to a variable called it. The it variable is how ghci refers to your current statement in the REPL, so you won't see it in errors you are building from a source file.

Going through this information line by line gives you all of the information you need to understand what your error was, where it was introduced in the source file, and what expressions it was a part of. Now let's move on to the next error and see how it compares to this one:

```
λ (True, False) :: (Bool, Int)

<interactive>:2:8: error:
    • Couldn't match expected type 'Int' with actual type 'Bool'
    • In the expression: False
      In the expression: (True, False) :: (Bool, Int)
      In an equation for 'it': it = (True, False3) :: (Bool, Int)
```

In this line of code we've mistakenly used False as the second element of a tuple, where our type annotation says that it should be an Int. You can see that the shape of the error message is similar to the previous error message, but there are a few key differences. Let's walk through this message, and note where there are similarities or differences so you can get a better handle on the subtleties of how error messages are displayed.

```
<interactive>:2:8: error:
```

The first obvious change in our new error message is in the line and column number. Note that column 8 is the start of the second tuple element, False. The error location is helpfully giving you the location of the start of the innermost expression where the error occurred.

```
• Couldn't match expected type 'Int' with actual type 'Bool'
```

The second line of our new error message calls out that we've tried to use a Bool where the compiler expected an Int. Notice in this case that the compiler doesn't consider the entire tuple type, (Bool,Int) as a single type, but is able to look inside of the tuple and identify the part of it that doesn't match. In many cases this can be extremely helpful, since it will allow you to see what specific part of a larger type doesn't match.

```
• In the expression: False
```

This line is giving you a narrow view of the specific part of the expression that contains the error. In this case, the error tells you that you had an expression False that caused the error. Thankfully, the next line of the error message adds some additional detail that can make it easier for us to understand what's going on.

```
In the expression: (True, False) :: (Bool, Int)
```

The previous two lines of our error message were quite specific about the part of the code that had an error in it. In some cases, such a specific view into the code might not be helpful because it can be hard to see what the nature of the error is. The next line here is providing us with some additional context by giving us a view into the expression that contains our erroneous expression. Since our first error message didn't have any nested expressions, we didn't get this additional line.

```
In an equation for 'it': it = (True, False) :: (Bool, Int)
```

The final line of our second error message again contains a reference to our interactive session.

Now let's take a look at the last of our error messages. In this error, we've defined a function named f that performs addition on two Int values. We are calling this function with a type-inferred Int value and a Float. Unlike the previous examples we've looked at, the function and the values we're passing it are all well typed. The error here is that we're calling f with a Float value when it expects an Int.

```
λ let f = (+) :: Int -> Int -> Int in f 1 (2 :: Float)

<interactive>:3:42: error:
    • Couldn't match expected type 'Int' with actual type 'Float'
    • In the second argument of 'f', namely '(2 :: Float)'
      In the expression: f 1 (2 :: Float)
      In the expression:
        let f = (+) :: Int -> Int -> Int in f 1 (2 :: Float)
```

Once again, the general shape of this error message follows the pattern of the other errors you've seen, with the first line showing the location of the error, the second explaining the nature of the error, and the remaining lines giving you some context about where in the source code the error was found. Let's walk through this last error line by line to look at how it compares to the errors you've seen before.

```
<interactive>:3:42: error:
    • Couldn't match expected type 'Int' with actual type 'Float'
```

Just like all of the other errors that you've seen so far, this one starts with the line number and column of the error. Based on the column number of this error, we can see that the problem starts at the number 2.

The second line of the error message shows the specific type mismatch. Just like with the error caused by an invalid tuple field, our function call error starts by focusing on the inner-mode expression that contains the error, in this case the use of a Float where it expected an Int.

```
• In the second argument of ‘f’, namely ‘(2 :: Float)’
```

In this line of our error we have something different than we've seen before. The compiler is giving us the information that the error was in the second argument of our call to f. This might seem a bit odd given our focus on understanding currying, but it certainly results in much more readable error messages.

```
In the expression: f 1 (2 :: Float)
In the expression:
  let f = (+) :: Int -> Int -> Int in f 1 (2 :: Float)
```

The remainder of the function call error again follows the familiar pattern of providing some additional context clues to where the error ocurred. You might notice that in this case we didn't get any reference to ghci's it value. Error messages have an upper limit to the amount of context provided in the error, so as you add more expressions you might no longer see the outermost expression.

Working with Polymorphic Functions

So far we've looked at types that represent a specific sort of value like an Int or a String. A value with a single type like this is called *monomorphic*. Monomorphic functions are great when you know exactly what kind of values you'll be working with, but in many cases they're unnecessarily restrictive. You can get around these restrictions and write more general functions by using *polymorphism*. In this section, you'll learn about *parametric polymorphism*, which is the most common sort of polymorphism that you'll encounter while writing Haskell. Later on in this book, you'll be introduced to another kind of polymorphism called *ad hoc polymorphism*.

To understand how polymorphism works and how it can help us write better code, let's start by looking at a problem that we can't solve without polymorphism. There's a standard library function called id that will return any value you pass into it unmodified. This might sound a bit useless, but it turns out to have some utility, for example, when you're working with higher-order functions that can optionally transform your data when you don't want any transformation. We'd like to implement a version of this function ourselves; we'll call ours identity. Without using polymorphism there's no way we can implement a single function like this. To prove this to yourself, try to write the identity function yourself without polymorphism.

No matter what monomorphic type we assign to the function, you're limiting yourself to only working with that particular type of data. To implement a single function that works with any type, we'll need to use polymorphism. Let's take a look at the implementation with the type signature first, and then dive in to understand the type annotation and what it tells us about polymorphic functions in Haskell.

```
identity :: a -> a
identity val = val
```

The type of identity function, `a -> a` is making use of a *type variable*, in this case `a`. Type variables in Haskell are a way of representing polymorphic types. Just like a regular variable in Haskell can represent any value of the appropriate type, a type variable in Haskell can represent any type of the appropriate *kind*. You'll learn more about kinds later. Just like regular variables, type variables in Haskell start with a lowercase letter. You can use longer names for type variables in Haskell:

```
identity :: someValue -> someValue
```

Although you can use longer names for type variables, you'll find that single-letter variable names are quite common in Haskell, with the vast majority of type variable names in most Haskell code bases being between one and three letters long. In most cases, because type variables are representing very abstract concepts, it's hard to come up with a better variable name than you get with a single-letter identifier anyway.

The scope of a type variable is the type annotation in which it appears. That means that if you have two different functions, each with type variables, they can refer to different types, but within a single type expression, a given variable will always refer to the same type. Let's look at a couple of examples of type annotations:

```
len :: [a] -> Int
identity :: a -> a
uncurry :: (a -> b -> c) -> (a, b) -> c
```

You'll notice that we're using the type variable `a` in each of these functions, but they aren't related. The scope of `a` is limited to each individual type annotation. The `a` in the type annotation for `len` is completely unrelated to the `a` in `identity` or `uncurry`. On the other hand, within the type for `identity` or `uncurry`, each time a type variable appears we know that it has to hold the same type.

The fact that a type variable has to always represent the same type within a type expression means that we know some information about how a function behaves, even though we don't know what type it might be operating on for any given call. In the identity function for instance, we know that the type of the value that is returned will always be the same as the type of the value applied to it.

This is an important concept to understand, so let's take a deeper look at another example. In this example, we'll write a function that takes a function and a value and applies the function to the value and returns the results:

```
apply :: (a -> b) -> a -> b
apply f val = f val
```

In this example, our first parameter is a function from a to b, and our second parameter is a value of type a. The a in the first parameter and the a in our second parameter can be anything as long as they are the same. Likewise, the return value of the first parameter and the return value of our function are both b; again, they can be anything as long as they match.

Keep in mind that in apply :: (a -> b) -> a -> b the occurrences of a have to refer to the same type, and the occurrences of b have to refer to the same type, but a and b may or may not be the same type. It's easy to think at first glance that they have to to be different.

Let's look at a short example. We'll start by adding a new function, incrementInt, and then using it with apply:

```
incrementInt :: Int -> Int
incrementInt n = n + 1

incremented :: Int
incremented = apply incrementInt 1
```

If you replace the type variables in the type of apply with the types from incrementInt, you'll end up with this:

```
(Int -> Int) -> Int -> Int
```

So in this case, the a and b in apply are both Int.

A type variable can stand in for any type. In the examples you've seen so far, we've used basic types like Int and String as examples for what a type variable might be standing in for, but a type variable can also be satisfied by more sophisticated types, like lists or function types.

An easy way to demonstrate this is by looking back at the id function, which has the type id :: a -> a. The a in the type signature can stand in for a list if we pass one into id.

```
λ id ([1,2,3] :: [Int])
[1,2,3]
```

Exploring the Type Space of an Application with Undefined

As you get more accustomed to using types to help you write correct programs, you'll start to find that sometimes you want to test if the types for your functions are right before you spend the time implementing them. To help with that, Prelude includes the undefined function, which has the type undefined :: a. In other words, undefined is a value that inhabits all types. Of course it's impossible to actually write a pure function that can have any value of any type, given no inputs, and indeed, if you try to use an undefined value you'll get a runtime error:

```
λ undefined
*** Exception: Prelude.undefined
CallStack (from HasCallStack):
  error, called at libraries/base/GHC/Err.hs:80:14 in base:GHC.Err
  undefined, called at <interactive>:63:1 in interactive:Ghci6
```

This might seem like it would make undefined useless, but it turns out that it can be far more helpful than you might expect, thanks to Haskell's laziness and strong type system. In this section, you'll learn how to make use of undefined to iterate on the design of your application before you invest a large amount of time implementing your code.

We'll start with a problem: we need to write a program that will take a list of lists of numbers. We want to return a string with a comma-separated list of numbers, where each number is the sum of all occurrences of the biggest number, minus the sum of all occurrences of the smallest number. We'll call our function sumBiggest.

There are a lot of sub-computations that we'll want to do with this function, and we'll be juggling types a lot throughout. To avoid having to deal with too many different things at once, we'll use undefined to help us incrementally work on this function.

Let's start by defining the basic function as an undefined stub:

```
sumBiggest :: [[Int]] -> String
sumBiggest allNums = undefined
```

You can now compile the program, or load it into ghci. You can also write a function that uses sumBiggest:

```
showBiggest =
  let biggestInfo = sumBiggest [[1,1,2,3,4,4],[1,2,5,5],[-1,-2,5,-10,5]]
  in print $ "sumBiggest says: " <> biggestInfo
```

Although this will still fail if you try to call sumBiggest, either directly or indirectly through showBiggest, we've still gained the ability to typecheck our program while deferring writing the full implementation.

The next step is to think through the steps of the transformations that we want to make on the list, and add some intermediate functions in a let or where binding. We know that we'll need a way to get the biggest and smallest values, so let's start there:

```
sumBiggest :: [[Int]] -> String
sumBiggest allNums =
  let
    getBiggests :: [Int] -> [Int]
    getBiggests = undefined

    getSmallests :: [Int] -> [Int]
    getSmallests = undefined
  in undefined
```

We can also create some intermediate values that use these functions, even if we can't actually run them yet:

```
allBiggests :: [[Int]]
allBiggests = map getBiggests allNums

allSmallests :: [[Int]]
allSmallests = map getSmallests allNums
```

We need to calculate the difference of the sums of the biggest and smallest values, so the next step is to create another function that will give us a tuple of the biggest and smallest values. Let's call that zipSizes and add another value that uses it:

```
zipSizes :: [[Int]] -> [[Int]] -> [([Int],[Int])]
zipSizes = undefined

sizePairs :: [([Int],[Int])]
sizePairs = zipSizes allBiggests allSmallests
```

At this point, you can look at the type of zipSizes and realize that [[Int]] -> [[Int]] -> [([Int],[Int])] is a special case of [a] -> [b] -> [(a,b)], which is the type of zip. Let's fix that now:

```
sizePairs :: [([Int],[Int])]
sizePairs = zip allBiggests allSmallests
```

By stubbing out our intermediate functions first, we've been able to see an opportunity to use a built-in function that we might not have seen right away. Next, we'll want a way of actually calculating the sum of differences, and we'll want to convert those sums to strings:

```
differences :: ([Int],[Int]) -> Int
differences = undefined

differences' :: [String]
differences' = map (show . differences) sizePairs
```

Finally, we'll use the intercalate function from Data.List to join the strings together with commas and return our overall string. At this point, your full function should look something like this:

```
sumBiggest :: [[Int]] -> String
sumBiggest allNums =
  let
    getBiggests :: [Int] -> [Int]
    getBiggests nums = undefined

    getSmallests :: [Int] -> [Int]
    getSmallests nums = undefined

    differences :: ([Int],[Int]) -> Int
    differences pairs = undefined

    allBiggests :: [[Int]]
    allBiggests = map getBiggests allNums

    allSmallests :: [[Int]]
    allSmallests = map getSmallests allNums

    sizePairs :: [([Int],[Int])]
    sizePairs = zip allBiggests allSmallests

    differences' :: [String]
    differences' = map (show . differences) sizePairs
  in Data.List.intercalate "," differences'
```

As an exercise, work through the remaining functions and implement them. If you add any additional intermediate values, try to start with having them be undefined.

Getting Help from Type Holes

Throughout this chapter, we've put types and type annotations at the forefront of our examples. Adding explicit type annotations to all our let and where has been helpful as a learning exercise, but it's not a common style in real-world applications. Most Haskell code you'll see in the wild will include explicit type-level annotations for top-level bindings, but it's common to leave off the annotations inside of a function body and instead rely on type inference.

Omitting the type annotations inside of a function offers some substantial benefits. First, it means that we don't have to spend time updating type annotations when we're refactoring our code. In a larger code base this can be a substantial win for refactoring speed. Second, when we don't have to worry about adding annotations for all of our intermediate values, we often end up creating fewer intermediate values, and the resulting code ends up shorter and, in practice, is often easier to read and maintain.

All of these benefits also come with one major drawback: the compiler is good at doing type inference and figuring out what the type of any particular expression should be, but the human brain sometimes isn't. It's easy to get lost in a larger function and find yourself struggling to keep track of what types are what. *Type holes* solve this problem by giving us a way to use Haskell's type inference system more interactively, letting us ask the compiler directly what the type should be for a particular expression.

You can create a type hole by replacing any expression with an underscore (_), or a name that starts with an underscore. When you compile the code, the compiler will notice the type hole and will give you an error message that tells you exactly what the type of the expression should be in order to fill in the type hole. You can create type holes in regular source files, or add them into expressions in ghci. Similarly, you can get information about type holes by compiling a program or loading it into ghci.

Let's start by creating a new file, TypeHoleDemo.hs:

```
module TypeHoleDemo where

exampleNumbers :: [Int]
exampleNumbers = [1..10]

getFiveNumbers :: [Int]
getFiveNumbers = take 5 _
```

In this example, we've created a list of numbers, exampleNumbers, and a function, getFiveNumbers, which is using a type hole in place of the second argument to take. If we load this into ghci we can see that, as we expect, we'll get an error message telling us about the type hole:

```
λ :load TypeHoleDemo.hs
[1 of 1] Compiling TypeHoleDemo     ( TypeHoleDemo.hs, interpreted )

TypeHoleDemo.hs:7:25: error:
    • Found hole: _ :: [Int]
```

```
    • In the second argument of 'take', namely '_'
      In the expression: take 5 _
      In an equation for 'getFiveNumbers': getFiveNumbers = take 5 _
    • Relevant bindings include
        getFiveNumbers :: [Int] (bound at TypeHoleDemo.hs:7:1)
      Valid hole fits include
        getFiveNumbers :: [Int] (bound at TypeHoleDemo.hs:7:1)
        exampleNumbers :: [Int] (defined at TypeHoleDemo.hs:4:1)
        [] :: forall a. [a]
          with [] @Int
          (bound at <wired into compiler>)
        mempty :: forall a. Monoid a => a
          with mempty @[Int]
          (imported from 'Prelude' at TypeHoleDemo.hs:1:8-19
           (and originally defined in 'GHC.Base'))
  |
7 | getFiveNumbers = take 5 _
  |                         ^
Failed, no modules loaded.
```

At first glance the type hole error that we get looks similar to the type errors we've already seen, but there are some differences. Let's walk through this and see what we can learn about type hole errors:

```
TypeHoleDemo.hs:7:25: error:
```

The first thing you'll notice is that, just like standard type errors, our type hole error message starts with the line and column of our error. In this case, the type hole was in the file TypeHoleDemo.hs on line 7 and started in column 25.

```
• Found hole: _ :: [Int]
```

In the type errors we've looked at up until now, the compiler has typically given us two pieces of information: the type it expected, and the type it actually saw. When we create a type hole, there's no actual type found, so the compiler only needs to tell us what type it expects. In practice, this can make error messages a lot easier to follow by removing some extraneous information.

```
• In the second argument of 'take', namely '_'
  In the expression: take 5 _
  In an equation for 'getFiveNumbers': getFiveNumbers = take 5 _
```

Like other type errors, the compiler gives us some information about the expression where our error has occurred. In this case, it's showing us which argument of take had the type hole, along with some expressions to help us spot where the type hole is.

```
• Relevant bindings include
    getFiveNumbers :: [Int] (bound at TypeHoleDemo.hs:7:1)
```

The type hole error also shows us information about any other bindings that have been defined. In our simple example, we haven't created any let bindings, so the only thing in scope that is relevant is the function we're trying to define. If we added a let binding, we would also see it show up here. For example, we can change the definition of our function to this:

```
getFiveNumbers :: [Int]
getFiveNumbers = let quantity = 5 in take quantity _
```

If we reload our file in ghci now, you'll see that quantity is now also a relevant binding included in the error message:

```
• Relevant bindings include
    quantity :: Int (bound at TypeHoleDemo.hs:7:22)
    getFiveNumbers :: [Int] (bound at TypeHoleDemo.hs:7:1)
```

The final part of the error message is a list of values that are defined that have the right type, and so could be potential values to make the program typecheck:

```
Valid hole fits include
  getFiveNumbers :: [Int] (bound at TypeHoleDemo.hs:7:1)
  exampleNumbers :: [Int] (defined at TypeHoleDemo.hs:4:1)
  [] :: forall a. [a]
    with [] @Int
    (bound at <wired into compiler>)
  mempty :: forall a. Monoid a => a
    with mempty @[Int]
    (imported from 'Prelude' at TypeHoleDemo.hs:1:8-19
     (and originally defined in 'GHC.Base'))
```

In this example, the compiler is telling us that both getFiveNumbers and exampleNumbers from our module are values that would let our program typecheck. An empty list would work too, along with mempty, which comes from Prelude.

Using type holes like this to figure out the particular type of an argument to a function can be particularly helpful when you are dealing with polymorphic functions. Let's write a bit more code to see exactly how we can get some value out of type holes when we're dealing with polymorphism.

We'll start by adding two functions, one that computes the permutations of a thruple, and another that combines the first two elements of a thruple using some combining function:

```
permuteThruple ::
  (a,b,c) ->
  ((a,b,c),(a,c,b),(b,a,c),(b,c,a),(c,a,b),(c,b,a))
permuteThruple (a,b,c) =
  ((a,b,c),(a,c,b),(b,a,c),(b,c,a),(c,a,b),(c,b,a))
```

```
mergeFirstTwo :: (a,b,c) -> (a -> b -> d) -> (d,c)
mergeFirstTwo (a,b,c) f = (f a b, c)
```

Working with functions like this could be tricky. Although the functions themselves are polymorphic, the code that calls them might introduce some constraints that narrow down the possible types. With so many type variables, we can start to get lost. Using a type hole can help us recover some helpful information. Let's add a new function that uses a type hole to help us figure out what's going on:

```
showFields :: String
showFields =
  let (a,b) = combinePermutations . permuteThruple $ _
  in unlines [fst a, fst b]
  where
    joinFields a b = show a <> " - " <> b
    combinePermutations (a,b,c,d,e,f) =
      ( mergeFirstTwo a joinFields
      , mergeFirstTwo c joinFields
      )
```

You can try to manually review this code to figure out what type we should use in the type hole, but it quickly becomes apparent that it's going to be a lot of work. If we load the code up in ghci, the compiler immediately tells us what we need to know:

```
TypeHoleDemo.hs:20:54: error:
    • Found hole: _ :: (String, String, c)
      Where: 'c' is a rigid type variable bound by
               the inferred types of
                 a :: (String, c)
                 b :: (String, c)
               at TypeHoleDemo.hs:20:7-54
    • In the second argument of '($)', namely '_'
      In the expression: combinePermutations . permuteThruple $ _
      In a pattern binding:
        (a, b) = combinePermutations . permuteThruple $ _
    • Relevant bindings include
        combinePermutations :: forall {a1} {a2} {c1} {b} {c2} {d} {e} {f}.
                               (Show a1, Show a2) =>
                               ((a1, String, c1), b, (a2, String, c2), d, e, f)
                               -> ((String, c1), (String, c2))
          (bound at TypeHoleDemo.hs:24:5)
        joinFields :: forall {a}. Show a => a -> String -> String
          (bound at TypeHoleDemo.hs:23:5)
        showFields :: String (bound at TypeHoleDemo.hs:19:1)
   |
20 |   let (a,b) = combinePermutations . permuteThruple $ _
   |                                                      ^
Failed, no modules loaded.
```

In the second line of the error, the compiler tells us exactly what kind of tuple we should pass in:

```
• Found hole: _ :: (String, String, c)
```

The first two elements of our tuple need to be strings, and the final element appears to not be used at all, and so it can be any type that we want. Let's test it out by adding some hardcoded thruple argument:

```
showFields :: String
showFields =
  let (a,b) = combinePermutations . permuteThruple $ ("hello", "world", 10)
  in unlines [fst a, fst b]
  where
    joinFields a b = show a <> " - " <> b
    combinePermutations (a,b,c,d,e,f) =
      ( mergeFirstTwo a joinFields
      , mergeFirstTwo c joinFields
      )
```

If we load this in ghci and run it, we'll get a message back:

```
λ putStrLn showFields
"hello" - world
"world" - hello
```

Another case where type holes can come in handy is when the compiler finds a type error in your program, but attributes the error to the wrong part of the expression. Let's add some more code to our example file. This time we'll write code that has a type error, but we won't use a type hole just yet:

```
showStringPair :: (String,String) -> String
showStringPair (a,b) = "fst: " <> a <> ", snd: " <> b

doubleField :: a -> (a,a)
doubleField a = (a,a)

showValues :: String
showValues = unlines $ map (showStringPair . doubleField) [1..10]
```

If we load this into ghci we'll get a type error, but it's not the one we'd expect:

```
λ :load TypeHoleDemo.hs
[1 of 1] Compiling TypeHoleDemo     ( TypeHoleDemo.hs, interpreted )

TypeHoleDemo.hs:36:59: error:
    • No instance for (Enum String)
        arising from the arithmetic sequence '1 .. 10'
    • In the second argument of 'map', namely '[1 .. 10]'
      In the second argument of '($)', namely
        'map (showStringPair . doubleField) [1 .. 10]'
```

```
    In the expression:
      unlines $ map (showStringPair . doubleField) [1 .. 10]
   |
36 | showValues = unlines $ map (showStringPair . doubleField) [1..10]
   |                                                          ^^^^^^^

TypeHoleDemo.hs:36:60: error:
    • No instance for (Num String) arising from the literal ‘1’
    • In the expression: 1
      In the second argument of ‘map’, namely ‘[1 .. 10]’
      In the second argument of ‘($)’, namely
        ‘map (showStringPair . doubleField) [1 .. 10]’
   |
36 | showValues = unlines $ map (showStringPair . doubleField) [1..10]
   |                                                           ^
Failed, no modules loaded.
```

In this example, the actual bug that we have is due to the function we're passing to map. It should call show before it calls doubleField. The compiler is assuming this is well typed, and instead thinks we're passing the wrong value into map. With type inference, this is a problem you'll encounter from time to time. Two types don't match, but the compiler makes the wrong decision about which one is correct, and tries to suggest that you change the wrong thing.

When this happens, we can sometimes use a type hole to narrow down the problem. In this case, let's try turning doubleField into a type hole. Rather than replacing it entirely with an underscore, we can add an underscore prefix. This gives us a named type hole, and it will be easier when we want to remove the type hole and go back to the actual function call later:

```
showValues :: String
showValues = unlines $ map (showStringPair . _doubleField) [1..10]
```

When we load this version of the program into ghci, our error is much more clear:

```
λ :load TypeHoleDemo.hs
[1 of 1] Compiling TypeHoleDemo     ( TypeHoleDemo.hs, interpreted )

TypeHoleDemo.hs:36:46: error:
    • Found hole: _doubleField :: Integer -> (String, String)
      Or perhaps ‘_doubleField’ is mis-spelled, or not in scope
    • In the second argument of ‘(.)’, namely ‘_doubleField’
      In the first argument of ‘map’, namely
        ‘(showStringPair . _doubleField)’
      In the second argument of ‘($)’, namely
        ‘map (showStringPair . _doubleField) [1 .. 10]’
    • Relevant bindings include
        showValues :: String (bound at TypeHoleDemo.hs:36:1)
```

```
      Valid hole fits include
        mempty :: forall a. Monoid a => a
          with mempty @(Integer -> (String, String))
          (imported from 'Prelude' at TypeHoleDemo.hs:1:8-19
           (and originally defined in 'GHC.Base'))
   |
36 | showValues = unlines $ map (showStringPair . _doubleField) [1..10]
   |                                              ^^^^^^^^^^^^
Failed, no modules loaded.
```

Now that we've told the compiler where to look, the type hole is telling us that for our code to be valid, doubleField would need to have the type Integer -> (String,String):

```
• Found hole: _doubleField :: Integer -> (String, String)
```

Of course, doubleField returns a tuple of whatever type we pass into it, so we'll need to replace doubleField with a new function that both converts the value to a String and then creates the tuple. Let's try keeping our type hole around, but adding show to our function:

```
TypeHoleDemo.hs:36:46: error:
    • Found hole: _doubleField :: String -> (String, String)
      Or perhaps '_doubleField' is mis-spelled, or not in scope
    • In the first argument of '(.)', namely '_doubleField'
      In the second argument of '(.)', namely '_doubleField . show'
      In the first argument of 'map', namely
        '(showStringPair . _doubleField . show)'
    • Relevant bindings include
        showValues :: String (bound at TypeHoleDemo.hs:36:1)
      Valid hole fits include
        doubleField :: forall a. a -> (a, a)
          with doubleField @String
          (bound at TypeHoleDemo.hs:33:1)
        return :: forall (m :: * -> *) a. Monad m => a -> m a
          with return @((,) String) @String
          (imported from 'Prelude' at TypeHoleDemo.hs:1:8-19
           (and originally defined in 'GHC.Base'))
        pure :: forall (f :: * -> *) a. Applicative f => a -> f a
          with pure @((,) String) @String
          (imported from 'Prelude' at TypeHoleDemo.hs:1:8-19
           (and originally defined in 'GHC.Base'))
        read :: forall a. Read a => String -> a
          with read @(String, String)
          (imported from 'Prelude' at TypeHoleDemo.hs:1:8-19
           (and originally defined in 'Text.Read'))
        mempty :: forall a. Monoid a => a
          with mempty @(String -> (String, String))
          (imported from 'Prelude' at TypeHoleDemo.hs:1:8-19
           (and originally defined in 'GHC.Base'))
```

```
   |
36 | showValues = unlines $ map (showStringPair . _doubleField . show) [1..10]
   |                                              ^^^^^^^^^^^^
```

Now the type hole needs to have the type String -> (String,String):

```
• Found hole: _doubleField :: String -> (String, String)
```

That lines up perfectly with the type of doubleField, and in fact the compiler even recognizes that and suggests that it might be a valid fit:

```
Valid hole fits include
  doubleField :: forall a. a -> (a, a)
    with doubleField @String
    (bound at TypeHoleDemo.hs:33:1)
```

Let's take the compiler's advice and fill our type hole in with doubleField:

```
showValues :: String
showValues = unlines $ map (showStringPair . doubleField . show) [1..10]
```

If we load this in ghci it seems to work, and we can call showValues:

```
λ :load TypeHoleDemo.hs
[1 of 1] Compiling TypeHoleDemo     ( TypeHoleDemo.hs, interpreted )
Ok, one module loaded.
λ putStrLn showValues
fst: 1, snd: 1
fst: 2, snd: 2
fst: 3, snd: 3
fst: 4, snd: 4
fst: 5, snd: 5
fst: 6, snd: 6
fst: 7, snd: 7
fst: 8, snd: 8
fst: 9, snd: 9
fst: 10, snd: 10
```

As you are working through the examples in this book or trying out the exercises, be sure to keep type holes in mind as a helpful tool for narrowing down type errors and figuring out how to fix code that doesn't compile.

Looking at the Type of main

So far we've skimmed past the type of one important function: main. In all Haskell executables, there should be a single main function and it should have the type main :: IO (). This is called an *IO action*. You'll learn more about IO actions on page 263. For now, it's sufficient to know that functions with the type IO a are functions that do some sort of interaction with the real world, like printing a value to a screen or reading a file.

Summary

In this chapter, you've seen how Haskell's type system is integrated into the language. You've learned how to add type annotations to your own programs to help them be more readable and easier to use correctly, and you've learned how to use the type system to look up information about how functions work, and to troubleshoot your own programs using type holes. As you spend more time with Haskell, and improve your understanding of the type system and its capabilities, you will learn to see types as an invaluable tool to help you understand and express your code. Much of the rest of this book will be devoted to understanding how to best make use of Haskell's type system to write effective and maintainable programs, and investing early in making sure that you are comfortable with types and how to use them will pay dividends as you continue on your path toward mastering Haskell.

In the next chapter, you'll learn how to create your own types and how the way you define types can profoundly impact the way you write your programs. Having a good understanding of the way Haskell's built-in types work will be instrumental in being able to easily combine them when you build your own types, and will give you an effective starting point when you start to think about how you want to design and build your own types.

Exercises

Undefined

Consider a function that takes three integers but hasn't been defined:

```
addThree :: Int -> Int -> Int -> Int
```

There are several different ways that you could write a function like this. For example, here are two possible definitions:

```
-- definition 1
addThree = undefined

-- definition 2
addThree a b c = undefined
```

There are many other ways we could use undefined to write a version of `addThree` that type checks. Why are there so many different versions?

Understanding Functions by Their Type

The behavior of the following functions from base can be easily predicted based on their type. Review the type of each of these functions and try to guess at how they are implemented. Use ghci to see if you were right. Are there other ways you could have implemented them? Why or why not?

- Data.Tuple.swap :: (a,b) -> (b,a)
- concat :: [[a]] -> [a]
- id :: a -> a

Filling In Type Holes

Consider the following example code:

```
mapApply :: [a -> b] -> [a] -> [b]
mapApply toApply =
  concatMap (\input -> map ($ input) toApply)

example :: [Int] -> String
example = mapApply undefined
  where
    letters :: [Char]
    letters = ['a'..'z']

    lookupLetter :: Int -> Char
    lookupLetter n = letters !! n

    offsets :: [Int -> Int]
    offsets = [rot13, swap10, mixupVowels]

    rot13 :: Int -> Int
    rot13 n = (n + 13) `rem` 26

    swap10 :: Int -> Int
    swap10 n
      | n <= 10 = n + 10
      | n <= 20 = n - 10
      | otherwise = n

    mixupVowels :: Int -> Int
    mixupVowels n =
      case n of
        0 -> 8
        4 -> 14
        8 -> 20
        14 -> 0
        20 -> 4
        n' -> n'
```

Try to fill in the value of undefined so that you get the following output:

```
λ example [5..15]
"spftqgurhvsuwtjxukyblzcmadnteacfp"
```

Use type holes to help you figure out the type of the value you'll need to use.

CHAPTER 4

Creating New Types

In the last chapter, you learned the basics of how Haskell's type system works, and you wrote some programs that made use of some of the common predefined types available in the standard library. Those fundamentals are an important building block to making effective use of Haskell's type system, but the real power comes in creating your own types that let you precisely describe the structure and behavior of the data in your application. In this chapter, you'll learn how to create your own types that accurately represent the structure of your data. Later, on page 209, you'll learn to go a step further and describe the behavior of your types as well.

Creating Data Types and Records

One of the most common reasons to make your own data types in Haskell is to create named and structured collections of some other types. For example, you might want to create a type that represents some information about a customer like their first and last name, the number of products they've ordered, and their current outstanding account balance. You can create a new type with the `data` keyword. For example, to create a new `CustomerInfo` you can simply say:

```
data CustomerInfo
```

This defines the existence of a new type called `CustomerInfo`. Unfortunately, as we've written the code, the *only thing* it does is define a new type. We don't have any way to create a value of our new type, in other words we've created a type that doesn't have any inhabitants. That might sound a little bit useless, but there's a commonly used type that doesn't have any inhabitants called `Void` and its definition is simply:

```
data Void
```

Later on in this book, you'll learn about some cases where types that don't have any inhabitants can come in handy. For now we need to a way to create some customer information. We'll start by creating a *value constructor*. A value constructor is a special function that lets us create a new value of a certain type.

Like types, value constructors in Haskell start with a capital letter. Let's create a new value constructor for our type:

```
data CustomerInfo = CustomerInfo
```

Here we've created a new value constructor for our CustomerInfo type and called it CustomerInfo. Although the names are the same, it's important to remember that the identifier on the left is the name of a type, and the one on the right is a normal (*value level*) function. This is an example of *punning*, and it's quite common in most Haskell code bases.

You can use your new value constructor to create a value with the type CustomerInfo:

```
someCustomerInfo = CustomerInfo
```

Unfortunately, right now our CustomerInfo type only has a single inhabitant, which is the value we create when we call CustomerInfo. Values with a single inhabitant can also be quite useful in practice. The type with a single inhabitant in Haskell is often called *Unit*, or (). Although we can't actually define () ourselves since it's special syntax that's built into the language, you can think of it as being defined like this:

```
data () = ()
```

To add some inhabitants to our new type, we can add some parameters to our value constructor function. For example, if we wanted to add a single boolean flag to say whether the user was active or not, we could say:

```
data CustomerInfo = CustomerInfo Bool
```

Now our CustomerInfo value constructor becomes a function that takes a single Bool and returns some new CustomerInfo value:

```
λ :type CustomerInfo
CustomerInfo :: Bool -> CustomerInfo
λ :type CustomerInfo True
CustomerInfo True :: CustomerInfo
λ :type CustomerInfo False
CustomerInfo False :: CustomerInfo
```

When we add a single parameter, the number of inhabitants for our new type is equal to the number of inhabitants of the value it contains. In our example, we can have two different CustomerInfo values, one that we created by passing in True and one we created by passing in False.

You can add more parameters to your constructor by listing them after the first. Let's add another boolean value:

```
data CustomerInfo = CustomerInfo Bool Bool
```

Our new type now contains two boolean values, and it has four inhabitants:

```
CustomerInfo True True
CustomerInfo True False
CustomerInfo False True
CustomerInfo False False
```

In fact, each time you add a new parameter to your value constructor, the number of inhabitants of your type gets multiplied by the number of inhabitants of the new type. Because the number of inhabitants of a type increases multiplicatively, we often refer to these types in Haskell as *product types*.

Let's dump our booleans and create a CustomerInfo that holds data for our customer's first and last name, the number of items they've ordered, and their account balance:

```
data CustomerInfo = CustomerInfo String String Int Int
```

Next, let's create a useful example customer that we can work with, by applying some values to our value constructor function:

```
customerGeorge :: CustomerInfo
customerGeorge =
  CustomerInfo "Georgie" "Bird" 10 100
```

Creating a new CustomerInfo value like this doesn't do much good if we can't look at or do anything with the data once we've created it. To do anything useful with our new value, we need to be able to get at the data that we passed in to create it in the first place.

You've used pattern matching already with lists and values like numbers and strings. Pattern matching for data types works much the same way. To pattern match the fields of a type you can use the type data name, followed by the names you want to bind to each type field, or an underscore for fields you want to ignore. Let's look at an example where we use pattern matching to extract the fields of a customer type and generate a string:

```
showCustomer :: CustomerInfo -> String
showCustomer (CustomerInfo first last count balance) =
  let fullName = first <> " " <> last
      name = "name: " <> fullName
      count' = "count: " <> (show count)
      balance' = "balance: " <> (show balance)
  in name <> " " <> count' <> " " <> balance'
```

```
λ showCustomer customerGeorge
"name: Georgie Bird count: 10 balance: 100"
```

You can also match values in specific fields. For example, let's write a function that applies a discount to certain customers based on their first and last name:

```
applyDiscount :: CustomerInfo -> CustomerInfo
applyDiscount customer =
  case customer of
    (CustomerInfo "Georgie" "Bird" count balance) ->
      CustomerInfo "Georgie" "Bird" count (balance `div` 4)
    (CustomerInfo "Porter" "Pupper" count balance) ->
      CustomerInfo "Porter" "Pupper" count (balance `div` 2)
    otherCustomer -> otherCustomer
```

This approach to pattern matching out fields works well for small data types where you will generally want access to all or most fields, but as you can imagine it can become cumbersome for larger types or cases where you frequently only want to access a single field. You can work around this by writing a function to access each field of your value:

```
firstName :: CustomerInfo -> String
firstName (CustomerInfo name _ _ _) = name

lastName :: CustomerInfo -> String
lastName (CustomerInfo _ name _ _) = name

widgetCount :: CustomerInfo -> Int
widgetCount (CustomerInfo _ _ count _) = count

balance :: CustomerInfo -> Int
balance (CustomerInfo _ _ _ balance) = balance
```

Updating values follows a similar pattern. An example function that updates a customer's first name is provided here. As an exercise, implement update functions for the rest of the fields in CustomerInfo.

```
updateFirstName :: CustomerInfo -> String -> CustomerInfo
updateFirstName (CustomerInfo _ lastName count balance) firstName =
  CustomerInfo firstName lastName count balance
```

Thankfully, although this process of adding getter and setter functions for each field of a datatype is a good learning experience, it isn't necessary in practice because Haskell has a special syntax for dealing with product types with named parameters. These data types are called *records*, and you'll often see the syntax used to work with records referred to as *record syntax*.

In record syntax you create a product type, but each field of the datatype is assigned a name as well as a type. The names are used to automatically generate functions to get fields from the record. These functions are called *field selectors*, or often just *selectors*. There is also special syntax to generate a record with new fields. Let's rewrite our CustomerInfo type using record syntax:

```
data CustomerInfo = CustomerInfo
  { firstName :: String
  , lastName :: String
  , widgetCount :: Int
  , balance :: Int
  }
```

When using record syntax we follow the name of the data constructor with curly braces, and then a list of each named record field, with an annotation for its type. The type annotations in the record aren't optional here; you need them for the expression to be valid. When you define a record this way, you once again get a function named after your data constructor, in this case CustomerInfo, whose arguments are the fields of the record in the order they appear:

```
CustomerInfo :: String -> String -> Int -> Int -> CustomerInfo
```

Additionally, you get a new way of constructing a value using named arguments. To construct a value using named arguments, you follow the data constructor name with curly braces, and then list the fields that you want to assign and the values:

```
customerGeorge :: CustomerInfo
customerGeorge =
  CustomerInfo
  { balance = 100
  , lastName = "Bird"
  , firstName = "George"
  , widgetCount = 10
  }
```

Notice here the named arguments appear in a different order than they do when you defined the record. One advantage to using named arguments is you don't have to remember the positions of individual arguments. A disadvantage to constructing records this way is you can't partially apply fields to the data constructor using record syntax. For example, if we wanted to create some function to initialize new customers with some bonus items using record syntax, we would need to manually accept the missing fields as parameters:

```
customerFactory :: String -> String -> CustomerInfo
customerFactory fname lname =
  CustomerInfo { balance = 0
               , widgetCount = 5
               , firstName = fname
               , lastName = lname
               }
```

Record field names can also be used to access fields of a record. Each record field becomes a function to extract that field from your record. This means that you no longer need to manually write functions to extract record fields. We can see this in action by looking at fields from customerGeorge in ghci:

```
λ firstName customerGeorge
"George"
λ lastName customerGeorge
"Bird"
λ widgetCount customerGeorge
10
λ balance customerGeorge
100
```

These record field functions are ordinary functions that can be composed, passed as arguments to higher-order functions, and so on. For example, if we wanted to write a function that calculated the total number of widgets that we needed to assemble for a group of customers we could write:

```
totalWidgetCount :: [CustomerInfo] -> Int
totalWidgetCount =
  sum . map widgetCount
```

Updating records can also be done easily using *record update syntax*. With record update syntax you can update a specific field of your record based on its name. Let's use record update syntax to write a function that clears out a user's widget count and balance:

```
emptyCart :: CustomerInfo -> CustomerInfo
emptyCart customer =
  customer { widgetCount = 0
           , balance = 0
           }
```

You can see in this example that record update syntax mirrors other record syntax. Keep in mind that, in spite of the name, record update syntax does not change the original record value. The record update syntax returns a new record with the specified fields updated to their new values. You can see this in action in ghci:

```
λ george = emptyCart customerGeorge
```

```
λ balance george
0
λ balance customerGeorge
100
```

Creating Bindings for All Record Fields with Wildcards

Record syntax can make it easier to deal with cases where you want to work with small records, or only want to regularly access a couple of record fields. For functions that need to regularly access all of the fields of a record, pattern matching out all of the fields, or using record syntax to construct new records, can start to feel like it involves a lot of boilerplate. You can reduce some of this boilerplate by enabling a *language extension* to add a new feature to Haskell.

A language extension lets you turn on features that extend the core Haskell language, giving you new ways to write programs. GHC supports over a hundred different language extensions as of version 9.4. As new features are added to the compiler, they are almost always enabled through a language extension to start with. Over time, some extensions have become quite popular and are used in nearly all new Haskell projects. Other extensions are deprecated, superseded by newer extensions that provide expanded capabilities, or no longer in favor. Finally, many of the extensions you'll see throughout this book are popular but only useful in particular circumstances. Throughout this book you'll learn about several new language extensions you might want to enable. You can refer to the GHC manual[1] for a complete list of all language extensions.

For now, let's enable the RecordWildCards extension. There are several different ways that we can enable extensions in GHC. For now we'll look at two.

RecordWildCards

The RecordWildCards extension has been available since GHC 6.8.1. It isn't enabled by default in either GHC2021 or Haskell2010 so you'll need to enable it manually. Simply enabling this extension extension shouldn't break any existing code, however, be aware that in some cases, introducing record wildcards into an existing application might introduce unexpected bugs due to name shadowing. Many projects either enable this extension globally, or prohibit its use altogether. Enabling this extension on a module-by-module basis can end up causing a maintenance burden on the application long term since applications that use RecordWildCards need to be somewhat more careful about naming conventions and name shadowing.

1. https://ghc.gitlab.haskell.org/ghc/doc/users_guide/exts.html

The first way to enable extensions is on a per-file basis using a *language pragma*. Language pragmas should be placed at the top of each source file, and they will enable the extensions listed only for the current file. To use a language pragma to enable the RecordWildCards extension, add this to the top of your source file:

```
{-# LANGUAGE RecordWildCards #-}
```

You can also enable language extensions in ghci with :set or :seti. When you are enabling a language extension from ghci (or on the command line) prefix the extension name with -X, for example:

```
λ :seti -XRecordWildCards
```

Using :set will enable the extension for both code that you are typing directly into ghci as well as new code that you load; :seti will only apply the extension to the code that you type into ghci. In general, it's best to use :seti for enabling language extensions. If you use :set you might forget to include a language extension needed to compile a file in the file itself, and then you'll find that your program fails to compile even though you can load it interactively.

Now that you have the RecordWildCards extension enabled, let's use it to refactor two of our existing functions: customerGeorge and showCustomer. The RecordWildCards extension allows you take all of the fields of a record and turn them into variables that are bound inside of an expression by using TypeConstructor {..}. You can use this to either destructure a record or to construct one. We'll do both during our refactoring.

Let's start by refactoring showCustomer. Now instead of pattern matching out all of the fields, we'll use the record wildcards to automatically bring all of the fields into scope:

```
showCustomer :: CustomerInfo -> String
showCustomer CustomerInfo{..} =
  firstName
  <> " "
  <> lastName
  <> " "
  <> show widgetCount
  <> " "
  <> show balance
```

You can see in this example that we're bringing into scope all the fields of our record as variables that we can use however we like. We can also use record wildcards to create a new value. In that case, we still need to use bindings to define our variables with names that match the record fields, but by using record wildcards we can forgo explicitly setting each field. Let's refactor our customerGeorge function to use record wildcards to create the value that we're returning:

```
customerGeorge =
  let firstName = "George"
      lastName = "Bird"
      widgetCount = 10
      balance = 100
  in CustomerInfo {..}
```

The field names don't necessarily need to be defined as let bindings; you can also use names bound to function parameters in wildcards. As an example, let's refactor our customer factory function:

```
customerFactory firstName lastName =
  let widgetCount = 10
      balance = 100
  in CustomerInfo {..}
```

Record wildcards can be handy, especially in longer functions or functions where you have large records that you are working with. They also can make code somewhat harder to read because it becomes less clear where variables are being defined, and it requires that the reader be familiar with the fields of any given record. Try it out and decide for yourself if or when it works best in your applications.

Dealing with Duplicate Record Fields

In some cases, you might find yourself wanting to have two records in a module that share some or all of their field names. Imagine that we wanted to add a new record that would keep track of employee information; we'll call it EmployeeInfo. This record will also need to have an employee's first and last name, along with their timezone and their preferred contact info:

```
data CustomerInfo = CustomerInfo
    { firstName   :: String
    , lastName    :: String
    , widgetCount :: Int
    , balance     :: Int
    }

data EmployeeInfo = EmployeeInfo
    { firstName   :: String
    , lastName    :: String
    , timezone    :: String
    , contactInfo :: String
    }
```

If we try to build a module with both of these records, we'll get an error:

```
[1 of 1] Compiling CustomerInfoDuplicateFields
         ( src/CustomerInfoDuplicateFields.hs, interpreted )

src/CustomerInfoDuplicateFields.hs:11:7: error:
    Multiple declarations of ‘firstName’
    Declared at: src/CustomerInfoDuplicateFields.hs:4:7
                 src/CustomerInfoDuplicateFields.hs:11:7
   |
11 |     { firstName   :: String
   |       ^^^^^^^^^

src/CustomerInfoDuplicateFields.hs:12:7: error:
    Multiple declarations of ‘lastName’
    Declared at: src/CustomerInfoDuplicateFields.hs:5:7
                 src/CustomerInfoDuplicateFields.hs:12:7
   |
12 |     , lastName    :: String
   |       ^^^^^^^^
Failed, no modules loaded.
```

The compiler is telling us here that the error is caused by multiple declarations of the same two fields, firstName and lastName. Helpfully, it also tells us where the declarations are.

The reason we're getting an error here is that field selectors are treated as normal functions, so if we define two records with two field selectors that have the same name, it's effectively the same as if we'd tried to create two regular functions with the same name. We can't give two functions in the same module the same name.

The problem of duplicate record fields is a common one in larger Haskell applications, and there are a few different approaches that people have come up with to work around the problem. You'll learn how to use Haskell's module system on page 155 to work around the problem of duplicate record fields, but for now let's focus on one of the more common ways to address the problem of duplicate record fields: using naming conventions to avoid collisions.

Naming Record Fields

The choice of how to name your record fields can have a big impact on the way that you write your code. As you just learned, choosing overly generic names can lead you to refactoring the structure of your source code so that you can use qualified imports to disambiguate names. Another way to disambiguate names is to choose different names for your record fields. A common idiom in Haskell applications is to simply prefix the record field name with the name of the type, so for example, your CustomerInfo record would become:

```
data CustomerInfo = CustomerInfo
    { customerInfoFirstName   :: String
    , customerInfoLastName    :: String
    , customerInfoWidgetCount :: Int
    , customerInfoBalance     :: Int
    }
```

Creating Sum Types

Records are a useful feature of Haskell's type system, and you'll use them regularly in the code you write, but they are just a small part of the power of types in Haskell. In this section, you'll learn about several other useful features of Haskell's type system, which broadly fall under the term *algebraic datatypes*, or *ADTs*.

The name *algebraic datatype* comes from the formal study of types and type systems. We won't get into the details of the name or the underlying theory in this book, but we'll continue to use the term, along with some related terms like *sum type* and *product type* when we're referring to particular types of features. These are commonly used terms when working with Haskell, but you can learn what they mean and how to use them in the context of writing Haskell programs without needing to understand the theory that gave them their names.

Using Sum Types as Enums

Earlier in this chapter, you learned about product types and records. Product types let you combine many other types together. Another way you can use types to help you better structure data is to use them to represent a choice between two types. We call these types *sum types*. Let's work through a simple example by looking at an implementation of Bool, which is one of the simplest sum types that we can define.

```
data Bool = True | False
```

In this example, we've defined a new type, Bool, which has *two* value constructors, True and False. Neither of these value constructors take any parameters, so they each have a single inhabitant

A Bool can be either True *or* False, and so the type has two inhabitants.

Of course, we can extend this beyond a choice between two options. Haskell programs frequently use sum types to enumerate all of the inhabitants of a specific type. For example, if we wanted to create a type to represent the cardinal directions, we can easily list out all of them as a sum type:

```
data Direction = North | South | East | West
```

Creating Sum Types with Data

In many cases, we don't want to choose between product or sum types. Consider the problem of storing some contact information for a user who might want to provide a phone number for receiving text messages or, alternatively, a mailing address for receiving written correspondence. As with the examples of sum types you've already looked at, we have a clear choice between two different value constructors, which in this case we can call TextMessage and Mail. However, each of these value constructors need to take some parameters: a phone number for text messages, or a mailing address for sending mail. The syntax for doing this follows naturally from the syntax of sum and product types. We create a value constructor for each branch as we've done for previous sum types, but for each of these value constructors we can add any number of parameters, just like we did for product types.

Let's look at a concrete example:

```
data PreferredContactMethod = Email String
  | TextMessage String
  | Mail String String String Int

emailContact :: PreferredContactMethod
emailContact = Email "me@example.com"

textContact :: PreferredContactMethod
textContact = TextMessage "+1 307 555 0100"

mailContact :: PreferredContactMethod
mailContact = Mail "1123 S. Road St." "Suite 712" "Examplesville, OH" 98142
```

This pattern of combining multiple product types into a single new type is sometimes referred to as a *sum of products*, although the pattern is so common that in practice most Haskell developers will casually just refer to sum, product, or sum-of-product types as "a type."

Using Sum Types in Practice

Now that you've created some contact information, it would be useful to be able to do something with it. Let's continue with the example by writing a function called confirmContact that will generate some confirmation text that we could display to a user, letting them know that we'll use their preferred contact method for future communications.

Just like the data types you created in the previous section, you can use pattern matching to extract the values from your new type. When you were working with a single data constructor, you only needed to pattern match for it, and so it made sense to use a pattern to match values at the function argument level. When you are working with sum types you can still pattern match function arguments directly, but it's more common to use a case statement. In this example, we're using a case statement to both select the specific constructor as well as to extract its arguments.

```
confirmContact :: PreferredContactMethod -> String
confirmContact contact =
  case contact of
    Email emailAddress ->
      "Okay, I'll email you at " <> emailAddress
    TextMessage number ->
      "Okay, I'll text you at " <> number
    Mail street1 street2 citystate zip ->
      "Okay, I'll send a letter to\n"
      <> street1 <> "\n"
      <> street2 <> "\n"
      <> citystate <> " " <> show zip
```

In some circumstances, you might not care about all of the fields when pattern matching in sum types. In that case, you can use a pair of empty brackets to represent the parameters to the data constructor without having to type them all out. Although this looks similar to the syntax for record wildcards, it doesn't require any language extensions. Let's look at an example. If you did not want to print out a user's actual contact information for privacy reasons, you could write a variant of confirmContact that only looks at the constructor:

```
confirmContact' :: PreferredContactMethod -> String
confirmContact' contact =
  case contact of
    Mail{}        -> "Okay, I'll send you a letter!"
    Email{}       -> "Okay, I'll email you!"
    TextMessage{} -> "Okay, I'll text you!"
```

You might find yourself wondering what the benefit is of using a single sum type here rather than three different data types. You could, after all, write each branch of the case statement in our example as a function that takes some unique type and generates the right output:

```
data Email = Email String
data TextMessage = TextMessage String
data Mail = Mail String String String Int

emailContact :: Email
emailContact = Email "me@example.com"

textContact :: TextMessage
textContact = TextMessage "+1 307 555 0100"

mailContact :: Mail
mailContact = Mail "1123 S. Road St." "Suite 712" "Examplesville, OH" 98142
```

```
confirmEmailContact  (Email emailAddress) =
  "Okay, I'll email you at " <> emailAddress

confirmTextContact (TextMessage number) =
  "Okay, I'll text you at " <> number

confirmMailContact (Mail street1 street2 citystate zip) =
  "Okay, I' ll send a letter to\n"
  <> street1 <> "\n"
  <> street2 <> "\n"
  <> citystate <> " " <> show zip
```

This second approach might look appealing, and seems to offer even better type safety, but now consider the problem of writing a function that returns a preferred contact method for several different users. Using distinct types for each contact method makes this difficult because the function would need to return a value with a different type depending on the preferred contact method. Using sum types, however, we can easily express this function since all of our different values are still of type PreferredContactMethod:

```
contactForUser :: String -> PreferredContactMethod
contactForUser username =
  case username of
    "George" ->
      Email "george@example.com"
    "Porter" ->
      TextMessage "+1 307 555 0100"
    "Remmy"  ->
      Mail "1123 S. Road St." "Suite 712" "Examplesville, OH" 98142
    name ->
      Email $ name <> "@example.com"
```

Another example where sum types can help you get around restrictions you might face with multiple types is when dealing with lists. You know that you can only store a single type in a list, but if you have different types of values that you need to store, you can wrap them in a sum type.

Let's look at one more example, using sum types to store a list of strings and numbers:

```
data StringOrNumber = S String | N Int

stringsAndNumbers :: [StringOrNumber]
stringsAndNumbers =
  [ S "This list has"
  , N 2
  , S "different types of values"
  ]
```

Summing Records

Just as you were able to use record syntax to provide field names and get field selectors for data types with a single constructor, you can also use record syntax for sum types. The syntax for this is a combination of the record syntax you've seen using curly braces and field names, and the sum type syntax using |. Let's look at an example of combining sum types and records to create a sum type over customers and employees, along with a couple of example values:

```
data Person = Customer
    { name    :: String
    , balance :: Int
    }
    | Employee
    { name        :: String
    , managerName :: String
    , salary      :: Int
    }

george =
  Customer { name = "Georgie Bird"
           , balance = 100 }

porter =
  Employee { name = "Porter P. Pupper"
           , managerName = "Remi"
           , salary = 10 }
```

Using sum types with records gets you the same benefits as using records. As you saw in the example, you can use record syntax to make use of named fields when you construct a value. You can also use the field names to access values:

```
λ name george
"Georgie Bird"
λ name porter
"Porter P. Pupper"
```

Unfortunately, record syntax when combined with sum types introduces a source for potential errors. Record fields that exist only for certain data constructors are partial functions—if you try to access a field that doesn't exist for the value you've constructed, you'll get a runtime exception:

```
λ balance george
100
λ balance porter
*** Exception: No match in record selector balance
λ managerName porter
"Remi"
λ managerName george
"*** Exception: No match in record selector managerName
```

The risk of runtime errors from these partial record selectors means that most Haskell developers generally avoid directly combining sum types and records. Instead of directly mixing records and sum types, we can create a new record for each constructor. This will prevent us from ever trying to access fields that don't exist in a particular branch of our sum type. Let's look at an example:

```
data CustomerInfo = CustomerInfo
  { customerName :: String
  , customerBalance :: Int
  }

data EmployeeInfo = EmployeeInfo
  { employeeName :: String
  , employeeManagerName :: String
  , employeeSalary :: Int
  }

data Person
  = Customer CustomerInfo
  | Employee EmployeeInfo

george = Customer $
  CustomerInfo { customerName = "Georgie Bird"
               , customerBalance = 100 }

porter = Employee $
  EmployeeInfo { employeeName = "Porter P. Pupper"
               , employeeManagerName = "Remi"
               , employeeSalary = 10
               }
```

In this example, we've added records to hold the particular values associated with customers and employees independently. This avoids problems with partial field selectors, but now getting at any of our data means that we need to pattern match on Person and then call the appropriate field selector.

One way that we can work around this is to add functions to our API to make it easier to get at data that exists for all of the different potential values in our sum type. For example, since both customers and employees have names, we can add a function getPersonName to get the name for any person:

```
getPersonName :: Person -> String
getPersonName person =
  case person of
    Employee employee -> employeeName employee
    Customer customer -> customerName customer
```

What about functions to access fields that only exist in one constructor? Let's take a look at the employeeManager field to start with. The employeeManager field is a String, and it only exists in EmployeeInfo, which we have when we've constructed a person using the Employee constructor.

```
getPersonManager :: Person -> String
getPersonManager person =
  case person of
    Employee employee -> employeeManagerName employee
    Customer customer -> undefined
```

Now it seems like we're back in the land of partial functions. As long as we get an employee passed in, we can get the manager, but as soon as we get a customer we'll fail, because we'll encounter an undefined value. What we need to do is return the name of a manager if the person is an employee, but if they are a customer we need some value that says "nothing to see here, move along." That sounds a lot like a sum type! Let's create a new type called MaybeString to capture this:

```
data MaybeString = NoString | SomeString String
```

With the new type in hand, you can write a function that returns SomeString if there's a valid value, or NoString if there isn't:

```
getPersonManager :: Person -> MaybeString
getPersonManager person =
  case person of
    Employee employee -> SomeString (employeeManagerName employee)
    Customer _customer -> NoString
```

We can take the same approach with customerBalance and employeeSalary. You can imagine that we could create a new type named MaybeInt that works just like MaybeString, and use it to create functions to get a person's balance and salary:

```
getPersonBalance, getPersonSalary :: Person -> MaybeInt
```

As an exercise, implement the MaybeInt type and the getPersonBalance and getPersonSalary functions yourself. When you're finished, you can move on to the next section where you'll learn about another more general way to implement this pattern.

Creating Polymorphic Types

Having separate implementations for optional values of each type that we might return works, but it can quickly get out of hand. Not only do we have to create, and export, many new types, we also must write variations of many utility functions several times, require that our users learn about and remember the name of several types, and in general make a lot of extra work for ourselves. Thankfully we can avoid all of this additional work by making use of *type parameters*. Type parameters allow you to make a *type constructor* that takes some types as parameters. When you pass some parameters to a type constructor, you end up with a type. You have already worked with parameterized types when you've created lists and tuples, but until now we've glossed over the details.

Let's start by looking at the definition of the Maybe type. This will already be defined for you when you start a new program, since it's part of the Prelude. The Prelude is a module that's imported by default in all Haskell programs, and it contains all of the things from the standard library that are available by default. If you want to write this yourself as you follow along, you can pick another name, like MyMaybe.

```
data Maybe a = Nothing | Just a
```

In this example, Maybe by itself isn't a full type, so we call it a *type constructor*. When we pass a parameter to Maybe, we'll end up with a type like Maybe Int or Maybe String. The *type variable* a is a *type parameter*. Just like with polymorphic functions, the type variable a here can represent any type, but it will always represent the same type everywhere in our type definition. In many cases, you'll want to work with some specific instance of a type, like in the following examples where we implement balance, salary, and manager in terms of Maybe:

```
getPersonBalance :: Person -> Maybe Int
getPersonBalance person =
  case person of
    Customer customerInfo ->
      Just $ customerBalance customerInfo
    _ ->
      Nothing

getPersonSalary :: Person -> Maybe Int
getPersonSalary person =
  case person of
    Employee employeeInfo ->
      Just $ employeeSalary employeeInfo
    _ ->
      Nothing

getPersonManager :: Person -> Maybe String
getPersonManager person =
  case person of
    Employee employeeInfo ->
      Just $ employeeManagerName employeeInfo
    _ ->
      Nothing
```

In other cases, however, you may want to work with polymorphic versions of parameterized types. In this case, you can use a type variable just like you would with any other polymorphic function. For example, we can write a function that will take any type of Maybe value and convert it to a list of the appropriate type:

```
maybeToList :: Maybe a -> [a]
maybeToList (Just val) = [val]
maybeToList Nothing = []
```

The Maybe type generalizes a single optional value. It's frequently used both to signal optional inputs to a function as well as to make partial functions safe by indicating that there might not be a valid output for some input. Although useful, sometimes we want a slightly richer choice between two types, especially when we might want to represent success or detailed failure, or a choice between two paths. In this case, you can use another common type defined in Prelude, the Either type. Either takes two type parameters, representing the types of a left and right value. By convention in Haskell applications, Left typically represents an error case, and Right represents a success case.

```
data Either a b = Left a | Right b
```

Let's look at a couple of examples. We'll start by writing a function that tries to get the Right value of an Either:

```
eitherToMaybe :: Either b a -> Maybe a
eitherToMaybe e =
  case e of
    Left _    -> Nothing
    Right val -> Just val
```

In some cases, you might want to pass a parameterized type as an argument to another parameterized type. In that case, you need to use parentheses to group the types. Let's look at a concrete example by writing a function that takes an Either value to its Right constructor.

```
handleMissingRight :: Either String (Maybe a) -> Either String a
handleMissingRight e =
  case e of
    Left err           -> Left err
    Right (Just val)   -> Right val
    Right Nothing      -> Left "Missing value"
```

Of course you can keep adding parameters as you need. Most of the time one or two parameters are enough, but you'll occasionally see types with three, four, or even five parameters in some common Haskell libraries.

Creating Inductively Defined Data Structures

Data types in Haskell are also how we express data structures. Thanks to laziness, writing data structures in Haskell can present some interesting opportunities for thinking about new ways to express the structures of data. Most data structures that you'll build in Haskell are recursive, or as we sometimes call them, *inductively defined*. In this section, you'll implement several different inductively defined data structures.

Counting With Peano Numbers

The simplest type of inductively defined data structure that you can implement is a type that represents a *peano number*. Peano numbers are a way of representing whole numbers as a recursive function, where a given peano number is either "zero" or "a successor to a peano number." Peano numbers will have some use later on in this book when you learn about writing more advanced programs inside of the type system, but for now we won't focus on a practical use for them. Instead, they'll serve as a simple introduction to the idea of inductively defined data structures.

You can implement peano numbers as a sum type with two constructors. We'll call our data type Peano and we'll begin by adding a single value constructor. The first constructor we'll call Z, and it represents zero. It won't need to have any values associated with it, since it represents the single unit value of zero:

```
data Peano = Z
```

The successor constructor, which we'll call S will have a value, which is the peano number that it's a successor to:

```
data Peano = Z | S Peano
```

With this definition you can write functions like toPeano and fromPeano to walk the inductively defined data structure to get a numeric value. Let's implement those two functions to start with, so that it's easy to test with different values:

```
toPeano :: Int -> Peano
toPeano 0 = Z
toPeano n = S (toPeano $ n - 1)

fromPeano :: Peano -> Int
fromPeano Z = 0
fromPeano (S p) = succ (fromPeano p)
```

If you look closely, you'll see that there's a lot of similarity between the two functions. Both are recursive functions with a base case at zero. The successor functions in both cases reduce their input while growing their output. In toPeano each recursive call adds a new S constructor. In fromPeano we're using the succ function, from Prelude, which increments an enumeration. In our case we're using Int values, so succ n is another way of saying n + 1, but the name in this case serves to illustrate the similarities between the two functions.

You can load these functions up into ghci and play around with them, but it's hard to do much when you're limited to just converting back and forth between the different ways of representing a number. Let's add a couple of functions to make things a little more interesting. We'll start by adding an equality test for two peano numbers. Although we could of course convert them to Int and compare them with (==), it will be more illustrative to instead implement equality by traversing the data structure.

To test for equality, we'll create another recursive function that will traverse our data structure, but in this case we're taking two parameters, and we'll want to traverse them at the same time. By definition, Z values are always equal to one another, so we'll use that as our base case:

```
eqPeano :: Peano -> Peano -> Bool
eqPeano p p' =
  case (p,p') of
    (Z,Z) -> True
```

If we have two non-zero values, we can't directly test them for equality, but we can test whether their predecessors are equal recursively. Since at each step we're reducing each side by one, if they are equal, the call should terminate at zero for both values at the same time:

```
(S n, S n') -> eqPeano n n'
```

Finally, if one of the values is Z, but not the other, then they are not equal, because Z is only equal to Z. With that change, the full function will look like:

```
eqPeano :: Peano -> Peano -> Bool
eqPeano p p' =
  case (p,p') of
    (Z,Z) -> True
    (S n, S n') -> eqPeano n n'
    _ -> False
```

Lastly, let's add a function to add two peano numbers. Try to implement this function yourself as an exercise before continuing on to the solution:

```
addPeano :: Peano -> Peano -> Peano
addPeano Z b = b
addPeano (S a) b = addPeano a (S b)
```

In this example, we're recursively destructuring the first parameter and for each successor constructor we remove from the left-hand side, we add one to the right-hand side.

Inductively Defined Lists

The structure of the peano numbers, and the patterns you used for working with them, might have brought to mind the patterns that you've used when writing functions that work with lists. In fact, the structure of a linked list in Haskell very closely resembles that of the peano numbers. An inductively defined list will have two constructors, one representing an empty list, and another representing the value of the head of the list, and the tail of the list. One big difference is that for lists, we'll want to add an additional type parameter so that we can hold any sort of value. Let's write a linked list implementation to see it in action:

```
data List a = Empty | Cons a (List a)
```

You can implement toList and fromList functions using a similar pattern to the one that you used to implement toPeano and fromPeano. Try to write these functions yourself before you look at the example implementations:

```
toList :: [a] -> List a
toList [] = Empty
toList (x:xs) = Cons x (toList xs)

fromList :: List a -> [a]
fromList Empty = []
fromList (Cons x xs) = x : fromList xs
```

Manually implementing recursion on our lists is fine for these two functions, but if you were going to use them to write a longer program, it would start to get frustrating. Let's try to refactor the recursion out of these implementations and, in the process, look at how we can implement our own higher order functions on top of inductively defined data structures. We'll start with toList, which we can write using our friend foldr from Prelude:

```
toList :: [a] -> List a
toList = foldr Cons Empty
```

Going the other way, writing fromList, the algorithm that we want is the same:

```
fromList :: List a -> [a]
fromList = listFoldr (:) []
```

The problem here is that we haven't defined a fold function for our custom list type. Let's write one now. You can try to implementing this yourself before you look at the example:

```
listFoldr :: (a -> b -> b) -> b -> List a -> b
listFoldr _ b Empty = b
listFoldr f b (Cons x xs) =
  f x $ listFoldr f b xs
```

You can see in your implementation of the fold function, just like when you were working with peano numbers or manually implementing your list conversion functions, that the structure of the functions matches the structure of the recursion in the data types. This is a pattern that you'll see repeated across many different data structures as you work with Haskell applications.

For the sake of completeness, try implementing the following functions based on their type signatures and the behavior of the list functions in Prelude:

```
listFoldl :: (b -> a -> b) -> b -> List a -> b
listHead :: List a -> Maybe a
listTail :: List a -> List a
listReverse :: List a -> List a
listMap :: (a -> b) -> List a -> List b
```

Building a Calculator

Now that you have some experience working with sum types and implementing inductively defined data structures, let's put that knowledge into action and build a more sophisticated application. In this section, you'll build a small program to parse and evaluate arithmetic expressions in prefix notation. Before you start building the program, let's look at some examples of the application running:

```
λ run "+ 3 5"
"The answer is: 8"
λ run "/ 16 4"
"The answer is: 4"
λ run "* 2 / 16 4"
"The answer is: 8"
λ run "- 10 + 1 * 2 / 8 4"
"The answer is: 5"
```

As you can see in the examples, you'll need to support four different operations: addition, subtraction, multiplication, and division. Whenever you find yourself wanting to work with a fixed number of operations, like your arithmetic operations in this case, a sum type is a good first thing to start thinking about. Let's start by building a basic sum type that will capture these operations. Our type represents an arithmetic expression, so we'll call it Expr:

```
data Expr = Add | Sub | Mul | Div
```

Next, let's think about what fields we might want to associate with each of the constructors. These constructors all represent a binary operation. For now we'll only worry about Int types, so we can add the operands as fields to each constructor:

```
data Expr = Add Int Int
  | Sub Int Int
  | Mul Int Int
  | Div Int Int
```

This is a step forward. We have a data type that we could put data in and get data out of, but it's pretty limiting because we can't nest expressions. In our examples we were able to express several different operations in a single expression. To do that we'll want to make our data type recursive, meaning the operands for each constructor are themselves sub-expressions. That means that we need a base case. Luckily, there's one sitting in front of us that we overlooked when we originally enumerated our operations. Not only do we have our four binary operations, we also have literal numbers as part of the grammar of our arithmetic expression. Let's add a new Lit constructor to represent a literal integer, and update the rest of our type to recursively reference sub-expressions:

```
data Expr = Lit Int
    | Sub Expr Expr
    | Add Expr Expr
    | Mul Expr Expr
    | Div Expr Expr
```

Just like you did with peano numbers, you can write a recursive function that will take one of these recursive values and compute a number. Instead of incrementing the number, you'll decide on an operation based on the constructor for the value:

```
eval :: Expr -> Int
eval expr =
  case expr of
    Lit num -> num
    Add arg1 arg2 -> (eval arg1) + (eval arg2)
    Sub arg1 arg2 -> (eval arg1) - (eval arg2)
    Mul arg1 arg2 -> (eval arg1) * (eval arg2)
    Div arg1 arg2 -> (eval arg1) `div` (eval arg2)
```

You might notice some duplication here. Except in the case of literal numbers, all our case matches follow the same pattern where we recursively parse each of the two arguments and combine the results with some operation. We can refactor this to reduce the duplication by moving the recursion into a second function, which we'll call eval'. The eval' function will take the two arguments, along with our operator, and handle recursively parsing the two arguments:

```
eval :: Expr -> Int
eval expr =
  case expr of
    Lit num   -> num
    Add arg1 arg2 -> eval' (+) arg1 arg2
    Sub arg1 arg2 -> eval' (-) arg1 arg2
    Mul arg1 arg2 -> eval' (*) arg1 arg2
    Div arg1 arg2 -> eval' div arg1 arg2
    where
      eval' :: (Int -> Int -> Int) -> Expr -> Expr -> Int
      eval' operator arg1 arg2 =
        operator (eval arg1) (eval arg2)
```

With your new eval function in hand, you can start writing some expressions and evaluating them to numbers. Try loading your program up in ghci and evaluating a few expressions:

```
λ eval $ Add (Lit 1) (Lit 2)
3
λ eval $ Sub (Lit 10) (Div (Lit 10) (Lit 2))
5
λ eval $ Add (Lit 5) (Sub (Lit 10) (Div (Lit 10) (Lit 2)))
10
```

Remember that value constructors are normal functions, so you can use backticks to make them work as infix functions. If you find infix notation easier to read, give it a try:

```
λ eval $ Lit 5 `Add` (Lit 10 `Sub` (Lit 10 `Div` Lit 2))
10
```

You'll quickly notice that entering expressions by manually writing out all of the constructors is pretty obnoxious. Let's create a parser that will allow us to write nice expressions, like we did in the example we used to start this section. We'll call our parse function parse and it'll take a string as input. In the best-case scenario, we'd like to return an Expr value, but we'll need to account for erroneous input, since not every string is a valid arithmetic expression. Let's give our function the type: parse :: String -> Either String Expr.

We'll build our parser out in a few separate pieces, focusing on one step at a time. The first part of our parser will tokenize our input string, hand off the majority of the parsing to a second function, parse', and then do some final error handling before returning a value. In particular, we'll look for errors where parse' gives us back a Left value, because it found an error, or the case where it gives us a Right value, but tells us that it didn't parse all of the tokens.

Let's start by writing parse and then we'll move on to filling in some additional details by writing parse':

```
parse :: String -> Either String Expr
parse str =
  case parse' (words str) of
    Left err       -> Left err
    Right (e,[])   -> Right e
    Right (_,rest) -> Left $ "Found extra tokens: " <> (unwords rest)
```

The two functions that we're using from Prelude, words and unwords, work with strings. The words function takes an input string and splits it up along blank space boundaries, returning a list of strings. The unwords function, intuitively, does the opposite, taking a list of strings and joining them all with spaces.

With the top level function written, it's time to move on to the next part of the parser. Because these functions are helpers that are highly coupled to the implementation of parse, add them as let or where bindings rather than top level functions.

The parse' function is where we'll handle individual tokens. The shape of this function is quite similar to eval function that you have already written. We'll start with a case statement to look at the specific token that we're parsing.

To parse a literal value, we can use a function from the standard library named readEither from the Text.Read module. This function will try to parse a String value into some other value, in our case an Int. As you can imagine, not all strings can be converted into numbers. To handle errors, readEither will either return Right with our converted value, or Left with an error message.

Even though readEither is part of the standard library, it's not in scope by default. We'll need to import a new module to use it. You'll learn more about modules, and how to import things, in the next chapter. For now you can copy the import statement from the example directly into your code:

```
module Calculator where

import Text.Read (readEither)
```

For the operators in our expression, we'll need to recursively parse the arguments to the expression by looking at the rest of the string. Just like in eval, we'll factor the recursive function out into a helper. We'll call our helper function parseBinary, since it's parsing a *binary operator*, which is an operator that takes two arguments:

```
parse' :: [String] -> Either String (Expr,[String])
parse' []  = Left "unexpected end of expression"
```

```
parse' (token:rest) =
  case token of
    "+" -> parseBinary Add rest
    "*" -> parseBinary Mul rest
    "-" -> parseBinary Sub rest
    "/" -> parseBinary Div rest
    lit ->
      case readEither lit of
        Left err -> Left err
        Right lit' -> Right (Lit lit', rest)
```

You might wonder why we're returning a tuple of an expression and a list of strings here. This is a common pattern when implementing recursive parsers. The idea is that each recursive call will consume some part of the input, and will return the remainder of the input, allowing the caller to make forward progress through the list of tokens. This will make a bit more sense after you implement the parseBinary function, so let's move on to that next:

```
parseBinary ::
  (Expr -> Expr -> Expr)
  -> [String]
  -> Either String (Expr, [String])
parseBinary exprConstructor args =
  case parse' args of
    Left err -> Left err
    Right (firstArg,rest') ->
      case parse' rest' of
        Left err -> Left err
        Right (secondArg,rest'') ->
          Right $ (exprConstructor firstArg secondArg, rest'')
```

You can see that parseBinary looks similar to the eval' function that you wrote earlier. Instead of some arithmetic operator, it receives one of your Expr constructors. Instead of evaluating arguments recursively, it parses them. We've also had to add some error handling to account for the fact that parsing might fail.

Looking through the implementation of this function, we can now start to understand the reason for returning a tuple rather than an expression. As we parse the arguments for our operators, we have to know where to start parsing the second argument. To handle that, when we start parsing the first argument, we have it give us back the remainder of the string that it hasn't parsed, and we can use that remainder to start parsing the second argument.

Finally, as a matter of convenience, let's write one more function to make it easier to call our parser and evaluate the result. We'll call this function run and it will have the type run :: String -> String:

```
run :: String -> String
run expr =
  case parse expr of
    Left err -> "Error: " <> err
    Right expr' ->
      let answer = show $ eval expr'
      in "The answer is: " <> answer
```

Functions as Values

You've learned how to create data types and records that hold regular Haskell values, and build data types like List that hold recursive values. Another type of value you might sometimes want to hold inside of a data type is a function.

Creating a data type that holds a function looks much like creating any other data type. For example, we can make a data type that holds a function from a String to a pair of strings by saying this:

```
data StringParser = StringParser (String -> (String, String))
```

More often than not, when you see data types that hold a single function, they'll be records with a field that gives the function some useful name:

```
data StringParser =
  StringParser { runStringParser :: String -> (String, String) }
```

The first time you see something like this it can be a little bit hard to understand why you might want to create a data type that holds a function, when we already have first class functions in Haskell without needing to wrap them in a data type. Later on in this book, you'll learn some Haskell features that will make storing functions in data types more useful, but for now let's look at a small example of how keeping functions inside of data can help you build abstractions that could be easier for consumers of your code to use.

Sticking with our string parser example, we can imagine that there are any number of different functions that someone might want to write that could split a string into two different parts. One common example might be that we want to take some number of characters off the front of a string. If we were writing a plain function to do that, we might just use the splitAt function. In newer versions of GHC, this will already be defined for you. If you're using an older version of GHC, you'll need to import it from the Data.List module by adding import Data.List at the beginning of your module.

Let's look at a quick non-parser example first, and then we'll look at how we can turn it into a parser. We'll start by writing a function called takeCharacters that will take some number of characters off the front of a string. We don't just want to return those characters though, we also want to return the remainder of the string that we haven't dealt with yet, so we'll return a tuple. The first element of the tuple will be the data we just parsed, and the second element will be the data we haven't yet parsed:

```
module ParserExample where
import Data.List (splitAt)

takeCharacters :: Int -> String -> (String,String)
takeCharacters numCharacters inputString =
  splitAt numCharacters inputString
```

If we test this out in ghci we can see that our output is a tuple of strings, just as we'd expect:

```
λ takeCharacters 3 "abc12345"
("abc","12345")
```

Before we turn this into a StringParser let's do a little bit of a refactor on this code. We'll start by adding some parentheses back into the type signature. We can normally leave these out, but they'll make it easier for us to understand how we'll turn this version of our function into a StringParser:

```
takeCharacters :: Int -> (String -> (String,String))
takeCharacters numCharacters inputString =
  splitAt numCharacters inputString
```

Next, let's remove inputString from the definition of takeCharacters. Instead, we'll create a new function from the input string to our parsed tuple, and return that:

```
takeCharacters :: Int -> (String -> (String,String))
takeCharacters numCharacters = stringParser
  where
    stringParser :: String -> (String,String)
    stringParser inputString =
      splitAt numCharacters inputString
```

Now, let's rewrite stringParser to use a lambda abstraction rather than binding inputString as an argument:

```
takeCharacters :: Int -> (String -> (String,String))
takeCharacters numCharacters = stringParser
  where
    stringParser :: String -> (String,String)
    stringParser = \inputString ->
      splitAt numCharacters inputString
```

It's a small change to go from this refactored version of takeCharacters to a full StringParser version. We can create a StringParser value from a function with the type String -> (String,String) and that happens to be exactly the type of stringParser function we've already defined. We just need to pass the stringParser function into the StringParser value constructor:

```
takeCharacters :: Int -> StringParser
takeCharacters numCharacters = StringParser stringParser
  where
    stringParser :: String -> (String,String)
    stringParser = \inputString ->
      splitAt numCharacters inputString
```

Finally, let's refactor this function one last time to be a little bit less verbose. We can remove the intermediate definition of stringParser altogether and pass the lambda directly to the StringParser constructor:

```
takeCharacters :: Int -> StringParser
takeCharacters numCharacters = StringParser $ \inputString ->
  splitAt numCharacters inputString
```

This version of our parser is functionally equivalent to the original version, except now we've wrapped the part of the function that transforms strings inside of a StringParser, which will make it somewhat easier to work with.

Next, let's look at another example of a StringParser we might want to implement: parsing a string by extracting one space-separated word at a time. We can use the break function for this. The break function breaks a string into two parts at the first location where some predicate function that we pass in is true. In this example, we're breaking the string apart at the first space we encounter. Like splitAt we'll get back a tuple of lists. The first list will contain everything up until the first space, and the second list will contain everything after the first space.

```
getNextWord :: StringParser
getNextWord = StringParser $ \someString ->
  case break (== ' ') someString of
    (nextWord, "") -> (nextWord, "")
    (nextWord, rest) -> (nextWord, tail rest)
```

At this point you might be wondering what value StringParser is giving us in exchange for the added complexity of having to wrap part of our functions up in a value constructor. You'll learn about some more advanced ways we can use these kinds of values later. For now, let's look at one good example: making it easy to combine our parsers in a general way. For example, we can write a function that runs two parsers, one after another:

```
combineParsers :: StringParser -> StringParser -> StringParser
combineParsers firstParser secondParser = StringParser $ \someString ->
  let (_firstPart, firstResult) = runStringParser firstParser someString
  in runStringParser secondParser firstResult
```

This lets us easily re-use existing functions that we've already written, combining them in interesting ways to create new parsers that we could also join together if we wanted to. For example, let's look at two different ways that we could combine takeCharacters and getNextWord:

```
getNextWordAfterTenLetters :: StringParser
getNextWordAfterTenLetters =
  combineParsers (takeCharacters 10) getNextWord

tenLettersAfterTheFirstWord :: StringParser
tenLettersAfterTheFirstWord =
  combineParsers getNextWord (takeCharacters 10)
```

In all of these examples, the first string of our tuple is the one that we're really interested in. The second string is just holding the rest of the data in case we want to do something else with it, like use it with a different parser. When we're building things like this, we'll usually make a helper function that will run a parser for us and just give us the value we're interested in:

```
parseString :: StringParser -> String -> String
parseString parser inputString =
  fst $ runStringParser parser inputString
```

Now that we have all of these functions, let's explore them a little bit in ghci. First, we can run our basic parsers to get the values out of them:

```
λ parseString (takeCharacters 5) "Hello, World"
"Hello"
λ parseString getNextWord "Haskell Is Fun"
"Haskell"
```

And we can call our combined versions just as easily:

```
λ parseString tenLettersAfterTheFirstWord "AVeryLongWord 0123456789abcdef"
"0123456789"
λ parseString getNextWordAfterTenLetters "123456 hello world"
"lo"
```

We can even create new ways to parse things ad hoc in the REPL as we're exploring our code:

```
λ secondWord = combineParsers getNextWord getNextWord
λ thirdWord = combineParsers getNextWord secondWord
λ parseString thirdWord "one two three four"
"three"
```

Of course everything that we've done in these examples could have been done without putting our functions into a data type, but the data type has made our code a bit easier to work with. We no longer have to keep track of many layers of higher-order functions directly, or pass around a lot of parameters all the time. We can think in terms of the abstract idea of something that parses a string.

Creating Type Aliases

Throughout this chapter, you've learned how to create new data types from scratch to describe the values in your program, but there are some cases where creating an entirely new type from scratch isn't necessary. In some cases, you might just want to provide a new name to some existing type. In these cases, rather than creating a new type, you can use a *type alias*.

Type aliases can be a useful way to improve the readability of your code while retaining a degree of flexibility and avoiding introducing the overhead of constructing new data types, but they can also be misused in ways that remove some of the protections you can get with proper types. In this section, we'll look first at one of the cases where type aliases might make your code quality worse. Once you have had a chance to see how to not use type aliases, we'll look at a couple of examples of cases where they can be useful.

Wrapping Basic Data Types

Type aliases allow you to provide a new name for some existing type. You've already been using one type alias throughout this book, perhaps without realizing it: the String type is a type alias for a list of Char values. If you look at the info for String in ghci you can see precisely how it's defined:

```
λ :i String
type String = [Char]    -- Defined in ‘GHC.Base’
```

From this example you can see that a type alias is defined with the type keyword, followed by the alias name. The type on the right-hand side is the type that is being aliased. Note that, unlike with a data type, there is no data constructor on the right-hand side of the equals sign here.

Defining a type alias is a handy way to be able to give some general type a name that's more semantically meaningful in your application. String is a great example of providing a more meaningful name, but let's build our own function that makes use of type aliases as well. We'll write a program that will let us calculate the average velocity of an object given the distance that it has traveled, in meters, over some period of time, given in seconds. We could start with a version that doesn't use type aliases:

```
velocity :: Double -> Double -> Double
velocity meters seconds = meters / seconds
```

```
speedLimit :: Double
speedLimit =
  let
    meters = 299792458 :: Double
    seconds = 1.0 :: Double
  in velocity meters seconds
```

If someone is looking at the implementation of our function, it's fairly straightforward how to use it, but imagine that our function was made available in some library and a user wants to call it. They might start by checking its type signature:

```
λ :type velocity
velocity :: Double -> Double -> Double
```

Without looking at the implementation, or reading the documentation, it's hard to use this function. Our users will have no idea what the order of the arguments should be, nor the units to use for input or what units to expect for output. Let's look at what happens when we use type aliases to provide a more human readable name for the Doubles in the type signature:

```
type Meters = Double
type Seconds = Double
type MetersPerSecond = Double

velocity :: Meters -> Seconds -> MetersPerSecond
velocity meters seconds = meters / seconds
```

We haven't changed the implementation of velocity here at all, instead we've simply created some aliases for Double and used them in the type annotation for velocity. We can rebuild our program and you'll see that it builds and even the speedLimit function continues to work, although we are passing it Doubles instead of the new type aliases.

```
λ :type velocity
velocity :: Double -> Double -> Double
λ :type speedLimit
speedLimit :: Double
λ speedLimit
9.8
```

The flexibility with type aliases that allows our speedLimit method to continue working after we've refactored velocity has worked out for us in this case, but it hints at one of the cases where type aliases can cause us some problems: because all type aliases that resolve to the same type are equivalent, the compiler gives us no extra help if we misuse them.

One straightforward example of this is that since Meters and Seconds are both aliases for Double, we can use them arbitrarily in ways that don't make sense for what the values should semantically represent. For example, the compiler will happily let us add meters to seconds, or pass seconds in as the first parameter of velocity:

```
λ oneMinute = 60 :: Seconds
λ oneKilometer = 1000 :: Meters
λ someMeters = (velocity (oneMinute + oneKilometer) oneKilometer) :: Meters
λ :type someMeters
someMeters :: Meters
```

Similarly, if we refactor velocity to swap the order of the arguments, our speedLimit function would continue to compile but return incorrect results:

```
λ :type velocity
velocity :: Seconds -> Meters -> MetersPerSecond
λ speedLimit
0.1020408163265306
```

It's worth noting that all of these errors would have been possible if we'd never created a type alias in the first place. We could just as easily add a double that was supposed to represent Meters with one that was supposed to represent Seconds. Introducing type aliases hasn't allowed any new errors as far as the compiler is concerned, but it has provided us with a false sense of safety, and in making the choice to use type errors over data types, we've given up the opportunity for the compiler to help detect some of these errors for us.

As you can see, type aliases offer some benefits over using built-in types, but they can sometimes make code a bit more error prone, or at the very least we give up the opportunity to get better type safety from using a proper data type. So when is the right time to use a type alias?

Type aliases are best reserved for cases where the aliased type really does have the same meaning as the type it's aliasing. String as an alias for [Char] is a good example of this. A String makes sense as a list of characters, and it's intuitive that any operation that would work on one would work on the other. On the other hand, an alias like Seconds has a very different meaning from a plain Int, so it's not a good example of when to use a type alias.

Using Type Aliases with Type Parameters

One of the most common ways to make use of type aliases is to use them to fix some type parameters. In other words, you can use a type alias as a way to give a name to some partially applied type. This avoids some of the problems you ran into in the last section where you create type aliases that have some distinct semantic meaning from their underlying type, and instead encourages you to create aliases that do have some logical mapping to the underlying type.

In fact, the String alias that we looked at in the previous section as an example of a "good" type alias is an example of this pattern. Recall that a String is an alias for a list of characters, which we typically write:

```
type String = [Char]
```

Let's rewrite this using our own list type, to help clarify what's happening. We'll call our string type String' to differentiate it from the standard string type:

```
data List a = Empty | List a
type String' = List Char
```

It's easier to see here that a String is just applying the Char type to List or [].

You can extend this pattern to types that have more than one parameter. For example, consider the Either type. Imagine that you have some specific error type that you've defined for your application. It might have an error message along with some additional context:

```
data AppError = AppError
  { errorMessage :: String
  , errorContext :: [String]
  , errorWrapped :: Maybe AppError
  }
```

You could write all of the functions in your program so they return Either AppError a. For example, imagine you were writing a small inventory management program and you had some functions that all might fail in some way:

```
parseUserOrder :: String -> Either AppError Order
generateInvoice :: Order -> Either AppError Invoice
updateInventory :: [Order] -> [(Widget,Int)] -> Either AppError [(Widget,Int)]
```

There's nothing necessarily wrong with the repetition of Either AppError here, but if you are going to consistently use this pattern throughout your program, making use of a type alias can make the program both more readable, and also can make it a little bit easier for you to avoid mistakenly writing a function that returns some other error value. Let's take a look at how we could do this.

We'll start by creating a type alias for Either AppError. Type aliases can have parameters just like regular data types, so we could write this:

```
type AppValue a = Either AppError a
```

Alternatively, and more idiomatically, you can η-reduce this and write:

```
type AppValue = Either AppError
```

With the type alias, you can rewrite your functions:

```
parseUserOrder :: String -> AppValue Order
generateInvoice :: Order -> AppValue Invoice
updateInventory :: [Order] -> [(Widget,Int)] -> AppValue [(Widget,Int)]
```

Using a type alias here makes our code a little bit more readable, by removing some of the noise of having Either AppError repeated everywhere in the code. Instead, we have AppValue which is shorter and conveys a bit of useful meaning. We also get the benefit that we ensure that anyone using an AppValue will consistently use our AppError type for errors. If we had continued to use Either directly, someone working in the code base might have reasonably decided to use some other value instead of AppError. By fixing that parameter to Either, we're making it more clear that we intend to standardize on that as our error value in all of the functions we're using in our application.

Summary

Although we call Haskell a *functional* programming language, data and the way that we represent it is at the heart of how to write effective Haskell programs. Creating the right data types will help the compiler help you by finding bugs and helping you write more reliable code, but more than that, the way that you structure data in your programs will influence everything about how you work with your code, and how it evolves over time. Data is, in essence, the real heart of functional programming. As you work through the rest of this book you'll see many other ways that data impacts that way we think about code.

Exercises

Planting Trees

Consider a binary tree with a type:

```
data BinaryTree a = Leaf | Branch (BinaryTree a) a (BinaryTree a)
```

Write the definition of the binary tree type, and then add the following functions:

```
-- Turn a binary tree of strings into a pretty-printed string
showStringTree :: BinaryTree String -> String

-- Add a new integer into a binary tree of integers
addElementToIntTree :: BinaryTree Int -> Int -> BinaryTree Int

-- Check to see if an int value exists in a binary tree of ints
doesIntExist :: BinaryTree Int -> Int -> Bool
```

Eval Division by Zero

Write a new version of your eval function named safeEval that will return an error if the user tries to divide by zero. It should have the type:

```
safeEval :: Expr -> Either String Int
```

Here's an example of the output you should expect when using safeEval:

```
λ> eval $ Lit 10 `Div` Lit 0
*** Exception: divide by zero
λ> safeEval $ Lit 10 `Div` Lit 0
Left "Error: division by zero"
λ> safeEval $ Lit 10 `Div` Lit 10
Right 1
```

Hint: You may need to make quite a few changes to your eval function to complete this exercise, but no changes to your Expr type should be necessary, and you should not need to write any additional functions.

Calculator Pretty Printer

Write a new function, prettyPrint, with the type:

```
prettyPrint :: Expr -> String
```

The function should take any expression and return a human readable string that shows the calculation as someone might write it themselves.

```
λ putStrLn $ prettyPrint $ Lit 5 `Add` Lit 10
5 + 10 = 15
λ putStrLn $ prettyPrint $ Lit 5 `Add` (Lit 10 `Div` Lit 2)
5 + ( 10 ÷ 2 ) = 10
λ putStrLn $ prettyPrint $ Lit 14 `Mul` (Lit 5 `Add` (Lit 10 `Div` Lit 2))
14 × ( 5 + ( 10 ÷ 2 ) ) = 140
```

CHAPTER 5

Creating And Structuring Haskell Projects

So far, all the programs that you've built have been small applications that fit in a single source file. To run these programs you've compiled your source file with `ghc`, or ran them directly from `ghci`. As you start to do more with Haskell, your programs will grow, and you'll want to have applications that are organized across several files. You'll also want to start bringing in external dependencies beyond what's available in the standard library.

There are several popular Haskell build tools that will help you organize projects and manage dependencies. In this chapter, you'll learn about how Haskell projects are organized, and how to build applications and manage external dependencies. We'll focus on building projects using *cabal*, one of the most popular Haskell build and dependency management tools.

Creating Haskell Projects

Cabal is something of a Swiss army knife in the Haskell ecosystem, and it serves several purposes, including: package and dependency management, building, and running your program. In this section, we'll take a quick tour of these features and you'll learn how to get started using cabal to define a new project, manage dependencies, and build the project.

Your Output Might Look Different

This chapter contains some example output you might see when creating new projects with cabal. Since cabal is getting active updates to add new features, you might notice minor differences between the examples here and the output you see when you follow along. Don't worry though, even though some things will change as cabal improves, the examples in this chapter should continue to work as expected for a long time, even if the output you see from the tool changes a bit.

Using Cabal as a Haskell Package Manager

Cabal works as a package manager and you can use it to manage Haskell libraries and applications. You can install libraries and applications for your user with cabal by running cabal install. For example, let's install the stylish-haskell that will let you automatically format your Haskell source files. Start by running cabal update to update the package cache. This tells cabal what packages and versions are available for you to install:

```
user@host$ cabal update
Downloading the latest package list from hackage.haskell.org
To revert to previous state run:
    cabal v2-update 'hackage.haskell.org,2020-10-13T23:04:28Z'
user@host$ cabal install stylish-haskell
```

When you run cabal install, cabal will download and compile the latest version of the application for you. The resulting binary will be available in ${HOME}/.cabal/bin. It's a good idea to add that path to your environment's default search path. For example, you can add the following to your .bashrc file if you are using bash on a *nix system:

```
export PATH=${HOME}/.cabal/bin:${PATH}
```

You can also install Haskell libraries on your system with cabal by passing it the --lib flag. For example, you can install the very popular text library with cabal:

```
user@host$ cabal install --lib text
```

Most of the time you'll manage dependencies and install libraries on a per-project basis, and won't need to install packages directly like this, however, it may be handy if you want to ensure some libraries are always available for quickly writing small scripts for doing ad hoc work in ghci.

Starting a Cabal Project

The way you'll use cabal most of the time is for building and running projects that are managed using cabal. When you're creating a new project, you can use cabal to initialize the project by running cabal init.

To see all the options available when running cabal init you can run:

```
user@host$ cabal help init
```

There are a lot of options, but for now we'll just pass in the --interactive flag. Let's walk step by step through each prompt to understand what cabal is asking. These examples come from cabal version 3.2.0.0. The text might look slightly different if you're using a newer version of cabal.

```
user@host$ mkdir learn-cabal
user@host$ cd learn-cabal
user@host$ cabal init --interactive
Should I generate a simple project with sensible defaults? [default: y] n
What does the package build:
   1) Executable
   2) Library
   3) Library and Executable
Your choice? 3
```

This first prompt is asking you what kind of project you'd like to create. For libraries, pick the *Library* option. If you're building an application, however, it's common to use the *Library and Executable* project rather than just *Executable*. This supports the common Haskell idiom of creating a very small minimal executable application and putting most of the application logic in a library. Separating out the logic into a library makes testing easier.

```
What is the main module of the executable:
 * 1) Main.hs (does not yet exist, but will be created)
   2) Main.lhs (does not yet exist, but will be created)
   3) Other (specify)
Your choice? [default: Main.hs (does not yet exist, but will be created)] 1
```

The next option you are presented with asks you what the name of the Main module should be for your application. By convention this is named Main and may be a regular Haskell source file called Main.hs or a *literate Haskell* file named Main.lhs. You can also select your own filename if you choose (App.hs is a popular alternative). We won't cover literate Haskell in this book, so go ahead and select the default option to create a file named Main.hs.

```
Please choose version of the Cabal specification to use:
 * 1) 1.10   (legacy)
   2) 2.0    (+ support for Backpack, internal sub-libs, '^>=' operator)
   3) 2.2    (+ support for 'common', 'elif', redundant commas, SPDX)
   4) 2.4    (+ support for '**' globbing)
Your choice? [default: 1.10   (legacy)] 4
```

Now you are given an option to select which type of cabal configuration file you want to use. The default option here is the legacy cabal file format, which is the most widely supported option and is a good choice if you don't need newer features. In this chapter, you'll be learning about newer cabal features, so go ahead and select the most recent option:

```
Package name? [default: learn-cabal] learn-cabal
```

The next prompt gives you a chance to name your package. The default package name is the name of the current working directory. You can select the default here or pick a different package name:

```
Package version? [default: 0.1.0.0] 0.1.0.0
```

You can also pick an initial version number for your package. This should follow the Haskell *Package Versioning Policy* (*PVP*). The PVP uses a four-part numbering system, generation.major.minor.patch. Changes to the *generation* number indicate very large, perhaps philosophical, changes to the API design. *Major* version number changes indicate backwards-incompatible changes. *Minor* changes indicate backwards-compatible changes such as additions to the library or bugfixes. *Patch* level changes indicate that only bugfixes have been added. You can refer to the PVP documentation[1] for a detailed summary of the package versioning policy and how to use it when creating and publishing packages.

```
Please choose a license:
   1) GPL-2.0-only
   2) GPL-3.0-only
   3) LGPL-2.1-only
   4) LGPL-3.0-only
   5) AGPL-3.0-only
   6) BSD-2-Clause
 * 7) BSD-3-Clause
   8) MIT
   9) ISC
  10) MPL-2.0
  11) Apache-2.0
  12) LicenseRef-PublicDomain
  13) NONE
  14) Other (specify)
Your choice? [default: BSD-3-Clause] 7
```

After setting a version, you can choose a license for your application. You can choose one of the suggested options or pick your own. If you are picking your own license, cabal uses *SPDX* license identifiers. Most open source code in the Haskell community is released under the BSD-3 license. If you select a license that cabal knows about, it will automatically create a file named LICENSE that contains the text of the selected license.

```
Author name? [default: Haskell Programmer] Haskell Programmer
Maintainer email? [default: haskeller@example.com] haskeller@example.com
Project homepage URL? http://example.com
Project synopsis? A sample project to learn how to use cabal
```

The next several questions give you an opportunity provide your name and email address, along with a homepage for your project and a synopsis. If you don't otherwise have a homepage for your project, it's common to use a link

1. https://pvp.haskell.org

to where the project is hosted, such as on github[2] or gitlab.[3] You can change these values later, so don't worry if you don't have a good synopsis or a homepage yet.

```
Project category:
 * 1) (none)
   2) Codec
   3) Concurrency
   4) Control
   5) Data
   6) Database
   7) Development
   8) Distribution
   9) Game
  10) Graphics
  11) Language
  12) Math
  13) Network
  14) Sound
  15) System
  16) Testing
  17) Text
  18) Web
  19) Other (specify)
Your choice? [default: (none)] 1
```

The project category is used to help organize projects in Hackage. If any of the suggestions seem appropriate, select one, or you can choose *none* if nothing seems like a good fit.

```
Application (Main.hs) directory:
 * 1) (none)
   2) src-exe
   3) app
   4) Other (specify)
Your choice? [default: (none)] 3
Library source directory:
 * 1) (none)
   2) src
   3) lib
   4) src-lib
   5) Other (specify)
Your choice? [default: (none)] 2
```

The next two questions will help cabal create the appropriate directories to organize your application. A common convention that you'll see throughout

2. https://github.com
3. https://gitlab.com

the examples in this book is to use a directory called app to hold the source file for the executable portion of the application and a directory called src to hold the source code to the library portion of the application.

```
Should I generate a test suite for the library? [default: y] y
```

Cabal can generate a test suite for you if you ask it to. This is a good way to make sure that there is less friction to writing tests as you start developing your application.

```
Test directory:
 * 1) test
   2) Other (specify)
Your choice? [default: test] 1
```

Just like the executable and library portions of your application, the directory where you store your test files is configurable. A directory named test is the most common choice.

```
What base language is the package written in:
 * 1) Haskell2010
   2) Haskell98
   3) Other (specify)
Your choice? [default: Haskell2010] 1
```

Next you have the opportunity to select a language standard that should be used with your project. For all of the examples in this book you'll want to select Haskell2010.

```
Add informative comments to each field in the cabal file (y/n)? [default: n] n

Guessing dependencies...

Generating LICENSE...
Generating Setup.hs...
Generating CHANGELOG.md...
Generating src/MyLib.hs...
Generating app/Main.hs...
Generating test/MyLibTest.hs...
Generating learn-cabal.cabal...

You may want to edit the .cabal file and add a Description field.
```

The final choice you'll have to answer is whether or not you'd like the generated cabal configuration file to contain helpful comments. These comments can be a great way to learn more about the fields. In the example cabal file in the next section we'll omit the comments, but you should try generating a file with the comments enabled to get a chance to read the documentation on what the fields are doing.

Understanding the Cabal File Format

Whether you are generating a file using cabal init or starting from scratch or an existing project, your cabal projects will need a cabal file. Cabal files use the .cabal extension, and by convention will share the name of your project.

In the last section, you should have generated a new cabal file named learn-cabal.cabal. It should look something like the example:

```
cabal-version:       2.4
-- Initial package description 'learn-cabal.cabal' generated by 'cabal
-- init'.  For further documentation, see
-- http://haskell.org/cabal/users-guide/

name:                learn-cabal
version:             0.1.0.0
synopsis:            A sample project to learn how to use cabal
-- description:
homepage:            http://example.com
-- bug-reports:
license:             BSD-3-Clause
license-file:        LICENSE
author:              Haskell Programmer
maintainer:          haskeller@example.com
-- copyright:
-- category:
extra-source-files:  CHANGELOG.md

library
  exposed-modules:     MyLib
  -- other-modules:
  -- other-extensions:
  build-depends:       base ^>=4.13.0.0
  hs-source-dirs:      src
  default-language:    Haskell2010

executable learn-cabal
  main-is:             Main.hs
  -- other-modules:
  -- other-extensions:
  build-depends:       base ^>=4.13.0.0, learn-cabal
  hs-source-dirs:      app
  default-language:    Haskell2010

test-suite learn-cabal-test
  default-language:    Haskell2010
  type:                exitcode-stdio-1.0
  hs-source-dirs:      test
  main-is:             MyLibTest.hs
  build-depends:       base ^>=4.13.0.0
```

In this section, you'll learn about the syntax of cabal files and about some of the package properties and fields that are generated when you initialize a new cabal project. Most of the fields we'll look at in this section relate to Haskell features you will learn about later in this book, so we'll only touch briefly on them now, and we'll revisit them later as the relevant features are introduced.

The generated cabal file is a good demonstration of the basic syntax of a cabal file. Most cabal files consist primarily of some top-level package properties along with some build target stanzas and target-level fields. The properties and fields are both key-value pairs separated by a colon:

```
key: value
```

A cabal stanza, usually with a name, and some fields:

```
stanza-type name
  field-key-1: field-val-1
  field-key-2: field-val-2
```

In most cases, the stanzas that you'll see in a cabal file will refer to some build target. In our generated example, we have library, executable, and test-suite target stanzas. You'll learn about some additional stanzas later in this book as you start to incorporate new features into your programs. You can refer to the cabal documentation[4] for a complete description of all of the stanzas and fields that are available.

Comments are also supported in cabal files. Like Haskell comments, cabal comments start with two dashes. A comment can start at the beginning of a line, or after indentation, but it can't trail any other expressions:

```
-- This is a comment top level comment
library
  -- this is an indented comment
  exposed-modules: MyLib -- This comment will cause an error
```

At the top of the generated cabal file you'll see several package-level properties that have been set based on the answers you gave during the initialization process. The name and version properties are the only two properties that are strictly required for all cabal files. For the generated example file, the cabal-version property is also required, since otherwise cabal will default to an earlier version of the cabal file format that doesn't support all of the features used in the generated example.

4. https://cabal.readthedocs.io/en/3.4/index.html

Try running cabal init several times with different answers to the prompts, or generate the file with additional helpful comments, to get a complete description of all of the properties that are provided when you generate a new cabal file. Next we'll turn our attention to the target stanzas and the fields that are set for them.

After the package-level properties, you can see we have three stanzas in the generated file, for each of the three targets that we can build. The first of these is the library stanza. The library target needs to be present when you're building a library from your package. Unlike the other targets you'll see later on in this section, the default library target doesn't take a name parameter—the name of the library will always be the same as the name of your package. Newer versions of cabal do allow you to define some additional private libraries that can help you better organize your project, and those libraries must be named just like other targets.

Within the library target, you can see that we have a few fields already set, as well as a couple of optional fields that have been commented out.

```
library
  exposed-modules:     MyLib
  -- other-modules:
  -- other-extensions:
  build-depends:       base ^>=4.13.0.0
  hs-source-dirs:      src
  default-language:    Haskell2010
```

The first two fields in the library target, exposed-modules and other-modules, are the only ones that are library specific. These fields are responsible for listing which parts of the library are public and available to all consumers of the library, and which parts are private to the library itself. The exposed-modules field is required and lists the publicly available parts of the library. other-modules is optional, and you can see that it's been commented out in our example. This field will allow you to list parts of the library that are for internal use only. You'll revisit these fields later on in this chapter once you've learned more about modules and added some to your example project.

other-extensions is another optional field that's been added to the cabal file for us. It's often used with another optional field, default-extensions. These fields let you configure language extensions you want to enable for an entire project. The default-extensions lists language features that you want to enable across the entire build target, and other-extensions lists the ones that you'll want to enable on a case-by-case basis. Language extensions must be supported by a compatible compiler, and cabal may use these fields to solve for the minimal required compiler versions to build the package.

build-depends lists the libraries, internal or external, that the build target depends on. It's a comma-separated list with an optional version restriction. For example, if you wanted to depend on any version of base along with the text and bytestring libraries you would set the field to:

```
build-depends:   base
               , text
               , bytestring
```

In some cases, you might not want to specify version dependencies in the cabal file. This might happen during active development when you want to make sure you're always using the most up-to-date packages, when you're using a *freeze file* to manage dependencies, or when an external tool is managing dependencies and versioning for you, for example, if you're using nixpkgs to manage your build environment.

More often, especially for libraries that you're going to publish, you'll want to add version constraints to your dependencies. Version constraints help cabal download a compatible version of your dependencies when building your library and help make sure that all the dependencies in a project work together.

Cabal supports all of the usual equality and inequality operators for comparing versions: >, >=, ==, <= and < all work as you would expect, allowing you to require an exact version of a package, or depending on newer or older versions. For example to depend on base version 4.13.0.0 or newer you can write:

```
build-depends: base >=4.13.0.0
```

Hackage's package versioning policy, the PVP, specifies that a change in the the two leftmost fields of a version number indicate backwards-incompatible changes. For example, going from version 1.0.0.0 to 2.0.0.0 would indicate a substantial redesign of the library, whereas going to version 1.1.0.0 would indicate that a small backwards-incompatible change has been introduced. Similarly, going to 1.0.1.0 or 1.0.0.1 should be a compatible change. This versioning policy means that it's usual to depend on a range of compatible versions. You can combine version constraints using && or ||, and so it's common to see constraints like *at least version 4.13.0.0, but less than 4.14*:

```
build-depends: base >=4.13.0.0 && < 4.14
```

This pattern is common enough in fact that cabal supports special syntax to express constraints like this. The so-called *carrot operators* limit a constraint to only the range of packages that should be compatible per the PVP guidelines. The constraint `base ^>= 4.13.0.0` inequality in the example file is doing exactly that.

Changing How Your Program Gets Built

After adding dependencies and updating the list of modules you are providing, one of the most important things you'll want to do in your cabal files is to configure the way `ghc` will build your programs. You can do this by adding options to the `ghc-options` field for each target in your cabal file. Here's an example of a common set of compiler flags that you might enable by default in a library:

```
ghc-options: -O1 -Wall
```

If you are compiling an executable program instead of a library, you might instead have this:

```
ghc-options: -O1 -threaded -rtsopts -with-rtsopts=-N
```

The GHC manual[5] contains an extensive list of all of the flags that you can provide to fine-tune how your program is compiled. In this section, we'll look at a couple of the most common options that you might want to configure for your programs. All of these flags can be set in the `ghc-options` field of your cabal file, or passed to GHC directly if you are compiling your program without cabal.

Optimizations

The most common option you'll want to set when you compile your program is to turn on optimizations. Enabling optimizations will generally make your program run faster and possibly use less memory. You can control the level of optimization with the `-O` flag. If you don't pass an optimization flag at all, or pass in `-O0`, the compiler will not do any optimizations at all. The first optimization level, `-O1` will turn on a number of individual optimization options. You can get even more optimizations, at the cost of slower compile times, by enabling `-O2`. In most cases, you should enable `-O1` when you start a new project. This will give you a good balance of performance and faster compile times. If you want better performance you should try `-O2` and, then fine tune the specific set of optimizations later on a case-by-case basis if you have evidence that you need to enable or disable them.

5. https://downloads.haskell.org/~ghc/latest/docs/html/users_guide/flags.html

Warnings and Errors

By default, Haskell is fairly conservative about the kinds of code that it will warn you about. The -Wall flag turns on many more warnings, making it easier to find potential bugs in your program. Although the "all" in -Wall might make you think this flag enables all warnings, it actually only enables common and safe warnings. You can enable every warning that GHC knows about by passing in -Weverything.

It's a common practice in mature projects enable the -Werror flag. This flag will turn warnings into errors, meaning that your program will fail to compile if there are any warnings at all. Forcing yourself to fix any warnings before your program will compile can help improve the quality of your code in the long-run, but it can also slow you down enormously when you are actively developing code and find that you can't load your code into ghci or run some tests until you fix all of the warnings in your project.

Profiling

Sometimes your program runs more slowly or requires more memory than you expect. In these situations, it can be helpful to profile your program to see how it's being run. GHC supports profiling your programs at runtime, but to enable that feature you need to compile your program, and all of its dependencies, with profiling enabled. You can enable profiling for your particular target by adding the -prof option to GHC. If you want complete profiling information, you should also configure cabal to download the profiling information for all of your dependencies by running:

```
cabal configure --enable-profiling
```

Building and Running Your Program

Once you have a cabal file written that defines what your project should look like, you can also use cabal to compile or run any target in your cabal file. For small projects like the ones you'll build while working through this book, you can compile your applications by running cabal build. This is a quick way to compile all the targets in your cabal file to see if you have any errors. If you are missing any dependencies, cabal will download and install them for you when you compile your application.

For larger applications with long compile times, you can specify a single target from your cabal file. In some cases, like if you have an executable and library target with the same name, the name of the target by itself might be ambiguous, and so you need to give cabal some additional information by prefixing the target name with lib or exe:

```
user@host$ cabal build lib:learn-cabal
Up to date
user@host$ cabal build exe:learn-cabal
Up to date
```

After you've compiled an application you can run it with cabal exec. You'll need to provide the name of an executable target to tell cabal which application you want to run. You can only run executable targets, so you don't need to worry about prefixing your target names with exe:

```
user@host$ cabal exec learn-cabal
Hello, Haskell!
someFunc
```

When you're actively working on a project and iteratively testing your program, it's inconvenient to have to compile and then run your program repeatedly. The cabal run command combines both compilation and execution into a single command, letting you easily run the latest version of your program:

```
user@host$
cabal run learn-cabal
Up to date
Hello, Haskell!
someFunc
```

Using Code from Other Modules

It's rare to write programs that are entirely self contained. Nearly all programs that we write will depend on some some code that's been defined elsewhere in some other module. To make use of code defined in some other module, we have to *import* the code from that module. When we import a module, we can get access to all of the code that it has *exported*. In this section, we'll focus on using libraries, and you'll learn how to import code from modules defined inside of libraries that you depend on. Later on in this chapter, you'll learn how to define your own modules and control what they export.

Importing a Module

You can import a module using the import keyword. You need to write an import declaration for each module you want to import, and all of your imports should be at the top of your module, immediately after the module declaration. Once you import a module, everything that module exports will be available to use.

As an example, let's create a cabal project named import-demo. You can write the cabal file yourself or use cabal init to create an executable project:

```
cabal-version:      2.4
name:               import-demo
version:            0.1.0.0
license:            NONE

executable import-demo
    main-is:          Main.hs
    build-depends:    base
    hs-source-dirs:   app
    default-language: Haskell2010
```

Now that we have a new project, let's write an application that can benefit from using some parts of the standard library that aren't normally available to us without importing an extra module. For this example, we'll write a program that will count the number of non-printable characters, like tab and newline characters, in a string.

In order to count the number of non-printable characters, we need to know whether a particular character is printable or not. The standard library includes a function named isPrint that returns True if a character is a printable Unicode character, and False otherwise.

Until now, the functions you've used from the standard library have always been available to you without needing to import anything. That's because Haskell includes a special module named Prelude that's imported by default into every module. The Prelude module exports a large, commonly used portion of the standard library. For things in the standard library that aren't included with Prelude, we need to import the modules explicitly.

The isPrint function, along with several other functions for dealing with Char data, is exported by the module Data.Char module. Let's start by importing it:

```
module Main where
import Data.Char
```

In this example, you can see the syntax of a basic import, and notice that we've included it immediately after the start of our module. You're free to include empty lines or comments between the start of your module and your import list, but you can't include any other code.

Now that we've imported Data.Char, we can use isPrint and implement the rest of our program:

```
module Main where
import Data.Char

countNonPrintableCharacters :: String -> Int
```

```
countNonPrintableCharacters =
  length . filter (not . isPrint)

main :: IO ()
main =
  print $ countNonPrintableCharacters "\v\t\aHello\r\n"
```

Let's use cabal to run our program and make sure it's working:

```
user@host$ cabal run
Up to date
5
```

We can also test our program out in ghci. Let's use the cabal repl command to start an interactive session that will inherit all of the settings we've configured in our cabal file:

```
user@host$ cabal repl
```

When we use cabal repl, our Main module will be loaded automatically into our session automatically, so we don't need call :load explicitly. We can run main, or pass some strings directly to countNonPrintableCharacters:

```
λ main
5
λ countNonPrintableCharacters "123"
0
λ countNonPrintableCharacters "123\t\r\t"
3
```

Let's try calling isPrint directly from our ghci session to test whether a couple of characters count as being printable or not:

```
λ isPrint '\n'
False
```

Although we haven't imported Data.Char into our ghci session, the code that it exports is still available in our interactive session. When you load a file into ghci, all of the modules that it imports will be available in your session. To see this in action, let's quit our current ghci session and start a new one using the ghci command rather than cabal repl so that Main isn't loaded automatically:

```
λ :t isPrint

<interactive>:1:1: error: Variable not in scope: isPrint
λ :load app/Main.hs
[1 of 1] Compiling Main             ( app/Main.hs, interpreted )
Ok, one module loaded.
λ :t isPrint
isPrint :: Char -> Bool
```

You can see in this example that until we load Main.hs we don't have access to isPrint. As soon as we load Main, isPrint becomes available.

Loading Files in ghci

Keep in mind that a module's imports will only be available in ghci if you load it with :load. If you import a module, then you'll only get access to whatever that module exports. This is one of the key differences between :load and import in ghci.

If you don't want to load a file, you can also import modules directly in-line in ghci. For example, let's try using the permutations function from Data.List to look at all of the different permutations of the list [1,2,3].

If we try to call permutations right now, it won't be available because we haven't imported Data.List:

```
λ permutations [1,2,3]

<interactive>:6:1: error:
    Variable not in scope: permutations :: [a0] -> t
```

Once we import Data.List, the function will be available:

```
λ import Data.List
λ permutations [1,2,3]
[[1,2,3],[2,1,3],[3,2,1],[2,3,1],[3,1,2],[1,3,2]]
```

Local Module Aliases

As you've seen, when you import a module all of the code that it exports becomes available for you to use. At times this can present a problem, for example if a module exports something with a name that conflicts with something already defined in your program. Let's continue with our character counting example by expanding our code to support another string type that's commonly used in Haskell programs. The Text type comes from the text package, and it gives us a more efficient way to work with human-readable Unicode text. We'll start by adding text as a dependency in our project:

```
cabal-version:       2.4
name:                import-demo
version:             0.1.0.0
license:             NONE

executable import-demo
    main-is:           Main.hs
    build-depends:     base
                     , text
    hs-source-dirs:    app
    default-language: Haskell2010
```

Next, let's return to Main.hs and work on updating our code to support counting the non-printable characters in a Text value. We'll start by importing the Data.Text module, which exports the Text type along with some useful functions for dealing with Text values:

```
module Main where
import Data.Char
import Data.Text
```

Unfortunately, it turns out that merely importing Data.Text is enough to cause our program to fail to compile. Let's try running cabal build and looking at the error messages before going on:

```
app/Main.hs:7:3: error:
    Ambiguous occurrence 'length'
    It could refer to
       either 'Prelude.length',
              imported from 'Prelude' at app/Main.hs:1:8-11
              (and originally defined in 'Data.Foldable')
          or 'Data.Text.length',
              imported from 'Data.Text' at app/Main.hs:3:1-16
  |
7 |   length . filter (not . isPrint)
  |   ^^^^^^

app/Main.hs:7:12: error:
    Ambiguous occurrence 'filter'
    It could refer to
       either 'Prelude.filter',
              imported from 'Prelude' at app/Main.hs:1:8-11
              (and originally defined in 'GHC.List')
          or 'Data.Text.filter',
              imported from 'Data.Text' at app/Main.hs:3:1-16
  |
7 |   length . filter (not . isPrint)
  |            ^^^^^^
```

It looks like the length and filter functions that we were using have now been defined twice. Both Prelude and Data.Text export functions with the same name, and the compiler has no way to know which one we intended to use.

One way we can address this is to include the name of the module along with the ambiguous functions. In this case, we want to continue using the versions from Prelude so we'll replace length with Prelude.length and filter with Prelude.filter:

```
countNonPrintableCharacters :: String -> Int
countNonPrintableCharacters =
  Prelude.length . Prelude.filter (not . isPrint)
```

Now that our function calls aren't ambiguous anymore, let's go ahead and add a new version of our function to work with Text values. Our algorithm will remain the same, but we'll work on Text values and use the versions of length and filter defined in Data.Text:

```
countNonPrintableCharactersInText :: Text -> Int
countNonPrintableCharactersInText =
  Data.Text.length . Data.Text.filter (not . isPrint)
```

Next, let's add a function that will call both the String and Text versions of our function, just to make sure they always return the same value:

```
countNonPrintableCharactersStringAndText :: String -> (Int,Int)
countNonPrintableCharactersStringAndText input =
  ( countNonPrintableCharacters input
  , countNonPrintableCharactersInText $ pack input)
```

You'll notice that we're using the pack function in our call to countNonPrintableCharactersInText. This function comes from Data.Text and it's how we can convert a String into a Text value. With this function in place, the last thing we need to do is to update main. Let's look at our entire program as it currently stands:

```
module Main where
import Data.Char
import Data.Text

countNonPrintableCharactersInText :: Text -> Int
countNonPrintableCharactersInText =
  Data.Text.length . Data.Text.filter (not . isPrint)

countNonPrintableCharacters :: String -> Int
countNonPrintableCharacters =
  Prelude.length . Prelude.filter (not . isPrint)

countNonPrintableCharactersStringAndText :: String -> (Int,Int)
countNonPrintableCharactersStringAndText input =
  ( countNonPrintableCharacters input
  , countNonPrintableCharactersInText $ pack input)

main :: IO ()
main =
  print $ countNonPrintableCharactersStringAndText "\v\t\aHello\r\n"
```

At this point our program compiles, since we've included the full name of the functions that were previously ambiguous. One drawback to our current approach is that in a longer program it can start to get tiresome to type the full module name every time we want to use a function that would otherwise be ambiguous. This would be an even bigger problem if the module name were long.

Thankfully, we can give each module an alias when we import it using the as keyword. As an example, let's import Data.Text but give it the alias T:

```
import Data.Text as T
```

Using an alias, we can still call any unambiguous functions without the module name, but when we need to include the module name we can use the shorter alias instead of the full module name. For example, with an alias our countNonPrintableCharactersInText will become:

```
import Data.Text as T

countNonPrintableCharactersInText :: Text -> Int
countNonPrintableCharactersInText =
  T.length . T.filter (not . isPrint)
```

You can also import the same module several times with different aliases. This will let you use any of the aliases that you've assigned to the module interchangably. For example, we can assign Data.Text the aliases T and Text and use them in countNonPrintableCharactersInText:

```
import Data.Text as T
import Data.Text as Text

countNonPrintableCharactersInText :: Text -> Int
countNonPrintableCharactersInText =
  Text.length . T.filter (not . isPrint)
```

In practice, the only time you're likely to import a module with multiple aliases is as an incremental step when refactoring your code, for example, when you are merging two previously separate modules, or splitting a module into several new smaller modules.

More commonly, you can also assign the same alias to several modules. For example, the module Data.Text.Encoding provides utility functions for dealing with text encoding, like encodeUtf8 and decodeUtf8 that will let you encode and decode raw UTF-8 encoded text. In these cases, it's sometimes desirable to import several related modules under a single alias. Let's import Data.Text.Encoding and then encode and re-decode our text before we count the characters:

```
import Data.Text as T
import Data.Text.Encoding as T

countNonPrintableCharactersInText :: Text -> Int
countNonPrintableCharactersInText =
  T.length . T.filter (not . isPrint) . T.decodeUtf8 . T.encodeUtf8
```

In this example, we've combined all of the functions that have been exported by Data.Text and Data.Text.Encoding into a single alias, T.

Qualified Imports

So far, whenever we've imported a module the entire contents of the module have been made available to us. Even when we've assigned an alias to some modules, using the alias name is optional except when the name would otherwise be ambiguous. This is great for keeping our code short and easy to read, but it comes with a maintenance cost: code that works today might stop working in the future when we accidentally introduce some ambiguity into a call. This can happen in two different ways. First, you might add a new function without realizing that the name conflicts with something that's already exported by a module that you are importing. This can be irritating, but at the very least you'll quickly get feedback from the compiler and have the opportunity to rename your function. A worse outcome is that you have some code that has been working for some time, and then it starts to fail when you update your dependencies, and a module that you have been importing begins to export something with a conflicting name. In this scenario, you might find yourself having to make changes to code that you haven't touched in some time, and perhaps making changes throughout your entire code base to address unexpected name conflicts.

Qualified imports give us one way to avoid this problem. When we use the `qualified` keyword in our import statement, we require that anything exported by the module be referenced using either the full name of the module, or the module alias if we've given one. Let's look at an example of this by modifying our character counting application. We'll change our import of `Data.Char` to be a qualified import:

```
module Main where
import qualified Data.Char
import Data.Text as T
import Data.Text.Encoding as T

countNonPrintableCharactersInText :: Text -> Int
countNonPrintableCharactersInText =
  T.length . T.filter (not . isPrint) . T.decodeUtf8 . T.encodeUtf8

countNonPrintableCharacters :: String -> Int
countNonPrintableCharacters =
  Prelude.length . Prelude.filter (not . isPrint)

countNonPrintableCharactersStringAndText :: String -> (Int,Int)
countNonPrintableCharactersStringAndText input =
  ( countNonPrintableCharacters input
  , countNonPrintableCharactersInText $ pack input)

main :: IO ()
main =
  print $ countNonPrintableCharactersStringAndText "\v\t\aHello\r\n"
```

If we try to compile our program now, we'll get an error. We've updated the import of Data.Char to be qualified, and so our references to isPrint are no longer valid:

```
app/Main.hs:8:30: error:
    • Variable not in scope: isPrint :: Char -> Bool
    • Perhaps you meant 'Data.Char.isPrint' (imported from Data.Char)
  |
8 |   T.length . T.filter (not . isPrint) . T.decodeUtf8 . T.encodeUtf8
  |                              ^^^^^^^

app/Main.hs:12:42: error:
    • Variable not in scope: isPrint :: Char -> Bool
    • Perhaps you meant 'Data.Char.isPrint' (imported from Data.Char)
   |
12 |   Prelude.length . Prelude.filter (not . isPrint)
   |                                          ^^^^^^^
```

You'll notice here that, thankfully, the compiler has pointed out not only what function is no longer valid, but also found that the version we want is now called Data.Char.isPrint. Typing Data.Char everywhere we call isPrint might be a little annoying, but we can combine qualified imports with aliases. This will allow us to require that we use a qualified name every time we reference something imported from a module, but still allow us to use a shorter and more readable module alias. Let's change our qualified import to give it the alias Char and then update our code to use the qualified name when we call isPrint:

```
module Main where
import qualified Data.Char as Char
import Data.Text as T
import Data.Text.Encoding as T

countNonPrintableCharactersInText :: Text -> Int
countNonPrintableCharactersInText =
  T.length . T.filter (not . Char.isPrint) . T.decodeUtf8 . T.encodeUtf8

countNonPrintableCharacters :: String -> Int
countNonPrintableCharacters =
  Prelude.length . Prelude.filter (not . Char.isPrint)

countNonPrintableCharactersStringAndText :: String -> (Int,Int)
countNonPrintableCharactersStringAndText input =
  ( countNonPrintableCharacters input
  , countNonPrintableCharactersInText $ pack input)

main :: IO ()
main =
  print $ countNonPrintableCharactersStringAndText "\v\t\aHello\r\n"
```

Once again, our program compiles. Now, thanks to our use of qualified imports, we're also protected against any accidental name collisions with Data.Char.

Choosing What to Import

Normally, when you import a module you are importing everything that the module makes available. Sometimes this is a useful feature, like when you want to use most of what a module exports. Other times, you might want to only import a subset of the things that a module exports. When you want more fine-grained control over what you import, you can use import lists.

There are two types of import lists. Most commonly, import lists allow you to list explicitly the things that you want to import from a particular module. To add an import list, you need to list everything that you want to import inside of parentheses after the import statement. Let's give it a try by modifying our character counting function. Instead of a qualified imports of Data.Text.Encoding and Data.Char we'll import only the particular functions that we want to use from those modules:

```
import Data.Char (isPrint)
import Data.Text as T
import Data.Text.Encoding (decodeUtf8, encodeUtf8)

countNonPrintableCharactersInText :: Text -> Int
countNonPrintableCharactersInText =
  T.length . T.filter (not . isPrint) . decodeUtf8 . encodeUtf8
```

In this example, you can see how we've specified the exact functions that we want to import from each of the two modules. We don't have to qualify the modules, but we can still be assured that we're not going to have any accidental name collisions, since nothing except what we've listed in the import list will be available. We can see this in practice in ghci. Let's import isPrint from Data.Char into a fresh ghci session:

```
λ import Data.Char (isPrint)
```

Now we can call isPrint as you'd expect, but we'll get an error if we try to call a different function exported by Data.Char that we haven't listed in our import list. For example, we can try to call isSpace:

```
λ isPrint ' '
True
λ isSpace ' '

<interactive>:3:1: error:
    Variable not in scope: isSpace :: Char -> t
```

In ghci, if you've imported a particular function from a module and decide that you want some other functions, you can add more import statements with import lists to get the extra functions. Let's add isSpace to our session to see for ourselves:

```
λ import Data.Char (isSpace)
λ isPrint ' '
True
λ isSpace ' '
True
```

You'll notice here that when we write another import statement it adds the new function to our environment, but we still have access to the isPrint function that we imported earlier. If you decide you want everything from the module, you can still write an import statement without an import list. For example, if we try to call isHexDigit we'll get an error, but when we import all of Data.Char we'll have access to it, along with everything else exported by the module:

```
λ isHexDigit '0'

<interactive>:7:1: error:
    Variable not in scope: isHexDigit :: Char -> t
λ import Data.Char
λ isHexDigit '0'
True
```

You can use import lists alongside qualified imports and module aliases too. Returning to our character counting example, let's update our import of Data.Text. We'll make it a qualified import, keep our module alias, and also use an import list to limit ourselves to only importing the pack, length, and filter functions that we're intending to use:

```
module Main where
import Data.Char (isPrint)
import Data.Char (isSpace)
import qualified Data.Text as T (pack, length, filter)
import Data.Text.Encoding (decodeUtf8, encodeUtf8)

countNonPrintableCharactersInText :: Text -> Int
countNonPrintableCharactersInText =
  T.length . T.filter (not . isPrint) . decodeUtf8 . encodeUtf8

countNonPrintableCharacters :: String -> Int
countNonPrintableCharacters =
  Prelude.length . Prelude filter (not . isPrint)

countNonPrintableCharactersStringAndText :: String -> (Int,Int)
countNonPrintableCharactersStringAndText input =
  ( countNonPrintableCharacters input
  , countNonPrintableCharactersInText $ T.pack input)

main :: IO ()
main =
  print $ countNonPrintableCharactersStringAndText "\v\t\aHello\r\n"
```

If you build this, you'll notice that we have an error:

```
app/Main.hs:7:38: error:
    Not in scope: type constructor or class 'Text'
  |
7 | countNonPrintableCharactersInText :: Text -> Int
  |                                      ^^^^
```

Functions aren't the only thing that are imported, or not, when we use import lists. It looks like we've forgotten to import the Text type. One option that we have is to add it to the import list for our qualified import of Text:

```
module Main where
import Data.Char (isPrint)
import qualified Data.Text as T (Text, length, filter, pack)
import Data.Text.Encoding (decodeUtf8, encodeUtf8)

countNonPrintableCharactersInText :: T.Text -> Int
countNonPrintableCharactersInText =
  T.length . T.filter (not . isPrint) . decodeUtf8 . encodeUtf8

countNonPrintableCharacters :: String -> Int
countNonPrintableCharacters =
  Prelude.length . Prelude.filter (not . isPrint)

countNonPrintableCharactersStringAndText :: String -> (Int,Int)
countNonPrintableCharactersStringAndText input =
  ( countNonPrintableCharacters input
  , countNonPrintableCharactersInText $ T.pack input)

main :: IO ()
main =
  print $ countNonPrintableCharactersStringAndText "\v\t\aHello\r\n"
```

In this example, we've added Text to our import list, and we've also changed the reference to Text in the type of countNonPrintableCharactersInText. Since Data.Text is a qualified import, we need to reference it with the alias we've given to the module, in this case T.

You've already seen that you can import a module more than once with different import lists. You can also import a module more than once using other combinations of features. One pattern that you'll see somewhat frequently is to use an unqualified import with an import list to import the types defined in a module, and to use a qualified import for everything else. We can apply this pattern in our example by adding an unqualified import of Data.Text to import just the Text type, but keeping everything else in Data.Text under a qualified import:

```
module Main where
import Data.Char (isPrint)
import Data.Text (Text)
```

```
import qualified Data.Text as T
import Data.Text.Encoding (decodeUtf8, encodeUtf8)

countNonPrintableCharactersInText :: Text -> Int
countNonPrintableCharactersInText =
  T.length . T.filter (not . isPrint) . decodeUtf8 . encodeUtf8

countNonPrintableCharacters :: String -> Int
countNonPrintableCharacters =
  Prelude.length . Prelude.filter (not . isPrint)

countNonPrintableCharactersStringAndText :: String -> (Int,Int)
countNonPrintableCharactersStringAndText input =
  ( countNonPrintableCharacters input
  , countNonPrintableCharactersInText $ T.pack input)

main :: IO ()
main =
  print $ countNonPrintableCharactersStringAndText "\v\t\aHello\r\n"
```

Choosing What Not to Import

Import lists are a great way to include just a few items from a module, but the syntax you've used so far can be inconvenient if you want all but a few things from a module. In cases where you want to import all but a few things, you can use the hiding keyword before your import list. As you might expect, this inverts the import list, causing you to import everything from the module except what you've listed. As you might expect, you can combine imports that hide certain elements with qualified imports and aliases. Let's take another look at our character counter, but this time instead of using a qualified import for all of Data.Text, we'll do an unqualified import, but we'll hide the length and filter functions that were conflicting with Prelude. For those two functions specifically, we'll do a qualified import so that we still have access to them:

```
module Main where
import Data.Char (isPrint)
import Data.Text hiding (length, filter)
import qualified Data.Text as T (length, filter)
import Data.Text.Encoding (decodeUtf8, encodeUtf8)

countNonPrintableCharactersInText :: Text -> Int
countNonPrintableCharactersInText =
  T.length . T.filter (not . isPrint) . decodeUtf8 . encodeUtf8

countNonPrintableCharacters :: String -> Int
countNonPrintableCharacters =
  Prelude.length . Prelude.filter (not . isPrint)

countNonPrintableCharactersStringAndText :: String -> (Int,Int)
countNonPrintableCharactersStringAndText input =
  ( countNonPrintableCharacters input
  , countNonPrintableCharactersInText $ pack input)
```

```
main :: IO ()
main =
  print $ countNonPrintableCharactersStringAndText "\v\t\aHello\r\n"
```

Hiding imports can be particularly useful if you want to define your own implementation of a function from a module. For example, imagine that we wanted to define our own length function. Since length is defined in Prelude we'd get a conflict, but we can explicitly import Prelude and hide the length function:

```
module Main where
import Prelude hiding (length)

length :: [a] -> Int
length [] = 0
length (_:xs) = 1 + length xs

main :: IO ()
main =
  print $ "the length of 'hello' is: " <> show (length "hello")
```

As you might expect, you can also use an exclusion list with qualified imports, and with local module aliases.

Common Practices for Importing Modules

With so much flexibility in how you import things, you might find yourself wondering how to approach imports in your applications. Each style of import offers its own benefits and drawbacks.

Standard imports are often the easiest place to start. When you import a module without any import list, aliases, or qualification, you simply get access to everything exported from that module and you can start writing code right away. Name collisions are the biggest drawback of standard imports. In some cases, libraries use standard names by design and most imports will cause collisions. In other cases, you may simply want to avoid accidental name collisions. In either case, the next step is often to use qualified imports with an alias.

Qualified imports without an alias can be extremely verbose. From time to time you'll come across libraries with short module names, but long module names are common in Haskell, and repeatedly typing a long module name can become tiresome. Aliases, without qualification, give you a way to disambiguate name collisions, but they invite inconsistency. You may have some code that uses the alias and other code that doesn't. For these reasons, you'll see that qualified imports and local aliases are frequently used together. Qualified imports with a short readable module alias provide some additional documentation by letting readers know exactly where a given function was imported from, avoid the problem of accidental name collisions, and with well-chosen module aliases they minimize the impact of repeatedly typing the module name.

You'll see import lists being used with both qualified and unqualified imports. In some cases, import lists can serve as an additional form of documentation. When you list everything that you want to import from a particular module, it's easier to understand why the module has been imported. In some larger projects, you'll also notice the use of import lists as a way to improve compile times. Since GHC attempts to only recompile code that has changed, using an import list may allow you to avoid some extra work. That's because your module will need to be recompiled if a function you import has changed. If you import everything from a module, then your module will need to be recompiled every time that dependency changes. If you only import a particular function, then the compiler might be able to avoid recompiling your module if that function didn't change in your dependency.

Creating Your Own Modules

Importing modules defined by libraries is a great starting point when you are building an application, but as your programs start to grow larger, you'll also quickly realize that you'll need to use them in your own application to help you organize and re-use your own code. Modules are the basic unit of organization in Haskell applications, and in this section, you'll learn how to write modules, control what they export, and how to design an application to make the best use of modules so that your code is easy to use and re-use.

Let's start by looking at how we can create a module. Haskell modules are closely related to individual source files. Each file contains one module, and each module is defined by a single file. Generally, the name of the file that defines a module should match the name of the module itself. For example, if you have a module named `Example`, it should be defined in a file named `Example.hs`. Modules exist in a hierarchy that mirrors the organization of your source files. If you have a directory named `Examples` and that directory contains a file named `ExampleOne.hs` then the module defined in that file should be named `Examples.ExampleOne`. Each subdirectory adds a new section to the module name.

The relationship between file path and module name should be relative to the source directory for your application. For example, if you have a new application called `HaskellBook` and you've set the source directory for the project to `src`, then a file at the path `src/HaskellBook/Examples/Introduction/CreatingModules.hs` should define a module named `HaskellBook.Examples.Introduction.CreatingModules`. The `src` is omitted because that's the root source code directory for the project.

To get a first-hand feel for how we can use modules to organize our code, let's use cabal-init to create a new cabal project called module-examples. We'll make it a library, and set the source directory to src.

Once you've created the project, we'll add our first new module. Create a new file at src/HaskellBook/Examples/Introduction/CreatingModules.hs. You'll need to create all of the intermediate subdirectories as well. Inside of the file, add a new module header. We'll name the module HaskellBooks.Examples.Introduction.CreatingModules:

```
module HaskellBook.Examples.Introduction.CreatingModules where
```

The syntax for creating a module should look familiar. We've been using the module and where keywords to define module headers since the beginning of the book. You've also seen the hierarchical naming module convention a couple of times when you've imported libraries as part of some of the examples in the book. This is, however, the first time that we've created a module with a longer name like this. You've likely noticed that the path to the file we created matches the name of the module. Each directory in the path to the file became a segment of the module name, separated by dots (.). This is the standard way for organizing source files and modules names in Haskell projects. These conventions aren't strictly required. You can name your files and modules whatever you like, but most developers and most Haskell tooling will assume you're following the standard naming conventions.

Now that we have a module to work with, we should also add it to our cabal file. You learned earlier that the cabal files give us two ways to add modules: we can add our new module to the exposed-modules section of the cabal file to make it available to any consumers of our library, or we can add it to the other-modules section if we want our new module to only be used internally within our library. For now, let's add our new module to the exposed-modules section of the cabal file:

```
cabal-version:      2.4
name:               module-examples
version:            0.1.0.0
license:            NONE
extra-source-files: CHANGELOG.md

library
    exposed-modules:  MyLib
                    , HaskellBook.Examples.Introduction.CreatingModules
    build-depends:    base ^>=4.16.0.0
    hs-source-dirs:   src
    default-language: Haskell2010
```

Note that, depending on the version of cabal that you used to create the project, and the options you selected, your cabal file might look slightly different from the example.

Making Code Available for Re-Use

Now that we have a module, let's add some code to it. By default, everything we define at the top level of our module will be exported. As an example, let's add a function that will add some excitement to a message:

```
module HaskellBook.Examples.Introduction.CreatingModules where

excitingMessage :: String -> String
excitingMessage message =
  "Exciting news: " <> message <> "!!!"
```

Now let's load our library up into ghci. Since we want to load modules from the library that we're writing, we'll use cabal repl to start our ghci session instead of calling ghci directly. This will start up ghci with our library loaded, alongside any other dependencies we've added to our cabal file:

```
user@host$ cabal repl
```

Although our library will be loaded in ghci, we'll still need to import the modules we want to use. If you try to call excitingMessage without importing the module that defines it, we'll get an error:

```
λ excitingMessage "Modularity"

<interactive>:1:1: error:
    Variable not in scope: excitingMessage :: t0 -> t
```

We can import our new module, which will make our function available:

```
λ import HaskellBook.Examples.Introduction.CreatingModules
λ excitingMessage "Modularity"
"Exciting news: Modularity!!!"
```

Functions aren't the only thing that get exported from a module. In the last section, you saw an example of how the Text type was exported by the Data.Text module. By default, any top-level functions, variables, and types will exported. To help illustrate this, let's expand our example module by building a small library to let us create greeting messages.

We want our library to format greetings that include some particular salutation, for example, "hello" or "happy birthday." The message will be to someone, and it might be from one or several people. Both the salutation and the names of the people in the message will be String data, but we don't want to confuse a name for a salutation, so let's start by creating pair of types so that we can keep the names and salutations separate:

```
data Name = Name { getName :: String }
data Salutation = Salutation { getSalutation :: String }
```

Next, let's create a new record that holds all of the information about a greeting. We'll call it GreetingMessage:

```
data GreetingMessage = GreetingMessage
  { greetingSalutation :: Salutation
  , greetingTo :: Name
  , greetingFrom :: [Name]
  }
```

We can make our library more convenient for our users by providing a default greeting. If our users only want to change part of the default message, they can use record update syntax to change the fields they want to modify. Since our message only has three fields, this pattern won't be as useful as it would be with larger records, especially records with more sensible defaults, but it'll still serve as a good example of creating default values when we're writing Haskell libraries:

```
defaultMessage :: GreetingMessage
defaultMessage = GreetingMessage
  { greetingSalutation = Salutation "Hello"
  , greetingTo = Name "Friend"
  , greetingFrom = []
  }
```

Finally, let's add a function to turn our GreetingMessage into a message we can print on the screen. You're welcome to pick your own message formatting as you follow along with the example:

```
formatMessage :: GreetingMessage -> String
formatMessage (GreetingMessage greetingSalutation greetingTo greetingFrom) =
  greetingWithSuffix
  where
    basicGreeting =
      getSalutation greetingSalutation <> " " <> getName greetingTo

    greetingWithSuffix =
      case greetingFrom of
        [] ->
          basicGreeting <> "!"
        [friend] ->
          basicGreeting <> ", from: " <> getName friend
        [friendA, friendB] ->
          basicGreeting <> ", from: " <>
            getName friendA <> " and " <> getName friendB
```

```
        friends ->
          basicGreeting <> ", from your friends: " <>
            formatFriendList friends

    formatFriendList friends =
      case friends of
        [] ->
          ""
        [friend] ->
          "and " <> getName friend
        (friend:moreFriends) ->
          getName friend <> ", " <> formatFriendList moreFriends
```

In this example, we've used pattern matching to extract all the fields of our GreetingMessage record. Let's do a small refactor to make use of the RecordWildCards extension. Once you've done that, the final version of your greeting module should look like the example:

```
{-# LANGUAGE RecordWildCards #-}
module HaskellBook.Examples.Introduction.CreatingModules where

data Name = Name { getName :: String }
data Salutation = Salutation { getSalutation :: String }

data GreetingMessage = GreetingMessage
  { greetingSalutation :: Salutation
  , greetingTo :: Name
  , greetingFrom :: [Name]
  }

defaultMessage :: GreetingMessage
defaultMessage = GreetingMessage
  { greetingSalutation = Salutation "Hello"
  , greetingTo = Name "Friend"
  , greetingFrom = []
  }

formatMessage :: GreetingMessage -> String
formatMessage GreetingMessage{..} =
  greetingWithSuffix
  where
    basicGreeting =
      getSalutation greetingSalutation <> " " <> getName greetingTo

    greetingWithSuffix =
      case greetingFrom of
        [] ->
          basicGreeting <> "!"
        [friend] ->
          basicGreeting <> ", from: " <> getName friend
        [friendA, friendB] ->
          basicGreeting <> ", from: " <>
            getName friendA <> " and " <> getName friendB
```

```
      friends ->
        basicGreeting <> ", from your friends: " <>
          formatFriendList friends

  formatFriendList friends =
    case friends of
      [] ->
        ""
      [friend] ->
        "and " <> getName friend
      (friend:moreFriends) ->
        getName friend <> ", " <> formatFriendList moreFriends
```

Now that we've turned our module into a small library, let's load it back up into ghci with cabal repl so that we can see what is available to us when we import it. We'll start by formatting the default message:

```
λ import HaskellBook.Examples.Introduction.CreatingModules
λ formatMessage defaultMessage
"Hello Friend!"
```

As you would expect, both formatMessage and defaultMessage are available now that we've imported our library. What if we wanted to customize the message?

```
λ george = Name "George"
λ remi = Name "Remi"
λ porter = Name "Porter"
λ formatMessage $ defaultMessage {greetingFrom = [george, remi, porter]}
"Hello Friend, from your friends: George, Remi, and Porter"
```

We can use record update syntax, so it would appear that the field selectors for GreetingMessage have been exported, along with the type constructor for Name. In fact, all the top-level functions and variables we've defined in our module are available. So are the types we've defined, along with their field selectors and constructors.

Types and values that we define in our module are available when we import it, but language extensions that we've enabled in a module are not carried over. We can see this for ourselves if we try to write a function that depends on the RecordWildCards extension. For example, let's try to write a function that counts the number of people who sent a message:

```
λ import HaskellBook.Examples.Introduction.CreatingModules
λ countSenders GreetingMessage{..} = length greetingFrom

<interactive>:2:14: error:
    Illegal `..' in record pattern
    Use RecordWildCards to permit this
```

Even though the extension was enabled in our module, we can't use it outside of the module unless we enable the extension where we want to use it:

```
λ :set -XRecordWildCards
λ countSenders GreetingMessage{..} = length greetingFrom
λ countSenders defaultMessage
0
```

There are benefits and drawbacks to the fact that language extensions are only enabled in the module where they are defined. A benefit is that you can choose what extensions you want to enable on a case-by-case basis without requiring that users of your module make the same choice. On the other hand, a major drawback is that you may find yourself repeatedly adding the same handful of extensions across all, or most, of your modules. If you notice that you are enabling the same extensions in most modules, you might want to consider adding them to the default-extensions section in your cabal project. Let's add RecordWildCards as a default extension for our library:

```
cabal-version:      2.4
name:               module-examples
version:            0.1.0.0
license:            NONE
extra-source-files: CHANGELOG.md

library
    exposed-modules:  MyLib
                    , HaskellBook.Examples.Introduction.CreatingModules
    build-depends:    base ^>=4.16.0.0
    hs-source-dirs:   src
    default-language: Haskell2010
    default-extensions: RecordWildCards
```

Now we can use the RecordWildCards extension in any other module we add to our project without adding a LANGUAGE pragma. Similarly, if we start ghci using cabal repl, all of our default extensions will be enabled and we don't need to use :set to turn them on individually.

Choosing What to Export

By default, all of the top-level bindings that you define in a module are exported and available to any code that imports your module. This is convenient since it means that we can start writing modules without needing to think about what should or shouldn't be visible to consumers of our module, but frequently we'd like to have more control over what we choose to export. For example, we might want to hide some functions we've written that shouldn't be part of our public API. Export lists are a way to get fine-grained control over what is, and isn't, exported from the modules that you define.

In this section, you'll learn how to use export lists to control what is visible to consumers of your module, and work through several different use-cases where export lists can help you define a better API for your module.

Export Lists

Just like import lists, which let you choose what should be imported from a module, export lists let you choose what should be exported by your module. The syntax for an export list is similar to the syntax for an import list. To add an export list to your module, you need to add a comma-separated list of what you want to export. The export list should come after the module name before the where keyword. For example, let's add a new value, testMessage, to our example module. We'll also update our export list to specifically export testMessage:

```
{-# LANGUAGE RecordWildCards #-}
module HaskellBook.Examples.Introduction.CreatingModules
 ( testMessage
 ) where

data Name = Name { getName :: String }
data Salutation = Salutation { getSalutation :: String }

data GreetingMessage = GreetingMessage
  { greetingSalutation :: Salutation
  , greetingTo :: Name
  , greetingFrom :: [Name]
  }

defaultMessage :: GreetingMessage
defaultMessage = GreetingMessage
  { greetingSalutation = Salutation "Hello"
  , greetingTo = Name "Friend"
  , greetingFrom = []
  }

formatMessage :: GreetingMessage -> String
formatMessage GreetingMessage {..} =
  greetingWithSuffix
  where
    basicGreeting =
      getSalutation greetingSalutation <> " " <> getName greetingTo

    greetingWithSuffix =
      case greetingFrom of
        [] ->
          basicGreeting <> "!"
        [friend] ->
          basicGreeting <> ", from: " <> getName friend
        [friendA, friendB] ->
          basicGreeting <> ", from: " <>
            getName friendA <> " and " <> getName friendB
```

```
        friends ->
          basicGreeting <> ", from your friends: " <>
            formatFriendList friends

    formatFriendList friends =
      case friends of
        [] ->
          ""
        [friend] ->
          "and " <> getName friend
        (friend:moreFriends) ->
          getName friend <> ", " <> formatFriendList moreFriends

testMessage :: String
testMessage =
  formatMessage $ defaultMessage { greetingFrom = [Name "test example"] }
```

You'll notice in this example that we've moved the export list down onto a separate line. This syntax is allowed for both import and export lists, but it's more common with export lists, since they tend to be longer than import lists. With our export list in place, let's run cabal repl again and import our module. When we do, you'll see that while testMessage is available, nothing else that we've defined in our module is visible:

```
λ import HaskellBook.Examples.Introduction.CreatingModules
λ putStrLn testMessage
Hello Friend, from: test example
λ defaultMessage

<interactive>:3:1: error: Variable not in scope: defaultMessage
λ :type formatMessage

<interactive>:1:1: error: Variable not in scope: formatMessage
```

When we add an export list, nothing is exported by default anymore. We need to add anything that we want to be available into the export list.

Although export lists can be a useful way of controlling what part of your code makes up the visible external API, we don't necessarily want to give up the benefits of interactive development with ghci. You can comment out the export list while you're in development, and then uncomment it when you're done, but that's not a particularly satisfying solution. Thankfully, if you open your code in ghci with :load rather than import, everything defined in the module will be available whether you included it in your export list or not. For example, if you :load your module without changing the export list, you'll see that you can still reference everything in your module:

```
λ :load src/HaskellBook/Examples/Introduction/CreatingModules.hs
[1 of 1] Compiling HaskellBook.Examples.Introduction.CreatingModules (
  src/HaskellBook/Examples/Introduction/CreatingModules.hs, interpreted)
```

```
Ok, one module loaded.
λ :type defaultMessage
defaultMessage :: GreetingMessage
λ :t Name
Name :: String -> Name
```

Dealing with Constructors and Field Selectors

Now that you know how to create an export list, let's update our example to export the remaining parts of our module. Start by copying the example:

```haskell
{-# LANGUAGE RecordWildCards #-}
module HaskellBook.Examples.Introduction.CreatingModules
 ( Name
 , Salutation
 , GreetingMessage
 , defaultMessage
 , formatMessage
 , testMessage
 ) where

data Name = Name { getName :: String }
data Salutation = Salutation { getSalutation :: String }

data GreetingMessage = GreetingMessage
  { greetingSalutation :: Salutation
  , greetingTo :: Name
  , greetingFrom :: [Name]
  }

defaultMessage :: GreetingMessage
defaultMessage = GreetingMessage
  { greetingSalutation = Salutation "Hello"
  , greetingTo = Name "Friend"
  , greetingFrom = []
  }

formatMessage :: GreetingMessage -> String
formatMessage GreetingMessage {..} =
  greetingWithSuffix
  where
    basicGreeting =
      getSalutation greetingSalutation <> " " <> getName greetingTo

    greetingWithSuffix =
      case greetingFrom of
        [] ->
          basicGreeting <> "!"
        [friend] ->
          basicGreeting <> ", from: " <> getName friend
        [friendA, friendB] ->
          basicGreeting <> ", from: " <>
            getName friendA <> " and " <> getName friendB
```

```
        friends ->
          basicGreeting <> ", from your friends: " <>
            formatFriendList friends

    formatFriendList friends =
      case friends of
        [] ->
          ""
        [friend] ->
          "and " <> getName friend
        (friend:moreFriends) ->
          getName friend <> ", " <> formatFriendList moreFriends

testMessage :: String
testMessage =
  formatMessage $ defaultMessage { greetingFrom = [Name "test example"] }
```

Now that we've expanded our export list, let's load our program up again with cabal repl and try to generate a few messages. We'll start with a default message:

```
λ import HaskellBook.Examples.Introduction.CreatingModules
λ putStrLn $ formatMessage defaultMessage
Hello Friend!
```

So far, so good! Next, let's modify our default message:

```
λ putStrLn $ formatMessage $
    defaultMessage {greetingTo = Name "Module Demo"}

<interactive>:3:46: error: Not in scope: 'greetingTo'
```

Unfortunately, we can't use our API as designed with our current export list. Although we exported our GreetingMessage type, that doesn't seem to have extended to exporting the field selectors that were created when we defined the record. We can go back and update our export list momentarily, but for now we ought to be able to create a GreetingMessage without referencing the record fields. Let's try that to see if we can still create a custom message:

```
λ msg = GreetingMessage (Salutation "Hello") (Name "Module Demo") []
```

Unfortunately, it turns out that we can't create a message this way either. Depending on the version of GHC that you are using, you might see different error messages. In GHC 9.2, you will see this error:

```
<interactive>:5:7: error:
  • Illegal term-level use of the type constructor 'GreetingMessage'
    imported from 'HaskellBook.Examples.Introduction.CreatingModules'
    (and originally defined
    at src/HaskellBook/Examples/Introduction/CreatingModules.hs:(14,1)-(18,3))
  • In the expression:
      GreetingMessage (Salutation "Hello") (Name "Module Demo") []
```

```
    In an equation for 'msg':
        msg = GreetingMessage (Salutation "Hello") (Name "Module Demo") []
```

In GHC 8.10, the error message will look a little different:

```
<interactive>:2:7: error:
    Data constructor not in scope:
      GreetingMessage :: t0 -> t1 -> [a0] -> t

<interactive>:2:24: error:
    Data constructor not in scope: Salutation :: t2 -> t0

<interactive>:2:45: error:
    Data constructor not in scope: Name :: t3 -> t1
```

In both cases, the error is caused by the same underlying issue: we've exported the *types* for Name, Salutation, and GreetingMessage but we haven't exported their *constructors*, or any field selectors.

You can export field constructors just like any other function. In this case, we could add greetingSalutation, greetingTo, and greetingFrom to our export list, but we still wouldn't be able to create a GreetingMessage value. To update the values in defaultMessage we need to provide either Name or Salutation values, and creating those means we need to call the Name or Salutation constructors. If we want to export a value constructor for our types, we need to include those alongside the types that we're exporting. The syntax for this looks like an export list within an export list. We add a comma-separated list of all of the constructors that we want to export for a particular type. In our case, we only have a single value constructor for each of these types. Let's go ahead and add the value constructors for all of our types. Our export list will look like this:

```
module HaskellBook.Examples.Introduction.CreatingModules
 ( Name (Name)
 , Salutation (Salutation)
 , GreetingMessage (GreetingMessage)
 , greetingSalutation
 , greetingTo
 , greetingFrom
 , defaultMessage
 , formatMessage
 , testMessage
 ) where
```

With the field selectors and constructors added to the export list, you can freely create new message values now:

```
λ putStrLn . formatMessage $
    defaultMessage { greetingTo = Name "Module Demo" }
Hello Module Demo!
```

You can also include any field selectors in the export list for a particular type. Let's update our export list again to include the field selectors for each of our types in their respective export lists:

```
module HaskellBook.Examples.Introduction.CreatingModules
  ( Name (Name, getName)
  , Salutation (Salutation, getSalutation)
  , GreetingMessage ( GreetingMessage
                    , greetingSalutation
                    , greetingTo
                    , greetingFrom
                    )
  , defaultMessage
  , formatMessage
  , testMessage
  ) where
```

For types with many constructors, or large records, it can be inconvenient to type out everything that you might want to export for a type. Even for types with only a single constructor and a small number of field selectors you might not want to update the export list every time you make a change for the type. To help with that, there's a special syntax that you can use to export all of the constructors and field selectors associated with a particular type. Let's update our export list so we can see an example:

```
module HaskellBook.Examples.Introduction.CreatingModules
  ( Name (..)
  , Salutation (..)
  , GreetingMessage (..)
  , defaultMessage
  , formatMessage
  , testMessage
  ) where
```

You can use the same syntax for importing types, constructors, and field selectors. Let's open up a fresh `ghci` session with `cabal repl` and try out a few more imports using this current version of our module. We'll start by importing the `Name` type and its constructor, but not the `getName` field selector:

```
λ exampleName = Name "haskeller"
λ getName exampleName

<interactive>:5:1: error:
    Variable not in scope: getName :: Name -> t
```

Smart Constructors

It might seem inconvenient to need to export constructors and field selectors explicitly when you export the types you've defined in a module, but being able to keep these internal to a module is an important part of a common pattern you'll see in Haskell applications: *smart constructors*. A smart constructor is an ordinary function that lets you construct a value. Unlike a standard value constructor, smart constructors can include some additional logic. One of the most common ways to use a smart constructor is to perform some additional validation before creating a value. When you export a smart constructor for a type, but don't export the actual constructor, then you can guarantee that the only way a user could have gotten a value for your type is having gone through the smart constructor. This lets you make simplifying assumptions throughout the rest of your code by performing your basic validation once, at the time that you'd be creating the value.

Let's look at this in practice with a small example. Imagine that we are writing a program that needs to deal with a list of numbers, and we regularly want to find the smallest element in the list. We could use the minimum function in Prelude, but that's a partial function that will fail if we call it with an empty list. Since it needs to work with any list, it also has to go through the entire list to make sure it's found the smallest element.

In our program, we can write a much better minimum function if we can be sure that we're always working with a list that has at least one element, and if we always know the list we're working with will be sorted. To do that, let's add a new module to our project called HaskellBook.Examples.SortedList. We'll import the sort function from Data.List and we'll hide the minimum function from Prelude since we want to define our own:

```
module HaskellBook.Examples.SortedList where

import Data.List (sort)
import Prelude hiding (minimum)
```

Now, let's define a new SortedList type. Rather than re-inventing the list type from scratch, we'll define our sorted list in terms of the standard list type:

```
data SortedList = SortedList { getSorted :: [Int] }
```

Finally, we can write a minimum function that takes advantage of the fact that we know we're dealing with non-empty sorted lists:

```
minimum :: SortedList -> Int
minimum (SortedList numbers) = head numbers
```

You might have already spotted the problem, but let's use cabal repl to load this module into ghci and test it out:

```
λ import qualified HaskellBook.Examples.SortedList as SortedList
λ SortedList.minimum $ SortedList.SortedList [1,2,5,10]
```

So far, so good. Unfortunately, the assumptions that we're making about our list being non-empty and sorted aren't being enforced right now, so we're entirely free to pass in bad data:

```
λ SortedList.minimum $ SortedList.SortedList []
*** Exception: Prelude.head: empty list
λ SortedList.minimum $ SortedList.SortedList [10,9..]
10
```

The problem is that we're allowing ourselves to create a SortedList with any list we want, sorted or not, and we're not doing anything to validate that the list is well formed. We can fix this with a smart constructor and an export list. We'll start by creating a smart constructor called makeSortedList:

```
makeSortedList :: [Int] -> Maybe SortedList
makeSortedList [] = Nothing
makeSortedList numbers = Just $ SortedList (sort numbers)
```

Our smart constructor takes a list in and tries to generate a sorted non-empty list. If we get a non-empty list, we can do that by sorting whatever the user gives us. If they give us an empty list, we can't do anything with it, so we have to return Nothing. This might seem like it's a less convenient API, since the user now has to deal with a Maybe value whenever they want to construct a SortedList, but it allows us to handle all of the validation once when the list is initially created. This simplifies the rest of our code, and it also pushes the error handling up to the user at the time that they are creating the value in the first place, and are most likely to be able to make a sensible decision about what to do next when faced with an error.

Let's take another look at our module, this time with our export list in place:

```
module HaskellBook.Examples.SortedList
  ( SortedList (getSorted)
  , makeSortedList
  , minimum
  ) where

import Data.List (sort)
import Prelude hiding (minimum)

data SortedList = SortedList { getSorted :: [Int] }

makeSortedList :: [Int] -> Maybe SortedList
makeSortedList [] = Nothing
makeSortedList numbers = Just $ SortedList (sort numbers)

minimum :: SortedList -> Int
minimum (SortedList numbers) = head numbers
```

As you can see, with our smart constructor in place, the only way the user will have to create a SortedList value is by going through our makeSortedList function. This lets us ensure that we're always working with valid data.

Phantom Types and Export Lists

Before we move on from export lists, let's look at another example of how we can use export lists to create a safer interface into our code. This time, we'll build a small model of an API that you might use to manage user profile information for a social media application.

Let's start with a straightforward implementation of our API. We'll enable the RecordWildCards extension now, since we'll be using it later on in this section:

```
{-# LANGUAGE RecordWildCards #-}

module HaskellBook.Examples.UserInfo
  ( User
  , lookupUser
  , getUserName
  , getUserScore
  , getUserEmailAddress
  ) where
import Data.List (find)

data User = User
  { userName :: String
  , userInternetPoints :: Int
  , userPassword :: String
  , userEmailAddress :: String
  }

users :: [User]
users = [george, porter]
  where
    george = User
      { userName = "george"
      , userInternetPoints = 1000
      , userPassword = "secret"
      , userEmailAddress = "gbird2015@example.com"
      }
    porter = User
      { userName = "porter"
      , userInternetPoints = 500
      , userPassword = "hunter2"
      , userEmailAddress = "woofwoof@example.com"
      }

lookupUser :: String -> Maybe User
lookupUser name =
  find (\user -> userName user == name) users
```

```
getUserName :: User -> String
getUserName = userName

getUserScore :: User -> Int
getUserScore = userInternetPoints

getUserEmailAddress :: User -> String
getUserEmailAddress = userEmailAddress
```

In this example, we've defined a very small user query API. Given a username, we can look for the user in a hardcoded list. Once we have a user, we can get some information about them, like their username, how many internet points they've earned, and their email address. Since we're not exporting the User constructor, or the userPassword field selector, we've also made use of our export list to ensure we can't accidentally leak password information outside of the module. Of course, in a real-world application we'd want to avoid storing passwords in plain text altogether, but we'll stick with it to simplify our example.

One problem we have with the API for our application is it treats all user data equally. Although usernames and internet point counts are public information that should be available to anyone, a user's email address is private and we shouldn't display it to anyone except for the user themselves, after they've logged in. It turns out that we can use export lists to help us build an API that enforces this. Let's refactor our example so that we can see how this works.

First, we need a way to keep track of whether a user has been authenticated or not. We'll add two types to keep track of this information. We're only going to track whether a user has been authenticated or not at the type level, so we don't need to add a value constructor for our types:

```
data Authenticated
data Unauthenticated
```

Importantly, we're not going to add either of these types to our export list. We want to keep these two types entirely internal to our module.

Next, we'd like to keep track of whether a particular user is authenticated or not. We'll do that by adding a new type parameter to User. We're not going to have any values of this type, we're just using it keep track of whether a particular value has been authenticated or not. We call these types that don't have any corresponding values *phantom types*:

```
data User isAuthenticated = User
  { userName :: String
  , userInternetPoints :: Int
  , userPassword :: String
  , userEmailAddress :: String
  }
```

Now we can update the types of our functions. For example, when we first look up a user by name, we want the user to be unauthenticated until they log in:

```
lookupUser :: String -> Maybe (User Unauthenticated)
lookupUser name =
  find (\user -> userName user == name) users
```

We should be able to get a user's username or score regardless of whether they are logged in or not, so we'll make the type parameter polymorphic for those functions:

```
getUserName :: User isAuthenticated -> String
getUserName = userName

getUserScore :: User isAuthenticated -> Int
getUserScore = userInternetPoints
```

Finally, getting a user's email address should only work if they are authenticated:

```
getUserEmailAddress :: User Authenticated -> String
getUserEmailAddress = userEmailAddress
```

You'll notice that we didn't have to change the implementation of any of our functions, only their types. Our phantom type only exists as the type level, so there's nothing that we need to do at the value level to restrict when we can call a function. Even though we haven't changed anything at the value level, we can load our code up into ghci with cabal repl and see that it's working as intended. We can look up a user and get their name and score:

```
λ import HaskellBook.Examples.UserInfo
λ (Just george) = lookupUser "george"
λ getUserName george
"george"
λ getUserScore george
1000
```

If we try to get an email address from our unauthenticated user, we'll get a type error:

```
λ getUserEmailAddress george

<interactive>:5:21: error:
    • Couldn't match type ‘HaskellBook.Examples.UserInfo.Unauthenticated’
                     with ‘HaskellBook.Examples.UserInfo.Authenticated’
      Expected type: User HaskellBook.Examples.UserInfo.Authenticated
        Actual type: User HaskellBook.Examples.UserInfo.Unauthenticated
    • In the first argument of ‘getUserEmailAddress’, namely ‘george’
      In the expression: getUserEmailAddress george
      In an equation for ‘it’: it = getUserEmailAddress george
```

If we want to be able to get access to a user's email, we will need a way to authenticate them.

Let's add an authenticate function that will return an authenticated user if given a correct password:

```
authenticate :: User Unauthenticated -> String -> Maybe (User Authenticated)
authenticate User{..} password
  | userPassword == password = Just User{..}
  | otherwise = Nothing
```

You'll notice in this example that we're finally making use of the RecordWildCards extension. First, we get all of the fields out of the unauthenticated User value that's been passed into our function. If the password matches the one that we're trying to authenticate with, we construct a new User value, this time one that's been authenticated. We need to construct a new User value here since the newly constructed value has a different type from the one that was passed in, which was unauthenticated.

Like with our earlier sorted list example, our authentication API puts the burden of error handling on the user by returning a Maybe handle, but it simplifies the rest of our code by letting us assume that no authenticated users can exist unless they've successfully passed through the authentication step.

Now that we've implemented authentication, let's take a look at the final version of our code:

```
{-# LANGUAGE RecordWildCards #-}
module HaskellBook.Examples.UserInfo
  ( User
  , lookupUser
  , authenticate
  , getUserName
  , getUserScore
  , getUserEmailAddress
  ) where
import Data.List (find)

data Authenticated
data Unauthenticated

data User isAuthenticated = User
  { userName :: String
  , userInternetPoints :: Int
  , userPassword :: String
  , userEmailAddress :: String
  }
```

```
users :: [User a]
users = [george, porter]
  where
    george = User
      { userName = "george"
      , userInternetPoints = 1000
      , userPassword = "secret"
      , userEmailAddress = "gbird2015@example.com"
      }
    porter = User
      { userName = "porter"
      , userInternetPoints = 500
      , userPassword = "hunter2"
      , userEmailAddress = "woofwoof@example.com"
      }

lookupUser :: String -> Maybe (User Unauthenticated)
lookupUser name =
  find (\user -> userName user == name) users

authenticate :: User Unauthenticated -> String -> Maybe (User Authenticated)
authenticate User{..} password
  | userPassword == password = Just User{..}
  | otherwise = Nothing

getUserName :: User isAuthenticated -> String
getUserName = userName

getUserScore :: User isAuthenticated -> Int
getUserScore = userInternetPoints

getUserEmailAddress :: User Authenticated -> String
getUserEmailAddress = userEmailAddress
```

By carefully choosing what we want to export from our module, and adding some additional information at the type level that is only accessible from within our module, we've been able to enforce an authentication policy at the type level using phantom types. Now, any user who chooses to write code against our API will get a type error if they write code that might accidentally leak private information to an unauthenticated user. In this way, we've used Haskell's type system and modules to improve the security of our application at compile time. This is an example of a larger pattern that you'll see used in some Haskell applications where "resources" of various sorts are locked away behind smart constructors and unexported types. It can sometimes be challenging to figure out how to approach designing APIs this way, and not every problem lends itself to this type of solution, but when you have the opportunity, it can be a highly effective way of building APIs that are safe by default.

Re-Exporting Code from Other Modules

So far we've looked at examples of how to export code defined in a module from that module. We're not limited to only exporting things where they are defined though. A module can export anything from a module that's in scope, including code we've imported from other modules. As an example, let's build a demo of some of the things we've built while working on this section.

We'll start by making it easier to import all of the examples that we've built. A common pattern that you'll see in Haskell codebases is that there will be several small independent modules that exist at some point in the module hierarchy, along with a parent module that re-exports all, or the most relevant parts, of those modules. We can see this in action by creating our own Examples module that will re-export some of our code from the various modules we've already defined.

Create a new module named HaskellBook.Examples at src/HaskellBook/Examples.hs:

```
module HaskellBook.Examples where
```

We won't define any new functions in this module to keep the example small, although in real-world codebases you'll sometimes see these parent modules include helper functions that are either useful across all of the modules that they re-export, or help ease interoperability between the modules. We'll just focus on re-exporting code from our example modules. Let's start with UserInfo.

Our UserInfo module is fairly large, and has quite a bit of code and it would be nice to make all of it available for our demo. We can do that by re-exporting the entire module. In order to re-export a module, we can list it, along with the module keyword in our export list. We can only export code that's in scope in our module, so we'll *also* need to import the module:

```
module HaskellBook.Examples
  ( module HaskellBook.Examples.UserInfo
  )
where

import HaskellBook.Examples.UserInfo
```

Next, let's look back at our original module, HaskellBook.Examples.Introduction.CreatingModules. It's a very long module name to type out repeatedly, so let's import it with a local alias. While we're at it, the testMessage we're exporting from that module isn't very interesting for demo purposes, so let's hide it from our import:

```
module HaskellBook.Examples
  ( module HaskellBook.Examples.UserInfo
  , module CreatingModules
  )
where

import HaskellBook.Examples.UserInfo
import HaskellBook.Examples.Introduction.CreatingModules
  as CreatingModules hiding (testMessage)
```

In this example, you can see that when we re-export a module that we've imported using a local alias, we also use the local alias to refer to it when we re-export it. You'll also notice that we've broken up the import statement onto two lines. You can break up import statements into as many lines as you like, so long as you indent all of the additional lines with at least one space.

Finally, let's add an import for SortedList. As you may recall from when we originally wrote SortedList, it exports its own version of the minimum function that conflicts with the version defined in Prelude. To help avoid any potential name conflicts, let's import SortedList both qualified and with a local alias:

```
import qualified HaskellBook.Examples.SortedList as SortedList
```

Unfortunately, since we've used a qualified import we can't directly export the entire module. When you use a qualified import of a module, you'll need to explicitly list everything from that module you want to export in your export list:

```
module HaskellBook.Examples
  ( module HaskellBook.Examples.UserInfo
  , module CreatingModules
  , SortedList.SortedList(..)
  , SortedList.makeSortedList
  , SortedList.minimum
  ) where

import HaskellBook.Examples.UserInfo
import HaskellBook.Examples.Introduction.CreatingModules
  as CreatingModules hiding (testMessage)
import qualified HaskellBook.Examples.SortedList as SortedList
```

Now that we've create a module that exports everything we might want to use, we can build a demo. Let's create a new module named ModuleDemo:

```
module ModuleDemo where
import qualified HaskellBook.Examples as Examples

georgesEmailAddress :: Maybe String
georgesEmailAddress =
  case Examples.lookupUser "george" of
    Nothing ->
      Nothing
```

```
    Just unathenticatedGeorge ->
      case Examples.authenticate unathenticatedGeorge "secret" of
        Nothing -> Nothing
        Just george ->
          Just $ Examples.getUserEmailAddress george

friendlyEmail :: String -> String
friendlyEmail emailAddress =
  Examples.formatMessage Examples.GreetingMessage
      { Examples.greetingSalutation = Examples.Salutation "Hello"
      , Examples.greetingTo = Examples.Name emailAddress
      , Examples.greetingFrom = [Examples.Name "mailer daemon"]
      }

demo :: String
demo =
  maybe "unknown user" friendlyEmail georgesEmailAddress
```

As you can see from our demo example, when we are importing a module we do not need to be concerned with whether something that's exported by the module was defined in that module, or was re-exported from a different module. This makes re-exports a useful tool for refactoring, since we can change where things are defined while maintaining a compatible API at the module level.

Documenting Modules

Now that you've learned how to create modules that other developers can use, we should look at how to make modules that other developers *want to use*, by ensuring that our code is well documented. Haddock[6] is the most popular way to document Haskell programs. Haddock generates HTML-formatted documentation from your source code and specially formatted comments. All of the documentation on Hackage[7] is generated using Haddock. In this section, you'll get a quick introduction to using Haddock to document your modules. We won't cover all of the functionality of Haddock here, so be sure to read the official documentation to learn more about how you can document your code.

Let's start by running `cabal haddock`, generating some documentation on our project in its current state. When you run this command, you'll see quite a lot of output as `haddock` tells us about all of the things that are undocumented. In the end, you should see `cabal` print out a message telling you that it's generated the documentation at some long path. The specific path will depend

6. https://haskell-haddock.readthedocs.io/en/latest/
7. http://hackage.haskell.org

on your operating system, user name, and the version of ghc you are using, but it might look something like this example:

```
Documentation created:
/home/user/module-examples/dist-newstyle/build/x86_64-linux/
  ghc-9.2.2/module-examples-0.1.0.0/doc/html/module-examples/index.html
```

If you open this path in a web browser, you'll see a page with a list of all of the modules you've added to the project. You can click some of the links and see that Haddock has generated some documentation with the information available. By default, Haddock will generate a file per module, and each file will have an entry for everything that's exported by the module. Unfortunately, without any comments, the generated documentation isn't all that useful. Let's start adding some doc comments to HaskellBook.Examples.Introduction.CreatingModules so that we can get more useful documentation.

We'll start by adding some module-level documentation at the top of the file:

```
-- |
-- This module serves as an example of how you can create a
-- module. This comment will be placed at the top of the generated
-- documentation.

{-# LANGUAGE RecordWildCards #-}
module HaskellBook.Examples.Introduction.CreatingModules
  ( Name (..)
  , Salutation (..)
  , GreetingMessage (..)
  , defaultMessage
  , formatMessage
  , testMessage
  ) where
```

You'll notice in this example that our module-level documentation looks like a typical Haskell comment, except that we've added a line with a pipe character (|) at the start of our comment. In general, Haddock comments are normal Haskell comments that start with a pipe character. You can use either single-line comments, like in the example, or multiline comments. Let's rewrite our documentation with a multiline Haddock comment so you can see how that looks as well:

```
{- |
This module serves as an example of how you can create a module. This
comment will be placed at the top of the generated documentation.
-}
```

There's no benefit to choosing one style of comment over another, and you can pick whichever you prefer.

We can use the same style of comment to add documentation to functions and variables as well. Let's start by adding some documentation to testMessage:

```
{-|
A test message that you can use to see how messages are formatted.
-}
testMessage :: String
testMessage =
  formatMessage $ defaultMessage { greetingFrom = [Name "test example"] }
```

This comment is *okay*. It tells the user what to expect, but it would be a lot more useful if they could see what the actual test message is. Let's add some extra formatting to show the user what they'd expect to see if they typed testMessage into ghci:

```
{-|
A test message that you can use to see how messages are formatted:

>>> testMessage
"Hello Friend, from: test example"
-}
```

The three arrows (>>>) tell Haddock to render the next line as though it were typed into a REPL, and to treat the next line as output from the REPL. This lets you show users how to use your code with examples they can try themselves.

You're not limited to code that might be run in a REPL. You can also include more general code snippets in your documentation using the at-symbol (@) to mark the beginning and end of a code block. We can use this to add some documentation for defaultMessage that makes it more clear what the defaults are. Let's try this:

```
{- |
A default greeting message that isn't attributed to anyone:

@
GreetingMessage
  { greetingSalutation = Salutation "Hello"
  , greetingTo = Name "Friend"
  , greetingFrom = []
  }
@
-}
defaultMessage :: GreetingMessage
```

Unfortunately, if you look at the generated documentation after adding this comment, you'll notice that it isn't quite what we'd hoped. The code block that's generated looks *almost* right, but the strings "Hello" and "Friend" have lost their quotes and instead become broken links. This is happening because Haddock treats quoted strings as references that it should follow. Specifically, surrounding something with double quotes (") tells Haddock to treat it as a reference to a module. Surrounding something with single quotes (') makes it a reference to a function or type. We can insert literal quotes by escaping them with a backslash (\). Let's take advantage of this ability to link to things by making the type constructor and field selectors in our example link to their definitions in the documentation:

```
{- |
A default greeting message that isn't attributed to anyone:

@
'GreetingMessage'
  { 'greetingSalutation' = 'Salutation' \"Hello\"
  , 'greetingTo' = 'Name' \"Friend\"
  , 'greetingFrom' = []
  }
@
-}
defaultMessage :: GreetingMessage
```

Finally, since our documentation is now pointing users to GreetingMessage, let's document it as well. We'll add some documentation for the type, plus documentation for each of the individual fields in the record:

```
{- |
A GreetingMessage contains all of the information needed to generate a
greeting using 'formatMessage'. You can get a default greeting without
attribution from 'defaultMessage'. This makes it convenient to use
record update syntax to construct a new greeting:

>>> formatMessage defaultMessage { greetingFrom = [ Name "A Haskeller"] }
"Hello Friend, from: A Haskeller"
-}
data GreetingMessage = GreetingMessage
  { greetingSalutation :: Salutation
    -- ^ A 'Salutation', like \"Hello\"
  , greetingTo :: Name
    -- ^ 'Name' of the person that should be greeted
  , greetingFrom :: [Name]
    -- ^ 'Name's of the people who are sending the greeting
  }
```

In this example, you'll notice that we've introduced a new type of comment. We can use a comment starting with a caret symbol (^) to add comments for specific fields in a record. These comments can appear at the end of the line with the field they are documenting, or immediately after it. If you prefer, you can also use the pipe comment notation, putting a comment before each record field:

```
data GreetingMessage = GreetingMessage
  { -- | A 'Salutation', like \"Hello\"
    greetingSalutation :: Salutation
  , -- | 'Name' of the person that should be greeted
    greetingTo :: Name
  ,  -- | 'Name's of the people who are sending the greeting
    greetingFrom :: [Name]
  }
```

Knowing these basics, you can start to add documentation to all of the modules you write, making it easier for anyone (including you, in the future) who wants to use your modules to do so without needing to review all of the source code. You can read the official Haddock documentation[8] for a more complete overview of the supported syntax for writing documentation.

Summary

In this chapter, you learned how to create larger Haskell projects that depend on external libraries, and are made up of more than one module. Being able to re-use code, including both external libraries and code you've written, is key to being able to effectively build larger and more sophisticated applications.

Throughout the rest of this book, we will not spend much on the specific structure of the applications you are building, or the setup of particular projects. You can refer back to this chapter each time you need to start a new project until you're more comfortable setting up a project from scratch. At first, you're likely to find that your projects have a relatively flat organization, and you're unlikely to make extensive use of features like export lists, smart constructors, or re-exporting things you've imported from other modules. Don't go looking for ways to complicate the structure of your projects unnecessarily. Instead, as you're using external libraries, take note of common patterns and think about what problems that they might solve, and consider adopting more sophisticated organizational approaches slowly so that you can get a feeling for the pros and cons of different approaches to organizing your code.

Exercises

The ways that you choose to document and organize your code are more subjective than most of the topics we'll cover in this book. As you start to

8. https://haskell-haddock.readthedocs.io/en/latest/index.html

work on these exercises you'll realize there are several reasonable ways to approach them. For each of the exercises, try out a few different approaches to get a feel for the pros and cons of each, and to start developing your own personal style.

Refactoring UserInfo

Refactor the `HaskellBook.Examples.UserInfo` module into smaller modules. Try to look at different ways that you can separate out the concerns of authentication, looking up a particular user, and getting information about a user.

Old New Projects

Use cabal and create projects for all of the examples that you've already worked on as you've been working through this book. Consider how you might organize the modules to maximize re-use in cases where we worked through several variations of a single example.

Document Your Modules

Review the projects that you created in this chapter, as well as any cabal projects you created while working through previous examples, and document them. Make sure to check out the official Haddock documentation[9] to find out about more ways that you can effectively format your documentation.

---

9. https://haskell-haddock.readthedocs.io/en/latest/index.html

CHAPTER 6

Type Classes

Earlier in this book, you learned about a type of polymorphism called *parametric polymorphism* that allows you to write a single implementation of a function that can work with many different types using type variables. This style of polymorphism is when you are concerned with data structures and the shape of the data you are working with, but don't need to directly inspect values. Unfortunately, parametric polymorphism falls short when we need to deal with the polymorphic values in a non-generic way. As soon as we need to carry out specific operations on a polymorphic value, we run into the problem that our operations depend on what type the value happens to be.

Object-oriented programming languages let you solve this problem using inheritance or interfaces to write different implementations of functions depending on their type. The idea that we can provide a different implementation of a function depending on its type is called *ad hoc polymorphism*. Haskell provides its own approach to ad hoc polymorphism with *type classes*.

In this chapter, you will learn more about the limitations of parametric polymorphism and how to use type classes to write more expressive interfaces and how to build polymorphic functions that behave differently based on the type of their inputs. You will also learn to use Haskell's powerful *deriving* mechanism to get the benefit of ad hoc polymorphism without needing to write boilerplate code.

Using Ad Hoc Polymorphism with Type classes

Before we dive into using type classes, let's take a look at a small motivating example. Imagine that we wanted to write a function that could remove duplicate elements from a list. If we're only making use of parametric polymorphism we're a little bit limited in how we can write a function like this. To remove duplicates from the list we need to compare elements to find out if they match. The problem here is that our elements could be *anything*. We might even be dealing with functions or some other value that doesn't have a regular notion of equality.

Your first thought might be to just use the (==) function that we've been making use of throughout this book, but as you'll see shortly, the (==) function uses type classes, which defeats the purpose of our motivating example.

It turns out that the only way we could write a function like this using only parametric polymorphism is to ask the user to pass in a function to let us test equality. When we do this, we no longer have to be concerned about the problem of how to compare values, or even whether they are comparable. If they can tell us how to compare values we can remove duplicates, and if they can't tell us how to compare values then they can't call our function. In the end, if you write this function out, you might end up with something very similar to the example:

```
unique :: (a -> a -> Bool) -> [a] -> [a]
unique _ [] = []
unique f (elem:elems) =
  let
    f' a b = not $ f a b
    elems' = filter (f' elem) elems
  in elem : unique f elems'
```

We can allow ourselves to cheat for a moment and use (==) so that we can see this in action. If you prefer, you can define some types and write your own equality test for them to prove that this works without relying on a function that makes use of type classes:

```
λ unique (==) [1,2,3,2,1]
[1,2,3]
λ unique (==) ["hello","george","george","hello"]
["hello","george"]
```

This approach works well for small things, and you'll see it used in practice quite often when the only thing we need is a single function, especially when we only need that single function in one place. Unfortunately, the approach doesn't scale well as our code gets more complicated. For one thing, although a single additional function isn't too hard to add to our function, it can get a lot more challenging if you have several functions. Imagine that you wanted to calculate the sum of the unique numbers in a list. To do that you'll need to accept another function to allow you to add the elements, as well as a default value to use in case the list is empty:

```
sumOfUniques ::
  (a -> a -> a)
  -> (a -> a -> Bool)
  -> a
  -> [a]
  -> a
sumOfUniques add compare zero =
  foldr add zero . unique compare
```

As you can see, even adding one more function here starts to make the size of the functions working with these values quite long. Furthermore, the functions have become highly coupled, because sumOfUniques needs to accept a comparison function that it doesn't use directly, but just hands off to unique. Calling this function can also start to get a bit awkward, as we have to pass in multiple higher-order functions, leading to statements like sumofUniques (+) (==) 0 [1,2,3,2,1].

So what is to be done? One useful approach, if you have a set of related functions that you might want to use, is to store them in a record, allowing you to pass around a single parameter. As an example, let's create a record to hold some functions that work for natural numbers:

```
data Natural a = Natural
    { equal                  :: a -> a -> Bool
    , add                    :: a -> a -> a
    , multiply               :: a -> a -> a
    , additiveIdentity       :: a
    , multiplicativeIdentity :: a
    , displayAsString        :: a -> String
    }
```

With the record defined, we can also create values that define the Natural operations for various types. As an example, let's create one for Int values:

```
intNatural :: Natural Int
intNatural = Natural
  { equal = (==)
  , add = (+)
  , multiply = (*)
  , additiveIdentity = 0
  , multiplicativeIdentity = 1
  , displayAsString = show
  }
```

The definitions for the operations on Int values is pretty straightforward. Let's look at a more interesting example by returning to the Peano numbers example on page 136 that we built earlier in this book:

```
data Peano = Z | S Peano

toPeano :: Int -> Peano
toPeano 0 = Z
toPeano n = S $ toPeano (n - 1)

fromPeano :: Peano -> Int
fromPeano Z = 0
fromPeano (S n) = 1 + fromPeano n

peanoNatural :: Natural Peano
peanoNatural = Natural
  { equal = comparePeano
  , add   = addPeano
  , multiply = multiplyPeano
  , additiveIdentity = Z
  , multiplicativeIdentity = S Z
  , displayAsString = show . fromPeano
  }
  where
    comparePeano Z Z = True
    comparePeano (S a) (S b) = comparePeano a b
    comparePeano _ _ = False
    addPeano Z b = b
    addPeano (S a) b = addPeano a (S b)
    multiplyPeano Z _ = Z
    multiplyPeano (S a) b =
      addPeano b (multiplyPeano a b)
```

Now that you have defined a record that contains all of the functions necessary to do some operations on natural numbers, and have defined values for both Int and Peano numbers, let's rewrite our two functions to use this new record:

```
unique :: Natural a -> [a] -> [a]
unique _ [] = []
unique n (elem:elems) =
  let
    compare a b = not $ (equal n) a b
    elems' = filter (compare elem) elems
  in elem : unique n elems'

sumOfUniques :: Natural a -> [a] -> a
sumOfUniques n =
  foldr (add n) (additiveIdentity n) . unique n
```

The most immediate difference in our updated code is that the type signatures are much shorter, and more importantly, have become somewhat more readable thanks to the use of Natural a helping to highlight what kind of functions we're wanting to use.

The idea that you often want to group a set of related functions together with a name, and then accept them as part of a polymorphic function, is very common in Haskell, and you'll frequently run across code in the wild that's implemented just as you've done here, with a record full of function values. For one special case of this pattern, however, Haskell provides us with a powerful tool to solve the problem, called *type classes* (or, frequently, *typeclasses*).

Type classes provide support for *ad hoc* polymorphism, and are often used in a similar way to interfaces in object-oriented languages. In this section, you'll learn about the basics of type classes and how to use them. Throughout the first half of this book, you'll be introduced to several common type classes that are defined in base and by the core libraries. Later in the book, we'll return to the subject of type classes and you'll learn about some related features that make them much more powerful.

Creating a Type Class for Natural

At their most basic, type classes work a lot like the Natural type that you built in the previous section. With type classes you can give a name to a group of related functions, and this will allow you to provide an implementation for those functions for different types. As an example, you can rewrite your Natural record as a type class:

```
module NaturalClass where

class Natural n where
  equal :: n -> n -> Bool
  add :: n -> n -> n
  multiply :: n -> n -> n
  additiveIdentity :: n
  multiplicativeIdentity :: n
  displayAsString :: n -> String
```

You can see in this example how similar the type class approach is to defining the Natural as a record. In both cases, you have some type variable, in this case n, that you use as you're writing out the type annotations for the functions that belong to the type class.

Creating an instance of a type class is similar to creating a value of the Natural record. As an example, let's create an instance of the Natural type class for the Int type:

```
instance Natural Int where
  equal = (==)
  add = (+)
  multiply = (*)
  additiveIdentity = 0
  multiplicativeIdentity = 1
  displayAsString = show
```

You can see that the way we've defined the instance of this type class looks remarkably similar to the way that you defined intNatural earlier in this chapter. Following this same pattern, try to create an instance of Natural for Peano yourself.

Composing Type Classes

When creating a type class, it's common that you'd like to include the constraints of some other type class. Our Natural type class, for instance, has re-created the functionality that's already available in the Eq type class, which is exported by Prelude.

You've already used Eq extensively; it's where the (==) function comes from. In fact, Eq is a very small class, and (==) is the only function we need to define to create an instance:

```
class Eq a where
  (==) :: a -> a -> Bool
```

Eq Changes

At the time of this writing, Eq also defines a function named (/=) that defines inequality. An upcoming version of GHC will remove (/=) from the Eq type class and replace it with a regular function. Since (/=) is currently optional if you have provided a definition of (==), we will ignore it.

Since there are a lot of existing functions that are written for us and work if we have an instance of Eq, we would be better served by using Eq to define equality, and then adding the extra functionality we need to Natural. We can do this by adding a constraint on Eq when we define our type class:

```
class Eq n => Natural n where
  add :: n -> n -> n
  multiply :: n -> n -> n
  additiveIdentity :: n
  multiplicativeIdentity :: n
  displayAsString :: n -> String
```

With this constraint, we're requiring that anything that has an instance of Natural should also have an instance of Eq. Typically, you'd include a restriction like this if you want to use some functions from another type class in the default implementation of functions that are part of the type class that you're defining, but it's also possible to include the restriction because the type classes form a natural hierarchy.

You're not limited to a single constraint. It seems as though we've also duplicated the functionality of another common class exported by Prelude: the Show type class represents values that can be displayed as text. The version of Show that's exported by Prelude defines several possible functions that you can implement, but we can get by with a single function, show. You'll learn more about how to create type classes with default implementations in the next section, but for now we can imagine that the Show type class is defined like this:

```
class Show a where
  show :: a -> String
```

The Show Type Class

The Show type class is frequently used as a way to create generic human-readable text from Haskell values. It's also how ghci displays values. When the compiler creates an instance of Show for you automatically, it will generate a string that is valid Haskell code and can be parsed by the read family of functions from the Read type class. It's a good practice, especially in larger code bases, to stick with simple or automatically generated definitions for Show. You should define your own custom classes for more richly formatted ways of displaying values. Still, we will use Show instances as a shortcut occasionally in this book to make the examples easier to follow, and you'll see other projects where people take this particular shortcut.

Let's refactor Natural one more time. This time we'll also add a Show constraint to replace our old displayAsString function:

```
class (Show n, Eq n) => Natural n where
  add :: n -> n -> n
  multiply :: n -> n -> n
  additiveIdentity :: n
  multiplicativeIdentity :: n
```

Now that we've removed some extraneous functions and replaced them with constraints, we need to refactor our instance. Thankfully, Int already has instances of both Eq and Show defined, so we don't need to do anything but remove the definitions of equal and displayAsString:

```
instance Natural Int where
  add = (+)
  multiply = (*)
  additiveIdentity = 0
  multiplicativeIdentity = 1
```

While we're at it, let's also add an instance for our Peano type:

```
instance Natural Peano where
  add a Z = a
  add a (S b) = add (S a) b
  multiply Z _ = Z
  multiply (S a) b = add b (multiply a b)
  additiveIdentity = Z
  multiplicativeIdentity = S Z
```

If we try to load this version of our program, we'll get an error:

```
NaturalClass.hs:34:10: error:
    • No instance for (Show Peano)
        arising from the superclasses of an instance declaration
    • In the instance declaration for 'Natural Peano'
   |
34 | instance Natural Peano where
   |          ^^^^^^^^^^^^^

NaturalClass.hs:34:10: error:
    • No instance for (Eq Peano)
        arising from the superclasses of an instance declaration
    • In the instance declaration for 'Natural Peano'
   |
34 | instance Natural Peano where
   |          ^^^^^^^^^^^^^
Failed, no modules loaded.
```

The errors here are pointing us in the right direction. Our type class has constraints on Eq and Show, so we can't create an instance of Natural without also defining Eq and Show instances. The compiler is telling us we need to provide instances for those two classes if we want to create a Natural instances for Peano. Let's update our example one last time to add instances for Eq and Show and verify that everything works as expected:

```
module NaturalClass where

data Peano = Z | S Peano

toPeano :: Int -> Peano
toPeano 0 = Z
toPeano n = S $ toPeano (n - 1)

fromPeano :: Peano -> Int
fromPeano Z = 0
fromPeano (S n) = 1 + fromPeano n

class (Show n, Eq n) => Natural n where
  add :: n -> n -> n
  multiply :: n -> n -> n
  additiveIdentity :: n
  multiplicativeIdentity :: n
```

```
instance Natural Int where
  add = (+)
  multiply = (*)
  additiveIdentity = 0
  multiplicativeIdentity = 1

instance Eq Peano where
  (==) Z Z = True
  (==) (S a) (S b) = a == b
  (==) _ _ = False

instance Show Peano where
  show Z = "Z"
  show (S a) = "(S " <> show a <> ")"

instance Natural Peano where
  add a Z = a
  add a (S b) = add (S a) b
  multiply Z _ = Z
  multiply (S a) b = add b (multiply a b)
  additiveIdentity = Z
  multiplicativeIdentity = S Z
```

Now, if we reload our code in ghci, we can see that everything is working as we'd expect:

```
λ :load NaturalClass.hs
λ add (1 :: Int) (2 :: Int)
3
λ multiply multiplicativeIdentity (100 :: Int)
100
λ add additiveIdentity (S (S (S (S Z))))
(S (S (S (S Z))))
```

Creating Default Implementations and Minimal Definitions

Type classes can do more than collect a set of functions for you to implement for your own type. One useful feature when writing a type class is that you can provide a default implementation of a function. As an example, let's consider the Ord type class for things that have an ordering. This type class is defined in Data.Ord and is normally exported by Prelude. For our examples, we'll hide the default implementations so we can see how to build it ourselves. There are quite a few functions provided by Ord:

```
module OrdExample where
import Prelude hiding (Ord(..), Ordering(..))

data Ordering = LT | EQ | GT
```

```
instance Show Ordering where
  show LT = "LT"
  show EQ = "EQ"
  show GT = "GT"

class Eq a => Ord a where
  compare :: a -> a -> Ordering
  (<)  :: a -> a -> Bool
  (<=) :: a -> a -> Bool
  (>)  :: a -> a -> Bool
  (>=) :: a -> a -> Bool
  max  :: a -> a -> a
  min  :: a -> a -> a
```

You might notice that we've created a new type, Ordering, and added an instance of the Show type class here. Like Ord, Ordering is normally defined in Data.Ord and exported by Prelude. We've redefined it in our example to help make the examples easier to follow.

There are quite a few useful functions here that will let us do all sorts of useful comparisons on ordered values. The downside to all of this functionality is that we're asking our users to implement quite a few functions, and in many cases we might be asking them to implement those functions unnecessarily. For example, let's define our own instance of Ord. We'll use Word8 values from Data.Word since our example will be simpler when we we're dealing with unsigned values:

```
module OrdExample where
import Prelude hiding (Ord(..), Ordering(..))
import Data.Word (Word8)

data Ordering = LT | EQ | GT

instance Show Ordering where
  show LT = "LT"
  show EQ = "EQ"
  show GT = "GT"

class Eq a => Ord a where
  compare :: a -> a -> Ordering
  (<)  :: a -> a -> Bool
  (<=) :: a -> a -> Bool
  (>)  :: a -> a -> Bool
  (>=) :: a -> a -> Bool
  max  :: a -> a -> a
  min  :: a -> a -> a

instance Ord Word8 where
  compare a b
    | a == b = EQ
    | a == 0 = LT
```

```
    | b == 0 = GT
    | otherwise = compare (a - 1) (b - 1)
  a < b =
    case compare a b of
      LT -> True
      _ -> False
  a <= b =
    case compare a b of
      GT -> False
      _ -> True
  a > b =
    case compare a b of
      GT -> True
      _ -> False
  a >= b =
    case compare a b of
      LT -> False
      _ -> True
  max a b =
    case compare a b of
      GT -> a
      _ -> b
  min a b =
    case compare a b of
      LT -> a
      _ -> b
```

Not only is there a lot of typing involved here, but you'll also notice that all of the functions we're providing implementations for are done in terms of the compare function. We've done a lot of typing, and it seems like the work we've done here is something that the compiler could have done for us.

Thankfully, we can make our type classes easier for users who need to create instances by providing default implementations of the functions we define in the type class. You've already seen how we can implement the other functions in terms of compare for Word8; let's take the same idea and use it to create a default in our type class:

```
class Eq a => Ord a where
  compare :: a -> a -> Ordering
  (<)  :: a -> a -> Bool
  a < b =
    case compare a b of
      LT -> True
      _ -> False
```

```
  (<=) :: a -> a -> Bool
  a <= b =
    case compare a b of
      GT -> False
      _ -> True

  (>)  :: a -> a -> Bool
  a > b =
    case compare a b of
      GT -> True
      _ -> False

  (>=) :: a -> a -> Bool
  a >= b =
    case compare a b of
      LT -> False
      _ -> True

  max  :: a -> a -> a
  max a b =
    case compare a b of
      GT -> a
      _ -> b

  min  :: a -> a -> a
  min a b =
    case compare a b of
      LT -> a
      _ -> b
```

When we have defaults in place, we're free to provide our own implementations when we're creating instances of a type class, but if we don't provide one the default will be used. Let's look at an example of this in practice. We can start by changing the instance definition for Word8 to only provide the necessary compare function:

```
module OrdExample where
import Prelude hiding (Ord(..), Ordering(..))
import Data.Word (Word8)

data Ordering = LT | EQ | GT

instance Show Ordering where
  show LT = "LT"
  show EQ = "EQ"
  show GT = "GT"

class Eq a => Ord a where
  compare :: a -> a -> Ordering
  (<)  :: a -> a -> Bool
  a < b =
    case compare a b of
      LT -> True
```

```
      _ -> False

  (<=) :: a -> a -> Bool
  a <= b =
    case compare a b of
      GT -> False
      _ -> True

  (>)  :: a -> a -> Bool
  a > b =
    case compare a b of
      GT -> True
      _ -> False

  (>=) :: a -> a -> Bool
  a >= b =
    case compare a b of
      LT -> False
      _ -> True

  max  :: a -> a -> a
  max a b =
    case compare a b of
      GT -> a
      _ -> b

  min  :: a -> a -> a
  min a b =
    case compare a b of
      LT -> a
      _ -> b

instance Ord Word8 where
  compare a b
    | a == b = EQ
    | a == 0 = LT
    | b == 0 = GT
    | otherwise = compare (a - 1) (b - 1)
```

We can test this ourselves in ghci. We'll need to add some extra type annotations for now to test this, but you'll learn how to make this a bit more ergonomic later in this chapter when you learn how to use *visible type applications*.

```
λ compare (1 :: Word8) (0 :: Word8)
GT
λ max (3 :: Word8) (5 :: Word8)
5
λ min (3 :: Word8) (5 :: Word8)
3
```

If we provide our own implementation of a function with a default implementation, ours will take precedence. For example, we could write our own incorrect versions of `min` and `max` that always return the first argument:

```
instance Ord Word8 where
  compare a b
    | a == b = EQ
    | a == 0 = LT
    | b == 0 = GT
    | otherwise = compare (a - 1) (b - 1)
  min a b = a
  max a b = a
```

If we run this in ghci you can see that the behavior changes, and we always get back the first argument we pass to these functions:

```
λ :reload
λ min (5 :: Word8) (3 :: Word8)
5
λ max (3 :: Word8) (5 :: Word8)
3
```

Something you might have noticed as we've been working through this section is that we've provided default implementations of all of the functions in Ord in terms of the compare function, but that's not the only function we could have picked. For example, instead of implementing (<=) in terms of compare, we could have implemented compare in terms of (<=). When we have more than one option for a function that a user can provide, we can provide default implementations of them in terms of one another. For example, let's add a default implementation of compare in terms of (<=):

```
class Eq a => Ord a where
  compare :: a -> a -> Ordering
  compare a b
    | a == b = EQ
    | a <= b = LT
    | otherwise = GT

  (<)  :: a -> a -> Bool
  a < b =
    case compare a b of
      LT -> True
      _ -> False

  (<=) :: a -> a -> Bool
  a <= b =
    case compare a b of
      GT -> False
      _ -> True

  (>)  :: a -> a -> Bool
  a > b =
    case compare a b of
      GT -> True
      _ -> False
```

```
  (>=) :: a -> a -> Bool
  a >= b =
    case compare a b of
      LT -> False
      _ -> True

  max  :: a -> a -> a
  max a b =
    case compare a b of
      GT -> a
      _ -> b

  min  :: a -> a -> a
  min a b =
    case compare a b of
      LT -> a
      _ -> b
```

Now we can create an instance of Ord using either compare or (<=), or both. A good starting point is to simply reload our existing code with our old definition of our Word8 instance using compare to see that it continues to work:

```
λ compare (1 :: Word8) (5 :: Word8)
LT
λ compare (10 :: Word8) (5 :: Word8)
GT
λ (1 :: Word8) <= (5 :: Word8)
True
λ min 1 5 :: Word8
1
λ max 1 5 :: Word8
5
```

Next, let's update our instance of Ord. Instead of compare we'll provide a definition of (<=):

```
instance Ord Word8 where
  a <= b
    | a == b = True
    | a == 0 = True
    | b == 0 = False
    | otherwise = (a - 1) <= (b - 1)
```

Once again, if we reload our code we'll see that we're getting the exact same behavior, even though we've provided a different function:

```
λ :reload
λ compare (1 :: Word8) (5 :: Word8)
LT
λ compare (10 :: Word8) (5 :: Word8)
GT
```

```
λ (1 :: Word8) <= (5 :: Word8)
True
λ min 1 5 :: Word8
1
λ max 1 5 :: Word8
5
```

Being able to provide a default implementation of all the functions in the type class is convenient, but unfortunately, at the moment we've made the interface a little easier to use than it actually should be. Since we've provided a default implementation of all of the functions, what will happen if we try to create an instance without defining anything? Let's try it:

```
instance Ord Word8 where
```

Now let's load our code up into ghci:

```
λ :reload
[1 of 1] Compiling OrdExample       ( OrdExample.hs, interpreted )
Ok, one module loaded.
```

Everything looks good so far, but if we try to use any of the functions defined by Ord, our program will hang forever. You can try it yourself; just press control-c to stop the process when you're tired of waiting.

```
λ max 1 5 :: Word8
```

The reason that this hung forever was that we've created an infinite recursion. Each time we call compare, we hit the default implementation that references (<=). Each time we call (<=) we hit the default implementation that sends us back to compare. This will continue forever. We need a way to tell the compiler, and any other developers who will create instances of our type class, what the minimal complete definition of a type class should be.

Haskell gives us a way to do this using the MINIMAL pragma. Like LANGUAGE pragmas you've already seen, the MINIMAL pragma is surrounded by a block comment, but unlike LANGUAGE it doesn't go at the top of a file, instead it goes at the end of your type class.

To use a MINIMAL pragma, you need to pass it a list of the type class functions that should be implemented by the user. Comma-separated functions must all be implemented, and one of any set of vertical pipe (|) separated functions must be implemented. For our Ord type class we can add a pragma to say that at a minimum, either compare or (<=) should be implemented:

```
class Eq a => Ord a where
  compare :: a -> a -> Ordering
  compare a b
```

```
    | a == b = EQ
    | a <= b = LT
    | otherwise = GT

  (<)  :: a -> a -> Bool
  a < b =
    case compare a b of
      LT -> True
      _ -> False

  (<=) :: a -> a -> Bool
  a <= b =
    case compare a b of
      GT -> False
      _ -> True

  (>)  :: a -> a -> Bool
  a > b =
    case compare a b of
      GT -> True
      _ -> False

  (>=) :: a -> a -> Bool
  a >= b =
    case compare a b of
      LT -> False
      _ -> True

  max  :: a -> a -> a
  max a b =
    case compare a b of
      GT -> a
      _ -> b

  min  :: a -> a -> a
  min a b =
    case compare a b of
      LT -> a
      _ -> b
  {-# MINIMAL compare | (<=) #-}
```

If we reload our code in ghci we'll get an error telling us that we haven't provided the minimal complete definition of the type class:

```
λ :reload
OrdExample.hs:52:10: warning: [-Wmissing-methods]
    • No explicit implementation for
        either 'compare' or '<='
    • In the instance declaration for 'Ord Word8'
   |
52 | instance Ord Word8 where
   |          ^^^^^^^^^
Ok, one module loaded.
```

Although the MINIMAL pragma is only needed when you have circular definitions, it's good practice to include them any time you have default implementations. Not only will MINIMAL ensure that GHC generates a warning for missing functions, but Haddock will also extract these pragmas and use them when generating type class documentation, making it easier for users who are browsing the online documentation for your module.

Signatures for Default Instance Definitions

Providing default implementations of functions in your type class can make them much nicer to use, but when we try to design our type classes to provide as much as possible "out of the box" for our users, we're often faced with a problem. Frequently, we can provide sensible default implementations for a function, but doing so would require that we depend on some other type class.

As an example, let's imagine that we're writing a logging library. One feature we might want to support is giving users the ability to log some data that might need to be redacted. For example, we might want to log that a user provided a password, but we don't want to include the value of that password in our plain text log files.

Our first approach to writing this type class might not provide any default at all, since we won't know if something should be redacted:

```
module DefaultSignaturesDemo where

class Redacted a where
  redacted :: a -> String
```

Next, let's create a new UserName type that will hold a username. We'd like to have a Show instance of this type so that we can work with it on the command line as we're testing, but for production purposes we might want to log user names, so we'll also create a Redacted instance:

```
module DefaultSignaturesDemo where

class Redacted a where
  redacted :: a -> String

data UserName = UserName String

instance Show UserName where
  show (UserName name) = name

instance Redacted UserName where
  redacted (UserName name) = name
```

Reading through this example, you might notice that our instances of Show and Redacted are identical. We can take what we've learned from this chapter so far to make our API easier to use. Let's add a Show constraint onto our class, and provide a default implementation of redacted that calls out to show:

```
class Show a => Redacted a where
  redacted :: a -> String
  redacted = show

data UserName = UserName String

instance Show UserName where
  show (UserName userName) = userName

instance Redacted UserName
```

You'll notice in this example that we're still creating an instance of Redacted, but now we aren't providing any functions to it. We can drop the where keyword in situations like this where we don't need to define any functions for our instance. You'll learn about some other ways to handle this scenario later on in this chapter, but this is still an improvement. We now only need to define a single function to format our value, and we get a 'Redacted' instance for free.

So far, so good; we can load this up into ghci and everything is working as we'd hope:

```
λ UserName "George"
George
λ redacted $ UserName "George"
"George"
```

Unfortunately, this breaks down as soon as we start to think about data where we can't, or don't, want to define a Show instance. For example, we may want to log some redacted information about a user's password so we can know if they attempted to log in or not, but we don't want to provide a Show instance because we don't want to risk mistakenly printing a user's password in plain text.

What should we do in this case? It would seem that if we need to remove the Show constraint from our type class, then our only other choice is to force our users to write the same code for show and redacted whenever they could have otherwise used the default implementation.

DataKinds

The DefaultSignatures extension has been available since GHC 7.2.1. It's not enabled by default in either GHC2021 or Haskell2010, so you'll need to enable it manually. This is generally a safe extension that shouldn't interfere with any existing code.

One way that we can solve this problem is to make use of the DefaultSignatures language extension. This extension allows us to add a type signature to the default implementation of a function in a type class. When we add a signature to the default implementation, we can also add type class constraints. Let's take a look at this in action and then we'll see what it means for us as we're creating type classes. We'll start by adding the language extension and updating our type class to provide a default signature for redacted:

```
{-# LANGUAGE DefaultSignatures #-}
module DefaultSignaturesDemo where

class Redacted a where
  redacted :: a -> String
  default redacted :: Show a => a -> String
  redacted = show
```

You'll notice that we've dropped them Show constraint on the type class. We'll no longer require that every Redacted have an instance of Show. Instead, we're using the default keyword to add a type signature to our default implementation of redacted that is more specific than the general type that's part of the type class. This means that any instance that wants to provide a definition of redacted only needs to satisfy the general type redacted :: a -> String. If an instance wants to use the default implementation though, then it needs to also provide a Show instance.

Let's look at this in action by adding a new Password type. We won't add a Show instance for Password, but we can try to define an instance of Redacted that uses the default definition of redacted just to verify that we get an error:

```
λ :reload
DefaultSignaturesDemo.hs:17:10: error:
    • No instance for (Show Password)
        arising from a use of 'DefaultSignaturesDemo.$dmredacted'
    • In the expression: DefaultSignaturesDemo.$dmredacted @(Password)
      In an equation for 'redacted':
          redacted = DefaultSignaturesDemo.$dmredacted @(Password)
      In the instance declaration for 'Redacted Password'
   |
17 | instance Redacted Password
   |          ^^^^^^^^^^^^^^^^^
Failed, no modules loaded.
```

As we would expect, we're getting an error because we haven't defined an instance of Show for Password. If we provide our own implementation that doesn't rely on Show, then everything will work as expected. Let's create our own implementation of redacted for our instance:

```
{-# LANGUAGE DefaultSignatures #-}
module DefaultSignaturesDemo where

class Redacted a where
  redacted :: a -> String
  default redacted :: Show a => a -> String
  redacted = show

data UserName = UserName String

instance Show UserName where
  show (UserName userName) = userName

instance Redacted UserName

data Password = Password String

instance Redacted Password where
  redacted _ = "<redacted>"
```

Thanks to our default signature, we can fall back to using a Show constraint when one is available, and otherwise require that the user provide their own implementation of a function. Before we move on, let's load this up in ghci just to verify that it's working as expected:

```
λ UserName "george"
george
λ redacted $ UserName "george"
"george"
λ Password "hunter2"

<interactive>:110:1: error:
    • No instance for (Show Password) arising from a use of 'print'
    • In a stmt of an interactive GHCi command: print it
λ redacted $ Password "hunter2"
"<redacted>"
```

Just as we'd hoped, UserName provides both a Show and Redacted instance that work the same, since we fall back to show when we haven't provided a new definition for redacted. When we're working with Password values we don't have a Show instance, and so we can't print the values out in plain text, but we can use our own definition of redacted to get a safe masked value.

Specifying Type Class Instances with Type Applications

A common problem when you're using type class constraints is ambiguity about which specific type class instance should be used. Consider, for example, a program you want to have print out the additive and multiplicative identities of some Natural numbers. You might write something like this:

```
showIdentities =
  let mul = multiplicativeIdentity
      add = additiveIdentity
      msg = "The additive identity is: "
            <> show add
            <> " and the multiplicative identity is: "
            <> show mul
  in print msg
```

Unfortunately, this fails to compile! The problem is that multiplicativeIdentity and additiveIdentity both return a type that depends on the type class instance that we're using, but the compiler doesn't have a way to pick any particular instance, and so it has to give up and raise an error. One way we could get around this for our example function is to add a type annotation:

```
showIdentities =
  let mul = multiplicativeIdentity :: Peano
      add = additiveIdentity :: Peano
      msg = "The additive identity is: "
            <> show add
            <> " and the multiplicative identity is: "
            <> show mul
  in print msg
```

This gets us past our error, but it's not an ideal solution. The first problem is that we're assuming that the return type of the function is sufficient to tell the compiler which type class to use. It works out for our small example here, but if the return type of the function had been polymorphic, we'd be back in the same situation. The second problem is that type annotations can be a little syntactically awkward in some places, especially in pointfree code. It would be ideal in cases like this if we could directly tell the compiler which type class to use, just like we did when we passed in a value of our original Natural record type.

TypeApplications

The TypeApplications extension has been available since GHC 8.0.1. This extension is enabled by default in GHC2021 but you'll need to enable it manually if you are using Haskell2010. This is a safe extension, and shouldn't introduce any problems with existing code.

The TypeApplications language extension allows us to do exactly that. Type applications gives you the ability to pass type names as arguments to polymorphic functions, to select the type class instance that's used. To see it in action, let's start up a ghci session. TypeApplications is enabled with GHC2021, but if you're using a version of GHC older than 9.0, you'll need to enable the extension manually:

```
λ :set -XTypeApplications
```

With the language extension enabled we can use @TypeName to pass a type name into a polymorphic function. A good way to see this quickly is by using read. The read function has type read :: Read a => String -> a, and so by controlling the Read instance it uses to parse the string, we can control the return type. Let's run through a few examples:

```
λ read @Integer "1"
1
λ read @Float "1"
1.0
```

You can see in these examples how the output of the function call depends only on the type parameter. You can partially apply type applications as well, just like regular arguments:

```
λ readInt = read @Int
λ readFloat = read @Float
λ :type readInt
readInt :: String -> Int
λ :type readFloat
readFloat :: String -> Float
λ
```

You can use multiple type applications in functions that have more than one variable with a type class constraint. For example, let's write a function that takes a string and returns an Either value that depends on the length of the input:

```
showLeftRight :: (Read a, Read b) => String -> Either a b
showLeftRight s
  | length s > 5 = Left (read s)
  | otherwise = Right (read s)
```

Just like before, we'll need to use type applications to tell the compiler which instance of the Read type class to use, but now we have two type variables to work with, a and b. We'll use two type applications; the first will select the type to use for a, and the second will select the type to use for b:

```
λ showLeftRight @Float @Int "3.1415"
Left 3.1415
λ showLeftRight @Float @Int "321"
Right 321
```

You'll notice that since we're using an Either here, only one of the two type applications will ever be relevant. If we're returning a Left value, we don't care about the second type variable's instance, since we'll never use it. In that case, you can just provide one type application:

```
λ showLeftRight @Float "3.1415"
Left 3.1415
```

If you only want to provide the second type, you can use @_ as a placeholder. This allows us to skip type applications when they aren't relevant, so for example, if you know that you'll only be using the Right constructor you can say:

```
λ showLeftRight @_ @Int "123"
Right 123
```

Type applications themselves can also be polymorphic. Using polymorphic type applications allows you to create some types of abstractions that would otherwise be difficult to express. Understanding how these work will be easier when working in a source file, since we'll be wanting to write type annotations for functions, so create a new file. In addition to TypeApplications, we'll need to enable another extension, ScopedTypeVariables. We'll look at the new features that this extension enables as we're working through the examples.

ScopedTypeVariables

The ScopedTypeVariables extension has been available since GHC 6.8.1. It's enabled by default in GHC2021 but you'll need to enable it manually if you are using Haskell2010. This extension changes the way type checking works, and may cause some existing programs to stop compiling. It may be beneficial to consider trying to enable this extension project wide in Haskell2010 codebases to identify any problems before upgrading to GHC2021. This extension implies ExplicitForAll. If you are using ScopedTypeVariables you don't need to manually enable ExplicitForAll.

```
{-# LANGUAGE ScopedTypeVariables #-}
{-# LANGUAGE TypeApplications    #-}
```

Next, let's write a function that will guarantee that the Read and Show instances behave as we expect. One of the generally implied contracts about the behavior of these two type classes is that when we show a value, and then read it, we should get the original value back. We can start testing this by writing a function like adheresToReadShowContract:

```
adheresToReadShowContract val =
  let a  = show . read . show $ val
      b = show val
  in a == b
```

Unfortunately, a construct like show . read . show is too much for GHC to be able to handle with type inference, and we'll get a couple of errors where the compiler tells us that it can't figure out what type it should use to instantiate the type class instances. If you haven't already, try to compile your code so that you can see the error yourself.

We could solve this problem by using explicit type application to provide some type like Int or Bool or whatever to read, but that is overly restrictive. One of the benefits of our function is that right now it should allow us to test any type that has a Read and a Show instance. We don't want to give that up!

If our program compiled, we would expect the type signature for it to be something like:

```
adheresToReadShowContract :: (Read a, Show a) => a -> Bool
```

We'd like to be able to tell GHC that, whatever type it uses to instantiate a, that should also be the instance that it uses for the calls to read and show. To do that we'll need to use some syntax that is available thanks to the ScopedTypeVariables extension that we've added. Let's take a look at the code first and then break down what's happening:

```
adheresToReadShowContract :: forall a. (Read a, Show a) => a -> Bool
adheresToReadShowContract val =
  let a = show . read @a . show $ val
      b = show val
  in a == b
```

The first thing you'll notice is that we've added a new element to our type signature, forall a.. The use of forall here is introducing explicit *universal quantification*. This isn't a term you'll often need to use, except perhaps when reading some specific GHC documentation. More generally, it's simply referred to as *explicit forall*. In the code that you've written so far, the forall has been implied when you've used type variables. Writing it explicitly will not generally change the way your program works, but with the ScopedTypeVariables language extension, using an explicit forall brings the type variables into scope in the body of the function. That means that we can refer to the type variable when we're using explicit type applications.

Since our use of ScopedTypeVariables has allowed us to bring our type variable a into scope, we can apply it to read, which gives GHC enough information to successfully compile the program.

Specified and Inferred Types

Compiler Version Differences

This section describes a feature that was introduced in GHC 9 and is not available in GHC version 8.10. If you're using GHC 8.10, you can either skim this chapter now, or revisit it later when you upgrade to a newer compiler version. Since this feature isn't available in GHC 8.10, we won't use it in any examples in the rest of this book. If you're using GHC 9.4, feel free to experiment with this feature as you work through some of the exercises in the book to get a feel for how it can improve the ergonomics of your APIs.

Although type applications can be helpful in a lot of circumstances, you might find that there are some common situations where they don't work as expected. One example that you might run into is trying to use type applications with code that you've defined in ghci. For example, let's imagine that we are writing some code interactively to convert between numbers by way of an intermediate conversion to an Int. We might experimentally define this in ghci and then try to call it at some specific types to see what we get:

```
λ convertViaInt input = fromIntegral $ fromIntegral @_ @Int input
λ :t convertViaInt
convertViaInt :: (Integral w, Num b) => w -> b
λ convertViaInt @Int 5
```

Unfortunately, the result we get back isn't what we'd hope:

```
λ convertViaInt @Int 5

<interactive>:148:1: error:
    • Cannot apply expression of type 'w0 -> b0'
      to a visible type argument 'Int'
    • In the expression: convertViaInt @Int 5
      In an equation for 'it': it = convertViaInt @Int 5
```

What's going on here? We have a function with some polymorphic types, but when we try to use a visible type application we're getting back a fairly unintuitive error.

The problem is that GHC tracks two different sorts of type variables: *specified types* and *inferred types*. In all of the examples so far where we've used visible type applications, we've been writing out a type annotation for the functions that we're going to call with a visible type application. When we manually write out the type variables, we're specifying them, and they become *specified types*. When we have polymorphic type variables that we've never directly referenced, they are tracked by the compiler as *inferred types*. It turns out, we're only allowed to use visible type applications to select specified types. An inferred type is one that we *must* allow the compiler to infer for us.

This is particularly hard to understand with the default ghci settings because by default, the way that the types are displayed, we can easily find ourselves in a situation where we can't see the difference between a function where we can use visible type applications and one where we can't. For example, let's re-define convertViaInt and give it a type annotation:

```
λ :{
> convertViaInt :: (Integral w, Num b) => w -> b
> convertViaInt a = fromIntegral $ fromIntegral @_ @Int a
> :}
λ :t convertViaInt
convertViaInt :: (Integral w, Num b) => w -> b
λ convertViaInt @Int 5
5
```

In this example, the type of convertViaInt *appears* to be exactly the same as the earlier version, but suddenly our visible type application is accepted. Let's turn on the print-explicit-foralls option. This will ask ghci to print out the forall part of the type that it normally hides:

```
λ :set -fprint-explicit-foralls
λ :t convertViaInt
convertViaInt :: forall w b. (Integral w, Num b) => w -> b
```

So far, so good. The type of the working version of convertViaInt looks like we'd expect it to. Let's go back to our earlier version and look at its type to see if we can spot a difference:

```
λ convertViaInt a = fromIntegral $ fromIntegral @_ @Int a
λ :t convertViaInt
convertViaInt :: forall {w} {b}. (Integral w, Num b) => w -> b
```

You might notice that in this version of our function, our type variables have gained brackets. This is how we indicate that a particular type is inferred, rather than specified. In this case, both of the type variables are in brackets, so they are both inferred. Since visible type applications always apply starting with the first specified type, but there aren't any specified types in this version of the function, the compiler doesn't have much to do except throw its hands in the air and raise an exception.

At first, the idea of inferred types might seem like nothing more than a nuisance that prevents us from selecting the types that we want to use in our code. Thankfully, we can still control the types that our function is called at using normal type annotations:

```
λ convertViaInt @Integer @Double 5

<interactive>:177:1: error:
    • Cannot apply expression of type 'w0 -> b0'
      to a visible type argument 'Integer'
    • In the expression: convertViaInt @Integer @Double 5
      In an equation for 'it': it = convertViaInt @Integer @Double 5
λ (convertViaInt :: Integer -> Double) 5
5.0
```

We can also explicitly mark type variables as inferred when we're writing code. For example, let's say that we wanted to provide a library with our convertViaInt function, and we wanted to make it easy for users to specify the type of value that it should return while keeping the input polymorphic. We can mark our type variables inferred to be explicit about the expectation:

```
module InferredTypeDemo where

convertViaInt :: forall {a} b. (Integral a, Num b) => a -> b
convertViaInt input =
  fromIntegral $ fromIntegral @_ @Int input
```

If we load this into ghci you'll see that we can now easily use a visible type application to control the output type:

```
λ convertViaInt @Double 100
100.0
λ convertViaInt @Int 100
100
λ convertToDouble = convertViaInt @Double
λ :t convertToDouble
convertToDouble :: forall {a}. Integral a => a -> Double
```

Wrapping Types with Newtype

One of the key limitations that you've seen when working with type classes is that each data type must have at most a single instance of the type class. Having more than one implementation of show or read for a type would not only make it impossible for the compiler to select an implementation to use, it would also make the program unmaintainably confusing as the intention behind what a type class means for any given type would be obscured. As with the MyResult type that you built in the last section, which was structurally identical to Either, it's common that you might want to have some underlying data structure represented by more than one type, each with its own name and perhaps its own type class instances as well.

To address this problem, Haskell gives us another way of creating a type using the newtype keyword. Types created with newtype are often referred to as *newtype wrappers* because a newtype is simply a way of wrapping an existing type. Unlike data types, newtypes are "zero-cost" abstractions. The compiler guarantees that using a newtype will not introduce any additional computational or memory overhead, and the underlying data structure will share the same representation as the type that it wraps.

Creating a newtype looks very similar to creating a new data type, except that you'll use the newtype keyword instead of data. Let's create a new wrapper around Either to see an example:

```
newtype MyEither a b = MyEither (Either a b)
```

Although this looks very similar to a data declaration, newtypes are limited in ways data declarations are not. Newtypes must always have exactly one constructor, which itself must have exactly one field. You can't use sum types or have multiple fields for a newtype. It's typical for newtype wrappers to use record syntax to name their field. To make our example more idiomatic, we would say:

```
newtype MyEither a b = MyEither { getEither :: Either a b }
```

In this example, MyEither takes two type parameters, which we pass on directly to the underlying type, but this isn't an inherent restriction. Newtypes can take more or fewer type parameters. All of the following would also be valid newtype definitions for example:

```
newtype MyEither = MyEither { getEither :: Either String Int }
newtype MyEither a = MyEither { getEither :: Either String a }
newtype MyEither a = MyEither { getEither :: Either a a }
newtype MyEither a b c = MyEither { getEither :: Either a b }
```

Even though a newtype is just a wrapper around some other type at the lowest level, it is a "real" type. Unlike a type alias, you can't directly substitute a newtype with the type that it's wrapping. This can be very helpful if you want to maintain a clean logical separation between different types in your code, while still benefiting from having a single optimized underlying data structure. Newtypes also allow you to provide different type class instances for a single representation of a data structure. Type aliases, since they aren't actually their own distinct types, don't have their own type class instances. Finally, newtypes allow you to express certain things that aren't otherwise directly allowed due to limitations in the type checker. In the rest of this section we'll explore each of these use-cases for type classes.

Using Type Classes with Newtypes

One of the biggest reasons for using newtype wrappers is to provide type class instances for a type that you're wrapping. There are two reasons that you might want to use a newtype to create type class instances rather than creating instances for the underlying type: to avoid *orphan instances*, and to support multiple different type class instances for an underlying type. In this section, we'll look at a single example that demonstrates both of these reasons for using newtype wrappers.

An orphan instance is a type class instance that you define in a module where you didn't define either the type class you're creating an instance of, or the underlying type that you're creating an instance for. In other words, it's an "orphan instance" because the instance doesn't "belong to" the implementation of the type class or the data type. Although orphan instances aren't an error that will stop your program from building, they will generate a warning, and they are considered bad style and a risk to the long term maintainability of your application. The biggest risk with orphan instances is that in the future, the library that defined the type class, or the underlying type, might choose to add an instance. In Haskell there's a rule that in your entire program there can only ever be one single instance of a type class for each type. That means it's very easy for an update to a library to break your code if it started providing an instance of something that you've already defined an orphan instance for. Not only do you risk your program failing to compile because of conflicting instances, it also makes your code harder to maintain because you will have a non-standard implementation of the type class.

Even when you have defined your data type or the type class you want to create an instance of, it's not uncommon to have more than one plausible way of creating an instance for a type class. Since you're limited to a single instance per type, using newtype wrappers allows you to define multiple instances of a type class while still using a single underlying data definition and not introducing any unnecessary overhead.

Let's turn our attention to a pair of type classes that you've been making use of already: Semigroup and Monoid. We can look at their definitions in ghci:

```
λ :info Semigroup
class Semigroup a where
  (<>) :: a -> a -> a
  GHC.Base.sconcat :: GHC.Base.NonEmpty a -> a
  GHC.Base.stimes :: Integral b => b -> a -> a
  {-# MINIMAL (<>) #-}
```

```
λ :info Monoid
class Semigroup a => Monoid a where
  mempty :: a
  mappend :: a -> a -> a
  mconcat :: [a] -> a
  {-# MINIMAL mempty #-}
```

You'll recognize the (<>) operator from Semigroup, which is how you've been concatenating lists and strings throughout this book. The Monoid type class builds on Semigroup by adding mempty, which represents some initial starting or empty value. One good way of seeing what the behavior of values and functions defined by type classes should be is to look at them in ghci. As an example, let's look at several different mempty values:

```
λ mempty @[Int]
[]
λ mempty @String
""
λ mempty @(Maybe [Int])
Nothing
```

You can see that mempty returns some sort of zero or initial value. In fact, the contract for mempty says that it should always be true that (mempty <> a) == a. Later on in this book, you'll learn more about laws for different kinds of type classes and how to think about them. For the moment, let's return to the idea of a "zero" or "initial" value. It's intuitive to realize that the "empty" value for a list is an empty list, and it's not a huge leap to recognize that Nothing is a kind of starting point for a Maybe value. This is a bit misleading though, because we're thinking about mempty as some value of a particular type. In reality, mempty is related to a particular *operation*. For numeric types like Int, we have more than one choice in how we might want to combine values, and each of those choices gives us a different mempty value. Let's look at some concrete examples. First we'll look at addition. Addition lets us combine two numbers by adding them together, so the "empty" starting point is 0, since anything added to 0 gives us back the original number. Next, multiplication is another way that we can merge two numbers into a single number, but the "empty" value for multiplication is 1. In other words, (<>) defines some operation for a type, and mempty is the identity for that operation.

As you can imagine, having two very clear choices for how we might define Semigroup and Monoid for a type like Int presents us with a bit of a problem. How do we pick which one to use? Thankfully, with newtype we can avoid the question and provide users with both options. To do that, we'll need to start by adding a newtype for each operation we want to support:

```
newtype Product =  Product { getProduct :: Int }
newtype Sum = Sum { getSum :: Int }
```

Next, we'll need to create instances of Semigroup and Monoid for each newtype. This example will show you how to do this for Product. As an exercise, define the instances for Sum on your own:

```
instance Semigroup Product where
  (Product a) <> (Product b) = Product (a * b)

instance Monoid Product where
  mempty = Product 1
```

Understanding Higher Kinded Types and Polymorphism

You've seen that data and newtypes can accept type parameters, and even how those type parameters can be used polymorphically, for example, with the reverse function:

```
reverse :: [a] -> [a]
```

Types like this that accept type parameters are called *higher kinded types*. Higher kinded types are a powerful feature that differentiate Haskell types from the generics of many other popular languages. When combined with type classes, higher kinded types allow you to write highly generic and expressive code quickly and easily. In this section, you'll learn how to make use of higher kinded types to write highly re-usable code, and how to make use of a new language extension, KindSignatures, to allow the compiler to catch a new class of errors that you might encounter when writing code with higher kinded types.

KindSignatures

The KindSignatures has been available since GHC 6.8.1. It's enabled by default in GHC2021 but you'll need to enable it manually if you are using Haskell2010. This extension is generally safe and shouldn't interfere with any existing code.

Before diving into what higher kinded types are, it's helpful to stop and ask what a *kind* is. In short, a kind is the type of a type. Although the underlying idea here is straightforward, when you first encounter the idea of "types of types" it can seem a bit overly abstract, so let's look at a couple of examples.

Most types in Haskell, like Int, [a], or Maybe String, have the kind *. You can see the kind of a type in ghci by using the :kind or :k command.

```
λ :k Int
Int :: *
λ :k Int -> String
Int -> String :: *
λ :k Maybe Int
Maybe Int :: *
```

The kind of polymorphic types is also *, which you can see after enabling ExplicitForAll:

ExplicitForAll

The ExplicitForAll extension was first available in GHC 6.12.1. It's enabled by default in GHC2021, but you'll need to enable it manually if you are using Haskell2010. This is generally a safe extension that shouldn't cause problems with any existing code.

```
λ :set -XExplicitForAll
λ :k forall a b. [(a,b)]
forall a b. [(a,b)] :: *
```

The ExplicitForAll extension allows you to make explicit use of forall. If you have ScopedTypeVariables enabled from some earlier exercises you won't need to add this extension, since ScopedTypeVariables turns on ExplictForAll automatically.

For types like Maybe and Either that take a type parameter though, things are a little bit different. If Maybe Int is a type, and we know that Int is a type, then we might be able to infer that Maybe must be something that takes a type as an argument and returns a type. Indeed, when we look at the kind of Maybe we see just that:

```
λ :k Maybe
Maybe :: * -> *
```

Similarly, Either, which takes two type parameters, has the kind * -> * -> *. Applying types works like you would expect:

```
λ :k Either
Either :: * -> * -> *
λ :k Either Int
Either Int :: * -> *
λ :k Either Int Int
Either Int Int :: *
```

As a matter of vocabulary, in the Haskell world we often refer to types with the kind * as being *fully saturated types*. Non-fully saturated types are also called *type constructors*.

A powerful feature that the kind system allows in Haskell that isn't often available in other languages is the ability to be polymorphic over a parameterized types. Imagine, for example, that you have a function that will convert a list of showable items into a comma-separated string. You know how to write this function for a list:

```
toCSV :: Show a => [a] -> String
toCSV =
  let
    addField :: Show a => String -> a -> String
    addField s a = s <> "," <> show a

    dropLeadingComma :: String -> String
    dropLeadingComma s =
      case s of
        ',':s' -> s'
        _ -> s

  in dropLeadingComma . foldl addField ""
```

There are other types, though, that we might want to convert to CSV. One example is the NonEmpty list type from Data.List.NonEmpty. It allows you to create a list that you know won't ever be empty. Thanks to kinds, and higher kinded types, we can make our function polymorphic over the type constructor. In fact, we don't even have to change our implementation!

To get support for multiple kinds of lists, and other things, we only need to make use of the Foldable type class. As you might expect, the Foldable type class represents "things that can be folded." In fact, the type of foldl and foldr in base already makes use of this type class, although so far we've only used it with standard lists:

```
λ :type foldl
foldl :: Foldable t => (b -> a -> b) -> b -> t a -> b
λ :type foldr
foldr :: Foldable t => (a -> b -> b) -> b -> t a -> b
```

Notice in the type signatures for these fold functions that we have a type class constraint on t, but in our type signature we're *applying* the type a to t. That's because t is a higher kinded type variable, with the kind t :: * -> *.

We'll need to take this same approach to make our toCSV function generic. To make some of the details a bit more visible, let's add two language extensions to help us write our type signature more clearly. First we'll add ExplicitForAll, which will allow us to use the forall syntax in our type signatures. We'll also add KindSignatures to allow us to write the kind signatures for types in our type annotations:

```
{-# LANGUAGE KindSignatures #-}
{-# LANGUAGE ExplicitForAll #-}
module HKTDemo where
```

Next, let's import the module Data.Kind from base. This module exports a single kind, named Type, which is an alias for *. It will allow us to make our kind signatures look a little nicer:

```
import Data.Kind
```

We'll also import Data.List.NonEmpty so that we can test out our new function with both regular and non-empty lists:

```
import qualified Data.List.NonEmpty as NonEmpty
```

Next, we'll add our new version of toCSV along with its new type signature. In this example, we're going to be a more explicit than is strictly necessary to help illustrate how higher kinded types are used in our programs. We'll begin by using an explicit forall to introduce two type variables: a Foldable type named t, and an element type named a. We're also going to add a *kind signature* to each of these new type variables:

```
toCSV ::
  forall (t :: Type -> Type) (a :: Type)
  . (Foldable t, Show a)
  => t a -> String
```

You can see in this example how we add the kind signature to each type variable as it's introduced. (t :: Type -> Type) tells the compiler that t should be passed some type as an argument, and a :: Type says that a should be some ordinary type. In most situations, the compiler is able to infer the correct higher kinded types for us in our type signatures, so in this example, the explicit kind signature is only serving to add some documentation and to make it easier for you to understand how higher kinded types are used. Later on in this book, you'll work through some examples where the kind signatures are actually required to make your programs work.

Foldable Naming Conventions

You might find t to be an odd naming choice for a Foldable type, but it's a common naming convention. That's because f is usually reserved for another class called Functor that you'll learn about later in this book. The Foldable class is closely related to a commonly used class called Traversable, so it's likely that the name t has stuck around due to that association.

Now that we have figured out the type of toCSV, the implementation is straightforward:

```
toCSV ::
  forall (t :: Type -> Type) (a :: Type)
  . (Foldable t, Show a)
  => t a -> String
toCSV =
  let
    addField :: Show a => String -> a -> String
    addField s a = s <> "," <> show a

    dropLeadingComma :: String -> String
    dropLeadingComma s =
      case s of
        ',':s' -> s'
        _ -> s
  in dropLeadingComma . foldl addField ""
```

Before we move on, let's write a function that we can use to test our new function in ghci:

```
csvThings :: String
csvThings =
  let
    plainList = toCSV [1,2,3]
    nonEmptyList = toCSV $ 1 NonEmpty.:| [2,3]
  in unlines [plainList, nonEmptyList]
```

You can also load your new module up in ghci and experiment with some other types that have Foldable instances to see what you get:

```
λ toCSV Nothing
""
λ toCSV $ Just 1
"1"
λ toCSV $ Right 3
"3"
λ toCSV $ Left 4
""
```

You might notice in the last two examples that we're passing an Either value to toCSV. Clearly we're allowed to do this, since ghci accepted our code and gave us back a sensible answer, but it might not be immediately clear why we're allowed to do this. After all, Either takes *two* type parameters. Let's revisit these examples and use visible type applications to see if we can narrow down what's going on here. First, let's use visible type applications for our first two examples that use Maybe values to get a baseline:

```
λ toCSV @Maybe @Int Nothing
""
λ toCSV @Maybe @Int $ Just 1
"1"
```

You can see here that we're passing along two type values, Maybe takes a type so it matches up nicely with t :: Type -> Type from the type of toCSV. Next we pass in Int; that's an ordinary type and fits in with the a :: Type part of toCSV. If we naively follow this pattern with an Either value, we'll run into some trouble. Let's give it a try:

```
λ toCSV @Either @Int $ Right 3

<interactive>:6:8: error:
    • Expecting one more argument to 'Either'
      Expected kind 'Type -> Type',
        but 'Either' has kind 'Type -> Type -> Type'
    • In the type 'Either'
      In the first argument of '($)', namely 'toCSV @Either @Int @Int'
      In the expression: toCSV @Either @Int @Int $ Right 3
```

Just as we expected, we're getting an error. The wording the compiler is using here is pretty direct, but the first time you see it it's not always clear what you should do. Let's break it down:

```
• Expecting one more argument to 'Either'
```

The compiler starts by telling us that it's expecting us to pass something to Either. Instead of using Either by itself, we should be applying it to one type. The reason for this is given in the next part of the error:

```
Expected kind 'Type -> Type',
  but 'Either' has kind 'Type -> Type -> Type'
```

This part of the message tells us that our error is caused by the fact that the first argument to toCSV should be a type that takes one argument, but Either takes two arguments. The fix to this problem is, as the compiler has suggested, to pass one of the types to Either before we use it as an argument to toCSV. Let's take a look at this in ghci:

```
λ toCSV @(Either Int) @Int $ Right 3
"3"
```

Using parentheses, we can pass the first argument to Either before we pass the resulting type, which now just needs one more argument, to toCSV.

Using Higher Kinded Types with Your Own Types and Classes

You can also use higher kinded types when creating your own data types and type classes. Let's look at an example of a type class we can create using higher kinded types, called Select. The Select type is a simplified version of a type class called Alternative that you'll learn about later in this book. Our simplified version will have two functions, empty and pick. The empty function should return some sort of empty or zero value, and pick will allow us to pick between two options.

Like the Foldable type class, our Select type class will work for a higher kinded type. This allows us to create a type class that works for any parameterized type. We'll add the kind signature to our type variable when we're defining the type class.

```
{-# LANGUAGE KindSignatures #-}
module Selector where
import Data.Kind

class Select (f :: Type -> Type) where
  empty :: f a
  pick :: f a -> f a -> f a
```

Next, let's define a couple of instances of our new type class:

```
instance Select Maybe where
  empty = Nothing
  pick Nothing a = a
  pick a _ = a

instance Select [] where
  empty = []
  pick = (<>)
```

In our instances, you can see that we're using the higher kinded types Maybe and [], rather than fully saturated types like Maybe a or [a]. If that seems nonintuitive, remember that we're implementing the type class for the thing with the kind Type -> Type, in other words, we're implementing the type class for a type that hasn't yet had its parameter applied. This means that whatever instance we define will be used for all lists, or all Maybe types, regardless of the type parameter that's applied to them. This tells us that the type class and its instances expect to be implemented in terms of the shape of the data.

As a final step, let's load up ghci and run a few commands using our new type class instances:

```
λ :l Selector.hs
λ pick Nothing (Just 1)
Just 1
```

```
λ pick [1,2] [3,4]
[1,2,3,4]
λ foldl1 pick [Nothing,Nothing,Just "first!",Nothing,Just "second!"]
Just "first!"
```

Be sure to keep this file around. In the next section, you'll learn about how to automatically derive instances of type classes without having to write the instances yourself. After that, you'll return to your Selector type class when you use it to help you automatically derive instances.

Deriving Instances

You've seen how type classes allow you to create abstractions in your programs. A problem with type classes that you might have already run into is that most of the time you're doing a lot of work to create instances, but the code is uninteresting and often redundant. As an example, let's imagine a simple record to hold some customer info:

```
data Customer = Customer
  { name  :: String
  , mail  :: String
  , email :: String
  }
```

For our application, we'd like to provide implementations for three common type classes, Show, which will allow us to convert a customer record to a string, Eq, which will let us test equality between two records, and Ord, which will allow us to sort our records. We can manually implement the type classes:

```
instance Eq Customer where
  (==)
    (Customer name  mail email)
    (Customer name' mail' email') =
    name == name' &&
    mail == mail' &&
    email == email'

instance Ord Customer where
  compare
    (Customer name mail email)
    (Customer name' mail' email') =
    compare name name'
    <> compare mail mail'
    <> compare email email'

instance Show Customer where
  show (Customer name mail email) =
    "Customer {name = " <> show name <> ", "
    <> "mail = " <> show mail <> ", "
    <> "email = " <> show email <> "}"
```

Our manual implementations of the type classes are straightforward, but it can become pretty tedious. Thankfully, for cases like this where the implementation of a type class is fairly straightforward, Haskell has a mechanism to allow us to get an instance of a type class for free, using the deriving keyword.

In most cases, you'll derive an instance of a type class using the deriving keyword at the end of your data or newtype definition. For instance, in our Customer example we could instead have used automatically derived instances that would behave like our manual implementations:

```
data Customer = Customer
  { name  :: String
  , mail  :: String
  , email :: String
  } deriving (Eq, Show, Ord)
```

Deriving a type class automatically is a very powerful technique, but it only works in certain circumstances. The first requirement is that the type class has to be derivable. In standards compliant Haskell, only a few type classes are derivable:

- Eq for types that can be compared for equality
- Ord for types that have a total ordering
- Ix for types that support indexing into a range
- Show for types that can be converted into strings
- Read for types that can be parsed from strings
- Enum for types that can be converted to and from integers
- Bounded for types with finite upper and lower bounds

There are several GHC extensions that give you more options for deriving instances automatically. You'll learn about a couple of those extensions in this section, and others throughout the book.

Not every derivable class can be derived for every data type or newtype. One of the most common requirements when deriving a type class for a record is that all of the types within the record must also have instances of the type class you are trying to derive. For example, consider if instead of a String, we'd used a newtype wrapper for storing a customer's name in our earlier example:

```
module DerivingExample where

newtype Name = Name String

data Customer = Customer
  { name  :: Name
  , mail  :: String
  , email :: String
  } deriving (Eq, Show, Ord)
```

If we try to load this module, you'll see that the compiler will helpfully point out that we can't derive Eq, Show, or Ord instances for our type classes because the Name type doesn't have instances for those types:

```
λ :l DerivingExample.hs
DerivingExample.hs:9:15: error:
    * No instance for (Eq Name)
        arising from the first field of `Customer' (type `Name')
      Possible fix:
        use a standalone 'deriving instance' declaration,
          so you can specify the instance context yourself
    * When deriving the instance for (Eq Customer)
  |
9 |   } deriving (Eq, Show, Ord)
  |               ^^

DerivingExample.hs:9:19: error:
    * No instance for (Show Name)
        arising from the first field of `Customer' (type `Name')
      Possible fix:
        use a standalone 'deriving instance' declaration,
          so you can specify the instance context yourself
    * When deriving the instance for (Show Customer)
  |
9 |   } deriving (Eq, Show, Ord)
  |                   ^^^^

DerivingExample.hs:9:25: error:
    * No instance for (Ord Name)
        arising from the first field of `Customer' (type `Name')
      Possible fix:
        use a standalone 'deriving instance' declaration,
          so you can specify the instance context yourself
    * When deriving the instance for (Ord Customer)
  |
9 |   } deriving (Eq, Show, Ord)
  |                         ^^^
Failed, no modules loaded.
```

Unfortunately, in this case the error message that the compiler gives us is a little bit more general than we really want. The compiler in this case is recommending that you enable the StandaloneDeriving language extension. You'll learn a bit more about this extension later in the book, but for the moment let's return to addressing the error at hand. Looking past the compiler's suggested fix, you can use what you know about deriving to fix the issue at hand by providing instances of the Eq, Show, and Ord type classes for Name:

```
newtype Name = Name String deriving (Eq, Show, Ord)
```

StandaloneDeriving

The StandaloneDeriving extension has been available since GHC 6.8.1. This extension is enabled by default in GHC2021 but you'll need to enable it manually if you are using Haskell2010. This is a safe extension that shouldn't cause any problems with existing code.

With this change, you can now load your code. Next, let's look at some language extensions GHC provides to extend the deriving mechanism to make it.

Deriving More Things

The standard deriving mechanism in Haskell is quite useful but limited, which is why GHC has introduced several language extensions to make deriving more powerful and useful in more circumstances. In this section, you'll learn about a few of them that have the largest impact on the way you approach writing code. Throughout this book, you'll learn about others that are useful but less drastic in how they shape the way you approach writing your programs.

Deriving in Newtypes with Generalized Newtype Deriving

One of the first limitations that you'll run into with deriving in type classes is the problem of having a limited number of type classes that you're allowed to derive instances for. It makes sense that you might not be able to derive an instance of any given type class for a new data type, but for newtypes the limitation often means that you start writing very redundant code. As an example, imagine that you were writing a program that needed to work with currency. In order to make use of the type system to ensure that you are only ever adding compatible forms of currency, you might define a newtype wrapper to represent some unit of currency. For example, we'll define the USD type as representing 0.001 USD:

```
newtype USD = USD { getMillis :: Integer } deriving (Eq,Ord,Show)
```

Of course, you'd like to be able to add and subtract units of currency without having to unwrap the newtype for every operation, so it would be convenient to be able to use all the normal math functions that we could use with an Integer. Let's add instances for Num, Real, Enum, and Integral.

```
instance Num USD where
  (USD a) + (USD b) = USD (a + b)
  (USD a) * (USD b) = USD (a * b)
  abs (USD a) = USD (abs a)
  signum (USD a) = USD (signum a)
  fromInteger = USD
  negate (USD a) = USD (negate a)
```

```haskell
instance Real USD where
  toRational (USD a) = toRational a

instance Enum USD where
  toEnum a = USD (toEnum a)
  fromEnum (USD a) = fromEnum a

instance Integral USD where
  quotRem (USD a) (USD b) =
    let (a',b') = quotRem a b
    in (USD a', USD b')
  toInteger (USD a) = a
```

As you look through all of these type class instances, you'll notice that we're not adding any additional logic here; in every case, we're simply deferring to the type class instance of the type we're wrapping.

Thankfully, the GeneralizedNewtypeDeriving extension allows us to automate away this boilerplate. This language extension allows newtype wrappers to derive any type class instances that are implemented by the type they are wrapping, and it does so by mechanically applying the same algorithm we've just used: unwrap the type, apply the type class function, and rewrap the result.

Let's enable our language extension and look at the result:

```haskell
{-# LANGUAGE GeneralizedNewtypeDeriving #-}

newtype USD = USD { getMillis :: Integer }
  deriving (Eq, Ord, Show, Enum, Num, Real, Integral)
```

Much better! Generalized newtype deriving makes using newtype wrappers much more convenient because you are no longer required to implement type classes manually if you're only interested in using the underlying type's instance.

GeneralizedNewtypeDeriving

The GeneralizedNewtypeDeriving extension has been available since GHC 6.8.1. It's enabled by default in GHC2021 but you'll need to enable it manually if you are using Haskell2010. This is a generally safe extension that shouldn't interfere with any existing code.

Deriving Via a Compatible Type

The last extension to deriving that you'll learn about in this chapter turns some of what you've learned about type classes on its head. You've learned about how to use newtypes to add a new distinct type class instance to a type, but thanks to GHCs DerivingVia extension, you can also use newtypes as a template for how to define a type class for other types. This allows you to reduce boilerplate in your code by writing a derivation once and then re-using it in several different ways.

DerivingVia

The DerivingVia extension has been available since GHC 8.6.1. It's not enabled by default in either GHC2021 or Haskell2010 so you'll need to enable it manually. This is generally a safe extension that shouldn't interfere with any existing code.

To see an example of how this works in action, we'll return to a couple of our old friends, in particular Monoid and Maybe.

In base, Maybe has an instance of Monoid that allows you to combine the underlying values of the Maybe. For example, if you have some values with the type Maybe [Int] you can combine them with (<>):

```
λ (Just [1]) <> (Just [2]) <> Nothing <> (Just [3])
Just [1,2,3]
```

This default monoid instance is quite useful, since it makes it very easy for us to combine optional values, but it's not the only instance that we might want to use. One common pattern when working with Maybe values is selecting the first non-empty value from a set of values. As an example, consider an application that will select the first of several possible contact methods that's available:

```
selectContact ::
  Maybe String -> Maybe String -> Maybe String -> Maybe String
selectContact email sms phone =
  case email of
    Just email' -> Just email'
    Nothing ->
      case sms of
        Just sms' -> Just sms'
        Nothing -> phone
```

It would be quite convenient if we could have a version of Maybe that offered a Monoid instance that made this easier. Since we can't add a new instance to an existing type, we'll use a type class called MyMaybe for which we can add the instance:

```
newtype MyMaybe a = MyMaybe (Maybe a) deriving Show

instance Semigroup (MyMaybe a) where
  (MyMaybe Nothing) <> b = b
  a <> _ = a

instance Monoid (MyMaybe a) where
  mempty = MyMaybe Nothing
```

If the implementation of Semigroup and Monoid looks familiar to you, it's because it's very similar to the instance of our Select type class that we defined for Maybe:

```
instance Select Maybe where
  empty = Nothing
  pick Nothing a = a
  pick a _ = a
```

In order to reduce code duplication, let's rewrite our Semigroup and Monoid instances to take advantage of the Select instance that we've already defined for Maybe:

```
instance Semigroup (MyMaybe a) where
  (MyMaybe a) <> (MyMaybe b) = MyMaybe (pick a b)

instance Monoid (MyMaybe a) where
  mempty = MyMaybe empty
```

This looks a lot nicer than our previous version that contained a lot of duplicated code, but something here still isn't quite right. The first thing you might realize is nothing here is actually specific to either our MyMaybe newtype or to Maybe itself. We can actually define a valid Semigroup and Monoid instance for any Select instance. Along the same lines, these handwritten instances aren't actually adding any value. They're simply unwrapping and rewrapping a newtype and using the underlying Select instance we've already defined for Maybe.

To deal with this kind of duplication, GHC offers a new type of *deriving strategy* called deriving via, which you can enable with the DerivingVia language extension. Deriving via is a little bit like the mirror version of the newtype wrappers that you've already written. So far, you've used newtype wrappers in a "one to many" kind of way, where for some given underlying type you can define many different newtype wrappers that each have their own different instances of some type classes. With deriving via you can instead use a "many to one" strategy for deriving. To use deriving via you'll need to create a type with one or more instances that will act like a template. Once you have your base type and instances defined, you can use deriving via to re-use the instance definitions for other types.

Let's look at an example of how this works in practice.

We'll start by creating a newtype wrapper that we'll use to define the template for how we'd like to derive Semigroup and Monoid instances from a Select instance. We'll call our newtype wrapper Sel because its job is basically wrapping Select. The wrapper itself is going to be very straightforward:

```
newtype Sel (f :: Type -> Type) (a :: Type) = Sel (f a)
```

In plain English, Sel is parameterized by two types, and it wraps the type given by applying its second type parameter to the first.

It's worth remembering here that when we defined our Select type class it was over a type with the kind Type -> Type:

```
class Select (f :: Type -> Type) where
```

Similarly, the first argument of Sel is a parameter with the kind f :: Type -> Type.

Next, let's create instances of Semigroup and Monoid for our Sel type. We're going to use the underlying Select instance, so we'll add a type class constraint to our first type parameter, f:

```
instance (Select f) => Semigroup (Sel f a) where
  (Sel a) <> (Sel b) = Sel (pick a b)

instance (Select f) => Monoid (Sel f a) where
  mempty = Sel empty
```

So now, for any type with the kind Type -> Type and a Select instance, we have a monoid instance. Before we move on, let's look at this in practice from ghci. We haven't derived a Show instance for Sel in our example code, so for debugging purposes we'll first make use of StandaloneDeriving to make it easier for us to see the values while we're testing things out:

```
λ :set -XStandaloneDeriving
λ deriving instance (Show (f a)) => Show (Sel f a)
λ a = Sel (Just 1)
λ b = Sel (Nothing)
λ a <> b
Sel (Just 1)
λ b <> a
Sel (Just 1)
λ (Sel [1,2]) <> (Sel [3,4,5])
Sel [1,2,3,4,5]
```

Before we move on, let's take a moment to look at the definitions of Sel and MyMaybe side by side:

```
newtype Sel (f :: Type -> Type) (a :: Type) = Sel (f a)
newtype MyMaybe a = MyMaybe (Maybe a) deriving Show
```

Roles

Roles describe different ways that two types can be equal. GHC supports three different kinds of equality. *Notional equality* requires that two types are exactly the same. *Representational equality* requires that they have the same runtime representation. Finally, *Phantom equality* allows any two types to be considered equal. It's

Roles

> rare that you'll need to think too much about type roles, and we won't cover them in more detail in this book. You can refer to the GHC users guide for more information if you find that you need to deal with the role system directly.

When you first learned about newtype, you learned that they offered a zero-overhead abstraction, and that the compiler guarantees that the newtype will store its value in the same way as the underlying type that it's wrapping. In GHC, two types that have the same underlying runtime representation are considered *representationally equal*. When two types are representationally equal, the compiler can figure out how to safely *coerce* values from one type to the other.

In our example, both Sel Maybe a and MyMaybe a are representationally equal to Maybe a, which means that the compiler knows how to convert back and forth between Sel Maybe a and MyMaybe a. We can use this to our advantage to avoid writing boilerplate type class instances, because deriving via allows us to derive a type class instance for one type using the instance defined for another type that is representationally equal. Let's look at it in action:

```
{-# LANGUAGE DerivingVia #-}

newtype MyMaybe a = MyMaybe (Maybe a)
  deriving Show
  deriving (Semigroup, Monoid) via (Sel Maybe a)
```

You'll notice that we needed to add a new extension at the start of our file. The DerivingVia extension is necessary for us to use the deriving via strategy. With this new deriving via statement, we're telling the compiler to use Sel as a template for how to derive the instances for Semigroup and Monoid. To do that, it will create an instance that converts our MyMaybe value into Sel Maybe, then calls the appropriate type class function, and converts the result back to a MyMaybe value.

Let's look at our new type in action:

```
λ (MyMaybe $ Just [1,2,3]) <> (MyMaybe $ Just [3,4,5])
MyMaybe (Just [1,2,3])
λ (MyMaybe Nothing) <> (MyMaybe $ Just [3,4,5])
MyMaybe (Just [3,4,5])
```

You're not limited to using deriving via with types that already have an instance of the type class. For example, there's no default Semigroup or Monoid instances for integral types, but we can use deriving via to borrow the instances defined by the Sum and Product types from Data.Semigroup:

```
{-# LANGUAGE DerivingVia #-}
module MyNumericMonoids where
import Data.Semigroup

newtype MySum = MySum { getMySum :: Int }
  deriving (Eq, Show)
  deriving (Semigroup, Monoid) via (Sum Int)

newtype MyProduct a = MyProduct { getMyProduct :: a }
  deriving (Eq, Show)
  deriving (Semigroup, Monoid) via (Product a)
```

```
λ :l MyNumericMonoids.hs
λ mconcat $ map MySum [1..10]
MySum {getMySum = 55}
λ mconcat $ map Product [1..10]
Product {getProduct = 3628800}
```

Anyclass Deriving

Earlier in this chapter, you saw some examples of type classes that provided default definitions for all of their functions. For example, our Redacted type class could provide a default definition of its only function so long as we also provided a Show instance. Even though we could create instances of those type classes without providing an implementation for any of their functions, we still needed to explicitly add an instance. This can start to get inconvenient, especially when you have a large number of types that you need to write empty instances for.

DeriveAnyClass

The DeriveAnyClass extension has been available since GHC 7.10.1. It's not enabled in either GHC2021 or Haskell2010 so you'll need to enable it manually. This is generally a safe extension, although it's best enabled alongside the DerivingStrategies extension to avoid ambiguity about what strategy is being used to drive instances.

The DeriveAnyClass language extension can help. When we enable this extension, we can derive any classes that we want, and GHC will add an empty instance declaration for us. Let's take another look at our Redacted example from earlier in this chapter to see how we can use DeriveAnyClass to make our code a little shorter and nicer to read.

We'll start by adding our new language extension:

```
{-# LANGUAGE DefaultSignatures #-}
{-# LANGUAGE DeriveAnyClass #-}
module AnyclassDemo where
```

```
class Redacted a where
  redacted :: a -> String
  default redacted :: Show a => a -> String
  redacted = show
```

Next, let's define UserName. Now that we know about deriving we can skip the instance of Show and derive it. We'll also make use of DeriveAnyClass to let us derive an instance of Redacted:

```
{-# LANGUAGE DefaultSignatures #-}
{-# LANGUAGE DeriveAnyClass #-}
module AnyclassDemo where

class Redacted a where
  redacted :: a -> String
  default redacted :: Show a => a -> String
  redacted = show

newtype UserName = UserName String deriving (Show, Redacted)
```

Let's load this up into ghci. If you are using a newer version of GHC, you may get a warning about using DerivingStrategies. If you see this warning, you can ignore it for now. We'll cover this extension and when to use it in the next section.

```
λ UserName "george"
UserName "george"
λ redacted $ UserName "george"
"UserName \"george\""
```

Using a derived instance of Show has changed our output slightly from the earlier examples, but overall we can see that our new version of the code is working exactly as we'd hoped, and with substantially less code.

Next, let's see what happens if we try to use our new extension to derive an instance of Redacted for our Password type, while still avoiding creating a Show instance:

```
newtype Password = Password String deriving (Redacted)
```

If we try to load this into ghci you'll see that once again we get an error because we've failed to provide either a Show instance or a definition of redacted:

```
λ :load AnyclassDemo
AnyclassDemo.hs:11:46: error:
    • No instance for (Show Password)
        arising from the 'deriving' clause of a data type declaration
      Possible fix:
        use a standalone 'deriving instance' declaration,
          so you can specify the instance context yourself
```

```
    • When deriving the instance for (Redacted Password)
   |
11 | newtype Password = Password String deriving (Redacted)
   |                                              ^^^^^^^^
Failed, no modules loaded.
```

Deriving Strategies

The ability to derive an empty instance for any class is useful, but as you may have seen in the last section, if you are using a newer version of GHC, this extension can sometimes be a source of confusion. The problem is the interaction between GeneralizedNewtypeDeriving and DeriveAnyClass can be unexpected. To see an example of why, let's imagine that we're going to add another user type, called an AdminUser, that is a newtype wrapper around our existing UserName. We'll also change our Redacted instance for UserName to add some extra formatting. Finally, we'll turn on GeneralizedNewtypeDeriving since we may want to use it as we're developing our program:

```
{-# LANGUAGE DefaultSignatures #-}
{-# LANGUAGE DeriveAnyClass #-}
{-# LANGUAGE GeneralizedNewtypeDeriving #-}
module AnyclassDemo where

class Redacted a where
  redacted :: a -> String
  default redacted :: Show a => a -> String
  redacted = show

newtype UserName = UserName String deriving Show
instance Redacted UserName where
  redacted (UserName user) = "UserName: " <> user

newtype AdminUser = Adminuser UserName deriving (Show, Redacted)
```

Now, let's load this program up into ghci and look at some redacted values to see what we get. We'll start by looking at a redacted user:

```
λ redacted $ UserName "george"
"UserName: george"
```

As we'd expect, we're using our new Redacted instance to get some nicer formatting when we show off our username. What if we create an admin user? It turns out that there are two possibilities. If GHC uses GeneralizedNewtypeDeriving, then it will use the instance that we've provided in UserName to generate an instance for AdminUser. On the other hand, if we use the approach enabled by DeriveAnyClass, we'll get the instance provided to use based on our Show instance, and get the somewhat less readable formatting. Let's try it out in ghci:

```
λ redacted $ Adminuser (UserName "george")
"Adminuser (UserName \"george\")"
```

As you can see, in this case we're using the default definition of redacted that we get from an empty instance when we use the DeriveAnyClass approach. It turns out that, whenever it's presented with the option between generalized newtype deriving and anyclass deriving, GHC will pick the anyclass approach to deriving instances. Knowing the rule lets us avoid surprises, but it would be helpful if we could choose which approach we want it to take when generating instances.

DerivingStrategies

The DerivingStrategies extension has been available since GHC 8.2.1. It's not enabled by default in either GHC2021 or Haskell2010 so you'll need to enable it manually. This is a safe extension that shouldn't interfere with any existing code.

We can choose the strategy GHC takes by enabling the DerivingStrategies extension. With this extension, we can specifically tell the compiler how we want it to try to generate our type class instances. Let's turn it on and use it for AdminUser, and then we'll look a bit more closely at how it works:

```
{-# LANGUAGE GeneralizedNewtypeDeriving #-}
{-# LANGUAGE DefaultSignatures #-}
{-# LANGUAGE DeriveAnyClass #-}
{-# LANGUAGE DerivingStrategies #-}
module AnyclassDemo where

class Redacted a where
  redacted :: a -> String
  default redacted :: Show a => a -> String
  redacted = show

newtype UserName = UserName String deriving Show
instance Redacted UserName where
  redacted (UserName user) = "UserName: " <> user

newtype AdminUser = Adminuser UserName
  deriving stock Show
  deriving newtype Redacted
```

In this example, we now have two different deriving clauses associated with our single AdminUser type. We've also added two new keywords, stock and newtype.

With the DerivingStrategies extension we can add several deriving clauses when we define a type, and each of those can have an associated deriving strategy. There are four strategies that you can use:

- stock can be used if you are trying to derive one of the standard derivable type classes and want to use the standard approach defined in the Haskell standard.

- newtype tells the compiler to use the generalized newtype deriving strategy to create an instance based on a newtype wrapper.
- anyclass tells the compiler to generate an empty instance declaration, which is the default when DeriveAnyClass is enabled.
- via uses the deriving via strategy that you learned about earlier in this chapter.

In newer versions of GHC, the GeneralizedNewtypeDeriving extension is enabled automatically, and the compiler now emits more warnings encouraging users to enable the DerivingStrategies extension and make use of explicit deriving strategies. In the rest of this book, we'll typically omit deriving strategies to keep the examples compatible with older Haskell versions, but you are encouraged to start using deriving strategies in your own code, since this style is likely to become more popular in newer Haskell code.

Summary

Type classes are an essential building block for nearly all large Haskell applications. You'll use them extensively throughout the rest of the book, and they will be common in both library and application code that you encounter. Unlike parametric polymorphism, you should be judicious in your use of type classes. Most large applications and libraries will introduce a few new type classes, but only a few. Overuse of type classes in your application can be a cause of excess abstraction that makes your program more difficult to work with and reason about, rather than easier.

Well-designed type classes should be narrowly focused on a specific feature, and will generally only define a small handful of functions. It's common to have type classes that only introduce a single new function, and the Natural type class you built in this chapter is fairly close to the natural upper limit for how big most type classes should be. It's better to introduce a few extra type classes and add dependencies, like making Natural depend on Eq, instead of having a large class.

Here are some good rules of thumb for knowing when to reach for a type class, or when to reach for some other techniques:

1. If you're modeling something that exists outside your program, like a real-world object, a mathematical object, or a business process with well-defined operations, then you might want to define a type class.
2. If your type class would only be used in one or two places, consider passing a function instead of defining a new type class.

3. If you would only have one instance of your type class, wait to define the class until you need at least one more instance. The "rule of threes" is a good one to follow—consider abstracting the behavior into a type class after the third time you would rewrite code.

4. If you find that most of your instances are newtype wrappers around some underlying type, then consider using a record that holds functions instead of a type class. In the long run this will be easier to work with, and it more correctly models the API you've designed.

Exercises

Writing Type Classes Representing Emptiness

Imagine that we wanted to create a type class that represents things that can be "empty" for some definition of empty that will depend on the particular type. In this exercise, we'll call the type class Nullable and give it two functions:

- isNull should return True if a value is "empty".
- null should return an "empty" value.

```
module Nullable where
import Prelude hiding (null)

class Nullable a where
  isNull :: a -> Bool
  null :: a
```

Create instances of this type class for:

1. Any Maybe a where a is Nullable
2. Any tuple, (a,b) where a and b are Nullable
3. Any list type

Adding a Default Null Test

Add a new Eq constraint to the definition of Nullable:

```
class Eq a => Nullable a
```

With this change in place, create a default implementation of isNull.

Deriving Nullable

In the first exercise in this chapter, you should have created an instance of Nullable for Maybe and list values. There are a few ways that you could have approached writing these instances, but let's look at some reasonable definitions you might have used:

```
module DerivingNullable where
import Prelude hiding (null)
import qualified Prelude (null)

class Nullable a where
  isNull :: a -> Bool
  null :: a

instance Nullable [a] where
  isNull = Prelude.null
  null = []

instance Nullable (Maybe a) where
  isNull Nothing = True
  isNull _ = False
  null = Nothing
```

These instances use a fairly intuitive definition of what should be considered `null`: empty lists are null, as are `Nothing` values. What if we have an optional list though?

```
λ isNull Nothing
True
λ isNull []
True
λ isNull (Just [])
False
```

In this case, it's not clear whether `Just []` should be considered a null value or not; it depends entirely on the program we are writing. You can even imagine that we might want different behavior in different parts of the same program.

In this exercise, try to create an API so that a user can make use of `deriving via` to create `Nullable` instances of their own types. A user should be able to decide whether `Just []` should be considered a null value or not by selecting which type they derive their instance from.

CHAPTER 7

Understanding IO

Up to now, we've been glossing over one of the most fundamental operations in programming and one of the major stumbling blocks people run into when they start learning Haskell: getting information into and out of your program.

One of the most common reasons that people struggle with understanding IO in Haskell is that the mechanics for how to do IO are taught without a thorough explanation of the reasoning behind them. Without understanding the reason for IO working the way it does, it can seem unreasonably complicated. In this chapter, you'll learn why IO in Haskell needs to work a bit differently than it does in other languages. You'll also develop intuition for how to work with it so that it doesn't feel so alien.

We'll start this chapter by looking at the challenges that come with IO in Haskell. You'll learn how laziness and purity require a different approach to IO in Haskell compared to other languages you might have used, and how Haskell's approach to IO manages to turn those challenges into a useful and powerful framework for IO. After that, you'll work through several short examples of IO in Haskell to help you develop an intuition for how to work with IO and make it seem less weird. Finally, you'll learn how to use lazy IO in practice. In the next chapter, we'll move from these small examples to building complete applications that make use of IO.

Talking About IO

"IO" can mean a lot of different things, so let's start the discussion by establishing a bit of terminology. In this book, there are three different ways that we'll use the term "IO." In the most general sense, we'll use the term IO to talk about the general concept of a program interacting with the outside world by doing things like reading files or writing stuff to the screen. Exactly what you'd expect.

Slightly more specifically than general IO are *IO Actions*. You'll learn more about these throughout this chapter, but for now you can think of it like this: IO is a general concept of doing some input or output. An IO action is a specific example of your program taking some action to do IO. In other words, "reading a file" is IO, but a specific function that reads the contents of a file is an IO action.

Finally, you'll learn about the `IO` type. A value of type `IO a` represents some computation that may have some side effects and will result in a value of type `a`.

Performing IO in a Pure, Lazy Language

Haskell's approach to IO is different from other languages you might have worked with because, as a pure and lazily evaluated language, it has some constraints that don't exist in other languages. Understanding the challenges that come with doing IO in a pure and lazy language is the first step to understanding how to do IO in Haskell. In this section, you'll first learn about how purity and laziness present challenges to doing IO. After that, you'll learn about `IO` and IO actions and how they address the challenges introduced by purity and laziness.

Understanding the Problems with IO

Laziness and purity are interesting and useful properties of Haskell, but they make IO particularly tricky. You learned about purity and laziness back in Chapter 1, Getting Started with Haskell, on page 1, but at the time we didn't take the time to look more deeply at why they made IO challenging. Now that you're learning about IO, it's going to be helpful to think about the challenges that come about with pure lazy IO.

When we can't interact with anything except our input values, or affect anything except our output values, then reading or writing data from the world outside of our program is going to present a challenge. Even if we were to cheat just a little bit and say that we'll allow a impurity just for the sake of letting us do IO, we still have the problem of laziness. Since laziness requires that we always use the result of some work before the work is actually done, there's a lot of IO that might never get executed, or might not get executed in the order that we'd expect.

Haskell's combination of laziness and purity present an interesting challenge for managing IO. In fact, early versions of Haskell used an entirely different approach to solving the problem of how to do IO. The solution that you'll learn about throughout the rest of this chapter has been part of Haskell since

Haskell 98.[1] The first time you see how IO is handled in Haskell programs it can seem a bit complex, but as you work through the next few chapters you'll start to learn how IO works and it will eventually feel quite natural.

Keeping IO Pure

The IO type is how we keep track of the state of the real world in a Haskell program. Understanding how IO works is an important insight that will help you work with Haskell more effectively even when you aren't actually doing IO.

Haskell being a pure language means we can't just change the value of things, and that includes changing the external environment. Instead of changing the value of the external environment in place, we need to keep track of all the changes we wanted to make. The changes that IO is keeping track of have a special name: *side effects*. A side effect is anything that happens outside of the function. For example, writing a file might return the number of bytes written, but it has the side effect of changing the contents of the file on disk. Even things like reading a file or looking at an environment variable have side effects, because they rely on information outside of the function.

Generally you won't see IO used by itself. Instead, it's common to pair the side effects with the value they were used to calculate. For example, if we wanted to read the contents of a file as a string we would represent that as IO String. The IO keeps track of the fact that the file is open and has been read, and the String has the actual value of the data. We call values like this *IO Actions*. Most of the time when we want to refer to any sort of IO action we'll use a type variable and write it IO a.

The way that IO keeps track of this is an implementation detail that we won't dive into in this book, but throughout this chapter you'll learn enough about IO to build a good intuition for how to use it effectively.

Keeping IO Lazy

Laziness can present some unique challenges for working with IO when we want to do more than one IO Action. If you remember from back in Chapter 1, Getting Started with Haskell, on page 1 when we first introduced laziness, you learned about how Haskell expressions are only computed when the value is needed. This can make doing IO tricky because it means we need to be careful about using the values from our IO actions to ensure that the computations are actually carried out in the order we expect.

1. https://www.haskell.org/onlinereport/index98.html

Let's look at an example. Say that we wanted to write a program that writes the string "Hello, Haskell" to `/tmp/hello`, then it reads the contents of `/tmp/hello` and prints that to the screen. In a lot of languages we could write something like:

```
writeReadFile =
  writeFile "Hello, Haskell" "/tmp/hello"
  let contents = readFile "/tmp/hello"
  print contents
```

Ignoring the incorrect syntax for a moment, we have a basic problem with writing code like this. Since we never look at the result of `writeFile` there's no way to be sure it would be called before `readFile`, so we could print whatever data happened to be in the file when we started our program—or even worse, our program might crash because the file didn't already exist.

We can get around the problem of not knowing what order our IO operations will run in if we ensure that the returned value of an IO action is used. To do that, we have to make computing the value of an IO action necessary to run the next IO action. To do that, we need to do two things: we need a way to combine IO actions, and a way to sequence them.

Combining IO actions lets us build up a single IO action from smaller pieces. If we wanted to copy a file, for example, we would want to perform two separate IO actions: reading the contents of the source file, and writing that to the destination file. Combining IO actions lets us represent those as a single larger IO action.

When we combine our IO actions, it's important that we keep in mind that we care about the order in which we combine our IO actions. Sometimes, when we're adding or multiplying numbers for example, we don't care which order we do things in. If we compute `a + b` we'll always get the same thing as `b + a` for any numbers we care to choose for `a` and `b`. We call functions like `(+)` where we can provide the arguments in any order *commutative*. Other times, joining strings for instance, we do care about the order. The string `"hello, " <> "world"` is going to be quite different from `"world" <> "hello, "`. Combining IO actions isn't commutative. When we copy a file, like in our earlier example, it matters quite a lot that we read the contents of the source file *before* we write the contents to our destination file.

So how do we go about doing this combining and sequencing of our IO actions?

Let's start by writing a function that needs to sequence some IO actions, with a comment representing the part we need to fill in. For this example, we'll use a simple file copy function that reads data from an input file and writes it to an output file:

```
copyFile :: FilePath -> FilePath -> IO ()
copyFile src dst =
  (readFile src) {- interesting stuff here -} (writeFile dst)
```

In this example, we're reading the contents of our file with readFile, and we're trying to write something with writeFile, but there's clearly an interesting middle bit that we're missing.

We can get an idea of what needs to go in the middle of our function by looking at the types of the functions we do know about. In this case, we have this:

- readFile :: FilePath -> IO String
- writeFile :: String -> IO ()

We can also use a type hole to help us figure out what should go into our missing part of the code:

```
copyFile :: FilePath -> FilePath -> IO ()
copyFile src dst =
  (readFile src) `_` (writeFile dst)
```

The compiler gives us a lot more detail than we might want from this particular type hole, but the most relevant bit tells us what we might have expected from the types of readFile and writeFile:

```
• Found hole: _ :: IO String -> (String -> IO ()) -> IO ()
```

We might not know how to write our missing function, but at least now we know what its type signature should be. We'll need to come up with a name for our function too, so that we can write it. Since we want to use this function to provide sequential ordering to our IO actions, let's call it andThen. After all, it makes a certain intuitive sense to read the code and say "read the source file contents *andThen* write the destination file contents."

We could start by making a function with exactly the type that our read and write functions use, and the type hole suggested:

```
andThen :: IO String -> (String -> IO ()) -> IO ()
```

This is a little bit too restrictive though. As you might have guessed, this general problem of making sure we can do one IO action and then another comes up frequently, so we'll pick a more general type for our function:

```
andThen :: IO a -> (a -> IO b) -> IO b
andThen = undefined
```

You'll learn how to implement `andThen` yourself in Ordering and Combining IO Actions, on page 270, but for now let's leave it undefined so that we can focus on what we can learn from the types. Learning how to reason about the behavior of a function based on its type signature is a very useful skill when you're working with Haskell.

Our type signature can tell us a lot about how our function needs to behave. The first thing we can understand about it comes from looking at its return type, `IO b`. The fact that it's an IO action tells us that we're doing something that involves side effects, even if we don't know for sure yet what those side effects are. Even more enlightening is the fact that we're returning an `IO b`.

Returning a type variable in a Haskell function tells us a lot about the structure of our function. Because `b` could be any sort of value, our function can't actually make one directly. *We can only create an output value of type `b` if we were passed in a `b` or a function returning a `b`.*

If you think about a function that returns an `Int`, we might not necessarily have to depend on any input in particular to return one. We could always just return 5 or 42 or 197 no matter what input we were given. To return a `b` though, what should we return? There's no way our function can actually decide.

Being unable to create a `b` directly takes us to our second parameter, a function `a -> IO b`. We can't create an `a` any more than we could create a `b`, but now we know that if we do have an `a` we could create an `IO b` from it. Luckily for us, the first parameter of our function is an IO action, `IO a`.

So we must return an `IO b`, but the only way for our function to possibly create one of those is by passing the `a` from our `IO a` into the function `a -> IO b`. Somehow we need to separate out the value from an IO action and pass it to a function that generates a new IO action, and then return an IO action with the value we got back from the function call.

What does this have to do with sequencing? As long as the value of `b` depends on the value of `a`, we have to actually compute `a` first. Since our `a` is part of an IO action, all of the side effects that go along with `a` are going to be computed before we can use it to generate our `IO b`. This dependency ensures that our IO actions have to happen in the right sequence.

If our `andThen` function provides a way for us to sequence IO operations by forcing values to depend on one another, what about combining them? It turns out that the nature of IO means that we don't actually have to do much to combine the values at all, instead we can rely on the language runtime, operating system, and hardware hosting our program. In other word, side effects are things that happen on the system in the real world. They are combined implicitly by virtue of being part of a program that is running on that system.

So, with our andThen function providing both a way to ensure our IO actions happen in the right order, and trusting that they are combined the way that we would expect, let's use it in our copy function:

```
copyFile :: FilePath -> FilePath -> IO ()
copyFile src dst =
  (readFile src) `andThen` (writeFile dst)
```

We can even string together many different actions into a much longer statement. Imagine that instead of using readFile and writeFile we wanted to be more explicit about how we were doing our file operations:

```
longCopy :: FilePath -> FilePath -> IO ()
longCopy src dst =
  openFile src ReadMode `andThen`
  hGetContents `andThen`
  \contents ->
    openFile dst WriteMode `andThen`
    flip hPutStr contents
```

You might find yourself wondering, if we can combine and order our IO actions, how we ever actually get a new IO action in the first place.

Let's consider another example program. In this example, we're going to write a program that might print the contents of a file to the screen, but if the path is /etc/passwd, we want to print out a special message:

```
noPassword :: FilePath -> IO String
noPassword path =
  case path of
    "/etc/passwd" -> newIO "hey, that's a secret!"
    fname -> readFile fname

showFile path = noPassword path `andThen` putStrLn
```

In our example, if the user provides a valid filename we can use the IO action that we get out of readFile, but if they ask us for the contents of /etc/passwd we want to return the string "hey, that's a secret!" The return type of our function is IO String, so we have to return our message as part of an IO action, even though in our special case we don't actually have any side effects. To do that, we'll need to introduce a new function, newIO. In our example program, newIO has the type newIO :: String -> IO String, but just like we did with andThen, we'll want to make our version a bit more generic than that:

```
newIO :: a -> IO a
newIO = undefined
```

In the next section, we'll talk about how IO works in real Haskell programs, and you'll learn how to write your own version of newIO and andThen using the standard libraries that come with Haskell for doing IO.

Ordering and Combining IO Actions

In the last section, you learned how we could use a function like andThen :: IO a -> (a -> IO b) -> IO b and newIO :: a -> IO a to work with IO in a pure lazy language. Now you'll have the opportunity to see how functions like this are implemented, and if you follow along with the example you can write them yourself:

```
andThen :: IO a -> (a -> IO b) -> IO b
andThen = (>>=)

newIO :: a -> IO a
newIO = return
```

That might have been a little bit anticlimactic. It turns out that our implementations are actually just providing new names to the existing >>= operator (pronounced *bind*) and the return function.

If you look at the types of (>>=) and return in ghci you'll see that they are actually more general than just IO. In fact, these functions are defined for the Monad type class. We'll talk more about monads in Chapter 9, Introducing Monads, on page 333, but for now let's just focus on how they are useful for IO specifically.

Before we dive into using >>= and return in a larger example, let's look at a couple of trivially small examples to get a feel for what it's like to use them.

Let's start with a simple function that works like read, but that returns the parsed value inside of an IO action (the built-in readIO function from System.IO provides a more robust version of this, but we'll stick to our version for the sake of demonstration right now).

Return and Pure

You may run across code that uses a function named pure instead of return. You'll learn more about the relationship between pure and return later on in this book. For now, it's enough to know that pure is more general than return, but for IO they'll behave the same way.

```
ioRead :: String -> IO Int
ioRead numString = return (read numString)
```

We can use this function along with return to turn a String into an IO Int:

```
λ return "4" >>= ioRead
4
λ return "10" >>= ioRead
10
```

We can chain more than two functions together. If we write another function to take our IO Int and turn it back into an IO String then we can translate back and forth as many times as we want:

```
ioShow :: Int -> IO String
ioShow = return . show
```

Again, let's go back over to our REPL and test out our new function. Now that we can go from a string to an int and back, we can join our functions together as much as we want:

```
λ return "4" >>= ioRead >>= ioShow >>= ioRead >>= ioShow
"4"
λ return "4" >>= ioRead >>= ioShow >>= ioRead >>= ioShow >>= ioRead
4
```

Adding more and more conversions between an int and a string is a pretty good way to waste energy if your office is getting a bit chilly, but it's hard to really know that we're actually doing anything since we're always getting back the same value we put in. Let's write another function that will let us increment our integer. We'll use the succ function from Prelude to increment our number:

```
ioSucc :: Int -> IO Int
ioSucc = return . succ
```

```
λ return "1" >>= ioRead >>= ioSucc
2
λ return "1" >>= ioRead >>= ioSucc >>= ioSucc >>= ioShow
"3"
```

Look! We've just invented addition! As neat as addition is though, let's turn our attention to a more practically useful example: printing the contents of a file to the screen. We'll use a couple of functions from System.IO that we glossed over in the last section:

- *openFile :: FilePath -> IOMode -> IO Handle*

  takes a path to a file, and a mode like ReadMode or WriteMode, and returns a *Handle* to a file

- *hClose :: Handle -> IO ()*

  Closes a file Handle. You should use hClose to close every handle that you open with openFile. There are a number of utility functions to manage this for you.

- *hGetContents :: Handle -> IO String*

  takes a file handle and returns a string with the contents of that file

We'll also be using putStrLn :: String -> IO () to write the contents of the string to the screen.

Now that you understand how >>= works and how to chain together IO commands, it's not to hard to follow a real working example of how to print a file's contents to the screen:

```
doSomeFileStuff =
  openFile "/tmp/foo.txt" ReadMode
  >>= \handle -> hGetContents handle
  >>= \contents -> putStrLn contents
  >>= \_ -> hClose handle
```

Independently Sequencing IO Actions

The >>= function gives you a way to pass a value through some functions while making sure that they are executed in some specific sequence, but sometimes you might find that you don't actually care about the value.

Imagine that you have several functions that have the type IO (), and you wanted to run them in order. As an example, say we wanted to print several different lines of text to the screen. At first we might try to use >>= to do this, but we'll get an error:

```
λ putStrLn "hello world" >>= putStrLn "nice to meet you" >>= putStrLn "goodbye"

<interactive>:16:28: error:
    • Couldn't match expected type ‘() -> IO a0’
                  with actual type ‘IO ()’
    • Possible cause: ‘putStrLn’ is applied to too many arguments
      In the second argument of ‘(>>=)’, namely
        ‘putStrLn "nice to meet you"’
      In the first argument of ‘(>>=)’, namely
        ‘putStrLn "hello world" >>= putStrLn "nice to meet you"’
      In the expression:
        putStrLn "hello world" >>= putStrLn "nice to meet you"
          >>= putStrLn "goodbye"

<interactive>:16:60: error:
    • Couldn't match expected type ‘a0 -> IO b’
                  with actual type ‘IO ()’
```

```
    • Possible cause: 'putStrLn' is applied to too many arguments
      In the second argument of '(>>=)', namely 'putStrLn "goodbye"'
      In the expression:
        putStrLn "hello world" >>= putStrLn "nice to meet you"
          >>= putStrLn "goodbye"
      In an equation for 'it':
          it
            = putStrLn "hello world" >>= putStrLn "nice to meet you"
                >>= putStrLn "goodbye"
    • Relevant bindings include
        it :: IO b (bound at <interactive>:16:1)
```

The problem here is that >>= wants something of type a -> IO b, but putStrLn has the type IO (). One way to solve this is to use an intermediate function that ignores its input. You saw an example of this in the last section when you needed to ignore the output of putStrLn so that you could close the file handle. As you can imagine, this is a common situation. For example, we will have the same problem if we want to print two messages to the screen:

```
λ putStrLn "hello world" >>= \_ -> putStrLn "good night world"
hello world
good night world
```

This works when we just have one or two functions to join together, but it gets tedious if we have too many things that we want to run in sequence. Imagine if we had to write code like this:

```
showSomeText :: IO ()
showSomeText =
  putStrLn "this is just some text"
  >>= \_ -> putStrLn "there are many lines of it"
  >>= \_ -> putStrLn "each one a new function"
```

You may start wondering if we could write a function to make this pattern less verbose. In fact, we can do just that. Let's call it thenCall:

```
thenCall :: IO a -> IO b -> IO b
thenCall a b = a >>= \_ -> b

showWithThenCall :: IO ()
showWithThenCall =
  putStrLn "this is just some text"
  `thenCall` putStrLn "there are many lines of it"
  `thenCall` putStrLn "not one a new function"
```

This is a much nicer way of sequencing our IO actions, but it turns out that we've once again recreated an existing wheel. The >> function, which also comes from the Monad type class, works exactly like our thenCall function. Let's look at a final version of our example just to visualize how it works:

```
showWithSeq :: IO ()
showWithSeq =
  putStrLn "this is just some text"
  >> putStrLn "there are many lines of it"
  >> putStrLn "not one a new function"
```

Mapping IO Values with fmap

So far we've talked a lot about combining functions that both do IO, but we haven't talked about a common problem: what do you do when you have a function that doesn't know (or care) about IO, and you want to use it on an IO value?

Let's think about command line parsing, which can be one of the most common cases where we might run into this situation. Say we wanted to write an application that would add up a list of integers the user provides as command line arguments. We can use the getArgs function from the System.Environment module in base to get a list of all of the command line arguments as a list of strings, but we'll still need to convert those strings to integers and add them up. Let's say that we have a function that already knows how to take a list of strings and give us back the sum of them:

```
sumArgs :: [String] -> Maybe Int
```

We'll look at the full definition of sumArgs a bit later, but for now let's just focus on how we could call it with our command line arguments.

The first approach to come to mind is probably the one that we've been using so far throughout this chapter. We can use a lambda function to unwrap our IO value so that we can work with it:

```
module SumArguments where
import System.Environment (getArgs)

main :: IO ()
main =
  getArgs
  >>= \args -> return (sumArgs args)
  >>= print
```

This works, but it's a little bit verbose. We are forced to unnecessarily introduce a new variable, and we're dedicating a large portion of our code to the ceremony of unwrapping and rewrapping our argument list in an IO action.

Next, you might think that we could make this a little shorter by eliminating our explicit function. We can write this in a shorter, more pointfree style:

```
main :: IO ()
main =
  getArgs >>= return . sumArgs >>= print
```

This is shorter and a little bit easier to read but we're still not clearly expressing our intention. We use >>= for ordering IO actions, and combining their side effects. Our sumArgs function is a pure function. It doesn't rely on the state of the real world when we call it, and it doesn't cause any side effects, so most of what we get from calling >>= is completely superfluous!

Bind and Return

Whenever you see return being used with >>= it's a sign that you might want to refactor your code. We'll learn more about the relationship between these two functions in Chapter 9, Introducing Monads, on page 333, and you'll be able to understand exactly why this is. Until you've finished with that chapter, just remember that whenever you see >>= return it's a hint that you might want to think about using fmap instead.

The fmap function comes from the Functor type class, and it helps us solve exactly this problem, by giving us a way to apply a pure function to a value inside of an IO action without having to use >>=. Let's take a minute to review how map works:

```
λ :type map
map :: (a -> b) -> [a] -> [b]
λ map (+1) [1..5]
[2,3,4,5,6]
λ map show [1..5]
["1","2","3","4","5"]
λ :type map show [1..5]
map show [1..5] :: [String]
```

The fmap function works almost exactly the same way, but it works on all sorts of Functor instances, not just on lists. Let's look at an example:

```
λ :type fmap
fmap :: Functor f => (a -> b) -> f a -> f b
λ :type fmap (+1) (return 1 :: IO Int)
fmap (+1) (return 1 :: IO Int) :: IO Int
λ fmap (+1) (return 1 :: IO Int)
2
λ :type fmap show (return 1 :: IO Int)
fmap show (return 1 :: IO Int) :: IO String
λ fmap show (return 1 :: IO Int)
"1"
```

We will talk more about functors in Mapping Functors, on page 333, but for now we'll just look at how we can use fmap to make our IO actions more readable.

We can use fmap to make our function more clear by expressing exactly what we're trying to do:

```
main =
 fmap sumArgs getArgs >>= print
```

Not only is this code slightly shorter than our previous version, it more clearly communicates what we want to do: get a list of arguments, transform the list using a pure function, and print the transformed list to the screen.

We can use fmap for things other than IO too. In our actual implementation of sumArgs, we can use fmap to avoid having to use an if statement or pattern matching to deal with a Maybe value:

```
import Text.Read (readMaybe)

sumArgs :: [String] -> Maybe Int
sumArgs strArgs =
  let intArgs = mapM readMaybe strArgs
  in fmap sum intArgs
```

In this simple function, we are taking a list of strings and using readMaybe, from base's Text.Read module, to get back a Maybe [Int]. mapM is a utility function that lets us take lists of monad values like [Maybe a] and [IO a] and convert them to values like Maybe [a] and IO [a]. You'll learn more about monad values soon on page 333.

To keep consistency with other seemingly unpronounceable operators being used for important things in Haskell, the operator (<$>) is a commonly used alias for fmap. We can use it to rewrite our main function:

```
main =
  sumArgs <$> getArgs >>= print
```

One thing you might notice about this example is how (<$>) here has a nice symmetry with the ($) operator. In both cases you are applying a value to a function. With $, the value you are applying is a normal Haskell value, and with (<$>), the value being applied to the function is something like the result of an IO action, or some other functor value.

You'll notice both fmap and (<$>) are used regularly in Haskell programs. Some code bases adopt a style of preferring one function or the other, but it's common to mix and match them to maximize readability. Throughout this book we'll use (<$>) more frequently than fmap. This is a purely stylistic choice, and you are encouraged to try writing your code with both variations of the function to see which style you prefer.

Running IO in Real Applications

At the beginning of this chapter, you learned about laziness and what that means for performing IO in Haskell applications. After that we looked at several small examples of how to work with IO in Haskell, building up more complex IO actions from smaller ones and creating programs that have useful side effects. Although the examples we looked at should have helped you gain an intuition for working with IO, so far we've managed to get away with avoiding having to understand too much about the details of how IO is working, and without having to think too much about the performance of our application. In Haskell applications that do a lot of IO, it's likely that sooner rather than later you'll encounter a scenario where laziness and performance are significant concerns for how you structure your program.

In this section, we'll look in more detail at how IO actions are evaluated in Haskell applications, and what that means for the stability and performance of your programs. You'll also get some hands-on experience working with lazy IO, and some of the bugs that can arise when laziness and IO interact in unexpected ways.

When we have a basic IO action, like we might get from the `getArgs` function we've been working with, it's tempting to think like we're working with a strictly evaluated language and say that the function performs some IO and returns a value. In the cases that we've seen so far that intuition even appears to hold. In reality, this view of IO in Haskell is slightly incorrect and if we don't work to counter our first intuition we can introduce subtle bugs in our program. Having a better understanding of IO will also make it easier to fully understand the way IO is working as we continue through this chapter.

Let's begin by taking a look back at some examples of how laziness works in Haskell, and in particular what that means for IO actions in general. After that we'll look at some real-world examples of the interaction betwen laziness and IO, and you'll learn how to avoid errors introduced when IO actions are too lazy.

Haskell expressions have a type that's evaluated by the compiler when we're building the program, and it has a value that will be computed by the running program when it's needed. This is different from strict languages where the value of an expression is calculated as soon as the expression is encountered or assigned to a variable. Remember from Chapter 1, Getting Started with Haskell, on page 1 when we used this example:

```
ignoreUnevaluated :: Int
ignoreUnevaluated =
  let infinity = sum [1..] in 12
```

We were able to create a the variable infinity and assign it to a computation that would never finish, but we could still run the function. It turns out we can do exactly the same thing with IO actions:

```
ignoreUnevaluatedIO :: IO ()
ignoreUnevaluatedIO =
  let screamIntoTheVoid = putStrLn "quack"
  in return ()
```

If you try running ignoreUnevaluatedIO you'll notice that you don't get any output. Since we're never looking at the value of screamIntoTheVoid it never gets computed, never becomes part of the history of the real world that we're returning, and never outputs anything to the screen.

It's not only the entire IO a that can go unevaluated. The side effects captured in the IO action are evaluated separately from the value associated with the IO action. Sometimes that value isn't even evaluated at all. Let's look at another example to highlight how this works:

```
lazyIODemo :: IO ()
lazyIODemo =
  let sayHello :: IO ()
      sayHello = putStrLn "Hello"
      raiseAMathError :: IO Int
      raiseAMathError = putStrLn "I'm part of raiseAMathError"
                        >> return (1 `div` 0)
  in sayHello
  >> raiseAMathError
  >> sayHello
```

In this example, we're creating two IO actions, sayHello and raiseAMathError. We use >> to sequence them into a single new IO action. The IO action that we've named raiseAMathError is interesting. The IO portion is nothing unusual, but the value we're associating with it is an uncomputable value of type Int. If we actually try to evaluate the expression 1 `div` 0 we would get a runtime exception caused by our attempt to divide by zero. Since we use (>>) we disregard the value inside of the IO action, and so we never need to actually calculate it. That means the error is never raised. The end result is that raiseAMathError is an IO action that has perfectly normal every day side effects and also a unevaluated expression for an uncomputable value.

If you run lazyIODemo you might be surprised to find that there's no exception raised at all even though the side effects of raiseAMathError are evaluated and the message is printed to the screen. This is because >> and >>= require that any previous IO actions are evaluated before the current one. This makes intuitive sense if you think about how we can't read the contents of a file before we open it. Less intuitively is that the >> and >>= functions don't force the evaluation of the value contained in the IO action. If you think about reading a very large file from disk, this starts to make a little bit more sense. While we want to make sure that the file exists and that we can open it, it is reasonable to make sure we really need the contents of the file before we actually do the work of reading it. After all, why should we read the whole file if we only need to use the first few characters.

Understanding Laziness

It can be hard to understand exactly when and how values are evaluated in Haskell. If you're finding these examples a little challenging to follow, consider bookmarking this section and revisiting it after you've finished the chapter on mutable data on page 365 where you'll learn about how Haskell expressions are evaluated in much more detail.

Next let's look at an example of a program that might unexpectedly crash, and see how better understanding IO actions and lazy evaluation can help us rewrite this program so it no longer crashes. We'll start by creating a simple program that will create 500 files in /tmp/test/, creatively named with the numbers 1 through 500, whose contents will be the file names. The important parts here are that we have a lot of files, and they have some data in them that we want to read. Our program will create the files, then read them and write their contents to the screen. We're using readFile and writeFile, which are both provided by System.IO as part of the standard library, and as you might guess they read and write a file. We're also using mapM, which is a function we'll talk more about later in this chapter. For now, just know that it works a lot like a special version of map that we can use for our IO actions. Instead of getting [IO a] like we would with a regular map, mapM gives us IO [a], so instead of getting many small IO actions containing a single value, we get one big IO action and all of the values. In this example, we'll include a few extra type annotations that would normally be unnecessary, but they'll help you make sense of what's going on as you are learning about IO.

```
makeAndReadFile :: Int -> IO String
makeAndReadFile fnumber =
  let fname = "/tmp/test/" <> show fnumber
  in writeFile fname fname >> readFile fname
```

```
unsafe :: IO ()
unsafe =
  let files = mapM makeAndReadFile [1..50000] :: IO [String]
  in files >>= (putStrLn . show)
```

If you try to run this function, you are likely to get an error that looks something like this:

```
*** Exception: getCurrentDirectory:getWorkingDirectory:
  resource exhausted (Too many open files)
```

The exact behavior of this example will depend on your system. You may be able to reproduce the error with fewer files, or you might need more. On some systems you might not be able to reproduce the error at all. The important part of this example is demonstrating that what should have been a straightforward program crashed unexpectedly. Isn't that exactly what Haskell is supposed to prevent?

This unexpected bug is caused because we didn't account for the way that lazy IO works in Haskell. When we call readFile we're not actually going out to the real world and reading the file at all; instead, we're creating an unevaluated expression that represents the contents of the file, and associating them with a state in the real world where the file has been opened. None of the actual work has been done yet. When we bind files to our expression putStrLn . show we suddenly need to evaluate all of our strings, which means we need to actually do the work of trying to open all of our files at once. Since readFile doesn't close the file handle until the contents of the file have been read, and we're now trying to open all of the files before we print them out, we end up opening more files than the system will allow and crashing.

So what can we do about this? We are running out of file handles because we are trying to open all of the files at once before we print anything out. If we refactor our code so that each IO action both gets the file data and writes it to the screen, then we can close the file before we move on to the next IO action. We'll start by creating a helper function, makeAndShow, that gets the file contents and writes it to the screen:

```
makeAndShow :: Int -> IO ()
makeAndShow n =
  makeAndReadFile n >>= putStrLn
```

You might at first think about making a very simple modification to our unsafe function to use this new function:

```
safe :: IO ()
safe =
  mapM makeAndShow [1..500]
```

If you try to build that, you'll realize it doesn't quite work, because mapM wants to give us a list of values. Since all of our values are just () there's not much sense in that. We could change the type of our function to IO [()] but that's a bit of a code smell. Let's see if we can do better. We know that >> lets us sequence IO actions without caring about the value, and we can use foldl to reduce a list of values. We can put those two ideas together to reduce a list down to a single IO action:

```
safe :: IO ()
safe =
  foldl (\io id ->
           io >> makeAndShow id
        ) (return ()) [1..500]
```

We start our fold with an empty IO action containing an initial value of (). Then we reduce our list with >>, each time sequencing the previous IO action with the current one, and discarding the results. In the end, we're left with a single IO action.

This pattern turns out to be a very common one, and there's a built-in function for it, called mapM_. We can use it to implement the final version of our function:

```
safe :: IO ()
safe = mapM_ makeAndShow [1..500]
```

Lazy IO, especially lazy file IO, is a common source of errors in Haskell applications. Once you understand how IO works, and the impact of laziness, you can proactively design your applications to avoid many of the common pitfalls.

Summary

In this chapter, you learned about how to do IO in a purely functional lazy language, including what IO actions are, how to combine them into larger and more complex actions, and how to understand the way that they are evaluated in running programs. In the next chapter, we'll take these concepts and put them to use to build a full application. Before you move on, take some time to review the exercises at the end of the chapter and work through a few of them. Understanding the basics of how IO works will be important for your understanding of the rest of the content in this book.

Exercises

Thinking About IO Types

1. Write a function that returns a value of type `IO (IO String)`. What happens if you try to use >>= with that? What if you want to print the string?
2. Using your function from the previous example, create a function that has the type signature: `IO (IO a) -> IO a`.
3. Write a function that returns a value of type `[IO a]`, and a second function with the type `[IO a] -> IO [a]`. When might you use a function like that?

Building a Command Line Calculator

1. Write a program that reads in numbers from the command line and prints the sum of the provided values.
2. Modify your previous program so that the first argument is an operation (+, -, or *) and performs the supplied operation on the list of numbers.

Building a Word Replacement Utility

Write an application that will accept three arguments on the command line:

- `path`: The path to a file
- `needle`: A word to find in the input file
- `replacement`: A word to use as a replacement when printing the file

When a user runs your program, you should print out the contents of the file at `path`, but replace all occurrences of `needle` with `replacement` in the output. To make things easier, assume that you can use the `words` function and don't need to worry about handling multiple spaces or words that span lines.

CHAPTER 8

Working with the Local System

With all programs, at some point or another you'll find yourself needing to interact with the local system. You've already done some of it in previous chapters when we wrote a program that asked a user to type something in, or when we printed some text to the screen, and in the last chapter, you learned a lot about how IO really works in Haskell. But reading and writing data from a terminal is just one small example of the many ways that you'll find yourself wanting to have your program interact with the real world.

In this chapter, we'll focus on the most common ways that you might want to have your program interact with the outside world. As we're working through the chapter, we'll explore practical matters like how to read files from disk and how to get command line arguments, and we'll also explore the way that Haskell handles these types of operations (you've already seen some hints of this with the `IO ()` type signature in `main`).

Building Applications with IO

In the last chapter, you learned about how Haskell handles IO by working through several small examples, but it can be hard to understand how to move from these smaller examples to building a complete application that includes IO. In this chapter, we'll use all of the material that we've covered so far in this book and built a complete application, including IO. First, we'll look at a common design pattern for organizing IO in functional programs. Next, we'll build a complete Haskell application that does several different kinds of IO, including command line argument handling, dealing with environment variables, file IO, and interacting with external processes.

Procedural Shell, Functional Core

One of the most common problems that people encounter when they first start trying to write larger Haskell is programs is understanding how to handle IO architecturally. Even when you understand the mechanics of how IO works in the language, it can be hard to figure out how to apply those ideas when you are building a complete program. The problem is that when you are coming from a language where you can do IO at any time, you get accustomed to writing programs that do IO as needed. If you visualize your program as a call graph, any individual function in the call graph might do a little bit of IO because it needs to look up a value from the environment, make a network request, or write a file. In many cases, this is even considered good architecture—encapsulating the implementation details of what type of IO a function is doing means that the user doesn't need to know, or think about, any of those details.

In Haskell, this approach to designing applications can become a problem. The issue is that IO actions in Haskell aren't regular values. An IO action can be combined with another IO action, but once we've introduced some IO we can't go back to the world of normal pure functions. In some ways this is a terrible inconvenience, since most real applications will depend on a little bit of IO, and in fact that IO is often used to bootstrap the application. On the other hand, each call to IO is a potential failure scenario, and the inconvenience that we're experiencing is often a case of Haskell focusing us to honestly face the risk of failure that was always there in our programs anyway.

Thankfully, the problem of structuring a pure functional program that needs to do some IO isn't as hard as it might seem. There are several different approaches to managing applications that need to mix pure code with side effects. One of the most useful approaches is to make use of a common design pattern that is frequently called *"Procedural Shell, Functional Core."*

The "Procedural Shell, Functional Core" is aptly named. The idea is that most of the IO that we do in our programs tends to happen at the "edges" of our application. That is to say, we typically need to do some IO to collect the data that we're going to start processing in our program. Some examples of this are things like reading the command line arguments, reading files, or making some network requests. At the other end of our program, once it's finished, we want to do something with the output. This might mean writing some data to the screen, writing a file, or sending some information to a database. This

IO-heavy input and output forms the "procedural shell" of our application. Between these two parts of our program, we need to do some work on the input to translate it to the output. If we are careful to ensure that we are collecting all of our input up front, and we don't write any output until the end, then this computation in the middle can be purely functional. This is the "functional core" of our program.

This pattern of having a procedural shell and a functional core doesn't just happen once at the very top of our program though. As you'll see in this chapter, we can sometimes build the larger procedural shell by composing IO actions that are themselves built using the same "procedural shell, functional core" approach. Although we still need to consume these IO actions as IO actions, by internally separating them out into procedural and functional pieces we can reason about, and test, the code more easily.

Creating a Pager

A *pager* is a program that lets a user display text from a file one page at a time. The term "pager" isn't used very frequently these days, but if you've ever used common command-line programs like less or man you've used a pager.

A pager is a great example of a small utility that will let you apply all of the different concepts that you've been learning about to build a single complete application that does something recognizable while still being small enough to start and finish as you work through this chapter.

Fundamentally, our pager needs to let us do three things:

1. Output the contents of an ASCII or UTF8 encoded text file to the screen
2. Scroll the output backwards and forwards one page at a time
3. Display some metadata, like the file name and creation time

Setting Up the Application

We'll start working on our application by creating a new project that has both a library, where most of our logic will be, and an executable that will call out to the library. There are a few additional dependencies we'll need as we're working through this application. You can add the dependencies now and we'll look at them in more detail as we start to make use of them throughout the chapter.

```
cabal-version:      2.4
name:               hcat
version:            0.1.0.0
```

```
library
  hs-source-dirs:      src
  exposed-modules:     HCat
  build-depends:       base
                     , bytestring
                     , text
                     , process
                     , directory
                     , time
  default-language:    Haskell2010

executable hcat
  hs-source-dirs:      app
  main-is:             Main.hs
  build-depends:       base, hcat
  default-language:    Haskell2010
```

Next, we need to create our basic application outline. That means we need to create the files that we've listed in our cabal project: src/HCat.hs and app/Main.hs.

We'll start our library, since we will be importing it into our executable. For now, we'll define a single function named runHCat. This function isn't doing anything yet, but adding it now ensures that we can call something from Main and that will let us verify that our build environment is set up and working correctly before we start writing more code:

```
module HCat where

runHCat :: IO ()
runHCat = return ()
```

Finally, let's write Main. Like HCat this module is going to be pretty empty. The only thing we want to to is to write a main function that calls runHCat:

```
module Main where
import HCat (runHCat)

main :: IO ()
main = HCat.runHCat
```

Once you have all of the pieces in place, you should be able to compile and run your program with cabal run hcat. This will let you know that all of the pieces are in place and working.

Viewing the Contents of an ASCII or UTF8 Encoded Text File

Now that you have a basic application up and running, it's time to make it do something useful. We'll add several features to our program throughout this chapter, but for now let's focus on a single feature: displaying the contents of a file to the screen. To do that we'll need to:

1. Know which file the user wants to view
2. Read the contents of the file
3. Write the contents of the file to the screen

We'll take each of these requirements in order. Once we're done you'll have a program that works like a minimal version of the Unix cat command.

Reading a Filename from the Command Line

Before we can do anything with a file, like reading it, we need to know what file we're working with. For a command line pager, the most convenient way to get a filename is to have the user pass it along as the first argument when they run our program.

If you run the program directly, you can pass command line arguments to a Haskell program the same way that you pass arguments to any other application: by listing them right after the name of the program you want to run:

```
user@host$ hcat filename.txt
```

When you are actively working on a program, it's more common to run the application with cabal run. This lets you easily ensure that the program gets recompiled when it needs to, so you don't find yourself accidentally running an older version. There are few things more frustrating than spending time trying to figure out why a new feature isn't working, or a bug didn't get fixed, only to realize that you forgot to recompile the program.

Passing command line arguments to a program you are running with cabal run works almost exactly the same as passing command line arguments to any other program. The difference is that when you are running a program with cabal you need to handle both the arguments that you might want to pass to cabal and the arguments that you might want to pass to your program.

Cabal handles this by treating all arguments as arguments to the cabal process up until it encounters two dashes (--). Everything after the two dashes are arguments to the program you are running:

```
user@host$ cabal run hcat -- filename.txt
```

Here, cabal is getting two arguments: run and hcat. Next, we pass in -- to end the list of arguments to cabal and then add filename.txt which will be the first argument to the program we're running.

We can pass in as many arguments as we'd like, but it won't do us any good until we update our program to look at them, so let's update HCat to read the arguments that have been passed into our program and print them out.

The System.Environment module from base comes with all of the functions that we need to get information from the environment, including the command line arguments that were passed in. Let's add it to the import list:

```
import qualified System.Environment as Env
```

This module gives us getArgs, which is an IO action that'll give us a list of strings holding all the command line arguments that were passed in. Its type is:

```
getArgs :: IO [String]
```

We can see this in action by getting the list of arguments and then printing them out:

```
runHCat :: IO ()
runHCat = Env.getArgs >>= print
```

Let's run through a couple of examples just to get a feel for how this works. We'll start by passing in no arguments, and as you might expect we get back an empty list. In some languages, when you get the list of command line arguments, the first argument is always the name of the executable that was called, but getArgs doesn't do that; you'll only get the list of arguments that were passed to the program, not the name of the program. If we don't pass any arguments, our program will print out an empty list:

```
user@host$ cabal run hcat
[]
```

The specifics of how arguments are handled is an implementation detail of your shell. Generally arguments are separated by spaces. Let's pass in a couple of arguments so that we can see that the list that gets printed out does indeed match the argument list we're providing:

```
user@host$ cabal run hcat -- foo 123
["foo","123"]
```

The getArgs function can handle arguments that contain spaces and special characters. The ways you have to send arguments with spaces and special characters will vary a bit depending on the shell that you're using, but generally if you pass in escaped or quoted arguments they'll be handled as you would expect.

```
user@host$ cabal run hcat -- foo 123 \"quoted\" "embedded space"
["foo","123","\"quoted\"","embedded space"]
```

If you want to try testing this from ghci you might quickly run into a problem: how can you pass commands to the program from ghci? The withArgs function function will help you with both of those problems.

withArgs takes a list of strings and an IO action, for example, our runHCat action that prints the arguments:

```
user@host$ cabal repl lib:hcat
λ import qualified System.Environment as Env
λ Env.withArgs ["foo", "123", "embedded spaces"] runHCat
["foo","123","embedded spaces"]
```

Being able to quickly test some of our code in ghci even when we're dealing with command line argument processing will make it easier to iterate on your code as you are working through some of the examples early on in this chapter.

Handling Command Line Arguments

Being able to read arguments from the command line is great, but printing them out to the screen doesn't help us much. We need to handle the arguments that were passed in so we can do something useful with the filename.

Command line argument processing can turn into a complicated problem, and for most applications you would write it makes sense to turn to one of the several command line parsing libraries. These libraries often make use of features that you won't learn about until later on in this book, and the process of building command line handling ourselves is instructive, so for this example we'll handle the parsing manually.

For now the only thing we want our program to do is to accept the name of a file, read that file, and print its contents to the screen. To do that, we only need to accept a single argument: the name of the file that we want to print. Let's start our implementation by writing a new function, handleArgs, that will look at our command line arguments and return the path to the file that we should open:

```
handleArgs :: IO FilePath
handleArgs =
  head <$> Env.getArgs
```

The very first thing you might notice in this example is that the type of our function is IO FilePath, not IO String. We can do this because FilePath is a type alias for String. Using FilePath in our type here lets us remind ourselves that we're expecting the argument we get to be a path to some file, and not just an arbitrary string.

You might also notice that we're again making use of the (<$>) function you learned about earlier in this book. Like before, we're using this so we can apply a regular pure Haskell function, head in this case, to the value our IO action will compute.

The end result is that handleArgs is an IO action that should get the first element from the list of command line arguments that were passed into the program when it was started.

Let's update runHCat to call handleArgs so that we can see it in action.

```
runHCat :: IO ()
runHCat = handleArgs >>= print
```

With our new argument handling code in place, we expect that our program will print out the first, and only the first, argument that gets passed to it. Although we're using the FilePath type, that's just an alias for a regular String, so we can still test our program for now using some placeholder values:

```
user@host$ cabal run hcat -- foo
"foo"
user@host$ cabal run hcat -- foo bar baz
"foo"
```

This is looking good. Whether we pass a single argument or several arguments, we're always printing out the first thing that was passed in. We do have a problem with our current program though:

```
user@host$ cabal run hcat
hcat: Prelude.head: empty list
```

If we run our program with no arguments, we get a runtime error. An error of some kind isn't really a problem here—after all, there's really no correct behavior for the program to do if we don't give it a file as input. Unfortunately, the error that we're generating isn't at all helpful for the user. Let's try to figure out the problem with our program and then try to make some changes to make our program more robust and able to provide better error messages.

The error that we're seeing is a runtime exception that's being raised because we've tried to call the head function on an empty list. You may recall from earlier in this book that this won't work. The head function is *partial* and it's not well defined for empty lists. That means instead of getting some well-defined error out when we call head, the whole program just blows up and we're left showing our users an exception. Let's revisit handleArgs and see if we can come up with a better approach.

The problem we should think about is the exception that's being raised. We're getting an error because we're trying to pass an empty list to head. This makes perfect sense; if the list we're getting is the list of arguments, and we don't provide any arguments, then naturally the argument list will be empty.

Let's think about the solution to our problem starting with the types. If we think just about the part of the function that's working correctly, it's a function from a non-empty list of strings to a FilePath. Unfortunately, we can't ensure that the user will always enter something at the command line, so we need to expand the valid range of input values to account for potentially empty lists. We don't actually have to change anything here since we're already getting those empty lists—and that's what's causing our bug.

On the output side of our function, we can't create a FilePath from an empty list, but we can create an error message. That means we need to change our return type. The values we are returning will be *either* an error message, or the path to the file. With this change, the type of our function will become:

```
handleArgs :: IO (Either String FilePath)
```

Now we have a type for our function, and we need to write the code to make it happen. Let's start by adding a helper function as a where binding. This will let us keep the code a bit more readable for now by keeping the part dealing with IO separate from the part of the code doing error handing. We will call our helper function parseArgs and it will handle the pure functional core of our function:

```
handleArgs :: IO (Either String FilePath)
handleArgs =
  -- placeholder
  where
    parseArgs argumentList =
      case argumentList of
        [] -> Left "Error: No arguments provided!"
        (arg:args) -> Right arg
```

This version of parseArgs will use pattern matching to detect if the argument list is empty. If so, we return an error message, and otherwise we return the front of the list.

The last thing we have to do is call parseArgs with the input list that we get when our program is running. We can call it with (<$>), the same way we were previously calling head:

```
handleArgs :: IO (Either String FilePath)
handleArgs =
  parseArgs <$> Env.getArgs
  where
    parseArgs argumentList =
      case argumentList of
        (arg:args) -> Right arg
        [] -> Left "no filename provided"
```

We still have one last problem to think about. We will return an error message to our user if they don't give us any files. If the user gives us more than one file path though, we'll silently discard all but the first item. That's not a crash, but it's unexpected behavior that might not make a user very happy. Luckily, now that we have a version of our argument handler that can safely deal with the case where we don't get any arguments, we also have a natural way to extend our program to also handle the case where we got more than one argument. See if you can update your version of the function to handle the case where we get more than one argument, and then check to see if it matches the example:

```
handleArgs :: IO (Either String FilePath)
handleArgs =
  parseArgs <$> Env.getArgs
  where
    parseArgs argumentList =
      case argumentList of
        [fname] -> Right fname
        []      -> Left "no filename provided"
        _       -> Left "multiple files not supported"
```

With these changes we no longer crash, and we can provide the user with helpful feedback if they give us some input that our program can't handle. Let's look at it in action:

```
user@host$ cabal run hcat
Left "no filename provided"

user@host$ cabal run hcat -- file1 file2
Left "multiple files not supported"

user@host$ cabal run hcat -- file1
Right "file1"
```

This version of our program is certainly an improvement over the earlier version. The program no longer crashes when we give it bad input, and the messages we get are helpful. We can still improve the quality of the output though. One problem with the current version of our program is that we're printing out the Left and Right constructors from our Either value. The meaning of these values are clear to us since we built the program, but it might confuse a user. Let's make one more change to the output so our messages are more meaningful to a casual user.

Just like with handleArgs we'll start by adding a new helper. Instead of a pure function though, this helper will be a function that takes our result value and returns IO action to print an appropriate message to the screen:

```
runHCat :: IO ()
runHCat =
  -- placeholder, we'll fill this in shortly
  where
    displayMessage parsedArgument =
      case parsedArgument of
        Left errMessage ->
          putStrLn $ "Error: " <> errMessage
        Right filename ->
          putStrLn $ "Opening file: " <> filename
```

In order to call displayMessage, we first need to parse our arguments, *and then* we need to pass the parsed argument to displayMessage and print out the appropriate value. That means we need to sequence the two IO actions using (>>=).

The final version of our newly updated runHCat function will look like this:

```
runHCat :: IO ()
runHCat =
  handleArgs >>= displayMessage
  where
    displayMessage parsedArgument =
      case parsedArgument of
        Left errMessage ->
          putStrLn $ "Error: " <> errMessage
        Right filename ->
          putStrLn $ "Opening file: " <> filename
```

Let's see it in action by running through our list of examples:

```
user@host$ cabal run hcat -- file1
Opening file: file1

user@host$ cabal run hcat -- file1 file2
Error: multiple files not supported

user@host$ cabal run hcat
Error: no filename provided
```

Reading the Contents of a File

Now that we've updated our program to allow us to get a file name from the command line, it's time to start taking a look at how we can print the file to the screen. In the last chapter, you've already seen how we can use functions like readFile to get the contents of a file. We can apply what we've learned pretty trivially to get a working version of our application by reading the file that we get passed in and then printing it out.

```
runHCat :: IO ()
runHCat =
  handleArgs
  >>= \fnameOrError ->
  case fnameOrError of
    Left err ->
      putStrLn $ "Error processing: " <> err
    Right fname ->
      readFile fname >>= putStrLn
```

That's it! If you build this you'll see that program prints out the contents of the file, or an error message, just as we expected. There are still a couple of improvements that we can make to this program. In the rest of this section, we'll look at some ways that we can improve our application, including making our code a bit more readable, handling IO errors, and using more efficient strings.

Dealing with IO Exceptions

Let's start by looking at handling IO exceptions. If you try running your application and give it a path to a file that doesn't exist, you might get something like this:

```
user@host$ cabal exec hcat -- /tmp/missing.file
*** Exception: /tmp/missing.hs:
    openFile: does not exist (No such file or directory)
```

It shouldn't be surprising that we'd get some kind of error when we try to read a file that doesn't exist. In this case, the error that we get is a particular type of exception called an IOError. We've seen other kinds of exceptions before in some of our examples earlier in this book, but until now we haven't had a good way to deal with them. In this section, we'll focus specifically on IOError type exceptions.

When we're talking about IO errors there are two separate modules that we care about. System.IO.Error is where the IOError type is defined, along with several functions for creating, modifying, and handing IO errors. If you only care about IO errors, you can get by with just this module.

The Control.Exception module provides a much more general set of tools for working with all sorts of exceptions. The Exception type class is defined in this module, and we can use it for IO errors as well as exceptions defined by other libraries, exceptions raised in pure functions, or even exceptions we want to define ourselves.

In this section, we'll focus on the exception handling tools provided by Control.Exception, but for now we're going to limit ourselves to just looking at handling IO exceptions. We'll also look at how to generate custom IO exceptions using the tools in System.IO.Error.

We'll start by importing our modules:

```
import qualified Control.Exception as Exception
import qualified System.IO.Error as IOError
```

We'll add some basic error handling to our runHCat. We're not going to worry about recovering from our error, but instead of a nasty message, we'll make the output friendlier and a bit nicer for the user to read.

The function that we want to use to catch an exception is, appropriately, called catch. Its type is catch :: Exception e => IO a -> (e -> IO a) -> IO a. The Exception type class is defined in Control.Exception. As you might expect, there is an instance for IOError provided for us. The catch function takes an IO action and an error handler. The error handler function tells catch what you want to do to recover from the error. It needs to take the error as input, and return some IO action that represents the recovered state.

Let's take a look at how it works in practice:

```
runHCat :: IO ()
runHCat = Exception.catch
  ( handleArgs
    >>= \arg ->
      case arg of
        Left err ->
          putStrLn $ "Error processing: " <> err
        Right fname ->
          readFile fname >>= putStrLn
  ) handleErr
  where
    handleErr :: IOError -> IO ()
    handleErr e = putStrLn "I ran into an error:" >> print e
```

In this example, we've taken our existing code and wrapped it in a call to catch. If any error, like a failure to open a file, happens during that IO action our handler, handleErr, will get called. Note that while we sometimes add type annotations purely for readability, in this example the annotation is required for handleErr so that the compiler knows what kind of Exception we're catching.

Code like our previous example is common in production Haskell applications, but let's look at some ways that we can refactor it to be a little nicer to read. We'll start by adding a second helper function called handleIOError:

```
handleIOError :: IO () -> IO ()
handleIOError ioAction = Exception.catch ioAction handleErr
```

Now we can pass our IO action into this handler function and have errors caught and handled automatically:

```
runHCat :: IO ()
runHCat =
  withErrorHandling $
      handleArgs
      >>= \arg ->
        case arg of
          Left err ->
            putStrLn $ "Error processing: " <> err
          Right fname ->
            readFile fname >>= putStrLn
  where
    withErrorHandling :: IO () -> IO ()
    withErrorHandling ioAction = Exception.catch ioAction handleErr
    handleErr :: IOError -> IO ()
    handleErr e = putStrLn "I ran into an error:" >> print e
```

The way that we've refactored the code here allows us to easily add some context—in this case a context for error handling—to our function while still keeping the body of our function focused on the logic we care about. This sort of refactoring to add some context using a function like withSomeContext $ is a common technique for making programs more readable. We'll see some more examples of this later on in this book.

We have one more refactoring opportunity that we can take to make the code a bit nicer to read. Our handleArgs function isn't raising an exception. Instead, it's returning an Either value to let us know if there's been an error or not. Using Either is a great way to handle errors, but in our case it leaves us with a situation where we're handling errors in two different ways. We could edit handleArgs to raise an exception, but instead, let's look at another option that we could use even if we were using a function from a library that we don't control. We'll create a function to turn an Either into an IO Error.

We'll call our example function eitherToErr and give it the type eitherToErr :: Show a => Either a b -> IO b. Handling our happy path where we have a Right value will be straightforward, so let's add that as well:

```
eitherToErr :: Show a => Either a b -> IO b
eitherToErr (Right a) = return a
```

If we have a Left value, we'll need to construct an IO exception. To do that, we'll use two functions from System.IO.Error. First, we need to add an IOError value. We can do that with the userError function, which creates one from a string. Once we have an error value, we need to throw it. When it comes to raising an exception, we have three separate options:

1. ioError :: IOError -> IO a
2. throwIO :: Exception e => e -> IO a
3. throw :: Exception e => e -> a

The first of our functions, ioError, comes from the System.IO.Error module. It takes an IOError and returns an IO action. The type of IO action that it returns can be anything, since we'll be raising an exception and never actually generating a value of that type.

The second of our functions, throwIO, is a bit more general than ioError. Instead of being limited to just IOError exceptions, throwIO can accept any type of exception, but it still returns an IO action.

The throw function from Control.Exception is the most general of our functions. It takes any kind of exception and raises it. Although we can use throw in place of throwIO and our program will still compile, the functions work a bit differently. The difference is tricky and we'll gloss over the specifics for now, but in general if you're working with IO it's best to use throwIO, since it will behave the way you'd expect. Calls to throw may not always evaluate predictably when you're dealing with IO actions.

Now that we know how to raise an exception, we can write the last part of our function. Since we want an IO error, we'll call throwIO:

```
eitherToErr (Left e) =
  Exception.throwIO . IOError.userError $ show e
```

Putting this all together, we can use eitherToErr to make our program look a bit nicer. Notice in this final example we've also refactored our code to use the TypeApplications extension to eliminate the need for a separate handleErr function:

```
runHCat :: IO ()
runHCat =
  handleIOError $
      handleArgs
      >>= eitherToErr
      >>= readFile
      >>= putStrLn
```

```
  where
    handleIOError :: IO () -> IO ()
    handleIOError ioAction =
      Exception.catch ioAction $
      \e -> putStrLn "I ran into an error:" >> print @IOError e

eitherToErr :: Show a => Either a b -> IO b
eitherToErr (Right a) = return a
eitherToErr (Left e) =
  Exception.throwIO . IOError.userError $ show e
```

Using this approach to handling exceptions, we can now write nice looking compact and expressive code while still handling potential errors and corner cases in our application.

Using Efficient Strings

The last change we'll make to our basic application is a matter of efficiency. So far, we've been using functions from the System.IO module to read and write files using String values. This works for small applications without memory or performance constraints, but for real-world applications, strings can introduce unnecessary performance overhead. There are two common libraries that are used in many Haskell applications that make it easier and more efficient to work with strings.

The text[1] package gives us access to tools for representing and processing textual data. Working with Text is much more efficient than working with String values, and Text works natively with Unicode text data, which can be a source of errors when dealing with text represented as a String. In this chapter, we'll be using two modules from the text package:

```
import qualified Data.Text as Text
import qualified Data.Text.IO as TextIO
```

The bytestring[2] package can help us deal with files more efficiently. Whereas the text package is focused on representing textual data, bytestring provides us with an efficient implementation of packed arrays of bytes. Byte arrays are the way that strings are represented in languages like C, and strict bytestrings can let us write Haskell applications with performance characteristics similar to C applications, while still having access to an API that gives us functions very similar to what we'd have when working with built-in String types.

1. http://hackage.haskell.org/package/text
2. http://hackage.haskell.org/package/bytestring

The bytestring package provides a few different modules that we'll use occasionally in this book. These are the ones that you're most likely to see:

1. Data.ByteString
2. Data.ByteString.Lazy
3. Data.ByteString.Char8

These modules all provide very similar interfaces over slightly different sorts of values, but with important differences. Data.ByteString.Lazy provides a lazily evaluated bytestring. These are useful when you're not sure how much data you want to read off disk, or when you might not want all the data at once. This module provides the functions toStrict and fromStrict to convert back and forth between the standard strict ByteString values and the lazy ones. The bytestrings defined in Data.ByteString.Char8 are defined as a set of Char values instead of Word8 values. This means that you can easily convert back and forth between a String and a Data.ByteString.Char8.ByteString.

ByteStrings and Unicode

It's important to remember that ByteStrings only work with raw bytes and ASCII text. This makes Data.ByteString.Char8 dangerous because it gives you an interface that seems to work well with string data, but can be subtly incorrect when you need to deal with Unicode or other character encodings. In most cases, when dealing with text you should use the text package. You can encodeUtf8 and decodeUtf8 from Data.Text.Encoding to convert back and forth between ByteString and Text values. That said, Data.ByteString.Char8 can be useful when dealing with things like file formats that use ASCII text.

For the rest of this chapter we'll mostly be using Text values, with a couple of exceptions that we'll note as we come across them. For the moment we'll add Data.ByteString to our import list and we'll get around to using it later on:

```
import qualified Data.ByteString as BS
```

The functions that we get from text and bytestring typically look and act the same as their equivalent functions from System.IO except that they work with Text and ByteString values instead of String values. For example, instead of readFile :: FilePath -> IO String we can use TextIO.readFile :: FilePath -> IO Text.Text, and instead of putStrLn :: String -> IO () we can use BS.putStrLn :: BS.ByteString -> IO (). In fact, with just a couple of small changes we can update runHCat to be more efficient:

```
runHCat :: IO ()
runHCat =
  handleIOError $
      handleArgs
      >>= eitherToErr
      >>= TextIO.readFile
      >>= TextIO.putStrLn
  where
    handleIOError :: IO () -> IO ()
    handleIOError ioAction =
      Exception.catch ioAction $
      \e -> putStrLn "I ran into an error:" >> print @IOError e
```

We'll continue to use bytestrings and text values throughout the rest of this book. Using these more efficent libraries for handling binary and text data can greatly improve the speed and memory requirements of any application that you build.

Viewing Text One Page at a Time

Now that we have a program that can display the contents of a file directly to the screen, it's time to start adding pagination. In this section, we'll update our program so that we can scroll forward through the contents of a file one page at a time. We need to let the user scroll at their own speed, so we'll let them press the spacebar to advance one page forward through the document. When they scroll past the last page of the document we should exit the program. We also want to let the user exit the program earlier if they find what they are looking for, so we'll let them press the `q` key at any point while they are scrolling through the document to quit immediately.

You probably already have an intuitive idea for what we mean when we talk about a "page of text," but as we're working on implementing pagination it'll help us to think more carefully about what a page of text is in the context of our application. We're not going to do any raw or low-level terminal IO, so we'll be working with individual lines of text. Most terminal emulators have some notion of a dimension measured in a number of rows and columns of fixed-width characters. When we are doing normal high-level terminal IO, each row of text corresponds to a line of printed output, and each line of output can have as many characters as the terminal has columns. If a line of text has more characters than there are columns in the terminal, most terminal emulators will do their own word wrapping. Terminal word wrapping means that our program will have fewer visible lines of text available, since some of the rows will have been taken up by wrapped lines, so we will need to manually track the wrapping in our program to avoid bugs.

When we put all of this togther, we can think of a page of text as a collection of lines of text, each of which are at most some fixed number of characters long.

Let's start by writing a function to group the lines of text into individual pages. We'll call our function groupsOf. In order to group our lines of text into pages, we need two things. First, we need to know how many lines of text there are on a page. Second, we need a list of the lines of text that we want to group into pages. We'll represent a page of text as a list of lines on that page, and we'll return a list of pages, so the return type of our function will be a list of lists of lines of text.

If we picked a concrete type for our function, we could end up with a type like:

```
groupsOf :: Int -> [Text.Text] -> [[Text.Text]]
```

Of course we might very well want to re-use this code to work with String values, or some other type of text, so we'll use a polymorphic type:

```
groupsOf :: Int -> [a] -> [[a]]
```

The algorithm that we're going to use to group the pages together is pretty straightforward. The splitAt function from Prelude will do the heavy lifting for us. This function takes a number, n and a list, l, and returns a tuple containing the first n elements of l and the remainder of the elements. We can see this in action in ghci:

```
λ splitAt 0 [1..10]
([],[1,2,3,4,5,6,7,8,9,10])
λ splitAt 5 [1..10]
([1,2,3,4,5],[6,7,8,9,10])
λ splitAt 9 [1..10]
([1,2,3,4,5,6,7,8,9],[10])
λ splitAt 20 [1..10]
([1,2,3,4,5,6,7,8,9,10],[])
```

You can see from this example that, thankfully, splitAt handles the case where we want to split at a point past the end of the list by just returning all of the elements in the first element of the tuple, and an empty list in the second element. This will simplify our code quite a bit.

Let's start writing our groupsOf function by looking at the base case: an empty list. If we don't have any text to show, our list of pages of text will also be empty:

```
groupsOf :: Int -> [a] -> [[a]]
groupsOf n [] = []
```

Next let's define the recursive case. We can think of the recursive definition of our function like this: our paginated text is a page made up of the first n lines of text, and the rest of the pages are the result of paginating the remainder of the text:

```
groupsOf n elems =
  let (hd, tl) = splitAt n elems
  in hd : groupsOf n tl
```

Let's open up ghci and test this out to make sure it works like we expect:

```
λ groupsOf 3 [1,2,3]
[[1,2,3]]
λ groupsOf 3 [1,2,3,4,5,6]
[[1,2,3],[4,5,6]]
λ groupsOf 3 [1,2,3,4,5,6,7]
[[1,2,3],[4,5,6],[7]]
λ groupsOf 10 [1,2,3,4,5,6,7]
[[1,2,3,4,5,6,7]]
```

There's one edge case here that we haven't tested: if we try to create groups of size zero, our function will return an infinite list of empty lists. This behavior makes sense; a group of size zero is an infinite list, and if we're never consuming any elements of the input list then we'll never complete the process of paginating it. You have a couple of options to deal with this. You can choose to leave the behavior as is, pattern match and return an empty list if the group size is zero, make the function a partial function and error to return an error if the caller tries to pass in a group size of zero, or you could change the type of the function to something like this:

```
groupsOf :: Int -> [a] -> Maybe [[a]]
```

Throughout this chapter, we'll stick with the definition of the function as is, but you are encouraged to experiment with other ways of writing this and see if you find one that you like better.

Word Wrapping

Now we have a function that can group lines of text into pages, but it doesn't account for the fact that any given input string that it gets could be wider than the terminal that we want to write to, leading to word wrapping. The next thing that we'll need to do is write something that will let us wrap a string, or a Text in our case, so that it takes as many lines as needed to fit into the available width.

We'll implement word wrapping by adding a new function named wordWrap. The function will take in the maximum width of a line of text, in characters, and will return a list of rows of text that are each at most that length. The type of our function will be:

```
wordWrap :: Int -> Text.Text -> [Text.Text]
```

We'll start by writing a "hard-wrapping" algorithm. This will simply break apart lines of text at the maximum line length without respect for word boundaries. The base case for this function will be when the length of the line of text we have is less than, or equal to, the maximum length of a line. In that case, our word-wrapped line of text will just be a single-element list containing the original line of text:

```
wordWrap :: Int -> Text.Text -> [Text.Text]
wordWrap lineLength lineText
  | Text.length lineText <= lineLength = [lineText]
```

If our line is longer than the maximum allowed line length, then we want to take as many characters as we can, and then wrap the rest of the text recursively. You might notice that the implementation here is similar to the groupsOf function you implemented earlier:

```
wordWrap :: Int -> Text.Text -> [Text.Text]
wordWrap lineLength lineText
  | Text.length lineText <= lineLength = [lineText]
  | otherwise =
    let (wrapped, unwrapped) = Text.splitAt lineLength lineText
    in wrapped : wordWrap lineLength unwrapped
```

One problem with this version of the code is that it will word wrap without respect to individual word boundaries. It would be convenient if we could preferentially break lines apart on word boundaries so that a word would only get separated if it were actually longer than the allowed width of the text. Let's look at how we can update our wrapping function to better handle word boundaries.

The algorithm we'll use is going to be a small modification to our existing hard-wrapping algorithm. Our base case will remain the same, and for lines that need to be wrapped we'll still start by splitting the text at the maximum word boundary. After we've split our input in the current line of text, we'll attempt to "soft wrap" the line. This helper function, which we'll implement soon, will try to find the last word boundary in the text. If it can find one, it will return a tuple of the text before and after the word boundary. For example, if we are going to try to soft wrap the string "word wrapping is tricky" we would end up with the tuple ("word wrapping is", "tricky"). The wrapped part of the line will be the first element of our tuple. The remainder of the line will get prepended to the leftover text that we'll wrap recursively.

The soft wrapping itself will recursively walk "backwards" through the input string. If the character we're currently looking at is a space, then we're at the last possible word boundary and we'll split the string. If we get all the way to the beginning of the string and haven't found a space, then the string must not have any natural word boundaries, and we'll have to fall back to using the hard-wrapped input without any additional splitting.

Let's look at the code, and then walk through an example:

```
wordWrap :: Int -> Text.Text -> [Text.Text]
wordWrap lineLength lineText
  | Text.length lineText <= lineLength = [lineText]
  | otherwise =
    let
      (candidate, nextLines) = Text.splitAt lineLength lineText
      (firstLine, overflow) = softWrap candidate (Text.length candidate - 1)
    in firstLine : wordWrap lineLength (overflow <> nextLines)
  where
    softWrap hardwrappedText textIndex
      | textIndex <= 0 = (hardwrappedText,Text.empty)
      | Text.index hardwrappedText textIndex == ' ' =
        let (wrappedLine, rest) = Text.splitAt textIndex hardwrappedText
        in (wrappedLine, Text.tail rest)
      | otherwise = softWrap hardwrappedText (textIndex - 1)
```

To make it easier to understand this code, let's step through what would happen when we call this function and try to wrap the string "word wrapping is tricky" to a length of six characters.

At first we'll call our function with the two parameters:

```
wordWrap 6 "word wrapping is tricky"
```

Our base case will fail to match, because our text is more than six characters long. That means we'll begin by splitting our input into a candidate line of six characters, and everything else that still needs to be wrapped. We can see this in ghci:

```
λ Text.splitAt 6 "word wrapping is tricky"
("word w","rapping is tricky")
```

At this point, candidate is our candidate wrapped line, and it's set to "word w". The value of nextLines is "rapping is tricky". The next thing we do is call softWrap with our candidate string and an index, which we'll set to point at the end of the string.

```
softWrap "word w" 5
```

When we call softWrap our index is not less than, or equal to, zero, which would indicate that the string can't be soft wrapped. Next we'll check to see if the element at our current index is a space. Again, we can test this out in ghci:

```
λ Text.index "word w" 5
'w'
```

The index isn't a space, so we'll decrement the index and call softWrap recursively:

```
softWrap "word w" 4
```

This time, our index test will find a space:

```
λ Text.index "word w" 4
' '
```

That means we've found a word break that we can soft wrap at. We'll split the string here into our new line that is soft wrapped at a line break, and the rest of our text. If we test this out in ghci, we can see that the space we were just looking for is at the start of our leftover string:

```
λ Text.splitAt 4 "word w"
("word"," w")
```

It would look bad to have all wrapped lines of text have a preceding space, so we'll drop that space off the string before we return it. Now we have firstLine set to "word" and overflow set to "w". Now it's time for our recursive call. If we fill in the values for our variables we have:

```
"word" : wordWrap 6 ("w" <> "rapping is tricky")
```

Now we need to handle our recursive call to wrap the remainder of our text, "wrapping is tricky". Once again, our initial string is too long and so we need to split it:

```
λ Text.splitAt 6 "wrapping is tricky"
("wrappi","ng is tricky")
```

In this case, the first word of our line of text is longer than the entire length of a line—it's a good thing we accounted for that edge case! When we call softWrap we'll step backwards through the entire string looking for a space, but of course we won't find one this time, so we'll hit our base case and return the hard wrapped version, "wrappi". We'll add that to our list of wrapped words and make another recursive call:

```
"word" : "wrappi" : wordWrap 6 ("" <> "ng is tricky")
```

The next two words that we handle will follow the same recursive process, and in the end we'll end up with a wrapped string:

```
λ wordWrap 6 "word wrapping is tricky"
["word","wrappi","ng is","tricky"]
```

Handling Terminal Dimensions

The last piece of our functional core is going to combine wordWrap and groupsOf into a single function that will paginate text. To do this we'll need to take in both the width and height of the screen. To handle that, let's create a new record called ScreenDimensions to hold the rows and columns of the screen:

```
data ScreenDimensions = ScreenDimensions
  { screenRows :: Int
  , screenColumns :: Int
  } deriving Show
```

Now we'll create a function called paginate that takes our screen dimensions and the text that we want to show and breaks it into a list of pages that will each fit on the screen comfortably. To do this, we'll use Text.lines to turn our large bytestring into a list of individual lines of text. concatMap, which you've seen before, will let us map each of our lines of text into one or more lines of word-wrapped text, which we can then group into pages worth of lines. As a last step we'll use Text.unlines to combine each of our pages back into a single bytestring for easy printing:

```
paginate :: ScreenDimensions -> Text.Text -> [Text.Text]
paginate (ScreenDimensions rows cols) text =
  let unwrappedLines = Text.lines text
      wrappedLines = concatMap (wordWrap cols) unwrappedLines
      pageLines = groupsOf rows wrappedLines
  in map Text.unlines pageLines
```

Now that we've finished implementing the pure core of our feature, which will let us easily paginate some text, it's time to work on the procedural shell of our application.

Calling External Applications

We've built a program that can fit some text to a screen given its dimensions, but we've got one major missing piece: how do we get the dimensions of the screen in the first place? One way that we could approach this is to simply ask the user to input the information when they open the file, but this would be an awful user experience. In most cases, there's no easy way for a user to have that information available, so they'd need to tediously count rows and columns, or use a tool to give them the information. Another option would be to look for a library that gives us detailed terminal information. Low-level terminal libraries can be complicated though, and building something that works cross-platform can be a real challenge.

System Dependent Code Ahead

Some aspects of this section are not entirely portable across all operating systems and configurations. When we call out to external applications or interact with a shell in this section we will necessarily have to make some assumptions about what kind of environment the application is running in, and what tools are available. All of the examples in this section have been tested on Linux and should work well in most typical Linux, MacOS, and BSD environments. If you are using Windows, most of these examples should work if you are using the Linux Subsystem for Windows. If you find yourself in an environment where some of these examples do not run as expected, you can experiment with the code to find something that works better for your system, or use a virtual machine so that you can experiment with the applications in a supported environment.

There's a tool named tput that's available out of the box on most Unix-like systems that we can use to look up the size of the terminal in a platform independent way. Unfortunately for us though, tput is an executable program and not a library, so to call it we'll need to run the application and parse its output. Dealing with calling external applications is something that comes up from time to time when building systems, and so in this section, we'll look at how to create and manage the life cycle of external applications using the process[3] package.

At the core of the process package is a module, System.Process, that gives you the tools to spawn and interact with subprocesses. This module defines a few data types and includes several functions to help you work with external processes. Most of the functionality provided by the System.Process is concerned with giving you fine-grained control over processes, how they are spawned, and how they run. For our purposes, we don't need fine-grained control and can make use of one of the higher level utility functions provided by the library, readProcess:

```
readProcess :: FilePath -> [String] -> String -> IO String
```

3. https://hackage.haskell.org/package/process

The readProcess function let's us run a program by providing it the name of a program or a path to the application we want to run, a list of arguments that it should receive, and any input that should be available to it over stdin. When readProcess is evaluated, the IO action will wait until the program has finished executing and will return all of the output that the program wrote to stdout as a String. Let's look at an example in ghci:

```
λ import System.Process
λ readProcess "cal" ["01", "1972"] "" >>= putStrLn
    January 1972
Su Mo Tu We Th Fr Sa
                   1
 2  3  4  5  6  7  8
 9 10 11 12 13 14 15
16 17 18 19 20 21 22
23 24 25 26 27 28 29
30 31
```

In this example, we're calling the cal program to generate a calendar for January of the year 1972. You'll notice that the first argument that we're passing, "cal", isn't a full path. Most functions from the process library will use system-specific conventions for handling calls to programs. For example, on Unix-like systems, if you don't provide a full path to a program, then it will look at the PATH environment variable to figure out what directories should be searched for applications. The second argument that we pass in is a list of arguments. The cal program can be optionally given a date and it will generate a calendar for the given month or year. Here we're printing out a calendar of January, 1972, so we pass two arguments, "01" for January, and "1972" for the year 1972. Finally, running an external program is an IO action, and so we are binding the output of that IO action to the input of putStrLn using >>=.

For our pager application, we'll need to use readProcess to call tput so that we can get the size of our terminal. We also want to make sure that we're only going to call the command on systems where we expect it to be available. In our application we'll concern ourselves with Darwin and Linux systems. For other systems, we'll return a hard-coded default terminal size. The System.Info package exports a string named os that contains the name of the current OS. Putting all that together, here's an example function to get the dimensions of a terminal:

```
import System.Process (readProcess)
import qualified System.Info as SystemInfo
```

```
getTerminalSize :: IO ScreenDimensions
getTerminalSize =
  case SystemInfo.os of
    "darwin" -> tputScreenDimensions
    "linux" -> tputScreenDimensions
    _other -> pure $ ScreenDimensions 25 80
  where
    tputScreenDimensions :: IO ScreenDimensions
    tputScreenDimensions =
      readProcess "tput" ["lines"] ""
      >>= \lines ->
        readProcess "tput" ["cols"] ""
        >>= \cols ->
              let lines' = read $ init lines
                  cols'  = read $ init cols
              in return $ ScreenDimensions lines' cols'
```

It's a little bit unwieldy! Later on in this chapter, in Improving Readability with Do Blocks, on page 321, you'll learn how to refactor this function so that it's more readable. For now, we can still get a good idea of what's happening here. We're starting out looking at the current OS, and returning a default value if we're not running on Darwin or Linux. Once the OS check is out of the way, we call Process.readProcess twice, once to get the number of lines in the terminal, and a second time to get the columns.

Like most processes, tput returns its output with a trailing newline. That's handy on an interactive terminal because it makes sure that the cursor gets set back to the start of a line before your prompt is displayed, but when you're calling a process programatically you need to strip it off. The init function is part of the standard library. It takes a list and returns all but the last element, which in this case is the newline character. The last thing we do is pass our string to read to convert the string into a number.

Our implementation is a bit fragile. The exercises section at the end of this chapter has some opportunities for how you can make this code more robust.

Getting User Input

The final challenge that we have with getting our pager working is being able to show a page based on user input. To do this, we'll need to be able to read keypresses to control what the application does and then take an action based on the keypress. Let's start by looking at how we can deal with representing the user input, and then we'll look at how to get the input. Finally, we'll bring it all together into a function that gets user input and acts on it accordingly.

We've decided that we want to control our application by using space to go to the next page and typing q to quit, so we'll need to handle two separate keypresses. For the sake of simplicity, we'll ignore any other keypresses.

Once we've displayed a page of text, our program won't do anything until the user enters some text. Once we've gotten the text, if it's input that we accept, we'll use that input to decide if we should continue on to the next page, or cancel the application. We'll encode those two choices into a new type called ContinueCancel:

```
data ContinueCancel = Continue | Cancel deriving (Eq, Show)
```

Next we need to build a function that gets a ContinueCancel value inside of an IO action. It won't have any input (aside from what the user gives it), so its type will be getContinue :: IO ContinueCancel.

Now that you understand how IO works, and have some experience reading files and writing things to the screen, implementing this function shouldn't be too hard. We've worked with handles before to read and write to files. Working with the shell is essentially the same thing. Instead of getting a file handle by calling openFile we'll just use the special handle stdin. The System.IO module gives you three handles when your application starts: stdin, stdout, and stderr. These all connect to the standard file descriptions for your application just like you'd expect.

Since we're concerned with keypresses instead of entire lines or files of text, we'll use the hGetChar function to get a single character at a time from stdin. These are both exported by the System.IO module in base. A naive implementation of our function might look something like this:

```
import System.IO

getContinue :: IO ContinueCancel
getContinue =
  hGetChar stdin
  >>= \input ->
    case input of
      ' ' -> return Continue
      'q' -> return Cancel
```

In the next section, we'll bring everything together and start using this function to display our paginated data. For now, we can temporarily modify our runHCat function to call getContinue so that we can see it in action:

```
runHCat :: IO ()
runHCat =
  putStrLn "do you want to Continue (space) or quit (q)" >>
  getContinue >>=
```

```
  \cont ->
    case cont of
      Continue -> putStrLn "okay, continuing!" >> runHCat
      Cancel -> putStrLn "goodbye!"
```

If you run the application right now you might notice that it doesn't behave like you would expect. You can press space or the q key as many times as you want and nothing will happen. If you press enter, you might see several lines of output come across the screen all at once, and then the program will crash!

The spaces in this example are rendered as underscores to make it more obvious what's happening:

```
user@host$ cabal run hcat
do you want to Continue (space) or quit (q)

___
okay, continuing!
do you want to Continue (space) or quit (q)
okay, continuing!
do you want to Continue (space) or quit (q)
okay, continuing!
do you want to Continue (space) or quit (q)
hcat: src/HCat.hs:(338,7)-(340,24): Non-exhaustive patterns in case
```

The first problem we have is that the application isn't reacting to our input until we press enter. This is due to the fact that most terminals by default are *line buffered*, which means that our program will get an entire line of text at a time, and the terminal won't actually send us anything that the user has typed until they press enter. We can disable that by calling the hSetBuffering function to configure the type of buffering that we want to use. We want to get the keypresses as soon as the user enters them, so we'll set it to NoBuffering. With that change in place our function will now be:

```
getContinue :: IO ContinueCancel
getContinue =
  hSetBuffering stdin NoBuffering
  >> hGetChar stdin
  >>= \input ->
    case input of
      ' ' -> return Continue
      'q' -> return Cancel
```

If we run our program again we'll see slightly different behavior. Just like before, let's press the spacebar three times, and then press enter:

```
user@host$ cabal run hcat
do you want to Continue (space) or quit (q)
 okay, continuing!
```

```
do you want to Continue (space) or quit (q)
 okay, continuing!
do you want to Continue (space) or quit (q)
 okay, continuing!
do you want to Continue (space) or quit (q)

hcat: src/HCat.hs:(338,7)-(340,24): Non-exhaustive patterns in case
```

It's looking a little better, but we still have a few problems. We display a message to the user each time we press the spacebar now, but we're still crashing whenever we press enter. There's also something wrong with the output. Let's address the crash first.

The crash message is telling us that we have a non-exhaustive pattern in our case statement. The pattern that it's referring to is at the end of our function, where we're looking for the space or q characters. It turns out by not including anything to match the other characters that might get entered we've added a bug, and not ignored them like we intend. Let's make a small change to our program. Instead of ignoring those characters, we'll use a wildcard pattern to match any other letters, and in that case we'll simply recursively call getContinue, which will again wait for another keypress:

```
getContinue :: IO ContinueCancel
getContinue =
  hSetBuffering stdin NoBuffering
  >> hGetChar stdin
  >>= \input ->
    case input of
      ' ' -> return Continue
      'q' -> return Cancel
      _   -> getContinue
```

Let's run the program again:

```
do you want to Continue (space) or quit (q)
 okay, continuing!
do you want to Continue (space) or quit (q)

qgoodbye!
```

If we press space we again see the message right away, and if we press enter our program no longer crashes! The output is still getting corrupted by our keypresses though. The extra space in front of our "okay, continuing!" message might be easy to overlook, but the "q" in front of our "goodbye!" message is harder to ignore. The problem that we have is *terminal echoing*. By default, a terminal will output any characters that the user types to the screen. In the normal case that's what we want, but for a tool like hcat where we are building a more interactive UI, we want to suppress that. We can change this behavior by disabling terminal echoing, so the users keypresses don't show up on the screen. Just like with buffering, we can disable echo on stdin by calling hSetEcho:

```
getContinue :: IO ContinueCancel
getContinue =
  hSetBuffering stdin NoBuffering
  >> hSetEcho stdin False
  >> hGetChar stdin
  >>= \input ->
    case input of
      ' ' -> return Continue
      'q' -> return Cancel
      _   -> getContinue
```

If you run the program now you'll see that everything should behave as expected. We can get user input without buffering, hide the keypresses so that they don't corrupt the output, and silently ignore any keypresses that we're not expecting. Now that we can control our pager, let's move on to connecting all of the pieces of our application togther.

Paging Our File

Now that we've gotten all of the individual components of our functional core and procedural shell built, we can finally put everything together and paginate a file for our user! In this section we'll add one more function, and then make some updates to runHCat to bring everything together.

Let's start with our new function. We haven't yet written a function to actually print a page of text to the screen. We'll create a new function called showPages to show all of the pages of our document. Let's take a look at the code first, and then we can walk through it:

```
showPages :: [Text.Text] -> IO ()
showPages [] = return ()
showPages (page:pages) =
  TextIO.putStrLn page
  >> getContinue
  >>= \input ->
    case input of
      Continue -> showPages pages
      Cancel   -> return ()
```

We're using pattern matching here to detect when we've shown all of our pages. For cases where we still have a page, our algorithm is pretty simple: we print out the page, and then we wait for the user to make a keypress. If they want to continue, we show the next page, and otherwise we just finish our IO action.

There's one small quirk of our implementation that might be inconvenient: when we view a short file, we don't clear the screen. That means it might be hard for a user to tell how much of the text they are looking at is from the current file, and how much is just left from previous output to their terminal.

We can address this by clearing the screen before we print any page of text. This can be done using ANSI terminal escape sequences, which are supported in Linux, BSD, MacOS, and recent versions of Windows. You can look up the details of the ANSI escape sequences online, or copy the example to get an IO action that will print out the correct escape sequence to clear the screen and reset the cursor position to the top-left of the console:

```
clearScreen :: IO ()
clearScreen =
  BS.putStr "\^[[1J\^[[1;1H"
```

There are a couple of things that might get your attention when you look at this code. First, you'll notice we're using a ByteString rather than a Text value. We could use Text here, since both ByteString and Text support the types of values that we want to use. In this case though, ByteString is semantically a better choice. Even though we're typing in a string, our escape sequence is logically a raw byte sequence. We wouldn't want it to be interpreted as Unicode if we were to try to do something with the string later on.

OverloadedStrings

The OverloadedStrings extension has been available since GHC 6.8.1. This extension isn't enabled by default in either GHC2021 or Haskell2010 so you'll need to enable it manually. This is a popular extension, and many projects enable it by default in their cabal files so that it can be used across an entire codebase. This extension does introduce some changes that can make errors harder to understand and, since it changes the meaning of string literals, some existing projects might not compile when this extension enabled.

Speaking of typing in a byte sequence, you might also notice that we've typed in a literal string value here, but the compiler is accepting it as a ByteString value rather than a normal String. If you copy this code into your example as-is, you will find that you'll get an error. Being able to type literal values for string types like Text and ByteString is extremely convenient, and so we have a language extension, OverloadedStrings, which allows us to do just that. Let's add it to the top of our file:

```
{-# LANGUAGE OverloadedStrings #-}
```

Now that we have a way to clear the screen, we can update showPages:

```
showPages :: [Text.Text] -> IO ()
showPages [] = return ()
showPages (page:pages) =
  clearScreen
  >> TextIO.putStr page
  >> getContinue
  >>= \input ->
    case input of
      Continue -> showPages pages
      Cancel   -> return ()
```

Updating our main runHCat function is likewise pretty straightforward. We just need to get the contents of our file, then paginate it before passing it to showPages:

```
runHCat :: IO ()
runHCat =
  handleArgs
  >>= eitherToErr
  >>= flip openFile ReadMode
  >>= TextIO.hGetContents
  >>= \contents ->
    getTerminalSize >>= \termSize ->
      let pages = paginate termSize contents
      in showPages pages
```

If you build your application and run it now you'll see how you can combine a procedural shell with a functional core to combine pure functions, like our word wrap and pagination function, with IO actions like getting user input, handling errors, or calling external processes.

Take a moment to spend some time running the program and watching it work. In the next section, we'll build on the program to add some new capabilities, and then we'll look at ways that we can refactor the code to make it easier to work with.

Adding a Status Line with Metadata

In the last section, you finished the second version of your file viewing application. This version added the ability to scroll through a document a page at a time, and would allow you to exit the program at any time. In this section, we're going to expand on our example program by including some additional information in a status bar. There are a lot of pieces of information that we could potentially add to a status bar, and you can choose to add some extra information if you'd like while you are working through this section, but we'll focus our example on adding these:

1. The name of the file
2. The size of the file, in bytes
3. The last time the file was modified
4. The read, write, and execute permissions on the file
5. The current page that we're viewing
6. The total number of pages in the document

To get some of this information we'll need to add a dependency on couple of common packages. The directory package will give us some cross-platform tools for getting information about files and directories. We'll use this package to get information like the modification time and permissions. The time package will give us the ability to format a timestamp to make it human readable.

```
import qualified Data.ByteString as BS
import qualified Data.Time.Clock as Clock
import qualified Data.Time.Format as TimeFormat
import qualified Data.Time.Clock.POSIX as PosixClock
import qualified System.Directory as Directory
```

Collecting Information

The first thing that we need to do is to create a record to hold all of the data about our file that we want to show in the status line. In this example, we'll call our record FileInfo:

```
data FileInfo = FileInfo
  { filePath  :: FilePath
  , fileSize  :: Int
  , fileMTime :: Clock.UTCTime
  , fileReadable :: Bool
  , fileWriteable :: Bool
  , fileExecutable :: Bool
  } deriving Show
```

This record will hold all of the basic information about our file that we want to display in the status bar. You'll notice that we're not including the current or total page count. By omitting those fields, we can calculate a single FileInfo for each file that we're looking at, without having to regenerate a new value for each page.

Next, let's write a function to create a new FileInfo value. We'll call the function fileInfo. Let's look at the implementation and then step through what it's doing:

```
fileInfo :: FilePath -> IO FileInfo
fileInfo filePath =
```

```
  Directory.getPermissions filePath >>= \perms ->
    Directory.getModificationTime filePath >>= \mtime ->
      BS.readFile filePath >>= \contents ->
        let size = BS.length contents
        in return FileInfo
           { filePath = filePath
           , fileSize = size
           , fileMTime = mtime
           , fileReadable = Directory.readable perms
           , fileWriteable = Directory.writable perms
           , fileExecutable = Directory.executable perms
           }
```

You'll notice our function returns an IO action with a FileInfo, since all the things we're doing to get information about the file are themselves IO actions. Most of the work we're doing in this function is calling some IO actions and packing their results into a FileInfo record. We use getPermissions to get the permissions of the file, and getModificationTime to get the time the file was last changed. There isn't an easy cross-platform way to look up the size of a file without reading it, but we can read the contents into a ByteString and then look at the length of the ByteString to get the size of the file. We're using ByteString here instead of Text because we are specifically interested in the number of *bytes* in the file. If we used Text here we'd get the number of *characters*, which could be a lot smaller than the number of bytes, especially if we were dealing with text in a language that typically requires more than a single byte to represent a character. The last thing we do is to use the helper functions readable, writable, and executable to get the specific capabilities out of the Permissions type that is returned from getPermissions.

We can start manually testing our code now by calling fileInfo on different paths. Let's run through a couple of examples:

```
λ fileInfo "HCat.hs"
FileInfo { filePath = "HCat.hs"
         , fileSize = 17033
         , fileMTime = 2022-01-24 05:09:57.532796141 UTC
         , fileReadable = True
         , fileWriteable = True
         , fileExecutable = False
         }
λ fileInfo "../hcat.cabal"
FileInfo { filePath = "../hcat.cabal"
         , fileSize = 731
         , fileMTime = 2022-01-24 04:20:48.234890708 UTC
         , fileReadable = True
         , fileWriteable = True
         , fileExecutable = False
         }
```

This function is serving its purpose of getting information about the contents of a file, but the way it's being displayed in ghci isn't going to work for us if we want to show a status line. For one thing, the formatting is all wrong to fit onto a single line. For another, we are missing the current page that we're viewing and the overall page count, both key pieces of information we'll want to display on the status line.

Formatting the Status Line

For each page of our file output, we'd like to create a status line at the bottom of the screen that shows some information from our FileInfo record, plus the current and total page count. The status line also needs to be formatted to take up only the amount of space available in a single row of text no matter how wide or small the user's terminal is.

To handle this, let's add a new function that will take a FileInfo along with a terminal width, total page count, and the current page. We'll return a new Text value that contains all the status information. Let's call our function formatFileInfo:

```
formatFileInfo :: FileInfo -> Int -> Int -> Int -> Text.Text
```

Since we need to access all of the fields in our FileInfo record, we'll use the RecordWildCards extension to create bindings for all of them automatically:

```
formatFileInfo FileInfo{..} maxWidth totalPages currentPage =
```

We'll use the printf function from the Text.Printf module in base to format our actual status line string. Let's start there and define all the fields we want to show, and then work backwards and define them one at a time:

```
statusLine = Text.pack $
  printf
  "%s | permissions: %s | %d bytes | modified: %s | page: %d of %d"
  filePath
  permissionString
  fileSize
  timestamp
  currentPage
  totalPages
```

If you've used printf style functions in other languages, the syntax here might look familiar to you. The printf function takes a *format string* that uses special formatting symbols to represent values in a formatted string. You can find a comprehensive list of the format specifiers in the Haddock documentation.[4] In our status line we're using %s, which is a placeholder for a String, and %d,

4. https://hackage.haskell.org/package/base-4.16.0.0/docs/Text-Printf.html#v:printf

which is a placeholder for an Integral value, in our case Int. After the format string we provide a list of values that will be used to fill in the format specifiers in the order that they appear.

Several of these fields are freebies. The filePath and fileSize fields are taken directly from our FileInfo record, and both currentPage and totalPages are being passed into the function. That means we need to work backwards to define both permissionString and timestamp.

Getting a value for permissionString is just a matter of a few if expressions:

```
permissionString =
  [ if fileReadable then 'r' else '-'
  , if fileWriteable then 'w' else '-'
  , if fileExecutable then 'x' else '-' ]
```

If you find this confusing, remember that a String is just a list of Char values.

The next field we need to prepare is timestamp. This is going to be a human-readable timestamp based on the modification time that's stored in our FileInfo. We'd like to show the timestamp in YYYY-MM-DD HH:MM:SS format. To do that we'll use the formatTime function from the Data.Time.Format module in the time package. The formatTime takes a format string, a locale, and a UTCTime value and returns a human-readable timestamp. Like printf, the format string we pass to formatTime uses percent signs to indicate different kinds of values. You can look at the full list in the Haddock documentation.[5] We'll use %F %T as our format string. This will give us our desired YYYY-MM-DD HH:MM:SS formatted timestamp:

```
timestamp =
  TimeFormat.formatTime TimeFormat.defaultTimeLocale "%F %T" fileMTime
```

With these two values, we can generate a status line. Let's take a look in ghci to see how our status line will look:

```
λ info <- fileInfo "./ex"
λ TextIO.putStrLn $ formatFileInfo info 100 5 2
./ex|permissions: r-x|5 bytes|modified: 1970-01-01 00:00:01|page: 2 of 5
```

This isn't too bad, it gives us a lot of information in a pretty readable format. There are a couple of changes we still should make: first, the status line could potentially be wider than the size of the terminal that we are writing to. In this case, we should truncate the status line so that we don't accidentally cause word wrapping. Second, we should do something to make the status line more visually distinctive so that it's easy for the user to tell the difference between the status bar and the rest of the text.

5. https://hackage.haskell.org/package/time-1.12.1/docs/Data-Time-Format.html

Let's start by truncating the text in the status bar if it's too long. Here's the algorithm that we'll use:

- If the terminal is three or fewer characters wide, don't display a status line at all.
- If the length of the status line text is not longer than the width of the display, show the text unmodified.
- If the length of the status line is longer than the display, replace the last three characters in the status line with ellipses.

This algorithm translates pretty naturally to code:

```
truncateStatus statusLine
  | maxWidth <= 3 = ""
  | Text.length statusLine > maxWidth =
    Text.take (maxWidth - 3) statusLine <> "..."
  | otherwise = statusLine
```

Finally, we can decorate our text to make the status line more visually distinctive. One way we can do that is to once again use ANSI terminal escape sequences to invert the colors of the text. As before, feel free to copy the literal escape codes from the example:

```
invertText inputStr =
  let
    reverseVideo = "\^[[7m"
    resetVideo = "\^[[0m"
  in reverseVideo <> inputStr <> resetVideo
```

Now that we can truncate and highlight the status bar, we just need to call those functions on our printf formatted string. The final version of formatFileInfo is:

```
formatFileInfo :: FileInfo -> Int -> Int -> Int -> Text.Text
formatFileInfo FileInfo{..} maxWidth totalPages currentPage =
  let
    timestamp =
      TimeFormat.formatTime TimeFormat.defaultTimeLocale "%F %T" fileMTime
    permissionString =
      [ if fileReadable then 'r' else '-'
      , if fileWriteable then 'w' else '-'
      , if fileExecutable then 'x' else '-' ]
    statusLine = Text.pack $
      printf
      "%s | permissions: %s | %d bytes | modified: %s | page: %d of %d"
      filePath
      permissionString
      fileSize
      timestamp
```

```
      currentPage
      totalPages
  in invertText (truncateStatus statusLine)
  where
    invertText inputStr =
      let
        reverseVideo = "\^[[7m"
        resetVideo = "\^[[0m"
      in reverseVideo <> inputStr <> resetVideo
    truncateStatus statusLine
      | maxWidth <= 3 = ""
      | Text.length statusLine > maxWidth =
        Text.take (maxWidth - 3) statusLine <> "..."
      | otherwise = statusLine
```

Improving Readability with Do Blocks

Now that we have a way to get information about a file and format it nicely, the next step in building our application will be to integrate our new fileInfo function into our pagination code. Before we move on to this next step though, we're going to take a slight detour and look at some ways that we can refactor our code to be easier to read and write using a common Haskell feature called do notation.

So far in this chapter we've built up IO actions using functions like >>= and fmap that we learned about in the previous chapter. As our programs have gotten longer and more sophisticated, you might have thought that our applications have also grown less readable. If we look back at fileInfo as an example, you'll notice that each time you add a new field to the overall collection of information, you are following the same pattern of adding a new function so that you can bind the result of an IO action:

```
fileInfo :: FilePath -> IO FileInfo
fileInfo filePath =
  Directory.getPermissions filePath >>= \perms ->
    Directory.getModificationTime filePath >>= \mtime ->
      BS.readFile filePath >>= \contents ->
        let size = BS.length contents
        in return FileInfo
           { filePath = filePath
           , fileSize = size
           , fileMTime = mtime
           , fileReadable = Directory.readable perms
           , fileWriteable = Directory.writable perms
           , fileExecutable = Directory.executable perms
           }
```

For three values that works well enough, but you can easily imagine how adding a few more items to the file info would start to make the code completely unreadable. As the procedural shells of our application start to do more, we need a better way to write the code. In fact, you might find yourself writing procedural style IO-heavy code and wishing that Haskell was a more procedural language, or at least supported the syntax of common imperative programming languages.

Haskell gives us the ability to do just that with *do notation*. do notation allows us to use the do keyword to write imperative style blocks called "do blocks". The do notation is *syntactic sugar*. It doesn't add new capabilities to the language, but it gives you a nicer and more convenient way to write some types of code. In fact, the Haskell compiler will automatically translate imperative style code inside of do blocks into code that uses (>>=). There's nothing that you can write with do notation that you can't write by calling >>=, but the syntax of do blocks can be quite a bit nicer in some cases.

The quickest way to understand what a do block is doing is with a short example. Let's write a small function that uses do notation, and then we'll *desugar* it into the >>= style that you've been using throughout this chapter. We'll create a small function that will read the contents of two files, and then write the lines back out to a third file, interleaving the lines from the first two:

```
interleaveLines :: String -> String -> String
interleaveLines a b =
  unlines . concat . Data.List.transpose $ [lines a, lines b]

interleaveFiles :: FilePath -> FilePath -> FilePath -> IO String
interleaveFiles file1 file2 outFile = do
  content1 <- readFile file1
  content2 <- readFile file2
  putStrLn "I've read two files"
  let content3 = interleaveLines content1 content2
  writeFile outFile content3
  return content3
```

Even without digging into the details of do notation, you should be able to follow what's going on in the interleaveFiles function. The most obvious difference in this code from code that we've been writing is the use of <- for variable assignment. You might also have noticed that we have statements like putStrLn and writeFile that just appear like they would in a procedural program. Finally, you might notice the use of let without a corresponding in when we say let content3 = interleaveLines content1 content2.

So why the new type of assignment, and why *two different styles* of assignment? Before we dig into that, let's look at a desugared version of the same function:

```
bindInterleave :: FilePath -> FilePath -> FilePath -> IO String
bindInterleave file1 file2 outFile  =
  readFile file1
  >>= \content1 ->
  readFile file2
  >>= \content2 -> putStrLn "I've read two files"
  >>= \_ ->
        let content3 = interleaveLines content1 content2
        in writeFile outFile content3
        >> return content3
```

Comparing these two versions of the function, we can see the syntactic sugar of the do notation is just wrapping the pattern of using bind with anonymous functions. In do blocks we use <- style assignment to bind a variable. Saying foo <- bar inside of a do block is the same as saying bar >>= \foo -> ... in normal Haskell notation.

In simple cases like this, do blocks can slightly improve the readability of our program by removing the >>= \var -> from each line of our code, allowing us to focus on the important parts of our application.

do blocks can also be nested, allowing us to create more complex applications where using bind notation would quickly get unwieldy.

Refactoring fileInfo

Now that we know about do blocks, we can clean up some of our code. Let's start by looking at how we can refactor our fileInfo function to use do notation. We will start by mechanically replacing the anonymous functions with do bindings:

```
fileInfo :: FilePath -> IO FileInfo
fileInfo filePath = do
  perms <- Directory.getPermissions filePath
  mtime <- Directory.getModificationTime filePath
  contents <- BS.readFile filePath
  let size = BS.length contents
  return FileInfo
    { filePath = filePath
    , fileSize = size
    , fileMTime = mtime
    , fileReadable = Directory.readable perms
    , fileWriteable = Directory.writable perms
    , fileExecutable = Directory.executable perms
    }
```

This version of the code is much more readable. We've removed a large amount of indentation, and it's easier to follow the important parts of the program since we've removed some extra syntax that made it a little harder to follow along with the important parts of the program.

One additional small change we can make is to combine reading the contents of the file and calculating its size, turning that into a single expression:

```
size <- BS.length <$> BS.readFile filePath
```

Using (<$>) this way is a common pattern that you'll see frequently throughout this book and in production Haskell code.

This style of do notation that we've just used follows the usual Haskell convention of using significant whitespace to manage the structure of our program. All of the code inside of the do block is indented by a consistent number of spaces to group the expressions together. If we are writing several let bindings inside of a do block, we need to add an additional level of indentation to differentiate the let bindings from the do expressions:

```
letBindingDo :: IO (Int,Int,Int)
letBindingDo = do
  let
    a = 1
    b = 2
    c = 3
  return (a,b,c)
```

Uncommonly, you might also see code that uses an alternative form of do notation that makes use of braces and semicolons instead of significant whitespace. This style of code is equivalent to the more usual style with significant whitespace, but it more closely resembles imperative code in a C-family language. As an example:

```
fileInfo :: FilePath -> IO FileInfo
fileInfo filePath = do
  { perms <- Directory.getPermissions filePath;
    mtime <- Directory.getModificationTime filePath;
    size <- BS.length <$> BS.readFile filePath;
    return FileInfo
      { filePath = filePath
      , fileSize = size
      , fileMTime = mtime
      , fileReadable = Directory.readable perms
      , fileWriteable = Directory.writable perms
      , fileExecutable = Directory.executable perms
      };
  }
```

In this style of notation, each expression is terminated with a trailing semicolon, and the entire do block is wrapped in braces.

Let expressions are also wrapped in braces:

```
letBindingBrackets :: IO (Int,Int,Int)
letBindingBrackets = do
  {
    let {
    a = 1;
    b = 2;
    c = 3;
    };
    return (a,b,c);
  }
```

The use of braces and semicolons here eliminates the need for significant whitespace, although whitespace for the sake of formatting and making the code more readable is still recommended.

This style of do notation is rarely used, and throughout the rest of the book we'll use the much more common significant whitespace style of code. This bracket-and-semicolon style is mentioned here because you may run across it in some popular papers and other pieces of documentation, and it does occasionally show up in some open source projects.

In the next section, we'll finish up our application by putting all of our new functions together and using do notation to refactor runHCat. As you're working through that last section, keep an eye out for other refactoring opportunities.

Showing the Status Bar and Refactoring runHCat

Before we took a detour to learn about do notation, we had just finished adding support for collecting metadata about the files that we are going to view, and writing a function to display that information in a status bar. Now that we know about do notation we'll be able to take on a small bit of refactoring work to make integrating this feature into our application easier.

The first thing that we need to do is to update our paginate function to add the status bar to the end of each page of text that we generate. Let's take a look at the refactored version of paginate and then we can briefly walk through what it's doing:

```
paginate :: ScreenDimensions -> FileInfo -> Text.Text -> [Text.Text]
paginate (ScreenDimensions rows cols) finfo text =
  let
    rows' = rows - 1
    wrappedLines = concatMap (wordWrap cols) (Text.lines text)
    pages = map (Text.unlines . padTo rows') $ groupsOf rows' wrappedLines
    pageCount = length pages
    statusLines = map (formatFileInfo finfo cols pageCount) [1..pageCount]
```

```
  in zipWith (<>) pages statusLines
  where
    padTo :: Int -> [Text.Text] -> [Text.Text]
    padTo lineCount rowsToPad =
      take lineCount $ rowsToPad <> repeat ""
```

Our underlying pagination function remains the same as before, but we've made a couple of changes. First, we're taking the input text and generating pages that are each a single line shorter than the size of our screen, using rows'. This gives us room for the status bar at the bottom.

The next change is that we're adding padding to the bottom of each page, using padTo. In this example, we're simply adding as many empty lines as necessary to ensure that we have enough rows to fill the available vertical space. Once we've padded out the list of rows, we use Text.unlines to transform the collections of rows into a single page of text with newlines.

After generating the individual pages, we count the total number of pages and use that count to generate a unique status line for each page. The line zipWith (<>) pages statusLines will go through the list of pages and status lines and append each status line to its corresponding page.

So far, so good; we can generate pages using file metadata now, but we need to actually get the metadata and pass it into paginate. Right now we're calling paginate from runHCat, and runHCat has gotten a little hard to work with.

Recall from earlier in this chapter that our current version of runHCat is:

```
runHCat :: IO ()
runHCat =
  handleArgs
  >>= eitherToErr
  >>= flip openFile ReadMode
  >>= Text.hGetContents
  >>= \contents ->
    getTerminalSize >>= \termSize ->
      let pages = paginate termSize contents
      in showPages pages
```

We could continue with our current implementation and add a call to fileInfo so that we can pass it along to paginate:

```
runHCat :: IO ()
runHCat =
  handleArgs
  >>= eitherToErr
  >>= \targetFilePath ->
    openFile targetFilePath ReadMode
```

```
    >>= TextIO.hGetContents
    >>= \contents ->
      getTerminalSize >>= \termSize ->
        fileInfo targetFilePath >>= \finfo ->
          let pages = paginate termSize finfo contents
          in showPages pages
```

If you run this, you might notice a bug: the status line in our program should be displaying, but on most systems it will actually be invisible until you try to exit the program, at which point it will appear. The problem here is terminal buffering. By default, our terminal will be using line-buffered output, which means that each line of text will be printed when the terminal encounters a newline. Our status line doesn't end with a newline. If it did, we'd end up losing an extra line in our terminal to displaying an empty line for the cursor. Unfortunately, this means that the terminal won't render our status line until we exit the program. When our program exits, the shell takes back control over standard output and flushes the output buffer of our program.

This is an easy fix. We can use hSetBuffering on stdout just like we did for stdin when we wanted to read keypresses without forcing the user to press enter. The problem is that our function is already quite unwieldy and we're just adding more layers to it. Without a refactor, the fixed version of runHCat will have yet another layer of nesting:

```
runHCat :: IO ()
runHCat =
  handleArgs
  >>= eitherToErr
  >>= \targetFilePath ->
    openFile targetFilePath ReadMode
    >>= TextIO.hGetContents
    >>= \contents ->
      getTerminalSize
      >>= \termSize ->
        hSetBuffering stdout NoBuffering
        >> fileInfo targetFilePath
        >>= \finfo ->
          let pages = paginate termSize finfo contents
          in showPages pages
```

It's clear that this is starting to get unmanageable, so use what we've learned about do notation to refactor our function. We'll start with a completely mechanical translation, replacing >>= \var -> with var <- and otherwise not changing the structure of the code. That leaves us with this version which is already looking quite a bit more readable:

```
runHCat :: IO ()
runHCat = do
  args <- handleArgs
  targetFilePath <- eitherToErr args
  fileHandle <- openFile targetFilePath ReadMode
  contents <- TextIO.hGetContents fileHandle
  termSize <- getTerminalSize
  hSetBuffering stdout NoBuffering
  finfo <- fileInfo targetFilePath
  let pages = paginate termSize finfo contents
  showPages pages
```

We've eliminated a lot of the nesting and it's easier to focus on the calls that are being made. There are still some small improvements that we can make though. For one thing, we've completely eliminated all uses of >>= in this version of the function, but we can combine do notation with >>= to make code that's easier to read than using either style alone.

For example, let's consider the process of opening our file and reading the contents. We are creating fileHandle as an intermediate variable, and then using it immediately to pass as an argument to TextIO.hGetContents. We could use TextIO.readFile here and eliminate the need for a file handle, but for the sake of the example, let's say we want to keep each step of this explicit.

In this case, the intermediate variable isn't adding any value, but it does add visual noise that can make it harder for us to see what's going on. In an ideal world, each binding in our do block would correspond to a meaningful IO action that we want to do. We can often make that happen by combining related IO actions using >>= and then binding the output.

The big drawback to using >>= in a do block is that we can naturally read do bindings right to left, from the IO action to the variable being bound to its output. On the other hand, we'll typically read >>= from left to right. Switching the direction that we need to read the code in the middle of a line introduces some mental overhead.

To make this easier, we can use =<<. As you might expect from looking at it, =<< behaves exactly like >>= but with the arguments reversed. This lets us write a do binding that can entirely be read from right to left.

Let's refactor our program again using this approach to see how it works in practice:

```
runHCat :: IO ()
runHCat = do
  targetFilePath <- eitherToErr =<< handleArgs
  contents <- TextIO.hGetContents =<< openFile targetFilePath ReadMode
```

```
  termSize <- getTerminalSize
  hSetBuffering stdout NoBuffering
  finfo <- fileInfo targetFilePath
  let pages = paginate termSize finfo contents
  showPages pages
```

In cases where you have several IO actions that you want to chain together, using =<< can also be difficult to use while keeping your code readable. In cases like this, it can be convenient to use nested do blocks:

```
runHCat :: IO ()
runHCat = do
  targetFilePath <- do
    args <- handleArgs
    eitherToErr args

  contents <- do
    handle <- openFile targetFilePath ReadMode
    TextIO.hGetContents handle

  termSize <- getTerminalSize
  hSetBuffering stdout NoBuffering
  finfo <- fileInfo targetFilePath
  let pages = paginate termSize finfo contents
  showPages pages
```

Nesting do blocks is an effective way to keep all relevant code in a single function, but avoid having too many bindings in scope at the top level of your function.

Summary

This has been a long chapter, and you should take a moment to congratulate yourself for making it through. In this chapter, we've tackled some of the biggest obstacles that people encounter when trying to learn how to use Haskell in the real world, and we did it by focusing on real-world problems and how to solve them practically using the tools that Haskell provides us. Many of the concepts that you learned in this chapter will come up many more times throughout the rest of the book, and throughout the programs that you write. Take time to work through the exercises at the end of the chapter, and to review the content if there are areas where you feel like you might need a review. This stuff can be a little tricky and it's okay to come back later for a refresher!

Exercises

Now that you've built a complete application that handles IO and does some real work, take a some time to work through these exercises. The concepts you learned in this chapter will be critical as you work through the rest of the book, so it will be beneficial to ensure that you have a solid understanding of the concepts here.

If you run into an exercise that you are having trouble completing, try going back and reviewing this chapter, as well as some previous chapters. If you are still having difficulty, move on to the next chapter but plan to come back and revisit the exercise again later.

Handling Terminal Size Edge Cases

In our `getTerminalSize` function, there were several potential bugs that could have occurred. Try addressing these edge cases:

- `tput` is missing
- `tput` doesn't return a number
- `tput` output doesn't contain a trailing newline

Do-ing Some Refactoring

Throughout most of this chapter we used bind syntax to implement our IO actions. Look through some of the code you've written for opportunities to refactor this application to use `do` notation where appropriate.

Refactoring to Use Text and ByteString

Many of the earlier exercises in this book used `String` instead of `ByteString` or `Text`. Refactor some of your existing code to use these more efficient types instead.

Viewing Multiple Files

Expand your application to allow the user to pass more than one file in on the command line, and view them in order. Make sure to update the status line when you go from showing one file to another.

Scrolling Backwards

Instead of just scrolling forward, update your application to allow the user to scroll backwards as well.

Add a Help Screen

Allow the user to view help text on how to use the program by entering `?` while viewing a file. The program should clear the screen and display a help message.

Once the user scrolls past the end of the help text or presses `q`, the program should return them to where they were in the document.

Terminal Resizing

Sometimes users will want to resize their terminals while viewing a document. This is a problem for our pager since we calculate the size of the terminal exactly once at the start of the program. Update your program to allow the user to resize the terminal while retaining their current place in the document (the first word on the screen before resizing should still be the first word on the screen after resizing, regardless of how much the screen space has increased or decreased).

Note that detecting changes to the size of the terminal automatically will be unreasonably difficult with the knowledge that you have learned so far in this book, so you should handle terminal resizing by allowing the user to press a key to reflow the text.

CHAPTER 9

Introducing Monads

Over the last two chapters, you learned about the the `Functor` and `Monad` type classes by writing code that interacted with the real world using `IO`. Although `IO` is a great introduction to these type classes, there are many other ways that `Functor` and `Monad` are useful that have nothing to do with side effects or `IO`.

`Monad` in particular has a bit of a reputation in Haskell as being both extremely important as well as difficult to learn. Throughout this chapter, you'll work your way up to creating your own `Monad` type class and writing your own `Monad` instances incrementally. In the process, you'll learn the hows and whys that will remove some of the mystery from the type class.

Before we can dive into the details of monads though, we'll need to spend some time with two other other important type classes, `Functor` and `Applicative`. These three type classes form a hierarchy. All `Monad` instances must also have an `Applicative` instance, and all `Applicative` instances must in turn also have a `Functor` instance. We'll start by working our way through these three type classes from bottom to top, starting with `Functor`. You'll have the chance to create your own definitions for these type classes, and reimplement the instances for several common types to get a handle on how they work. Finally, at the end of the chapter we'll look at the rules that govern how these instances should be implemented so that they are well behaved and work as you would expect.

Mapping Functors

A `Functor` is a simple type class that has just two functions, `fmap` and `<$`. As you'll see throughout the rest of this book, `Functor` instances are extremely common in Haskell, and you're likely to work with this type class in nearly every program you write. Before we dive into what a `Functor` is, let's take a look at how we could define the type class ourselves if it wasn't already provided for us in `base`:

```
class Functor f where
  fmap :: (a -> b) -> f a -> f b
  (<$) :: a -> f b -> f a
  (<$) a fb = fmap (const a) fb
```

In addition to the functions defined in the type class, the <$> function is also defined in the standard library as an infix version of fmap. In most Haskell code, you'll see <$> being used at least as often as fmap, if not more so. Let's go ahead and add it to our example code:

```
infixl 4 <$>
(<$>) :: Functor f => (a -> b) -> f a -> f b
(<$>) = fmap
```

To understand what a Functor is, let's start by looking at what it *does*. The fmap function is the important function to think about when we're trying to understand Functor. Although (<$) is useful from time to time, it can be implemented in terms of fmap and understanding it doesn't really bring us a lot closer to understanding what a functor is.

The type of fmap is:

```
fmap :: (a -> b) -> f a -> f b
```

The type of fmap might look familiar; it's very similar to the type of the map function that you've been using for some time now:

```
map :: (a -> b) -> [a] -> [b]
```

This isn't a coincidence at all! In fact, lists are functors and the definition of fmap for a list is just map.

What can this similarity between map and fmap start to tell us about Functor? For one thing, it can help us start to understand that, just like map is about being able to work with the individual elements of a list without needing to be concerned about the overall shape or structure of the list, fmap gives us a way to work with values of anything that has a valid Functor instance without having to worry about whatever definition of structure is meaningful to the type we happen to be dealing with at the time.

Another equivalent way of thinking about Functor is to think of values as representing a "computation" or a "program." A value like [Int] is a computation that will generate several outputs, whereas Maybe Int is a computation that might not generate a value at all, and IO Int is a computation that will generate an Int but might also have some real-world side effects. In this view of the world, a Functor is a computation that allows us to change the type of result that it will generate by passing it a function.

Structure of Types

You can think of the structure of a value as its general "shape." For example, if you think of a list, the number and order of its elements provide its shape. If we have a list of numbers, we can convert them to strings, or add five to all of them without changing the number or order of the arguments. Another name for pattern matching is "destructuring," and you can use this to get an intuition about what structure means. When you could pattern match on something, for example, on a Maybe value, you're often matching on the structure.

The "structural" and "computational" views of Functor, as well as Applicative and Monad, are interchangeable. Whichever view of the problem you take, it won't change the way you approach code. Picking one view or another can, however, make it a bit easier to figure out what code to write, since different problems might lend themselves better to one view or another. Generally, in this book we'll prefer to take the structural view of things when we can, but throughout this chapter we'll examine both the structural and computational meaning of the type classes we're looking at so that you'll be prepared no matter what sort of problem comes along.

So, now that we have a general understanding of what they are, let's look at a couple of examples of creating instances of the Functor type class. We'll start with our old friend Maybe. If we think about what it would mean to "map" over a Maybe, we could say that one reasonable definition would be to apply a function to a value if we have one. Let's take a look at how we could write fmap for Maybe:

```
data Maybe a = Nothing | Just a
instance Functor Maybe where
  fmap _ Nothing = Nothing
  fmap f (Just a) = Just (f a)
```

Our implementation of fmap lines up with our idea of what mapping means for a Maybe value. If we have Nothing then we just return Nothing, but if we have some value, then we apply our function to that value. If you load up ghci we can test this out (don't worry about writing this code yourself, the standard library provides a Functor instance for Maybe for you already). In the following examples, we'll use a mixture of both fmap and <$> so you can see how they each look when they are being used:

```
-- Show the value, if there is one
λ show <$> Just 1
Just "1"
```

```
-- Increment the value, if there is one
λ (+1) <$> Just 1
Just 2

-- If there's a value, create a tuple of that value and its successor
λ  (\a -> (a, succ a)) <$> Just 9
Just (9, 10)

-- If we try to increment the value inside of Nothing, we still get Nothing
λ fmap (+1) Nothing
Nothing

-- Reverse the worder of words in a string, if we have one
λ (unwords . reverse . words) <$> Just "hello, world"
Just "world hello,"

-- Reversing the words in Nothing safely returns Nothing
λ fmap (unwords . reverse . words) Nothing
Nothing

-- The <$ function replaces the value with a different value
λ True <$ Just 4
Just True

-- If we replace the value inside of Nothing, we still get nothing
λ ("peanut butter", "jelly") <$ Nothing
Nothing

-- Even if we operate on a Nothing value, the types still change as expected
λ let nothing = Nothing :: Maybe Int
λ :type nothing
nothing :: Maybe Int
λ :type (True <$ Nothing)
(True <$ Nothing) :: Maybe Bool
```

Let's look at another example of something that implements the Functor type class in a similar way: lists. The standard library provides an implementation of Functor for lists using map, but let's write our own so that we can better get a feel for what's happening. We'll begin by creating a new list type, and adding a couple of utility functions to make it easier to work with:

```
data List a = Empty | List a (List a)

toList :: [a] -> List a
toList [] = Empty
toList (a:as) = List a (toList as)

fromList :: List a -> [a]
fromList Empty = []
fromList (List a as) = a : fromList as
```

The Functor instance for our list ends up looking quite a lot like the one we defined for Maybe. Calling fmap on an Empty list returns an Empty list, just like calling fmap on Nothing returns Nothing. When we have a non-empty list, we apply our function to the head of our list, and then fmap the rest of the list recursively. Let's see what it looks like in code:

```
instance Functor List where
  fmap _ Empty = Empty
  fmap f (List a as) = List (f a) (fmap f as)
```

Like with our Maybe example, we'll use the built-in standard library list and its Functor instance to visualize how this works in practice. Try it out with your own custom List type too.

```
-- map the successor function over all the elements in the list
λ succ <$> [1..5]
[2,3,4,5,6]

-- map then show function over all the elements in the list
λ show <$> [1..5]
["1","2","3","4","5"]

-- replease every element in the list with True
λ True <$ [1..5]
[True,True,True,True,True]

-- Replicate each element of the list 3 times
λ  replicate 3 <$> [1,2,3]
[[1,1,1],[2,2,2],[3,3,3]]

-- Replicate each element of the list and map the successor function to it
λ (succ <$>) . replicate 3 <$> [1,2,3]
[[2,2,2],[3,3,3],[4,4,4]]

-- Replicate each element of the list and map the successor function to it
-- then show the list
λ show . (succ <$>) . replicate 3 <$> [1,2,3]
["[2,2,2]","[3,3,3]","[4,4,4]"]

-- Replicate each element of the list and map a function that shows the the
-- successor of it
λ (show . succ <$>) . replicate 3 <$> [1,2,3]
[["2","2","2"],["3","3","3"],["4","4","4"]]
```

Another common type that has Functor instances is Either. As a reminder, we can write our own definition of Either this way:

```
data Either a b = Left a | Right b
```

The instance for Either is a little bit different from what we've seen so far with Maybe and lists. Both of those types have a single type parameter, but Either has *two* type parameters. What does that mean for our Functor instance? It means that we can't just go and create an instance of Functor directly, or we'll get an error that looks something like this:

```
Either.hs:12:18: error:
    • Expecting one more argument to ‘Either’
      Expected kind ‘* -> *’, but ‘Either’ has kind ‘* -> * -> *’
    • In the first argument of ‘Functor’, namely ‘Either’
      In the instance declaration for ‘Functor Either’
   |
12 | instance Functor Either where
   |                  ^^^^^^
```

This error might look a bit weird at first, because it's the first time we've run into a problem with *Kinds*. You can think of a Kind as "the type of a type." Just like functions have different types if they take different numbers of parameters, a type will have a different Kind if it has a different number of type parameters.

We can look at the kind of a type in ghci using the :kind command. Let's look at the kinds of a couple of types to understand what's going on a bit better.

The kind of a normal type with no parameters, like an Int or a String is *:

```
λ :kind Int
Int :: *

λ :kind String
String :: *
```

The kind of a type that has been given all of its type parameters is also *. You'll sometimes see types like this be referred to as *fully saturated*:

```
λ :kind Maybe Int
Maybe Int :: *

λ :kind [String]
[String] :: *

λ :kind Either String Int
Either String Int :: *

λ :kind (Int -> Bool)
(Int -> Bool) :: *
```

On the other hand, a type that still needs a type parameter will have the kind * -> *. You'll notice that this looks a lot like the syntax we use for functions, and that's a good intuition. We can think of types like this as functions that take a type as a parameter and return a type:

```
λ :kind Maybe
Maybe :: * -> *

λ :kind []
[] :: * -> *
```

```
λ :kind Either String
Either String :: * -> *

λ :kind (forall a. a -> Int)
(forall a. a -> Int) :: *
```

And just like a function that takes two parameters will have a different type than a function that takes one parameter, a type constructor that takes two parameters will have a different kind than a type constructor that takes a single parameter. For example, let's compare the kinds of Maybe, which take a single type parameter, to the kind of Either, which takes two type parameters:

```
λ :kind Maybe
Maybe :: * -> *

λ :kind Either
Either :: * -> * -> *
```

If we look at the type of fmap, we're talking about a type that takes a single type parameter, and that means that its kind has to be * -> *.

```
fmap :: (a -> b) -> m a -> m b
```

So, when we try to create an instance of Functor using Either, which has the kind * -> * -> *, the compiler will let us know that we can't do that, because the kind of Either doesn't match the kind that it was expecting.

So, what do we do? If we apply a type to Either then we'll get a type with the kind that we need. Of course, we don't want to pick any specific type, but we can use a type variable to allow anything for the first type parameter:

```
instance Functor (Either a) where
```

If we think back to the type of fmap, we had a type variable, m, that had the kind * -> *. In this case, we're going to substitute m for Either a, so the type of fmap would be:

```
fmap :: (b -> c) -> (Either a) b -> (Either a) c
```

The parentheses around (Either a) here are to illustrate how we've replaced m with Either a. Normally we'd write:

```
fmap :: (b -> c) -> Either a b -> Either a c
```

So, applying a type variable lets us get the right kind, and create a Functor instance for Either. What, if anything, does this mean about how we will implement the instance?

In the case of Either, where the first type parameter corresponds to Left values, and the second type parameter corresponds to Right values, it means that fmap is only going to operate on Right values. Much like how fmap ignores Nothing values for Maybe, it will ignore Left values for Either a. Knowing that, our implementation is short and looks a lot like the instance we defined for Maybe:

```
instance Functor (Either a) where
  fmap f (Left a) = Left a
  fmap f (Right a) = Right (f a)
```

After all of this, you might find yourself asking, "What if we wanted to define a version of fmap that worked on Left values instead of Right ones?" Or more generally, "What if we want to define an instance on some type parameter other than the last one?"

Unfortunately, there's not an easy way to handle this. When we're working with functions and values, we have ways of easily applying a value to the second argument of a function; for type class instances we're limited to applying types left-to-right in order.

If you do find yourself in a situation where you need to do this, generally the best approach is to use a newtype wrapper with the order of the type parameters reversed:

```
newtype ReverseEither a b = ReverseEither (Either b a)
  deriving Show

instance Functor (ReverseEither a) where
  fmap f (ReverseEither (Left a)) = ReverseEither (Left (f a))
  fmap f (ReverseEither (Right a)) = ReverseEither (Right a)
```

Finally, before we move on to Applicative let's look at one final example of a Functor that might not be quite so intuitive at first: functions. The normal everyday (->) style functions that we've been using since the very beginning of the book are another example of Functors. We'll implement our own version as an example shortly, but before we do, let's use ghci to look at an example:

```
-- create a new function that we can fmap. Its type is: Int -> Int
λ addOne n = n + 1

-- show has type Int -> String, addOneAndShow is also Int -> String
λ addOneAndShow = show <$> addOne

-- reverse here has type String -> String, as does addOneShowAndReverse
λ addOneShowAndReverse = reverse <$> addOneAndShow

-- it works just like function composition would have
λ addOneShowAndReverse 50
"15"

-- And for good measure, let's redefine both right next to one another
λ withComposition = reverse . show . (+1)
λ withFmap = reverse <$> show <$> (+1)
```

```
-- See, they work just the same!
λ withComposition 1024
"5201"
λ withFmap 1024
"5201"
```

To see how this works, we'd like to implement it ourselves. Reimplementing (->) would be a bit tricky, so let's use a newtype to recreate the same behavior for our own definition of function.

We'll start by creating a type called Function:

```
newtype Function a b = Function
  { runFunction :: a -> b }
```

Just like with Either, Function is a type with two type parameters. In this case, the first parameter is the input type to the function, and the second parameter is the output type. Just like with Either, we'll need to apply a type variable Function first so that we can create a Functor instance:

```
instance Functor (Function a) where
```

When we applied a type variable Either it meant that fmap couldn't access Left values, but functions don't have left and right values, so what's the implication for functions?

Calling fmap might change the type of the second type parameter, but it won't ever touch the first type parameter. For Function that means fmap might change the return type of the function, but won't ever change the type of its argument.

Let's look at an example of the type of fmap when we're talking about Function values:

```
fmap :: (b -> c) -> Function a b -> Function a c
```

This might still make it a little hard to see what's going on. Let's look at the type of fmap for a regular (->) function:

```
fmap :: (b -> c) -> (a -> b) -> (a -> c)
```

If that looks familiar, it's because if we strip some unnecessary parentheses then we can see it's exactly the same type as the function composition operator, (.):

```
(.) :: (b -> c) -> (a -> b) -> a -> c
```

So, writing a Functor instance for Function is nothing more than function composition:

```
instance Functor (Function a) where
  fmap f (Function g) = Function (f . g)
```

Applying Applicatives

Now that you've seen several different examples of types that can have a lawful Functor instance, let's move on and take a look at Applicative:

```
class Functor f => Applicative f where
  pure   :: a -> f a

  infixl 4 <*>
  (<*>)  :: f (a -> b) -> f a -> f b
```

One thing that is new here is the use of => to define a constraint as part of our type class definition. This works just like it does when you use type constraints in functions. In this case, it allows us to express that anything that can be an instance of Applicative must also provide an instance for Functor. We won't see any examples of this until later chapters, but you can also introduce constraints when you define instances.

The Applicative type class that we've defined has two functions that we really care about: pure, and the unfortunately hard to pronounce (<*>). The real Applicative type class also has three extra functions: liftA2, (*>) and (<*). We'll ignore those last three for now, because they can all be implemented in terms of pure and (<*>).

So, what is an Applicative? In the structural view of the world, we said that Functor represents a class of things that allow us apply a function that would change the type or value of the Functor without changing its underlying structure. In this structural view of things, an Applicative allows you to use pure to introduce a plain value while giving it some new structure, and it allows you to use (<*>) to take two values that each have their own structure and to combine those structures in some way.

Alternatively, in the computational view of the world we said that a Functor was something that would allow us to provide a function to modify the result that we would eventually end up computing. In this computational view of the world, pure allows us to introduce some pure value into a new computation. IO is a great example of this. If we create an IO action using pure, we get back a pure IO action that will result in the value we originally passed in without having any other side effects. In the computational view of (<*>), we can create a new computation that will generate its result by evaluating two other computations and combining their results. For example, if we view Maybe as a computation that might or might not complete, then when we say f <*> a, we are creating a new computation that will return a value if, and only if, it can run the computation f and get a function, and run the computation a to get a value to apply to that function. If either of those computations fail, then the entire computation fails.

Let's look at a couple of complete examples of creating Applicative instances so that we can get a better feel for how they work. We'll start again with Maybe. The Applicative instance for Maybe is short and simple:

```
instance Applicative Maybe where
  pure = Just
  Nothing <*> _ = Nothing
  Just f  <*> a = f <$> a
```

As you learned earlier, pure is typically defined by a constructor. In the case of Maybe, we can use Just, which already does exactly what we need. Our definition of <*> is also pretty straightforward. The applicative instance of Maybe lets us apply an optional function, so if the function we want to apply is Nothing, then we return Nothing. If we have a real function value, then we apply it using fmap.

Like we did with functors, let's run through a few examples of using the applicative instance for Maybe so that we can get a feel for how it works:

```
-- Pure returns Just value
λ pure 1 :: Maybe Int
Just 1
-- <*> Applies Just func to Just val giving Just (func val)
λ Just (+1) <*> pure 1
Just 2
-- Just func <*> Nothing returns Nothing
λ Just (unwords . reverse . words)  <*> Nothing
Nothing
-- Create a function that returns an optional function
λ let addSome x = if x < 5 then Just (+x) else Nothing
-- If we get a function then we can apply it
λ addSome 3 <*> Just 1
Just 4
-- If we get Nothing then we return Nothing
λ addSome 5 <*> Just 1
Nothing
```

Just like with functor, Either a also has an Applicative instance, and it is quite similar to the instance we've just defined for Maybe:

```
instance Applicative (Either a) where
  pure a = Right a
  (Left err) <*> _ = Left err
  (Right f) <*> g = f <$> g
```

Not all of the Applicative instances we can define are quite as straightforward as their Functor counterparts though. Lists, for example, have a bit more structure to them than Either or Maybe, and so we have to do a little bit more work to write a reasonable Applicative instance.

Let's continue with our own List type and look into what an Applicative list instance looks like. We'll start with pure:

```
instance Applicative List where
  pure a = List a Empty
```

The definition of pure does turn out to be fairly straightforward: we have a value and we create the minimal required structure to hold that value, which is a single-element list.

What about (<*>)? To write an implementation of <*>, we need to think about what it means to merge the structure of two lists. With Maybe we returned Nothing if we had no function. The equivalent for lists would be to return an empty list if we have an empty list of functions, so let's start there:

```
Empty <*> _ = Empty
```

So far, so good, but if we have a non-empty list on the left, then that's a structure that we somehow have to combine with the list, empty or not, on the right. How can we do this?

Each element of our left-hand list is a function. One place to start with would be to fmap each of those functions over the right-hand list. We could try by writing this:

```
a <*> b = fmap (`fmap` b) a
```

Unfortunately this won't work. The type of the function we've just defined is:

```
List (a -> b) -> List a -> List (List b)
```

But our fmap implementation is required to have the type:

```
fmap :: (a -> b) -> List a -> List b
```

The only reasonable thing we can do is to concatenate each of the lists that we are generating by fmaping the elements of our first list onto our second list. That means we'll need to write a function to concatenate lists:

```
-- Equivalent to (<>) on regular lists
concatList :: List a -> List a -> List a
concatList Empty as = as
concatList (List a as) bs = List a (concatList as bs)
```

Now that we have a way of combining lists, we can use it to write the rest of our applicative instance. For each function in our left-hand list, we'll want to fmap the function over the right-hand list, and then concatenate that list to the result of calling <*> on the rest of the left-hand operand:

```
List f fs <*> vals =
  (fmap f vals) `concatList` (fs <*> vals)
```

Here's the final version of our applicative instance with everything put together:

```
instance Applicative List where
  pure a = List a Empty
  Empty <*> _ = Empty
  List f fs <*> vals = (f <$> vals) `concatList` (fs <*> vals)
```

Finally, let's again run through a few examples of how we can use the applicative instance for List so that we can start to develop an intuition for how it works:

```
-- define funcList and numList to use throughout these examples
λ let funcList = toList [id, succ, (*2)]
λ let numList = toList [1..5]
-- the result of <*> is the concatenation of each function fmapped to the list
λ fromList $ funcList <*> numList
[1,2,3,4,5,2,3,4,5,6,2,4,6,8,10]
-- Using an empty list as the left-hand operand returns and empty list
λ fromList $ Empty <*> numList
[]
-- Using an empty list as the right-hand operand returns and empty list
λ fromList $ funcList <*> Empty
[]
-- We can combine pure with <*> to apply a single function to our list
λ fromList $ pure (replicate 2) <*> numList
[[1,1],[2,2],[3,3],[4,4],[5,5]]
```

As a final example, let's also consider Function and what an Applicative instance for it might look like. Just like all of our examples so far, pure is fairly easy: we can lift a pure value into a function by writing a function that always returns that value:

```
instance Applicative (Function a) where
  pure a = Function $ const a
```

Our definition of (<*>) will be trickier. Let's start by looking at the types involved. Remember that the general type of (<*>) is:

```
(<*>) :: f (a -> b) -> f a -> f b
```

For Function in particular, that means:

```
(<*>) :: Function a (b -> c) -> Function a b -> Function a c
```

The first thing we have to ask ourselves is, what does Function a (b -> c) even mean? If we strip away the newtype wrapper, it means we have a function of the type:

```
a -> (b -> c)
```

Of course we can remove the parentheses here and see that what we're really talking about is just:

```
a -> b -> c
```

To make things a little bit more clear, let's also look at the unwrapped version of (<*>) for plain functions:

```
fmap :: (a -> b -> c) -> (a -> b) -> a -> c
```

That's a little bit of something to try to wrap our heads around! Thankfully, we can get some help if we let the type drive our implementation. Let's start writing this with some blank spots, and fill them in as we think through what we need to do to satisfy the required type. We'll start by just writing the left-hand side of the implementation:

```
Function f <*> Function g =
```

Here, f will have the type f :: a -> b -> c and g will have the type g :: a -> b. Let's keep those in mind as we take a step forward. We need to return a value with the type Function a c. That means we need to return a function that takes a value of type a:

```
Function f <*> Function g = Function $ \value ->
```

We need to return a value of type c and the only way to get one is to call f with a value of type a and a value of type b. value has type a so we can start there:

```
Function f <*> Function g = Function $ \value ->
  f value _
```

We also need to pass f a value of type b. The only way to get one of those is to apply value to g. That gives us the final version of our (<*>) implementation for Function:

```
instance Applicative (Function a) where
  pure a = Function $ const a
  Function f <*> Function g = Function $ \value -> f value (g value)
```

In reality, the Applicative instance of functions doesn't come up all that often in this form, but it's helpful to understand that there is a valid instance so that you don't get overly fixated on the idea of these type classes as "containers." The Applicative instance of functions does give rise to one particularly interesting piece of code golf though. We can use it to define an extremely terse implementation of the Fibonacci sequence:

```
λ fibs = 0 : 1 : (zipWith (+) <*> tail) fibs
λ take 10 fibs
[0,1,1,2,3,5,8,13,21,34]
```

Now that we've looked at functors and applicatives, we can look at monads. In the next section, we'll talk about monads and how they relate to IO and interacting with the local system.

Working with the Monad Type Class

For all of the virtual ink spilled in pursuit of monad tutorials, the reality is that monads aren't actually as complicated or terrible as everyone makes them out to be. Monad is actually just a type class, with a few rules about how the functions defined in the type class should work.

```
class Applicative m => Monad m where
  infixl 1 >>=
  (>>=)  :: m a -> (a -> m b) -> m b

  infixl 1 >>
  (>>)   :: m a -> m b -> m b
  a >> b = a >>= \_ -> b

  return :: a -> m a
```

These functions should all look pretty familiar! Nearly everything that we've been doing so far with IO in this chapter comes from its Monad type class instance! You'll also recognize Applicative from the last section, so with every monad you'll also get functions that work with Functor and Applicative like fmap and <*>.

The return function from the Monad type class looks very similar to pure, and as you'll see later, these should generally be implemented in the same way. Like <*>, the >>= function is how monads manage structure while applying a function. Unlike Applicative though, monads focus on the relationship between the structure of the input value and the structure of the output value of the applied function. That probably sounds pretty abstract, so let's look at a couple of concrete examples to help cement our understanding of what's going on. Like with functors and applicatives, we'll start with the Monad instance for Maybe and then we'll look at List.

```
instance Monad Maybe where
  return = Just
  Nothing >>= _ = Nothing
  Just a >>= f = f a
```

Our Monad instance for Maybe is pretty simple. Just like with pure, our return function lifts a value into Maybe by calling Just to construct a Maybe value. The implementation of >>= is almost but not quite the same as our fmap implementation. When we have Nothing we return Nothing. If we get Just a though, we simply pass the inner value into our function.

Let's look at a few examples of how we can use this. We'll need to start by defining a few functions that will return a Maybe. We'll use readMaybe from the Text.Read module that's part of the standard library. It's a safer version of read that returns Nothing if it can't parse the value. We'll also define two functions ourselves to let us play around with the Monad instance of Maybe:

```
import Text.Read (readMaybe)

-- Return half of a value if it's even, otherwise Nothing
half :: Int -> Maybe Int
half num =
  if even num
  then Just (num `div` 2)
  else Nothing

-- Takes a boundry.  Returns Just the value if it's within the range,
-- and Nothing otherwise
bound :: (Int, Int) -> Int -> Maybe Int
bound (min, max) num =
  if (num >= min) && (num <= max)
  then Just num
  else Nothing
```

Now that we have some utility functions to use, let's use them to look at some ways we can use Maybe as a monad:

```
-- Every function returns a Just value
λ readMaybe "10" >>= half >>= bound (0,5)
Just 5
-- Trying to parse "Ten" fails, giving a Nothing for the entire expression
λ readMaybe "Ten" >>= half >>= bound (0,5)
Nothing
-- parsing succeeds, but we get Nothing from calling `half 11`
λ readMaybe "11" >>= half >>= bound (0,10)
Nothing
-- we can use return to put a pure function into a series of >>= calls
λ readMaybe "11" >>= bound (0,20) >>= return . succ >>= half
Just 6
```

Like we've seen earlier in this chapter with IO, we can use >>= to help us build a sequence of functions that are evaluated in order. Let's write an Applicative instance for our List type next so we can look at another example of writing a monad.

Like with our definition of pure, our definition of return just needs to create a new single element list:

```
instance Monad List where
  return a = List a Empty
```

For our definition of >>= we'll return an empty list if we get one as input, just like we did with our definition of <*>:

```
Empty >>= f = Empty
```

Now, we just need to write the rest of our implementation of >>=. Just like we did with our implementation of <*>, we'll work with one element at a time. We'll apply our function to each element of the list, and concatenate the result with a call to >>= for the rest of the list. In fact, our implementation of >>= is almost exactly like our implementation of pure, except that we can use regular function application an element at a time instead of needing to fmap our function over an entire list.

Let's look at what a complete Monad instance for List looks like:

```
instance Monad List where
  return a = List a Empty
  Empty >>= f = Empty
  List a as >>= f =  (f a) `concatList` (as >>= f)
```

Just like we did for Maybe, we'll add a few utility functions to make it easier for us to experiment with the Monad instance of List.

The first thing we'll do is define a Show instance for List so that we can work with it more easily from ghci. We'll just convert our List to a regular Haskell list and use its instance of Show for convenience:

```
instance Show a => Show (List a) where
  show = show . fromList
```

For this example, we'll need to add the OverloadedStrings extension. We'll also need to add a new extension, FlexibleInstances:

```
{-# LANGUAGE OverloadedStrings #-}
{-# LANGUAGE FlexibleInstances #-}
```

If you've been following along with ghci instead of using source files you can enable these with the :set command:

```
λ :set -XFlexibleInstances -XOverloadedStrings
```

We've previously used the OverloadedStrings extension to make it easier for us to create ByteString or Text values. In this example, we're going to use OverloadedStrings so that we can use string literals to create values of our own List type.

Once OverloadedStrings is enabled, we can use the string literal syntax to create a value for any type that has an instance of the IsString class from Data.String.

Before we can create a sensible instance of IsString, we'll also need to add the FlexibleInstances extension to remove some restrictions on how we can create instances of type classes. For our use-case, it will allow us to define an instance of a type class for one specific instance of a parameterized type. Since we only want to implement IsString for List Char, we'll need this language extension. FlexibleInstances is a generally safe language extension. It can sometimes require you to add additional type signatures where you wouldn't need to, and in rare cases can make your programs fail to compile. As a general rule of thumb, it's fine to include it if you need it.

FlexibleInstances

The FlexibleInstances extension has been available since GHC 6.8.1. It's enabled by default in GHC2021 but you'll need to enable it manually if you're using Haskell2010. This is a generally safe extension that shouldn't cause problems with any existing programs.

With those two language extensions, we can create an instance of IsString:

```
import Data.String

instance IsString (List Char) where
  fromString = toList
```

With this instance added, we can now create List Char values just like we would regular strings. Thanks to our Show instance we'll be able to view them too. Go ahead and try it out in ghci:

```
λ "Hello, Haskell" :: List Char
"Hello, Haskell"
```

Writing out List Char is going to get a little tedious so let's create a type alias to make it a little easier to work with in our examples:

```
type StringL = List Char
```

Finally, let's write a couple of functions to work with. Let's start by defining just the type signatures for the additional functions that we'd like to have:

```
replicateL :: Int -> a -> List a
wordsL     :: StringL -> List StringL
unwordsL   :: List StringL -> StringL
```

Try to create your own implementations of these functions based on the type signature before looking at the examples:

```
replicateL :: Int -> a -> List a
replicateL 0 _ = Empty
replicateL n a =
    let tail = replicateL (pred n) a
    in List a tail

wordsL :: StringL -> List StringL
wordsL = toList . map toList . words . fromList

unwordsL :: List StringL -> StringL
unwordsL = toList . unwords . fromList . (fromList <$>)
```

```
-- Create a nested list of numbers
λ let ll = toList (map return [1..5]) :: List (List Int)
-- Print it out so we know what we're staritng out
λ ll
[[1],[2],[3],[4],[5]]
-- (>>= id) will concatonate elements of a list
λ ll >>= id
[1,2,3,4,5]
-- We can mix pure from Applicative with >>= from Monad.
λ pure "hello haskell" >>= wordsL
["hello","haskell"]
-- Get the words from a string, repeat them 3 times
λ pure "hello haskell" >>= wordsL >>= replicateL 3
["hello","hello","hello","haskell","haskell","haskell"]
-- We can concat them by binding them to id again
λ pure "hello haskell" >>= wordsL >>= replicateL 3 >>= id
"hellohellohellohaskellhaskellhaskell"
-- But we can also call unwords to put them back into a string
λ unwordsL $ pure "hello haskell" >>= wordsL
"hello haskell"
-- If we pass our values into a function that returns an empty list,
-- we get an empty list back
λ unwordsL $ pure "hello haskell" >>= wordsL >>= const Empty
""
-- Same if we have an empty list in the middle
λ unwordsL $ pure "hello haskell" >>= const Empty >>= wordsL
""
```

That's it! You've been using the IO monad throughout this book, and now you've created instances of monads for two different types. You've also learned about functors and applicatives, which are closely related to monads, and created instances of those too. In the next section, we'll move beyond how to use this and look a little bit at some of the rules you should follow to make sure that your own functor, applicative, and monad instances are well behaved and work with all of the tooling the standard library provides to work with these sorts of types.

Understanding the Laws of the Land

Haskell functors, applicatives, and monads are more than just the functions given by their type classes. Each of these type classes also come with a set of laws that govern what the implementations should look like. While "laws" might sound rigid and formal, in reality, understanding these laws can be very helpful because they can often lead you to better understanding of how to create instances of these type classes in the first place. Many of these laws originated in pure mathematics, but you don't need to have a strong math background to follow this section. We'll walk through all of the laws purely using what you've learned about Haskell so far in this book. If you encounter unfamiliar math-y sounding terminology, don't worry about it too much. You can make a quick note of any unfamiliar terms and look them up later if you like. Understanding the terminology used in this section will be a little bit helpful in deepening your understanding, but a lack of familiarity shouldn't impede your ability to follow along.

There's nothing in the language that will give you an error if you violate these laws, and sometimes libraries do, so it's good to think of them more like guidelines that can lead you toward writing better code. Following the laws for functors, applicatives, and monads will make it much easier for you to reason about what your code is doing and will allow you to make use of all of the different functions that work with those type classes. In this section, we'll go over the laws that govern functors, monads, and applicatives. This section will be useful not only to help you understand the rules that govern how common types like IO work, but also to help you get practice in reading and understanding some of the more formal looking parts of the standard library documentation. If you find yourself having trouble with this section, bookmark it and come back to it after you've finished a few more chapters, and read through it again.

Using the Functor Laws

Functors are the simplest of our trio of type classes, and also have the simplest laws, so we'll start with them. There are two laws that well-behaved functors should adhere to, and they are both documented in the standard library documentation. There are two functor laws, *identity* and *composition*:

```
-- Identity
fmap id = id
-- Composition
fmap (f . g) = fmap f . fmap g
```

The identity law of functors is pretty simple: mapping the identity function shouldn't change the value of the functor. The implication is that fmap should only ever be a mapping function and shouldn't change anything in the functor except for the value that it's mapping. The second law, composition, follows naturally from the first. The law of composition says that it shouldn't matter whether we compose calls to fmap, or we fmap a composed function. Put simply, these two laws together state that fmap should "do nothing but simply apply the mapping to the value(s) inside the functor."

Both our Maybe and List implementations satisfied the functor laws, so let's look at an example of a Functor instance that violates the laws so that we can get a full picture of what sort of behavior they disallow. We'll create an Outlaw type that contains a value and a counter. Our outlaw will increment the counter every time we call fmap:

```
data Outlaw a = Outlaw Int a deriving (Eq, Show)

instance Functor Outlaw where
  fmap f (Outlaw cnt val) = Outlaw (cnt + 1) (f val)
```

Let's create a sample outlaw and a couple of helper functions to use when we look at testing our functor laws. We'll use the toUpper function from Data.Char to let us convert a String to uppercase

```
bang = (<> "!")
upcase = map Data.Char.toUpper
billyTheKid = Outlaw 0 "bank robber"
```

Now we can test our our identity law. We'll write a simple function that should return true if our identity law holds:

```
testIdentity =
  fmap id billyTheKid == id billyTheKid
```

If we run this, we'll see that we actually get back False, because our outlaw is violating the functor laws. We can see why if we run each side of our comparison in ghci:

```
λ testIdentity
False
λ fmap id billyTheKid
Outlaw 1 "bank robber"
λ id billyTheKid
Outlaw 0 "bank robber"
```

Since our outlaw's fmap function has the side effect of changing the counter, our functor law fails to hold. We can see a similar problem when we test the second functor law:

```
testComposition  =
  fmap (bang . upcase) billyTheKid == (fmap bang . fmap upcase $ billyTheKid)
```

```
λ testComposition
False
λ fmap (bang . upcase) billyTheKid
Outlaw 1 "BANK ROBBER!"
λ fmap bang . fmap upcase $ billyTheKid
Outlaw 2 "BANK ROBBER!"
```

Just like the case with our identity function test, the side effect of incrementing a counter causes us to get back a different value when we compose the functions before mapping compared to composing the calls to fmap.

The functor laws are useful guidelines that help us write programs that behave consistently and are easy to reason about. Whenever you're creating an instance of a type class like Functor, Applicative, or Monad, it's helpful to encode the laws as unit tests so that you can make sure that you've written an instance that adheres to the laws. In the rest of this section, we're going to look at the laws for monads and applicatives. As we go along, try to write some unit tests to ensure that your List instances for these type classes adhere to the laws.

Using the Monad Laws

Although Applicative comes before Monad in our type class hierarchy, the Monad laws are shorter and easier to understand, so let's focus on them before we conclude this section by looking at the laws for applicatives. There are three monad laws: left and right-hand identity laws, and a law of associativity. Let's look at how they are shown in the documentation for the standard library, and then we'll dig into them in detail:

```
-- identity (left)
return a >>= m = m s

-- identity (right)
m >>= return = m

-- Associativity
(a >>= b) >>= c = a >>= (\x -> b x >>= c)
```

The similarity between the monad and functor identity laws aren't as obvious written this way as they could be, so let's rewrite them slightly, and show them next to the functor identity law, to help make the parallel a bit easier to see:

```
-- Functor Identity law
fmap id f = id f
```

```
-- Monad Identity (Left) law
(>>=) (return a) f = f a
-- Monad Identity (Right) law
(>>=) m return = m
```

In the functor identity law, we said that we had restrictions around what we chould change when we called fmap. The monad identity laws are similar, telling us what we can change when we call >>=. Unlike our functor, the values inside of our monad can change when we call >>=. These laws also relate to what kind of a value we should get out of calling return.

This all sounds a little bit abstract, but if we think about it in terms of the IO monad, it's easier to reason about what the laws are trying to say.

Let's start by looking at one specific manifestation of the first law:

```
return "filename" >>= getcontents = getContents "filename"
```

If we put our filename into an IO action, and then use >>= to pass it to getContents we shouldn't expect it to behave any differently than if we'd just passed the filename in directly in the first place. This should make sense if you recall back on page 264 where we talk about how IO represents some changes that have happened out in the real world. The return function creates a blank slate where we haven't actually made any changes, and >>= makes sure that our changes happen in order. Looking at it this way, it should make sense that "First do these no changes at all, and then read the file" shouldn't behave any differently from just reading the file.

The second identity law is pretty similar to the first one. Let's restate it the same way that we did the first law:

```
getContents "filename" >>= return = getContents "filename"
```

Here we call getContents on our file, and then pass the contents to return with >>=. Our right-hand identity law basically says that the call to return shouldn't change anything. In IO terms, saying "open the file and then do nothing" should be the same as saying "open the file."

Our Maybe and List instances also obeyed these identity laws. Just like we did with Functor, let's look at an example of an outlaw monad that breaks the identity laws. We'll continue the trend of tracking how often fmap was called by adding a number to our counter every time we call >>=:

```
instance Monad Outlaw where
  return summary = Outlaw 0 summary
  (Outlaw cnt a) >>= f =
    let (Outlaw cnt' v) = f a
    in Outlaw (cnt + cnt' + 1) v
```

Like we did before we'll write a couple of manual test functions to see how the laws hold up with our outlaw monad. We'll also add a utility function to make it easier to test >>= operations.

```
stoleAHorse :: String -> Outlaw String
stoleAHorse = return . (<> " and horse robber")

testLeftIdentity =
  (return "robbed a bank" >>= stoleAHorse) == stoleAHorse "robbed a bank"

testRightIdentity =
  (billyTheKid >>= return) == billyTheKid
```

If we load these up into a REPL, we can see the same sorts of failures we had with our outlaw functor—introducing changes to our counter that didn't come from either of the operands to >>= cause our laws to be violated:

```
λ testLeftIdentity
False
λ return "robbed a bank" >>= stoleAHorse
Outlaw 1 "robbed a bank and horse robber"
λ stoleAHorse "robbed a bank"
Outlaw 0 "robbed a bank and horse robber"
λ testRightIdentity
False
λ billyTheKid >>= return
Outlaw 1 "bank robber"
λ billyTheKid
Outlaw 0 "bank robber"
```

Now that we've looked at how the first two monad laws work, and when they are violated, let's move on to the final monad law: associativity. Associativity is related to the order that we evaluate values. The most familiar example of associativity that you've probably seen is in arithmetic. Both addition and multiplication are associative, meaning that you can omit or move around parentheses however you want, but division and subtraction aren't associative, so changing the order of evaluation can change the output:

```
λ (2 + 3) + 4 == 2 + (3 + 4)
True
λ (2 * 3) * 4 == 2 * (3 * 4)
True
λ (2 - 3) - 4 == 2 - (3 - 4)
False
λ (2 / 3) / 4 == 2 / (3 / 4)
False
```

The associativity law for monads is really getting to the same point: the way that we group the monadic actions doesn't matter in the end, because >>=

ensures that they'll be evaluated in a consistent order. Let's look at this one in terms of IO actions to make it a little easier to understand:

```
λ openFile "/tmp/example.txt" ReadMode >>= hGetContents >>= putStrLn
Hello from "example.txt"

λ :{
*System.IO| openFile "/tmp/example.txt" ReadMode
*System.IO| >>= (\handle -> hGetContents handle >>= putStrLn)
*System.IO| :}
Hello from "example.txt"
```

We can't use == to compare IO actions, but if we look at what's happening in these examples, we can still understand what's going on with the associativity law. In both examples, we're opening a file handle, then reading the contents and printing them out. The law of associativity says that it doesn't matter how we group these IO actions. This might seem a little counterintuitive at first; after all, how can it *not matter* if we try to read the contents of a file and print them out before we open the file? This sort of composability is available thanks to lazy evaluation. If you look back on page 277 and remember how IO is evaluated, you'll understand how the particulars of the way Haskell treats evaluating IO allows it to fulfill this property.

Using the Applicative Laws

The last of the type class laws that we'll look at are the laws for Applicative. Applicative has four laws, and they are a bit trickier than the laws for Functor and Monad. In particular, the names of the laws might sounds a bit more intimidating, but as we've seen in the last two sets of laws, we can follow the code and write tests to get a feel for how our particular instances are holding up to the laws without having to delve too deeply into the underlying mathematical theory. Let's start with the applicative laws as they are documented in the standard library:

```
-- Identity
pure id <*> v = v
-- Composition
pure (.) <*> u <*> v <*> w = u <*> (v <*> w)
-- Homomorphism
pure f <*> pure x = pure (f x)
-- Interchange
u <*> pure y = pure ($ y) <*> u
```

The applicative identity law is pretty much like the identity laws for monads and functors. Since we've seen two similar examples already, you should be able to work through this example yourself.

The composition law of applicatives looks a little bit more complicated than the composition law for functors, but it's actually pretty similar. Let's take a minute to unpack it and try to really understand what's happening.

Recall that the type for <*> is `Applicative f => f (a -> b) -> f a -> f b`, and the type for `.` is `(.) :: (b -> c) -> (a --> b) -> a -> c`. So when we say `pure (.)` we're getting back something like: `f ((b -> c) -> (a -> b) -> a -> c)`. That means that the `u` and `v` in our law need to be functions. So we could rewrite our law so it looks like this:

```
pure ((b -> c) -> (a ->b) -> a -> c)
  <*> f (b -> c)
  <*> f (a -> b)
  <*> f a
  == f (b -> c)
  <*> (f (a -> b) <*> f a)
```

Wow! That's a lot of arrows! Let's see if we can simplify this a little bit more so it's easier to parse.

The first part of this law is that we're composing two functions inside of our applicative. We've got two functions to start with:

```
u :: f (b -> c)
v :: f (a -> b)
```

And we have a single value:

```
w :: f a
```

We want to get out a value with the type `f c`. The most obvious way we might do that is to first call `v` on `w` with <*>:

```
w' :: f b
w' = v <*> w
```

Then we can call `u` on `w'`:

```
result :: f c
result = u <*> w'
```

If we write it all together as a single expression we get:

```
result :: f c
result = u <*> (v <*> w)
```

If we were dealing with regular functions instead of applicatives, we could write this quite simply:

```
result :: c
result = g (f a)
```

And if we were writing it with functors we might say:

```
result :: f c
result = fmap g . fmap f
```

We might naturally think that it would be nice to compose functions with . instead of calling them one after another. Since we're working inside of an applicative, we'll start by lifting composition into our applicative:

```
apCompose :: f ((b -> c) -> (a -> b) -> a -> c)
apCompose = pure (.)
```

Now we can compose our two applicative functions. We start with u:

```
u' :: f ((a -> b) -> a -> c)
u' = apCompose <*> u
```

And next we bring in v:

```
v' :: f (a -> c)
v' = u' <*> v
```

And finally we can apply our newly composed function to get a value:

```
result :: f c
result = v' <*> w
```

If we write all that as a single expression, we get the left-hand side of our composition law:

```
result :: f c
result = pure (.) <*> u <*> v <*> w
```

So our applicative law of composition says that no matter which way we want to go about trying to apply our functions, we should always get the same value back out.

The next applicative law is the law of *homomorphism*. Homomorphism is one of those words that can sometimes make Haskell sound scary and overly formal, but we're not going to spend any time on formally defining it. Instead, we'll just look at the law and show how it follows from the intuition that we've built up around how some of these laws work. The law of homomorphism says that:

```
pure f <*> pure x = pure (f x)
```

To put it in English: lifting a function and a value into our applicative with pure and then applying the function with <*> should give us the same value as just lifting the result of calling the function on the value. This is another law that formalizes the notion that <*> really shouldn't be doing much except for applying the mapping, and that pure should be giving us some sort of reasonable initial value.

We can use lists as a good example of how this works. Let's look at an example:

```
λ pure succ <*> pure 1 :: [Int]
[2]
-- This is the same as if we'd said
λ [succ] <*> [1]
[2]
-- Our monad law says this should be the same
λ (pure succ <*> pure 1 :: [Int]) == (pure (succ 1))
True
-- The same thing words with Maybe Int too
λ pure succ <*> pure 1 :: Maybe Int
Just 2
λ (pure succ <*> pure 1 :: Maybe Int) == (pure (succ 1))
True
```

These examples show that well-behaved applicatives follow the law of homomorphism, and how following these laws makes our code easy to reason about. Thanks to this law, we can either lift a function and its argument using `pure` before applying them with `(<*>)`, or we can use ordinary function application and lift the result with `pure` afterwards.

The last applicative law is the law of *interchange*. Interchange is related to commutivity, and the law of interchange provides a way that we can sort of flip the operands of `<*>` in a predictable way. The law is given as:

```
u <*> pure y = pure ($ y) <*> u
```

The left-hand side of the law is the usual application with applicatives. The right-hand side might look a bit weird, so let's break it down.

We'll start using the left-hand side to fill in some things that we know:

```
result :: f b
result = u <*> pure y

u :: f (a -> b)
y :: a
pure y :: f a
```

So, we know that the right-hand side needs to evaluate to a type of `f b`:

```
result :: f b
result = pure ($ y) <*> u
```

Let's take a minute to recall that the type of `$` is `($) :: (a -> b) -> a -> b`. Since we already know `y :: a`, then we know that the expression `($ y)` must have the type `(a -> b) -> b`. When we lift that into our applicative with `pure` we get:

```
pure ($ y) :: f ((a -> b) -> b)
```

When we apply u to that expression with <*> we're effectively applying a value of type f (a -> b) to a function of type f ((a -> b) -> b), giving us a result value of f b.

Let's look back at the law one more time now that we've walked through all of the parts, and then we'll look at a simple example of it in practice:

```
u <*> pure y = pure ($ y) <*> u
```

We can demonstrate this law with Maybe:

```
λ let u = pure succ :: Maybe (Int -> Int)
λ u <*> pure 3
Just 4
λ pure ($ 3) <*> u
Just 4
λ (u <*> pure 4) == (pure ($ 4) <*> u)
True
```

The law of interchange allows us to compose functions in different ways while still being able to reason effectively about the results.

The functor, monad, and applicative laws will make it easier for you to figure out how to write instances for your own types. In fact, you may find that frequently there's only one implementation that actually follows all of the laws. As you spend more time working with these type classes, having an understanding of the underlying laws will also make it easier to reason about what your code is doing. As you're working through that section, and the rest of this chapter, keep an eye out for how code we write and decisions that we make are influenced by these laws.

Summary

In this chapter, you learned about the Functor, Applicative, and Monad type classes, and how to work with *lawful* type classes. You'll work with these type classes regularly, so getting a good understanding of how they work and why they work they way they do is useful. Of equal importance, in this chapter you got a chance to see first hand how to design and implement type classes that have a wide variety of uses with highly divergent behavior that still adhere to the basic laws of the classes.

Later on in this book on page 435 you'll build your own parser and define new Functor, Applicative, and Monad instances for a brand new type of computation. After that, you'll learn how build new Monad instances by composing the behaviors of existing instances using Monad Transformers on page 467.

Exercises

Flipping the Script

Try to write instances of Functor, Applicative, and Monad for List where Functor is defined in terms of Applicative, and Applicative is defined in terms of Monad. Is this possible? Why or why not?

Not a Functor

Imagine that we've created a new type to represent a *sorted* list of values:

```
{-# LANGUAGE DerivingStrategies #-}
module SortedListFunctor (SortedList, insertSorted) where

data SortedList a = Empty | Cons a (SortedList a)
  deriving stock (Eq, Show)

insertSorted :: Ord a => a -> SortedList a -> SortedList a
insertSorted a Empty = Cons a Empty
insertSorted a (Cons b bs)
  | a >= b = Cons b (insertSorted a bs)
  | otherwise = Cons a (Cons b bs)
```

Although SortedList might be useful, it turns out that you can't write a *correct* instance of Functor for a SortedList. Try to define Functor yourself and experiment with its behavior. See if you can figure out why you can't write a correct instance.

The Extended Functor Family

In addition to the standard Functor class that you've used in this chapter, there are other type classes that are related to Functor but with somewhat different behaviors.

Bifunctors

A Bifunctor is like a Functor but even more so, because a Bifunctor lets you map two different fields. The Bifunctor class is defined in Data.Bifunctor. Let's take a look at a definition for it:

```
class Bifunctor f where
  bimap :: (a -> c) -> (b -> d) -> f a b -> f c d

  first :: (a -> c) -> f a b -> f c b
  first f = bimap f id

  second :: (b -> d) -> f a b -> f a d
  second f = bimap id f
```

Try to write an instance of Bifunctor for Either.

Contravariant Functors

The Contravariant class from Data.Functor.Contravariant in base defines a _contravariant_ functor. Although we don't normally refer to them this way, the Functor class that you've been working with so far is a *covariant* functor. You don't need to worry about the terminology too much though. You can think of this as a "backwards" functor. Let's look at its definition:

```
class Contravariant f where
  contramap :: (b -> a) -> f a -> f b
```

Try to create a new version of the Function type that you defined earlier, and then write an instance of Contravariant for it. Can you also create an instance of Contravariant for your original definition of Function? Why or why not?

Profunctors

A Profunctor is a combination of a Bifunctor and a Contravariant functor. Profunctor isn't defined in base, but you'll see it defined by some other popular libraries. Like a Bifunctor, it works on types with two arguments. Like Contravariant functors, the first argument to a Profunctor works "backwards." Let's take a look at a definition for Profunctor:

```
class Profunctor f where
  dimap :: (c -> a) -> (b -> d) -> f a b -> f c d

  lmap :: (c -> a) -> f a b -> f c b
  lmap f = dimap f id

  rmap :: (b -> d) -> f a b -> f a d
  rmap f = dimap id f
```

Try to create an instance of Profunctor for your original Function type. Can you write a valid instance? Why or why not? How does this differ from trying to create a instance of Contravariant for Function?

CHAPTER 10

Mutable Data in the Real World

Using Mutable References in a Pure Language

Mutable data, that is, data that has a value that you can change over time as your program is running, is an idea that comes up more or less frequently in most programming languages. Mutability can allow you to write algorithms that are more efficient or more clear than their equivalents built without mutable data, but this mutability comes at a high cost, introducing a potential for any number of bugs that can cause programs to crash, or worse, to continue running while behaving incorrectly. Haskell, as a pure functional programming language, avoids mutability by default, but in some cases you'll find that considered use of mutability can improve your programs.

When you decide to use mutable data in your Haskell program, you have a choice between several different approaches. Throughout the rest of this chapter you'll see some motivating examples for when mutability can help you write functional programs, see some pitfalls to avoid when dealing with mutability, and learn how to use some of the different tools Haskell gives you for creating and working with mutable values.

Working with IORefs

In Haskell, rather than storing a value that is directly mutable, we store an immutable reference to some data that we can change using the reference. There are several different types of mutable references that you can use, depending on the specific needs of your application. You'll learn about several different types of references throughout this chapter, but for the moment we'll focus on particular type of reference, the `IORef`.

A value with the type `IORef a` is a normal Haskell value that holds an immutable pointer to some internal data that is managed by the GHC runtime.

You can use an IORef like any other normal Haskell value. You can pass it into a function, return it, store it in a record, or capture the value in a closure. Creating a new IORef, or using one to read or write the value at the reference, is always an IO action. Let's dive into some basics of how to use IORefs, and then we'll move on to some ways that you can use IORefs in real-world applications.

Creating IORefs

You can create a new IORef a by calling newIORef from Data.IORef and giving it an initial value to store at your reference. In this example, we'll create a new IORef that will hold an Int and initialize it to 0:

```
λ import Data.IORef
λ numRef <- newIORef @Int 0
```

Since you need to initialize any newly created reference, there's no chance of accidentally getting a null or uninitialized reference. If you have a reference that may not have a value, you can use a Maybe value, just like you would with a non-reference value.

```
λ optionalNumRef <- newIORef @(Maybe Int) Nothing
```

Reading and Writing IORefs

Data.IORef is a small module with only a few exported functions that let you create, read, write, and modify IORefs in place. You've already learned how to create a new IORef, so let's work through an example of how to modify them. We'll start by using writeIORef :: IORef a -> a -> IO () and readIORef :: IORef a -> IO a to first write a value to an IORef and then to read it back:

```
{-# LANGUAGE TypeApplications #-}
module Main where
import Data.IORef

readWriteRef :: IO Int
readWriteRef = do
  myRef <- newIORef @Int 0
  writeIORef myRef 7
  refValue <- readIORef myRef
  pure refValue

main :: IO ()
main = readWriteRef >>= print
```

In this example, the readWriteRef function is an IO action that creates a new IORef, writes a value to it, and then reads the value and returns it.

Using IORefs to Traverse a Directory Tree

To see an example of how to use IORefs in a real-world application, let's write a function that will allow us to traverse part of a filesystem. We'll make use of two libraries from Hackage for this application:

- directory gives us functions to deal with files and directories.
- containers provides the Set data structure.

Create a new project and add the directory and containers dependencies. We'll start by adding the TypeApplications extension and importing a few modules that we'll be using:

```
{-# LANGUAGE TypeApplications #-}
module Main where

import Control.Exception (IOException, handle)
import Control.Monad (join, void, when)
import Data.Foldable (for_)
import Data.IORef (modifyIORef, newIORef, readIORef, writeIORef)
import Data.List (isSuffixOf)
import System.Directory
  ( canonicalizePath
  , doesDirectoryExist
  , doesFileExist
  , listDirectory
  )
import qualified Data.Set as Set (empty, insert, member)
import Text.Printf (printf)
```

Since we'll be using several new functions throughout this example, we've listed each function in our import statement. You may choose to import the entire modules here if you want to experiment with the examples as you work through them.

Next, we need to define a couple of helper functions that will make it easier for us to implement our directory traversal. The first helper function we'll write, dropSuffix, will let us easily strip off any trailing slashes from a path provided by a user:

```
dropSuffix :: String -> String -> String
dropSuffix suffix s
  | suffix `isSuffixOf` s =
    take (length s - length suffix) s
  | otherwise = s
```

As we're traversing the contents of a directory, we need to classify the files that we find. We'll want to identify subdirectories that we want to descend into, plain files that we want to work with, and special files (for example, named pipes, Unix sockets, or block and character devices) that we'll ignore. To make this easier we'll add a new type, FileType, and a function, classifyFile, which will take the path to a file and return the file's type:

```
data FileType
  = FileTypeDirectory
  | FileTypeRegularFile
  | FileTypeOther

classifyFile :: FilePath -> IO FileType
classifyFile fname = do
  isDirectory <- doesDirectoryExist fname
  isFile <- doesFileExist fname
  pure $ case (isDirectory, isFile) of
           (True, False) -> FileTypeDirectory
           (False, True) -> FileTypeRegularFile
           _otherwise    -> FileTypeOther
```

Let's start by looking at a naive traversal implementation that doesn't make use of IORefs:

```
naiveTraversal :: FilePath -> (FilePath -> a) -> IO [a]
naiveTraversal rootPath action = do
  classification <- classifyFile rootPath
  case classification of
    FileTypeOther ->
      pure []
    FileTypeRegularFile ->
      pure $ [action rootPath]
    FileTypeDirectory -> do
      contents <- map (fixPath rootPath) <$> listDirectory rootPath
      results <- concat <$> getPaths contents
      pure results
  where
    fixPath parent fname = parent <> "/" <> fname
    getPaths = mapM (\path -> naiveTraversal path action)
```

In our naive example function, we start traversing a directory structure by classifying the file we're given. If it's some special file, we don't do anything and return an empty list. If it's a plain file, we construct a singleton list by applying the user-provided function to the file. If we're looking at a directory, we recursively traverse each file in the directory. You'll notice that listDirectory returns a *relative file name* (without a trailing /), so we prefix our current path to it.

This function works, but we have two problems. The first problem that we have is an inefficiency—we're constructing a large number of intermediate lists that we're concatenating together. For large directories with many files and subdirectories also containing many files, this can lead us to making a lot of allocations and holding a lot of data in memory as we're trying to create our final result. The second problem is a bug. We are not accounting for circular references that we might encounter while traversing the directory structure, so there's a risk that we could end up waiting forever—or at least until our program runs out of memory and crashes.

IORefs can help us address both of these problems. We'll still use the same basic algorithm, but now we'll keep some history of directories we've visited, and we'll avoid creating intermediate lists as we're building up our set of results.

Our new function, traverseDirectory, will have the same type as our naive traversal function:

```
traverseDirectory :: FilePath -> (FilePath -> a) -> IO [a]
traverseDirectory rootPath action = do
```

Next, let's consider the problem of encountering loops in our filesystem. A loop will occur when a directory contains a symbolic link to a directory that is an ancestor of the current directory. In other words, imagine the following directory structure:

```
user@host:/tmp$ tree hasLoop/
hasLoop/
└── foo
    └── theLoop -> /tmp/hasLoop

2 directories, 0 files
```

If we begin traversing in hasLoop we will eventually decend into theLoop. After a few iterations, we'll start to see paths like:

```
user@host:/tmp$ tree /tmp/hasLoop/foo/theLoop/foo/theLoop/foo/theLoop
/tmp/hasLoop/foo/theLoop/foo/theLoop/foo/theLoop
└── foo
    └── theLoop -> /tmp/hasLoop
```

One way to fix this is to use the canonicalizePath function from System.Directory. This function will look at the path to a file, and if the file is a symbolic link, it will give us the path that the link references:

```
λ canonicalizePath "/tmp/hasLoop/foo/theLoop"
"/tmp/hasLoop"
```

We can use this function to keep track of the canonical path of all of the directories that we've ever tried to descend into, we just need a way to keep a list of every directory that we've seen. We'll manage that using a Set from the containers library. Let's create a new IORef to reference an empty set:

```
seenRef <- newIORef Set.empty
```

We're also going to create a new IORef to hold the list of results that we want to eventually return. We'll make use of this a bit later in our function:

```
resultRef <- newIORef []
```

Now that we have a way to hold a set of the directories we've already dealt with, it'd be nice to have a couple of helper functions to make it easy for us to test whether we've already dealt with a directory, and to say we've already dealt with one. We want these functions to have access to the seenRef reference we just defined, so we'll define our new functions inside of a let block:

```
let
  haveSeenDirectory canonicalPath =
    Set.member canonicalPath <$> readIORef seenRef

  addDirectoryToSeen canonicalPath = do
    seen <- readIORef seenRef
    writeIORef seenRef $ Set.insert canonicalPath seen
```

In the example, we've added two new helper functions. The first, haveSeenDirectory, takes a canonical path and looks to see whether it is a member of the set that is currently in the IORef.

The second function, addDirectoryToSeen, takes a canonical path and updates the set of paths that we've seen to include this new path. We first extract the set of paths we've seen, then add our new one and update the reference. This pattern of extracting a value from a reference, updating it, and writing it again can start to get a little tedious. The modifyIORef has the type modifyIORef :: IORef a -> (a -> a) -> IO (), and it allows you to apply a function to the value at a reference. Let's refactor addDirectoryToSeen to use it:

```
addDirectoryToSeen canonicalPath =
  modifyIORef seenRef $ Set.insert canonicalPath
```

With the helper functions in place, we can start implementing our traversal logic. Like haveSeenDirectory and addDirectoryToSeen, we'll add our new function to the our let block:

```
traverseSubdirectory subdirPath = do
```

The first thing we'll want to do when we're looking at any directory is to get a list of all of the contents:

```
contents <- listDirectory subdirPath
```

Once we have a list of the contents of the current directory, we want to iterate over them so that we can either handle the files, or decend into the subdirectories. Instead of using a map or fold here, we're going to make use of a new function from Data.Foldable, for_.

for_ is handy function that lets you apply some Applicative or Monad computation to each item in a collection of elements. For example, you can print out a list of numbers with:

```
λ for_ [1..10] $ \num -> putStr $ show num <> " "
1 2 3 4 5 6 7 8 9 10
λ
```

For our directory traversal function we're going to iterate over the contents that we've just gotten from the current directory.

```
for_ contents $ \file' ->
```

Dealing with file IO on a live system is tricky—a lot of things can go wrong. Files may be deleted between when we list the directory contents and when we try to access them, broken symbolic links might point to files that no longer exist, or parts of the filesystem could become unmounted. All of these cases could lead to IO Exceptions being raised.

In some cases, handling IO exceptions can be quite challenging, but thankfully in this case, if we run into an error with handling a file, we can safely skip it and move on to the next file.

We'll handle our potential errors with the handle function from Control.Exception. This function works just like the catch function that you've already used, except the arguments are reversed and we provide our error handler first. In cases like our current function with very simple error handling this can make our code easier to read:

```
handle @IOException (\_ -> pure ()) $ do
```

The first thing we'll want to do as we're processing any given file is to fix up the name and classify the file type. After that, we'll match on the file classification. For any nonstandard file type, we'll ignore it and move on:

```
let file = subdirPath <> "/" <> file'
canonicalPath <- canonicalizePath file
classification <- classifyFile canonicalPath
case classification of
  FileTypeOther -> pure ()
```

Finally, we can add in the code to handle files and directories while making use of our IORef-based approach. For an individual file, we no longer return a value, instead we'll just cons the result of applying our user-supplied function directly onto our reference list:

```
FileTypeRegularFile ->
  modifyIORef resultRef (\results -> action file : results)
```

For directories, we no longer have to keep an intermediate list of results and concatenate them together, we do however need to ensure that we add our directory to the list of directories we've already processed. We'll use when from Control.Monad. This function has the type when :: Applicative f => Bool -> f () -> f (), and it allows us to conditionally run a computation:

```
FileTypeDirectory -> do
  alreadyProcessed <- haveSeenDirectory file
  when (not alreadyProcessed) $ do
    addDirectoryToSeen file
    traverseSubdirectory file
```

The last thing we need to do is call traverseSubdirectory with the root path (and remove the trailing '/' if present), and then return the contents of our list. The final function is:

```
traverseDirectory :: FilePath -> (FilePath -> a) -> IO [a]
traverseDirectory rootPath action = do
  seenRef <- newIORef Set.empty
  resultRef <- newIORef []
  let
    haveSeenDirectory canonicalPath =
      Set.member canonicalPath <$> readIORef seenRef

    addDirectoryToSeen canonicalPath =
      modifyIORef seenRef $ Set.insert canonicalPath

    traverseSubdirectory subdirPath = do
      contents <- listDirectory subdirPath
      for_ contents $ \file' ->
        handle @IOException (\_ -> pure ()) $ do
        let file = subdirPath <> "/" <> file'
        canonicalPath <- canonicalizePath file
        classification <- classifyFile canonicalPath
        case classification of
          FileTypeOther -> pure ()
          FileTypeRegularFile ->
            modifyIORef resultRef (\results -> action file : results)
          FileTypeDirectory -> do
            alreadyProcessed <- haveSeenDirectory file
            when (not alreadyProcessed) $ do
              addDirectoryToSeen file
              traverseSubdirectory file

  traverseSubdirectory (dropSuffix "/" rootPath)
  readIORef resultRef
```

We still have some opportunities to refactor this function a bit, but before we do, let's load it up in ghci and test it to see how it works. In the following examples we'll use this directory structure:

```
user@host:~$ tree /tmp/test/
/tmp/test/
├── a
│   └── b
│       └── c
│           └── d
│               └── d-file
├── fizz
│   ├── buzz
│   │   └── buzz-file.1
│   └── fizz-file
└── foo
    ├── bar
    │   ├── bar-file.1
    │   └── baz
    │       └── baz-file.1
    └── foo-file.1

9 directories, 6 files
```

We can start testing our directory traversal function by using it to give us a list of all of the files that it encounters:

```
λ :type traverseDirectory "/tmp/test/" id
traverseDirectory "/tmp/test/" id :: IO [FilePath]
λ traverseDirectory "/tmp/test/" id
[ "/tmp/test/foo/bar/bar-file.1"
, "/tmp/test/foo/bar/baz/baz-file.1"
, "/tmp/test/foo/foo-file.1"
, "/tmp/test/a/b/c/d/d-file"
, "/tmp/test/fizz/fizz-file"
, "/tmp/test/fizz/buzz/buzz-file.1" ]
```

We can also do some transformations on the filenames. For example, if we wanted to get the length of the filenames:

```
λ traverseDirectory "/tmp/test/" length
[28,32,24,24,24,31]
```

Imagine though that instead of simply working with the names of the files themselves, we wanted to do something that involved the contents of the file, like reading the file in and counting the number of bytes:

```
import Data.ByteString (ByteString)
import qualified Data.ByteString as BS

countBytes :: FilePath -> IO (FilePath, Integer)
countBytes path = do
  bytes <- fromIntegral . BS.length <$> BS.readFile path
  pure (path, bytes)
```

Let's try passing in countBytes to our traversal function to see what we get back:

```
λ traverseDirectory "/tmp/test/" countBytes
λ
```

Nothing! If that's unexpected, we might get some help from looking at the type of the expression:

```
λ :type traverseDirectory
traverseDirectory :: FilePath -> (FilePath -> a) -> IO [a]
λ :type traverseDirectory "/tmp/test/" countBytes
traverseDirectory "/tmp/test/" countBytes
  :: IO [IO (FilePath, Integer)]
```

When we call traverseDirectory with countBytes we're getting back a computation that itself contains a list of computations which, if evaluated, will give us the number of bytes in a file. We can work around this by evaluating all the computations in the list. The sequence and join functions will take care of this for us:

```
λ :type sequence
sequence :: (Traversable t, Monad m) => t (m a) -> m (t a)
λ :type join
join :: Monad m => m (m a) -> m a
λ join . fmap sequence $ traverseDirectory "/tmp/test/" countBytes
[("/tmp/test/foo/bar/bar-file.1",0)
,("/tmp/test/foo/bar/baz/baz-file.1",0)
,("/tmp/test/foo/foo-file.1",0)
,("/tmp/test/a/b/c/d/d-file",0)
,("/tmp/test/fizz/fizz-file",0)
,("/tmp/test/fizz/buzz/buzz-file.1",0)]
```

This approach still has the problem of causing us to accumulate a potentially large number of unevaluated computations. It would be ideal if our traverseDirectory function could evaluate an IOAction for us as it's doing its other work. Let's take on a small refactor to see this in action:

```
traverseDirectory :: FilePath -> (FilePath -> IO ()) -> IO ()
traverseDirectory rootPath action = do
  seenRef <- newIORef Set.empty
  let
    haveSeenDirectory canonicalPath =
      Set.member canonicalPath <$> readIORef seenRef

    addDirectoryToSeen canonicalPath =
      modifyIORef seenRef $ Set.insert canonicalPath

    traverseSubdirectory subdirPath = do
      contents <- listDirectory subdirPath
      for_ contents $ \file' ->
        handle @IOException (\_ -> pure ()) $ do
        let file = subdirPath <> "/" <> file'
```

```
        canonicalPath <- canonicalizePath file
        classification <- classifyFile canonicalPath
        case classification of
          FileTypeOther -> pure ()
          FileTypeRegularFile ->
            action file
          FileTypeDirectory -> do
            alreadyProcessed <- haveSeenDirectory file
            when (not alreadyProcessed) $ do
              addDirectoryToSeen file
              traverseSubdirectory file
  traverseSubdirectory (dropSuffix "/" rootPath)
```

This version of our function no longer keeps a results reference around. Instead of appending a result to a list of results, we instead simply run some IOAction with the current file. This means that we don't, necessarily, need to store any intermediate files at all. If, for example, we wanted to print the file sizes out as we go, we can say:

```
λ traverseDirectory "/tmp/test/" $ \file -> countBytes file >>= print
("/tmp/test/fizz/buzz/buzz-file.1",0)
("/tmp/test/fizz/fizz-file",0)
("/tmp/test/a/b/c/d/d-file",0)
("/tmp/test/foo/foo-file.1",0)
("/tmp/test/foo/bar/baz/baz-file.1",0)
("/tmp/test/foo/bar/bar-file.1",0)
```

You can also recreate the capabilities of the original function by factoring out the use of an IORef to accumulate results into a new function:

```
traverseDirectory' :: FilePath -> (FilePath -> a) -> IO [a]
traverseDirectory' rootPath action = do
  resultsRef <- newIORef []
  traverseDirectory rootPath $ \file -> do
    modifyIORef resultsRef (action file :)
  readIORef resultsRef
```

These two functions, traverseDirectory and traverseDirectory', demonstrate one of the common ways that you'll use IORefs in real-world applications. By creating an IORef that is part of the closure of a function that you pass around, or call recursively, you can get data and run computations that would be awkward or expensive to do without external mutable state.

Let's look at one more example, just to drive the point home. Imagine that you want to get the contents of the largest file in our directory tree. We'll assume for the sake of the example that the filesystem does not allow any easier way to get the size of a file except for reading it into memory. If you were to use the original version of traverseDirectory that returns a list of values, you could read the contents of each file and then take the longest file, but that would mean that you'd need to possibly store all of the contents of all of the files in memory. That could put quite unreasonable memory pressure on the application. Alternatively, you could store a computation that returns the length and fold over it, but that requires traversing the entire directory structure twice. Using an IORef, we can re-use our existing traverseDirectory function and get the longest file in a single pass:

```
longestContents :: FilePath -> IO ByteString
longestContents rootPath = do
  contentsRef <- newIORef BS.empty
  let
    takeLongestFile a b =
      if BS.length a >= BS.length b
      then a
      else b

  traverseDirectory rootPath $ \file -> do
    contents <- BS.readFile file
    modifyIORef contentsRef (takeLongestFile contents)

  readIORef contentsRef
```

Using an IORef here allows us to re-use our existing traversal function, make a single pass through the directory structure, and keep at most two files worth of data in memory at a time.

Building a Basic Metrics System with IORefs

So far, you've learned how to create a reference that has the lifetime of some single IO action, but in some cases it would be convenient to have a reference that is available to your entire program, and for the lifetime of the application. Although global mutable data is often cast as inadvisable at best, and an antipattern at worst, there are situations where module-level global variables can be quite useful. One of these situations is when dealing with global concerns like logging or metrics. In this section, we'll look at how to build a minimal metrics system that you can use to instrument a program.

Let's start by defining a new record, AppMetrics, that we'll use to hold all of our different metrics. For our simplified application, we're going to hold three different metrics: successCount will count all of the times a function call succeeded, failureCount will return all the time a function failed, and callDuration will count the total amount of time that we have spent in each function. We'll be using Data.Map.Strict from the containers library for the examples in this section. A Map is a dictionary that lets us efficiently associate keys with values. For example, we'll use a Map String Int to let us efficiently look up Int values given String keys:

```
module Metrics where
import qualified Data.Map.Strict as Map
import Data.IORef

data AppMetrics = AppMetrics
  { successCount :: Int
  , failureCount :: Int
  , callDuration :: Map.Map String Int
  } deriving (Eq, Show)
```

In a real application, you would typically store the set of metrics dynamically rather than choosing a fixed set of things to measure upfront, but for this minimal example we'll stick with a few prechosen metrics.

Metrics present an interesting challenge to us when we're trying to design our software. Metrics must be mutable, since their entire purpose is to change as things in our program happen. They must also be available throughout our entire program, since we will ideally be instrumenting much of our application to track what is happening. It is inconvenient to pass around a pure metrics value that we return along with values in our program, so we'd like to have metrics that exist separately from our main application. These constraints make them good candidates for existing as an IORef.

Let's look at an example of how we might use an IORef to implement metrics for a small sample program.

We know that we want to have our metrics be global to our module so that we can track metrics from any function, and we know that our metrics value needs to be mutable, so a reasonable starting point might be to create a top-level IORef:

```
metrics :: IO (IORef AppMetrics)
metrics = newIORef AppMetrics
  { successCount = 0
  , failureCount = 0
  , callDuration = Map.empty
  }
```

Next, for the sake of testing, let's write a function that can print some metrics out to the screen so that we can easily verify that our metrics are working as expected:

```
printMetrics :: IO ()
printMetrics =
  metrics >>= readIORef >>= print
```

We'll also need some functions to update metrics. For the moment, let's be optimistic and we'll just implement a function to increment the success counter:

```
incrementSuccess :: IO ()
incrementSuccess =
    metrics >>= flip modifyIORef incrementSuccess
    where
      incrementSuccess m =
        m { successCount = 1 + successCount m }
```

Finally, let's write a couple of functions so that we can test our metrics out:

```
successfullyPrintHello :: IO ()
successfullyPrintHello = do
  print "Hello"
  incrementSuccess

printHelloAndMetrics = do
  successfullyPrintHello
  printMetrics
```

We can load our module into ghci to test it:

```
λ printHelloAndMetrics
"Hello"
AppMetrics
  {successCount = 0, failureCount = 0, callDuration = fromList []}
```

You might notice that this approach didn't work at all! What happened?

Let's take another look at our metrics function:

```
metrics :: IO (IORef AppMetrics)
metrics = newIORef AppMetrics
  { successCount = 0
  , failureCount = 0
  , callDuration = Map.empty
  }
```

The problem that we have right now is that metrics is a an IO action, and each time we run that action we get a new reference that is initialized with an empty set of metrics. In other words, every time we pass metrics into (>>=) or get a metrics value in a do block using <-, we're going to get a brand new empty collection metrics. Instead of getting the metrics when we need it by calling metrics we're going to need to create a single source of truth for metrics and pass it around through all of our computations.

We could, of course, directly pass around our IORef, but that leaks an implementation detail that we might want to change later. Instead, let's create a new type that represents an IORef that holds some metrics data.

At this point, we have two choices for how we could do this. One option would be to create a record that holds separate references to each of the things we'd like to potentially update. In this case, we'd replace our existing AppMetrics type with one like this:

```
data AppMetrics
  { successCount :: IORef Int
  , failureCount :: IORef Int
  , callDuration :: IORef (Map.Map String Int)
  }
```

This can be a great approach to take when you might want to have different threads updating metrics independently, or when want to pull out specific metrics and pass them around while hiding the rest of the metrics from some particular function. The down side to this approach is that it can be a little bit more work to manage, because we now have to implementing updating each reference separately. This can introduce performance problems if you have a lot of functions that want to work with several different metrics, since you'll have to read and write multiple references for each metrics update.

An alternative approach would be to keep our original AppMetrics definition, and add a newtype wrapper around a reference to the metrics:

```
newtype Metrics = Metrics { appMetricsStore :: IORef AppMetrics }
```

This approach makes it more efficient to update the entire set of metrics at once, but at the cost of some degree of parallelism. For now, we'll stick with our original AppMetrics definition and the Metrics wrapper, because it will let us write a bit less code as we're working through the examples. In an exercise at the end of this chapter, you'll have an opportunity to refactor some of your metrics code to make use of multiple references.

To go along with our newtype wrapper, let's rename metrics and have it actually return a Metrics value:

```
newMetrics :: IO Metrics
newMetrics =
  let
    emptyAppMetrics = AppMetrics
      { successCount = 0
      , failureCount = 0
      , callDuration = Map.empty
      }
  in Metrics <$> newIORef emptyAppMetrics
```

The idea behind using a newtype wrapper around our IORef is that we'd like users of our metrics API to be able to ignore the implementation detail that we're using an IORef to handle the metrics. So far, we've updated metrics by modifying the reference value directly, but that's not going to work if we want to hide the fact that we're dealing with a reference from the user. Instead, let's add some utility functions that allow us to modify the metrics. Let's start with a pair of functions to increment our success and failure counters:

```
tickSuccess :: Metrics -> IO ()
tickSuccess (Metrics metricsRef) = modifyIORef metricsRef $ \m ->
  m { successCount = 1 + successCount m }

tickFailure :: Metrics -> IO ()
tickFailure (Metrics metricsRef) = modifyIORef metricsRef $ \m ->
  m { failureCount = 1 + failureCount m }
```

Next, let's add a timeFunction call that will let us run an IO action with a given name and time how long it took to execute. For this function, we'll need to make sure we've added a dependency on the time library to our cabal file, and we'll import a few functions from Data.Time.Clock to let us do some time calculations:

```
import Data.Maybe (fromMaybe)
import Data.Time.Clock
  ( diffUTCTime
  , getCurrentTime
  , nominalDiffTimeToSeconds
  )

timeFunction :: Metrics -> String -> IO a -> IO a
timeFunction (Metrics metrics) actionName action = do
  startTime  <- getCurrentTime
  result     <- action
  endTime    <- getCurrentTime

  modifyIORef metrics $ \oldMetrics ->
    let
      oldDurationValue =
        fromMaybe 0 $ Map.lookup actionName (callDuration oldMetrics)

      runDuration =
        floor . nominalDiffTimeToSeconds $
          diffUTCTime endTime startTime

      newDurationValue = oldDurationValue + runDuration

    in oldMetrics {
      callDuration =
          Map.insert actionName newDurationValue $
            callDuration oldMetrics
      }

  pure result
```

Our timer function is a bit longer than tickSuccess and tickFailure, but not much more complicated. The majority of the work that we're doing here is to calculate the total amount of time being spent in a given function by first finding the time when we start and finish running the function that was passed in and then adding that time to any already accumulated time for this particular action.

Finally, to make things easier to test, let's add a displayMetrics function that will print our current metrics to the screen. Since we're going to want access to all of the fields in our metrics store, we'll enable RecordWildCards to make it easier:

```
{-# LANGUAGE RecordWildCards #-}

displayMetrics :: Metrics -> IO ()
displayMetrics (Metrics metricsStore) = do
  AppMetrics{..} <- readIORef metricsStore
  putStrLn $ "successes: " <> show successCount
  putStrLn $ "failures: " <> show failureCount
  for_ (Map.toList callDuration) $ \(functionName, timing) ->
    putStrLn $ printf "Time spent in \"%s\": %d" functionName timing
```

Now that we've got a few functions that we can use to collect metrics, we can start testing it out. Let's re-use our traverseDirectory code from earlier in this chapter, but now we'll collect metrics like how many times we succeeded or failed to open a file, and how long we spent in the various functions that we needed to call to process the files.

We'll start by modifying traverseDirectory to make use of our metrics code. The changes will be fairly minimal, so let's look at the final version of the function:

```
{-# LANGUAGE TypeApplications #-}
import qualified Data.Set as Set
import Control.Exception

traverseDirectory :: Metrics -> FilePath -> (FilePath -> IO ()) -> IO ()
traverseDirectory metrics rootPath action = do
  seenRef <- newIORef Set.empty
  let
    haveSeenDirectory canonicalPath =
      Set.member canonicalPath <$> readIORef seenRef

    addDirectoryToSeen canonicalPath =
      modifyIORef seenRef $ Set.insert canonicalPath

    handler ex = print ex >> tickFailure metrics

    traverseSubdirectory subdirPath =
      timeFunction metrics "traverseSubdirectory" $ do
        contents <- listDirectory subdirPath
        for_ contents $ \file' ->
          handle @IOException handler $ do
          let file = subdirPath <> "/" <> file'
          canonicalPath <- canonicalizePath file
          classification <- classifyFile canonicalPath
```

```
          result <- case classification of
            FileTypeOther -> pure ()
            FileTypeRegularFile ->
              action file
            FileTypeDirectory -> do
              alreadyProcessed <- haveSeenDirectory file
              when (not alreadyProcessed) $ do
                addDirectoryToSeen file
                traverseSubdirectory file
          tickSuccess metrics
          pure result
  traverseSubdirectory (dropSuffix "/" rootPath)
```

We've added a new parameter, bound to the name metrics, so we can actually keep track of the metrics we want to handle in the function. Additionally, we've changed the main loop in traverseSubdirectory so the function it calls is wrapped by timeFunction. This lets us keep track of the total amount of time we're spending traversing through the directory tree. We're also now incrementing our failure count if we catch an exception while trying to process a file, and incrementing the success count if we successfully process it.

Our new function will take the path to a directory and will traverse it using our new metrics-aware traverseDirectory function. For each file in the directory listing, we'll print out the number of words in the file, and we'll update a global histogram that counts the number of occurrences of each character across all of the files that we've processed. Once we're done traversing the directory we'll print out the histogram and a summary of our metrics.

We'll start by importing a couple of modules from the text library to help us deal with the contents of the files:

```
import qualified Data.Text as Text
import qualified Data.Text.IO as TextIO
```

Next we'll start defining our function. We'll begin by creating some new metrics and an IORef that we can use to keep track of the histogram that we'll be updating with each file that we process:

```
directorySummaryWithMetrics :: FilePath -> IO ()
directorySummaryWithMetrics root = do
  metrics <- newMetrics
  histogramRef <- newIORef Map.empty
```

Next, we'll call our new metric-aware traverseDirectory function, and we'll pass it in the empty metrics store that we've just created:

```
traverseDirectory metrics root $ \file -> do
```

The first thing we want to do for each file is to print out the name of the file we're trying to process. After that, we'll read the contents of the file into a Text value so that we can process it:

```
putStrLn $ file <> ":"
contents <- timeFunction metrics "TextIO.readFile" $
  TextIO.readFile file
```

You'll notice here that we're using the readFile function provided to use in Data.Text.IO. This is a *strict* function that will ensure we actually read the file right away. If you recall the example you worked through when you first started learning about IO on page 277, you saw how using laziness with IO could introduce errors, like accidentally exhausting the number of open file descriptors. Not only will using Text here give us a significant performance improvement over String, but using strict IO here will help us avoid some of the problems that can crop up when we are using laziness with IO. Another unexpected benefit of using TextIO.readFile in our case is that it will fail if it tries to read data that isn't valid Unicode text. Normally we wouldn't consider failure to be a benefit, but we have failure metrics we'd like to test and this gives us an easy way to populate a directory with files that will fail and let us see that we're counting those failures correctly.

Now that we have the contents of the file, let's do some things with it. We'll start by counting the number of words. As before, we'd like to time this so that we have an idea of how much time we're spending with this particular file. We'll start by printing out the number of words in the file:

```
timeFunction metrics "wordcount" $
  let wordCount = length $ Text.words contents
  in putStrLn $ "    word count: " <> show wordCount
```

Next, let's update the histogram. We'll start by reading the current histogram out of our reference. We'll use that as the starting point and fold over each of the characters in current text that we have:

```
timeFunction metrics "histogram" $ do
  oldHistogram <- readIORef histogramRef
  let
    addCharToHistogram histogram letter =
      Map.insertWith (+) letter 1 histogram
    newHistogram = Text.foldl' addCharToHistogram oldHistogram contents
  writeIORef histogramRef newHistogram
```

The insertWith function here allows us to provide a merge function to be used in case we happen to have a collision in the map. In our case, we're using this to let us increment the count of a letter each time we find one. The first time we see a new letter, Map.insertWith will add new entry with the letter as the key and the value 1. The next time we see that letter, it'll call our function, (+), with the old count and the new value that we want to insert, which is always 1, meaning that each time we see a character we'll increment the count at that position in the map.

As a final step, we'll print out the histogram data and then print out all of our metrics:

```
histogram <- readIORef histogramRef
putStrLn "Histogram Data:"
for_ (Map.toList histogram) $ \(letter, count) ->
  putStrLn $ printf "    %c: %d" letter count

displayMetrics metrics
```

The final version of our function is:

```
directorySummaryWithMetrics :: FilePath -> IO ()
directorySummaryWithMetrics root = do
  metrics <- newMetrics
  histogramRef <- newIORef (Map.empty :: Map.Map Char Int)
  traverseDirectory metrics root $ \file -> do
    putStrLn $ file <> ":"
    contents <- timeFunction metrics "TextIO.readFile" $
                  TextIO.readFile file
    timeFunction metrics "wordcount" $
      let wordCount = length $ Text.words contents
      in putStrLn $ "    word count: " <> show wordCount

    timeFunction metrics "histogram" $ do
      oldHistogram <- readIORef histogramRef
      let
        addCharToHistogram histogram letter =
          Map.insertWith (+) letter 1 histogram
        newHistogram =
          Text.foldl' addCharToHistogram oldHistogram contents
      writeIORef histogramRef newHistogram

  histogram <- readIORef histogramRef
  putStrLn "Histogram Data:"
  for_ (Map.toList histogram) $ \(letter, count) ->
    putStrLn $ printf "    %c: %d" letter count

  displayMetrics metrics
```

If you use this function to try to get information about a large directory, you might notice something unexpected. First, the output of the program will start out working like you'd expect: all of the files in the directory will be listed, along with the number of words in them. Once the program has finished outputting the word counts though, it will pause for a while. Depending on the size of the directory you were calculating metrics on, the pause might be anywhere from less than a second up to several seconds. Once it's done, you might see some metrics like this:

```
successes: 20611
failures: 43
Time spent in "TextIO.readFile": 24
Time spent in "histogram": 0
Time spent in "traverseSubdirectory": 91389
Time spent in "wordcount": 4304
```

Calculating the histogram should be a fairly time-consuming operation. The fact that we are waiting a while for the final histogram to be printed out is evidence that there is work there to do, but our metrics code seems to think that we're spending no time at all here. What's going on? It turns out that we've encountered a bug in our program caused by lazy IO. This is a common problem in Haskell programs, and in the next section, we'll dive into what causes these problems, how to troubleshoot them, and some techniques for fixing the problem.

Dealing with Laziness and IO

When we see the behavior of our program, our first instinct might be to look at how we're recording the time spent in the histogram code—perhaps we've accidentally introduced a bug that causes us to not record times correctly? The fact that we have more reasonable values for our other calls is evidence against this though.

The problem we've run into is writeIORef handles the value it's writing into the reference lazily. Although we're always writing *something* into the reference immediately each time we're calling writeIORef, the value we're writing isn't our newly updated histogram. Instead, we're writing a *thunk* that contains the computation that will give us an updated histogram when we need it. Creating a thunk is fast enough that at the millisecond-resolution we're rounding down to zero each time we call the function. It's only once we try to actually look at the values in the map that we finally have to compute them.

One way that we could work around this is by adding a new timer around the code that we're using to actually print out the histogram:

```
timeFunction metrics "print histogram" $ do
  histogram <- readIORef histogramRef
  putStrLn "Histogram Data:"
  for_ (Map.toList histogram) $ \(letter, count) ->
    putStrLn $ printf "    %c: %d" letter count
```

Now when we run our program, we'll see that while our histogram construction continues to not take any time, we can track the amount of time it takes to evaluate the histogram so that we can print it out:

```
successes: 20611
failures: 43
Time spent in "TextIO.readFile": 25
Time spent in "histogram": 0
Time spent in "print histogram": 5788
Time spent in "traverseSubdirectory": 3850
Time spent in "wordcount": 0
```

Unfortunately, the problem here goes deeper than just not having a correct accounting of the time that we spent computing the histogram. We've also introduced a type of problem known as a *space leak*.

Understanding Space Leaks

Space leaks are a type of error we can run into in Haskell when laziness starts to work against us, and we start to see a large number of thunks accumulated that are not evaluated. This can manifest in several different ways, including causing our programs to use too much memory, to have poor or unpredictable performance patterns, or more rarely, to crash at runtime with a stack overflow. What we've seen so far when trying to run our directory traversal program is an example of how space leaks can make themselves known when the performance isn't what we expect. Specifically, we would expect generating the character histogram to take a lot of time, but in fact it takes almost no time at all.

The idea that a space leak can show up as a problem with unexpected performance characteristics can be counterintuitive, but as we look into what happened with our program in this case it will start to be clear just why the unusual performance was an indicator of a space leak.

Before we dive into the code and start working on a fix, let's get some hard data. When we suspect that we have a space leak, it can be helpful to look at information about the amount of memory we're allocating, and what the garbage collector is doing. Even if the data doesn't initially tell us where to look for the error, it gives us a baseline to measure against, so we can see if the changes we're making are actually having a positive impact on the runtime characteristics of the application.

We can't get the kind of information that we need from ghci, so let's create a new file and make sure that we have main defined so that we can compile the application as a stand-alone program:

```
import System.Environment (getArgs)

main :: IO ()
main = getArgs >>= directorySummaryWithMetrics . head
```

If you haven't already created a new cabal project for this program, you can take a minute to do so now, or you can compile the program directly with ghc. In either case, make sure that you've enabled -O2 level optimizations. GHC is able to do a number of optimizations, and we want to avoid spending too much time chasing down optimizations that the compile will take care of for us anyway.

```
$ ghc -O2 DirectorySummary.hs -o DirectorySummary
```

Once you've built the program, we want to run it, but instead of running the program like normal, we're going to pass in some extra flags to the Haskell runtime so that we can ask it to collect some information about memory usage as our program is running. Flags like this that we use to control the way the Haskell runtime works, or to ask it for some extra information about our program, are called *RTS flags*. RTS flags are normal command line flags, but we need to differentiate between options we want to pass to the Haskell runtime and the options that we want to pass to our program. To do so, we start by passing in the special +RTS argument. This argument will cause the runtime to interpret all the arguments that it sees as arguments to the runtime system, until it sees the -RTS argument. This lets us pass in as many arguments as we want to the runtime system without our application having to know about or handle them.

In our particular case, we only want to pass a single RTS flag, -s. This flag will ask the runtime to generate summary statistics about the memory utilization of our application:

```
$ ./DirectorySummary +RTS -s -RTS ./example-dir/
```

When you run the program with this RTS flag you'll get all of the normal output you'd expect, and then at the end before your program exits you'll see some output like this:

```
 1,911,494,744 bytes allocated in the heap
    44,005,608 bytes copied during GC
    12,816,336 bytes maximum residency (10 sample(s))
     6,051,224 bytes maximum slop
            39 MiB total memory in use (3 MB lost due to fragmentation)

                                   Tot time (elapsed)  Avg pause  Max pause
Gen  0    1764 colls,  0 par     0.026s   0.026s     0.0000s    0.0004s
Gen  1      10 colls,  0 par     0.007s   0.007s     0.0007s    0.0012s

INIT    time    0.000s  (  0.000s elapsed)
MUT     time    0.363s  (  0.363s elapsed)
GC      time    0.033s  (  0.033s elapsed)
EXIT    time    0.000s  (  0.000s elapsed)
Total   time    0.396s  (  0.396s elapsed)

%GC     time       0.0%  (0.0% elapsed)

Alloc rate    5,262,713,737 bytes per MUT second

Productivity  91.7% of total user, 91.6% of total elapsed
```

There's a lot of information here that we won't cover in this book, but you can refer to the GHC User Guide[1] for comprehensive documentation on the meaning of all these fields. For the moment we're going to focus on the *maximum residency* field, which tells us the amount of memory that our program was actually using at its peak.

If you look at the total size, in bytes, of all of the data in your example directory, you'll notice that it is fairly similar to the total residency of our application. For example, if we look at the total number of bytes in all of the files in example-dir, we'll see that they total about 12.3 megabytes, which is a little bit less than the total residency of our application, but suspiciously close:

```
$ du -s -B 1 ./example-dir/
12365824        ./example-dir/
```

The fact that our maximum residency is so similar to the size of all of the files in our directory can start to give us a hint about what has happened. When we read the contents of a file in so that we can calculate the character histogram, we're not freeing that data right away. Instead, we're keeping all of the files in memory. The fact that we see observable delay before the histogram is printed out on the screen gives us a bit more information: we're reading all of the files, but not actually calculating the histogram until we're ready to print it out. It seems like, in this case, laziness might be causing trouble. Let's take a look at what's going on, and in the next section, we'll look at a few ways to address this particular type of problem.

1. https://downloads.haskell.org/ghc/latest/docs/html/users_guide/index.html

Laziness, Strictness, and IO

The root cause of the problem we've run into is that we're mixing lazy and strict values, and it's causing our program to act unexpectedly. Let's take a look at our histogram calculation code again for reference:

```
traverseDirectory metrics root $ \file -> do
  contents <- timeFunction metrics "TextIO.readFile" $
              TextIO.readFile file

  -- Omitting some things here

  timeFunction metrics "histogram" $ do
    oldHistogram <- readIORef histogramRef
    let
      addCharToHistogram histogram letter =
        Map.insertWith (+) letter 1 histogram
      newHistogram = Text.foldl' addCharToHistogram oldHistogram contents
    writeIORef histogramRef newHistogram
```

The first thing that we need to keep in mind here is that TextIO.readFile is a strict function. Whenever we call it, we're going to get the entire contents of the file brought into memory. Similarly, combining IO actions using (>>=) or in a do block is always strict. As we're traversing the directories, we're always going to read the contents of the file before we write an update to histogramRef or before we move on and read the contents of the next file.

The second thing that we have to keep in mind is that Haskell is lazy by default, so all of the things that don't have to be strict are going to generate *thunks* instead of strictly evaluated values. That means that whenever we create a new histogram, we're not really computing the value of a brand new histogram, we're just creating a new thunk that can compute a histogram when a histogram is needed:

```
newHistogram = Text.foldl' addCharToHistogram oldHistogram contents
```

Perhaps unintuitively, a value to an IORef is not strict. When we call writeIORef, we're not forcing the value newHistogram to be computed, instead we just write the thunk into the reference.

The last thing to keep in mind is a thunk keeps around references to everything that is needed to compute a value. In this case, each thunk we're writing into the reference is keeping a reference to the previous thunk that was stored in the IORef and a reference to the contents of the text file we've just read. Since we have a reference to the contents of the text file, that data can't be garbage collected. Since we have a reference to the previous thunk, which in turn has a reference to the contents of its text file, that text file can't be garbage collected either. By the time we've finished traversing the directory, we have a chain of thunks that are keeping open references to all the data from all the files we've opened—plus a bit of overhead for the other calculations we need to do.

The solution to this problem is to reduce the amount of laziness in our program. If we can compute the value of the histogram thunk immediately, then we will no longer need to keep references to the contents of the file or the previous thunk, and the garbage collector can clean everything up for us. This is a common enough problem in Haskell programs that we have not just one, but several different approaches we can use to solve the problem. Before we dive into reviewing the options though, let's take a slight detour to understand exactly what we mean when we're talking about strictness, laziness, and what it means to evaluate an expression. This will give us the tools to better understand when and how to introduce strictness, and also make sure we're better prepared to avoid this type of space leak in the future.

Thunks and Evaluation in Haskell Programs

Much earlier in this book you learned about how thunks can enable us to do creative things like creating infinitely linked lists on page 74, and more recently, you saw an example of how a thunk being created unexpectedly created a space leak that caused us to use far more memory than necessary when we were counting the frequency of characters in a directory full of files. Most of the time as we are writing Haskell, we don't have to think too much about the details of what thunks are being created and when, and thankfully, most of the time if we do think about them it's because they are helping us write things that might be harder to express in a strict language. Sometimes though, laziness causes problems, and when that happens we need to understand a little bit more about how our programs are actually being run. In this case, that means we need to know a bit more about what thunks are and how they work so that we can fix our space leak and ensure we don't have similar problems in the future.

So, what is a thunk? Up until now, we've used a pretty simple mental model of a thunk as a value that hasn't yet been computed. This is right, but there's a little bit more to it than is apparent from that explanation. To better explore what thunks are and how they impact the way our programs are run, let's work through an example. Our example will recreate the same space leak caused by writing into an `IORef` that we encountered when we were working with our timer function, but in a much smaller and simpler program so that we can avoid too many extraneous details.

Our example program will have two functions. Our first function, characterCounter, will read the contents of a file and return an IO action that will give us a way to count the number of occurrences of some character or substring inside of the contents of the file:

```
characterCounter :: FilePath -> IO (Text.Text -> Int)
characterCounter filePath = do
  haystack <- TextIO.readFile filePath
  pure $ \needle ->
    Text.count needle haystack
    + Text.count needle (Text.pack filePath)
```

Next, we'd like to call characterCounter. Our second function, someExample, is going to do some work to figure out what path we should open, and then count the number of spaces in the file at that path and write the count into an IORef:

```
someExample :: FilePath -> IO (IORef Int)
someExample path = do
  countRef <- newIORef 0
  let
    somePath = complicatedPathFinding path
  counter <- characterCounter somePath
  writeIORef countRef (counter " ")
  pure countRef
  where
    -- You can use any function you'd like here
    complicatedPathFinding = id
```

The first thing to think about when we're dealing with performance problems like space leaks or unexpected slowness in a Haskell program should be memory allocation. Allocations and freeing up memory are core to the way that Haskell programs are run. Space leaks, unexpectedly slow programs, stack overflows, and bugs like exhausting the number of file descriptors are all examples of problems that are closely tied to the way things are allocated.

Most of the things we're dealing with when we write programs end up existing at runtime as *heap objects*. Heap objects are how the Haskell runtime allocates memory for everything from literal values like numbers, to values we've created using value constructors, to functions and thunks. Understanding how heap objects work is the first step to understanding more about how thunks and laziness works in Haskell.

At a high level, all of the heap objects that we create in our program have the same structure: a header that contains some metadata about what kind of heap object we're dealing with, followed by some additional information that varies depending on the type of heap object, and finally, a payload that contains data, or references to data, that is needed by the heap object.

Some of the most common types of heap objects we deal with in most Haskell programs are called *thunks*. The GHC runtime keeps track of several different kinds of thunks internally, but for our purposes we don't need to differentiate between them, and for the sake of simplicity we'll collectively refer to all of them as "a thunk."

When a thunk is first created, it's going to have three different sets of data. First, the header will tell the GHC runtime what kind of thunk it's dealing with, and will have all of the other housekeeping information that all heap objects need. The next section contains the code that needs to run so that the thunk can be evaluated when and if the result of the thunk is needed. Finally, the payload section keeps around a table of references to the values that that the code section needs to refer to in order to calculate a value.

To help make this a bit more concrete, let's look at our example code and think about what happens when we define somePath. When we define somePath in our let binding, the runtime is going to manage that by creating a new thunk:

```
let
  somePath = complicatedPathFinding path
```

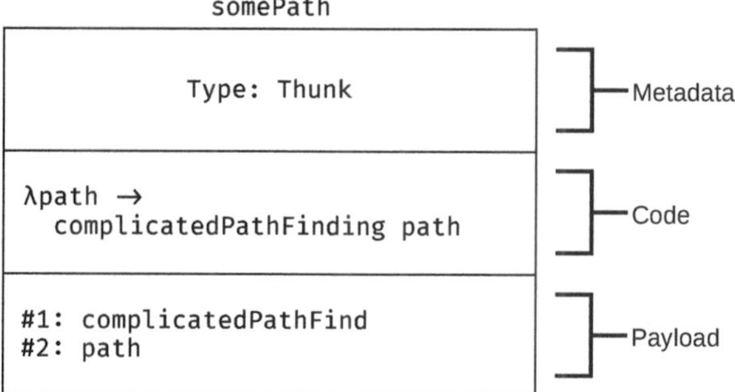

The header data for our new heap object will have a type that tells the runtime we're dealing with a thunk, and the code section will tell us we need to call a function named complicatedPathFinding, applying a value to it named path. A reference to the actual complicatedPathFinding function and a reference to the string we're applying are stored in the payload so that we can reference them if we need to run the code to get a value for the thunk.

This thunk by itself isn't doing much, so let's move on to the next thing we're defining: our character counter function, named counter. We're getting the function we're binding counter to by running an IO action. IO actions can be stored in thunks just like everything else, but since the implementation details of IO can be a little tricky and aren't relevant to the problem at hand, we're going to skip over that and instead focus on what's happening inside of characterCounter when it gets evaluated.

The first thing we do inside of characterCounter is read the contents of the file using the path that we passed in. Since the value we applied to this function is the somePath thunk from earlier, we're finally going to need to calculate a value for our path.

When we need the value of a thunk, the first thing that happens is we run the code in the code section of the heap object. Generally, that will result in some new value being created and stored as a brand new heap object. That new value is the actual value of our thunk. Once that's done, we need a way to get to the answer from the thunk, so the value of the thunk is updated. Any references we were holding onto in the payload section can be released, and thunk is updated with an *indirection*. The indirection tells us where to look for the value we calculated from the thunk. All this happens transparently and automatically the first time we try to read the value of the thunk, and all we see is the final result: the path to the file we want to open.

With our path available, we can read the contents of the file; again we'll skip over the details of IO for now. The last thing we do is to return a new function. Functions, like thunks, are allocated as heap objects, and just like a thunk, a function will store references to anything it needs to compute a value in the payload section of the heap object. Let's take another look at the function we're returning so we can figure out what references it would need to have in its payload:

```
\needle ->
    Text.count needle haystack
    + Text.count needle (Text.pack filePath)
```

There are quite a few different values that we're referencing in this function. First, we're calling the Prelude function (+), and we're calling both count and pack from the Data.Text module. Keeping references to top-level functions like this doesn't typically have much of a performance impact, since the same values can be referenced by everything in the program that needs to refer to them. In addition to the top-level functions that we're referencing, the body of our function is also referencing the value of its parameter, needle. Since this is a parameter to the function, and not a value that's referencing some existing heap object, we don't actually need to store anything for that now. The last two values we're referencing are filePath and haystack. These are both part of the function's *closure*. That's a fancy way to say that they are values that are in scope when we're defining this function, but they aren't top-level values or functions that can be shared across the entire program.

What we've just described is the information stored in the heap object for a function, but like anything else we're not going to start by generating a function. Instead, we'll return a thunk that when evaluated will compute a function. In practice, thunks and function heap objects are quite similar though, and all the values we had to store in the function object's payload will also be in the thunk's payload.

The last thing we do in our example is call 'writeIORef' to update our counter. The value that we pass to it is yet another thunk. This thunk contains the thunk that we created that will eventually evaluate to the counting function we returned from `characterCounter`, along with the parameter we want to pass to that function. Just as in our earlier example, we've created a small space leak here. The problem once again is that when we write the thunk into our IO reference, we're keeping around a reference to the contents of our text file, preventing that data from being garbage collected. Now that we understand a bit more about how thunks and heap objects work, we can start to formulate a solution to this type of problem.

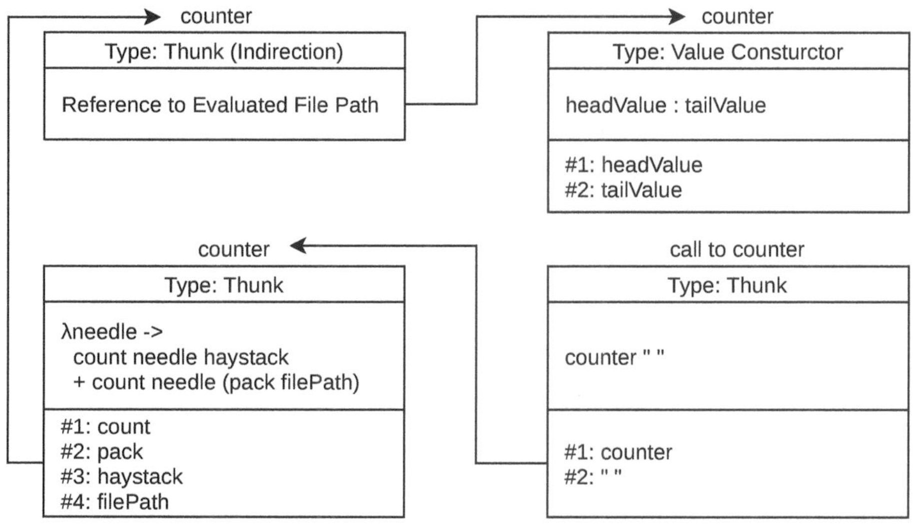

The crux of the problem in both our original code and our smaller example here is that when we write a value into our reference, what we're writing is a thunk that contains references to all of the data in its closure, including the contents of our file. If we could force the thunk to get evaluated, we might be able to let the garbage collector free the memory that we've allocated to hold the contents of our file, but only if we evaluate the thunk in the right way.

Right now we have a thunk that contains this code:

```
(counter ' ')
```

If we could naively evaluate this thunk, we'd replace the code in this thunk with a reference to a computed value that calls counter, which is just another thunk. Even if we evaluated the counter thunk, we'd still be left with a function heap object that contains the file contents in its closure. We need a way to get our thunk evaluated enough that we don't have to hold this kind of information anymore. To do that, we need to evaluate the value into *weak head normal form.*

A value in weak head normal form has to follow some very particular rules. First, it can't be a thunk, although it can have references to other thunks. Second, the heap object has to be either a function or a constructor. Finally, if the object is a function, we have to have applied any arguments to it that we could have applied.

Let's look at some examples. First, we'll look at some value constructors that are in weak head normal form:

```
100
'H' : <thunk>
\x -> x + 1
Just <thunk>
```

In these examples, 100 is in weak head normal form because a numeric literal is a value constructor for a numeric type. The list 'H' : <thunk> is in weak head normal form because the heap object contains a value constructor for a list, (:). Even though the tail of the list is a thunk, the expression is in weak head normal form because the actual heap object is a data constructor. Next, the function \x -> x + 1 is in weak head normal form because we don't have any values that we can apply to the function. Finally, Just <thunk> is in weak head normal form because it, like our list, is a value constructor, even though the actual value is a thunk.

On the other hand, we can also write some expressions that aren't in weak head normal form. Let's see some examples of those:

```
<thunk>
(\x -> x + 1) 5
5 + 1
```

The first example here is an unevaluated thunk. Even if the thunk would be evaluated to a function or value constructor, the thunk itself is neither, and so it's not in weak head normal form. In our second example, the expression (\x -> x + 1) 5 isn't in weak head normal form either. In this case, we have a value, 5, that we could apply to the function. If we did apply 5 to our function, we'd get to our final example, 5 + 1. This function is also not in weak head normal form, since (+) is a function. This is more obvious if we rewrite 5 + 1 using prefix notation, (+) 5 1. Since we have parameters we haven't yet applied, it isn't in weak head normal form.

Let's work through turning our thunk representing (counter " ") into weak head normal form manually to see what we'd get by doing the reduction.

First, let's expand counter, replacing it with its definition:

```
(\needle ->
  Text.count needle haystack
  + Text.count needle (Text.pack filePath)) " "
```

We can see right away that before we can have a value in weak head normal form we'll need to apply our parameter. That gives us this new expression:

```
Text.count " " haystack + Text.count " " (Text.pack filePath)
```

Next we have several other functions that haven't had all of their arguments applied. If we take yet another reduction that next step, we'd end up with something like this:

```
Text.count " " "haystack contents" + Text.count " " "/path/to/haystack"
```

We still need to apply our values to Text.count on both sides of our expression, which gives us: 1 + 0. That's still not in weak head normal form, so we need to apply our parameters one more time, and we're left with the value constructor 1.

By reducing the expression down to weak head normal form, we've removed any heap objects that need to hold references to the contents of the file we've opened, so that it can be safely garbage collected. We've also freed up several intermediate heap objects and removed a lot of indirection, potentially giving ourselves better performance. Of course, if we weren't ever going to use the results of our count, we might have done all of that work for nothing, so we wouldn't want to go reducing things for no reason.

The main problem we have left is that we've manually reduced our value down to weak head normal form as an example, but we need a way to tell the compiler to do it for us. Thankfully, we have a few ways to do it.

The first option that we have, and in this particular case the easiest, is to use a *strict* function to write data into our IORef. Some functions, like modifyIORef, offer strict versions that will reduce one of their arguments to weak head normal form when they are called. In this case, we can use the strict modifyIORef' to ensure our counter is reduced before it's written.

In this particular example, turning our lazy call to writeIORef into a strict call to modifyIORef' is a single line change that can drastically improve the performance of our program:

```
modifyIORef' countRef (const $ counter " ")
```

If we apply the same change to our metrics application, we'll also see a drastic reduction in the amount of memory being used. For example, by changing our timer function slightly, we can reduce both the total amount of memory in use and the maximum residency significantly:

```
timeFunction metrics "histogram" $ do
  oldHistogram <- readIORef histogramRef
  let
    addCharToHistogram histogram letter =
      Map.insertWith (+) letter 1 histogram
    newHistogram = Text.foldl' addCharToHistogram oldHistogram contents
  modifyIORef' histogramRef (const newHistogram)
```

If we run our example program from earlier with the single small change, we can see that we've significantly reduced the memory usage of our application:

```
 1,999,084,672 bytes allocated in the heap
    46,426,400 bytes copied during GC
     2,210,696 bytes maximum residency (26 sample(s))
       513,144 bytes maximum slop
             8 MiB total memory in use (0 MB lost due to fragmentation)

                                 Tot time (elapsed)  Avg pause  Max pause
Gen  0    1828 colls,  0 par     0.023s   0.023s     0.0000s    0.0003s
Gen  1      26 colls,  0 par     0.011s   0.011s     0.0004s    0.0005s

INIT    time    0.000s  (  0.000s elapsed)
MUT     time    0.422s  (  0.421s elapsed)
GC      time    0.034s  (  0.034s elapsed)
EXIT    time    0.000s  (  0.000s elapsed)
Total   time    0.456s  (  0.456s elapsed)

%GC     time       0.0%  (0.0% elapsed)

Alloc rate    4,739,720,785 bytes per MUT second

Productivity  92.6% of total user, 92.5% of total elapsed
```

Unfortunately, not all functions offer a strict version that works for us out of the box. If we need to implement strictness ourselves, there are several helper functions that are available in base and in some libraries. Most of these use one of two basic approaches to making data strict: calling the seq function, or using a popular GHC extension, BangPatterns.

BangPatterns

The BangPatterns extension has been available since GHC 6.8.1. It's enabled by default in GHC2021, but you'll need to manually enable it in Haskell2010. This is a safe extension and shouldn't generally cause any changes to code that doesn't directly use the feature.

The seq function is available in Prelude. Its type is seq :: a -> b -> b, and its purpose is to ensure that its first argument is evaluated to weak head normal and to return its second argument. It's typically used when you need to strictly evaluate an argument that you'll pass into a function. For example, we could replace our call to modifyIORef' with some code that uses seq directly instead:

```
newHistogram `seq` writeIORef histogramRef newHistogram
```

Here we have forced newHistogram to be reduced to weak head normal form before we pass it into writeIORef. In cases like this where the last parameter of a function is the one that we want to apply strictly, we can also use the strict function application operator from base, ($!). This function works just like the regular ($) operator that you're already familiar with, but it reduces its right-hand argument to weak head normal form before applying it to the function. For example, we can rewrite our somewhat verbose seq version much more tersely:

```
writeIORef histogramRef $! newHistogram
```

The use of the ! symbol in $! mirrors the last tool that we have for evaluating values to weak head normal form: using the BangPatterns extension. This extension allows us to add a *strictness annotation* by putting a ! symbol in front of let bindings and named parameters to ensure that they are evaluated to weak head normal form. Although they aren't usually used this way, we can use a bang pattern to ensure that newHistogram is evaluated to weak head normal form:

```
{-# LANGUAGE BangPatterns #-}

let
   addCharToHistogram histogram letter =
     Map.insertWith (+) letter 1 histogram
   !newHistogram = Text.foldl' addCharToHistogram oldHistogram contents
 writeIORef histogramRef newHistogram
```

More commonly, bang patterns are used with the parameters of functions to ensure one or more of the function's arguments are evaluated strictly, or with the fields in records to ensure that the data in the record is always reduced to weak head normal form before being stored. For example, instead of using modifyIORef' we could write our own writeIORef' function that ensures that the value we are writing is strict:

```
writeIORef' :: IORef a -> a -> IO ()
writeIORef' ref !val = writeIORef ref val
```

By including the bang pattern on the val parameter, we ensure the argument will always be evaluated to weak head normal form whenever the result of the function is evaluated. Since writeIORef' is an IO action that will generally be evaluated right away, we'll immediately evaluate the histogram thunk before we write it into the references.

Using bang patterns in records and data constructors follows the same pattern. Imagine if, instead of writing the histogram as a number, we had defined a new data type to hold the histogram:

```
data FileStats = FileStats (Map.Map Char Int)
```

Let's update the timer function of our code with the minimal changes required to use this new data type:

```
timeFunction metrics "histogram" $ do
  (FileStats oldHistogram) <- readIORef histogramRef
  let
    addCharToHistogram histogram letter =
      Map.insertWith (+) letter 1 histogram
    newHistogram =
      FileStats (Text.foldl' addCharToHistogram oldHistogram contents)
  writeIORef' histogramRef newHistogram
```

Running this version of the code with summary metrics, you'll notice we've regressed back to our original larger memory footprint, even though we are continuing to use our strict writeIORef' function that was previously giving us substantial improvements. The problem is our implementation of writeIORef' reduces its argument to weak head normal form. Now that we're writing a FileStats value instead of a map into our reference, reducing the argument to weak head normal form means we're only reducing the value down as far as the value constructor, and keeping the histogram calculation inside of a thunk. What we actually want is for the field of the record to be evaluated to weak head normal form when we construct the record.

Using BangPatterns we can add a strictness annotation to the types of fields in data types and records. Let's rewrite FileStats to ensure that our histogram will always be evaluated to weak head normal form:

```
data FileStats = FileStats  (Map.Map Char Int)
```

If we'd used a record for FileStats the syntax would be similar:

```
data FileStats = FileStats
  { fileHistogram :: !(Map.Map Char Int)
  }
```

With this small change, if we rebuild and re-run our program we can once again see that we're back to the lower memory footprint that we had before we added the value constructor.

Summary

Haskell programs tend to use mutability sparingly, but in the real world problems arise where mutable references can offer us a way to write substantially more simple or efficient code, and in most large applications there will be at least a few cases where mutable references are the best solution. In practice, many of the situations where you will find yourself wanting to use mutable references are also situations where you need to think carefully about laziness, and when and how parts of your program will be evaluated.

Exercises

traverseDirectoryIO

Write a new function, traverseDirectoryIO, that has the type:

```
traverseDirectoryIO :: FilePath -> (FilePath -> IO a) -> IO [a]
```

This function should behave like traverseDirectory' but should accept a function returning an IO action, rather than a value.

Timing Pure Functions

The timeFunction that you built as you worked through this chapter only supports timing IO actions. Try writing a version of this function that also works for pure values, with the type:

```
timePureFunction :: Metrics -> String -> a -> IO a
```

What are the limitations to your implementation function? Are there things that a user of the function could do to ensure that the timing information was better?

Metrics Strictness

Consider the MetricsStore type that you defined earlier in this chapter:

```
data MetricsStore = MetricsStore
  { successCount :: Int
  , failureCount :: Int
  , callDuration :: Map.Map String Int
  } deriving (Eq, Show)
```

How might you make use of strictness to improve the performance of metrics? Try writing some metrics collecting functions using several different approaches to strictness and profiling the results.

CHAPTER 11

Serializing Heterogenous Data

Heterogenous Data in Haskell

So far in this book, you've learned how to use polymorphism to create data structures and functions that can work with many different types. In all of the examples you've worked through so far, you've had to select a single type for any given instance of a polymorphic type. For example, while you can create a list that can hold any type, once instantiated, that list is restricted to only holding values of that one specific type that you selected.

In some cases, having data structures that are restricted to being uniform in the type they can hold can be quite inconvenient. In these situations, we turn to *heterogenous* data structures, which can hold values from an arbitrary collection of types. One particularly common example of a problem space where heterogenous data is helpful is in building tools to serialize and deserialize data. Throughout this chapter, you'll work through building a tool to archive and extract sets of files, similar to the standard Unix `tar` command. As you're working through this tool, you'll get a chance to learn about three common approaches to dealing with heterogenous data. First, you'll learn how to serialize and deserialize data using tools you are already familiar with, like sum types and records. Second, you'll learn about a more powerful technique for building a serializer using *existential quantification* that will allow you to build a library that can support serializing any arbitrary collection of types. Third, in the next chapter, you'll continue with this project by building tools to deserialize the archives that you've been creating.

A First Pass at a File Archiver

Throughout this chapter, you'll work through building a library for a tool called `filepack`. The FilePack library that we build will allow users to create archives of files that can be saved to disk, stored in a database, or sent over the internet. The examples you build as you work through this chapter will only support the programmatic creation and extraction of archives, but you are encouraged to create a complete application around this library as an additional example.

For maximum compatibility with third-party systems and tooling, we'll store the contents of our files as *base64 encoded* string data. Base64 encoding is a well-known approach to encoding binary data in plain ASCII text so that it can be handled in systems that assume they are dealing with plain text. Rather than implementing the base64 encoding algorithm ourselves, we'll import the base64-bytestring package. This package provides the Data.ByteString>Base64 module that we'll be using throughout the chapter.

Exploring the Base64 Encoding Package

We can see some examples of base64 encoding and decoding in ghci. We'll start by turning on the OverloadedStrings extension so that we can easily type ByteString literals, and we'll import both Data.ByteString and Data.ByteString.Base64:

```
λ :set -XOverloadedStrings
λ import qualified Data.ByteString as BS
λ import Data.ByteString.Base64 (encode,decode)
```

The two functions we'll be most interested in from the module are encode and decode, which allow us to encode a ByteString as base64, or decode it from base64 respectively. We can look at the types in ghci:

```
λ :type encode
encode :: BS.ByteString -> BS.ByteString
λ :type decode
decode :: BS.ByteString -> Either String BS.ByteString
```

To encode a ByteString we pass it to encode. The ByteString that we get back out will look nothing like the input. You can try running a few examples to see what base64 encoded strings look like:

```
λ encode "Hello, World"
"SGVsbG8sIFdvcmxk"
λ encode "String To Encode"
"U3RyaW5nIFRvIEVuY29kZQ=="
```

Decoding a string could fail if we pass in a value that isn't a valid base64 string. If the value is a valid base64 string, we should always get back precisely the same string that we originally encoded:

```
λ decode (encode "Hello, World")
Right "Hello, World"
```

```
λ decode "Hello, World"
Left "invalid character at offset: 5"
```

Creating the Basic Application

We'll start by creating a new project with cabal and adding a new module, FilePack, to the library. In this example, we're going to need to add the OverloadedStrings extension. Since we know that we're going to need them, we'll also go ahead and import the ByteString and Base64 encoding modules:

```
{-# LANGUAGE OverloadedStrings #-}

module FilePack where

import Data.ByteString (ByteString)
import qualified Data.ByteString as BS
import qualified Data.ByteString.Char8 as BC
import qualified Data.ByteString.Base64 as B64
import Data.Word
import System.Posix.Types (FileMode, CMode(..))
import Text.Read (readEither)
```

A file pack is really nothing more than a collection of files, so the next thing we need to figure out is how we want to represent an individual file. For now, let's start with something minimal, and we'll expand on what we can do with it throughout the chapter.

We'll create a new record, FileData, to store information about a file. We'll have four fields in our record:

- fileName will hold the name of the file on disk.
- fileSize will hold the size of the unpacked file.
- filePermissions will store the file's permissions.
- fileData will store the actual contents of the file.

Since a file size can never be negative, we'll store the size as a Word32. The Word types, from Data.Word, allow us to store unsigned numeric values.

System Dependent Code Ahead

In this chapter, we'll assume that a CMode is an alias for Word32. CMode might alias other numeric types depending on your operating system. In that case, you may need to define some additional type class instances to fully support your operating system.

We'll store the permissions using the CMode type from System.Posix.Types. This type will let us store a numeric representation of the file permissions in normal Unix permissions style as a three-digit octal number. We'll also bring in FileMode, which is an alias for CMode that has a more easily understandable name.

Finally, we'll store the contents of our file as a ByteString. This will make our lives easier since it is the native type that our base64 encoder wants to use, and can represent arbitrary binary data.

With these fields in place, we can create our new FileData record:

```
data FileData = FileData
  { fileName        :: FilePath
  , fileSize        :: Word32
  , filePermissions :: FileMode
  , fileData        :: ByteString
  } deriving (Eq, Read, Show)
```

The FileData record represents a single file. A FilePack is a collection of files that should be stored in an archive. We'll use a newtype wrapper for our file pack:

```
newtype FilePack =
  FilePack {getPackedFiles :: [FileData]} deriving (Eq, Read, Show)
```

Now we're ready to serialize our file pack into an archive. Sticking with the theme of starting with a minimal implementation, we'll use Show to serialize our file pack into a String, then BS.pack to convert the String into a ByteString, and finally we'll call B64.encode to generate the final archive:

```
packFiles :: FilePack -> ByteString
packFiles filePack =
  B64.encode . BC.pack . show $ filePack
```

We need to do a bit more work to unpack our file, but not too much. We'll start by importing another module from bytestring, Data.ByteString.Char8. This module has most of the same functions that are available in Data.ByteString, but they work with String and Char values rather than lists of bytes. Data.ByteString.Char8 re-exports the same ByteString type that is exported by Data.ByteString, so you don't need to worry about converting between Data.ByteString.ByteString and Data.ByteString.Char8.ByteString.

Next, we'll need to try to decode the serialialized data that we've gotten. If that fails we can give up, because there's nothing more that we can do. On the other hand, if we do get a decoded value, then we can try to use our Read instance to convert that value back to a FilePack.

We can't just call read though. There are two issues we'll need to solve. First, read might fail at runtime. It would be nice if we could get some better error reporting if something goes wrong. To do that, we can use the readEither function from Text.Read in base. This function works like read but returns an Either value rather than failing at runtime.

The other issue is that readEither and other similar functions all work with String values rather than bytestrings, so we'll call BC.unpack to convert our ByteString into a string before trying to parse it.

With all of that in place, here's what our unpack function looks like:

```
unpackFiles :: ByteString -> Either String FilePack
unpackFiles serializedData =
  B64.decode serializedData >>= readEither . BC.unpack
```

As a general rule, using Show and Read for important serialization work as we've done in this example is a bad idea. Both read and show are quite closely tied to the specific implementation of a record. The strings generated by show include the names of all of the record fields, in the order they are written in the code. Similarly, read will fail if any fields have been added, removed, renamed, or the order of fields in a record have changed. Later on in this chapter we'll stop depending on these and implement serialization and deserialization ourselves, but for now we'll keep using these as a quick way to develop our first prototype.

Writing In-Line Tests

As we're working through the development of our library, it'll be nice to test our code in ghci, but it can start to get a little annoying to rewrite the tests we want to run repeatedly. In cases like that, one handy approach is to add some tests in our module that will be available to run interactively each time we load the code into ghci. Once you've finished active work on the feature, you can delete your test code or use them as the foundation for unit tests.

```
testPackFile :: ByteString
testPackFile =
  packFiles sampleFilePack

testUnpackFile :: Either String FilePack
testUnpackFile = unpackFiles testPackFile

testRoundTrip :: FilePack -> Bool
testRoundTrip pack =
  (Right pack) == (unpackFiles $ packFiles pack)
```

These test functions will now let us look at the result of packing and unpacking FilePack values, as well as verifying that we can *round-trip* our data by ensuring that decoding some encoded data gives us back what we started with.

```
λ testRoundTrip
True
```

Supporting Multiple File Types

Our simple version of FilePack works remarkably well for being such a small library, but there are a few drawbacks to the approach that we've taken. The most immediate one is we're requiring our users to do the hard work of turning their data into a ByteString before they can ever create a file. It'd be nice if we could allow users to instead work with whatever types they are already using to represent their file data, but pack those files directly into a file pack.

The next incremental step that we could take to giving our users more flexibility in how they represent their data is to make use of a sum type. Instead of taking a ByteString to serialize data, we can take any of several different types of data that could represent the file.

For the moment, let's consider a couple of other popular ways to represent Haskell data. ByteString will allow us to easily support binary data, so next, let's add support for Text to support text content. We'll also add support for text stored as a String so that users who are working with strings don't need to pack and unpack their data.

We've already added bytestring into our cabal dependencies, and String support comes from base. We'll also need to add text as a dependency in our cabal file.

Next, we need to import a couple of modules. Data.Text will give us access to Text types. The Text type is an efficient way to represent and work with Unicode text data:

```
import Data.Text (Text)
import qualified Data.Text as Text
```

With our imports in place, we can move on to defining a type to represent our file contents. Since we have three different formats to choose from, we'll create a new *sum type*, FileContents:

```
data FileContents
  = StringFileContents     String
  | TextFileContents       Text
  | ByteStringFileContents ByteString
  deriving (Eq, Read, Show)
```

And next, let's update our our FileData record to use FileContents:

```
data FileData = FileData
  { fileName        :: FilePath
  , fileSize        :: Word32
  , filePermissions :: FileMode
  , fileData        :: FileContents
  } deriving (Eq, Read, Show)
```

Finally, we need to update our sampleFilePack to select a particular encoding of our data:

```
sampleFilePack :: FilePack
sampleFilePack = FilePack $
    [ FileData "stringFile" 0 0 $ StringFileContents "hello string"
    , FileData "textFile" 0 0 $ TextFileContents "hello text"
    , FileData "binaryFile" 0 0 $ ByteStringFileContents "hello bytestring"
    ]
```

Using a sum type here allows us to create a slightly more flexible API while having to write minimal code. In cases where you know ahead of time that you'll only need to support a few specific input types, making use of a sum type to represent all of the options is often the easiest way forward.

In the case of our file packer, however, we want to allow users of our library to package any sort of data into files without restricting them to a particular set of representations.

Serializing with Type Classes

Using Show and Read in our prototype certainly made things easier on us when we were serializing and deserializing things, but that wasn't the only benefit. It also meant that we didn't have to think much about how users would interact with our library. Show and Read are both common type classes that have implementations for most basic types, and our users might already have them implemented for their own data.

Now that we're going to be dropping these type classes in favor of something that works more reliably for our problem, we are going to need to ensure that we're still giving users the ability to interact with our library using whatever types they happen to be using to represent their own file data. We'll still handle this with type classes, but now instead of relying on preexisting type classes, we'll define our own.

We'll start with a class for encoding data into a bytestring:

```
class Encode a where
  encode :: a -> ByteString
```

Let's also create a type class for decoding things that we have encoded. You'll build a complete decoder for file packs in the next chapter, but defining the type class now will give you something that you can use to test with as you work through this chapter:

```
class Decode a where
  decode :: ByteString -> Either String a
```

Now that we have defined a type class, we need to start creating some instances for it. Eventually we'll want to create instances for things like FileData and FilePack, but we'll start by creating instances for more basic types, so that we can re-use them when we're implementing our bigger instances.

Creating Instances for Basic Types

Let's start creating instances for our basic types with ByteString. Since we're defining our own type classes for encoding and decoding things, we're free to pick any approach that we want. We're free to continue using base64 encoding for our fields, or to simply use the underlying bytestring directly. For now, let's just make our encode and decode functions for ByteString preserve the input string unmodified:

```
instance Encode ByteString where
  encode = id

instance Decode ByteString where
  decode = Right . id
```

We can create instances for Text and String with just a little bit more work. For Text we'll use the encodeUtf8 and decodeUtf8 functions fromData.Text.Encoding to do the conversion for us:

```
import Data.Text.Encoding (encodeUtf8, decodeUtf8)

instance Encode Text where
  encode = encodeUtf8

instance Decode Text where
  decode = Right . decodeUtf8
```

Similarly, our instances for String can simply re-use the work already done for us by pack and unpack from Data.ByteString.Char8. We'll need to add the FlexibleInstances extension for these instances. Without FlexibleInstances we're not allowed to create an instance of a type class that specifies a particular value for a type parameter. Since String is an alias for [Char], that means we wouldn't ordinarily be allowed to create an instance for it. Instead, we'd need to create a more general instance for [a]. With FlexibleInstances we're allowed to be more specific and restrict our instance to only [Char]:

```
{-# LANGUAGE FlexibleInstances #-}

instance Encode String where
  encode = BC.pack

instance Decode String where
  decode = Right . BC.unpack
```

With our various string types accounted for, let's turn our attention to a type that has a more interesting instance: Word32.

Serializing Word32

The Word32 type represents an unsigned four-byte (32-bit) number. Word32 is the first major departure from our serialization pattern so far, because it's not string data but instead raw binary data. Although we might naively choose to convert our number to a string and encode that string the same way we encoded Text and String values, in this example, we'll stick to our chosen approach of avoiding show and read and instead encoding the data ourselves. As you'll see later on in this chapter, the choice to encode the raw binary data now will end up paying dividends to us later when it's time to deserialize our files.

Thankfully, as its name implies, ByteString works under the hood with raw binary data. Specifically, raw individual bytes. Until now we've ignored the "binary-ness" of ByteString and worked with them through interfaces that let us think of them as textual string data, but we are perfectly free to skip these interfaces and work directly with the underlying bytes that make up a ByteString.

Earlier, when we wrote our Encode and Decode instances for String we used the pack and unpack functions from Data.ByteString.Char8. The pack function takes a list of characters and returns a new ByteString, and unpack takes a ByteString and returns a list of characters.

If we want to work with the underlying bytes instead of character strings, all we need to do is to use the pack and unpack functions from Data.ByteString instead of Data.ByteString.Char8:

```
λ :type BS.pack
BS.pack :: [Word8] -> ByteString
λ :type BS.unpack
BS.unpack :: ByteString -> [Word8]
```

This is pretty convenient, but the difficulty we're going to run into is that we're dealing with a four-byte Word32 value, and somehow we need to convert that to four one-byte Word8 values instead.

Let's write a function called Word32ToBytes that will handle the conversion for us. It'll have the type:

```
word32ToBytes :: Word32 -> (Word8, Word8, Word8, Word8)
```

We'll start our implementation by importing Data.Bits from base. This will give us access to some useful bitwise operators that we can use to split up our

Word32: The bitwise-and operator (.&.), the bitwise-or operator (.|.), and the bitwise shift function.

```
import Data.Bits ((.&.), (.|.), shift)
```

Bit Twiddling

If you haven't worked with bitwise operations in a while, you might find some of the examples in this section hard to follow. In that case, you should use ghci to experiment with the operations before you move forward. You can use the printf function from Text.Printf to easily display values in binary to make this easier: showBinary = printf "%b\n".

The implementation of our function makes use of some bit twiddling to get the underlying bytes out of our Word32 value:

```
word32ToBytes :: Word32 -> (Word8, Word8, Word8, Word8)
word32ToBytes word =
    let a = fromIntegral $ 255 .&. word
        b = fromIntegral $ 255 .&. (shift word (-8))
        c = fromIntegral $ 255 .&. (shift word (-16))
        d = fromIntegral $ 255 .&. (shift word (-24))
    in (a,b,c,d)
```

In this function, we take one-byte sections out of our Word32 one at a time by shifting the value to the right and then using 255 .&. to take only the lower byte of the shifted value. In the end, we'll have gotten each of the bytes one-by-one. If you haven't encountered this sort of bit twiddling before, or don't remember much about it, you don't need to worry. We'll revisit this one more time later on in this section when we reconstruct the values, and afterwards we won't need to return to the details of this function again.

We can get a better idea of how this works by writing a quick function in ghci to help us visualize this. We'll need to import Text.Printf so that we can easily print out hex digits, and then we can create a small helper function, printBytes, which takes a four-tuple of bytes and prints them out:

```
λ import Text.Printf
λ printBytes (a,b,c,d) = printf "%02x %02x %02x %02x\n" a b c d
```

And now we can print out some values:

```
λ printBytes $ word32ToBytes 0xAABBCCDD
dd cc bb aa
λ printBytes $ word32ToBytes 255
ff 00 00 00
```

```
λ printBytes $ word32ToBytes 65535
ff ff 00 00
λ printBytes $ word32ToBytes 0xffff0000
00 00 ff ff
```

The order of bytes in the output will depend on the native byte order (or "endianness") of your system. The previous examples are from a little endian x86-64 system, which puts the least significant bytes first.

Since we're not going to be working directly with the bytes in our application, other than encoding and decoding them, we don't need to be immediately concerned with the byte order in our data. We would, however, need to consider byte order if we were going to try to make our application work with files that were created on systems with a potentially different byte ordering.

Now that we have a way to get the individual bytes out of a Word32, we can pack them into a bytestring without too much extra work. We'll start by building a function that will let us create a new ByteString from a Word32:

```
word32ToByteString :: Word32 -> ByteString
word32ToByteString word =
  let (a,b,c,d) = word32ToBytes word
  in BS.pack [a,b,c,d]
```

We can also create a function that will let us add a Word32 to the beginning of an existing bytestring. This will come in handy later as we start to serialize our data:

```
consWord32 :: Word32 -> ByteString -> ByteString
consWord32 word bytestring =
  let packedWord = word32ToByteString word
  in packedWord <> bytestring
```

Now that we have a way to turn a Word32 into a ByteString we can encode one by calling word32ToByteString:

```
instance Encode Word32 where
  encode = word32ToByteString
```

Now that we have a working encoder, let's turn our attention toward decoding a value. Our decoder function needs to turn a bytestring back into a single Word32 by putting the individual bytes in the word back together. Before we start dealing with the ByteString data, let's first write a simpler function that will start with the raw bytes and put them back together into a Word32:

```
word32FromBytes :: (Word8, Word8, Word8, Word8) -> Word32
word32FromBytes (a,b,c,d) =
  let
    a' = fromIntegral a
```

```
    b' = shift (fromIntegral b) 8
    c' = shift (fromIntegral c) 16
    d' = shift (fromIntegral d) 24
  in a' .|. b' .|. c' .|. d'
```

This function is the inverse of our previous word32ToBytes function. Each value was originally shifted to the right by 0, 1, 2, or 3 bytes, so we shift them back to their correct position and then use bitwise-or (.|.) to combine them back into a single value.

Once you've written this function, you can validate that it's correct by writing a function to test Word32 values to ensure that converting a value to bytes and back returns the original value.

Turning a ByteString into a Word32 using our new word32FromBytes function isn't going to be very hard, but it does have the potential to fail. Unlike when we were created a ByteString, we now have to consider the possibility of failure. A Word32 must be made up of precisely four bytes, so we need to check the size of our input and return an error if we get more or less data than we expect.

We'll handle this by unpacking our bytestring and pattern matching on the resulting list. If we get exactly four bytes, we can convert them into a Word32 and otherwise we'll report an error:

```
bytestringToWord32 :: ByteString -> Either String Word32
bytestringToWord32 bytestring =
  case BS.unpack bytestring of
    [a,b,c,d] -> Right $ word32FromBytes (a,b,c,d)
    _otherwise ->
      let l = show $ BS.length bytestring
      in Left ("Expecting 4 bytes but got " <> l)
```

Finally, we can write our Decode instance for Word32 by directly calling bytestringToWord32:

```
instance Decode Word32 where
  decode = bytestringToWord32
```

Serializing FileMode

A FileMode is an alias for CMode, which is itself a newtype wrapper around Word32. This means we can easily re-use the work we've just done with Word32 to serialize and deserialize FileMode too:

```
instance Encode FileMode where
  encode (CMode fMode) = encode fMode

instance Decode FileMode where
  decode = fmap CMode . decode
```

Serializing FileData

Now that we've written instances to let us serialize all of the types that we're using inside of FileData, we can move on to serializing a FileData value itself. As a first step, let's refactor FileData. Instead using a sum type like FileContents to list a small set of supported files, we'll add a type parameter to keep track of the type of the contents in our file:

```
data FileData a = FileData
  { fileName        :: FilePath
  , fileSize        :: Word32
  , filePermissions :: FileMode
  , fileData        :: a
  } deriving (Eq, Read, Show)

newtype FilePack a =
  FilePack {getPackedFiles :: [FileData a]}
  deriving (Eq, Read, Show)
```

Next, let's move on to writing an Encode instance for FileData. Unlike our earlier examples, FileData is a record that has several values that will need to be packed together. Let's start with a relatively simple attempt at encoding file data:

```
instance Encode a => Encode (FileData a) where
  encode FileData{..} =
    encode fileName
    <> encode fileSize
    <> encode filePermissions
    <> encode fileData
```

In this example, we're depending on the Encode instance for whatever type we're using to store the contents of the file. We already have instances defined for the types we're using to store metadata. This is enough to let us encode each individual field in the record, and from there we can concatenate them together to get encoded file data. This approach will compile, and we can see it working to encode data in ghci. Now that we can support several different content types, we'll use a type application to tell the compiler what kind of contents we're intending to use:

```
λ encode $ FileData @String "testPath" 0 0 "Foo"
"testPath\NUL\NUL\NUL\NUL\NUL\NUL\NUL\NULFoo"
```

Unfortunately, we've created a problem for ourselves when we want to decode a value. If we try to implement an equally straightforward decoder we'll quickly see what happened:

```
instance Decode a => Decode (FileData a) where
  decode encodedFileData =
    case decode encodedFileData of
      -- ...
```

Do you see the problem yet? We get a single ByteString in as input, and the first thing that we try to decode will consume our entire bytestring. If all of our fields were of a fixed size, then we could just take enough data out of the bytestring for each field and decode that, but we're dealing with both string data from FilePath and unknown data with the field our user provides.

We need some way to separate out the individual fields so that we can decode them effectively. We could add a separator to our strings so that we can mark the end of one section of data and the start of another, but since we might be storing arbitrary data, there aren't any separators that we could use that couldn't also occur naturally in the data that we're encoding.

We can avoid this problem by prefixing each field with the size, in bytes, of the field. Then, when we're decoding things, we can always just take the exact amount of the string that we need and decode it.

To support adding size information to everything that we encode, let's add a second function to our Encode type class called encodeWithSize:

```
class Encode a where
  encode :: a -> ByteString
  encodeWithSize :: a -> ByteString
```

Of course, if we have a definition of encode we can always come up with a reasonable definition of encodeWithSize by looking at the length of the encoded value, so we can add a default implementation:

```
encodeWithSize :: a -> ByteString
encodeWithSize a =
  let s = encode a
      l = fromIntegral $ BS.length s
  in word32ToByteString l <> s
```

On the other hand, if we're provided a valid implementation of encodeWithSize, we can come up with a valid implementation of decode by dropping off the leading size field. So, we can add a default implementation for it as well:

```
encode :: a -> ByteString
encode = BS.drop 4 . encodeWithSize
```

As a last step, let's add a MINIMAL pragma to let our users know that they need to provide an implementation of at least one of these two functions. With that, our final type class definition will be:

```
class Encode a where
  encode :: a -> ByteString
  encode =
    BS.drop 4 . encodeWithSize

  encodeWithSize :: a -> ByteString
  encodeWithSize a =
    let s = encode a
        l = fromIntegral $ BS.length s
    in word32ToByteString l <> s
  {- MINIMAL encode | encodeWithSize #-}
```

We've already implemented encode for all of our values, so we could move on. For most of our instances, there's no way that we can do better than our default encodeWithSize implementation, so we only need to update our Word32 instance.

Since we know that Word32 will always take up four bytes when it's encoded, we don't need to look at the length of the encoded string at all. We can save some effort and hard-code the size ahead of time:

```
instance Encode Word32 where
  encode = word32ToByteString
  encodeWithSize w =
    let (a, b, c, d) = word32ToBytes w
    in BS.pack [ 4, 0, 0, 0
               , a, b, c, d]
```

This implementation should be significantly more efficient since we're only constructing a single ByteString.

Now that we have a way to keep track of the size of each field in FileData, we can return to our instance implementation. We'll use our new function to encode each of our fields with their size. We'll also encode the entire thing together as a single bytestring so we keep all the internal pieces together:

```
instance Encode a => Encode (FileData a) where
  encode FileData{..} =
    let
      encodedFileName = encodeWithSize fileName
      encodedFileSize = encodeWithSize fileSize
      encodedFilePermissions = encodeWithSize filePermissions
      encodedFileData = encodeWithSize fileData
      encodedData =
        encodedFileName
        <> encodedFileSize
        <> encodedFilePermissions
        <> encodedFileData
     in encode encodedData
```

For the moment we'll skip implementing Decode for our FileData. Later on in this chapter, we'll return to the subject of decoding records and other compound value types.

Serializing Tuples and Lists

Before we finish up with this section on serializing data, let's add two more instances that will come in handy later on in the chapter. As with FileData, we'll serialize them now, and add Decode instances later on.

We'll start by serializing tuples. As with FileData, we'll make use of encodeWithSize to let us differentiate between our first and second fields:

```
instance (Encode a, Encode b) => Encode (a,b) where
  encode (a,b) =
    encode $ encodeWithSize a <> encodeWithSize b
```

Next, we'll add an instance that will let us encode any list of encodable values. We don't know ahead of time how many elements we'll be processing, but we can still apply our pattern of encoding to every element of our list with its size, concatenating them together, and encoding the final result.

We'll use the foldMap function to do this. foldMap, like the name implies, is a combination of a fold and a map. It applies a function to each element in a list and combines the results with (<>):

```
instance Encode a => Encode [a] where
  encode = encode . foldMap encodeWithSize
```

Unfortunately, this instance doesn't work! If we try to compile it we'll get an error. Your error might look a bit different, but it should resemble this one:

```
FilePack.hs:49:10: error:
    • Overlapping instances for Encode String
        arising from a use of ‘FilePack.$dmencodeWithSize’
      Matching instances:
        instance Encode String -- Defined at FilePack.hs:49:10
        instance Encode a => Encode [a] -- Defined at FilePack.hs:85:10
    • In the expression: FilePack.$dmencodeWithSize @(String)
      In an equation for ‘encodeWithSize’:
          encodeWithSize = FilePack.$dmencodeWithSize @(String)
      In the instance declaration for ‘Encode String’
   |
49 | instance Encode String where
   |          ^^^^^^^^^^^^^
```

The important part here is the part that says *Overlapping instances*.

The problem is we've told the compiler to do the same thing in two different ways. In the instance we just wrote, we told it for any list it should use that instance's version of encode. When we created an instance for String we also told it to use that instance any time it had a list of characters. So the compiler throws up its arms, and an error, and refuses to compile our program.

Of course, to us it's obvious what we'd like to happen. We want our special case of String to be used when it can be, and we want to fall back to our general case of [a] otherwise. We can tell the compiler to do just that by telling it that our new instance is OVERLAPPABLE. The OVERLAPPABLE pragma is a way that we can tell GHC to always prefer a different instance if there happens to be a conflict.

With the pragma in place our instance now looks like this:

```
instance {-# OVERLAPPABLE #-} Encode a => Encode [a] where
  encode = encode . foldMap encodeWithSize
```

And with the conflict resolved, GHC will happily compile our code again and work as we'd like.

Overlapping instances are a common problem. If you run into them you can use the OVERLAPPABLE instance as we've done here to specify an instance that should not be chosen if there is a conflict, or you can use the OVERLAPS pragma to provide one that should be authoritative.

The OverlappingInstances extension enables overlapping on all instances without the pragma, but this extension is deprecated and you should not use it in new code.

Building a List of FileData Values

Now that we have created a way to hold information about a specific file, and to serialize it, we should turn our eyes toward representing a collection of files. The minimal implementation here is pretty easy thanks to the work that we've done with supporting encoding lists. We'll make a newtype wrapper around a list of values, and while we're at it, we'll go ahead and give it an Encode instance. We're manually specifying the instance here because if we use newtype deriving we'll once again run into an overlapping instances problem.

```
instance Encode a => Encode (FilePack a) where
  encode (FilePack a) = encode a
```

We can use this to create files pretty easily:

```
λ filePack = FilePack [ FileData "file1" 0 0 "data1"
                      , FileData "file2" 0 0 "data2"
                      , FileData "file3" 0 0 "data3" ]
λ :type filePack
filePack :: FilePack (FileData String)
```

This works great so long as we only ever want to pack a single kind of file into an archive, but what if our user has a file that contains text data stored as a Text and a file that contains some image data stored as a ByteString?

```
λ textFile = FileData @Text "textfile.txt" 0 0 "some text"
λ imageData <- BS.readFile "image.jpg"
λ imageFile = FileData "image.jpg" 0 0 imageData
λ filepack = FilePack [textFile, imageFile]

<interactive>:75:32: error:
    • Couldn't match type ‘ByteString’ with ‘Text’
      Expected type: FileData Text
        Actual type: FileData ByteString
    • In the expression: imageFile
      In the first argument of ‘FilePack’, namely ‘[textFile, imageFile]’
      In the expression: FilePack [textFile, imageFile]
```

As you might have expected, this failed because we're trying to put values with two different types into a list. Up until now, when we ran into this situation we'd throw our hands up in the air and think of a different way to represent our code, but in this example being able to represent files with different types of content is really fundamental to what we're trying to build. Surely Haskell can't be stymied by a requirement like this.

Supporting Multiple File Types with Sum Types

One way that we could solve this problem is by creating a new sum type that would let us hold different sorts of files. There are a couple of ways we could do this. We might try a fairly high-level and user-friendly approach, like enumerating different sorts of files a user might be dealing with:

```
data SomeFile
  = SomeTextFile (FileData Text)
  | SomeImageFile (FileData ByteString)
  | SomeAudioFile (FileData ByteString)
```

As you can imagine, that would start to become quite a long list, and it would be impossible to predict all of the different sorts of files that a user might want to store. Alternatively, we could use a lower-level representation and just wrap the file data type directly:

```
data SomeFile
  = SomeStringFile (FileData String)
  | SomeTextFile (FileData Text)
  | SomeByteStringFile (FileData ByteString)
```

This approach is more general, but even now we're limited to just a handful of file types, and we've completely defeated the work that we did earlier to allow users to create their own file content types.

Some Failed Attempts

If you stare at the problem for a while, the next thing that might come to your mind as a way to get around this problem is to use forall.

We'll start by looking at FilePack. We have a type parameter that we're using to keep track of what kind of data is in our list. This is a problem because it's limiting us to a single type of value. Let's remove it:

```
λ newtype FilePack = Filepack [a]

<interactive>:7:30: error: Not in scope: type variable ‘a’
```

This doesn't work because GHC doesn't have any idea what a is or where it came from. If a isn't a type parameter we need to introduce it somehow. We can use the forall keyword here to introduce a type variable. Let's try it:

```
newtype FilePack = FilePack (forall a. Encode a => [a])
```

Hey, that works! We can create a FilePack that can hold any sort of data that has an Encode instance. Let's create a value:

```
λ filepack = FilePack [FileData "file" 0 0 "file"]

<interactive>:22:22: error:
    • Couldn't match expected type ‘a’
                  with actual type ‘FileData [Char]’
      ‘a’ is a rigid type variable bound by
        a type expected by the context:
          forall a. Encode a => [a]
        at <interactive>:22:21-48
    • In the expression: FileData "file" 0 0 "file"
      In the first argument of ‘FilePack’, namely
        ‘[FileData "file" 0 0 "file"]’
      In the expression: FilePack [FileData "file" 0 0 "file"]
```

Foiled again. This time we're telling our newtype wrapper that it needs to hold some polymorphic value that can be any Encode value, but then we're trying to give it a value with a specific type. Since that specific type isn't polymorphic, it fails to typecheck.

Impredicative Polymorphism

One of the problems that we're going to run into with all of these attempts is that even if they would otherwise typecheck, we're using forall outside of our list. No matter how flexible we might be with picking a value, we're still going to come up with a list of values of the same type. What we'd really like to have is a list of anything, so long as it can be encoded. Let's try another approach:

```
λ data FilePack = FilePack [forall a. Encode a => a]

<interactive>:29:17: error:
    • Illegal polymorphic type: forall a. Encode a => a
      GHC doesn't yet support impredicative polymorphism
    • In the definition of data constructor 'FilePack'
      In the data type declaration for 'FilePack'
```

This still doesn't work…yet. As you might note from the error message here, impredicative polymorphism is on the roadmap for GHC and may even be available in newer releases of the compiler. If this works for you, congratulations! You can move on to the next section of this chapter. If, however, you are working with an older GHC version, or working in a code base that was written before impredicative types were added, we have a different approach we can use to work around this problem.

Existential Types

Existential types in Haskell give you a way to "weaken" a type into a representation that is more general, but about which you have less information. In our case, we'd like to take all of the different FileData types that we might have, like FileData String or FileData Text, and forget everything about them except that they are something we can encode. When we do that, what we end up with is an existential type that we can use in places where we have to use a single type—for example, in a list. To make use of them we have to add the ExistentialQuantification extension.

ExistentialQuantification

The ExistentialQuantification extension has been available since GHC 6.8.1. It's enabled by default in GHC2021 but you'll need to enable it manually in Haskell2010. This extension implies the ExplicitForAll feature, so you don't need to enable it if you've already enabled ExistentialQuantification. This is generally a safe extension that shouldn't cause problems with any existing code.

Let's look at an example to start with. We'll create a new type, Packable, that will hold values that we can put into a FilePack:

```
{-# LANGUAGE ExistentialQuantification #-}
data Packable = forall a. Encode a => Packable { getPackable :: FileData a }
```

You'll notice in this example that although we're using a type variable, a, we're not actually referring to that type variable anywhere in the type declaration. This means that our existential type, Packable, doesn't carry around any information about the type of the variable we used to construct it. Erasing this information is what lets us use Packable to do things like create a list that holds different sorts of file data.

Instead of holding the type information as a parameter to Packable, we've introduced it in our statement:

```
forall a. Encode a => Packable
```

This allows us to not only introduce the type variable, but also add in any constraints that we might need. Adding constraints at this point is important, because once we've constructed a value of our existential type we no longer have access to any information about the type of the value.

To understand this limitation a little bit better, let's try to write something that will get our FileData out of a Packable value:

```
getPackedFileData (Packable fileData) = fileData
```

Let's load this up in ghci and see what happens:

```
FilePack.hs:125:41: error:
    • Couldn't match expected type 'p' with actual type 'FileData a'
        because type variable 'a' would escape its scope
      This (rigid, skolem) type variable is bound by
        a pattern with constructor:
          Packable :: forall a. Encode a => FileData a -> Packable,
        in an equation for 'getPackedFileData'
        at FilePack.hs:125:20-36
    • In the expression: fileData
      In an equation for 'getPackedFileData':
          getPackedFileData (Packable fileData) = fileData
    • Relevant bindings include
        fileData :: FileData a (bound at FilePack.hs:125:29)
        getPackedFileData :: Packable -> p (bound at FilePack.hs:125:1)
    |
125 | getPackedFileData (Packable fileData) = fileData
    |                                         ^^^^^^^^
Failed, no modules loaded.
```

That's quite an error message. The internet is full of questions about "rigid skolem" variables from intrepid Haskell developers who have run into problems trying to work with existential types.

The problem here is that, as you've learned, when we create a new Packable value we erase any information we had about the type that we created it with, except that it is encodable.

When we try to pattern match with (Packable fileData) we're bringing into existence some variable, fileData. When we go to return that value, it needs to have a type, but there's no type that we can actually assign to it because we've already lost that information. Not only that, the limited information that we do have about our value, forall a. Encode a, is captured by our Packable value. The type can't exist outside of Packable, so we don't have any way of extracting that value.

The idea that the erased type information might somehow leak out of an existential type is sometimes referred to by saying that the variable might "escape its context," and you'll sometimes get error messages from GHC that refer to the error this way. For example, if we rewrite getPackedFileData to be pointfree we'll get a different error:

```
λ getPackedFileData = getPackable

<interactive>:39:21: error:
    • Cannot use record selector 'getPackable' as a function due to escaped
      type variables
      Probable fix: use pattern-matching syntax instead
    • In the expression: getPackable
      In an equation for 'getPackedFileData':
          getPackedFileData = getPackable
```

Although the error message in this case is different, the fundamental problem is the same. We can't leak any type information out of an existential type.

Just because we can't leak type information out of our existential type doesn't mean that we can't do anything useful with existential data. One way you can make use of existential types is to use a record that contains some functions you might want to call. As an example, let's create a new existential type that can hold a value and some functions:

```
{-# LANGUAGE ExistentialQuantification #-}
{-# LANGUAGE RecordWildCards #-}
module ExistentialDemo where

data SomeExistential b = forall a. SomeExistential
  { someValue :: a
  , modifyValue :: a -> a
  , combineValues :: a -> a -> a
  , consumeValue :: a -> b
  }
```

Although we have a type parameter here, b, we're still creating an existential type because we're erasing the existence of a. Inside of our record, we have several functions that reference both of our type variables, a and b. All of the normal typing rules apply here within our record, so someValue and the types of all of our functions are referring to the same type when they use the type variable a. Similarly, when we refer to b in consumeValue we're referring to the b type parameter that we've added to our type constructor, so if we have a value with the type SomeExistential Int then we know that consumeValue must take as input whatever type someValue happens to be, and it must return an Int.

Since the type of a gets erased when we create an existential, we can't ever get at it directly, but we are allowed to use the values and functions inside of our record as long as we never end up with a value whose type would leak out from the existential. Let's look at a concrete example.

We'll start by writing a function that will let us create one of our existential values that holds some numeric value:

```
addAndMultiplyInt :: Integral a => a -> SomeExistential Int
addAndMultiplyInt n = SomeExistential
  { someValue = n
  , modifyValue = (+n)
  , combineValues = (*)
  , consumeValue = fromIntegral
  }
```

We can't do much with this directly, but we can write a function to do some work with our existential value and give us back something that we can work with. Let's write one:

```
runExistential :: SomeExistential a -> a
runExistential SomeExistential{..} =
  consumeValue $
    combineValues (modifyValue someValue) someValue
```

In this function, we're referring to values that we don't, and can't, know the type of. We can do that, because we don't know what type someValue is, but we do know that whatever type it has, modifyValue can accept one and returns one. Similarly, combineValues takes two of them and returns one. At the end of our computation we're calling consumeValue. Once again, we don't know what type is going into consumeValue, but we do know the type that it will return. For example, if we pass runExistential, a value with the type SomeExistential Int, we don't know what the values are inside of the existential, but we do know that whatever we get out must be an Int, and if we look up the type information in ghci it will tell us as much:

```
λ :type runExistential . addAndMultiplyInt
runExistential . addAndMultiplyInt :: Integral a => a -> Int
λ runExistential $ addAndMultiplyInt 4
32
```

In this example, we're passing in a number and getting a number back out, but of course with our existential type we might be wrapping up anything. Let's create a version that holds a string:

```
reverseAndUnwordsString :: String -> SomeExistential String
reverseAndUnwordsString s = SomeExistential
  { someValue = s
  , modifyValue = reverse
  , combineValues = \a b -> unwords [a,b]
  , consumeValue = id
  }
```

And if we apply one of these to runExistential, we'll get back a string:

```
λ runExistential $ reverseAndUnwordsString "Hello, World"
"dlroW ,olleH Hello, World"
```

Since consumeValue has a known return type, we can also use that as an entry point to be able to modify our existential record. For example, we could start by saying:

```
modifyExistential :: (a -> b) -> SomeExistential a -> SomeExistential b
modifyExistential f SomeExistential{..} = SomeExistential
  { someValue = someValue
  , modifyValue = modifyValue
  , combineValues = combineValues
  , consumeValue = f . consumeValue
  }
```

If you look at the type of this function, you might recognize it from earlier in this book. It's the type of fmap, so we can define a Functor instance for our existential type as well:

```
instance Functor SomeExistential where
  fmap = modifyExistential
```

This makes it easy for us to start making some changes to the eventual value returned by runExistential, as you can see in the demo:

```
λ runExistential $ show <$> addAndMultiplyInt 7
"98"
λ runExistential $ length <$> reverseAndUnwordsString "hello"
11
```

Of course, we're not limited to a single function to evaluate an existential, we could write others as well. For example, this one returns the result of consumeValue directly:

```
λ runSimple SomeExistential{..} = consumeValue someValue
λ runSimple $ length <$> reverseAndUnwordsString "hello"
5
λ runSimple $ reverseAndUnwordsString "hello"
"hello"
```

You might have noticed at this point that what we've been doing is similar to another Haskell feature you've already used: type classes. In fact, much of what we have done so far could have been done with type classes instead of using an existential record, but with a little bit less flexibility.

For example, let's consider the type class equivalent to SomeExistential and addAndMultiplyInt:

First of all, we'll need to add a couple of additional language extensions:

```
{-# LANGUAGE MultiParamTypeClasses #-}
{-# LANGUAGE AllowAmbiguousTypes #-}
{-# LANGUAGE FlexibleInstances #-}
```

AllowAmbiguousTypes

The AllowAmbiguousTypes extension has been available since GHC 7.8.1. It isn't enabled by default in either Haskell2010 or GHC2021. Although this extension is generally safe to use, in some cases it can make it more difficult to track down errors in your program. As a general rule, it's best to enable this extension on a module-by-module basis when you need it rather than enabling it project-wide.

MultiParamTypeClasses

The MultiParamTypeClasses extension has been available since GHC 6.8.1. This extension is enabled by default in GHC2021, but you'll need to enable it explicitly if you are using Haskell2010. This is generally a safe extension that shouldn't cause problems with any existing code.

Our type class definition doesn't look much different than the definition of our existential, except that we don't need to actually store a value at all. Instead, we'll just add the functions:

```
class SomeClass a b where
  modifyClassValue :: a -> a
  combineClassValues :: a -> a -> a
  consumeClassValue :: a -> b
```

This type class has two parameters, a and b. This mirrors both the type parameter, b, and the quantified type, a in our existential type. We also need to add AllowAmbiguousTypes, since neither modifyClassValue nor combineClassValues ever refer to b; they are ambiguous—if we call them the compiler doesn't know which instance it should use, and so without this extension it will not try at all and will give us an error.

Next we can create an instance. Let's make one for integral types that output an Int, just like addAndMultiplyInt:

We'll need to enable FlexibleInstances so that we can tell GHC what type we want to use for our second type parameter. Otherwise, this instance looks quite similar to the existential version that we created earlier:

```
instance Integral a => SomeClass a Int where
  modifyClassValue a = a + a
  combineClassValues = (*)
  consumeClassValue = fromIntegral
```

Finally, let's write runSomeClass, a function that will be the type class equivalent to runExistential. We'll need to add another couple of extensions here as well:

```
{-# LANGUAGE TypeApplications #-}
{-# LANGUAGE ScopedTypeVariables #-}

runSomeClass :: forall a b. SomeClass a b => a -> b
runSomeClass val =
  let
    modified = modifyClassValue @a @b val
    combined = combineClassValues @a @b modified val
  in consumeClassValue combined
```

We've had to enable TypeApplications and ScopedTypeVariables here so that we can tell GHC exactly what types we want to use when we call modifyClassValue and combineClassValues. We have to do this for the same reason that we had to enable AllowAmbiguousTypes earlier when defining our class: since these types never refer to b explicitly, without a type annotation GHC can't figure out what versions of the function to call.

Other than our new type applications, runSomeClass again looks pretty similar to our existential version, and if we run it we'll see that it does indeed return the same values:

```
λ runSomeClass 5 :: Int
50
λ runExistential $ addAndMultiplyInt 5
50
λ runSomeClass 3 :: Int
18
λ runExistential $ addAndMultiplyInt 3
18
```

There are some cases where we can't trivially create a type class that's equivalent to an existential record. Let's imagine a different existential record that simply returns its input no matter what:

```
constExistential :: Int -> SomeExistential Int
constExistential n = SomeExistential
  { someValue = n
  , modifyValue = const n
  , combineValues = const $ const n
  , consumeValue = const n
  }
```

If we re-use our existing runExistential function here, you'll see that we do in fact always get out what we put in:

```
λ runExistential $ constExistential 7
7
λ runExistential $ constExistential 2
2
λ runExistential $ constExistential 0
0
```

On the other hand, if we try to redefine our SomeClass instance to do the same thing, you'll find that we can't really directly port our code. Ultimately, we can't create a consumeClassValue function that always returns our original input, because that input is part of runSomeClass and not the instance itself. Since we can only have one instance of a type class per type, or in the case of our SomeClass, per pair of types a and b, we'd need to either create a newtype wrapper and instance for every integer constant we wanted to use, or create a new type class. In fact, that we needed to try to redefine our existing type class at all shows one of the advantages of existential records. We can arbitrarily have many different existential records that we can pass around, whereas with type classes we are limited to a single instance per type.

From these examples, you can see that existential records can be useful in cases where you want something like a lightweight and ad hoc type class, or where you need some additional constant values associated with your functions without the overhead of defining multiple type classes. Even so, in most cases you can restructure your code to avoid using an existential record. When it's possible, you are usually going to be better served using a type class than an existential record because type classes are more idiomatic Haskell. Type classes give you nice things like constraints. They don't force you to lose track of type information, and the fact that they can only have a single implementation is often a feature for readers of your code who can better predict what is going to happen on any given function call, because they can understand the behavior of a type class once and re-use that knowledge.

Type Classes and Existential Constraints

You've just learned how you can use existential record types to recreate some of the flexibility of type classes, and why you usually shouldn't, but these two features aren't often in opposition. In fact, the most common way to use existential types in practice is in combination with type class constraints.

When you define an existential type, you can include type class constraints on the quantified variable. For example, we can create an existential type whose value must be showable:

```
data CanBeShown = forall a. Show a => CanBeShown a
```

Just like in our previous examples, we can't get a value out of CanBeShown directly, but because we know a must have an instance of Show we are free to use that to get information back out of our existential value. We could, for example, write a show function:

```
showWhatCanBeShown :: CanBeShown -> String
showWhatCanBeShown (CanBeShown value) = show value
```

And we can create type class instances for our existential type, so long as we don't rely on knowing the type of the value that is inside of it:

```
instance Show CanBeShown where
  show (CanBeShown a) = show a
```

Existential types like this are particularly useful because they give us a way of creating collections of things that share some common behaviors, like being able to be printed. Since we're erasing the type information of the values inside our existential, we can create collections of existential values that were created with different types:

```
print [CanBeShown "hello", CanBeShown 12, CanBeShown True]
["hello",12,True]
```

Let's take a moment to appreciate this. We've just created a list of a string, a number, and a boolean value and printed them out. Existential types helped us work around the "single type of element in a list" restriction by erasing the type information and only keeping around the relevant type class constraints that we needed.

Existential File Packing

Now that you understand existential types and how we can use them, you might already see how we can create a pack of files containing different types of underlying values. We will create a new existential type that represents any data that we can encode:

```
data Packable = forall a. Encode a => Packable { getPackable :: FileData a }

instance Encode Packable where
  encode (Packable p) = encode p
```

And now we can trivially define a FilePack as a list of Packable values:

```
newtype FilePack = FilePack [Packable]

instance Encode FilePack where
  encode (FilePack p) = encode p
```

One of the problems with using existential types this way is that it can be inconvenient for our users to have to manually wrap all of their values inside of our existential type. We can make this more ergonomic by giving users a way to easily add any 'FileData' to a file pack without having to wrap it themselves:

```
addFileDataToPack :: Encode a => FileData a -> FilePack -> FilePack
addFileDataToPack a (FilePack as) = FilePack $ (Packable a) : as
```

This is also a good opportunity to use an infix operator to recreate the convenience of creating lists:

```
infixr 6 .:
(.:) :: (Encode a) => FileData a -> FilePack -> FilePack
(.:) = addFileDataToPack

emptyFilePack :: FilePack
emptyFilePack = FilePack []
```

With that done, we've successfully built a system that will let us encode heterogenous file data into a single packed file. Let's look at a demo:

```
testEncodeValue :: ByteString
testEncodeValue =
  let
    a = FileData
      { fileName = "a"
      , fileSize = 3
      , filePermissions = 0755
      , fileData = "foo" :: String
      }
    b = FileData
      { fileName = "b"
      , fileSize = 10
      , filePermissions = 0644
      , fileData = ["hello","world"] :: [Text]
      }
    c = FileData
      { fileName = "c"
      , fileSize = 8
      , filePermissions = 0644
      , fileData = (0,"zero") :: (Word32,String)
      }
  in encode $  a .: b .: c .:  emptyFilePack
```

We'll skip showing the output here since it's just a blob of encoded binary data, but if you run this in ghci you may be able to pick out some of the key parts of these files in the encoded data now that you are familiar with exactly how everything is being encoded.

Summary

In this chapter, you learned how to make effective use of type classes, and how to use a new feature of Haskell's type system called existential types. While existential types are not a feature that you'll use frequently, they are a critical tool for working with certain types of real-world workloads where you can't otherwise easily deal with the variety and flexibility of the data that you need to support. The limitations that existential types put on how you can use your data will also be useful later on in this book when you learn how to work with certain types of mutable data.

Exercises

Nested FilePacks

Try building filepacks that contain other filepacks. Is there anything you can do to make the API more ergonomic? What do you notice about the API you've already built that makes this process easier or harder?

Building a Real Archival tool

Throughout this chapter, you've built a library that will help you create a file archive. Try using this library, along with what you've learned over the last few chapters, to build a command line tool that will let you pack up files.

Build a Trace Tool

In this chapter, we focused on building a file archival tool, but many of the ideas you learned here are applicable to other domains as well. Another area where you could use existential types is in building a tool to collect a trace of function calls.

Consider this example:

```
{-# LANGUAGE ExistentialQuantification #-}
{-# LANGUAGE RecordWildCards #-}
module CallTrace where
import Text.Printf

data TraceData -- fill me in
newtype Trace -- fill me in

emptyTrace :: Trace
emptyTrace = undefined

traceCall
  :: (Show a, Show b)
  => String
  -> (a -> (Trace, b))
  -> a
  -> (Trace, b)
traceCall = undefined

showTrace :: Trace -> String
showTrace = undefined

factor :: Int -> (Trace, [Int])
factor n =
  traceCall "factor" factor  (n, 2)
  where
    factor' :: (Int, Int) -> (Trace, [Int])
    factor' (num, curFact)
      | num == 1 = (emptyTrace, [])
      | (num `mod` curFact) == 0 =
        let nextNumber = num `div` curFact
            message = "consFactor " <> show curFact
            (trace, results) = traceCall message factor' (nextNumber, curFact)
         in (trace, curFact : results)
      | otherwise =
        let nextFactor = curFact + 1
         in traceCall "skipFactor" factor' (num, nextFactor)
```

```
verboseFactor :: Int -> IO ()
verboseFactor n = do
  let (trace, factors) = factor n
  putStrLn "factors: "
  print factors
  putStrLn "trace: "
  putStrLn (showTrace trace)
```

Try to implement the missing pieces so that your program compiles and gives you some appropriate output. Here are a couple of examples so that you can test your own code:

```
λ verboseFactor 3
factors:
[3]
trace:
stack depth: 3
factor (3,2) => [3]
  skipFactor (3,3) => [3]
    consFactor 3 (1,3) => []
```

```
λ verboseFactor 1080
factors:
[2,2,2,3,3,3,5]
trace:
stack depth: 11
factor (1080,2) => [2,2,2,3,3,3,5]
  consFactor 2 (540,2) => [2,2,3,3,3,5]
    consFactor 2 (270,2) => [2,3,3,3,5]
      consFactor 2 (135,2) => [3,3,3,5]
        skipFactor (135,3) => [3,3,3,5]
          consFactor 3 (45,3) => [3,3,5]
            consFactor 3 (15,3) => [3,5]
              consFactor 3 (5,3) => [5]
                skipFactor (5,4) => [5]
                  skipFactor (5,5) => [5]
                    consFactor 5 (1,5) => []
```

CHAPTER 12

Deserializing Heterogenous Data

Extracting Heterogenous Values from the Archive

In the last chapter, you built a library named FilePack that will allow you to combine files with various types of data into a single archive. Throughout that chapter, you learned about using existential types to deal with heterogeneous collections of data. Although you were able to build a library with a nice API for creating archives, there was one glaring problem: after creating a file pack you had no way of *unpacking* the data.

In this chapter, we'll work on the other half of the file packing program: decoding a file pack that can contain many different types of data. Just like when we were encoding data, we'll want to support arbitrary data types that can be defined by the user, and we'll want to support file packs that are made up of files with different types.

A File Archive Builder

Before we get started on the underlying problem of parsing our file archive, let's review the code that we built in the last chapter that we'll be re-using heavily throughout this chapter. If you already have a project with the code you built in the last chapter, then you can re-use that project in this chapter as well. If not, make sure to create a new project and copy the example code so that you'll have everything you need as you work through the project in this chapter.

We started by creating a new record, FileData, that would let us store a file with some metadata:

```
{-# LANGUAGE RecordWildCards #-}
{-# LANGUAGE FlexibleInstances #-}
{-# LANGUAGE ExistentialQuantification #-}
{-# LANGUAGE TypeApplications #-}
```

```
module FilePackParser where
import Data.Bits (shift, (.&.), (.|.))
import Data.ByteString (ByteString)
import qualified Data.ByteString as BS
import qualified Data.ByteString.Char8 as BC
import Data.Text (Text)
import Data.Text.Encoding (decodeUtf8, encodeUtf8)
import Data.Word
import System.Posix.Types (CMode (..), FileMode)

data FileData a = FileData
  { fileName :: FilePath
  , fileSize :: Word32
  , filePermissions :: FileMode
  , fileData :: a
  } deriving (Eq, Show)
```

To make it easier for us to encode and decode file archives, we defined two new type classes: Encode and Decode. We also created some short instances for many common types that we expected we'd be using throughout our code:

```
class Decode a where
  decode :: ByteString -> Either String a
instance Encode ByteString where
  encode = id
instance Decode ByteString where
  decode = Right
instance Encode Text where
  encode = encodeUtf8
instance Decode Text where
  decode = Right . decodeUtf8
instance Encode String where
  encode = BC.pack
instance Decode String where
  decode = Right . BC.unpack
instance Encode FileMode where
  encode (CMode fMode) = encode fMode
  encodeWithSize (CMode fMode) = encodeWithSize fMode
instance Decode FileMode where
  decode = fmap CMode . decode
```

We knew that we'd want to be able to encode Word32 values, but we decided to pack these directly into the ByteString, rather than printing them and storing the ASCII-encoded representations of the numbers. We wrote a couple of helper functions to help us write Encode and Decode instances for Word32:

```
word32ToBytes :: Word32 -> (Word8, Word8, Word8, Word8)
word32ToBytes word =
    let a = fromIntegral $ 255 .&. word
        b = fromIntegral $ 255 .&. shift word (-8)
```

```
        c = fromIntegral $ 255 .&. shift word (-16)
        d = fromIntegral $ 255 .&. shift word (-24)
    in (a,b,c,d)

word32FromBytes :: (Word8, Word8, Word8, Word8) -> Word32
word32FromBytes (a,b,c,d) =
  let a' = fromIntegral a
      b' = shift (fromIntegral b) 8
      c' = shift (fromIntegral c) 16
      d' = shift (fromIntegral d) 24
  in a' .|. b' .|. c' .|. d'

word32ToByteString :: Word32 -> ByteString
word32ToByteString word =
  let (a,b,c,d) = word32ToBytes word
  in BS.pack [a,b,c,d]

bytestringToWord32 :: ByteString -> Either String Word32
bytestringToWord32 bytestring =
  case BS.unpack bytestring of
    [a,b,c,d] -> Right $ word32FromBytes (a,b,c,d)
    _ ->
      let l = show $ BS.length bytestring
      in Left ("Expecting 4 bytes but got " <> l)

instance Encode Word32 where
  encode = word32ToByteString
  encodeWithSize w =
    let (a, b, c, d) = word32ToBytes w
     in BS.pack [4,0,0,0,a,b,c,d]

instance Decode Word32 where
  decode = bytestringToWord32
```

With all of our Encode instances in place, we were able to also define an Encode instance for FileData:

```
instance Encode a => Encode (FileData a) where
  encode FileData{..} = encode $
    encodeWithSize fileName
    <> encodeWithSize fileSize
    <> encodeWithSize filePermissions
    <> encodeWithSize fileData
```

Finally, to support packing more than one file into the archive, we also added Encode instances for lists and tuples, and created a new FilePack type that contains a list of Packable values that can describe a heterogeneous collection of encodable file data:

```
instance (Encode a, Encode b) => Encode (a,b) where
  encode (a,b) = encode $ encodeWithSize a <> encodeWithSize b
```

```
instance {-# OVERLAPPABLE #-} Encode a => Encode [a] where
  encode = encode . foldMap encodeWithSize

data Packable = forall a. Encode a =>
  Packable { getPackable :: FileData a }

instance Encode Packable where
  encode (Packable p) = encode p

newtype FilePack = FilePack [Packable]

instance Encode FilePack where
  encode (FilePack p) = encode p
```

Deserialization as Parsing

In the last chapter, you built a tool to encode a file archive as raw binary data. One of the biggest challenges that we ran into as we were developing that project was the fact that we wanted to support files with different types in a single archive. We were able to do this by using *existential types* to erase the information about a specific type but keep the important information that it had an Encode instance.

The fundamental reason that this approach worked for encoding was that, at some point, the user of our library had to create values that were loaded into a FilePack, and those values had to have instances that said how the data should be encoded. Our existential type allowed us to forget the other information about that type, but we still carried the particular implementation of encode that each type used along with its data. That meant that when it came time to call encode on the entire FilePack, our program was able to figure out which particular encode function it needed to call for every single piece of data.

Decoding a FilePack is going to bring in a new wrinkle: when we're loading in a new file archive and decoding it, all we have is some raw binary data. We don't know what type it should be, so we have no idea which Decode instance we should use to extract the data.

In order to extract data, we'll need the user to tell us what kind of data they want to extract, and then we can make a best effort at extracting the data into that type using the binary data we have. Of course, the user might be trying to deserialize some corrupt data, or might be wrong about the way the data was encoded originally, so we'll need to be able to report errors to them as well.

You might recognize that what we're talking about here is a *parsing* problem. Deserializing data, especially in the general way that we want to support for FilePack usually comes down to a parsing problem. We'll approach the problem of extracting our encoded data as a parsing problem. This means that as you work through this chapter, keep in mind that the techniques you're using here will apply equally well to parsing other types of data, like JSON or XML data, binary file formats, or text input you receive directly from a user.

Creating a Parsing Function

Before we can start unpacking an entire archive we need to think smaller. A filepack archive is made up of one or more different FileData values, and each of those FileData values are in turn made up of all of the individual values in the overall record. If we want to unpack a FileData, we'll need to start by being able to unpack each of the individual types that make up a FileData record.

Let's start by decoding Word32 values. Not only do we need to decode these because they are one of the types that make up a FileData record, but we're also going to need to deal with the Word32 size field prefixes that we added to help us encode compound values more easily.

We already have a Decode instance for Word32 that makes use of the bytestringToWord32 function that we built earlier to help us test our code. We'll keep using those functions, but we're going to need to do a little bit of extra work to extract an actual Word32 value our of our file pack. The first thing we need to account for is the fact that we're not just encoding the Word32 values directly into our FilePack. All of the data that we encoded was prefixed with an additional Word32 that told us the size of the next fields. Let's start by writing a function, naiveDecodeWord32, that will help us get a Word32 field:

```
naiveDecodeWord32 :: ByteString -> Either String Word32
naiveDecodeWord32 inputString =
  decode (BS.drop 4 inputString)
```

In this very naive version of our decoding function, we're simply dropping the first four bytes of our input string and then using our existing Word32 decode instance to try to parse the rest of it. We can try it out in ghci and see that it works not only to successfully parse a correctly encoded value, but it also gives us some degree of error handling against bad values:

```
λ naiveDecodeWord32 (encodeWithSize @Word32 255)
Right 255
λ naiveDecodeWord32 (encode @Word32 255)
Left "Expecting 4 bytes but got 0"
λ naiveDecodeWord32 (encode @String "Greetings")
Left "Expecting 4 bytes but got 5"
```

This is a pretty good starting spot, and works well for a naive function. The biggest problem with our current implementation is that we discard any of the input that we're not using to parse our Word32. It would be nice if that were all we had to do for our decoders, and in fact we'll get there in the end, but for now we can't rely on our upstream callers to know implementation details like how much data we need to decode our number. Instead, we should take what we need to parse a value from the input, and return the rest of it to be used for the next thing that needs to be parsed.

Sticking with our most naive possible implementation, we can do this by first dropping the four-byte size prefix, and then splitting the rest of the string into two parts: the encoded word that we want to parse, and everything else. The splitAt function from Data.ByteString does this for us, so it's pretty easy:

```
naiveDecodeWord32 :: ByteString -> Either String (Word32, ByteString)
naiveDecodeWord32 inputString =
  let
    (encodedWord, rest) = BS.splitAt 4 (BS.drop 4 inputString)
  in do
    decodedWord <- decode encodedWord
    pure (decodedWord, rest)
```

This is starting to look a bit better—we still have some error handling for free thanks to the Decode instance we wrote for Word32, and now we're returning the remainder of the string for additional parsing. This implementation is still a bit rough around the edges though. For one thing, our error messages could be better. We don't make it clear to the user the error is referring to the number of bytes after the size prefix, and we don't differentiate at all between the case where we didn't even get enough bytes for the size prefix, or where we did get enough for the prefix but didn't have enough leftover to parse the word. We're also making a blanket assumption the size prefix will always be four bytes. It's true it should always be four bytes if the input we're getting is indeed a correctly encoded Word32, but if our function is being called with some other kind of data then our user is probably already having a hard enough time and we can make their day a little easier by differentiating this error case from the others. In fact, all these improved error messages can go a long way toward helping a user who is trying to debug an encoder or decoder, or to troubleshoot why some data they want to parse isn't getting parsed as they expect.

Let's take one more pass at our function by adding more robust error handling for all of these edge cases:

```
import Control.Monad (when)

naiveDecodeWord32 :: ByteString -> Either String (Word32, ByteString)
naiveDecodeWord32 inputString = do
  when (BS.length inputString < 4) $
      Left "Error, not enough data to get the size of the next field"
```

```
  let (encodedSizePrefix, rest) = BS.splitAt 4 inputString
  sizePrefix <- fromIntegral <$> bytestringToWord32 encodedSizePrefix
  when (sizePrefix /= 4) $
    Left "the field size of a word should be 4"
  when (BS.length rest < fromIntegral sizePrefix) $
    Left "Not enough data for the next field size"
  let (encodedWord, rest') = BS.splitAt sizePrefix rest
  decodedWord <- decode encodedWord
  pure (decodedWord, rest')
```

The when Function

The when function in this example comes from the Control.Monad module, which is part of base. This function is quite useful when we're writing procedural style code in a do block as we've done here, since it lets us conditionally run some action without having to put the rest of our code into an if or case expression. In this example, we're only evaluating Left if the field size isn't what we expect. Since a Left value will terminate our Either action, it can be used as a way to early-abort on errors.

Now that we can decode Word32 values effectively, let's move on to strings. Once again, we'll aim to provide useful error messages when we can, and we'll return the remainder of the data that we didn't consume with our parsing.

Let's start by looking at the implementation for a naive String decoder:

```
naiveDecodedString :: ByteString -> Either String (String, ByteString)
naiveDecodedString inputString = do
  when (BS.length inputString < 4) $
    Left "Error, not enough data to get the size of the next field"
  let (encodedSizePrefix, rest) = BS.splitAt 4 inputString
  sizePrefix <- fromIntegral <$> bytestringToWord32 encodedSizePrefix
  when (BS.length rest < fromIntegral sizePrefix) $
    Left "Not enough data for the next field size"
  let (encodedString, rest') = BS.splitAt sizePrefix rest
  decodedString <- decode encodedString
  pure (decodedString, rest')
```

Do you notice anything? We've renamed a couple of things since we're working with strings instead of words now, and we've removed the check to verify the size of the field should always be exactly four bytes. Otherwise, these two functions are nearly identical. If we continued to implement other decoders, we could keep using the same pattern, but we're hiding almost all the interesting logic behind the same repetitive bits of code to deal with the mechanics of how we've encoded the format. It seems like it might be time to do a bit of refactoring to break this function up into some re-usable components.

One of the most fundamental things we're going to be doing with all of our decoding functions is taking some bytes out of the input string to parse, and returning the rest of the data unmodified. Let's start refactoring by writing a function to handle this for us:

```
extractBytes
  :: Int
  -> ByteString
  -> Either String (ByteString, ByteString)
extractBytes n byteString = do
  when (BS.length byteString < n) $
    Left $ "Error, extract bytes needs at least " <> show n <> " bytes"
  pure $ BS.splitAt n byteString
```

Another thing we'll want to do regularly is to look at the size of the next block of data by reading the size prefix at the start of the current input to figure out how much data we should extract for the next segment of input. We can re-use the extractBytes function that we just wrote to make that easier:

```
nextSegmentSize :: ByteString -> Either String (Word32, ByteString)
nextSegmentSize byteString = do
  (nextSegmentStr, rest) <- extractBytes 4 byteString
  parsedSegmentSize <- bytestringToWord32 nextSegmentStr
  pure (parsedSegmentSize, rest)
```

Most of the time when we want to parse a field, we're going to follow a pattern: first we'll get the size of the next segment, then we'll take however many bytes we need from the input string again. We can also write a function to do all of this for us and just give us the next segment of data that we need to decode:

```
nextSegment :: ByteString -> Either String (ByteString, ByteString)
nextSegment byteString = do
  (segmentSize, rest) <- nextSegmentSize byteString
  extractBytes (fromIntegral segmentSize) rest
```

Something still doesn't feel right here. We've refactored our code into very small functions, and yet in all of these examples, the majority of the code that we're writing is bookkeeping. We're still manually dealing with pattern matching out the value we care about and the remainder of the ByteString frequently. The work that we're doing to re-use our functions is starting to get a little tedious.

It turns out that we still have a significant refactoring opportunity that can greatly reduce the tedium of writing code like this for both us and users who want to use our parsing library: refactoring our ad hoc parser into a *monadic parser*.

Building a Monadic Parser

Monadic parsers are a common pattern in Haskell applications. The term *monadic* in a monadic parser is a little bit misleading, because as you'll see later on in this chapter, a lot of the benefit from this style of parsing comes from its Applicative instance, rather than its Monad instance. Still, creating a Parser monad allows users of our library to use the familiar do notation.

To get an idea of where we're going and what this will look like in practice, let's start with a short demo of what it will look like to decode the values that we encoded in testEncodeValue earlier:

```
testDecodeValue
  :: ByteString
  -> Either String
  ( FileData String
  , FileData [Text]
  , FileData (Word32,String)
  )
testDecodeValue = decodeAndParse $ do
  a <- extractValue
  b <- extractValue
  c <- extractValue
  pure (a,b,c)
```

So far we've been parsing things using one-off functions to parse different types of data, and each of our functions have had a slightly different type, depending on the particulars of what we were doing and what we were trying to parse. As we're building our monadic parsing library we'll still be building up a number of small functions, but we want those to capture the differences in the logic for the different things that we want to parse. To distill out the important differences, we should start by looking at the commonalities. One of the things that a lot of these functions had in common is that they have a very similar type. If we were to define a general parsing function, we might give it this type:

```
parseFunction :: Decode a => ByteString -> Either String (a, ByteString)
```

In other words, functions that take some input and return either an error, or a tuple of a parsed value and the remainder of the input that wasn't consumed parsing that value. Let's start building our monadic parser by creating a newtype wrapper around functions with that general type. We'll omit the Decode constraint for now to keep things more general:

```
newtype FilePackParser a = FilePackParser
  { runParser :: ByteString -> Either String (a, ByteString) }
```

You learned much earlier in this book, when you first started creating your own types on page 144 how creating a data type that held a function could let you write code that was easier to compose, and in the previous chapter, you learned how you could create an instance of Functor for a regular function. Now we'll build on some of those ideas as we're creating our monadic parser, starting with defining a Functor instance for FilePackParser.

If we want to eventually create a Monad instance for FilePackParser, we'll need to start by creating a Functor instance. Remember that creating a Functor instance requires that we define a single function, fmap. For our purposes, the type of fmap will be:

```
fmap :: (a -> b) -> FilePackParser a -> FilePackParser b
```

So, we want to take a function and a parser, and return a new parser that applies the function to the value that we've just parsed. Let's start with a bit of a naive implementation that makes it clear what's happening, and then we'll refactor it into something more idiomatic.

The function we call fmap with—let's name it changeParsedOutput—needs to work on a value we've actually already parsed. To get a parsed value, we need the parser we are mapping over—let's call that parseFunction—and we need some input data we can apply to parseFunction to get output out. We know what we need, so let's start our implementation by writing a helper function:

```
functorHelper
  :: (a -> b)
  -> (ByteString -> Either String (a, ByteString))
  -> ByteString
  -> Either String (b, ByteString)
functorHelper changeParsedOutput parseFunction input = do
  (parsedValue, remainder) <- parseFunction input
  pure (changeParsedOutput parsedValue, remainder)
```

So, our helper function tries to parse input with parseFunction and, if we fail, we propagate the error. If we succeed though, we take the result of our parsing and apply it to changeParsedOutput to get the new result that we want, and we return that along with the unmodified remainder leftover from when we parsed our original value.

Let's look at how we can use this to create a Functor instance:

```
instance Functor FilePackParser where
  fmap changeParsedOutput parser = FilePackParser $ \input ->
    functorHelper changeParsedOutput (runParser parser) input
```

As you can see, this definition of fmap offloads most of the work to the helper function we've just written. We pass along changeParsedOutput completely unmodified, along with the parse function that's inside of parser. We also need to pass along some input so we can actually run the parser. We get that input by passing along the input that is given when we run the FilePackParser we're returning. The first time you encounter this pattern it can be a bit confusing trying to understand where our input is actually coming from. It can seem like we're introducing input magically. The thing to remember is since FilePack-Parser holds a function, at some point our user will eventually give us an input string to start with, and that will become the value of input that we use.

To cement this idea, let's work through a short example. For the sake of simplicity we won't really parse much of anything in this example, but we'll start with a "parser" that tries to take the first ten characters out of an input, and counts the number of occurrences of the letter "a".

```
parseCount :: FilePackParser Int
parseCount = FilePackParser $ \input ->
  let
   countLetters letter =
     BS.length . BC.filter (== letter)
  in
    if BS.length input < 10
    then Left "Error: not enough input"
    else
      let (toParse, rest) = BS.splitAt 10 input
      in Right (countLetters 'a' toParse, rest)
```

In this example, we're using the same pattern of creating a FilePackParser by passing it a function that uses some input. We can run it with a few different inputs to see how it parses each of them:

```
λ runParser parseCount "aaaaaaaaaaaa"
Right (10,"aa")
λ runParser parseCount "bbbaaaaaaaaa"
Right (7,"aa")
λ runParser parseCount "bbbaaaaa"
Left "Error: not enough input"
```

If we use our Functor instance, you'll see that we're in a similar situation; we're getting back a FilePackParser that still needs some input in order to do anything.

```
λ showParseCount = fmap show parseCount
λ runParser showParseCount "aaaaaaaaaaaa"
Right ("10","aa")
λ reverseShowParseCount = reverse <$> show <$> parseCount
λ runParser reverseShowParseCount "aaaaaaaaaa00"
Right ("01","00")
```

In these examples, the FilePackParser that we're getting back when we call fmap (or (<$>), which is the infix operator version of fmap), is going to take whatever input we give it, and then pass that input along to the parser that we originally called fmap with, parseCount in this case.

Now that we've explored how our original fmap definition worked, let's make a quick refactor to remove our unnecessary helper function:

```
instance Functor FilePackParser where
  fmap f parser = FilePackParser $ \input -> do
    (parsedValue, result) <- runParser parser input
    pure (f parsedValue, result)
```

This version is less verbose and a bit easier to read for not having an extra function we have to keep track of. We're no longer passing along a bunch of values for no reason, and instead we're implementing the actual logic of fmap directly in its definition.

Next, let's move on to defining an Applicative instance. While our Functor instance was broadly similar to the instance we defined for functions, our Applicative instance for FilePackParser will be a bit different.

We'll start, as usual, by creating an instance and defining pure:

```
instance Applicative FilePackParser where
  pure a = FilePackParser $ \s -> pure (a, s)
```

Our pure function here is taking the entire input string that we get and moving it directly to the remainder, and setting the parsed value to the value passed into pure. If we take the computational view of our parser, where consuming some of the input is a side effect, then this definition of pure makes a lot of sense. We're inserting a pure value into the parser, which means that we don't have any side effects—we're not consuming anything from the input.

Let's stick with this computational view, where consuming values are side effects, as we start to think about how we can define (<*>). In this view of the world, we have two computations. One of them will consume some of the input to give us a function, and the other will consume some of the input to give us a value that we can apply to that function. We need to return a new computation that combines both of those side effects and returns the result:

```
instance Applicative FilePackParser where
  pure a = FilePackParser $ \input -> pure (a, input)
  f <*> s = FilePackParser $ \input -> do
    (f', initialRemainder) <- runParser f input
    (a, finalRemainder) <- runParser s initialRemainder
    pure (f' a, finalRemainder)
```

You can see here that the first thing we do is consume some of the input to get a function, f'. We take the state, in this case the remainder of our input, and thread that through into our call to s. We return *that* remainder—the remainder after consuming the input of both parsers—along with the result of calling our function.

You'll note here that order matters. Some types have Applicative instances that can be run in any order, or even in parallel, but for things like this where the order does matter, it's conventional to keep the order of operations left-to-right, as we've done here.

Parsing with Applicatives

Now that we've built an Applicative instance, we have everything we need to extract a FilePack value, and to allow our users to build their own decoding tools based on our decoder. Before we move on to writing a Monad instance, let's finish writing our decoders using what we have available so far from the Applicative type class. This will give you a chance both to see how far we can get with Applicative as well as an opportunity to see what restrictions we are under when we don't have a Monad instance.

As you know, Applicative types give us a way of combining some computations in a particular way. The general pattern you'll see for applicative parsers is we're combining a computation that's progressively building up a new fully parsed value with a second computation that's progressively consuming parts of an unparsed value. This'll be a bit easier to understand as we look at an example.

Since we've already written a few variations of it, let's start by writing the part of our parser that consumes individual parts of our larger unparsed input. The extractValue parser will combine a lot of the functionality we've already written into a single parser called extractValue:

```
extractValue :: Decode a => FilePackParser a
extractValue = FilePackParser $ \input -> do
  when (BS.length input < 4) $
    Left "Input has less than 4 bytes, we can t get a segment size"

  let (rawSegmentSize, rest) = BS.splitAt 4 input
  segmentSize <- fromIntegral <$> bytestringToWord32 rawSegmentSize

  when (BS.length rest < segmentSize) $
    Left "not enough input to parse the next value"

  let (rawSegmentValue, rest') = BS.splitAt segmentSize rest

  case decode rawSegmentValue of
    Left err -> Left err
    Right a  -> Right (a, rest')
```

This parser follows the same pattern of many other parsing functions that we've already built. The first thing that we do is to try to get the size of the next input field by reading the field prefix and then taking that many bytes out of the input. If we don't have enough input data, we generate an error. Next, we try to decode the segment that we've extracted, and we also return an error if that fails. Finally, we return the decoded value along with the remainder of the input that we didn't use.

Before we move on, let's try this out in ghci so that we can see it in action:

```
λ runParser (extractValue @Word32) $ encodeWithSize @Word32 12345
Right (12345,"")

λ runParser (extractValue @String) $ encodeWithSize @String "Parsing is fun"
Right ("Parsing is fun","")

λ runParser (extractValue @Word32) $ encodeWithSize @String "Errors aren't fun"
Left "Expecting 4 bytes but got 17"
```

You can see in these examples that we can encode and decode single values now using our applicative decoder. One minor inconvenience here is that when we run the parser this way, we're also getting back an empty string that's leftover from our processing. To make our lives a bit easier, let's add a helper function to make it easier for us to test our parsers as we're working through some more examples in this chapter:

```
execParser :: FilePackParser a -> ByteString -> Either String a
execParser parser inputString =
  fst <$> runParser parser inputString
```

This function will allow us, and other users of our library, to more easily get a value out of an encoded input without needing to manually discard the leftover data that is included with runParser. As we're testing our own code, this is just a small convenience, but for other users of our library this abstraction also serves to hide unnecessary implementation details from users who might not care about how we handle passing along the parse state.

The choice of how we want to order the arguments here can have a small but meaningful impact on how users will interact with our library. In fact, it's common to see libraries like this provide named functions for both functions that take a parser first, followed by input, and functions that take input first followed by a parser. As you're working through some of the examples in the rest of this chapter, think about how the ergonomics of parsing would be different if the order of arguments to execParser were flipped.

Before we look at how to decode larger data types, we need to define one. We'll return to our FileData and FilePack examples shortly, but for the moment let's create a small one-off record we can use to explore applicative style decoding:

```
data SomeRecord = SomeRecord
  { recordNumber :: Word32
  , recordString :: String
  , recordTuple  :: (Word32, String)
  } deriving (Eq, Show)

exampleRecord :: SomeRecord
exampleRecord = SomeRecord 1 "two" (3, "four")

packRecord :: SomeRecord -> ByteString
packRecord SomeRecord{..} =
  encodeWithSize recordNumber
  <> encodeWithSize recordString
  <> encodeWithSize (fst recordTuple)
  <> encodeWithSize (snd recordTuple)
```

Unlike some of our previous examples, we can't just call extractValue here, because we don't have a Decode instance defined for SomeRecord. We're also dealing with a more complicated record type with a number of different fields. So, how do we go about decoding a value?

Our goal is to get each of the fields we need to reconstruct our record out of the encoded input, one by one, and pass them into the SomeRecord value constructor. At each step of the process, we'll consume a bit more data from the unprocessed part of our input, and add that decoded value into our record.

We'll call our new parser someRecordParser:

```
someRecordParser :: FilePackParser SomeRecord
```

Rather than looking at how we can implement an entire parser for SomeRecord though, let's take it a piece at a time. We'll start by just parsing out the first field. As a refresher, remember that value constructors are functions that take in all of the elements in that type and return a new value, so the type of SomeRecord is:

```
SomeRecord :: Word32 -> String -> (Word32, String) -> SomeRecord
```

So, we'll start with a Word32 value. You've already extracted some Word32 values out of an encoded string using extractValue and that's exactly what we're going to do here:

```
someRecordParser = SomeRecord
  <$> extractValue
```

The first time you see this pattern you might have a hard time following the leap that we just made here, so let's take a moment to slow down and make sure that we've fully understood what's happening.

You'll recall from several examples throughout the book the type of (<$>) is:

```
(<$>) :: Functor f => (a -> b) -> f a -> f b
```

This might leave you wondering for a moment how we are able to say SomeRecord <$> extractValue when SomeRecord takes three arguments, but the first argument to (<$>) is a function of a single argument. The reason this work is our friend, currying. After all, we can rewrite the type of SomeRecord using some extra parentheses to be:

```
SomeRecord :: Word32 -> (String -> (Word32, String) -> SomeRecord)
```

So, SomeRecord really does fit the shape of a function (a -> b) it's just that the b is itself a function with the type (String -> (Word32, String) -> SomeRecord). This means that when we use (<$>), what we're going to end up with is a FilePackParser that parses a value and returns function:

```
SomeRecord <$> extractValue
  :: FilePackParser (String -> (Word32, String) -> SomeRecord)
```

Another way to look at this is that we're taking the Word32 value that we get as a result of running our parser and applying that to SomeRecord. We're keeping the leftover data that we didn't consume when we parsed the Word32 value unmodified, so now we have a parser that will give us back a partially applied value constructor, plus the remainder of the input that wasn't used to parse the value that we just applied.

Next up, we need to get a String. We already have a Decode instance defined for String, so we can use extractValue to get one of those too. The difference here is that when we started, SomeRecord was a normal function that we wanted to apply to a parsed value with fmap, but that left us with a parser. Of course, we just spent the last section building exactly what we need to handle this situation! The Applicative instance that we just defined will let us handle exactly this situation, with (<*>):

```
someRecordParser = SomeRecord
  <$> extractValue
  <*> extractValue
```

We can apply the same reasoning to using (<*>) that we did when we first used (<$>). Remember that the type of (<*>) is:

```
(<*>) :: Applicative f => f (a -> b) -> f a -> f b
```

In this case, a is String and b is ((Word32, String) -> SomeRecord). If we think about what this is doing, using what we know about both Applicative in general and the specific implementation that we've built, you can see that we're building up a new parser that will take some input and use it to run a computation that will generate a function. Next, we take the leftover input from running that computation and feed it into the extractValue parser to get a value, which we apply to the function we've just parsed.

The last parameter we need to pass into SomeRecord is again a little bit different. Instead of the plain single values we've passed in so far, we need to deal with a tuple: (Word32, String). So, how do we get a FilePackParser (Word32, String) out of the input? It's a compound value, and we can build it exactly the same way that we've been building our current parser: using (<$>) and (<*>):

```
{-# LANGUAGE TupleSections #-}

someRecordParser :: FilePackParser SomeRecord
someRecordParser = SomeRecord
  <$> extractValue
  <*> extractValue
  <*> extractTuple
  where
    extractTuple :: FilePackParser (Word32, String)
    extractTuple = (,) <$> extractValue <*> extractValue
```

TupleSections

The TupleSections extension has been available since GHC 6.12. It's enabled by default in GHC2010 but you'll need to enable it manually if you are using Haskell2010. This is a safe extension that shouldn't cause any problems with existing code.

Now that we have a parser, we can hand it over to execParser to get a function that will directly transform some input into our desired output (or fail with an error message at the very least).

```
parseSomeRecord = execParser someRecordParser
```

This gives us a nice function that we can use to evaluate any given input into a parsed output. It's handy if we have a bunch of different records that we want to parse:

```
getSeveralRecords :: [ByteString] -> Either String [SomeRecord]
getSeveralRecords = traverse (execParser someRecordParser)
```

Another way to use execParser is by defining our actual parser directly inline, instead of defining someRecordParser as a FilePackParser separately. For example, we can rewrite it as:

```
someRecordParser :: ByteString -> Either String SomeRecord
someRecordParser = execParser $ SomeRecord
  <$> extractValue
  <*> extractValue
  <*> ((,) <$> extractValue <*> extractValue)
```

Now that we've figured out how to deal with extracting compound data types, we can apply these ideas directly to a couple of our Decode instances for tuples and FileData:

```
instance (Decode a, Decode b) => Decode (a,b) where
  decode = execParser $ (,) <$> extractValue <*> extractValue

instance Decode a => Decode (FileData a) where
  decode = execParser $ FileData
    <$> extractValue <*> extractValue <*> extractValue <*> extractValue
```

You'll notice here that since decode should return an Either String value, we are able to again make use of execParser to get back a function that will take some input and immediately use it to try to decode the parser that we've defined in-line.

Now that we have everything we need to encode and decode FileData let's write one more function to help us use ghci to manually test that we can correctly *round-trip* our data. If you aren't familiar with it, *round-trip testing* is a term commonly used to describe tests that ensure encoding a value and then decoding it gets you back the same value that you originally started with.

```
testRoundTrip :: (Encode a, Decode a, Show a, Eq a) => a -> IO ()
testRoundTrip val =
  case decode (encode val) of
    Left err ->
      putStrLn $ "Failed to round-trip value: " <> err
    Right roundTripVal
      | roundTripVal == val ->
          putStrLn "It works!"
      | otherwise -> do
          putStrLn "Round-trip failed!"
          putStrLn $ "expected: " <> show val
          putStrLn $ "got:      " <> show roundTripVal

runRoundTripTest :: IO ()
runRoundTripTest =
  testRoundTrip $ FileData
  { fileName = "c"
  , fileSize = 8
  , filePermissions = 0644
  , fileData = (0,"zero") :: (Word32,String)
  }
```

If you try this out in ghci you should see that "It Works!" We can now make use of our Applicative parser to more easily decode compound types, including our FileData type. Unfortunately, the work we've done so far doesn't quite get us all the way to being able to fully decode an entire FilePack. In the next section, we'll expand the capabilities of our parser to allow us to fully parse an entire archive.

Parsing a List of Values

So far you've successfully unpacked a single FileData value using your Applicative parser, but to unpack an entire archive we need to support being able to decode an entire list of values. In theory, this shouldn't be too hard, as we've been working with lists since the first chapter of this book, but the fact that we're now dealing with parsers instead of plain lists means we need to think a bit differently about how we build support for decoding values.

Fundamentally, what we'd like to do is to have our user give us a way of parsing a single element, and we'd then like to use that parser to parse as many elements as there are in the input we're given.

One way to do this is build our own recursive parser that will call extractValue to get each element of our list, as long as we have some input. Let's write a function called extractValues that will handle this for us:

```
{-# LANGUAGE OverloadedStrings #-}

extractValues :: Decode a => FilePackParser [a]
extractValues = FilePackParser $ \input ->
  if BS.null input
  then Right ([], "")
  else do
    (val, rest) <- runParser extractValue input
    (tail, rest') <- runParser extractValues rest
    pure (val:tail, rest')
```

In this function we test to see if we're at the end of the input, and if so, we return an empty list. This is our base case. Otherwise we try to extract the next element, which will be the head of the list, and then recursively parse the remainder of the input. Aside from the small detail that we're running inside of a FilePackParser, this resembles a lot of other direct recursive functions that we've built throughout the book. This works, and we can test it out in ghci to see it in action:

```
λ execParser (extractValues @Word32) $ encode @[Word32] [1..10]
Right [1,2,3,4,5,6,7,8,9,10]
```

The first problem with this approach is that it's not very flexible. We're using extractValue to parse values, but that only works as long as we have a Decode instance. If we want to decode a list of values using some other parser, we'd need to define a brand new Decode instance, possibly using a newtype wrapper, or we'd need to write a new version of extractValues.

As a concrete example, let's imagine that we have a parser named decodeEven that will extract Word32 values that are even, but will fail on odd values:

```
parseEven :: FilePackParser Word32
parseEven = FilePackParser $ \input -> do
  (n, rest) <- runParser extractValue input
  when (odd n) $
    Left $ show n <> ": value is odd"
  pure (n, rest)
```

There's an easy way that we can deal with this without needing to change extractValues too much: instead of hard-coding extractValue we can pass in the parser that we want to use. Since we're not always calling extractValue, let's also rename our function to something a little bit more meaningful:

```
parseMany :: FilePackParser a -> FilePackParser [a]
parseMany parseElement = FilePackParser $ \input ->
  if BS.null input
  then Right ([], "")
  else do
    (resultHead, rest) <- runParser parseElement input
    (resultTail, rest') <- runParser (parseMany parseElement) rest
    pure (resultHead : resultTail, rest')
```

Now, we can turn any arbitrary parser for a single element into a list parser that will consume all of the input and give us back a list of values:

```
λ execParser (parseMany @Word32 parseEven) $ encode @[Word32] [2,4..10]
Right [2,4,6,8,10]
```

And, we can get some useful errors out if something goes wrong:

```
λ execParser (parseMany @Word32 parseEven) $ encode @[Word32] [1..10]
Left "1: value is odd"
```

This approach to parsing a list of values is a good one, so long as we always want to consume the entire input when we parse. Unfortunately, sometimes we'll run into situations where we need to consume an unknown number of inputs into a list without consuming the entire input. To handle this kind of situation we only have one option: keep parsing data until we encounter an error, and then move on.

One way to handle this is to continue to modify our existing function so that instead of passing back a failure when our element parser fails, we instead return an empty list:

```
parseMany :: FilePackParser a -> FilePackParser [a]
parseMany parseElement = FilePackParser $ \input ->
  case runParser parseElement input of
    Left _err ->
      pure ([], input)
    Right (val, rest) -> do
      (tail, rest') <- runParser (parseMany parseElement) rest
      pure (val:tail, rest')
```

This is fine, it will let us parse lists the way that we want, but let's consider a similar problem. Imagine if, instead of a list, we wanted to parse an optional value. We might follow the same pattern we just used for decoding lists and write a function called extractOptional that returns Nothing instead of an empty list if we fail to parse a missing value:

```
extractOptional :: FilePackParser a -> FilePackParser (Maybe a)
extractOptional parseElement = FilePackParser $ \input ->
  case runParser parseElement input of
    Left _err -> pure (Nothing, input)
    Right (val, rest) -> pure (Just val, rest)
```

It turns out that both of these functions are special cases of a more general problem that comes up regularly when we're dealing with things like parsers: trying one parser, and if it fails then trying an *alternative* parser. This pattern is common enough that it's defined by the Alternative type class in Control.Applicative in base.

The Alternative type class is defined in base like this:

```
class Applicative f => Alternative f where
  empty :: f a
  (<|>) :: f a -> f a -> f a
  some  :: f a -> f [a]
  many  :: f a -> f [a]
  {-# MINIMAL , (<|>) #-}
```

Alternative gives us a way to combine two different Applicative values, and it's frequently used when building parsers to represent the idea of choice between two options. If the first option succeeds, it's returned, otherwise the second option is returned. Before we dive into what that means for FilePackParser, let's use ghci to look at a couple of examples of Alternative instances that are already defined for us.

The empty function gives us back an "empty" value. The precise definition of empty can vary a lot depending on the type of thing we're dealing with. For example, the empty value of Maybe is Nothing:

```
λ empty @Maybe
Nothing
```

For lists, the empty value is, intuitively, an empty list:

```
λ empty @[]
[]
```

Another example of something with an Alternative instance is IO. This case is a little bit different, because the value we get back from an empty IO is an exception. This might seem counterintuitive at first, but shortly we'll look at why this ends up being convenient in practice.

```
λ empty @IO
*** Exception: user error (mzero)
```

The other required function we need to define for Alternative is the (<|>) operator. This operator will return the "sum" or "combination" of its left and right values. As with empty, the precise definition can vary depending on the specific type we're looking at. For lists, it simply combines the two lists:

```
λ [1,2,3] <|> []
[1,2,3]
λ [1,2,3] <|> [4,5,6]
[1,2,3,4,5,6]
λ [] <|> [4,5,6]
[4,5,6]
λ [] <|> []
[]
```

On the other hand, Maybe defines (<|>) to be the first non-Nothing value, if there is one:

```
λ Just "Hello" <|> Just "World"
Just "Hello"
λ Just "Hello" <|> Nothing
Just "Hello"
λ Nothing <|> Just "World"
Just "World"
λ Nothing <|> Nothing
Nothing
```

The definition of (<|>) for IO is similar. It returns the value of the first IO action that did not raise an exception:

```
λ putStrLn "Hello" <|> putStrLn "World"
Hello
```

```
λ ioError (userError "exception") <|> putStrLn "World"
World
λ putStrLn "Hello" <|> ioError (userError "exception")
Hello
λ ioError (userError "exception one") <|> ioError (userError "exception two")
*** Exception: user error (exception two)
```

For FilePackParser we can define our own instance that'll behave similarly to the IO instance: we'll return the first non-exception value we encounter. Of course, we don't have to worry about IO errors, only situations where our parser returns a Left value. Like IO, we'll consider an empty parser to be an error.

```
import Control.Applicative

instance Alternative FilePackParser where
  empty = FilePackParser $ const (Left "empty parser")
  parserA <|> parserB = FilePackParser $ \s ->
    case runParser parserA s of
      Right val -> Right val
      Left errA -> runParser parserB s
```

Although our Alternative instance here isn't much more complicated than a case statement, we can use it to rewrite a much nicer version of both extractOptional and parseMany.

We can rewrite extractOptional as a short one-line function:

```
extractOptional :: FilePackParser a -> FilePackParser (Maybe a)
extractOptional p = Just <$> p <|> pure Nothing
```

Or, in pointfree style:

```
extractOptional = (<|> pure Nothing) . fmap Just
```

Our new version of parseMany similarly becomes a short one-line function, but now we have a choice to make. In the very first version of our list parsing function, we wrote a list parser that would consume all of the input data. It would also helpfully give us an error if our parser failed, which can be highly desirable if we know that we're expecting at least some value. When we refactored that code to allow only parsing as much input as was available, we lost the ability to also ensure that we got at least one value. So, do we want to write a function that parses some (one or more) values, or a function that parses as many (zero or more) values as are available?

Now that we have an Alternative instance making it easier for us to be more expressive, we don't have to pick. Each of these new functions can be written as a one-liner. So, let's write them. parseSome will parse at least one element, up to as many as are available in the input. parseMany will parse as many as are available, but will successfully return an empty list if nothing can be parsed.

```
parseSome :: FilePackParser a -> FilePackParser [a]
parseSome p = (:) <$> p <*> parseMany p

parseMany :: FilePackParser a -> FilePackParser [a]
parseMany p = parseSome p <|> pure []
```

You'll notice that these two functions are *mutually recursive*. parseSome parses the head of the list, and then gets the tail of the list by calling parseMany. We define parseMany by first trying to parse one or more elements with parseSome, and if that fails then giving up and returning an empty list. Although we haven't seen this sort of mutual recursion across functions much, if you try it out you'll see that thanks to laziness it works exactly as we'd expect.

Let's load these new functions into ghci and watch them in action:

```
λ someEvens = encode @[Word32] [2,4,6,8]
λ someNums = encode @[Word32] [1,2,3,4,6,8]

λ execParser (extractOptional parseEven) someEvens
Right (Just 2)
λ execParser (extractOptional parseEven) someNums
Right Nothing

λ execParser (parseSome parseEven) someEvens
Right [2,4,6,8]
λ execParser (parseSome parseEven) someNums
Left "1: value is odd"

λ execParser (parseMany parseEven) someEvens
Right [2,4,6,8]
λ execParser (parseMany parseEven) someNums
Right []
```

Our functions work great, and thanks to Alternative they were easy to write. It turns out that we didn't actually need to write these functions at all. Our parseSome and parseMany functions are precisely the implementations of some and many that the Alternative type class defines for us when we create a new instance, and extractOptional is just our own implementation of the optional function that's already defined for us in Control.Applicative:

```
λ :t some
some :: Alternative f => f a -> f [a]
λ :t many
many :: Alternative f => f a -> f [a]
λ :t optional
optional :: Alternative f => f a -> f (Maybe a)
```

Using our new Alternative instance we can now write a Decode instance for lists, getting us a step closer to our FilePack decoder:

```
instance {-# OVERLAPPABLE #-} Decode a => Decode [a] where
  decode = execParser (many extractValue)
```

Now that we're able to decode an entire list of files, we can fully decode a FilePack:

```
testDecodeValue
  :: ByteString
  -> Either String
  ( FileData String
  , FileData [Text]
  , FileData (Word32,String)
  )
testDecodeValue = execParser $ (,,)
  <$> extractValue
  <*> extractValue
  <*> extractValue
```

You can test this yourself using the testEncodedValue function you wrote in the last chapter.

So, you can see that we've been able to write a complete parser thanks to Applicative and a little help from Alternative. A lot of the time these two type classes are all you need to write a parser. In some cases though, Applicative doesn't give us quite enough expressive power. In those cases, we need to also go ahead and stay true to the "Monadic Parser" name and implement a Monad instance as well. In the next section, we'll add a Monad instance and you'll see some of the benefits that you get from monadic parsing over applicative parsing.

Adding a Monad Instance

Before we dive into what we can do with Monad, let's start by writing out our instance. You might recall that the Monad type class requires that we implement two functions: return and (>>=). When you already have an Applicative instance, like we do, it's usually to define return in terms of pure. So, we'll start by defining our new class:

```
instance Monad FilePackParser where
  return = pure
```

Next we need to define (>>=). As you may recall, the general type of (>>=) is:

```
(>>=) :: m a -> (a -> m b) -> m b
```

Or, specialized to FilePackParser:

```
(>>=) :: FilePackParser a -> (a -> FilePackParser b) -> FilePackParser b
```

We'll start out defining a new FilePackParser and binding its input so that we can use it inside of the parser:

```
valParser >>= mkParser = FilePackParser $ \input -> do
{:language="haskell"}
```

(>>=) takes a parse action and a function from a value to a new parse action. We need to start by running the first parse action that we're given so that we can get a plain value that we can pass into our function. We can do that with runParser just like we did when we defined (<*>):

```
(val, rest) <- runParser valParser input
```

Finally, we'll call our function, mkParser, with the value we just parsed. We'll run *that* parser with the remainder of the input that we have left from getting the value. The result of running this second parser will be returned directly, since that's the result of our new parser.

```
runParser (mkParser val) rest
```

Overall, the whole type class definition is just a few lines long:

```
instance Monad FilePackParser where
  return = pure
  valParser >>= mkParser = FilePackParser $ \input -> do
    (val, rest) <- runParser valParser input
    runParser (mkParser val) rest
```

So, what does this Monad instance buy us? As you'd expect, we can now use do notation instead of manually using (<$>) and (>>=) to write parsers. This improves the ergonomics of writing parsers, but it doesn't directly give us a lot of new things we can do. More importantly is that having a Monad instance means that we have the ability to *join* parser actions. Joining values is best described by the join function, defined in Control.Monad. Its definition is:

```
join :: Monad m => m (m a) -> m a
join m = m >>= id
```

In short, join lets us take two nested monadic actions, and combine them into a single action. The ability to do this is one of the important differences between Monad and Applicative. We don't often call join directly; instead, the fact that we're joining values is implicit in the way we use (>>=), but the fact that we can join values, explicitly or implicitly, also means that we can compose monadic parsers in ways that we can't compose applicative parsers.

One example of where we need to use (>>=) or join when parsing is dealing with sub-parsers. As an example, let's imagine that we want to support images in the Netpbm format[1] in our file archive. The Netpbm file format lets us store image data as a collection of binary or ASCII characters using a few different encoding schemes. We're going to support two of them: PBM and PGM. Don't worry if you've never heard of this format though; the details don't matter too much for our specific example.

```
data FilePackImage
  = FilePackPBM Word32 Word32 [Word32]
  | FilePackPGM Word32 Word32 Word32 [Word32]
  deriving (Eq, Show)

instance Encode FilePackImage where
  encode (FilePackPBM width height values) = encode $
    encodeWithSize @String "pbm"
    <> encodeWithSize width
    <> encodeWithSize height
    -- The Encode instance for list already includes size info
    <> encode values

  encode (FilePackPGM width height maxValue values) = encode $
    encodeWithSize @String "pgm"
    <> encodeWithSize width
    <> encodeWithSize height
    <> encodeWithSize maxValue
    -- The Encode instance for list already includes size info
    <> encode values
```

In this example, we have a sum type that lets us represent the different kinds of Netpbm formats that we might want to store. We need a way to differentiate between them so that we can decode them properly, so we're prefixing the encoded data with a string tag. Without this tag, we wouldn't know which of the possible formats we should decode the data into.

Using tags like this to differentiate between different constructors in a sum type is a common pattern, and you'll see it regularly when dealing with all kinds of file formats, from image formats to other file archive formats, to commonly used serialization formats like JSON and XML. With a monadic parser we can deserialize this kind of data easily:

```
instance Decode FilePackImage where
  decode = execParser $ do
    tag <- extractValue @String
    case tag of
      "pbm" ->
        FilePackPBM
        <$> extractValue
```

1. http://netpbm.sourceforge.net/

```
        <*> extractValue
        <*> many extractValue
      "pgm" ->
        FilePackPGM
        <$> extractValue
        <*> extractValue
        <*> extractValue
        <*> many extractValue
      otherTag ->
        FilePackParser $ \_ -> Left $ "unknown image type tag: " <> otherTag
```

You'll notice in this example we're still making use of our Applicative instance to write the parsers for each of the specific constructors that we care about, but at the top level we're using do notation to first extract the tag and then match on its contents to decide which of our two parsers to invoke. At first it may be tempting to try to refactor this to use applicative style parsing as well. At first glance, it seems like it shouldn't be that hard to simplify the code to consistently use the applicative parsing style, but if we look more deeply at what the code is doing, we'll see that it would be impossible to implement this without a Monad instance.

To understand why, let's break this function up into a couple of pieces. First, we'll extract each of our case branches into their own functions, parsePBM and parsePGM:

```
parsePBM, parsePGM :: FilePackParser FilePackImage
parsePBM = FilePackPBM <$>
  extractValue <*> extractValue <*> many extractValue
parsePGM = FilePackPGM <$>
  extractValue <*> extractValue <*> extractValue <*> many extractValue
```

Next, let's move the logic from our case expression into a function:

```
getNetpbmParser :: String -> FilePackParser FilePackImage
getNetpbmParser tag =
  case tag of
    "pbm" -> parsePBM
    "pgm" -> parsePGM
    otherTag ->
      FilePackParser $ \_ -> Left $ "unknown image type tag: " <> otherTag
```

We need the tag value to pass into getNetpbmParser. This is really just going to be a call to extractValue, but let's make it its own function for now, just to help illustrate what's happening:

```
getNetpbmTag :: FilePackParser String
getNetpbmTag = extractValue
```

Finally, we need to compose all of these pieces into our final decoding function. Let's write a function to do that, but before we dive into the implementation we'll think through its type.

First, we'll need to pass in the tag, or at least a way to get the tag, so we know what to parse, so our function will have the type:

```
parseImage :: FilePackParser String -> ???
```

Next, let's pass in our getNetpbmParser function. That way we can call it with the tag as soon as we've parsed it out of the input. That means our type will be:

```
parseImage
  :: FilePackParser String
  -> (String -> FilePackParser FilePackImage)
  -> ???
```

The goal is to get a parser for a particular image, so let's return the parser that we get when we call getNetpbmParser directly, without any modifications. That means the final type of our composition is:

```
parseImage
  :: FilePackParser String
  -> (String -> FilePackParser FilePackImage)
  -> FilePackParser FilePackImage
```

Does this look familiar? We've just demonstrated exactly why we need a Monad instance, because the type we need turns out to be (>>=)!

There are two lessons to take away from this example. The first is that adding a Monad instance to a parser can offer some concrete value, especially when you might need to use information from the input you are parsing to make decisions about how to parse the rest of the document. The other lesson to take away is that even when we did have access to a Monad instance and could have used do notation, we still made use of the Applicative instance for some of our parsing as well. This is a good example of a broader pattern you'll see when parsing things in Haskell: Applicative, Alternative, and Monad instances all work together, and it's common to fluidly switch between the features of each when parsing things.

Adding a MonadFail Instance

Before we close out this chapter, let's address one more ergonomic inconvenience that has cropped up a few times dealing with parsers that might fail. When we were manually building the parsing functions inside of FilePackParser this wasn't such a big deal, but as we've been able to build more and more of our code out of smaller parsers that we are composing, having to manually construct a parser with a Left value starts to get inconvenient. Worse, it ties us to a specific representation of our errors. In the future, if we wanted to refactor our parser to not use Either, we'd need to change every single error in our code base.

One option here would be to factor out the error handing into its own function:

```
parseError :: String -> FilePackParser a
parseError errMsg = FilePackParser (const $ Left errMsg)
```

This works well enough, but it's specific to our particular parser. A better option is to re-use a well-known type class for monadic values that might fail: MonadFail. The MonadFail type class has a single definition:

```
class Monad m => MonadFail m where
  fail :: String -> m a
```

Instances of MonadFail should obey the law:

```
fail a >>= b == fail a
```

In other words, calling fail should end the computation at the first failure that we encounter. This is exactly the behavior we've already been using, and we can directly re-use parseError as the implementation of fail to create our own instance of MonadFail for FilePackParser:

```
instance MonadFail FilePackParser where
  fail errMsg = FilePackParser (const $ Left errMsg)
```

Let's use our new instance to make a small refactor to our Decode instance of FilePackImage:

```
instance Decode FilePackImage where
  decode = execParser $ do
    tag <- extractValue @String
    case tag of
      "pbm" ->
        FilePackPBM
        <$> extractValue
        <*> extractValue
        <*> many extractValue
      "pgm" ->
        FilePackPGM
        <$> extractValue
        <*> extractValue
        <*> extractValue
        <*> many extractValue
      otherTag ->
        fail $ "unknown image type tag: " <> otherTag
```

As you can see, having a MonadFail instance doesn't make a huge difference to our code, but being able to use fail when a parser fails is a small ergonomic nicety for users of our library. Since MonadFail is common for monadic parsers, using it will make our parser feel consistent with many of the common parsers provided by various libraries in the Haskell ecosystem.

Summary

In this chapter, you learned how to deal with parsing data using both applicative and monadic style parsing. Haskell's type system and ecosystem make it particularly well suited to building parsers, and you'll notice the patterns that you used throughout this chapter pop up regularly when you are writing Haskell code. In fact, it's not a stretch to say that Haskell programmers will often try to turn problems into a parsing problem in many cases, because the techniques we've developed in this chapter are so handy that it's always a good idea to see if we can use them when we're presented with some new problem.

This chapter has also served as an example of how to take the work you've done so far in this book, learning about many of the existing values with Monad and Applicative instances, and extend them to your own problems, leveraging the power of these type classes for expressing your own unique computations.

In the next chapter, we'll continue building on these ideas by looking at how you can move on from defining a single Applicative or Monad instance that defines the behavior of some type and instead start defining types through the composition of effects from several different Monad instances.

Exercises

A Configurable Status Line for HCat

Using what you've learned in this chapter, revisit the HCat application that you built earlier. Update HCat to support a configurable status bar that will show up at the bottom of the output. The status bar configuration should be stored on disk in a configuration file (for example ~/.config/hcat.conf). Allow users to specify which fields they want to see, what order they should appear in, and the maximum width of each field.

Command Line Argument Parsing

Several of the examples that you've worked on in this book have required you to deal with command line arguments. So far, we've dealt with this in an ad hoc manner. Using what you've learned in this chapter, try to build a library to make it easier to work with command line arguments. Use this library to improve the command line argument handling for your filepack parsing program and the HCat application you built earlier.

Pretty Printing and Parsing

Reversible parsing is a technique that lets you write a parser that can also be used to encode data. This is particularly useful when you want to impelement parsing for files like JSON, XML, or our own FilePack format. A common use for reversible parsing is to implement a "pretty printing" tool that will let users reformat a document so that it's more readable.

Using what you've learned in this chapter, try to implement a parser for a simple plain text format, and then make the parser reversible. Your reversible parser should reformat the original input so that it's easier to read.

CHAPTER 13

Building Applications with Many Effects

Throughout this book you've learned several different ways to build up monadic computations that have their own particular properties, from Maybe computations that might not return a value and Either values that could succeed or have an error, to IO actions that might have any number of externally visible side effects like printing messages to the screen or updating an IORef. As you saw in the last chapter, many of the programs that we want to build involve several different types of effects that can be combined to build more sophisticated applications. Until now, when we've encountered a problem that required a novel combination of effects, we've built a new solution from scratch. Building up our computations from scratch each time we want something that uses a particular combination of effects might be instructive, but it also burdens us with the need to frequently rewrite the same code.

Monad transformers give us a better way forward, by allowing us to compose different types of monadic computations. In this chapter, you'll learn how to break a more complex application down into smaller composable building blocks: individual monad transformers that you can combine in different ways, allowing you to re-use your code and combine your effects. First, we'll revisit the problem of building a parser and look at how we can separate out the individual effects into their own independent re-usable modules. Next, you'll learn about some of the challenges that you might encounter as you start combining monad transformers, including learning how to think carefully about the order that you compose transformers, and build some new modules to make it easier to combine functions that have different kinds of effects. Finally, we'll look at the two popular monad transformer libraries, transformers and mtl, and you'll how to use them together, and when you might prefer one or the other.

Revisiting the Parsing Problem

We've dealt with parsing several times in this book, most recently in the previous chapter where we focused on building a parser to extract data created by our FilePack tool. In all of these examples, we've addressed the parsing problems we were trying to solve specifically, tailoring our code to the particular application we wanted to build. Narrowly focusing on a particular problem let us keep the size of our application small, but it also meant that we've rewritten similar code several times. That's a good indication that we might want to look at ways that we can abstract away parts of the problem to avoid rework in the future.

Let's start thinking about how we can abstract away parts of a parser by revisiting the definition of the parser we built in the previous chapter:

```
newtype FilePackParser a = FilePackParser
  { runParser :: BS.ByteString -> Either String (a, BS.ByteString) }
```

The definition of FilePackParser that we settled on in the last chapter represents a parser computation as a function from some previous parse state to an error message or a value and a new parse state. The first thing that we can do to make this a bit more re-usable is to allow our user to pick their own types for the internal state and for errors. That way, if a user decides they want to parse Text or String data, or use a sum type to differentiate between different errors, they can do it without needing to write a brand new parser type:

```
newtype Parser e s a = Parser
  { runParser :: s -> Either e (a, s) }

type FilePackParser = Parser String BS.ByteString
```

Making the error and internal state type parameters is a clear benefit to the flexibility of our parser, and as you can see in the example, it doesn't require that we give up a more ergonomic definition of the particular parser we might want to build. We can use type aliases to preserve the ergonomics of working with a very general type like Parser with some particular types applied.

Now that we've stripped away some details, like the specific types of the internal state and the errors, we can start to look at the shape of a parser and think about where we might be able to break it down into more fundamental abstractions. When we do this, it turns out that our Parser type is really a combination of two other monadic computations: the Either monad that we use for handling errors, and a monad that we haven't seen before, State. Before we dive into how we can combine Either and State to make a parser, let's take a quick detour to learn about the State monad. Understanding how State works independently of parsing will help us better understand how to use it as a building block.

The State Monad

The State monad gives us a way to represent mutable state in Haskell programs. Although State is widely used in Haskell programs, we rarely encounter it by itself. The mtl and transformers libraries export a couple of different variations of State, but you're more likely to encounter it behind the scenes in a type like Parser rather than working with it directly. In fact, you've worked with a variation of State quite extensively already in this book: IO is essentially a version of State where the mutable state is a reference to the external state of the real world.

Fundamentally, State is a function from an old state to a value and a new state. After working with FilePackParser extensively in the last chapter, the definition of State should be familiar, so let's look at a complete implementation of a State module and then walk through the ways that this is different than our earlier parsers:

```
module State where

newtype State s a = State {runState :: s -> (a, s)}

instance Functor (State s) where
  fmap f g = State $ \lastState ->
    let (val, nextState) = runState g lastState
     in (f val, nextState)

instance Applicative (State s) where
  pure val = State $ \s -> (val, s)
  f <*> g = State $ \oldState ->
    let (h, funcState) = runState f oldState
        (val, valState) = runState g funcState
     in (h val, valState)

instance Monad (State s) where
  return = pure
  f >>= g = State $ \oldState ->
    let (val, valState) = runState f oldState
     in runState (g val) valState

evalState :: State s a -> s -> a
evalState stateAction initialState =
  fst $ runState stateAction initialState

execState :: State s a -> s -> s
execState stateAction initialState =
  snd $ runState stateAction initialState
```

```
put :: s -> State s ()
put state = State $ \_ -> ((), state)

get :: State s s
get = State $ \state -> (state, state)
```

The most obvious difference between State and our parser examples is that we're no longer handling any possibility of failure. Our Functor, Applicative, and Monad instances are a bit simpler now that they don't need to deal with error handling, but otherwise they are the same as the version we wrote for FilePackParser.

A less obvious difference is that we've included two functions that work with State: get and put. When we were building our parser from scratch, we created quite a few different parser actions that directly accessed the parse state. Usually these functions looked something like this:

```
someParserAction :: State s a
someParserAction = State $ \oldState ->
  let newState = transformState oldState
  in (makeSomeValue oldState, newState)
```

In other words, most of our parser functions took advantage of the implementation details of the parser itself to get the old state and put a new state by writing the step function manually. With get and put we won't need to directly call a State constructor. Instead, we can use do notation:

```
someParserAction :: State s a
someParserAction = do
  oldState <- get
  put (transformState oldState)
  pure (makeSomeValue oldState)
```

Being able to use get and put instead of directly constructing a State value might seem like a small thing that doesn't have any real impact, but it turns out to be an important part of being able to use monad transformers to compose different monadic effects. That's because we can combine monad transformers in many different ways, and we frequently will want to write code that should be re-usable no matter how we've brought State into the picture. As you'll see later in this chapter, if we're directly accessing the State constructor we end up severely limiting the flexibility that we can get from our transformers.

Before we move on and look at some bigger examples of how we can use State, let's try a small example. We'll write a function that will let us build up some lines of text, with each new line of text being indented more than the previous line. We'll keep the current level of indentation in the mutable state:

```
module BasicStateDemo where
import State

appendLineWithIndent :: String -> String -> State Int String
appendLineWithIndent message previousMessage = do
  indentLevel <- get
  let
    nextIndentLevel = indentLevel + 2
    indent = replicate nextIndentLevel ' '
    output = previousMessage <> indent <> message <> "\n"
  put nextIndentLevel
  pure output

appendLineDemo :: IO ()
appendLineDemo =
  putStrLn $ evalState message 0
  where
    message =
      appendLineWithIndent "hello" ""
      >>= appendLineWithIndent "world"
      >>= appendLineWithIndent "love,"
      >>= appendLineWithIndent "George"
```

If we load this up into ghci we can see that our stateful function does exactly what we'd expect:

```
λ appendLineDemo
  hello
    world
      love,
        George
```

Stateful Parsing

Now that we've learned a bit about State and how it works on its own, let's look at how we can use State to make our lives easier when we're writing parsers. We've seen enough examples now to know that we can't have a parser without needing to deal with parse failures. Although we dropped support for error handling when we defined State, we can still write a State-based parser that works the way we want it to. Since a State computation can return any kind of result that it likes, we can have our stateful computation output an Either value that will tell us if we encountered an error. Let's see if we can use this to write a basic parser we can use to parse someone's name:

```
module BasicStateDemo where
import Data.Text (Text)
import Data.Char (isSpace)
import qualified Data.Text as Text
import State

type Parser a = State Text (Either Text a)
```

```
data FullName = FullName
  { first :: Text
  , middle :: Text
  , last :: Text
  } deriving Show

takeUntil :: (Char -> Bool) -> Parser Text
takeUntil predicate = do
  oldState <- get
  let (nextVal, rest) = Text.break predicate oldState
  put rest
  pure (pure nextVal)

dropChar :: Parser ()
dropChar = do
  parseState <- get
  let newState = Text.tail parseState
  put newState
  pure (Right ())

word :: Parser Text
word = do
  nextWord <- takeUntil isSpace
  _ <- dropChar
  pure nextWord

parseFullName :: Parser FullName
parseFullName = do
  firstName <- word
  middleName <- word
  lastName <- word
  pure $ do
    firstName' <- firstName
    middleName' <- middleName
    lastName' <- lastName
    pure $ FullName firstName' middleName' lastName'
```

It works...kind of. We've written a parser that technically meets our requirements: it's using State for handling the internal parse state, and Either for handling parse errors, but this has come at a pretty high usability cost. The reason this approach ends up with code that feels so awkward to use is that we're accustomed to having a single unified interface for all of the effects that happen in a computation. When we use do notation, we don't want to think about each separate type of effect independently. When we defined Applicative and Monad instances from scratch, we could deal with all of the different effects all at once. When we try to compose effects, we're feeling the pain of having to do this manually.

Most of the tedium that we're experiencing with this parser comes from the fact that we have two nested monads. Everything that we want to do needs to be wrapped and unwrapped twice. Once to deal with the outer State action, and again to deal with the inner Either value. When we built out a parser from scratch, we didn't need to deal with that because our Functor, Applicative, and Monad instances all managed both the mutable state and error handling at the same time.

Just because we're now using State and Either together doesn't mean that we have to give up having an interface that lets us deal with them together. One way that we can do this is to make Parser a newtype wrapper and add our own Functor, Applicative, and Monad instances. Unlike our earlier stand-alone parser, this time we won't have to deal with the details of implementing State or error handing ourselves. Instead, we can rely on State and Either to handle their own effects, and our instances will only need to coordinate the interaction between the two. Let's look at an example of how we can do this:

```
module FailingStatefulParser where
import Control.Monad
import Data.Char (isSpace)
import Data.Text (Text)
import qualified Data.Text as Text
import State (State)
import qualified State

newtype Parser a = Parser
  {runParser :: State Text (Either String a)}

evalParser :: Parser a -> Text -> Either String a
evalParser = State.evalState . runParser

parse :: Parser a -> Text -> (Either String a, Text)
parse = State.runState . runParser

instance Functor Parser where
  fmap f parser =
    Parser $ (fmap . fmap) f (runParser parser)

instance Applicative Parser where
  pure a = Parser $ (pure . pure) a
  f <*> a = Parser $ do
    f' <- runParser f
    a' <- runParser a
    pure $ f' <*> a'

instance Monad Parser where
  return = pure
  a >>= f = Parser $ do
    val <- runParser a
    case val of
      Left err -> pure (Left err)
      Right val' -> runParser (f val')
```

The improved instances are only half of what we need to do if we want to present a unified interface into both 'State' and 'Either'. We will also need a way to run both State and Either actions. Functions like get and put will still return State actions, and that means we can't use them directly, since the rest of our code will be expecting Parser actions. There are two different approaches we can take. The first option is to create Parser-specific implementations of the basic operations that are supported by State and Either. We can use those in place of functions like get and put. The second option is to create a general purpose way of turning any State or Either value into a Parser value. This is called *lifting*. You'll see some examples of writing lifting functions later on in this chapter, but for now let's stick with writing a couple of helper functions to handle the basic operations we'll need to support in our parser:

```
parseError :: String -> Parser a
parseError errMsg = Parser $ pure (Left errMsg)

parseGet :: Parser Text
parseGet = Parser (Right <$> State.get)

parsePut :: Text -> Parser ()
parsePut newState = Parser $ Right <$> State.put newState
```

With our new type class instances and our basic operations reimplemented, our parsing functions become much nicer to read. We don't have to think about the fact that we have two nested computations, we can simply treat our Parser as a single cohesive type of computation that supports both errors and mutable state.

```
takeUntil :: (Char -> Bool) -> Parser Text
takeUntil predicate = do
  oldState <- parseGet
  let (nextVal, rest) = Text.break predicate oldState
  parsePut rest
  pure nextVal

optionally :: Parser () -> Parser ()
optionally originalParser = Parser $ do
  oldState <- State.get
  result <- runParser originalParser
  case result of
    Left _err -> State.put oldState
    _success -> pure ()
  pure $ Right ()

word :: Parser Text
word = do
  nextWord <- takeUntil isSpace
  when (Text.null nextWord) $
    parseError "unexpected end of input"
```

```
  optionally dropChar
  pure nextWord

dropChar :: Parser ()
dropChar = do
  parseState <- parseGet
  case Text.uncons parseState of
    Nothing -> parseError "unexpected end of input"
    Just (_, rest) -> parsePut rest

parseFullName :: Parser FullName
parseFullName = FullName <$> word <*> word <*> word
```

You'll notice that one tradeoff we've had to make with our new error-aware parser is that our examples are a bit more complicated. We've had to create a new function, optionally, to handle running parsers that might fail. In this example, we've added this to account for the fact that the final word in our name won't necessarily have a trailing character. We've also added some logic to word to account for the potentially empty input. Although these extra error checks are necessary for accurate parsing no matter what approach we're using to parse text, as we build up a more sophisticated parser these types of checks will get easier to implement.

Handling Errors in Other Computations

In the last section, we looked at how to add error handling to a parser that we built using State, but as you've seen throughout this book the problem of dealing with error handling in some sort of computation is common. Another example where you've already had first-hand experience with this is in handling failures inside of IO actions. We've previously handled errors inside of IO actions by raising exceptions using ioError. Although we've managed to get by with IO exceptions, they have a couple of problems. First, we're risking errors caused by unhandled exceptions. We can certainly argue that developers *should* be responsible and handle exceptions appropriately but there's nothing to force us to catch them, and so we're risking bugs. Second, using IO exceptions for errors in our application logic can confuse different sorts of errors that should be handled in different ways.

Let's see if we can add error handling to an IO action using the same approach we used with our parser. We'll start by creating a new type called EitherIO:

```
newtype EitherIO a = EitherIO
  {runIO :: IO (Either String a)}
```

Next we'll need to define Functor, Applicative, and Monad instances for EitherIO:

```
instance Functor EitherIO where
  fmap f exceptionalIO =
    EitherIO $ (fmap . fmap) f (runIO exceptionalIO)

instance Applicative EitherIO where
  pure a = EitherIO $ (pure . pure) a
  f <*> a = EitherIO $  do
    f' <- runIO f
    a' <- runIO a
    pure $ f' <*> a'

instance Monad EitherIO where
  return = pure
  a >>= f = EitherIO $ do
    val <- runIO a
    case val of
      Left err -> pure (Left err)
      Right val' -> runIO $ f val'
```

Looking at this example, you may notice something interesting: all of these type class instances are identical to the instances we defined for Parser. You can carefully read the examples line by line, or try copying the implementation you created for Parser and change the name of the type. That's because we're not relying on any implementation details of the computation we're embedding our error handling in. It also means that our approach to embedding error handling won't just work for State and IO, it'll work for any type that has a Monad instance.

As you can imagine, it would be tedious to copy and paste the same instance definitions every time we want to add error handling to some type. Thankfully, we don't have to. Instead of creating a new type and defining a new way to embed errors every time, we can create a more general type that lets us transform a plain type into a type that can fail. Types like this that let us transform one type of Monad into another with more capabilities are known as *monad transformers*. Throughout this chapter, you'll learn about several different monad transformers, but for now we'll limit ourselves to handling.

Exceptional Transformers

Let's start looking at how we can build a more general approach to error handling by creating a new module. Both the mtl and transformers libraries refer to the monad transformer we're building as ExceptT. We'll stick with that name for both the name of our module, and the name of the general error handling transformer that we're going to define:

```
{-# LANGUAGE KindSignatures #-}
module ExceptT where
import Control.Applicative
import Data.Kind (Type)
```

The definition of ExceptT is similar to the definitions of Parser and EitherIO, but instead of assuming we'll always use a String for error handling and a State or IO action for the underlying monad, we'll make those additional parameters to ExceptT:

```
newtype ExceptT (e :: Type) (m :: Type -> Type) (a :: Type) = ExceptT
  { runExceptT :: m (Either e a) }
```

In this example, we're using KindSignatures to help make it clear that one of the type parameters that we've added, m, is a *higher kinded type*. When you first learned about higher kinded types on page 240 we only looked at them when we were dealing with type classes and function types, but as you can see from the example, higher kinded types are also useful as type parameters. In the case of ExceptT, the higher kinded type m represents whatever monadic type we're adding exception handling to.

As you might expect, the Functor, Applicative, and monad instances for ExceptT are similar to the instances we defined for EitherIO and Parser. One difference is that, when we were writing those instances, we could freely use functions like fmap or use do notation because the IO and State actions that we were wrapping have Functor, Applicative, and Monad instances. Now that we're wrapping a generic m, we need to be explicit about adding constraints to our instances:

```
instance Functor m => Functor (ExceptT e m) where
  fmap f a = ExceptT $ (fmap . fmap) f (runExceptT a)

instance Monad m => Applicative (ExceptT e m) where
  pure a = ExceptT $ pure (pure a)
  f <*> a = ExceptT $ do
    f' <- runExceptT f
    a' <- runExceptT a
    pure $ f' <*> a'

instance Monad m => Monad (ExceptT e m) where
  return = pure
  a >>= f = ExceptT $ do
    val <- runExceptT a
    case val of
      Left err -> pure $ Left err
      Right val' -> runExceptT $ f val'
```

Now that we've added our instances, we need to define the fundamental operations of ExceptT. When we defined State, we identified two basic operations we could use to define all our other stateful computations: get and put. With monad transformers, we're instead going to define the basic operations we're adding to some computation. In our example, we'll add three basic operations:

1. throwError will let us raise a new exception if we encounter an error.
2. catchError will allow us to handle an exception that has been raised.
3. succeed will let us take a computation that can't fail and embed it inside of an ExceptT computation.

Try writing an implementation of these functions yourself. You should be able to write them using what you've already learned in this chapter. Once you've tried writing them yourself, take a look at the example and see how your versions compare:

```
throwError :: Monad m => e -> ExceptT e m a
throwError exception = ExceptT (pure $ Left exception)

catchError :: Monad m => (e -> ExceptT e m a) -> ExceptT e m a -> ExceptT e m a
catchError handler action = ExceptT $ do
  result <- runExceptT action
  case result of
    Left err -> runExceptT (handler err)
    Right val -> pure (Right val)

succeed :: Monad m => m a -> ExceptT e m a
succeed a = ExceptT (Right <$> a)
```

Now that we've implemented ExceptT and defined some basic operations for working with exceptions, let's revisit a couple of our earlier examples and take a look at how we can reimplement them using ExceptT. We'll start by revisiting Parser, and then look at some examples of using ExceptT to add error handling to IO actions.

Parsing with ExceptT

We'll start our next parsing example by creating a new module and yet another definition of Parser. This time, we'll use a type alias:

```
module ExceptTParser where
import ExceptT
import Control.Monad
import Data.Char (isDigit, isSpace)
import Data.Text (Text)
import qualified Data.Text as Text
import State

type Parser a = ExceptT String (State Text) a
```

Although using a type alias means that our Parser implementation is going to be transparent to our users, we can still make our parser easier to use by adding a utility function for parsing some text. This is a common pattern when building APIs that use monad transformers, since forcing users to manually run all of the nested computations has poor ergonomics.

```
runParser :: Parser a -> Text -> Either String a
runParser = evalState . runExceptT
```

The definition of the parsers won't need to change drastically compared to our earlier examples. Let's look at a few examples for now. You'll finish re-implementing a complete monad transformer-based parser at the end of this chapter as an exercise.

We'll start by looking at parseNextCharacter:

```
parseNextCharacter :: Parser Char
parseNextCharacter = do
  input <- succeed get
  when (Text.null input) $
    throwError "parseNextCharacter: unexpected end of input"
  succeed . put . Text.tail $ input
  pure $ Text.head input
```

As you can see, there are only a couple of differences between this new version and the previous one. First, we've replaced failParser with our new more general throwError function. The behavior is the same, but we're now using a more general purpose function that works with any ExceptT action. Second, we're using succeed to lift put into our exceptT action. The need to explicitly lift operations like get and put from State into our ExceptT-wrapped action is a little bit annoying. Later on in this chapter, you'll learn how to rewrite some basic operations like get and put so that you don't need to explicitly lift them as often, but the need to occasionally lift operations like this is one of the down sides of working with monad transformers.

Not every function implemented with ExceptT will end up looking so similar to our earlier versions. One function that we can write differently is word. Using ExceptT has simplified our how we can handle the expected dropChar failure at the end of our input. You'll define an Alternative instance for ExceptT as an exercise at the end of this chapter to make this even easier.

```
word :: Parser Text
word = do
  nextWord <- takeUntil isSpace
  when (Text.null nextWord) $
    throwError "unexpected end of input"
```

```
  ignoreException dropChar
  pure nextWord
  where
    ignoreException =
      catchError (const $ pure ())
```

Having seen the patterns, you should be able to continue reimplementing the remainder of your ExceptT-based parser on your own.

State, Transformed

Error handling is just one example of how we can use monad transformers to add capabilities to other our computations. Let's look at another example by revisiting the State monad that we defined earlier in this chapter. We defined State as a function from an old state to a value and some new state:

```
newtype State s a = State {runState :: s -> (a, s)}
```

The State monad was useful because it gave us a way to write pure functions that needed access to mutable state. It's not hard to imagine that we might have other computations that would benefit from the ability to deal with mutable state. We can do that by modeling a *state transformer* named StateT as a function from an input state to some monadic value that computes a value and a new state. Since we've seen a few examples already, let's take a look at the full definition of StateT:

```
{-# LANGUAGE TupleSections #-}
module StateT where

newtype StateT s m a = StateT { runStateT :: s -> m (a, s) }

evalStateT :: Monad m => StateT s m a -> s -> m a
evalStateT stateAction initialState =
  fst <$> runStateT stateAction initialState

execStateT :: Monad m => StateT s m a -> s -> m s
execStateT stateAction initialState =
  snd <$> runStateT stateAction initialState

instance Functor m => Functor (StateT s m) where
  fmap f s =
    StateT $ fmap (first f) . runStateT s
    where first g (a,b) = (g a, b)

instance Monad m => Applicative (StateT s m) where
  pure a = StateT $ \s -> pure (a, s)
  f <*> a = StateT $ \s -> do
    (g,s') <- runStateT f s
    (b,s'') <- runStateT a s'
    pure (g b, s'')
```

```
instance Monad m => Monad (StateT s m) where
  return = pure
  a >>= f = StateT $ \s -> do
    (b, s') <- runStateT a s
    runStateT (f b) s'

put :: Monad m => s -> StateT s m ()
put state = StateT $ \_ -> pure ((), state)

get :: Monad m => StateT s m s
get = StateT $ \state -> pure (state, state)
```

Once again, we can see that moving from State to StateT requires only a few minor changes to our existing code. The general shape of our Functor, Applicative, and Monad instances remain the same, but they now run inside of an m action. We still have the same basic operations, get and put, and their definitions are once again quite similar to the original definitions.

Monad Transformers and the Identity Monad

One way to look at StateT is that it's a more flexible version of State because it allows us to add mutable state to any sort of computation. A more pessimistic view of the situation is to say that, like all monad transformers, StateT *requires* that we have some other computation to host the new capabilities we're adding. This limitation is a bit of a problem, since we've already seen that there are some situations, like building parsers, where we might want to use State without any other underlying computation.

One way to handle this would be to define two separate modules. We could define one module for the original State, and another module for StateT that we can use if we have some other computation we're already working with. This approach would work in theory, but it has a couple of drawbacks. First, we'd be writing a lot of duplicate code, and that invites bugs. Second, we can easily imagine a user of our library starting out using State and then realizing that they have some other effects that they need to manage, and needing to refactor their application to use StateT. Having two separate modules would introduce a much larger refactoring burden on our users in this case, since they'd need to update their code in many more places.

Thankfully, we have another option: the Identity monad. Identity is defined for us in the Data.Functor.Identity module in base, but let's look at an example implementation so that we can understand what it does:

```
module Identity where

newtype Identity a = Identity { runIdentity :: a }
  deriving (Eq, Show)
```

```
instance Functor Identity where
  fmap f a = Identity $ f (runIdentity a)

instance Applicative Identity where
  pure = Identity
  f <*> a = Identity $ runIdentity f $ runIdentity a

instance Monad Identity where
  return = pure
  a >>= f = f (runIdentity a)
```

As you can see, Identity doesn't actually do much of anything by itself. All of the instances that we've defined are essentially just normal function application over regular values. At first Identity may seem useless, but it turns out to be quite useful when combined with monad transformers, because using Identity as the underlying monad lets us get access to the features that are added by a monad transformer without needing to have some other computation that might have side effects we don't want or need. This is hinted at by the name *identity*.

Now we can take advantage of Identity to avoid duplication by defining our original State monad in terms of StateT:

```
type State s = StateT s Identity

evalState :: State s a -> s -> a
evalState stateAction initialState =
  runIdentity $ evalStateT stateAction initialState

execState :: State s a -> s -> s
execState stateAction initialState =
  runIdentity $ execStateT stateAction initialState
```

Since State is just a type alias for StateT, all of our existing functions like get and put work exactly as we expect. We also have the flexibility to write our own new stateful functions that can be used with any underlying monad that our users might need. Let's look at a small example to help illustrate the idea. We'll start by creating a trivial stateful function. In the example, we'll define a function called duplicate that reads the mutable state and returns it twice, in a tuple. You can pick some other simple function as you work through the example if you like.

```
duplicate :: Monad m => StateT a m (a,a)
duplicate = do
  val <- get
  pure (val,val)
```

In this example, we're not depending on any particular inner monad; that means we are free to pick whichever type of computation we happen to need.

For example, let's write a function that uses duplicate as though it were a plain State action. We'll start with a more verbose implementation that makes it clear what particular type we're using for duplicate:

```
pureDuplicate :: Int -> (Int,Int)
pureDuplicate val = evalState getDuplicate val
  where
    getDuplicate :: State Int (Int,Int)
    getDuplicate = duplicate
```

The definition of getDuplicate here isn't necessary except to help make the types more clear. We can also write this more simply as:

```
pureDuplicate :: Int -> (Int,Int)
pureDuplicate = evalState duplicate
```

We can also pick some other monad, like IO. Let's start with a more verbose version again:

```
printDuplicate :: Int -> IO ()
printDuplicate val = evalStateT getDuplicate val >>= print
  where
    getDuplicate :: StateT Int IO (Int,Int)
    getDuplicate = duplicate
```

In this example, we're using IO as our inner computation. That means the result of evalStateT will be an IO action that we can easily pass to print.

Stacking Transformers Effectively

Now that we've seen how to combine different effects using monad transformers, and defined transformers for both ExceptT and StateT, we find ourselves with a bit of a problem: how should we nest them? Consider the parser example we've been using throughout this chapter. Should we define one by nesting a StateT inside of an ExceptT, or vice versa? Let's take a look at the two options to see what impact the choice we have might make.

Nesting State Inside of Except

Let's start by continuing the pattern we've used so far in this chapter, using State as the inner monad and adding ExceptT to give it the ability to handle errors. First, we'll create a new module, add some imports, and define a type alias for our parser:

```
{-# LANGUAGE OverloadedStrings #-}

module ExceptState where

import Control.Applicative
import Control.Monad (when, void)
```

```
import Data.Text (Text)
import qualified Data.Text as Text
import ExceptT
import StateT

type ParseError = Text
type ParseState = Text

type Parser = ExceptT ParseError (State ParseState)

runParser :: Text -> Parser a -> Either ParseError a
runParser input parser =
  evalState (runExceptT parser) input
```

So far, everything is looking very much like the other parsers that we've defined in this chapter. Let's go ahead and add two short parsing functions to build our example on. We'll start with a parser that will get the next character from the parse state, and return an error if we're at the end of our input:

```
parseChar :: Parser Char
parseChar = do
  parseState <- succeed get
  case Text.uncons parseState of
    Nothing -> throwError "end of input"
    Just (c, rest) -> do
      succeed $ put rest
      pure c
```

In this example, remember that we need to use succeed when we want to get or put a value to lift the State action into ExceptT. Next, let's add a parser that lets us say that we expect the next character of the parse state to be some particular character. If it is, then we'll discard it, otherwise we'll raise an error:

```
char :: Char -> Parser ()
char expectedChar = do
  actualChar <- parseChar
  when (expectedChar /= actualChar) $
    throwError "Invalid character"
```

So far, so good. We can load this parser up into ghci and see it working:

```
λ runParser "123" parseChar
Right '1'
λ runParser "123" (parseChar >> parseChar)
Right '2'
λ runParser "abc" (char 'a' >> parseChar)
Right 'b'
λ runParser "abc" (char '1' >> parseChar)
Left "Invalid character"
```

Next, let's say that we want to add a parser that will remove any leading spaces from our input. One way we can do that is to repeatedly match a single space and discard it, continuing to do so until trying to match a space fails. You may recall that we encountered a similar problem when building the FilePack parser on page 453. In that example, we defined an instance of the Alternative type class to help us parse a list of values. Let's see if we can do the same thing now.

We'll start by returning to our ExceptT module. We'll add an import for Control.Applicative, then we can start defining our instance. Let's look at the definition first and then walk through it:

```
instance (Monoid e, Monad m) => Alternative (ExceptT e m) where
  empty = ExceptT (pure $ Left mempty)
  a <|> b = ExceptT $ do
    a' <- runExceptT a
    case a' of
      Right val -> pure (Right val)
      Left err -> do
        b' <- runExceptT b
        case b' of
          Right val -> pure (Right val)
          Left err' -> pure (Left $ err <> err')
```

Like all of the instances we've defined for ExceptT, we're adding a constraint that m must be a Monad. This lets us use do notation, and it gives us a way to access values from the inner computation. We're also adding a new constraint, requiring that the error type be a Monoid. We're adding this constraint so that we can use mempty to create a new error when empty occurs. Since the error could be any type, we need some way to create a default value, and mempty is a reasonable choice. As an additional benefit, if both of the alternatives fail in (<|>), we can combine the errors and show the user both of them.

The implementation of empty is straightforward. We fail and set the error to some empty default error value. The definition of (<|>) is longer, but also fairly mechanical. First we try to run the left-hand computation. If it succeeds, we use that value. If not, we try to run the right-hand computation, returning that value if it succeeds, and otherwise returning both errors.

We can use our new instance directly in ghci to try out some alternative parsing. For example, if we try some simple examples throwing exceptions, we can see everything acting like we'd hope:

```
λ runParser "hello" $ throwError "bad" <|> pure "good"
Right "good"
λ runParser "hello" $ pure "good" <|> throwError "bad"
Right "good"
```

```
λ runParser "hello" $ pure "good" <|> pure "better"
Right "good"
λ runParser "hello" $ throwError "bad" <|> throwError "worse"
Left "badworse"
```

What if we try to use this with our parsing code? Let's try an experiment: if the first character of our input string is the letter a, we'll discard it and return the second character. Otherwise, we'll return the first character:

```
λ runParser "abc" $ (char 'a' >> parseChar) <|> parseChar
Right 'b'
```

So far, so good. We discarded the first character and returned the second. Let's try again with different input so we can exercise the other half of our expression:

```
λ runParser "123" $ (char 'a' >> parseChar) <|> parseChar
Right '2'
```

That doesn't look right at all...what's going on? We can get a hint as to the problem if we look back at the instance we defined for FilePackParser:

```
instance Alternative FilePackParser where
  empty = fail "empty parser"
  parserA <|> parserB = FilePackParser $ \s ->
    case runParser parserA s of
      Right val -> Right val
      Left _    -> runParser parserB s
```

In our FilePackParser instance, the very first line of our definition of (<|>) is:

```
parserA <|> parserB = FilePackParser $ \s ->
```

That means the rest of the body of our definition is happening *inside* of the function from the previous parse state to the next one. In other words, the exception handling for FilePackParser is embedded inside of the mutable state. In our new transformer-based parser we're doing things the other way around, embedding the mutable state inside of the exception handling.

The result of this decision is that each of our two alternative parsers are going to run inside of a single computation and share a single mutable state. When we run the first parser, even though it fails, the side effects persist as we move on to the second parser. In our ghci examples, even though char 'a' fails to match a character, it still consumes a value from the parse state.

The choice of how we define our monad transformer stack can have other implications too. Another example that we can easily demonstrate with Alternative is the order in which we nest our transformers is impacted by the laziness of the computations we're nesting. The many function, for example, won't terminate with our current Parser definition. You can see this yourself in ghci; remember you can press ctrl-c to stop a function that isn't terminating:

```
λ runParser "abc" (many parseChar)
Interrupted.
```

Why does this fail to run? Because our definition of StateT is strict, we end up accidentally trying to evaluate an infinite list of parser actions before we look for the ones that succeeded.

Nesting Except Inside of StateT

Nesting State inside of ExceptT has clearly not worked out as well as we might have hoped. Thankfully, we've got an easily available alternative. We can nest Except inside of StateT instead. To start, let's return to our example and add a new type alias, Except:

```
import Identity

type Except e = ExceptT e Identity

runExcept :: Except e a -> Either e a
runExcept = runIdentity . runExceptT
```

As you can see, Except is analogous to State; it uses Identity as an inner monad. In practice, Except is more or less identical to Either, but the new type alias lets us keep consistency with some of our earlier examples.

Next, we'll head over to the StateT module. Since StateT will be our outer monad transformer, we'll need to add an Alternative instance for it:

```
import Control.Applicative

instance (Monad m, Alternative m) => Alternative (StateT s m) where
  empty = StateT $ const empty
  a <|> b = StateT $ \s ->
    runStateT a s <|> runStateT b s
```

Unlike the Alternative instance we defined for ExceptT, this instance requires that our inner monad also have an Alternative instance. Thankfully, we defined one for ExceptT in the previous example, so we don't have any more work to do.

While we're editing the StateT module, there's another function that we'll need to add. When we were using ExceptT as our outer monad, we had to define the succeed function as a way to lift a State action like get or put into the transformer. Now that we're embedding Except inside of StateT we'll have a similar problem. We can use get and put directly, but we need a way to lift an Except computation, like throwError, into the StateT transformer. Let's call the function liftStateT:

```
liftStateT :: Monad m => m a -> StateT s m a
liftStateT a = StateT $ \s -> (, s) <$> a
```

Now that we have updated our transformer modules, let's create a new module for our new parser. Like before, we'll start with a type alias for our parser, and define functions to extract a single character, or to expect a particular character:

```
{-# LANGUAGE OverloadedStrings #-}

module StateExcept where

import Control.Applicative
import Control.Monad (when, void)
import Data.Text (Text)
import qualified Data.Text as Text
import ExceptT
import StateT

type ParseError = Text
type ParseState = Text

type Parser = StateT ParseState (Except ParseError)

runParser :: Text -> Parser a -> Either ParseError a
runParser input parser =
  runExcept $ evalStateT parser input

parseChar :: Parser Char
parseChar = do
  parseState <- get
  case Text.uncons parseState of
    Nothing -> liftStateT $ throwError "end of input"
    Just (c, rest) -> do
      put rest
      pure c

char :: Char -> Parser ()
char expectedChar = do
  actualChar <- parseChar
  when (expectedChar /= actualChar) $
    liftStateT $ throwError "Invalid character"
```

Let's give our newly refactored parser a try in ghci and see how it handles our parsing requirements. First, we'll re-try our alternative examples:

```
λ runParser "123" $ (char '1' >> parseChar) <|> parseChar
Right '2'
λ runParser "123" $ (char 'a' >> parseChar) <|> parseChar
Right '1'
```

Success! When the first parser succeeds in matching the character 1, we return the next character. More importantly, when it fails we no longer keep the side effects from the failed alternative. Instead, we compute the right-hand side using the pristine initial state.

Let's see how our new parser handles many:

```
λ runParser "123" (many parseChar)
Right "123"
```

Once again, refactoring our parser to embed exception handling inside of our state actions instead of the other way around has fixed our problem.

As you can see from these examples, when you are working with monad transformers it's important to be considerate about the order of composition. The particular requirements of your application, and the implementation of the transformers, will be important as you think about how to structure your application.

Building a File Archiver

Now that we've had a chance to see several different examples of how we can use monad transformers, let's try to put it together into a more useful example. In this section, we'll build a utility that will let us create archives of files. Along the way, we'll look for some opportunities to refine our approach to our monad transformer definitions to improve their ergonomics.

Our application allows users to define a file archive using a small language that we'll parse. The language will let our users create a new archive, add items to the archive by importing files from disk, and add items by defining them inline. Here's an example of an archive with three files:

```
archive "example.archive":

  import "./example1.txt"

  new-file "inline-example.txt":
    this is some text
    it can have newlines
    but it needs to be indented

  import "./example2.txt"
```

Two of the archive files, example1.txt and example2.txt, are imported the local filesystem. The third file, inline-example.txt, is defined inline.

Creating an Archiver

We'll start building our archiver by defining a new module. We'll continue using our existing StateT and ExceptT modules, as well as several other imports from base. We'll also go ahead and add two new types: Archive will be a record that holds our final parsed file archive, and ArchivedFile will hold the contents and metadata about each file that has been added to our archive.

```
{-# LANGUAGE DerivingStrategies #-}
{-# LANGUAGE GeneralizedNewtypeDeriving #-}
{-# LANGUAGE OverloadedStrings #-}

module Archiver where

import Control.Applicative
import Control.Monad (void, when)
import Data.ByteString (ByteString)
import qualified Data.ByteString as ByteString
import Data.Char (isSeparator)
import Data.Text (Text)
import qualified Data.Text as Text
import qualified Data.Text.Encoding as Enc
import ExceptT
import StateT

data Archive = Archive
  { archiveName :: Text
  , archivedFiles :: [ArchivedFile]
  } deriving stock (Show)

data ArchivedFile = ArchivedFile
  { archivedFileName :: Text
  , archivedFileContents :: ByteString
  } deriving stock (Show)
```

Next, let's define the type for our archiving computations. Previous examples in this chapter have used type aliases to make the examples easier to follow, but for most real-world applications we'll want to create a newtype wrapper around our monad transformer stack. This will let us add any additional type class instances we might want to define, and will also help us differentiate between our archival computations and other unrelated computations that happen to also use the same underlying monad transformer stack.

We'll call our archival computation type Archiver. While we're at it, we'll also add a utility function to make it easier to run an Archiver action:

```
newtype Archiver a = Archiver
  {unArchiver :: StateT Text (ExceptT Text IO) a}
  deriving newtype (Functor, Applicative, Monad, Alternative)

runArchiver :: Text -> Archiver a -> IO (Either Text a)
runArchiver inputText archiver =
  runExceptT $ evalStateT (unArchiver archiver) inputText
```

You'll notice in this example that we're now nesting *three* different types of computation. Like the other parsers we have built in this chapter, we are composing StateT and ExceptT so that we can track a parse state and handle failures. Now we're also adding in IO. This will allow us to interact with the filesystem so that we can read the contents of imported files as part of our Archiver actions.

Like our earlier examples, let's start off the implementation of our Archiver parser by adding a parser to extract a character from the parse state:

```
parseChar :: Archiver Char
parseChar = do
  parseText <- Archiver get
  case Text.uncons parseText of
    Nothing ->
      Archiver . liftStateT . throwError $ "end of input"
    Just (c, rest) -> do
      Archiver (put rest)
      pure c
```

This function should look familiar by now, it's similar to other implementations of the same function. The most notable difference is that all of our calls to any of our monad transformer actions now need to go through an Archiver constructor. In the case of throwError, we also need to lift the error into StateT before we wrap it in an Archiver.

The need to manually lift values, and to wrap and unwrap them, is a big ergonomic burden when using monad transformers. One option to address this would be to add helper functions that handle the work for any particular transformer stack, but that means we would end up rewriting the same helper functions every time we used a particular combination of transformers. It also means that any users of our API need to learn what helper functions we've defined, and possibly define new bespoke helpers if we've forgotten to add some common and useful ones.

Thankfully, there's another approach we can take. We can define type classes to help us manage both lifting computations into our transformers, and to help us with wrapping and unwrapping common operations. Before we continue with our file archiver, let's look at how we can define these type classes and use them to improve the ergonomics of our transformer stack.

Abstracting Over Lift with MonadTrans

The first type class that we'll build to help make working with monad transformers easier is called MonadTrans, and it's the type class that tells us something is a monad transformer. So, what is a monad transformer? We've already built a couple of examples, so let's see if we can work backwards from ExceptT and StateT and figure out how we should define MonadTrans.

The first common feature of our two transformers was that they both allowed us to take any given monad and add some extra operations and effects to it. In the case of StateT that meant adding some mutable state. With ExceptT we added the ability to raise exceptions. In both cases though, we could add those operations to *any* other monad. The second common feature was that, in addition to whatever operations each transformer supported, they both offered us a way to *lift* an operation. In ExceptT we called the lifting operation succeed. When we defined StateT we called it liftStateT. Let's look at their types:

```
succeed :: Monad m => m a -> ExceptT e m a
liftStateT :: Monad m => m a -> StateT s m a
```

Both of these two functions seem to take a monadic computation with the type m a and return a monadic computation that does the same action, but inside of the newly transformed monad. Since the type of these two functions is so similar, let's use that as a starting point for our type class:

```
module MonadTrans where

class MonadTrans t where
  lift :: Monad m => m a -> t m a
```

Implementing this type class for StateT and ExceptT is pretty straightforward—we just need to call, or copy the definitions of, the lift functions we already defined. You can add these instances to your StateT and ExceptT modules respectively:

```
import MonadTrans

instance MonadTrans (StateT s) where
  lift m = StateT $ \state -> (,state) <$> m

import MonadTrans

instance MonadTrans (ExceptT e) where
  lift m = ExceptT (Right <$> m)
```

At one time, we would have been done with our definition of MonadTrans at this point. It turns out that lifting other monadic computations is the only basic operation that is universally shared across all monad transformers, so the version of MonadTrans that we defined in our example was quite similar to the definition used by the transformers library. Unfortunately, it turns out that this implementation has its own ergonomic difficulties that start to show up when we want to write code that uses nested monad transformers. Let's look at a silly but illustrative example by writing a function that will evaluate some computation twice and return the results lifted into a monad transformer:

```
doSomethingTwice :: (Monad m, MonadTrans t) => m a -> t m (a,a)
doSomethingTwice something = do
  first <- lift something
  second <- lift something
  pure (first, second)
```

Although it seems like this ought to compile, if we try to build this module we'll get an error. The compiler doesn't like using do notation, because it doesn't think that our monad transformer is a monad. That's for a good reason—although we clearly intend that a monad transformer *should* itself have a Monad instance, there's nothing that forces that to be true. For example, let's create a bad monad transformer named Decepticon to demonstrate the problem:

```
newtype Decepticon m a = Decepticon { getUnit :: () }

instance MonadTrans Decepticon where
  lift _ = Decepticon ()
```

This definition of MonadTrans for our Decepticon satisfies the compiler, but it's clearly not what we intended. For type classes like Applicative and Monad we use constraints to avoid this problem. Any type with a Monad instance must have an Applicative instance as well, and any type with an Applicative instance needs to also have a Functor instance. Unfortunately, with MonadTrans it's not quite as easy to add a constraint. Let's try it and see what happens:

```
class Monad t => MonadTrans t where
  lift :: Monad m => m a -> t m a
```

If we try to load this into ghci we'll get a somewhat confusing error:

```
MonadTrans.hs:4:29: error:
    • Expected kind '* -> *', but 't' has kind '*'
    • In the type signature: lift :: Monad m => m a -> t m a
      In the class declaration for 'MonadTrans'
  |
4 |   lift :: Monad m => m a -> t m a
  |                             ^^^^^

MonadTrans.hs:4:31: error:
    • Expecting one more argument to 'm'
      Expected a type, but 'm' has kind '* -> *'
    • In the first argument of 't', namely 'm'
      In the type signature: lift :: Monad m => m a -> t m a
      In the class declaration for 'MonadTrans'
  |
4 |   lift :: Monad m => m a -> t m a
  |                               ^
Failed, no modules loaded.
```

The compiler seems to be getting confused about the kind of t and m. Let's add an explicit kind annotation to help the compiler, and hopefully get a better error message. A monad transformer has two type parameters: the monadic type that is embedded into the transformer, which should have the kind Type -> Type, and the type of value the monad transformer will compute, which should have kind Type. That means the kind of a monad transformer should be (Type -> Type) -> Type -> Type:

```
module MonadTrans where
import Data.Kind

class Monad t => MonadTrans (t :: (Type -> Type) -> Type -> Type) where
  lift :: Monad m => m a -> t m a
```

Now the error we get is a bit more useful:

```
[1 of 1] Compiling MonadTrans       ( MonadTrans.hs, interpreted )

MonadTrans.hs:5:13: error:
    • Expecting one more argument to 't'
      Expected kind '* -> *', but 't' has kind '(* -> *) -> * -> *'
    • In the first argument of 'Monad', namely 't'
      In the class declaration for 'MonadTrans'
  |
5 | class Monad t => MonadTrans (t :: (Type -> Type) -> Type -> Type) where
  |             ^
Failed, no modules loaded.
```

This error gets to the root of our problem: a monad transformer by itself doesn't actually have a Monad instance. We only get a Monad instance after we apply some particular inner computation to our transformer. In other words, m should be a Monad, and (t m) should also be a Monad, but there's no direct constraint on t by itself. We can reason about this using what we know about Monad, but the kind signatures help us too. Anything with a Monad instance needs to have the kind (Type -> Type). That excludes t by itself, but we can see that the kind of m neatly slots into the first argument to t, giving us back a type with the kind (Type -> Type). In pseudocode, you can imagine it like this:

```
-- t can't be a Monad because it doesn't have the kind (Type -> Type)
t :: (Type -> Type) -> Type -> Type

-- m has the right kind, so it can be a monad
m :: Type -> Type

-- In (t m), m "fills in" the (Type -> Type) argument
t m = ((Type -> Type) -> Type -> Type) (Type -> Type)
    = Type -> Type -- The new type also has the right kind to be a Monad
```

Since m isn't a parameter to our type class, we can't ordinarily reference it in a constraint. Thankfully, GHC offers a language extension that we can use for exactly this kind of scenario: QuantifiedConstraints. This extension uses universal quantification with the forall keyword inside of our type class constraints. Let's add this extension and rewrite our type class one more time:

```
{-# LANGUAGE QuantifiedConstraints #-}
module MonadTrans where

class (forall m. Monad m => Monad (t m)) => MonadTrans t where
  lift :: Monad m => m a -> t m a
```

QuantifiedConstraints

The QuantifiedConstraints extension has been available since GHC 8.6.1. This extension isn't enabled by default in either GHC2021 or Haskell2010 so you'll need to enable it manually. This is a generally safe extension that shouldn't cause problems with any existing code.

Using QuantifiedConstraints, we can introduce a new type variable into the constraint, and use that to give the compiler some additional information that will allow it to prohibit some otherwise bad instances. For example, if we revisit our Decepticon example now, we'll see that we get a type error since we can't define a valid Monad instance for Decepticon m:

```
MonadTrans.hs:9:10: error:
    • Could not deduce (Monad (Decepticon m))
        arising from the superclasses of an instance declaration
      from the context: Monad m
        bound by a quantified context at MonadTrans.hs:1:1
    • In the instance declaration for ‘MonadTrans Decepticon’
  |
9 | instance MonadTrans Decepticon where
  |          ^^^^^^^^^^^^^^^^^^^^^
Failed, no modules loaded.
```

At the same time, our doSomethingTwice function works exactly as we would have expected, because we've not told the compiler that any time we have a type t m where t is a MonadTransformer and m is a Monad, then t m must also be a Monad. Since t m must be a Monad then we are free to use do notation or any of the other capabilities we get from working with monads.

Transforming Monads with Class

Now that we've generalized the ability to lift one computation into another with lift, and we've added MonadTrans instances to ExceptT and StateT, we can address another one of the ergonomic problems that we've been dealing with as we're using monad transformers: the need to explicitly lift functions written for one of our inner computations. Let's take another look at parseChar from our Archiver example:

```
parseChar :: Archiver Char
parseChar = do
  parseText <- Archiver get
  case Text.uncons parseText of
    Nothing ->
      Archiver . liftStateT . throwError $ "end of input"
    Just (c, rest) -> do
      Archiver (put rest)
      pure c
```

In theory, our Archiver is supposed to represent a computation that can:

1. Have mutable state
2. Raise an exception
3. Perform IO

As soon as we use it though, we can see that it's not allowing us to do any of those effects directly. If we want to use mutable state, we need to use get or put, but those return a StateT that we need to pass to our Archiver constructor. Worse, when we want to throw an error we need to lift the ExceptT action into the StateT with liftStateT and then pass that to the Archiver constructor. If we want to do IO, the situation starts to get absurd. To write an Archiver action that reads a file from disk, we need to lift our IO action three separate times: once into ExceptT, again into StateT, and finally into Archiver. Thanks to MonadTrans we can make this code a little bit better by using lift rather than having to remember a different function to lift into each different transformer, but the result is still unsatisfying:

```
import MonadTrans

readArchiveContents :: FilePath -> Archiver ByteString
readArchiveContents =
  Archiver . lift . lift . ByteString.readFile
```

The problem that we have here is that the basic operations we've defined for our side effects, like get and put or throwError, are each defined for a particular type of computation. We define get specifically for StateT, and we define throwError specifically for ExceptT. This is all well and good as long as these functions are the basic operations we need for just those particular types, but using monad transformers means that we can define many different types that all use those same basic operations. Now get isn't just a basic operation for StateT, but it's also a basic operation for any other monad transformer that has embedded StateT.

One way that we can address this is to write some basic operations for each type that we define. For example, we could write variations of get, put, throwError, and readFile for Archiver and use them instead of having to lift the operations every time we need them:

```
archiveGet :: Archiver Text
archiveGet = Archiver get

archivePut :: Text -> Archiver ()
archivePut = Archiver . put

archiveError :: Text -> Archiver a
archiveError text = Archiver $ liftStateT (throwError text)

archiveReadFile :: FilePath -> Archiver ByteString
archiveReadFile = Archiver . lift . lift . ByteString.readFile
```

This is a completely viable approach, and it's sometimes the way we want to approach building our applications. It gives us precise control over the actions that can happen inside of our computation, and gives us some flexibility to refactor the implementation details of our side effects later with minimal impact to the rest of our application. This approach also has some down sides. Most notably, it means that each time we want to use some other StateT or ExceptT action we'll need to either lift it, or add a new wrapper.

Another option that we have is to decouple the particular monad transformers from their operations using type classes. Let's look at an example of how we can do this with StateT by creating a new module called MonadState. We'll begin by importing a few modules:

```
{-# LANGUAGE MultiParamTypeClasses #-}
{-# LANGUAGE FlexibleInstances #-}

module MonadState (
  MonadState (..),
  module X,
) where

import ExceptT
import MonadTrans
import StateT as X hiding (get, put)
import qualified StateT as State
```

Next, let's try to define a new type class called MonadState. We need to represent any monadic computation of type m that has a mutable state of any type s:

```
class Monad m => MonadState s m where
  get :: m s
  put :: s -> m ()
```

We can easily create an instance of MonadState for StateT by re-using the get and put instances that we defined in the StateT module:

```
instance Monad m => MonadState s (State.StateT s m) where
  put = State.put
  get = State.get
```

We can also save our users from needing to manually lift calls to get and put when a StateT is nested inside of some of our other monad transformers. For example, we can preemptively add an instance of MonadState for ExceptT as long as the monad embedded into it has a MonadState instance:

```
instance MonadState s m => MonadState s (ExceptT e m) where
  put = lift . put
  get = lift get
```

Now, if we want to create a transformer stack where we are embedding a StateT inside of an ExceptT, we can call get or put directly without needing to use lift or succeed. Let's compare two small examples to see this in action. Imagine we wanted to write a simple guessing game. Each round, the user will guess the current state. The game will set the next state to whatever their guess was, and then it will return True if they guessed the state. Without MonadState we could write that with manual calls to lift, but we're leaking the implementation detail that GuessingGame is using a monad transformer, and forcing our user to deal with that rather than working with the state we're handling directly.

```
module MonadStateDemo where
import StateT
import ExceptT
import MonadTrans

type GuessingGame a = ExceptT String (StateT String IO) a

evalGame ::
  String -> GuessingGame a -> IO (Either String a)
evalGame input =
  flip StateT.evalStateT input . runExceptT

guessTheState :: String -> GuessingGame Bool
guessTheState guess = do
  answer <- lift get
  lift $ put guess
  pure $ guess == answer
```

If we use MonadState instead, we can preserve the same application logic, but now we don't need to lift our function state operations. This makes the API much nicer:

```
module MonadStateDemo where
import MonadState
import ExceptT

type GuessingGame a = ExceptT String (StateT String IO) a
```

```
guessTheState :: String -> GuessingGame Bool
guessTheState guess = do
  answer <- get
  put guess
  pure $ guess == answer
```

The benefits of this approach go deeper than just avoiding explicit calls to lift. Since our basic operations like get and put now depend on the MonadState type class rather than a particular type, we can refactor our program to make GuessingGame newtype without having to change guessTheState at all. We can just ask the compiler to derive an instance of MonadState for us:

```
{-# LANGUAGE DerivingStrategies #-}
{-# LANGUAGE GeneralizedNewtypeDeriving #-}
module MonadStateDemo where
import MonadState
import ExceptT

newtype GuessingGame a =
  GuessingGame { runGame :: ExceptT String (StateT String IO) a }
  deriving newtype (Functor, Applicative, Monad, MonadState String)

guessTheState :: String -> GuessingGame Bool
guessTheState guess = do
  answer <- get
  put guess
  pure $ guess == answer
```

This is a pretty substantial refactor given that we had to change nothing about our implementation at all. As you can imagine, as our programs grow larger, the overhead of changing the way we represent our types can be large, so this approach to abstraction can save a lot of refactoring effort.

We still have a bit of a problem though. Before we dive into the details, let's make a quick change to our program. Imagine that users are playing our guessing game, decide it's too difficult, and ask us to make two changes. First, the state should stay the same no matter how many times the game is played. Second, instead of having to guess the exact state, a user should win if they guess how many characters are in the state. This seems like it should make our program much simpler, so let's try to make the changes:

```
guessTheState :: Int -> GuessingGame Bool
guessTheState guess = do
  answer <- length <$> get
  pure $ guess == answer
```

It turns out that this small change results in a pretty big compiler error. If we try to build this version of the program, we'll get a couple of errors:

```
MonadStateDemo.hs:23:13: error:
    • Ambiguous type variable ‘t0’ arising from a use of ‘length’
      prevents the constraint ‘(Foldable t0)’ from being solved.
      Probable fix: use a type annotation to specify what ‘t0’ should be.
      These potential instances exist:
        instance Foldable (Either a) -- Defined in ‘Data.Foldable’
        instance Foldable Maybe -- Defined in ‘Data.Foldable’
        instance Foldable ((,) a) -- Defined in ‘Data.Foldable’
        ...plus two others
        ...plus 29 instances involving out-of-scope types
        (use -fprint-potential-instances to see them all)
    • In the first argument of ‘(<$>)’, namely ‘length’
      In a stmt of a 'do' block: answer <- length <$> get
      In the expression:
        do answer <- length <$> get
           pure $ guess == answer
   |
23 |   answer <- length <$> get
   |             ^^^^^^

MonadStateDemo.hs:23:24: error:
    • Ambiguous type variables ‘t0’, ‘a0’ arising from a use of ‘get’
      prevents the constraint ‘(MonadState
                                  (t0 a0) GuessingGame)’ from being solved.
      Probable fix: use a type annotation to specify what ‘t0’,
                                                          ‘a0’ should be.
      These potential instance exist:
        instance MonadState String GuessingGame
          -- Defined at MonadStateDemo.hs:19:50
    • In the second argument of ‘(<$>)’, namely ‘get’
      In a stmt of a 'do' block: answer <- length <$> get
      In the expression:
        do answer <- length <$> get
           pure $ guess == answer
   |
23 |   answer <- length <$> get
```

The compiler is telling us that it can't figure out what type of value should be returned by get. Since it doesn't know what kind of value get is returning, it also doesn't know what instance of Foldable should be used for length. If we can solve the first problem—getting the compiler to understand what type should be returned by get—then the second problem will solve itself.

The reason that we're getting this error is that the MonadState type class is defined with two parameters: the state value, s, and the monad, m. The way we've defined the class, there's no relationship between them. As the programmer, it's obvious to us that the type of state for StateT String is going to be String, but we're not giving the compiler enough information to figure that out. We can use a type application to help the compiler out:

```
{-# LANGUAGE TypeApplications #-}

guessTheState :: Int -> GuessingGame Bool
guessTheState guess = do
  answer <- length <$> get @String
  pure $ guess == answer
```

This will get our program compiling again, but now we're hardly better off than when we had to call lift each time we wanted to use an operation that acted on the state. It would be better if we could tell the compiler that whenever it sees a type like MonadState String (StateT String) it should be able to derive the type of the state from the type of the computation. There are two ways that we can solve this problem. Later on in this book on page 565 you'll learn about type families, an extremely flexible tool that will let you solve problems like this. For now, we'll focus on the approach favored by the mtl library: *functional dependencies*.

A functional dependency is a way for us to tell the compiler that some types in a multiparameter type class have a direct dependency on some other types. For example, we can say that the type of the state in a MonadState instance depends on the type of the monad. To do that, we'll need to add two new language extensions: FunctionalDependencies will allow us to create a functional dependency, and UndecidableInstances will allow us to write some type class instances that are normally prohibited, because they could cause the compiler's type checker to not be able to check the type of the instances.

FunctionalDependencies

The FunctionalDependencies extension has been available since GHC 6.8.1. It isn't enabled by default in either GHC2021 or Haskell2010 so you'll need to enable it manually. This extension implies the MultiParamTypeClasses extension, so you won't need to enable it explicitly if you've already enabled FunctionalDependencies. Since FunctionalDependencies substantially changes the behavior of type classes, it's typically enabled on a case-by-case basis for modules that need the feature, rather than being enabled project wide. You only need to enable the extension in the module where you define the a type class with functional dependencies. It's not needed when you only want to create a new instance.

UndecidableInstances

The UndecidableInstances extension has been available since GHC 6.8.1. This extension isn't enabled by default in either GHC2021 or Haskell2010 so you'll need to enable it manually. Although this extension is safe in the sense that it should not cause any previously existing code to stop working, it's generally not a good idea to enable this extension for an entire project. Instead, you should enable this extension on a case-by-case basis when it's needed in a particular module. The UndecidableInstances extension lifts restrictions that ensure the type checker can actually complete type checking type class instances. These checks are helpful more often than not, and prevent you from writing code that might cause the compiler to hang during type checking. You should only enable the extension when you actually need to relax these checks.

With our new language extension added, we can update our type class to add the functional dependency:

```
{-# LANGUAGE FunctionalDependencies #-}
{-# LANGUAGE UndecidableInstances #-}

class Monad m => MonadState s m | m -> s where
  get :: m s
  put :: s -> m ()
```

The part of the instance declaration after the vertical pipe (|) is our functional dependency. When we say | m -> s we're creating a functional dependency that tells the compiler that the type of m should uniquely determine the type of s.

With this change in place, our simple definition of guessTheState will work without any need for a type application or annotation. Since the type of the state depends on the type of the monad, the compiler is able to figure out that it must be a String.

```
{-# LANGUAGE DerivingStrategies #-}
{-# LANGUAGE GeneralizedNewtypeDeriving #-}
module EffectiveHaskell.Chapter13.MonadStateDemo.V3 where

import EffectiveHaskell.Chapter13.MonadState
import EffectiveHaskell.Chapter13.ExceptT

newtype GuessingGame a =
  GuessingGame { runGame :: ExceptT String (StateT String IO) a }
  deriving newtype (Functor, Applicative, Monad, MonadState String)

evalGame :: String -> GuessingGame a -> IO (Either String a)
evalGame input = flip evalStateT input . runExceptT . runGame
```

```
guessTheState :: Int -> GuessingGame Bool
guessTheState guess = do
  answer <- length <$> get
  pure $ guess == answer
```

Before we move on, let's celebrate our effort and refactoring with a quick look at some of our new code running live in ghci:

```
λ> evalGame "four" $ guessTheState 4
Right True
λ> evalGame "four" $ guessTheState 3
Right False
```

MonadError

The same ideas that we used to build MonadState can be applied to any other problem where we might have several different types that implement a particular effect. Another example of this is failure. You've already seen examples of using MonadFail to handle some failures when building your parser. Although it's handy in some cases, MonadFail is intended to be used to handle failing pattern matches. It's not intended for more sophisticated error handling.

You've already seen how ExceptT gives us more control over how we define and handle errors. We can take these same capabilities and define them in a type class so that we have a general purpose way of talking about types that support exceptions and robust error handling. This type class is named MonadError in the mtl. We can implement MonadError using the same patterns we used for MonadState:

```
{-# LANGUAGE FunctionalDependencies #-}
{-# LANGUAGE UndecidableInstances #-}
{-# LANGUAGE FlexibleInstances #-}

module MonadError (
  MonadError (..),
  module X,
) where

import ExceptT as X hiding (catchError, throwError)
import qualified ExceptT as Except
import MonadTrans
import ReaderT
import StateT

class Monad m => MonadError e m | m -> e where
  throwError :: e -> m a
  catchError :: m a -> (e -> m a) -> m a

instance Monad m => MonadError e (Except.ExceptT e m) where
  throwError = Except.throwError
  catchError = flip Except.catchError
```

```
instance MonadError e m => MonadError e (StateT s m) where
  throwError = lift . throwError
  catchError action handler =
    StateT $ \s ->
      let innerAction = runStateT action s
          liftedHandler e = runStateT (handler e) s
       in catchError innerAction liftedHandler
```

Tagless Final Encoding

Now that we have a general way to use functions like get and put, and the compiler is better able to keep track of the type of the state based on the monad it's associated with, we have one more opportunity to add an additional level of flexibility. Instead of picking any particular monad that our code should run in, we can instead use constraints to tell the compiler what capabilities our code needs. For example, our guessing game doesn't need to raise any exceptions, nor does it need to do any IO. We can run the guessing game inside of any computation, so long as it has mutable state, and that state has a Foldable instance we can use to get the length of the state. Let's try rewriting our original guesser to be more generic using these constraints:

```
genericGuesser :: (Foldable t, MonadState (t a) m) => Int -> m Bool
genericGuesser guess = do
  answer <- length <$> get
  pure $ guess == answer
```

Using constraints like this gives us even more flexibility, because now we're not only able to refactor the type of computation that our code runs in, we can also use the same code with different types of computation. Let's create a second guessing game type that will hold a list of numbers instead of a String:

```
newtype GuessingGame2 a =
  GuessingGame2 { runGame2 :: ExceptT String (StateT [Int] IO) a }
  deriving newtype (Functor, Applicative, Monad, MonadState [Int])
```

We can only use our original guessTheState function with our original GuessingGame type, but genericGuesser can be used with either of these types of computation, or even types that we haven't thought of yet.

This constraint-first approach to representing applications with type classes is called *tagless final encoding*. In the particular case where we're using tagless final encoding with monad transformers, it's often referred to as *mtl style*. That's because mtl is the name of the popular library that provides type classes like MonadState that work with the concrete monad transformers defined in the transformers library. When a specific term is needed to differentiate it from MTL style, you'll sometimes hear the approach to writing monad transformer code explicitly using lift and the transformers themselves called *direct style*.

Writing programs using MTL style has a mixture of advantages and disadvantages, so it's useful to think about the requirements of your particular application. MTL style offers clear advantages for flexibility. You can refactor your application more easily, and you can more easily re-use code that was written in MTL style in ways that the author might not have foreseen. MTL style is also a useful way to handle dependency injection in Haskell applications. Using MTL style makes it easier to write tests that select a particular computation that was designed for testing. The same flexibility that makes MTL style useful can also be a burden at times. The biggest disadvantage is that using MTL style means that you can't make assumptions about the side effects that might be executed by your code. Using a direct style that forces a particular computation that you have written means that you have more control over the behavior of your program. Direct style also lends itself to more clear and concise error messages, and in larger applications it can reduce the time it takes to compile your programs.

MonadIO

Before we revisit our Archiver tool, let's look at one last type class that is frequently used with tagless final style programs in general, and with monad transformers in particular: MonadIO. This class is defined for us in base at Control.Monad.IO.Class, but it's simple enough that we can recreate the entire class in just a few lines of code:

```
module MonadIO where

class Monad m => MonadIO m where
  liftIO :: IO a -> m a

instance MonadIO IO where
  liftIO = id
```

Writing instances for MonadIO for monad transformers tends to be straightforward. Let's look at the instances for StateT and ExceptT:

```
import EffectiveHaskell.Chapter13.MonadIO
instance MonadIO m => MonadIO (StateT s m) where
  liftIO = lift . liftIO

import EffectiveHaskell.Chapter13.MonadIO
instance MonadIO m => MonadIO (ExceptT s m) where
  liftIO = lift . liftIO
```

As you can see, MonadIO isn't doing much more than calling lift. The value of MonadIO is not in having sophisticated implementations of liftIO, but in the ability to use tagless final style functions to create IO actions that are polymorphic and work with IO actions or with any monad transformer that, directory or indirectly, embeds IO. For example, imagine that we wanted to write a function that added some basic logging that would tell us when a function was called. Writing to the screen requires that we be able to do IO, but with MonadIO we can make our function work for any type that embeds IO:

```
runWithLog :: MonadIO m => (a -> m b) -> a -> m b
runWithLog action val = do
  liftIO $ putStrLn "Running the function..."
  result <- action val
  liftIO $ putStrLn "Finished running the function"
  pure result
```

If we load this function into ghci we can see that it's usable with any monad transformer stack that embeds IO:

```
λ s = const (pure "hello state") :: a -> StateT String IO String
λ evalStateT (runWithLog s 100) ""
Running the function...
Finished running the function
"hello state"

λ e = const (pure "hello except") :: a -> ExceptT String IO String
λ runExceptT $ runWithLog e 100
Running the function...
Finished running the function
Right "hello except"

λ i = const (pure "hello IO") :: a -> IO String
λ runWithLog i 100
Running the function...
Finished running the function
"hello IO"

λ n = const (pure "hello nested") ::
    a -> StateT String (ExceptT String (StateT String IO)) String
λ> evalStateT (runExceptT (evalStateT (runWithLog n 100) "")) ""
Running the function...
Finished running the function
Right "hello nested"
```

Deriving a Better Archiver

Now that we've added the extra type classes to make it easier to work with monad transformer stacks, let's revisit our Archiver application again, and update it to work with the new type classes that we've just added. The first change that we'll make is to the definition of Archiver itself. The way that we're representing the stack of monad transformers doesn't need to change, but we can now realize one of the biggest benefits of moving toward our type class-based approach to working with transformers: deriving instances of all of the relevant type classes automatically. Since we're using a newtype wrapper to define Archiver, we can benefit from the work we've done to get all of the instances we need for free. Now that we've done the work, let's take a look at the final monad transformer-based archiver tool. You'll notice as you review this example that we're able to mix basic operations like get and put with exceptions and IO actions all inside of a single Archiver computation:

```
{-# LANGUAGE DerivingStrategies #-}
{-# LANGUAGE GeneralizedNewtypeDeriving #-}
{-# LANGUAGE OverloadedStrings #-}

module ClassyArchiver where

import Control.Applicative
import Control.Monad (void, when)
import Data.ByteString (ByteString)
import qualified Data.ByteString as ByteString
import Data.Char (isSeparator)
import Data.Text (Text)
import qualified Data.Text as Text
import qualified Data.Text.Encoding as Enc
import MonadError
import MonadIO
import MonadState

data Archive = Archive
  { archiveName :: Text
  , archivedFiles :: [ArchivedFile]
  }
  deriving stock (Show)

data ArchivedFile = ArchivedFile
  { archivedFileName :: Text
  , archivedFileContents :: ByteString
  }
  deriving stock (Show)

newtype Archiver a = Archiver
  {unArchiver :: StateT Text (ExceptT Text IO) a}
  deriving newtype
    ( Functor
    , Applicative
    , Monad
    , Alternative
    , MonadState Text
    , MonadError Text
    , MonadIO
    )
```

```
runArchiver :: Text -> Archiver a -> IO (Either Text a)
runArchiver inputText archiver =
  runExceptT $ evalStateT (unArchiver archiver) inputText

parseChar :: Archiver Char
parseChar = do
  parseText <- get
  case Text.uncons parseText of
    Nothing ->
      throwError "end of input"
    Just (c, rest) -> do
      put rest
      pure c

dropSpaces :: Archiver ()
dropSpaces = void $ many (expectChar ' ')

isNewline :: Char -> Bool
isNewline = (== '\n')

expect :: Eq a => Archiver a -> a -> Archiver ()
expect getActual expected = do
  actual <- getActual
  when (expected /= actual) $ do
    throwError "expectation violated"

expectChar :: Char -> Archiver ()
expectChar = expect parseChar

expectText :: Text -> Archiver ()
expectText expected = do
  stripped <- Text.stripPrefix expected <$> get
  case stripped of
    Nothing -> throwError "missing expected string"
    Just rest -> put rest

takeUntil :: (Char -> Bool) -> Archiver Text
takeUntil predicate = do
  (result, rest) <- Text.break predicate <$> get
  put rest
  pure result

word :: Archiver Text
word = do
  nextWord <- takeUntil (\s -> isSeparator s || isNewline s)
  void . optional $ expectChar '\n' <|> dropSpaces
  when (Text.null nextWord) $
    throwError "end of input"
  pure nextWord

quotedString :: Archiver Text
quotedString = do
  expectChar '"'
  quotedText <- takeUntil (== '"')
  expectChar '"'
```

```
  pure quotedText

restOfLine :: Archiver Text
restOfLine = remainderOfLine <|> remainderOfText
  where
    remainderOfLine = do
      txt <- takeUntil isNewline
      expectChar '\n'
      pure txt
    remainderOfText = get

dropEmptyLines :: Archiver ()
dropEmptyLines =
  void $ many $ dropSpaces >> expectChar '\n'

parseIndentedLine :: Int -> Archiver Text
parseIndentedLine indentLevel = do
  expectText $ Text.replicate indentLevel " "
  restOfLine

runSubparser :: Archiver a -> Text -> Archiver a
runSubparser action subparserState = do
  oldText <- get
  put subparserState
  result <- action
  put oldText
  pure result

parseBlock :: Archiver a -> Archiver a
parseBlock blockParser =
  dropEmptyLines >> getBlock >>= runSubparser blockParser
  where
    getBlock = do
      firstLineSpacing <- takeUntil (not . isSeparator)
      let indentation = Text.length firstLineSpacing
      firstLine <- restOfLine
      restOfBlock <- many (dropEmptyLines >> parseIndentedLine indentation)
      pure $ Text.unlines (firstLine : restOfBlock)

parseImportStatement :: Archiver ArchivedFile
parseImportStatement = do
  expectText "import"
  dropSpaces
  path <- quotedString
  dropSpaces
  expectChar '\n'
  contents <- liftIO $ ByteString.readFile (Text.unpack path)
  pure $ ArchivedFile path contents

parseNewFileStatement :: Archiver ArchivedFile
parseNewFileStatement = do
  expectText "new-file"
  dropSpaces
  path <- quotedString
```

```
  dropSpaces
  expectText ":\n"
  body <- Enc.encodeUtf8 <$> parseBlock get
  pure $ ArchivedFile path body

parseArchiveStatements :: Archiver [ArchivedFile]
parseArchiveStatements =
  many $ dropEmptyLines >> (parseImportStatement <|> parseNewFileStatement)

parseArchive :: Archiver Archive
parseArchive = do
  expectText "archive"
  dropSpaces
  archiveName <- quotedString
  expectText ":\n"
  files <- parseBlock parseArchiveStatements
  pure $ Archive archiveName files
```

Summary

Monad transformers are one of the most important concepts to understand as you start to work with real-world Haskell applications. Not every production application uses monad transformers, but they offer a well-understood solution to solve the common problem of composing different side effects, and there is a rich ecosystem of Haskell libraries that make use of monad transformers. Now that you've worked through implementing a few of your own transformers, and gotten to see how to use both direct style and MTL style encodings, you will be prepared to work with many different Haskell applications.

Exercises

Building Out the Monad Transformer Library

In this chapter, we focused on two specific monad transformers: StateT and ExceptT. The transformers library provides several other commonly used monad transformers. One of the most common monad transformers is the ReaderT transformer. This monad transformer lets you write computations that have a read-only environment:

```
newtype ReaderT r m a = ReaderT {runReaderT :: r -> m a}
```

The two basic operations for a ReaderT monad are ask, which fetches the value from the read-only environment, and local, which lets you run a ReaderT action with a modified local read-only environment. Their types are:

```
ask :: Monad m => ReaderT r m r
local :: Monad m => (r -> r) -> ReaderT r m a -> ReaderT r m a
```

In this exercise, write Functor, Applicative, Monad, MonadIO, and MonadTrans instances for ReaderT, and provide a definition for both ask and local. Once you have created a working definition of ReaderT, add a new class called MonadReader:

```
class Monad m => MonadReader r m | m -> r where
  ask :: m r
  local :: (r -> r) -> m a -> m a
```

Next, finish writing the following instances:

```
instance Monad m => MonadReader r (Reader.ReaderT r m) where
instance MonadReader r m => MonadReader r (ExceptT e m) where
instance MonadReader r m => MonadReader r (StateT s m) where
```

A New FilePackParser

Refactor the FilePackParser application that you wrote earlier in this book to use the following monad:

```
newtype FilePackParser a = FilePackParser
  { runFilePackParser :: StateT Text (ExceptT Text IO) a }
```

CHAPTER 14

Building Efficient Programs

So far in this book, we've spent most of our time focused on designing programs at a high level, and making use of the features Haskell gives us to build useful abstractions. In most cases, we've been relying on the compiler to generate code that's "fast enough" while we focus on designing an application that's easy to write and maintain. Unfortunately, compilers aren't perfect, and we often have opportunities to change our implementation to get better performance from our programs. You've already seen a few small examples of writing code to be more mindful of performance requirements, like when you learned about space leaks and bang patterns on page 386.

In this chapter, you'll build a text processing library that can be used to implement spellchecking on large text documents. As we work through building this library, we'll run across several examples of patterns we can use for improving the performance of Haskell programs. By the end of the chapter, you'll have learned how to write programs with performance in mind, profile applications to find bottlenecks, and be able to strategically deploy some micro-optimizations to improve the performance of the most critical parts of your applications. The exercises at the end of this chapter will give you an opportunity to take the library you've built and integrate it into the HCat application you built in chapter 8 on page 283.

Building a Naive Spellchecker

Spellchecking is an easy feature to take for granted. Spellchecking has been available for personal computers since the 1980s, and most software we use to write text today has spellchecking available. Surprisingly, spellchecking continues to be both a relevant problem domain, and one that can present some interesting challenges when we need to write efficient code. In the first part of this chapter, we'll build a general purpose spellchecking library that can be used with any dictionary.

Let's start by creating a new cabal project. You'll want to add a few dependencies to your project so you can follow along with this chapter:

- base
- containers
- text
- vector

We'll start our project by building a performance naive spellchecking implementation, so let's make a module named SpellCheck.Naive and add a couple of imports:

```
module SpellCheck.Naive where
import Data.Text (Text)
import qualified Data.Text as T
```

To implement a spellchecker, we need to write two functions. First, we need a way to check to see how similar a misspelled word is to a correctly spelled word. This will help us identify the potential corrections we will suggest to the user when they have a typo. Second, we'll need to check the words in the document we want to spellcheck against a dictionary of correctly spelled words, so that we can find words that need correction.

We can find out how similar two words are to one another using an *edit distance metric*. There are a few well-known examples of these that you can find online. The one we'll use is called *Levenshtein distance*. It will tell us how many changes we'd need to make to turn one string into another string when we're allowed to

- Add a letter to the string,
- Delete a letter from the string, or
- Replace a letter in the string with a different one.

Before we move onto the implementation, let's look at a couple of examples to get a better idea of what's happening. First, we'll try looking at the edit distance between identical strings:

```
λ editDistance "hello" "hello"
0
```

Since there are no changes to be made, the edit distance is 0. If we add some letters to either string, we'll see that the edit distance increases with the number of letters that we've added:

```
λ editDistance "hello" "helloo"
1
λ editDistance "hello12345" "hello"
5
```

In these examples, we can see that for each extra letter, the edit distance increases by one. It doesn't matter whether we add letters to the first string or the second string, since inserting a character and deleting a character both have the cost of a single edit. Next, let's replace some letters with different letters:

```
λ editDistance "aaa" "aab"
1
λ editDistance "aaa" "abb"
2
```

Here, you can see that replacing the wrong letter with a correct letter costs a single edit. In the examples, each time we need to replace an "a" with a "b" it adds a single edit to the edit distance.

Finally, our algorithm should always return the smallest number of edits necessary to make the strings match up:

```
λ editDistance "bababa" "ababab"
2
```

At first you might be surprised that the edit distance is 2. If we swapped out every "b" for an "a", and every "a" for a "b" we'd have a total edit distance of 6. We can accomplish the same thing in two edits by deleting the initial "b", which costs one edit and gives us "ababa", and then adding a "b" back to the end of the string, which costs us one more edit and gets our strings matching.

Surprisingly, there's a pretty straightforward algorithm to find the edit distance between two strings. Let's start by looking at the implementation, and then step through how it works:

```
editDistance :: Text -> Text -> Int
editDistance stringA stringB
  | T.null stringA = T.length stringB
  | T.null stringB = T.length stringA
  | T.head stringA == T.head stringB = editDistance restOfA restOfB
  | otherwise = 1 + minimum [insertCost, deleteCost, swapCost]
  where
    restOfA = T.tail stringA
    restOfB = T.tail stringB
    deleteCost = editDistance restOfA stringB
    insertCost = editDistance stringA restOfB
    swapCost = editDistance restOfA restOfB
```

Our implementation is made up of three basic rules:

First, if either string is empty, then the edit distance is equal to the length of the other string. We're implementing this rule with the first two guard clauses in our function:

```
editDistance :: Text -> Text -> Int
editDistance stringA stringB
  | T.null stringA = T.length stringB
  | T.null stringB = T.length stringA
  -- ...
```

This rule is the base case of our recursive function, and it's how we deal with situations where one string is longer than another. The rule works because, if the first string is empty, we need to add all of the letters from the second string. On the other hand, if the second string is empty, we need to remove all of the letters from the first string. In either case, that's one edit per letter in the non-empty string.

Second, if the first letter of two strings are the same, then the edit distance is the distance between the remainder of the two strings:

```
editDistance :: Text -> Text -> Int
editDistance stringA stringB
  -- ...
  | T.head stringA == T.head stringB = editDistance restOfA restOfB
  -- ...
  where
    restOfA = T.tail stringA
    restOfB = T.tail stringB
```

In our implementation, we're taking the tail of the two strings and calculating the distance between them recursively. This lets us step through the string and, as long as our values match, we never add any unnecessary edits.

The final rule says that if the first letters of our strings don't match, we need to add one to the overall edit distance between the strings. Unlike our previous examples though, the recursive case isn't quite so straightforward. Since we want to always return the minimum number of edits, we need to use the least expensive of our three options: inserting, deleting, or replacing a character.

```
editDistance :: Text -> Text -> Int
editDistance stringA stringB
  -- ...
  | otherwise = 1 + minimum [insertCost, deleteCost, swapCost]
  where
    restOfA = T.tail stringA
    restOfB = T.tail stringB
    deleteCost = editDistance restOfA stringB
```

```
    insertCost = editDistance stringA restOfB
    swapCost = editDistance restOfA restOfB
```

We can figure out the costs of each approach by calculating the edit distance recursively. To find out the edit distance if we delete a character, we can drop the current character and recalculate the distance. Similarly, we can find the cost of inserting a character by removing a character from the target string, or the cost of replacing a character by dropping a character from both strings.

To help understand what's going on, let's step through a small example:

```
editDistance "aaa" "abab"
  | T.head "aaa" == T.head "abab" =
    editDistance "aa" "bab"
      | otherwise = 1 + minimum [deleteCost, insertCost, swapCost]
                  = 1 + minimum [2, 1, 1]
                  = 1 + 1
                  = 2
      where
        deleteCost = editDistance "a" "bab"
          | otherwise = 1 + minimum [deleteCost, insertCost, swapCost]
                      = 1 + minimum [3,1,2]
                      = 1 + 1
                      = 2
          where
            deleteCost = editDistance "" "bab"
              | T.null "" = T.length "bab" = 3
            insertCost = editDistance "a" "ab"
              | T.head "a" == T.head "ab" =
                editDistance "a" "b"
                  | otherwise = 1 + minimum [deleteCost, insertCost, swapCost]
                              = 1 + minimum [1, 1, 0]
                              = 1 + 0
                              = 1
                  where
                    deleteCost = editDistance "" "b"
                      | T.null "" = T.length "b" = 1
                    insertCost = editDistance "a" ""
                      | T.null "" = T.length "a" = 1
                    swapCost = editDistance "" ""
                      | T.null "" = T.length "" = 0
            swapCost = editDistance "" "ab"
              | T.null "" = T.length "ab" = 2
        insertCost = editDistance "aa" "ab"
          | T.head "aa" == T.head "ab" = editDistance "a" "b"
            | otherwise = 1 + minimum [deleteCost, insertCost, swapCost]
                        = 1 + minimum [1, 1, 0]
                        = 1 + 0
                        = 1
```

```
        where
          deleteCost = editDistance "" "b"
            | T.null "" = T.length "b" = 1
          insertCost = editDistance "a" ""
            | T.null "" = T.length "a" = 1
          swapCost = editDistance "" ""
            | T.null "" = T.length "" = 0
    swapCost = editDistance "a" "ab"
      | T.head "a" == T.head "ab" = editDistance "" "b"
        | T.null "" = T.length "b" = 1
```

The first thing we do in this example is strip off the leading "a" from both strings. Since they match, we know the distance between "aaa" and "abab" is going to be the same as the difference between "aa" and "bab". Next, we have a mismatch between "a" and "b" so we need to decide whether the cheapest way forward is to

- Delete "a" and add the distance from "a" to "bab",
- Insert the missing "b" and add the distance from "aa" to "ab", or
- Replace the "a" with "b" and add the distance from "a" to "ab".

In the first branch, we try deleting the first "a", but that puts us back into the same situation we just found ourselves in, with the remaining "a" not matching the initial "b" from "bab". Once again we need to choose the smallest number of edits out of our three choices:

- Delete the "a" and compare the empty string ("") to "bab".
- Insert the missing "b" and compare "a" to "ab".
- Replace the "a" with a "b" and compare the empty strings that are left.

This time, two of our branches, deletion and replacement, have empty strings and so they each end their recursion and give us back a value. We'll need to take another trip through the code for this branch to find the difference between "a" and "ab".

The recursion continues on for a while even with these relatively short strings. Before we move on with building our spellchecker, you should spend some more time with the example, and even walk through a few of your own examples. It will be helpful to have a good understanding of the mechanics of how the code works when we start to optimize it later in the chapter.

Spellchecking a Document

Now that we have a way to find the distance between two words, we can move on to spellchecking. The first thing we need to do is to decide on how we want to report a particular spelling suggestion back to the user. Let's head over to the Types module in our library and create a new SuggestedMatch record to hold a suggestion. While we're at it, let's add a utility function called showSuggestedMatch that will format the suggestions nicely:

```
{-# LANGUAGE RecordWildCards #-}
module Types where
import SpellCheck.Naive
import Data.Text (Text)
import Text.Printf

data SuggestedMatch = SuggestedMatch
  { matchWord :: Text
  , matchSearchedWord :: Text
  , matchDistance :: Int
  } deriving (Show, Eq)

showSuggestedMatch :: SuggestedMatch -> String
showSuggestedMatch SuggestedMatch{..} =
  printf "%s -> %s: %d" matchWord matchSearchedWord matchDistance
```

Next, let's head over to our top level SpellCheck and write a function that will spellcheck single words against a dictionary of words. We can start with a straightforward implementation:

```
module SpellCheck where
import SpellCheck.Types
import SpellCheck.Naive
import Data.Text (Text)

spellcheckWord :: [Text] -> Text -> [SuggestedMatch]
spellcheckWord dictionary word =
  [ SuggestedMatch dictWord word (editDistance dictWord word)
  | dictWord <- dictionary
  ]
```

Running this version of our spellchecker in ghci will show us that we are in fact getting some recommendations for misspelled words:

```
λ dictionary = ["yellow", "mellow", "hello", "goodbye"]
λ printMatches = putStrLn . showSuggestedMatch
λ checkWord word = mapM_ printMatches $ spellcheckWord dictionary word

λ checkWord "yello"
yellow -> yello: 1
mellow -> yello: 2
hello -> yello: 1
goodbye -> yello: 7

λ checkWord "mello"
yellow -> mello: 2
mellow -> mello: 1
hello -> mello: 1
goodbye -> mello: 7
```

```
λ checkWord "hello"
yellow -> hello: 2
mellow -> hello: 2
hello -> hello: 0
goodbye -> hello: 7
```

There are a couple of problems that we have right now. First, we're showing suggestions for words that are many edits away. If someone typed "mello" it's not very likely the word that they wanted was "goodbye". We can fix this by adding a threshold so we can only show users words that are a close match. Second, we're showing results for words that are correctly spelled. For our purposes, we only want to show suggestions for misspelled words, so if a word has an exact match in the dictionary we should avoid returning any suggestions for it.

Let's refactor our spellchecker to take an extra parameter to configure how many edits are allowed for suggestions. While we're at it, we'll avoid returning any suggestions for correctly spelled words:

```
spellcheckWord :: [Text] -> Int -> Text -> [SuggestedMatch]
spellcheckWord dictionary threshold word =
  getSuggestions dictionary []
  where
    getSuggestions [] suggestions = suggestions
    getSuggestions (dictWord:dict) suggestions
      | distance == 0 = []
      | distance > threshold = getSuggestions dict suggestions
      | otherwise = getSuggestions dict (suggestion : suggestions)
     where
       distance = editDistance dictWord word
       suggestion = SuggestedMatch dictWord word distance
```

Let's re-run this version of spellcheckWord with our same dictionary and test examples. We'll use a threshold of 3. Most spellcheckers use a threshold of either 2 or 3. For all of the examples in this chapter, we're going to use a threshold of 3. This will give us more results for each search, which in turn will give us more opportunities to identify and address performance problems in our code.

```
λ dictionary = ["yellow", "mellow", "hello", "goodbye"]
λ printMatches = putStrLn . showSuggestedMatch
λ checkWord word = mapM_ printMatches $ spellcheckWord dictionary 3 word
```

```
λ checkWord "yello"
hello -> yello: 1
mellow -> yello: 2
yellow -> yello: 1
```

```
λ checkWord "mello"
hello -> mello: 1
mellow -> mello: 1
yellow -> mello: 2
λ checkWord "hello"
```

That looks much better! We're only getting reasonable suggestions for our misspellings, and none at all for words that were spelled correctly.

The last feature we need to add to our SpellCheck.Naive module is a function to let us spellcheck an entire document. For most practical purposes, users will want to spellcheck an entire document for errors, rather than checking a word at a time. We'll add a spellcheck function to let them do just that:

```
spellcheck ::  [Text] -> Int -> [Text] -> [SuggestedMatch]
spellcheck dictionary threshold =
  concatMap (spellcheckWord dictionary threshold)
```

Now that you've implemented the spellchecking module, you should update your project so that you can pass in some options and run the spellchecker from the command line. It will be important to build an executable that you can call outside of ghci since we'll want to compile our program with optimizations and profile it to understand how to improve the performance.

For the examples in the rest of this chapter, we'll assume a version of the application that takes four arguments: a dictionary of correctly spelled words, a document to spellcheck, an optional verbosity flag, and the name of the algorithm that we're testing. You can customize the interface to your application however you like, but at a minimum you'll likely find it helpful to add an argument to choose between different implementations of the spellchecker so that you can profile different approaches without having to recompile your program.

Profiling the Spellchecker

Now that we've built our application, let's run it and see what kind of results we can get. A good place to start will be to take the test cases we were using manually in ghci and put those into files so that we can see how well our program runs.

Let's create two files. First, we'll create a dictionary of the words with correct spellings. In the examples we'll call this small-dictionary.txt:

```
yellow
mellow
hello
goodbye
```

Next, let's create a list of words we want to check. We'll call this small-test-list.txt:

```
yello
mello
hello
```

Finally, let's build the application and run it. We can use the time command to get a sense of how fast our program is running. Depending on your operating system, the output of time may look slightly different:

```
user@host$ time cabal exec spellcheck -- \
  ./small-dictionary.txt ./small-test-list.txt verbose spellcheck-naive
hello -> yello: 1
mellow -> yello: 2
yellow -> yello: 1
hello -> mello: 1
mellow -> mello: 1
yellow -> mello: 2

real    0m0.035s
user    0m0.020s
sys     0m0.007s
```

It looks like our application is running well enough that it's hard to imagine what could be left to optimize. Unfortunately, these results are a bit misleading. We're testing with a very small dictionary of words. If we want to implement a more complete spellchecking program, we'll need to use a more complete dictionary.

There are several different free dictionaries available, and you may already have one installed on your operating system. The rest of the examples in this chapter will use the words.txt file from the Spell Checker Oriented Word List (SCOWL)[1].

Preparing the Word List

If you download the SCOWL word list, there's some preparation work you should do before using the data in your programs. First, you'll need to re-encode the wordlist to utf8. The word list shipped with SCOWL uses the ISO-8859 (extended Latin) encoding. You can convert the file to utf8 using the iconv tool.

On Linux and WSL, you can convert the file by running iconv -t utf8 -o words.utf8 -f iso-8859-3 words.txt. The -o flag isn't available on macOS, so instead you can redirect the output to a file: iconv -t utf8 -f iso-8859-3 words.txt > words.utf8

1. https://github.com/en-wl/wordlist

Preparing the Word List

> Once you've converted the file to utf8, you should shuffle the contents of the file so they are no longer in alphabetical order. This will help us get more accurate data during our test. On all platforms, you can do this by typing `sort -R words.utf8 > words.txt`.

Now that we have a complete dictionary, let's create a new file named `helllo.txt` that holds a single typo, the word "helllo":

```
helllo
```

After all of the setup, let's test out our spellchecker on a larger list of words:

```
user@host$ time cabal exec spellcheck -- .\
  /words.txt ./helllo.txt quiet spellcheck-naive

found 173 suggested matches

real    2m46.115s
user    2m46.032s
sys     0m0.076s
```

We found 173 suggestions, which is obviously quite a lot of options for a single typo. In a full-fledged spellchecking program we would apply some heuristics to limit the number of potential matches, but for the moment the larger number of results is less of a problem than the fact that our program took nearly three minutes to find suggestions for a single word! This is pretty unusable for a single word, let alone spellchecking a real document. We'll need to do better.

If we want to improve the performance of our program, the first thing that we'll need to do is start collecting data about where we're spending our time. We can get that data by enabling *profiling*. We can enable profiling in our application by adding a *cabal project file* named `cabal.project.local`. Cabal project files give us a way to configure projects made up of one or more separate packages, and to configure them all together. They also offer a number of configuration options for tuning options like profiling for our packages. Let's create a project file that will enable profiling for our application and library, and let's pass in RTS options so we can collect profiling data when we run our program:

```
profiling: True
library-profiling: True
optimization: 2

package *
  ghc-options: -rtsopts -fprof-auto
```

The first part of our project file sets some global options:

- profiling controls whether or not profiling is enabled for our executable. We need to enable this to collect profiling data when we run the program.
- library-profiling enables us to collect profiling information from the library part of our project. Nearly all of our code lives in our library, so we need to turn this on to get useful data.
- optimization sets the -O flag. We want our program to run fast, so we're setting the optimization level to 2.

After setting our global options, we can also add some package-specific stanzas to our project file. You can have several of these stanzas that configure individual packages, several specific packages, or use a wildcard as we've done here. In this example, we're setting passing a couple of flags to ghc:

- -rtsopts will let us pass options to the runtime system, including options to configure profiling.
- -fprof-auto will ask the compiler to automatically collect profile data from each function we define in our program. This is the most expensive profiling option, but also gives us the most detailed results.

Now that we've configured some profiling options, let's recompile our program and then run it again:

```
user@host$ time cabal exec spellcheck -- \
  ./words.txt ./helllo.txt quiet spellcheck-naive

found 173 suggested matches

real    10m59.992s
user    10m59.765s
sys     0m0.166s
```

Even though we haven't actually turned on profiling for this particular run of our application, building our program with profiling enabled has caused a substantial impact on the performance of our application. Not all of the programs we run with profiling enabled will be slowed down so much, but collecting profiling data has exacerbated some of the inefficiencies that were already in our application. To get a look at what those are, let's run our program again, and this time we'll collect profiling data:

```
user@host$ time cabal exec spellcheck -- \
  ./words.txt ./helllo.txt quiet spellcheck-naive +RTS -s -p

found 173 suggested matches
2,448,464,651,528 bytes allocated in the heap
      10,243,120 bytes copied during GC
```

```
      12,391,304 bytes maximum residency (12 sample(s))
         786,984 bytes maximum slop
              37 MiB total memory in use (0 MB lost due to fragmentation)

                                     Tot time (elapsed)  Avg pause  Max pause
  Gen  0     592385 colls,     0 par    1.784s   1.864s     0.0000s    0.0001s
  Gen  1         12 colls,     0 par    0.021s   0.021s     0.0017s    0.0038s

  INIT    time    0.000s  (  0.000s elapsed)
  MUT     time  652.690s  (652.671s elapsed)
  GC      time    1.805s  (  1.885s elapsed)
  RP      time    0.000s  (  0.000s elapsed)
  PROF    time    0.000s  (  0.000s elapsed)
  EXIT    time    0.000s  (  0.000s elapsed)
  Total   time  654.495s  (654.556s elapsed)
  %GC     time       0.0%  (0.0% elapsed)
  Alloc rate    3,751,342,895 bytes per MUT second
  Productivity  99.7% of total user, 99.7% of total elapsed

real	10m54.616s
user	10m53.895s
sys	0m0.653s
```

Thanks to the -s flag that we passed to the RTS, our program will print summary statistics about memory usage when it's done running. You've already seen one example of using summary statistics when you learned about IORefs on page 365. In that chapter, we focused on the total memory usage of our application. In this case, the total memory usage might be a little high, but the overall number of bytes allocated and garbage collected is more interesting.

During the ten minutes our program was running, we allocated nearly 2.5 terabytes of memory. Haskell programs do tend to allocate a lot of memory, but that still seems unusually high. Summary statistics like these can sometimes help us identify unexpected space leaks, but in this case it doesn't seem like we have enough information to entirely narrow down what's happening, so let's look at the actual profiling data that was generated.

When you run your program with the -p flag, your program will write profiling data to a file named <your-program-name>.prof. In this case, the file will be named spellcheck.prof.

Profiler Output Formatting

The actual output generated by the profiler is too large to fit comfortably in this book. Instead, we will look at the format more generally and highlight particular sections of the profiler output.

At the top of the profiling data, you'll see a header that includes the time the program was run, what arguments were passed to it, and the total amount of time and memory that it used:

```
Tue May 31 01:41 2022 Time and Allocation Profiling Report  (Final)

spellcheck +RTS -s -p -RTS ./words.txt ./helllo.txt quiet spellcheck-naive

total time  =      681.24 secs   (681243 ticks @ 1000 us, 1 processor)
total alloc = 1,536,053,166,248 bytes  (excludes profiling overheads)
```

This gives you a high-level overview of the run of your application. It's not particularly useful for diagnosing a performance problem, but as you are working on different implementations of some code, you'll frequently accumulate many different profiling files that you want to compare. Having a header to quickly glance at to see what version of the program you ran, and how well it performed, can make it much easier to sort through several profiling files.

The next section of the profiling output shows you the most expensive parts of your program. There are five columns:

- COST CENTER: Cost centers are names assigned to a particular part of the code that we want to measure when we're profiling. Since we used -fprof-auto, the compiler automatically created a cost center for all of our functions. You'll notice that for things like deleteCost and insertCost, which are where bindings inside of editDistance, the cost center includes the top-level function as well as the name of the particular binding.
- MODULE: This is the module where the code is defined.
- SRC: This is the source file where the code is defined.
- %time: This field tells us what percent of the overall program runtime was spent inside of this particular cost center. For example, we can see that we spent 54 percent of our time in editDistance.
- %alloc: Similar to %time, this field tells us what percentage of memory allocations were done inside of a particular cost center. We can see here that while we only spent about half of our time in editDistance it was responsible for nearly 80 percent of the memory our program allocated.

In our example, the five most expensive cost centers are:

cost center	%time	% alloc
editDistance	54.2	78.2
editDistance.deleteCost	16.1	5.3
editDistance.swapCost	14.9	5.3

cost center	%time	% alloc
editDistance.insertCost	10.1	0.0
editDistance.restOfA	4.5	11.1

The most expensive of these cost centers is editDistance, which takes up about half of the time and about 80 percent of the allocations in our program. The rest of the cost centers are all where bindings that were defined inside of editDistance. When we enabled -fprof-auto to ask the compiler to insert cost centers for us, it added them to all of the let and where bindings in our program, so we can narrow down the costs to particular parts of a larger function.

Overall, the top cost centers are exactly what we'd expect from our application; almost all of the time and memory is being spent in the function that is doing almost all of the work. We still don't have a good explanation for why our program is so slow. Let's move a bit further down the file and look at the detailed profiling output.

The detailed output has a lot of the same information that was in our high level summary. We have the name of each cost center, along with the source file and module it's in, and a numeric identifier. We also now have two different pairs of time and allocation fields. The first pair of fields, labeled individual, tells us about the time and allocations in that particular cost center. The second pair of fields, labeled inherited, tell us how much time and memory were used by that function and all of its children in the call tree. The inherited cost can be a good way to spot functions that call several functions that don't individually cost very much, but cumulatively end up having a big performance impact.

Finally, the entries field is the field that will be most interesting to us right now. This field tells us how many times a particular cost center was entered—in other words, how many times a particular function was called, or a value was evaluated. Let's look at the profiling data, starting with the call to spellcheckWord in our profiler output, and see what it can tell us. The output here has been reformatted to make it easier to follow:

```
spellcheckWord
  entries: 1
  (individual) %time: 0.0,   %alloc: 0.0
  (inherited)  %time: 100.0, %alloc: 100.0

  spellcheckWord.getSuggestions
    entries: 123383
    (individual) %time: 0.0,   %alloc: 0.0
    (inherited)  %time: 100.0, %alloc: 100.0
```

```
spellcheckWord.getSuggestions.distance
  entries: 123382
  (individual) %time: 0.0    %alloc: 0.0
  (inherited)  %time: 100.0  %alloc: 100.0

  editDistance
    entries: 15590594654
    (individual) %time: 54.2, %alloc: 78.2
    (inherited)  %time: 100.0 %alloc: 100.0

    editDistance.restOfA
      entries: 5337541962
      (individual): %time: 4.6 %alloc: 11.1
      (inherited): %time:  4.6 %alloc: 11.1

    editDistance.restOfB
      entries: 5337541962
      (individual): %time: 0.1 %alloc: 0.0
      (inherited):  %time: 0.1 %alloc: 0.0

    editDistance.deleteCost
      entries: 5126464655
      (individual): %time: 15.9 %alloc: 5.3
      (inherited):  %time: 15.9 %alloc: 5.3

    editDistance.insertCost
      entries: 5126464655
      (individual): %time: 10.1 %alloc: 0.0
      (inherited):  %time: 10.1 %alloc: 0.0

    editDistance.swapCost
      entries: 5126464655
      (individual): %time: 15.1 %alloc: 5.3
      (inherited):  %time: 15.1 %alloc: 5.3
```

We can see from the profiling data that spellcheckWord is called just once. This is what we'd expect since our input file only contains a single word we want to spellcheck. Next, spellcheckWord.getSuggestions is called 123383 times. This matches the number of words in the SCOWL words corpus, so we can see it's also being called once for each of the dictionary words we're checking our single input word against. Similarly, spellcheckWord.getSuggestions.distance is also called 123383 times—again once per word in our dictionary. So far so good, but editDistance is being called an astounding 15590594654 times. That works out to almost 126359 calls per dictionary word! We might have expected our naive algorithm to do a bit of re-work, but the profiler is telling us the inefficiency of our algorithm is much worse than we might have expected. Let's go back to the algorithmic drawing board and see if we can improve our performance.

Over the next few sections, we'll look at several alternate ways we can avoid doing extra work and incrementally improve the performance of our algorithm.

Memoizing editDistance

We've narrowed down our immediate performance problem to recalculating the same edit distances many times. The question now is, what can we do about that? One option is to simply avoid recalculating distances that we've already calculated once. If we replace our editDistance function with a version that remembers arguments it's been called with, and the results that were returned, then we can use the cached values rather than recomputing the distance whenever we encounter a familiar pair of strings. This is a technique called *memoization*, and it's common in many different languages and styles of programming.

When we want to memoize a function, Haskell offers us both some benefits and some challenges. The most immediate benefit is that, being a pure language, most Haskell code lends itself to being memoized without having to do any extra work. The same purity that makes our functions good candidates for memoization also makes the memoization itself a bit more challenging, since we need to be thoughtful about how we do the memoization. In this section, we'll look at two different approaches that you can use for memoization: first through automatic memoization using thunks, and second by using internal mutability to manually cache values.

Memoization (Almost) for Free

The first approach to memoization that we'll look at takes advantage of laziness to create a list of edit distances between all of the different points in our two strings. When we first create this list, all of the elements will be unevaluated thunks, so we don't need to pay the cost of actually computing the distance up front. Once we've created a list of unevaluated thunks, we can replace the recursive calls inside of our edit function with a lookup into our list of values. Any time we come upon an unevaluated thunk, it will call our edit function again, completing the recursive call we would have made directly. If we find an evaluated thunk, then nothing needs to be evaluated, and we can simply return the distance that we've already calculated.

The only thing we need to do for this approach to work is to turn the arguments of our editDistance function into something that lends itself to being used to look up elements in the list of cached results. This isn't always possible; thankfully, in this case we have an obvious solution: rather than iterating over each character in our input strings, we can iterate over a numeric index into the strings. Before we move on to memoization, let's take an intermediate step and refactor our function to use indexes in our strings, rather than using the characters directly. Since we'll be working on a new implementation that you might want to compare to the original naive version, let's put this implementation in our SpellCheck.ListMemo module:

```
module SpellCheck.ListMemo where
import Data.Text (Text)
import qualified Data.Text as T
import Types

editDistance :: Text -> Text -> Int
editDistance stringA stringB =
  getEditDistance 0 0
  where
    aLen = T.length stringA
    bLen = T.length stringB
    getEditDistance idxA idxB
      | idxA == aLen = bLen - idxB
      | idxB == bLen = aLen - idxA
      | stringA `T.index` idxA == stringB `T.index` idxB =
        getEditDistance (idxA + 1) (idxB + 1)
      | otherwise =
        let
          deleteCost = getEditDistance (idxA + 1) idxB
          insertCost = getEditDistance idxA (idxB + 1)
          swapCost = getEditDistance (idxA + 1) (idxB + 1)
        in 1 + minimum [deleteCost, insertCost, swapCost]
```

As you can see, we haven't had to change much in our editDistance implementation. You'll notice that we're using the T.index function now rather than T.head. This function lets us access a character at a particular offset inside of a Text value. It's a partial function, but we're testing the index to make sure it's not out of bounds in an earlier guard clause, so we're safe to use it here. The only other notable difference is that our original editDistance code has been moved into a where clause. This will come in handy when we add memoization.

Before we move on, you can add another entry to your list of benchmarks and profile this index-based implementation of our naive algorithm. You should notice from the profiling results that our new index-based implementation is slightly faster and uses somewhat less memory. We're saving a little bit of work by avoiding creating copies of each substring that we're evaluating, but we haven't yet addressed the amount of duplicate work we're doing. Until we avoid recomputing the distance for the same strings, we're going to be severely limited in the performance we can get out of our program. So, let's update our function to start memoizing results.

The first thing we need to do is add a cache of values. Our edit distance function takes two arguments—the length of each string. We need to map that to a single cache. We'll do that by storing our cache as a list of lists. For each index in our first string, we'll store a list of cached distances to every point in our second string:

```
distances =
  map (\idxA -> map (getEditDistance idxA) [0..bLen]) [0..aLen]
```

Remember, when we first define distances it's a list of unevaluated thunks. When we evaluate a particular element of the list, it will return another list of unevaluated thunks. Each of those thunks will call getEditDistance the first time we need to get their value.

Now that we have a cache of values, we need a way to look up a particular value. Let's add a function to help make this easier:

```
lookupEditDistance idxA idxB =
  distances !! idxA !! idxB
```

The last thing we need to do is replace the recursive calls to getEditDistance with calls to lookupEditDistance. The final version of our memoized function looks like this:

```
editDistance :: Text -> Text -> Int
editDistance stringA stringB =
  lookupEditDistance 0 0
  where
    distances =
      map (\idxA -> map (getEditDistance idxA) [0..bLen]) [0..aLen]
    lookupEditDistance idxA idxB =
      distances !! idxA !! idxB
    aLen = T.length stringA
    bLen = T.length stringB
    getEditDistance idxA idxB
      | idxA == aLen = bLen - idxB
      | idxB == bLen = aLen - idxA
      | stringA `T.index` idxA == stringB `T.index` idxB =
        lookupEditDistance (idxA + 1) (idxB + 1)
      | otherwise =
        let
          deleteCost = lookupEditDistance (idxA + 1) idxB
          insertCost = lookupEditDistance idxA (idxB + 1)
          swapCost = lookupEditDistance (idxA + 1) (idxB + 1)
        in 1 + minimum [deleteCost, insertCost, swapCost]
```

As with the move to an index-based function, the overall impact to our code by adding a memoization cache is pretty small. We added a couple of new bindings and replaced calls to getEditDistance with calls to lookupEditDistance. Let's profile this version and see what kind of performance improvement we've gotten by putting our potentially repeated work behind a thunk:

```
user@host$ time cabal exec spellcheck -- \
  ./words.txt ./helllo.txt quiet spellcheck-list-memo +RTS -s -p

found 173 suggested matches
   3,716,439,504 bytes allocated in the heap
          21,632 bytes copied during GC
      12,084,472 bytes maximum residency (4 sample(s))
         781,064 bytes maximum slop
              27 MiB total memory in use (0 MB lost due to fragmentation)

                                     Tot time (elapsed)  Avg pause  Max pause
  Gen  0       897 colls,     0 par    0.012s   0.012s     0.0000s    0.0001s
  Gen  1         4 colls,     0 par    0.007s   0.007s     0.0018s    0.0048s
  INIT    time    0.000s  (  0.000s elapsed)
  MUT     time    1.573s  (  1.573s elapsed)
  GC      time    0.019s  (  0.019s elapsed)
  RP      time    0.000s  (  0.000s elapsed)
  PROF    time    0.000s  (  0.000s elapsed)
  EXIT    time    0.000s  (  0.000s elapsed)
  Total   time    1.593s  (  1.593s elapsed)
  %GC     time       0.0%  (0.0% elapsed)
  Alloc rate    2,361,897,083 bytes per MUT second
  Productivity  98.8% of total user, 98.8% of total elapsed

real    0m1.656s
user    0m1.623s
sys   0m0.027s
```

Amazingly, these few small changes have saved us around an order of magnitude in runtime! If we look at the profiling output, we can verify that we've also substantially reduced the number of calls to editDistance from 15590594654 calls in our original un-memoized version down to 8066319 calls in our new version. By taking advantage of laziness and the fact that each thunk is only evaluated ones, we were able to reduce the number of calls to editDistance by over 99%!

Using a list or other data structure to cache the results of thunks as a way of memoizing function calls is an extremely effective low-effort technique for improving performance in your Haskell code, but there are a couple of things to watch out for. One decision to be mindful of is the data structure you are using to hold the cached values. Using the wrong data structure, or using a data structure in a less-than-optimal way, can have a big impact on how much memoization improves your program's performance. For example, we stored the results of our function calls in a list, and it worked well enough because we are dealing with short strings, so the cost of traversing our list of cached values wasn't very high. Our cache is also fairly *dense*, meaning we didn't have very many elements of our list that we never evaluated. If we were spending more time traversing our list, or had a lot of elements we never looked at, the performance improvement wouldn't have been as impressive. For example, let's add 100 empty unevaluated thunks to the beginning of each of our cached lists:

```
where
  offset = 100
  distances =
    map
      (\idxA -> map
        (\idxB -> getEditDistance (idxA - offset) (idxB - offset)
        ) [0..bLen + offset])
      [0..aLen + offset]
  lookupEditDistance idxA idxB =
    distances !! (idxA + offset) !! (idxB + offset)
```

When we run this, we can see this version of the application increases both the total amount of allocated memory and the runtime by 10x.

You should also keep in mind that holding references to memoization caches longer than necessary can inflate the memory usage of your application. This happens most often if you create the cache as a top-level binding. Top-level bindings won't be garbage collected, so accumulating a large collection of cached values in a long-running program can cause a space leak. Even without creating top-level bindings, you can inadvertently hold onto a reference to a cache from an unevaluated thunk. This is similar to the behavior you saw when you learned about IORefs on page 365 earlier in this book.

One edge case that can come up when memoizing functions is caused by a compiler optimization called *let floating*. This is an optimization that GHC will sometimes perform that "lifts" a value outside of a function where it's defined so that it can be re-used. When a large cache is floated out, it won't get garbage collected between function calls and you can end up accumulating a lot of used memory. You can typically identify this by profiling your application and noticing that your cache is responsible for a larger percentage of allocations than you would have expected.

When you encounter this problem, one way to solve it is to disable let floating in the current module. You can do that on a per-module basis with the

OPTIONS_GHC pragma, which lets you set compiler options on a per-module basis, and passing it the -fno-full-laziness argument, which disables let floating:

```
{-# OPTIONS_GHC -fno-full-laziness #-}
```

Let-floating-induced space leaks aren't common, and you shouldn't necessarily avoid memoization or proactively disable let floating to avoid problems. Unfortunately, the infrequency of the problem also means it can be hard to remember to look for this as a cause if you find that your program is unexpectedly using too much memory.

Internal Mutability with ST

In the last section, you learned how to use a data structure to cache results from an expensive function call. That approach works extremely well for certain types of problems, but it lacks the flexibility we sometimes need when trying to optimize our programs. In some cases, we need a more general type of mutability.

Earlier in this book, you learned about IORefs on page 365 as a way to get mutability. IORefs do give us access to mutability, but at the steep cost of needing to move our entire function into an IO action. In general, we'd rather avoid putting otherwise pure functions into IO, and from the perspective of an outside caller, a function like editDistance should remain pure even if it happens to use some mutable state internally.

The idea that we might have a function that is referentially transparent and acts like a pure function from the outside, but uses mutable data as part of its implementation, is called *internal mutability*. We can get internal mutability in Haskell with ST actions. In this section, we'll refactor our spellchecker again to use internal mutability, and look at some of the new things we can do when we're using a more flexible approach to caching. First though, let's take a look at the ST type and how to use ST actions.

An Introduction to ST

In the first chapter of this book, you were introduced to the idea of *referential transparency*. This is the idea that, thanks to Haskell being a pure functional language, any time we have some expression that evaluates to a value, we can replace the expression with the value, and the behavior of our program shouldn't change. One of the reasons that IO allows us to write pure functional programs that have side effects is that they replace an expression that might not have referential transparency, for example, a function that uses a value inside of an IORef, with a referentially transparent function that returns an opaque IO action. We have to do this for IO because the real world is subject to external factors that we can't control in our program. We might read from a file that was changed by another process, or access a mutable variable that we changed in another thread.

The problem with IO is that, once something gets embedded in an IO action, there's no way to get it back into the world of pure Haskell values. We can't simply write a function to turn an IO a into an a, because that would break referential transparency.

unsafePerformIO

There is a family of functions that will let us turn IO actions back into ordinary Haskell values. For example, the unsafePerformIO function from System.IO.Unsafe has the type unsafePerformIO :: IO a -> a. These functions have some legitimate uses, but as their name implies, they are unsafe and can be be quite tricky to use correctly. In almost all cases, you should prefer ST over unsafePerformIO and friends when writing programs that need internal mutability.

What if we could though? Let's imagine a type called SafeIO that lets us make SafeIO actions and evaluate them in a referentially transparent way. We'll also create a SafeRef type that is similar to an IORef but can be used with SafeIO. For the moment we'll skip actually implementing any of these examples and fall back on undefined to help us sketch out the idea for our theoretical library without worrying about how to build it.

```
data SafeIO a = SafeIO a
data SafeRef a = SafeRef a

instance Functor SafeIO where
  fmap = undefined

instance Applicative SafeIO where
  pure = undefined
  (<*>) = undefined

instance Monad SafeIO where
  (>>=) = undefined

runSafeIO :: SafeIO a -> a
runSafeIO (SafeIO a) = a
```

What could we do with a function like this, and what limitations would we have to put on it?

First, SafeIO shouldn't be able to access the *outside* world. That is to say, we can't do things like read or write files. Why not?

```
appendToFile :: FilePath -> String -> SafeIO ()
appendToFile = undefined

readFile :: FilePath -> SafeIO String
readFile = undefined

unsafeAction :: String -> SafeIO String
unsafeAction contents =
  appendToFile "example.txt" contents >> readFile "example.txt"

notValid :: String
notValid =
  runSafeIO (unsafeAction "foo") <> runSafeIO (unsafeAction "foo")
```

In this example, the expression runSafeIO (unsafeAction "foo") isn't referentially transparent. If we assume that example.txt starts as an empty file, the first time we evaluate the expression, we'll get back foo, and the second time we evaluate, it we'll get back foofoo. Any example we can think of where our SafeIO actions are allowed to access the world outside of our program are at risk of the same problem. If we want to make SafeIO actions actually safe, we'll need to restrict them from accessing anything outside of our program.

That doesn't make SafeIO useless though. We can still allocate and free memory and have access to mutable references. Let's imagine that we wanted to use a SafeIO equivalent to an IORef for some program:

```
newSafeRef :: a -> SafeIO (SafeRef a)
newSafeRef = undefined

modifySafeRef :: SafeRef a -> (a -> a) -> SafeIO ()
modifySafeRef = undefined

readSafeRef :: SafeRef a -> SafeIO a
readSafeRef = undefined

safeAction :: String -> SafeIO Int
safeAction message = do
  safeRef <- newSafeRef 0
  traverse_ (\_ -> modifySafeRef safeRef (+1)) message
  readSafeRef safeRef

valid :: Int
valid =
  runSafeIO (safeAction "hello") + runSafeIO (safeAction "hello")
```

In this example, runSafeIO (safeAction "hello") is referentially transparent. Even though it has side effects and modifies a reference, from the outside it behaves like a pure function. So, perhaps our SafeIO can have mutable references and remain safe? Let's try another example:

```
updateRefWithCount :: SafeRef Int -> String -> SafeIO Int
updateRefWithCount safeRef message =
  modifySafeRef safeRef (+ length message) >> readSafeRef safeRef

stillSafe :: String -> SafeIO Int
stillSafe message = do
  ref <- newSafeRef 0
  len1 <- updateRefWithCount ref message
  len2 <- updateRefWithCount ref message
  pure $ len1 + len2

stillValid :: Int
stillValid =
  runSafeIO (safeAction "hello") + runSafeIO (safeAction "hello")
```

In this example, we're passing shared state from stillSafe to updateRefWithCount, but all access to our safe reference is still held inside of a single SafeIO action that's being evaluated. There's never any shared state between different SafeIO actions, so they can't interfere with one another. That means stillValid is still a safe function.

Unfortunately, a small change here could still break our code. If we call updateRefWithCount directly with a SafeRef then we'll still break referential transparency:

```
notSoSafe :: Int
notSoSafe =
  let someRef = runSafeIO (newSafeRef 0)
  in runSafeIO (updateRefWithCount someRef "hello") +
     runSafeIO (updateRefWithCount someRef "hello")
```

In this example, the first time we evaluate runSafeIO (updateRefWithCount someRef "hello"), the value in our reference will start at 0 and the function will return 5, but the second time we evaluate the expression, the reference will start out at 5 and the expression will return 10.

These examples help to demonstrate another restriction we'll need to put on SafeIO if we want to be safe—we need to prevent any mutable data from being shared between different SafeIO actions. The question then is, how can we allow the safe example where we can compose SafeIO actions and evaluate them when they don't share resources, but still prohibit the second case where resources would cross the boundaries between different SafeIO actions?

It turns out that there's a clever way that we can use the type system to do this. Let's take a look at the implementation and then untangle why it works.

We'll start by updating the types of SafeIO and SafeRef to add an extra type parameter that we'll call 's'. This is a phantom type parameter; we won't use it in the value of either of our types. Instead, this parameter will act as a sort of type level identifier of which SafeIO action generated a particular value.

```
data SafeIO s a = SafeIO a
data SafeRef s a = SafeRef a
```

We'll also need to update the types of the functions that work with SafeIO actions. In particular, let's look at the new type of runSafeIO and newSafeRef:

```
runSafeIO :: SafeIO s a -> a
runSafeIO (SafeIO a) = a

newSafeRef :: a -> SafeIO s (SafeRef s a)
newSafeRef = undefined
```

You can update the rest of your examples. You should notice that right now everything will continue to compile. Our identifier doesn't seem to be helping us at all yet. The problem is that we're ensuring that the identifier of a SafeIO and a SafeRef are the same, but we're not ensuring that they are unique. The compiler can give the same identifier to every single SafeIO action and every single SafeRef and that will make our code typecheck, but it isn't what we want.

Luckily there's a trick we can use to help ensure we can get unique identifiers when we run a particular SafeIO action. We just need to change the type of runSafeIO a bit. If we wanted to be a bit verbose, we could rewrite the current type of our function with an explicit forall quantifier as:

```
runSafeIO :: forall s a. SafeIO s a -> a
```

The forall here says that, essentially, the function should work for any types s and a, and we as the caller of the function can decide what values of s and a should be used. When we call runSafeIO we're not providing any particular value, so the compiler picks one that satisfies the requirements for us and builds the application. Thankfully, there is a feature of the type system we can use to prevent the compiler from being so "helpful": *higher ranked types*. In newer versions of GHC, this feature is enabled by default, but in older versions of the compiler you'll need to enable the RankNTypes extension. When enabled, this extension lets us "nest" layers of polymorphism, passing one polymorphic function into another. It's not obvious how this differs from the functions we have been working with throughout this book, so let's dive into a hands-on example. With RankNTypes enabled, we can rewrite runSafeIO with a higher ranked type:

```
runSafeIO :: forall a. (forall s. SafeIO s a) -> a
```

Or, less verbosely:

```
runSafeIO :: (forall s. SafeIO s a) -> a
```

RankNTypes

The RankNTypes extension has been available since GHC 6.8.1. This extension is enabled by default in GHC2021 but you'll need to enable it manually if you are using Haskell2010. This extension is generally safe, and shouldn't break any existing code. This extension also implies the ExplicitForAll extension. If you've enabled RankNTypes you don't need to explicitly enable ExplicitForAll.

This function uses "rank 2" polymorphism. That means we've got a polymorphic function called runIO that needs to be able to work with any type a. We're passing it in a value with the type (forall s. SafeIO s a). The forall here is inside of an argument that's being passed to the function. That means runSafeIO doesn't have to be polymorphic over any type s; instead, the function it's being passed needs to be polymorphic and able to work with any s that runSafeIO chooses. In other words, neither we nor the compiler have the option of selecting a convenient value of s because it's not decided by the caller of runSafeIO. Instead, we need to provide a SafeIO action that will itself work for any arbitrary state identifier. In practice, that means we can't make any assumptions about what the type is, so each time we evaluate runSafeIO it will be with a new unique identifier. If you try to compile this version of the program you'll see that we're getting an error:

```
SafeIO.hs:67:28-39: error: …
    • Couldn't match type ‘a’ with ‘SafeRef s Integer’
      Expected: SafeIO s a
        Actual: SafeIO s (SafeRef s Integer)
      ‘a’ is a rigid type variable bound by
        the inferred type of someRef :: a
        at /home/user/EffectiveHaskell/Chapter14/st/SafeIO.hs:67:7-40
    • In the first argument of ‘runSafeIO’, namely ‘(newSafeRef 0)’
      In the expression: runSafeIO (newSafeRef 0)
      In an equation for ‘someRef’: someRef = runSafeIO (newSafeRef 0)
    • Relevant bindings include
        someRef :: a
          (bound at /home/user/EffectiveHaskell/Chapter14/st/SafeIO.hs:67:7)
   |
Compilation failed.
```

The type error here is a little hard to untangle if you aren't accustomed to this kind of error, but we can see what's happening if we step through the code. In the expression runSafeIO (newSafeRef 0) we're taking a value with the type SafeIO s (SafeRef s Int) and passing it to a function with type (forall s. SafeIO s a) -> a. If we expand the type variables out, we'll get:

```
forall a. (forall s. SafeIO s (SafeRef s a)) -> SafeRef s a
```

The problem is, this can't typecheck, because the type of our identifier would escape the scope where it's defined. This turns out to be exactly what we need to ensure that none of our mutable resources leak outside of a particular SafeIO action. As long as any mutable resource carries around the state identifier for the SafeIO action that created it, we can prevent it from escaping.

As you might have expected, it turns out that what we've been calling SafeIO is actually a type that already exists in base. It's called ST, and it's defined in Control.Monad.ST:

```
data ST s a

runST :: (forall s. ST s a) -> a
```

The Data.STRef module from base gives us access to STRefs:

```
data STRef s a

newSTRef :: a -> ST s (STRef s a)
readSTRef :: STRef s a -> ST s a
writeSTRef :: STRef s a -> a -> ST s ()
modifySTRef :: STRef s a -> (a -> a) -> ST s ()
```

Edit Distance with ST

Now that we have a way to use mutable references in a pure function with ST, let's revisit our edit distance function and look at how we can make use of this to write a more composable optimized version of our function. We'll start by creating a newtype wrapper to hold a reference to a cache, and write some utility functions to make it easier to read and write from the cache. We're going to go back to caching the text values rather than numeric offsets in this example:

```
{-# LANGUAGE OverloadedStrings #-}
module SpellCheck.STMemo where
import Data.Foldable
import Control.Monad
import Data.Map.Strict (Map)
import qualified Data.Map.Strict as Map
import Data.STRef
import Control.Monad.ST
import Data.Text (Text)
import qualified Data.Text as T
import Types

newtype MemoCache s = MemoCache (STRef s (Map (Text,Text) Int))

readCache :: MemoCache s -> Text -> Text -> ST s (Maybe Int)
readCache (MemoCache ref) stringA stringB =
  Map.lookup (stringA, stringB) <$> readSTRef ref
```

```
updateCache :: MemoCache s -> Text -> Text -> Int -> ST s ()
updateCache (MemoCache ref) stringA stringB distance =
  modifySTRef ref $ Map.insert (stringA, stringB) distance

newCache :: ST s (MemoCache s)
newCache = MemoCache <$> newSTRef Map.empty
```

Next, let's update our editDistance function. In the last implementation of editDistance that we created, the memoization step was entirely self-contained inside of the editDistance function. That was by necessity—we needed to be able to map the arguments of our function to indexes in a list, and we could only do that for any two pairs of strings. Now that we have more flexibility in the type of cache that we're using, and how we access it, we can use the same cache across all of the calls to editDistance. This will save us some time if we encounter duplicate words, or even just duplicate suffixes, in the document we're spellchecking.

```
editDistance :: MemoCache s -> Text -> Text -> ST s Int
editDistance cache a b =
  memoizedEditDistance a b
  where
    memoizedEditDistance stringA stringB = do
      result <- readCache cache stringA stringB
      case result of
        Just distance ->
          pure distance
        Nothing -> do
          newDistance <- findDistance stringA stringB
          updateCache cache stringA stringB newDistance
          pure newDistance

    findDistance stringA stringB
      | T.null stringA = pure $ T.length stringB
      | T.null stringB = pure $ T.length stringA
      | T.head stringA == T.head stringB =
          memoizedEditDistance restOfA restOfB
      | otherwise = do
          deleteCost <- memoizedEditDistance restOfA stringB
          insertCost <- memoizedEditDistance stringA restOfB
          swapCost   <- memoizedEditDistance restOfA restOfB
          pure $ 1 + minimum [swapCost, deleteCost, insertCost]
     where
       restOfA = T.tail stringA
       restOfB = T.tail stringB
```

As you can see, the pattern of our function remains quite similar to the earlier memoized version. We're using do notation now, since we're running inside of ST actions, but otherwise we're accessing our code in the same way.

Before we move on to calling editDistance let's take advantage of the composability of ST actions to add some heuristics to help make our spellchecking even faster:

Imagine that we wanted to have our spellchecker detect common variations of words and suggest the stem of the word. For example, if we found the word "eating" we would suggest "eat," and if we found the word "jumps" we would suggest "jump." One way that we can do that is to insert the corrections into our cache before we ever start running through our algorithm:

```
cacheSuffixDistances :: MemoCache s -> Text -> [Text] -> ST s ()
cacheSuffixDistances cache dictWord suffixes =
  traverse_ cacheSuffix suffixes
  where
    cacheSuffix suffix =
      updateCache cache dictWord (dictWord <> suffix) (T.length suffix)
```

Now, when we want to spellcheck a word, we can add some suffixes:

```
spellcheckWord :: MemoCache s -> [Text] -> Int -> Text -> ST s [SuggestedMatch]
spellcheckWord cache dictionary threshold word =
  foldM getSuggestions [] dictionary
  where
    getSuggestions suggestions dictWord = do
      cacheSuffixDistances cache dictWord ["s","es","'s","ed","ing"]
      distance <- editDistance cache dictWord word
      let
        suggestion = SuggestedMatch dictWord word distance
      if distance > 0 && distance <= threshold
        then pure (suggestion : suggestions)
        else pure suggestions
```

The last thing we need to do is add our spellchecking function. Up until now we've been creating ST actions, but thanks to runST we can make spellcheck a pure function, just like it is in our other implementations:

```
spellcheck ::  [Text] -> Int -> [Text] -> [SuggestedMatch]
spellcheck dictionary threshold words = runST $ do
  cache <- newCache
  concat <$> traverse (spellcheckWord cache dictionary threshold) words
```

Unfortunately, if you build and profile this version of our application, you'll find that our new, more flexible version of spellchecking comes at a bit of a cost in both memory footprint and processing time. It's not surprising that we'd have a large memory footprint now that we're storing a single cache for all of our matches, but if we look at the profiling output we can see that we're spending a substantial amount of time in both updateCache and readCache, with updateCache additionally taking up over half of our memory allocations. It seems that as convenient as our choice of data structure was for representing the cache, we're paying a high cost for using a Map.

In the next section, we'll look at how we can improve the performance of our programs using more efficient data structures, with a particular look at efficient vectors from the vectors package.

Optimizing Memory Layout with Vectors

Memoization has gotten us quite far along the path of building a sufficiently fast spellchecker, but we're still not fast enough. In this section, we'll look at another factor that can impact the performance of our programs: the shape of our data structures and the way we store and access memory in our programs.

You saw in the last section that when we started using ST to memoize a map of results, we ended up taking a significant performance penalty. It turns out that when we're trying to get the best performance out of our applications, there are a few factors we need to think about beyond algorithmic complexity:

- Avoiding indirection by having too many thunks that need to be evaluated for any particular value
- Avoiding using mutable references to immutable data structures, creating a lot of unexpected copying when we update the value in the reference
- Being mindful of the cost of traversing our data structure to access particular elements

In this section, we'll look at the vectors library, and some of the efficient data structures that it provides for writing more high performance code.

What is a Vector?

Throughout this book, we've made heavy use of lists whenever we needed a simple flat collection of data. Lists are a popular choice in Haskell because they have a lot of library support, there's special syntax that makes working with them convenient, and in most cases code written with lists is fast enough we don't have to worry about performance. As we look to writing more compute-bound and data-intensive applications, lists start to show some weaknesses. Before we dive into the weaknesses of lists, and the ways other data structures can improve on lists, let's review a simplified definition of a list:

```
data List a = EmptyList | Cons a (List a)
```

In other words, each list is either an empty list, or it's a value and a reference to the tail of the list. When we want to write efficient programs, this data structure can cause a couple of problems. First, to get to any element in the list, we have to traverse the entire list. If you want to get to the 1000th element of a list, your only option is to start at the beginning and walk one element at a time until you get to the 1000th element. The second problem is that each time you move from the head of a list to its tail, you might end up moving into a completely different part of memory. In an average Haskell program, we might not care very much about the cost of traversing a few elements in a list, or even a few hundred, and we certainly won't concern ourselves with things like the physical layout of memory, but these factors can end up dominating the performance profile of certain applications.

When we care about efficiently storing and accessing memory, instead of linked lists we're better off to use a contiguous slab of memory. If we know how much memory every item in the array will take, then we can get to any particular element directly without having to walk through all of the other elements. If we're dealing with several elements of the array, we can fetch them all at once, and let the CPU cache them so that we don't have to wait for the data at each index to be fetched.

There are several different ways to create and work with arrays in Haskell. The GHC.Arr module in base provides a fairly basic interface to dealing with arrays of values, and the primitives core library offers another low-level interface to arrays. Both of these modules offer basic array functionality, but most applications use the vectors library, which offers a rich and well-optimized interface on top of arrays that allows you to write more idiomatic code while still getting good performance.

A Quick Intro to Working with Vectors

The vector library is fairly large because it supports many different kinds of vectors for different use-cases. We'll look at a couple of different kinds of vectors in the upcoming sections, but in most cases you can start with basic vectors by importing Data.Vector. This module exports a number of functions that conflict with list functions from Prelude, so it's common to use qualified imports for vector modules:

```
module VectorDemo where
import qualified Data.Vector as Vec
```

In most cases, this is all that you'll need to do. You can create a vector from a list using toList, or create a vector an element at a time using Vec.cons:

```
vectorOfNumbers :: Vec.Vector Int
vectorOfNumbers = Vec.fromList [1..10]
```

```
vectorRange :: Int -> Int -> Vec.Vector Int
vectorRange a b
  | a == b = Vec.empty
  | otherwise = Vec.cons a $ vectorRange (a + 1) b
```

In general, the functions to work with vectors are similar enough to the functions that you've already seen for working with lists that we won't spend much time on the specifics. You can review the vector documentation on Hackage[2] for a complete overview.

Spellchecking with Vectors

Now that you know a little bit about the vectors library, let's jump into the implementation:

```
module SpellCheck.STVec where
import Data.Text (Text)
import qualified Data.Text as T
import Prelude hiding (length, read, words)
import Data.Foldable (for_)
import Control.Monad.ST
import qualified Data.Vector.Mutable as MVec

editDistance :: Text -> Text -> Int
editDistance stringA stringB = runST $ do
  let
    aLen = T.length stringA
    bLen = T.length stringB
    as = zip [1..] (T.unpack stringA)
    bs = zip [1..] (T.unpack stringB)
    lookupIndex x y = (y * (aLen + 1)) + x
  cache <- MVec.new $ (aLen + 1) * (bLen + 1)
  for_ [0..aLen] $ \idx -> MVec.write cache (lookupIndex idx 0) idx
  for_ [0..bLen] $ \idx -> MVec.write cache (lookupIndex 0 idx) idx
  for_ as $ \(idxA, charA) -> do
    for_ bs $ \(idxB, charB) -> do
      let
        cost = if charA == charB then 0 else 1
      insertCost <- (1 +) <$>
        MVec.read cache (lookupIndex (idxA - 1) idxB)
      deleteCost <- (1 +) <$>
        MVec.read cache (lookupIndex idxA (idxB - 1))
      swapCost <- (cost +) <$>
        MVec.read cache (lookupIndex (idxA - 1) (idxB - 1))
      MVec.write cache (lookupIndex idxA idxB) $
        minimum [swapCost, insertCost, deleteCost]
  MVec.read cache $ lookupIndex aLen bLen
```

2. https://hackage.haskell.org/package/vector

You'll notice this version of our algorithm looks different on the surface than the previous versions we've looked at. Instead of using recursion, we've switched to an iterative implementation that steps through the strings character by character and calculates the cost of the current edit. We're also initializing some elements in our vector before we start looking at the edit distance. The initialization of the vectors is equivalent to the part of our recursive algorithm where, if one of our input strings is empty, we return the length of the remaining string. Instead of handling that in our inner loop, we precalculate those costs for each point in our two strings, and set them in the vector ahead of time.

The remainder of our algorithm isn't all that different from the previous versions we've implemented, but the order we access the elements will be slightly different. In part, this approach illustrates how we can apply more traditional procedural algorithms with mutable data when writing pure Haskell functions. An additional benefit to being mindful about how we access data inside of vectors is *locality*. When we're running code, it's better to work with data that's already cached by the CPU, since it'll take longer to fetch it from memory than to access the local cache. Modern CPUs are pretty good at prefetching data from memory and caching it, but it works best when the data we're accessing is physically close together in memory. When we're working with data structures like lists and maps, we're storing references to pieces of memory that may be further away. Unlike those structures, a `Vector` is stored in a contiguous block of memory. That means we can sometimes see some extra benefits from CPU caching if we're careful about how we access the elements of a vector.

Minor algorithmic differences aside, the major change from our previous map-based cache implementation is that we're no longer working with an `STRef` to an immutable data structure. Instead, we're able to take advantage of mutability directly in our vector. Rather than making a copy of the cache for each change, we can directly modify memory in our vector as we calculate the edit distances between different parts of our string. Hopefully this will help us reclaim some of the performance that we lost when we originally switched to `ST`, but let's compile and profile our application to find out:

```
found 173 suggested matches
   1,567,828,368 bytes allocated in the heap
           9,104 bytes copied during GC
      12,167,208 bytes maximum residency (4 sample(s))
         780,248 bytes maximum slop
              28 MiB total memory in use (0 MB lost due to fragmentation)
                                        Tot time (elapsed)  Avg pause  Max pause
  Gen  0       375 colls,     0 par    0.007s   0.007s     0.0000s    0.0001s
  Gen  1         4 colls,     0 par    0.006s   0.006s     0.0016s    0.0041s
  INIT    time    0.000s  (  0.000s elapsed)
```

```
  MUT     time    0.695s  (  0.695s elapsed)
  GC      time    0.013s  (  0.013s elapsed)
  RP      time    0.000s  (  0.000s elapsed)
  PROF    time    0.000s  (  0.000s elapsed)
  EXIT    time    0.000s  (  0.000s elapsed)
  Total   time    0.708s  (  0.708s elapsed)
  %GC     time       0.0%  (0.0% elapsed)
  Alloc rate    2,256,217,778 bytes per MUT second
  Productivity  98.1% of total user, 98.1% of total elapsed
real    0m0.775s
user    0m0.740s
sys     0m0.028s
```

That's much better! Compared to our fast list-based memoized implementation, our new ST-based function uses the same amount of total memory, but does half the total number of memory allocations, and runs almost twice as fast! We're still at over half a second per word that we want to spellcheck, so we're not quite fast enough, but the switch to a vector type we can update directly has had some clear benefits to the overall performance of our application.

The Fastest Edit Distance

So far in this chapter we've improved the implementation of our code by making changes to the algorithms and underlying data structures that we're using. Algorithms and data structures are always a good place to start when we need to make our programs more efficient, but once we've addressed those opportunities we can often still realize significant performance improvements by making use of micro-optimizations. These are optimizations that tend to have a small individual impact, but can add up collectively. In this section, we'll look at a version of the editDistance function that has had several different micro-optimizations applied. Before we look at the code though, let's take a moment to review the progress that we've made in optimizing our application, and see what we have to look forward to with this version:

Version	Runtime	Allocations
Naive	680.0s	1500 GB
List Memo	1.3s	2.6 GB
Vector Memo	0.5s	1.0 GB
Micro-Optimized	0.05s	0.1 GB

As you can see, the most substantial improvement by far came from using a better algorithm, but we have still gotten nearly an order of magnitude improvement in performance by adding the micro-optimizations we'll be looking at in this section. So, let's take a look at the implementation:

```
{-# LANGUAGE BangPatterns #-}
module SpellCheck.LowLevelUnboxed where
import Data.Text (Text)
import qualified Data.Text as T
import qualified Data.Text.Unsafe as TU
import Types
import Prelude hiding (length, read, words)
import Data.Foldable (for_)
import Control.Monad.ST
import qualified Data.Vector.Unboxed.Mutable as MVec

{-# INLINE editDistance #-}
editDistance :: Text -> Text -> Int
editDistance stringA stringB = runST $ do
  let
    aLen = T.length stringA
    bLen = T.length stringB
    {-# INLINE lookupIndex #-}
    lookupIndex x y = (y * (aLen + 1)) + x
  cache <- MVec.new $ (aLen + 1) * (bLen + 1)
  for_ [0..aLen] $ \idx -> MVec.write cache (lookupIndex idx 0) idx
  for_ [0..bLen] $ \idx -> MVec.write cache (lookupIndex 0 idx) idx
  let
    columnCost !idxA !textIdxA
      | idxA > aLen = pure ()
      | otherwise = do
        let
          (TU.Iter !a' !textIdxA') = TU.iter stringA textIdxA
          {-# INLINE rowCost #-}
          rowCost !idxB !textIdxB
            | idxB > bLen = pure ()
            | otherwise = do
              let
                (TU.Iter !b' !textIdxB') = TU.iter stringB textIdxB
                cost = if a' == b' then 0 else 1
              insertCost <- (1 +) <$>
                MVec.read cache (lookupIndex (idxA - 1) idxB)
              deleteCost <- (1 +) <$>
                MVec.read cache (lookupIndex idxA (idxB - 1))
              swapCost   <- (cost +) <$>
                MVec.read cache (lookupIndex (idxA - 1) (idxB - 1))
              let
                {-# INLINE newCost #-}
                newCost = min swapCost $ min insertCost deleteCost
              MVec.write cache (lookupIndex idxA idxB) newCost
              rowCost (idxB + 1) (textIdxB + textIdxB')
        rowCost 1 0
        columnCost (idxA + 1) (textIdxA + textIdxA')
  columnCost 1 0
  MVec.read cache (lookupIndex aLen bLen)
```

Inlining (0.60s Saved)

The first major change you might notice in this version of our code is the judicious use of inlining. If you aren't familiar with it, inlining is a common technique used by compilers, including GHC, to transform code that calls a function with code that directly implements the body of that function. For example, say we have a pair of functions, addTwo and addFour:

```
addTwo a b = a + b
addFour a b c d = addTwo a b + addTwo c d
```

If we chose to inline addTwo, the compiler would replace calls with the actual function body, giving us:

```
addFour a b c d = a + b + c + d
```

The choice to inline a particular piece of code or not is ultimately made by GHC, but when necessary we can make strong suggestions to the compiler about code that it might want to consider inlining (or not inlining). As you may have noticed in our example code, we can use the INLINE pragma to suggest to the compiler that it should consider trying to inline a particular piece of code if it can.

Suggesting and Allowing Inlining

When optimizations are enabled, GHC will try to make good choices about when to inline code within a single module. The INLINE pragma is a strong suggestion to the compiler that it should try to inline a particular function, both within the current module and when it's called from other modules. The INLINABLE pragma is similar, but a bit weaker. It tells the compiler to provide all the necessary information so that a function can be inlined outside of the module where it was defined, but it doesn't encourage the compiler to make any particular choice about whether to inline or not.

Inlining by itself isn't actually an optimization. Inlining can make your programs take longer to compile, and sometimes it can even make them less efficient. If the compiler has made a poor decision and tried to inline something it shouldn't have, you can persuade it of that by using the NOINLINE pragma.

Inlining can be quite helpful at getting the compiler to generate more efficient code for us. That's not because inlining is directly improving the code, but the process of inlining code can help the compiler uncover opportunities to apply other optimizations.

In our highly optimized edit distance function, we're inlining four functions. First, we're inlining editDistance itself. Second, we're inlining lookupIndex, which helps us find the offsets into the vector that we want to use when looking up cached edit distances, or setting the edit distance for our current part of the loop. Third, we're inlining the rowCost function, which is the innermost part of our edit distance loop. Finally, we're inlining the newCost binding that is used to find the actual minimum edit cost for the particular point in our string.

Why these particular examples and not some others? In general, the choice to inline some code or not lends itself better to profiling than thinking through the code and trying to make an informed decision, but in our case there are a couple of factors that make inlining worth the attempt. First, when we have tight inner loops we may find that inlining can help the compiler generate more efficient code by reducing the overhead of making a function call. In most cases, the overhead of calling a function is small enough to be irrelevant, but it can add up in very performance critical code. Second, when we're dealing with data-structure-heavy code, for example the lists and vectors that are at the core of our edit distance implementation, we want to give the compiler the opportunity to perform *fusion*. Fusion is an optimization technique where the compiler can remove intermediate stages of a series of transformations on a data structure. The most well-known example of this is calling map on lists. Imagine you have some inefficient code like this:

```
inefficient = map a . map b . map c $ someList
```

Without fusion, each call to map would allocate a new list and walk the entire list applying the function. With fusion, the compiler can rewrite the expression to:

```
inefficient = map (a . b. c) someList
```

In spite of the name, this version is much more efficient because it doesn't need to allocate any intermediate lists, and only needs to walk the length of the list a single time.

There are many other optimizations that GHC can do, and exhaustively listing them is outside of scope of this book, but many of them can be enabled in some cases through inlining.

Bang Patterns (0.05s Saved)

The second small optimization that we've done is enable the BangPatterns language extension and use it to make many of the parameters in our inner loop strict. You've already seen some examples earlier in this book of how we can improve performance and memory usage by forcing certain values to be evaluated strictly.

Avoiding Allocations with Unsafe Text (0.30s Saved)

The third notable change to this edit distance implementation is that we've moved away from unpacking or indexing into our strings. Instead, we're using the ominously named Data.Text.Unsafe module from the text package to directly iterate through the underlying text representation. As with most other examples of highly optimized code, this example trades off some amount of safety and ease of use for raw performance by using a library that does away with many of the conveniences of higher-level access to Text data. By directly iterating through the Text values, we've avoided having to traverse the string an extra time to unpack it, and we've avoided the overhead of allocating an additional data structure to keep track of the character data.

Unboxed Values (0.25s Saved)

Most Haskell values are *boxed* values. That is to say, a Haskell value is a thunk that, when evaluated, will reference some particular value in memory. Boxed values in Haskell can be lazily evaluated, and they can be undefined. For all of their convenience, they also come with the overhead of having to allocate extra memory to hold the reference to the underlying value, as well as the computational cost of following an extra layer of indirection when we want to access the value being referenced. When we're dealing with performance critical code, it's often beneficial to work with raw machine values instead of references to values. In that case, we can benefit from *unboxed* values.

Unboxed values are raw machine values, like words, ints, and doubles. GHC provides us with a low-level interface to working with unboxed values through the GHC.Exts module in base, but working with unboxed values this way can be quite challenging. Thankfully, unboxed vectors provide us with a fast and efficient way to deal with unboxed values with relatively low overhead, especially when we're dealing with collections of unboxed values.

The last major performance improvement we've added to our edit distance application is to change our import of Data.Vector.Mutable to Data.Vector.Unboxed.Mutable. You'll notice that nothing else in our implementation needed to change, and you can freely swap between the boxed and unboxed versions locally if you want to look at the performance characteristics of each approach.

Summary

In this chapter, you worked through several iterative improvements of an edit distance calculator for spellchecking, and in the process learned some common techniques for improving the performance of your applications. Optimization in Haskell is a large topic, and there are many techniques that we haven't touched on in this chapter. Importantly though, the examples in this chapter have introduced you to some of the major concerns that you should keep in mind when looking at improving the performance of your Haskell applications:

1. Use the profiler early and often to identify expensive parts of your program.
2. Address algorithmic inefficiencies before data structures and micro-optimizations.
3. Look at opportunities to avoid doing too many memory allocations, and try to avoid too much indirection.
4. Use tools like ST to write imperative algorithms when they offer well-known efficient solutions to common problems.

Exercises

Handling Correctly Spelled Words

Throughout this chapter, you've focused on building a spellchecker with the assumption most words would need to be compared against the entire dictionary to find misspellings. In reality, most words in most documents are spelled correctly, and we could avoid doing a lot of work if we identify correctly spelled words before calculating the edit distance to potential candidate corrections.

Use what you've learned in this chapter to update your spellchecker to skip looking for corrections for words that are already spelled correctly.

Hint: Consider using the hashable library to generate a unique identifier for each string in your dictionary.

Remembering Common Typos

When a user is typing a long document, it's common that they will make certain mistakes many times. For example, a user might habitually omit particular double letters, or be prone to transposing certain letter sequences (for example typing "teh" instead of "the"). Update your spellchecker to remember misspellings and their corrections, rather than doing a complete search each time the misspelling is encountered.

Spellchecking in HCat

Use what you've learned in this chapter to add interactive spellchecking to the HCat application you built earlier, when learning about IO on page 283.

CHAPTER 15

Programming with Types

As you come to the last chapter in this book, you've learned how to write useful Haskell applications using many features of the type system that help you write programs that are both safe and expressive. In nearly all the examples you've built throughout this book, we've approached Haskell's type system as a tool that lets us write some constraints in our source code that limit what our code can do. This top-down approach is typical of most Haskell programs, but sometimes we want to encode some rules about our programs that aren't so easy to express with simple static types. In those cases, we can turn to *type level programming*.

In this chapter, you'll learn what type level programming is, and how to use it effectively in your programs, by building a series of small independent examples that show different features of type level programming. Finally, we'll work through a capstone example where you can put all of these concepts together, along with the things you've learned throughout the rest of the book, to build an application that makes use of type level programming.

What Is Type Level Programming?

Nearly every example that we've worked through in this book has made use of the type system in one way or another, and many of the examples have focused on ways to use the type system to write better programs. Even though we've leaned heavily on the type system as we were programming, the types have been something that we decided on ahead of time, or left to the compiler to infer. Our programs have been well typed, but the *computations* that our programs carried out have all been runtime values.

Type level programming lets us expand beyond computing only with runtime values. With type level programming we can also write computations that work on *types*. This lets us create more sophisticated interfaces to our applications since we can write APIs that are, in a way, their own small programs. Since our type level code is run at compile time, the results are types that are still applied when the rest of our application is compiled, so we can write somewhat more dynamic code without giving up type safety. The tradeoff for being able to retain type safety is that we're limited in the programs that we can write at the type level. You'll get to see examples of the limitations we'll run into as you're working through this chapter.

Terms and Types

Using type level programming means that we can write computations over types. This presents a bit of vocabulary problem, because we now have two different sorts of computation that will live side by side in our code, but are executed separately and work on different values. To help keep things clear, when we're dealing with type level programming, we'll use the word *term* to refer to expressions and values that are going to be evaluated at runtime, and we will continue to use *type* to refer to any type values or expressions that evaluate to types at compile time. Similarly, we'll use phrases like *term level* to differentiate ordinary Haskell code that will be evaluated at runtime from type level code that will be evaluated at compile time.

Types and Kinds

Before we can start building out large type level programming examples, we need to spent some time looking at two of the most basic building blocks of type level code: types and kinds. In type level code, the types are the values that we are computing with, and the kinds of those types give us "type" safety in the same way types provide safety to our term level code. Although you've worked extensively with types in this book, and you've encountered kinds occasionally, the way that we work with them in type level code is frequently different from how we'd work with them in term level code. In this section, we'll look at how to work with types and kinds for type level code, and see some examples of types and kinds that you wouldn't encounter when writing term level code.

The Type Kind

So far in this book, every time we've needed to work with kinds it's been so that we can work with higher kinded types that we'll use in our term level code. Since all of the types we were working with were intended to eventually represent some term level values, the only kinds that we've worked with so far are `Type`, and kinds that accept `Type` parameters. Let's look at a couple of examples. In these examples, we'll turn on the `NoStarIsType` extension. As you may recall from some earlier examples, we imported Data.Kind to allow us to *write* Type instead of * when using kind signatures. NoStarIsType goes the other direction, telling GHC to use the word Type instead of * in both error messages and ghci output.

NoStarIsType

Technically speaking, NoStarIsType isn't actually a language extension. The StarIsType extension has been available since GHC 8.6.1. StarIsType is enabled by default in Haskell2010 and GHC2021. The NoStarIsType "extension" disables StarIsType. The StarIsType extension can introduce conflicts with the TypeOperators extension, and it generally breaks consistency with other kinds Nat and Symbol using proper names. There are proposals to make NoStarIsType the default in a future version of GHC.

```
λ :set -XNoStarIsType
λ import Control.Monad.State.Strict
λ :kind Int
Int :: Type
λ :kind Maybe
Maybe :: Type -> Type
λ :kind StateT
StateT :: Type -> (Type -> Type) -> Type -> Type
```

By now you've worked with higher kinded types enough that you have a reasonable intuition for how to read these kinds. The kind Type in all of these examples represents some type that we might want to pass in, like Int or Maybe String. One of the first things we need to do in order to start writing type level code is to move past the intuition here and get a better understanding of what Type is, and start to look at other kinds.

The Type kind appears so often in our earlier examples because it's the kind of all types of term level values. Whatever the type, if we can have a value of it, its kind must be Type. Although we can't have values of higher kinded types like Maybe or StateT, the type parameters that we pass to these higher kinded types are also going to be types that will represent runtime values, so even our higher kinded type examples so far have necessarily revolved around the Type kind.

As we start to write code at the type level, types themselves become the values we want to compute with and we're no longer restricted to working only with types of actual runtime values. This means that in type level code, we'll start to work with a wide variety of different kinds, including kinds we define ourselves, and even polymorphic kinds.

Type Level Natural Numbers

Nat and Natural

In earlier versions of GHC, type level natural numbers had the kind Nat. In more recent versions Natural is used instead, and Nat is an alias. We're using Natural in these examples, so if you are following along using an older version of GHC you can either rename Natural to Nat or define your own alias by adding type Natural = Nat.

Type level literals give us a way of writing values like numbers and strings and using those as values at the type level. Type level literals are also a great first example of types with a kind other than Type. Let's open up ghci and take a look at a few examples.

We'll start by importing the GHC.TypeLits module from base. This module defines the kinds we'll be working with, and a number of utility functions to help us integrate our type level code with term level code.

```
λ import GHC.TypeLits
```

Next, let's explore some of the type level literals that you'll be working with frequently in this chapter. We'll start by looking at an example of how we can work with numbers when we're doing type level programming, using *type level naturals*:

```
λ :kind 0
0 :: Natural

λ :kind 1
1 :: Natural

λ :kind 2
2 :: Natural
```

As you can see, we write type level naturals the same way we'd write numeric literals at the term level. Since we're dealing with natural numbers, we can't make negative type level naturals. Aside from this restriction, many of the basic mathematical operations that you can do at the term level are also available at the type level. Let's try to add a couple of numbers at the type level and see what happens:

```
λ :kind 1 + 2
1 + 2 :: Natural
```

As it turns out, using :kind to evaluate a type level expression will give us the kind of the expression, but it doesn't evaluate the expression like we had expected. This can be useful in some circumstances, for example, if you want to find the kind of an expression that is computationally expensive to evaluate, but in most cases we'd like to see the actual result of our type level expression computed. We can ask ghci to evaluate the type level expression using :kind! (note the extra ! at the end). Let's see a few examples:

```
λ :kind! (+) 1 1
(+) 1 1 :: Natural
= 2

λ :kind! 1 + 2 + 3 + 4
1 + 2 + 3 + 4 :: Natural
= 10

λ :kind! 2 + 3 * 4
2 + 3 * 4 :: Natural
= 14

λ :kind! (2 + 3) * 4
(2 + 3) * 4 :: Natural
= 20

λ :kind! 5 <=? 10
5 <=? 10 :: Bool
= 'True
```

There are a few different things that we can see in these examples. First, you can see how using :kind! shows you both the kind of the entire expression you enter, as well as the simplified type that you get after evaluating the expression. You can also see that these type level expressions are evaluated similarly to term level expressions, including things like order of operations and parentheses. Finally, you'll notice in the last of these examples that we've used a type level expression with two naturals that returns a *kind* of Bool and a *type* of True. You'll learn more about type level booleans later on in this section, but for now this serves as a good example that, just like at the term level, we can have type level expressions that compute a value with a different kind than the values in the expression.

Type Level Strings

In addition to natural numbers, GHC.TypeLits also gives us an easy way to deal with type level strings, which have the kind Symbol. It's common for them to be referred to as *symbols* or *type level strings* interchangeably. You can write type level string literals the same way you write term level string literals:

```
λ :kind! "Hello"
"Hello" :: Symbol
= "Hello"
```

There are only a few operations defined for us in symbols. We can combine them using AppendSymbol:

```
λ :kind! AppendSymbol "Hello, " "World"
AppendSymbol "Hello, " "World" :: Symbol
= "Hello, World"

λ :kind! "Hello, " `AppendSymbol` "World"
"Hello, " `AppendSymbol` "World" :: Symbol
= "Hello, World"

λ :kind! "a" `AppendSymbol` "b" `AppendSymbol` "c"
"a" `AppendSymbol` "b" `AppendSymbol` "c" :: Symbol
= "abc"
```

You'll notice in this example that we're using AppendSymbol as an infix function, just like we would do with a term level function. One key difference between type and term level code is that type level functions like AppendSymbol still start with a capital letter.

In addition to symbols, newer versions of GHC also have a Char kind that we can use to add and remove characters from a type level string:

```
λ :kind! 'a' `ConsSymbol` "bc"
'a' `ConsSymbol` "bc" :: Symbol
= "abc"

λ :kind! UnconsSymbol "abc"
UnconsSymbol "abc" :: Maybe (Char, Symbol)
= 'Just '('a', "bc")

λ :kind! UnconsSymbol ""
UnconsSymbol "" :: Maybe (Char, Symbol)
= 'Nothing
```

As you can see from all of the examples so far, type level expressions share a lot of similarities with the term level code you're already familiar with from working through this book. Some of the types you're used to, like Bool, Maybe, and tuples also have equivalents at the type level. It turns out that it's no accident that so many types that you're accustomed to from term level code make an appearance as kinds in type level code. In many cases we can automatically promote types to kinds using the DataKinds extension.

Data Kinds

The DataKinds extension lets us use the same types we've been writing at the term level as kinds when we're working at the type level. With this extension enabled, every type we've defined is also a kind, and the constructors for that type are its inhabitants. Let's look at an example by creating a new module and defining a simple sum type to represent some colors:

DataKinds

The DataKinds extension has been available since GHC 7.4.1. This extension isn't enabled by default in either GHC2021 or Haskell2010 so you'll need to enable it manually. This extension is generally safe, however it may change the way certain errors are displayed.

```
module ColorDemo where

data Color = Red | Green | Blue
```

If we load this into ghci we can look at the *type* of Red, Green, and Blue if we treat them as term level constructors, but if we try to treat them as types and look at their kind we'll get an error:

```
λ :type Red
Red :: Color

λ :kind Red

<interactive>:1:1: error:
    Not in scope: type constructor or class 'Red'
    Suggested fixes:
      • Perhaps you intended to use DataKinds
        to refer to the data constructor of that name?
```

Helpfully, the compiler is telling us that we need to add the DataKinds extension if we want to do this. Let's take the compiler's advice and try again with the extension enabled:

```
λ :set -XDataKinds

λ :type Red
Red :: Color
λ :kind Red
Red :: Color

λ :type Blue
Blue :: Color
λ :kind Blue
Blue :: Color

λ :type Green
Green :: Color
λ :kind Green
Green :: Color
```

In this example, you can see that with DataKinds enabled, each of our constructors is now both a *value* with the *type* Color as well as a *type* with the *kind* Color. This ends up being a fairly common source of confusion when working with type level code. Since the type and term level code share the same names, and are implemented with the same code, it's easy to get mixed up and start conflating type and term level meanings of things. The typical manifestation of this in your code is that you'll start seeing errors that the compiler expected the kind Type but instead got a kind like Color. For example, if we try to create a value Red with the *type* Red, we'll get an error:

```
λ r = Red :: Red
<interactive>:37:12-14: error:
    • Expected a type, but 'Red' has kind 'Color'
    • In an expression type signature: Red
      In the expression: Red :: Red
      In an equation for 'r': r = Red :: Red
```

One way to differentiate between the term level constructor and the type level value is to use a single quote (') to refer to the promoted type:

```
λ :kind 'Red
'Red :: Color

λ :kind 'Green
'Green :: Color

λ :kind 'Blue
'Blue :: Color
```

There are some circumstances where the quote is required to remove ambiguity, like when there is both a type and constructor with the same name. For example, imagine that we have a type with a single constructor whose name shadows the name of the type:

```
data Foo = Foo
```

If we try to look at the kind of Foo, the compiler will tell us that its kind is Type:

```
λ :kind Foo
Foo :: Type
```

This happens because the type name takes precedence over the promoted constructor when the compiler is trying to figure out the kind of a type. In this case, if we want to refer to the promoted constructor, we need to add a single quote:

```
λ :kind 'Foo
'Foo :: Foo
```

This situation will happen any time there's a constructor and a type in scope with the same name. To avoid this problem, it used to be a common recommendation to always explicitly use a quote to identify promoted constructors, and prior to GHC 9.4 the compiler will generate a warning if you enable -Wall and fail to use the quote. GHC 9.4 plans to remove this warning from -Wall and there is a bit less consensus on style these days. The examples in this chapter will only add the quote if it's required or greatly enhances the clarity of a particular example.

Although basic sum types like Color are a good introduction to defining your own kinds, there is a lot more that we can do. You've already seen an example of using tuples and Maybe at the type level when we called UnconsSymbol. Let's look at another example: building lists at the type level.

Let's start by revisiting the list implementation on page 138 you created much earlier in this book:

```
module TypeLevelList where

data List a = Empty | Cons a (List a)
```

With the DataKinds extension enabled, we can use this same list definition to create lists at the type level. Let's try it out in ghci:

```
λ :kind! Cons Int (Cons String (Cons Bool Empty))
Cons Int (Cons String (Cons Bool Empty)) :: List Type
= 'Cons Int ('Cons [Char] ('Cons Bool 'Empty))

λ data Color = Cyan | Magenta | Yellow | Black
λ :kind! Cons Cyan
  (Cons Magenta
    (Cons Yellow
      (Cons Black Empty)))
Cons Cyan
  (Cons Magenta
    (Cons Yellow
      (Cons Black Empty))) :: List Color
= 'Cons 'Cyan
    ('Cons 'Magenta
      ('Cons 'Yellow
        ('Cons 'Black 'Empty)))
```

Although it's nice we can create type level lists, it's annoying that we have to type out Cons every time we want to add an item to the list. It would be much nicer if we could have an operator similar to (:) that we use at the term level. If we enable the TypeOperators extension, we can define our own operators to use at the type level. One way that we can add type operators is to use a type alias to define the operator. For example, let's define a new right-associative operator named (:+) as an alias for Cons. You'll notice in the example that we write the fixity declaration for a type operator exactly the same way that we would write it for a term level operator. One key benefit of this is that operators that are lifted with DataKinds will use the same fixity at both the type and term levels. We'll also need need to enable the PolyKinds extension to opt into GHC's more powerful kind system.

PolyKinds

The PolyKinds extension has been available since GHC 7.4, although we'll be using newer features of the type system and versions prior to GHC 8.10 have not been tested with this chapter. The PolyKinds extension is enabled by default in GHC2021, but you'll need to enable it manually if you are using Haskell2010. This extension enables syntax and modifies type inference to support the more advanced features of GHC's kind system. This extension should be safe to enable in most existing code, although it changes type inference which may rarely break some existing code, or cause changes to error messages.

TypeOperators

The TypeOperators extension has been available since GHC 6.8.1. This extension is enabled by default in GHC2021 but you'll need to enable it manually if you are using Haskell2010. This is a safe extension that shouldn't introduce problems with any existing code.

```
{-# LANGUAGE DataKinds #-}
{-# LANGUAGE TypeOperators #-}
{-# LANGUAGE PolyKinds #-}
module TypeLevelList where

infixr 6 :+
type (:+) = Cons
data List a = Empty | Cons a (List a)
```

With our type operator enabled, we can create type level lists that are much easier to both read and write:

```
λ :kind! 0 :+ 1 :+ 2 :+ Empty
0 :+ 1 :+ 2 :+ Empty :: List GHC.Num.Natural.Natural
= 'Cons 0 ('Cons 1 ('Cons 2 'Empty))
```

Since we're using an alias, the evaluated version of our expression still uses the name Cons. If you don't want this behavior, then you can define your operator as a constructor and it'll be lifted like any other constructor when you use DataKinds. As an example, let's rewrite our list and replace Cons with (:+) directly:

```
infixr 6 :+
data List a = Empty | (:+) a (List a)
```

Now when we evaluate your list expression, we'll get back the more readable operator-based version:

```
λ :kind! 0 :+ 1 :+ 2 :+ Empty
0 :+ 1 :+ 2 :+ Empty :: List GHC.Num.Natural.Natural
= 0 ':+ (1 ':+ (2 ':+ 'Empty))
```

As you can see in these examples, we can construct type level lists the same way that we were able to create lists at the term level, using a recursively defined kind, with a kind parameter. In the first example, we created a type level list of types with the kind Type, and in the second example we created a list of Color types. Just like we can only have term level lists of a single type, we're also restricted to type level lists of a single kind. If we try to create a list with Int and Cyan for example, we'll get an error because we're trying to mix two different kinds:

```
λ :kind! Int :+ Cyan :+ Empty
<interactive>:1:8-20: error:
    • Couldn't match kind 'Color' with 'Type'
      Expected kind 'List Type',
        but 'Cyan :+ Empty' has kind 'List Color'
    • In the second argument of '(:+)', namely 'Cyan :+ Empty'
      In the type 'Int :+ Cyan :+ Empty'
```

As you might have come to expect by now, although we *can* define our own type level lists, we don't actually need to. The normal list type that we use at the term level is also available to us at the type level. We can create literal type level lists the same way we'd create term level lists:

```
λ :kind! [1,2,3]
[1,2,3] :: [Natural]
= '[1, 2, 3]

λ :kind! ["Hello", "World"]
["Hello", "World"] :: [Symbol]
= '["Hello", "World"]

λ :kind! [String, Bool, Int -> (Int, Int)]
[String, Bool, Int -> (Int, Int)] :: [Type]
= '[[Char], Bool, Int -> (Int, Int)]
```

We can also cons new values onto type level lists, just like we'd do with term level lists, but we need to explicitly lift our list up to the type level. Otherwise, the compiler will tend to get confused and give us surprising error messages. Let's look at an example:

```
λ :kind! 1 : []
<interactive>:1:5-6: error:
    • Expecting one more argument to '[]'
      Expected kind '[Natural]', but '[]' has kind 'Type -> Type'
    • In the second argument of '(:)', namely '[]'
      In the type '1 : []'
```

```
λ :kind! 1 : [2]
<interactive>:1:5-7: error:
    • Expected kind '[Natural]', but '[2]' has kind 'Type'
    • In the second argument of '(:)', namely '[2]'
      In the type '1 : [2]'

<interactive>:1:6: error:
    • Expected a type, but '2' has kind 'Natural'
    • In the second argument of '(:)', namely '[2]'
      In the type '1 : [2]'

λ :kind! 1 : [2,3]
1 : [2,3] :: [Natural]
= '[1, 2, 3]
```

In the first two examples here, we get an error because the compiler can't determine that [] should represent an empty type level list of Natural. Instead, the compiler is treating [] as though it's the term level list type with the kind Type -> Type. In the second example, the compiler is making the same assumption about the term level use of [], but it thinks we've now applied the type 2. In other words, it's treating [2] as a type of kind Type. In the final example, the list we're using has two elements. Since the term level [] only accepts a single parameter, the compiler is able to recognize we must be using the type level version of the list.

Using explicitly lifted lists will help us move past the errors in our first two examples. Although it's not necessary when we're consing onto a list of two or more elements, we can include the explicit lift for consistency and avoid introducing bugs if we change the code later to remove some elements. Let's take another look at the examples:

```
λ :kind! 1 : '[]
1 : '[] :: [Natural]
= '[1]

λ :kind! 1 : '[2]
1 : '[2] :: [Natural]
= '[1, 2]

λ :kind! 1 : '[2,3]
1 : '[2,3] :: [Natural]
= '[1, 2, 3]
```

We run into a similar situation using type level tuples. If we try to create a type level tuple without explicitly promoting it, the compiler will assume we're trying to create a term level tuple and give us an error:

```
λ :kind! (1, Cyan)
<interactive>:1:2: error:
    • Expected a type, but '1' has kind 'Natural'
    • In the type '(1, Cyan)'
```

```
<interactive>:1:5-8: error:
    • Expected a type, but 'Cyan' has kind 'Color'
    • In the type '(1, Cyan)'
```

Explicitly promoting the tuple will work just as we'd hope:

```
λ :kind! '(1, Cyan)
'(1, Cyan) :: (Natural, Color)
= '(1, 'Cyan)
```

As you can see, the DataKinds extension gives us a great deal of power to create data structures that exist at the type level. In many cases, we can even re-use code we defined at the term level without any changes. All this expressive power doesn't do us much good without being able to write computations on this data. In the next section you'll learn how to write type level functions to build computations on the type level data structures you've learned how to define.

Functions from Types to Types

In the last section, you learned how to work with a wide variety of type level data, including natural numbers, strings, and data structures like lists and tuples. Having all of this data available at the type level is of limited use without being able to write computations to transform the data. In Haskell, we can build type level functions using a feature called *Type Families*.

Type families are conceptually straightforward. A type family is a function that accepts some types and returns a type, just like a term level function accepts some term level values and returns a value. Unlike term level functions, there are different "varieties" of type family we'll look at. Although each of these sorts of type family ultimately acts as a type level function, the way we write them and the reasons we use them vary. In this section, we'll start by looking at the most commonly used sort of type family: *associated type families*, which let us associate a type family with a particular type class, and give an alternative to functional dependencies that're often easier to use. Next, we'll look at open type families. These are similar to associated type families, but can be used outside of a type class. Finally, we'll look at closed type families. Closed type families are more limited than associated and open type families, since users can't add new instances in their own code. This limitation also makes closed type families more useful for type level programming, since we're able to use them more easily for writing general purpose computations.

Associated Type Families

Associated type families are the most common way that type families are used. Before we dive into understanding exactly what they are and how they work, let's look at a short example. Imagine that we're writing a library for working with shell commands where we would like to represent each supported shell command as its own type. For example, imagine that we have two types, ListDirectory and Grep, to represent the ls and grep commands:

```
newtype ListDirectory =
  ListDirectory { listDirectoryName :: FilePath }

data Grep =
  Grep { grepMatch :: String, grepFiles :: [String]}
```

One way we might want to approach building this library is to define a type class, ShellCommand, for types that can be run at the command line. This will let us encapsulate both the way we generate command line arguments from a particular command, as well as how we handle the output generated by the shell. How should we define it? We might start with something like this:

```
class ShellCommand cmd where
  runCmd ::
    Monad m => cmd -> (String -> [String] -> m String) -> m String
```

In this example, our class defines a single function runCmd that will take a command, and a function from an executable path and list of arguments to some output, and we will return the output. Unfortunately, this isn't a very good abstraction since we're essentially returning whatever output the shell generates unmodified. It would be better if we could return something that better represented the particular output of each command, but then we're faced with a different problem: what type should we return?

Using what you've learned in this book so far, there are a couple of solutions you might see. One option would be to create a sum type, ShellCommandOutput, and add a constructor for each type of output that we wanted to parse. This would work as long as we only wanted to support a finite number of shell commands, but it's not extensible. Any time we wanted to add a new command, we'd need to add a new constructor to ShellCommandOutput.

A second option would be to use a multi-parameter type class. Since the type of output that's generated depends on the command that's run, we can use functional dependencies to define the relationship. Let's take a look at a complete example using functional dependencies as a starting point.

System.Process

Remember that the System.Process module comes from the process library that you used earlier in the Local System chapter.

```
{-# LANGUAGE FunctionalDependencies #-}
{-# LANGUAGE FlexibleInstances #-}

module ShellCommandFunDeps where
import System.Process (readProcess)

class ShellCommand cmd cmdOutput | cmd -> cmdOutput where
  runCmd ::
    Monad m =>
    cmd ->
    (String -> [String] -> m String) ->
    m cmdOutput

newtype ListDirectory =
  ListDirectory { listDirectoryName :: FilePath }

instance ShellCommand ListDirectory [FilePath] where
  runCmd (ListDirectory dir) run =
    lines <$> run "ls" ["-1", dir]

data Grep =
  Grep { grepMatch :: String , grepFiles :: [String]}

data GrepMatch = GrepMatch
  { grepMatchingFileName :: FilePath
  , grepMatchingLineNumber :: Int
  , grepMatchingLineContents :: String
  } deriving (Eq, Show)

parseGrepResponse :: [String] -> [GrepMatch]
parseGrepResponse = map parseLine
  where
    parseLine responseLine =
      let
        (fileName, rest) = span (/= ':') responseLine
        (matchNumber, rest') = span (/= ':') $ tail rest
        contents = tail rest
      in GrepMatch fileName (read matchNumber) contents

instance ShellCommand Grep [GrepMatch] where
  runCmd (Grep match grepFiles) run =
    parseGrepResponse . fixResponses . lines <$>
      run "grep" ("-n" : match : grepFiles)
    where
      fixResponses :: [String] -> [String]
      fixResponses responseLines =
        case grepFiles of
          [fname] -> (\l -> fname <> ":" <> l) <$> responseLines
          _ -> responseLines

data Pipe a r b r' = Pipe a (r -> b)
```

```
instance (ShellCommand a r, ShellCommand b r') =>
  ShellCommand (Pipe a r b r') r' where
  runCmd (Pipe a mkB) run = do
    result <- runCmd a run
    runCmd (mkB result) run

grepFilesInDirectory ::
  String ->
  FilePath ->
  Pipe ListDirectory [FilePath] Grep [GrepMatch]
grepFilesInDirectory match dir =
  Pipe (ListDirectory dir) $
    Grep match . map (\fname -> dir <> "/" <> fname)

runShellCommand :: ShellCommand cmd r => cmd -> IO r
runShellCommand cmd =
  runCmd cmd (\cmdName args -> readProcess cmdName args "")
```

As you can see in this example, using functional dependencies works well enough for individual commands like ListDirectory and Grep, but it starts to show some rough edges when we begin to compose our commands with Pipe. The extra type parameters add noise and reduce the ergonomics, but a bigger problem is that writing a function like grepFilesInDirectory requires that we write out the specific output type of our intermediate commands. That means we'll need to change the type signature if we decide to refactor our commands to change the types they use internally. Worse, refactoring our library might require the users to change their code because of an implementation detail in how we represent some of our commands.

TypeFamilies

The TypeFamilies extension has been available since GHC 6.8.1. This extension isn't enabled by default in GHC2021 or Haskell2010 so you'll need to enable it manually. This is a safe extension that shouldn't cause problems with any existing code.

Associated type families are a useful alternative to multi-param type classes with functional dependencies in circumstances like this, because they allow us to write a function from our input type to the output type as a type level function that is embedded directly into our type class. To use associated type families we'll need to enable the TypeFamilies extension. With this extension enabled, we can add an associated type family to our type class with the type keyword. Let's look at an example of a type family in our ShellCommand class:

```
{-# LANGUAGE TypeFamilies #-}
{-# LANGUAGE RecordWildCards #-}

module ShellCommand where
import Data.Kind
import System.Process (readProcess)

class ShellCommand cmd where
  type ShellOutput cmd :: Type
  runCmd ::
    Monad m =>
    cmd ->
    (String -> [String] -> m String) ->
    m (ShellOutput cmd)
```

In this example, ShellOutput is an associated type family that we use to map a particular instance of ShellCommand to the type of output that will be generated by running the command. In this example, ShellOutput takes a single argument, cmd, but it's possible for type families to have several arguments and you'll see some examples of that later on in this chapter. The kind signature, :: Type, specifies what the kind of the returned value should be. In this case, the return kind should be a normal type. Let's write an instance of ShellCommand so that we can see how to use our type family, and get a chance to try using it in ghci. We'll start by writing an instance for ListDirectory:

```
instance ShellCommand ListDirectory where
  type ShellOutput ListDirectory = [FilePath]
  runCmd (ListDirectory dir) run =
    lines <$> run "ls" ["-1", dir]
```

This tells the compiler that the ShellOutput type family, when when called with the type ListDirectory, returns a type of the value [FilePath]. If we load our module into ghci you can see that the kind of ShellOutput looks like a function from a Type to a Type:

```
λ :kind! ShellOutput
ShellOutput :: Type -> Type
= ShellOutput
```

When we apply a Type, in thise case ListDirectory, we get back a type, [FilePath]. We can validate that in ghci too:

```
λ :kind! ListDirectory
ListDirectory :: Type
= ListDirectory

λ :kind! ShellOutput ListDirectory
ShellOutput ListDirectory :: Type
= [[Char]]
```

Remember that FilePath is an alias for String, which is itself an alias for [Char], so you can see that ShellOutput ListDirectory is returning exactly what we told it to return.

You can see how we can call a type family in the definition of runCmd, where we're using the type family to find the return type of runCmd:

```
runCmd ::
  Monad m =>
  cmd ->
  (String -> [String] -> m String) ->
  m (ShellOutput cmd)
```

In this type annotation, cmd is a type variable, and we're going to call ShellOutput with whatever value we happen to have in that variable. This lets us get the proper output type for any input type we call runCmd with. Let's look at another example and see how we can write an instance for Grep using type families:

```
instance ShellCommand Grep where
  type ShellOutput Grep = [GrepMatch]
  runCmd (Grep match grepFiles) run =
    parseGrepResponse . fixResponses . lines <$> run "grep" grepArgs
    where
      grepArgs = "-n" : match : grepFiles
      fixResponses :: [String] -> [String]
      fixResponses responseLines =
        case grepFiles of
          [fname] ->
            (\l -> fname <> ":" <> l) <$> responseLines
          _ ->
            responseLines
```

Just like with ListDirectory, we can define an instance for Grep with minimal changes to our code. Instead of a second parameter telling us that the result of a Grep should be a list of matches, we're using a type family. As you would expect, we can load this up into ghci and see that we get the correct output from ShellOutput when called with Grep instead of ListDirectory:

```
λ :kind! ShellOutput Grep
ShellOutput Grep :: Type
= [GrepMatch]
```

Most developers these days prefer the syntax of type families over functional dependencies, but the two instances we've looked at so far haven't shown much clear benefit to type families other than a bit of a nicer syntax. We can see a more obvious benefit when we define Pipe. By eliminating the second parameter to our type classes, composing them becomes much easier. With type families, we can redefine Pipe to need only two type parameters, one for each command on either end of the pipe:

```
-- data Pipe a r b r' = Pipe a (r -> b)
data Pipe a b = Pipe a (ShellOutput a -> b)
```

This new definition is more readable thanks to being able to remove two of our type parameters. It also carries a much more precise definition. Our old definition of Pipe didn't enforce any particular relationship between all of its parameters. We might have known that r was *supposed to be* the output type of a and that r' was *supposed to be* the output type of b, but there was nothing that required that to be the case. Using type families, we can be more explicit that the output type of the command a must be used to generate the command b.

The definition of ShellCommand for Pipe is also a little bit simpler thanks to the removed parameters:

```
instance (ShellCommand a, ShellCommand b) =>
  ShellCommand (Pipe a b)
  where
  type ShellOutput (Pipe a b) = ShellOutput b
  runCmd (Pipe a mkB) run = do
    result <- runCmd a run
    runCmd (mkB result) run
```

This example also highlights another important property of working with type families. The definition of ShellOutput (Pipe a b) refers to ShellOutput b. The ability to recursively solve for type families is what lets us write more complex computations at the type level than we could do before.

We still have one more opportunity to benefit from refactoring our code to use type families: we're now able to define grepFilesInDirectory without needing to refer to the output types of either ListDirectory or Grep:

```
grepFilesInDirectory ::
  String ->
  FilePath ->
  Pipe ListDirectory Grep
grepFilesInDirectory match dir =
  Pipe (ListDirectory dir) $
    Grep match . map (\fname -> dir <> "/" <> fname)
```

Thanks to our new definition of Pipe, we're able to join commands without having to explicitly refer to the output type, meaning that our users will be free to compose commands with less risk of breaking changes in the future. Unfortunately, even though we're not explicitly naming the output type of ListDirectory we're still relying on the implementation detail that it's defined as

[FilePath]. We're able to do this because type families work similarly to type aliases. Any time we use ShellOutput ListDirectory it's essentially a synonym for [FilePath]. Like with type aliases, this can have the down side that it may allow us to accidentally write code that depends on what should have been an implementation detail.

Associated Data Families

One way to avoid this problem is to use *data families*. A data family works like a type family, except that every data family instance defines a brand new type, rather than creating an alias for some existing type. Data families otherwise work like type families, except we use the data keyword instead of type. Let's take one more pass at refactoring our shell library to use data families instead of type families. We'll start by refactoring our type class definition:

```
class ShellCommand cmd where
  data ShellOutput cmd :: Type
  runCmd ::
    Monad m =>
    cmd ->
    (String -> [String] -> m String) ->
    m (ShellOutput cmd)
```

You'll notice that the only change to the definition of our type class is that we're now using the keyword data instead of type. The changes to our instances will be a little bit more invasive, but not much. Let's look at our ListDirectory instance next.

In this example, rather than directly translating our earlier type family, we'll revisit what we return. One of the requirements we ran into was that we needed a way to add the parent directory to the name of the files in the directory listing. We can make that easier for ourselves by keeping the path to the directory alongside the directory listing. We can do that by defining a new record with our data family:

```
instance ShellCommand ListDirectory where
  data ShellOutput ListDirectory =
    DirectoryListing { containingDirectory :: FilePath
                     , filenamesInListing :: [FilePath]
                     } deriving (Show, Eq)
  runCmd (ListDirectory dir) run =
    DirectoryListing dir . lines <$> run "ls" ["-1", dir]
```

As you can see, creating a new data family instance follows the same pattern that you used to create type family instances, but now we're defining a brand new constructor called DirectoryListing and adding fields to it. The constructor we're creating works just like any other constructor. You can see in this example that we're deriving Show and Eq instances.

Before we move on to writing an instance for Grep using data families, let's take advantage of this extra information we're now storing to write a utility function to handle getting a list of files in a directory listing including the name of their parent directory.

```
directoryListingWithParent :: ShellOutput ListDirectory -> [FilePath]
directoryListingWithParent DirectoryListing{..} =
  map fixPath filenamesInListing
  where
    fixPath fname =
      containingDirectory <> "/" <> fname
```

You'll notice in this example that we're referring to the type of our record by the data family name, ShellOutput ListDirectory. Although the constructor and record field selectors are all visible like normal, our new record's type is only accessible by applying our data family. Let's take a quick look at ghci to get a feel for the types we have in scope so far:

```
λ :t DirectoryListing
DirectoryListing
  :: FilePath -> [FilePath] -> ShellOutput ListDirectory
λ :kind ShellOutput ListDirectory
ShellOutput ListDirectory :: Type
λ :t containingDirectory
containingDirectory :: ShellOutput ListDirectory -> FilePath
λ :t filenamesInListing
filenamesInListing :: ShellOutput ListDirectory -> [FilePath]
```

In addition to defining brand new data types, we can also use newtype with data families to get the extra type safety benefits of a data family without any additional runtime overhead. Let's create an instance of ShellCommand for Grep using a newtype wrapper instead of a brand new record type:

```
instance ShellCommand Grep where
  newtype ShellOutput Grep =
    ListOfGrepMatches { getListOfGrepMatches :: [GrepMatch] }

  runCmd (Grep match grepFiles) run =
    ListOfGrepMatches . parseGrepResponse . fixResponses . lines <$>
    run "grep" grepArgs
    where
      grepArgs = "-n" : match : grepFiles
      fixResponses :: [String] -> [String]
      fixResponses responseLines =
        case grepFiles of
          [fname] -> (\l -> fname <> ":" <> l) <$> responseLines
          _ -> responseLines
```

In this example, you can see when we want to use a newtype with a data family, we replace the data keyword with newtype. The instance of the data family is defined like any other newtype, and the constructor and our field selector are available just like they were when we defined our DirectoryListing record:

```
λ :t ListOfGrepMatches
ListOfGrepMatches :: [GrepMatch] -> ShellOutput Grep

λ :t getListOfGrepMatches
getListOfGrepMatches :: ShellOutput Grep -> [GrepMatch]
```

As you can imagine, refactoring Pipe follows the same pattern that we've used for ListDirectory and Grep. If you'd like, you can jump ahead to the first exercise at the end of this chapter and complete refactoring this module to use data families.

Open Data and Type Families

After learning about associated data and type families, you might find yourself in a situation where you want to create a new type class just for the sake of having a data or type family. For example, imagine that you wanted to write some code that would let you generate type level string representations of some types. We can do that with associated types, but it ends up being pretty verbose:

```
{-# LANGUAGE FlexibleInstances #-}
{-# LANGUAGE TypeOperators #-}
{-# LANGUAGE TypeFamilies #-}
{-# LANGUAGE DataKinds #-}
{-# LANGUAGE UndecidableInstances #-}

module EffectiveHaskell.Chapter15.OpenDataFamiliesDemo where
import GHC.TypeLits

class HasNamedType t where
  type NamedType t :: Symbol

instance HasNamedType Int where
  type NamedType Int = "Int"

instance HasNamedType Char where
  type NamedType Char = "Char"

instance HasNamedType String where
  type NamedType String = "String"

instance (HasNamedType a, HasNamedType b) =>
  HasNamedType (a -> b) where
  type NamedType (a -> b) =
    NamedType a `AppendSymbol` " -> " `AppendSymbol` NamedType b
```

Open type families give us the same functionality without the need to explicitly define a type class. We call them *open* type families because, like type classes and associated type families, they are *open to extension*. In other words, we, or the user, can always add more instances later on without having to change the definition of the open type family. We can define an open type family at the top level of our module with the type family keywords, and create instances of the family with type instance. Let's take a look at an open type family based version of NamedType:

```
{-# LANGUAGE TypeFamilies #-}
{-# LANGUAGE DataKinds #-}
{-# LANGUAGE UndecidableInstances #-}
{-# LANGUAGE TypeOperators #-}

module OpenDataFamilyDemo where
import GHC.TypeLits
import Data.Kind

type family NamedType (a :: Type) :: Symbol
type instance NamedType Int = "Int"
type instance NamedType Char = "Char"
type instance NamedType String = "String"
type instance NamedType (a -> b) =
  NamedType a `AppendSymbol` " -> " `AppendSymbol` NamedType b
```

In this example, you can see the open type family looks similar to the associated type family implementation, but it does away with some of the extra syntax we needed for defining the HasNamedType class. In fact, you can really think of associated type families as a special case of a more general open type family, where the type family has to be defined for every instance of a particular type class. This requirement lets us use the type family in the types of the functions defined inside of the class. If you don't need to use the type family as part of the type of any functions in the class, then an open type family is essentially the same as an associated type family. We've also added a kind signature to the parameter of NamedType. In theory, we could have omitted the kind signature here, but adding kind signatures can help make our type level code safer and easier to read. Of course, we could have also added kind signatures to the parameters of our associated type family, but it's more common to see the kind signatures omitted for the parameters of associated type familes since it will often be included in the definition of the type class.

Let's open up ghci and try running a few commands to experiment with our new NamedType family. If we call our type family for any of the types we've defined instances for, we get back the string we'd expect:

```
λ :kind! NamedType Int
NamedType Int :: Symbol
= "Int"

λ :kind! NamedType String
NamedType String :: Symbol
= "String"

λ :kind! NamedType (String -> Int)
NamedType (String -> Int) :: Symbol
= "String -> Int"
```

We can even call our type family with a function that takes more than one argument, since currying will turn it into a single argument function for us:

```
λ :kind! NamedType (String -> Char -> Int -> Char)
NamedType (String -> Char -> Int -> Char) :: Symbol
= "String -> String -> Int -> Char"
```

If we try to call our type family with a type that we haven't defined an instance for, you might expect that we'll get an error. Instead, something unexpcted happens. The command will succeed, but the result will be an unevaluated type family expression:

```
λ :kind! NamedType (Bool -> Bool)
NamedType (Bool -> Bool) :: Symbol
= AppendSymbol
    (AppendSymbol (NamedType Bool) " -> ") (NamedType Bool)
```

The problem here is that :kind! is telling ghci to do its best to run type checking and reduce our type level expression, but it's not able to do so far enough to actually know that we have an error. Instead, it throws up its hands and gives us back the unevaluated expression. This can end up being a particular problem when you are using :kind! to type check your code, but not looking closely at the output. Since the result isn't an error, it's easy to look past the fact that the result is partially unevaluated and realize that this means you may have a type family that isn't actually defined.

One way that we can get a more through test of our type level code is to use it to generate an actual term level value, but our type family is generating a purely type level string. How can we turn that into something at the term level that we can run, and use to test our type family instances?

We'll start by using one of the useful functions that is provided to use in GHC.TypeLits, the symbolVal function. It has the type:

```
symbolVal :: KnownSymbol n => proxy n -> String
```

The KnownSymbol constraint is a type class constraint that's defined for all Symbol types. This means we know that n must be some kind of type level string. Knowing we have a type level string is good, since we want to get a term level string that matches the type level string, but it presents a problem. We need to pass something into symbolVal so that it can keep track of the type information it needs to return a string value, but we can't actually create any term level values with a symbol type. This is a common problem when we're dealing with type level code, but there's a straightforward solution: phantom types. We don't need a value whose type is a symbol, we just need a value whose type carries the symbol information along with it. We typically call values like this *proxies*.

The Data.Proxy module from base gives us a useful default definition for a proxy that looks like this:

```
data Proxy a = Proxy
```

In other words, a Proxy is a type that only has a single inhabitant, Proxy, but it can carry around any type information that we want. If you're reading carefully though, you'll notice that symbolVal's proxy is a type parameter, with a lowercase p. Since we'll never use the value of a proxy type, there's no reason to restrict it to being an actual Proxy, even if that's what you'll use as a proxy value most of the time.

You can use a proxy value with either a visible type application or a type annotation. Let's look at a couple of examples in ghci:

```
λ symbolVal (Proxy :: Proxy "Hello")
"Hello"

λ symbolVal $ Proxy @"World"
"World"
```

As you can see, Proxy let's us carry around the type information for a symbol and pass it into symbolVal so that we can get back a runtime string representation of the type literal string that we passed in. If we use the ScopedTypeVariables extension, we can also create a proxy value to carry around the information about a polymorphic type. Let's put this all together and write a new function, showTypeName that will take a type with a NamedType instance and generate a term level string representation. We'll need to start by enabling the FlexibleContexts extension.

FlexibleContexts

The FlexibleContexts extension has been available since GHC 6.8.1. It's enabled by default in GHC2021 but if you're using Haskell2010 you'll need to enable it manually. This is generally a safe extension that shouldn't cause problems with any existing code.

```
{-# LANGUAGE AllowAmbiguousTypes #-}
{-# LANGUAGE ScopedTypeVariables #-}
{-# LANGUAGE FlexibleContexts #-}
{-# LANGUAGE TypeApplications #-}

showTypeName :: forall t. (KnownSymbol (NamedType t)) => String
showTypeName = symbolVal $ Proxy @(NamedType t)
```

In this example, our function's type says the return type of NamedType must be a known symbol. With FlexibleContexts, we're allowed to call the NamedType family directly inside of the KnownSymbol constraint. Without this extension, we can only have constraints on type names.

Whatever that type happens to be, we'll create a proxy value that holds that type information, and passes it into symbolVal so that we can get a runtime string. Let's try it out in ghci:

```
λ showTypeName @Int
"Int"

λ showTypeName @Char
"Char"

λ showTypeName @(Int -> Int -> String)
"Int -> Int -> String"
```

In these examples, we're sticking to types that have NamedType instances, and as we'd expect we're getting back term level strings. We can use these strings like any other string:

```
λ typeName :: String = showTypeName @(String -> Int)

λ putStrLn $
  "The type '" <> typeName <> "' is " <> show (length typeName) <> " chars"
The type 'String -> Int' is 13 chars
```

Unlike our examples using :kind!, if we try to pass a type that doesn't have a NamedType instance to showTypeName we'll get an error:

```
λ showTypeName @Bool
<interactive>:907:1-12: error:
    • No instance for (KnownSymbol (NamedType Bool))
        arising from a use of ‘showTypeName’
    • In the expression: showTypeName @Bool
      In an equation for ‘it’: it = showTypeName @Bool
```

Why does this function successfully give us an error when looking at the kind didn't? It's because in this function we're forced to actually pick a particular instance of the KnownSymbol type class so that we get a string out of it, and at that point we're forced to deal with the fact that there's no instance defined for NamedType Bool. As you'll see later in this chapter, type classes are an important part of writing type level code, because they give us a way to map the computed types back to term level values.

Now that we have a way to more easily test our type family, and we can get useful errors out of it, let's make a few quality of life improvements by adding a some additional compound types. Let's start by adding an instance for tuples:

```
type instance NamedType (a,b) =
  "(" `AppendSymbol` NamedType a `AppendSymbol` ","
  `AppendSymbol` NamedType b `AppendSymbol` ")"
```

This is starting to get a bit unreadable thanks to the repeated use of infix AppendSymbol calls. Thankfully, we can create type operator aliases for type families the same way we could for lifted data types. Let's try to add a new operator and then refactor our NamedType instance to use it:

```
type (:++:) = AppendSymbol

type instance NamedType (a,b) =
  "(" :++: NamedType a :++: "," :++: NamedType b :++: ")"
```

Unfortunately, when we try to compile this refactored example, we get a new error:

```
src/OpenDataFamilyDemo.hs:15:1-26: error: ...
  • The type family ‘AppendSymbol’ should have 2 arguments,
    but has been given none
  • In the type synonym declaration for ‘:++:’
   |
Compilation failed.
```

This error illustrates one of the biggest limitations that we have with type families compared to term level functions. We're not allowed to use partially applied type families. Although we're free to reference constructors without passing in all of their arguments, like we did when we created a type operator for Cons earlier, a type family must always have all of its arguments applied. This restriction can be particularly troublesome if you want to write higher order functions like map or fold at the type level. You'll learn how to handle this situation later on in the chapter. Thankfully, in this case we can work around that restriction without too much trouble by adding type parameters to both sides of our operator:

```
type (:++:) a b = AppendSymbol a b

type instance NamedType (a,b) =
  "(" :++: NamedType a :++: "," :++: NamedType b :++: ")"
```

With our new type family instance in place, we can now get nicely formatted versions of types that include tuples:

```
λ showTypeName @(Char -> String, String -> Int)
"(Char -> String,String -> Int)"

λ showTypeName @(String -> (Int, Char))
"String -> (Int,Char)"
```

Now that we've covered tuples, let's try to add an instance that will let us format list types. We'll follow the same pattern we used for tuples:

```
type instance NamedType [a] = "[" :++: NamedType a :++: "]"
```

Once again, if we compile this we're faced with an error. This time the compiler is letting us know that we have conflicting instances:

```
src/OpenDataFamilyDemo.hs:19:15-23: error: …
    Conflicting family instance declarations:
      NamedType String = "String"
        -- Defined at /examples/OpenDataFamilyDemo.hs:19:15
      NamedType [a] = ("[" :++: NamedType a) :++: "]"
        -- Defined at /examples/OpenDataFamilyDemo.hs:23:15
   |
Compilation failed.
```

The problem we're running into now is String is an alias for the type [Char], but our new instance defined for [a] will match *any* list type, including [Char]. Open type families are very particular about overapping instances. We're only allowed to have to instances that overlap if all of the overlapping instances would return *exactly* the same value in the overlapping cases. We can see that this is the case if we hardcode both our String and [a] instances to always return "":

```
type instance NamedType String = ""
type instance NamedType [a] = ""
```

In this case, since the overlapping instances always return the same type the compiler accepts the overlap. Relying on this exception can be tricky though, since the types that each of the overlapping instances return needs to be structurally equal. For example, imagine that we hadn't yet defined an instance for String, but we had a list instance defined like this:

```
type instance NamedType [a] = "[" :++: NamedType a :++: "]"
```

Now, let's call NamedType String and see what we get back:

```
λ :kind! NamedType String
NamedType String :: Symbol
= "[Char]"
```

Next, let's add our String instance back, but this time we'll hard-code the return type of "[Char]". That seems like it should work, since it's exactly what we got when we evaluated the type family in ghci:

```
type instance NamedType String = "[Char]"
```

The compiler seems to have a different idea of equality than we do. If we try to compile this we'll still get an error:

```
src/OpenDataFamilyDemo.hs:20:15-23: error: …
    Conflicting family instance declarations:
      NamedType String = "[Char]"
        -- Defined at /examples/OpenDataFamilyDemo.hs:20:15
      NamedType [a] = ("[" :++: NamedType a) :++: "]"
        -- Defined at /examples/OpenDataFamilyDemo.hs:24:15
   |
Compilation failed.
```

Even though it seems like these two expressions ought to be the same, the compiler still won't accept this, since our literal symbol is structurally different from the computed symbol we're generating in our list instance. Let's give this another try. This time we'll be a bit more explicit about replicating the same structure by using (:++:) to combine the different parts of our symbol:

```
type instance NamedType String = "[" :++: "Char" :++: "]"
```

Unfortunately that still doesn't seem to be sufficient. If you try to compile this version you'll see that you're getting a similar error: the compiler still doesn't consider these two types equal. We have one more option. Let's replace the symbol literal "Char" with a call to NamedType:

```
type instance NamedType String = "[" :++: NamedType Char :++: "]"
```

If you try to compile this version of the code you'll see that we've finally found an instance that can successfully overlap. In order to do that, we needed to make sure that we were returning exactly the same type that we would have returned in our list instance, without any additional normalization.

Closed Data and Type Families

Open and associated type families are certainly useful, but the fact that they can be arbitrarily extended by users of our library also puts some limitations on the computations that we can reasonably do with them. Closed data and type families give us another way to write type level functions that give up extensibility, and in exchange there are different sorts of computations that we can build with them. This is thanks to the fact that we'll know every instance of a closed type family that will exist at the time it's defined. That lets us handle our cases exhaustively. In this section, we'll look at two different examples of how we can used closed type families to write type level computations. First, we'll look at how we can use type families to implement some basic arithmetic on peano numbers to get a feel for the syntax and basics of using type familes. Next, we'll work through some examples of working with type level lists using open and closed type families together to give us even more flexiblity.

You first learned about peano numbers much earlier in this book, when you first learned about creating your own types on page 136. Although GHC already gives us convenient access to type level literals, peano numbers are still useful because they are a great example of how to work with closed type families. Let's revisit our peano numbers, but this time we'll use them at the type level.

The first thing we'll want to do is create a new module and add in our definition of peano numbers:

```
{-# LANGUAGE UndecidableInstances #-}
{-# LANGUAGE TypeFamilies #-}
{-# LANGUAGE DataKinds #-}
{-# LANGUAGE TypeOperators #-}

module ClosedTypeFamilyDemo where
import GHC.TypeLits

data Peano = Zero | Succ Peano
```

The first problem that we'll run into working with peano numbers, whether it's at the type or term level, is that it's annoying to type out the numbers when we have to manually nest the constructors. Since we know that GHC already provides us with a nice way of writing type level `Natural` values using numeric literals, let's create a new type family to convert a `Natural` to a `Peano`.

The algorithm we want to implement for this is straightforward:

- If the `Natural` number is `0`, then return `Zero`.
- If it's anything larger than zero, return the successor of converting the next smallest natural number to a `Peano`.

If we try to implement this using an *open* type family though, we'll run into a problem: the most natural way of expressing this algorithm runs into the dreaded overlapping instances problem. Let's try it and see for ourselves:

```
type family ToPeano (n :: Natural) :: Peano
type instance ToPeano 0 = Zero
type instance ToPeano a = Succ (ToPeano (a - 1))
```

If you try to compile this you'll quickly see the problem: a can match *anything*, including 0, so it will overlap the instance that should be acting as the base case of our recursion.

Thankfully, we have another option. We can write ToPeano using a closed type family. Overlap is allowed in closed type families. Like guard clauses and case expressions, overlap in a closed type family is resolved top-to-bottom. Let's rewrite ToPeano as a closed type family and see how it works:

```
type family ToPeano (n :: Natural) :: Peano where
  ToPeano 0 = Zero
  ToPeano a = Succ (ToPeano (a - 1))
```

The first thing to notice is that the closed type family version of our code works as expected. If we load it up into ghci we can successfully convert naturals into peano numbers:

```
λ :kind! ToPeano 3
ToPeano 3 :: Peano
= 'Succ ('Succ ('Succ 'Zero))

λ :kind! ToPeano 5
ToPeano 5 :: Peano
= 'Succ ('Succ ('Succ ('Succ ('Succ 'Zero))))
```

You'll notice that the syntax for creating a closed type family is similar to that of an open type family, but now we include all of the instances inside of a where clause rather than creating instances using type instance. Before we move on, let's write a FromPeano instance as well, so that we can easily convert back and forth between Natural and Peano representations of numbers:

```
type family FromPeano (a :: Peano) :: Natural where
  FromPeano Zero = 0
  FromPeano (Succ a) = 1 + FromPeano a
```

Now we can round trip between Peano and Natural representations of numbers:

```
λ :kind! FromPeano (ToPeano 10)
FromPeano (ToPeano 10) :: Natural
= 10

λ :kind! ToPeano (FromPeano (Succ (Succ (Succ Zero))))
ToPeano (FromPeano (Succ (Succ (Succ Zero)))) :: Peano
= 'Succ ('Succ ('Succ 'Zero))
```

Being able to convert back and forth between different representations of a number will be useful as we're working through some more examples, but it's not particularly interesting on its own. Let's make our Peano numbers more useful by adding some basic arithmetic operations for them. We'll start with addition and multiplication. Unlike our earlier type family examples, these will need to take two parameters. Luckily, adding extra parameters to a type family is straightforward:

```
type family Add (a :: Peano) (b :: Peano) :: Peano where
  Add a Zero = a
  Add a (Succ b) = Add (Succ a) b

type family Multiply (a :: Peano) (b :: Peano) :: Peano where
  Multiply a Zero = Zero
  Multiply a (Succ Zero) = a
  Multiply a (Succ b) = Add a (Multiply a b)
```

One thing to notice about all the examples we've looked at so far is we're defining total functions. We can add or multiply any two peano numbers and get a number back out. Not all operations we might want to support are this flexible though. If we want to support subtraction, we'll quickly run into a problem: we can't represent negative numbers with Peano, but there's nothing stopping our users from trying to subtract a bigger number from a smaller one.

If we try to naively define Subtract it will work for cases where the numbers are subtractable, but if a user tries to do an invalid operation, we'll run into the same situation we encountered with NamedType—we'll get an unnormalized type instead of a useful error. Let's try it out and see:

```
type family Subtract (a :: Peano) (b :: Peano) :: Peano where
  Subtract a Zero = a
  Subtract (Succ a) (Succ b) = Subtract a b
```

If we load this into ghci we'll get reasonable values for valid operations:

```
λ :kind! FromPeano (Subtract (ToPeano 10) (ToPeano 2))
FromPeano (Subtract (ToPeano 10) (ToPeano 2)) :: Natural
= 8
```

Now let's try to subtract 10 from 2 and see what we get:

```
FromPeano (Subtract (ToPeano 2) (ToPeano 10)) :: Natural
= FromPeano
    (Subtract
       'Zero
       ('Succ
          ('Succ ('Succ ('Succ ('Succ ('Succ ('Succ ('Succ 'Zero))))))))))
```

Just like when we were working with symbols, we have the option of trying to get a runtime value out of our invalid subtraction so that we can force an error. Let's use the natValue function from GHC.TypeLits:

```
λ :type natVal
natVal :: KnownNat n => proxy n -> Integer
λ natVal $ Proxy @(FromPeano (Subtract (ToPeano 10) (ToPeano 2)))
8
λ natVal $ Proxy @(FromPeano (Subtract (ToPeano 2) (ToPeano 10)))
<interactive>:2228:1-6: error:
  • No instance for
      (KnownNat
        (FromPeano
           (Subtract
              'Zero
              ('Succ
                 ('Succ
                   ('Succ
                     ('Succ
                       ('Succ
                         ('Succ
                           ('Succ
                             ('Succ 'Zero))))))))))))
      arising from a use of ‘natVal’
  • In the first argument of ‘($)’, namely ‘natVal’
    In the expression:
      natVal $
        Proxy @(FromPeano (Subtract (ToPeano 2) (ToPeano 10)))
    In an equation for ‘it’:
        it
          = natVal $
              Proxy @(FromPeano (Subtract (ToPeano 2) (ToPeano 10)))
```

Even though we can get a runtime error with natValue there are two problems. First, it would be preferable if we could get the type error at the type level, rather than requiring that we try to get a term level value. Second, and more notably, the error message that we're getting here is unreadable and larger numbers result in even less readable and more deeply nested error messages. Type level programming can easily lead to cases where you can end up with impossibly complex error messages.

Thankfully, we can address both the problem of unreadable errors and the lack of errors when working at the type level in ghci with a single change: creating a user-defined type error. We can create a user-defined type error using TypeError and Text from GHC.TypeLits. Let's add a type error to Subtract:

```
type family Subtract (a :: Peano) (b :: Peano) :: Peano where
  Subtract a Zero = a
  Subtract Zero b =
    TypeError (Text "Subtract: Cannot result in a negative number")
  Subtract (Succ a) (Succ b) = Subtract a b
```

In this example, TypeError is a type family that can be used to generate a compile time type error. We call it with an error message that we can generate with Text. Now if we try to evaluate an invalid subtraction in ghci we'll see that the result would be a type error, and if we try to get a runtime value we'll see that our error message is much easier to read:

```
λ :kind! Subtract (ToPeano 5) (ToPeano 10)
Subtract (ToPeano 5) (ToPeano 10) :: Peano
= (TypeError ...)
```

```
λ natVal $ Proxy @(FromPeano (Subtract (ToPeano 5) (ToPeano 10)))
<interactive>:2271:1-6: error:
  • Subtract: Cannot result in a negative number
  • In the first argument of '($)', namely 'natVal'
    In the expression:
      natVal $ Proxy @(FromPeano (Subtract (ToPeano 5) (ToPeano 10)))
    In an equation for 'it':
      it
        = natVal $
            Proxy @(FromPeano (Subtract (ToPeano 5) (ToPeano 10)))
```

You can also get a bit more creative with your error messages to make them even more useful. For example, ShowType lets you print the value of a type in the error message. You can also combine error messages onto the same line with (:<>:), or create multiple lines of error message output with (:$$:). Let's look at one more example of a more nicely formatted error message:

```
type family Subtract (a :: Peano) (b :: Peano) :: Peano where
  Subtract a Zero = a
  Subtract Zero b = TypeError (
    Text "Subtract: Cannot result in a negative number" :$$:
    Text "The result would be -" :<>: ShowType (FromPeano b))
  Subtract (Succ a) (Succ b) = Subtract a b
```

This version of our error will not only explain that we can't have a negative peano number, it will even tell the user what negative value they would have gotten if negative numbers were allowed:

```
λ natVal $ Proxy @(FromPeano (Subtract (ToPeano 5) (ToPeano 10)))
<interactive>:2274:1-6: error:
  • Subtract: Cannot result in a negative number
    The result would be -5
  • In the first argument of '($)', namely 'natVal'
    In the expression:
      natVal $
        Proxy @(FromPeano (Subtract (ToPeano 5) (ToPeano 10)))
    In an equation for 'it':
        it
          = natVal $
              Proxy @(FromPeano (Subtract (ToPeano 5) (ToPeano 10)))
```

User-defined type errors are common in closed type families. Since a closed type family should be exhaustive and supports overlap, it's often straightforward to have a "catch-all" error case to give the user information about unsupported calls to the type family. You can also use type errors with open and associated type families, and as you'll see later in this chapter, with type classes.

Now that you've learned the basics about type families using peano numbers, let's move on to some more advanced examples of the sort of computations that you can do with type level families.

Type Level List Operations with Type Families

Earlier in this chapter, you learned about type level lists, but so far we've been limited to using them in fairly simple ways. None of the common functions you've come to expect for term level lists are defined for us at the type level, so we'll need to write them ourselves if we want to get more use out of lists for type level computation. In this section, we'll build a few list functions to help make working with lists easier at the type level.

As usual, let's start by creating a new module and adding some language extensions:

```
{-# LANGUAGE UndecidableInstances #-}
{-# LANGUAGE TypeFamilies #-}
{-# LANGUAGE TypeOperators #-}
{-# LANGUAGE PolyKinds #-}
{-# LANGUAGE DataKinds #-}

module TypeFamilyListFuncs where
import GHC.TypeLits
import Data.Kind
```

Now that we have the necessary boilerplate in place, let's start by adding a new closed type family that will let us search to see if a particular value is inside of a type level list:

```
type family Member (needle :: a) (haystack :: [a]) :: Bool where
  Member a '[] = False
  Member a (a : as) = True
  Member a (b : as) = Member a as
```

If you look at this example closely, you'll notice one of the big differences between pattern matching in type families compared to term level code like case expressions. Let's look at the line in more detail:

```
Member a (a : as) = True
```

In this line of code we're testing to see if the element we're searching for matches the head of the list, and we do it by using the same variable, a. In term level code this would fail and the compiler would warn us that we were trying to bind the same name to two different expressions, but at the type level using the same variable in a pattern means that the pattern will only match if the value of the variable is equal in both places.

Unfortunately, this feature also invites a bug that we wouldn't have to worry about in the term level. Consider the very next line of our type family:

```
Member a (b : as) = Member a as
```

In this example, b is a distinct type variable, so a and b do not *need* to be equal, but the expression also does not prohibit them from being equal. In other words, our two type family instances will overlap in the case that the head of the list is the element we're searching for. If we reverse the order of these two lines of code, the behavior would change and we would never report that we'd successfully found a match. With -Wall enabled you'll get a warning about this, but otherwise it can be a confusing source of bugs.

Thankfully, we've done our overlap in the correct order, so we can load our code up into ghci and see it in action:

```
λ :kind! Member 1 '[]
Member 1 '[] :: Bool
= 'False

λ :kind! Member 1 '[1,2,3]
Member 1 '[1,2,3] :: Bool
= 'True

λ :kind! Member 1 '[2,3,4]
Member 1 '[2,3,4] :: Bool
= 'False
```

Knowing when a type level list contains a particular element is quite useful, and you'll see some examples of how we can apply this later on in the chapter, but it's a bit limited. It would be nice if we could find all of the elements that satisfied some particular predicate, like being even. Writing a function like this at the term level would be easy enough:

```
findElems :: (a -> Bool) -> [a] -> [a]
findElems _ [] = []
findElems p (x:xs) =
  if p x then x : findElems p xs else findElems p xs
```

At the type level, writing a function like this is challenging because we're dealing with a higher order function, and that means we need a way to pass a type level function into a type family. As you learned earlier in this chapter, we can't use partially applied type families, so we'll need to use some new techniques to work around the limitation.

Let's start by writing a version of FindElems that works the way we'd like it to work, imagining some features that we'd like to have along the way. Then we'll try to either build the features we've imagined, or refactor FindElems until we get to some code that actually works.

```
type family FindElems (p :: a -> Bool) (elems :: [a]) :: [a] where
  FindElems _ '[] = '[]
  FindElems p (a:as) =
    If p a Then (a : FindElems p as) Else (FindElems p as)
```

The imaginary implementation of FindElems in this example is relying on two major features that are missing from our knowledge so far. First, we're assuming the user can pass in a type family that hasn't been fully applied. Second, we're trying to use an if expression, even though there's nothing like that defined for us at the type level.

Before we tackle the harder problem of dealing with higher order type level functions, let's address the lack of conditionals at the type level. The lack of conditional expressions at the type level might seem like a major oversight, but it turns out that it's very easy for us to write our own as long as we're willing to compromise on the precise syntax. Instead of using If, Then, and Else as individual keywords, we can write a type family that takes three parameters and will handle branching for us. We'll call it IfThenElse:

```
type family IfThenElse (p :: Bool) (t :: a) (f :: a) :: a where
  IfThenElse True t _ = t
  IfThenElse False _ f = f
```

This type family will take a predicate value, and values for each branch. If the predicate is true, we return the true branch, and otherwise we will return the false branch. Let's refactor FindElems to use this new type family:

```
type family FindElems (p :: a -> Bool) (elems :: [a]) :: [a] where
  FindElems _ '[] = '[]
  FindElems p (a:as) =
    IfThenElse (p a) (a : FindElems p as) (FindElems p as)
```

Now that we've dealt with branching, we need to revisit the fact that FindElems needs to take a function. We can't pass a type family in, because we're not allowed to use type families that haven't had all of their arguments applied, but type families aren't the only way we can represent something like (a -> Bool) at the type level. Type constructors take arguments, and we are allowed to pass those into a type family without having applied all of their arguments. We need to figure out a way to represent a type level *function* as data.

Thankfully for us, there's a well-established technique for removing higher order functions and replacing them with data. It's called *defunctionalization*, and we can do it using things we've already learned about working with type families and data kinds.

The first step to defunctionalizing FindElems is to create a type constructor that will represent the computation we want to pass into FindElems. If we wanted to pass in a function that would select even numbers, we might start with something like this:

```
data Even (n :: Natural)
```

In this example we're creating a new type, Even. We don't need to define any constructors, since we'll only ever use this at the type level. You might have noticed the problem that we have here already, but if not, let's take a look at the kind of Even in ghci:

```
λ :kind Even
Even :: Natural -> Type
```

Even has the kind Type, but we originally wanted something that will return a type of kind Bool. Using defunctionalization means we're going to have to compromise on the exact kind of the value we pass into FindElems though. Any type that we create, once we've applied all of our arguments, will end up having the kind Type. That doesn't mean we can't capture the return type of the computation the data type represents though—we just need to add it as an extra parameter. Let's do another round of refactoring:

```
data Even (n :: Natural) (r :: Bool)
type family
  FindElems (p :: a -> Bool -> Type) (elems :: [a]) :: [a]
  where
  FindElems _ '[] = '[]
  FindElems p (a:as) =
    IfThenElse (p a) (a : FindElems p as) (FindElems p as)
```

Now if we look at the kind of Even in ghci we'll see that it matches up exactly with what we want to pass into FindElems:

```
λ> :kind Even
Even :: Natural -> Bool -> Type
```

Although our kinds line up, it's a little bit awkward to read. There are a couple of small quality of life refactors we can make so that our code will be easier to read. First, we can replace (Bool -> Type) with a type alias that will abstract away the implementation detail that our defunctionalized types have to have the kind Type. Second, we can use a kind signature rather than named parameters when we define Even so that it matches up with the argument to FindElems. Let's make one more refactoring pass:

```
type ReturnValue r = r -> Type
data Even :: Natural -> ReturnValue Bool
type family
  FindElems (p :: a -> ReturnValue Bool) (elems :: [a]) :: [a]
  where
  FindElems _ '[] = '[]
  FindElems p (a:as) =
    IfThenElse (p a) (a : FindElems p as) (FindElems p as)
```

We're getting closer to a working type family, but we've still got some work left to do. The most obvious problem we have right now is that we've created a new type that represents the function we want to pass in, but we haven't actually defined any sort of computation that we can do with it. In other words, we've turned our function into a type so that we can pass it into the type family, but now we need to turn it back into a function.

So, we have an input value that is a type with the kind a -> ReturnValue Bool and we need to get out a type with the kind Bool. We need a function from a type to a type, which means that we need *another type family*. Let's add a new type family called EvalEven that will perform the computation for the Even type that we're passing in:

```
{-# LANGUAGE UndecidableInstances #-}
{-# LANGUAGE TypeFamilies #-}
{-# LANGUAGE TypeOperators #-}
{-# LANGUAGE PolyKinds #-}
{-# LANGUAGE DataKinds #-}

module TypeFamilyListFuncs where
import GHC.TypeLits
import Data.Kind

type family IfThenElse (p :: Bool) (t :: a) (f :: a) :: a where
  IfThenElse True t _ = t
  IfThenElse False _ f = f

type ReturnValue r = r -> Type
data Even :: Natural -> ReturnValue Bool

type family
  FindElems (p :: a -> ReturnValue Bool) (elems :: [a]) :: [a]
  where
  FindElems _ '[] = '[]
  FindElems p (a:as) =
    IfThenElse (EvalEven (p a)) (a : FindElems p as) (FindElems p as)
```

```
type family EQ (a :: k) (b :: k) :: Bool where
  EQ a a = True
  EQ a b = False

type family EvalEven (expr :: Bool -> Type) :: Bool where
  EvalEven (Even n) = EQ 0 (n `Mod` 2)
```

In this example, we've added a closed type family to evaluate our Even type, and we've updated FindElems to call EvalEven to convert a ReturnValue Bool into a Bool. We also added a new helper type family, EQ, to help us test for equality between two types.

If we load this up into ghci you can see that it works as expected, and we're able to get all of the even numbers out of a type level list:

```
λ :kind! FindElems Even '[1,2,3,4,5,6]
FindElems Even '[1,2,3,4,5,6] :: [Natural]
= '[2, 4, 6]
```

There's still one lingering problem and one more refactor to make before we're ready to be finished with this application. Since EvalEven is a closed type family, we're limited to only ever using FindElems to find even numbers. If we want to give our users the ability to call FindElems with new functions we didn't anticipate ahead of time, then we should refactor EvalEven into an *open* type family. Since it'll be useful for computations other than testing for even values, we'll also rename it Even. While we're at it, let's also add a new type family we can use with FindElems to find elements that are less than, or equal to, some number:

```
type ReturnValue r = r -> Type
data LessThanOrEqual :: Natural -> Natural -> ReturnValue Bool
data Even :: Natural -> ReturnValue Bool

type family Eval (expr :: ReturnValue r) :: r
type instance Eval (LessThanOrEqual a b) = b <=? a
type instance Eval (Even n) = EQ 0 (n `Mod` 2)

type family
  FindElems (p :: a -> ReturnValue Bool) (elems :: [a]) :: [a]
  where
  FindElems _ '[] = '[]
  FindElems p (a:as) =
    IfThenElse (Eval (p a)) (a : FindElems p as) (FindElems p as)
```

By combining an open type family like Eval with a closed type family like FindElems, we can get the right kind of flexiblity and power that we need for more complicated type level computations. Let's give this a try in ghci:

```
λ :kind! FindElems Even '[1,2,3,4,5,6]
FindElems Even '[1,2,3,4,5,6] :: [Natural]
= '[2, 4, 6]
```

```
λ :kind! FindElems (LessThanOrEqual 3) '[1,2,3,4,5,6]
FindElems (LessThanOrEqual 3) '[1,2,3,4,5,6] :: [Natural]
= '[1, 2, 3]

λ :kind! FindElems Even (FindElems (LessThanOrEqual 3) '[1,2,3,4,5,6])
FindElems Even
  (FindElems (LessThanOrEqual 3) '[1,2,3,4,5,6]) :: [Natural]
= '[2]
```

Working with type families to build up computations that work at the type level is a critical part of writing type level code, but there are two more important parts to working with type level programming effectively. In the next section you'll learn about *GADTs*, which will let you build up type level data structures from the term level so that you can effectively generate inputs to your type level code. Finally, we'll look at how you can use type classes to return the outputs of your type level code back to the term level for use in the rest of your application.

GADTs: Functions from Terms to Types

GADTs are a new way to define data types that give us more flexibility in the ways we express our data types, and which remove some limitations in how we can define constructors that help us combine term and type level programming. They also give us a brand new syntax for defining data types. We can enable GADTs with the GADTs extension. In this section, we'll look at how to use GADTs to define some types you're already familiar with, and how they can be used to handle features like existential types more easily. After that, we'll look at how GADTs fit in with type level programming, and you'll see how to use GADTs to represent data types that couldn't be written with traditional types.

GADTs

The GADTs extension has been available since GHC 6.8.1. It isn't enabled by default in either GHC2021 or Haskell2010 so you'll need to enable it manually. This is generally a safe extension that shouldn't interfere with any existing code. If you want to use the basic syntax of GADTs without the new type system capabilities that they add, you can also use the GADTSyntax extension, which will only enable the new syntax. GADTSyntax is enabled by default in GHC2021 but will need to be enabled manually in Haskell2010.

Using GADT Syntax

Let's start learning about GADTs by rewriting a few types you'll already be familiar with using GADT syntax. We'll start with Maybe, Either, and a List type.

```
{-# LANGUAGE GADTs #-}
{-# LANGUAGE DataKinds #-}
{-# LANGUAGE StandaloneDeriving #-}
{-# LANGUAGE TypeOperators #-}
{-# LANGUAGE KindSignatures #-}

module GADTs where
import Prelude hiding (Either(..), Maybe(..))
import Data.Kind

data Maybe a where
  Nothing :: Maybe a
  Just :: a -> Maybe a
  deriving (Eq, Show)

data Either l r where
  Left :: l -> Either l r
  Right :: r -> Either l r

data List a where
  Empty :: List a
  Cons :: a -> List a -> List a
  deriving Show
```

You can see in this example that GADT syntax has a strong resemblance to the closed type family syntax worked with earlier in this chapter. With GADT syntax, the constructors for our type are all listed in a where clause, and each constructor is given a type annotation that represents the type of the constructor. If you want to go even further, we can also use a kind signature instead of a type parameter in the definition of the type:

```
data Maybe :: Type -> Type where
  Nothing :: Maybe a
  Just :: a -> Maybe a
  deriving (Eq, Show)
```

You'll notice in this example that we're referencing the type variable a in our constructors even though we didn't explicitly bind it to the parameter when we defined Maybe. That's because GADTs are much more flexible with the way we treat type variables.

GADT syntax makes working with existential types much more intuitive. For example, imagine that we wanted to define a heterogenous list of values that have a Show instance. With traditional data type syntax we'd write this:

```
data ShowList = ShowEmpty | forall a. Show a => ShowList a ShowList
```

Writing existential types with GADT syntax more closely resembles the way we'd use constraints with a normal function definition:

```
data ShowList where
  ShowEmpty :: ShowList
  ShowCons :: Show a => a -> ShowList -> ShowList
```

Even more conveniently, GADT syntax also allows us to use constraints with ordinary constructors, which saves us the need to create smart constructors if we want to restrict what values could be used with a particular type. For example, imagine we wanted to have an ordinary list that could only hold numeric values. We'd need to put our list in its own module, restrict the export list, and add a smart constructor. With GADT syntax we can simply add the constraints alongside each constructor. Unfortunately, using constraints like this means that we can't derive type class instances in the usual way, although we can still use StandaloneDeriving to derive instances for these types:

```
data NumList a where
  NumEmpty :: Num a => NumList a
  NumCons :: Num a => a -> NumList a -> NumList a

deriving instance Eq a => Eq (NumList a)
deriving instance Show a => Show (NumList a)
```

Although it's not very common, you can use records with GADT syntax:

```
data MultiRecord where
  Record1 ::
    { intField :: Int, stringField :: String } -> MultiRecord

  Record2 ::
    { intField :: Int, boolField :: Bool } -> MultiRecord

data SingleRecord a where
  SingleRecordGADT ::
    { gadtStringField :: String
    , gadtIntField :: Int
    , gadtBoolField :: Bool
    , gadtCustomField :: a
    } -> SingleRecord a
```

Like traditional data types, record fields with the same name must have the same type across different constructors. You're also not obligated to provide the same set of fields for records across each constructor. Using GADT syntax for traditional sum types with record fields can lead to the same problem of record field selectors that are partial functions. If we make use of the full features of GADTs however, we can get record field selectors that are type safe and won't fail. In the next section you'll learn more about how GADTs work and how they are different for regular data types, even ones defined using GADT syntax, and you'll get a chance to see this in action.

GADTs

The key difference between GADTs and regular data types is that the *type* of a GADT value can be determined by the constructor that was called to create it. This is the fundamental connection between GADTs and type level programming. Since the type of a GADT value is determined by the term level function called to create it, GADTs give us a way to connect term and type level code by letting us construct the inputs to a type level program from the term level.

Before we get too far down the path of using GADTs for sophisticated type level code though, let's look at some smaller examples to get a feel for how GADTs work. One of the best examples is the way that we can use records fields with GADTs more safely than we could with normal sum types. Imagine that we were writing a program that could recognize a user by their name or a user ID, and we wanted to get a list of all users that were identified by name and had a particular first name. Without GADTs we might write it like this:

```
data UserNameRecord =
  UserNameRecord { userFirstName :: String, userLastName :: String }
data UserIDRecord = UserIDRecord { userID :: Int }
data User = UserByName UserNameRecord | UserByID UserIDRecord

usersWithFirstName :: String -> [User] -> [User]
usersWithFirstName targetFirstName = filter matchingFirstName
  where
    matchingFirstName nameRecord =
      case nameRecord of
        UserByName (UserNameRecord first last)
          | first == targetFirstName -> True
        _otherwise -> False
```

This example should look familiar; we've used this pattern several times in the book. We first define two helper records that hold information about users with names and users with IDs, respectively, and then we create a sum type where each constructor holds one type of user record. This adds some extra code, but it helps us avoid partial functions by avoiding having record fields directly in a sum type. When we want to search our list of user records, we might know that all of our users will be identified by name, but we still need to go through the steps to pattern match against User and then unwrap the inner UserNameRecord constructor to get at the name. Overall, we're getting a type safe program, but paying a fairly high cost for it.

With GADTs we can encode the constructor that was used to create a UserRecord directly in the type that each constructor returns. Let's take a look at how it works:

```
data User a where
  UserByName ::
    { userFirst :: String, userLast :: String } -> User String
  UserByID ::
    { userID :: Int } -> User Int
```

Now that we're using a GADT, we've added a type parameter to User. Unlike the earlier examples of GADT syntax though, we're not using this type parameter to represent some field in our records. Instead, each of our constructors is selecting a different value for our parameter, a. Let's look at this in ghci to get a better understanding of what's going on.

We'll start by looking at the types of UserByName and UserByID:

```
λ :t UserByName
UserByName :: String -> String -> User [Char]
λ :t UserByID
UserByID :: Int -> User Int
```

As you can see, each of our constructors returns a value with a different type. If we create a value by calling UserByID we will always get a value with the type User Int. Similarly, calling UserByName will always give us a value with the type User String. One of the ways that this is useful is that the compiler can reason about this relationship backwards as well as forwards. If we have a value with the type User String then we know that *it must have been created by calling UserByName*. We can see this in practice if we look at the types of our field selectors:

```
λ :t userFirst
userFirst :: User String -> String
λ :t userLast
userLast :: User String -> String
λ :t userID
userID :: User Int -> Int
```

Being able to deduce the constructor, and available record fields, from the type of the user means that we can greatly simplify our filter code:

```
usersWithFirstName :: String -> [User String] -> [User String]
usersWithFirstName firstName = filter ((== firstName) . userFirst)
```

Although it's useful to be able to differentiate between different types of users at the type level, this also ends up presenting us with a different problem. Since constructing a user by name and by ID results in a different type, we also can't create a list of name and ID users.

A Heterogenous User List

Earlier in this book you learned about using existential types as a way of creating heterogenous lists, but that approach came with a substantial cost: once a value was inserted into a list of existential typed values, we could never recover the original type and were limited to accessing the values through type classes.

It turns out that GADTs can give us another option for working with heterogenous lists that don't limit us in the same way that existential-based lists do, although it comes at the cost of needing to do some type level programming.

Let's start by taking a look at how we can use GADTs to define a heterogenous user list:

```
{-# LANGUAGE DataKinds #-}

infixr 9 :++:
data Heterogenous a where
  EmptyUsers :: Heterogenous '[]
  (:++:) :: User a -> Heterogenous as -> Heterogenous (a : as)
```

Unlike existential-based heterogenous lists, our GADT approach uses a straightforward, if somewhat brute force, approach to retaining the detailed type information for every element in the list. Our list has a type parameter that is itself a list of the type of every element that has been inserted into the list. Each time we add a new value, we also add its type to the type of the list. Let's load up ghci and take a look to get an idea of what this means in practice:

```
λ byName = UserByName "Georgie" "Bird"
λ byID = UserByID 12345
λ :type EmptyUsers
EmptyUsers :: Heterogenous '[]

λ :type byName :++: EmptyUsers
byName :++: EmptyUsers :: Heterogenous '[[Char]]

λ :type byID :++: byID :++: byName :++: EmptyUsers
byID :++: byID :++: byName :++: EmptyUsers
  :: Heterogenous '[Int, Int, [Char]]
```

As you can see, each time we add a new user type to the list, the type of the list changes to keep track of the new information. That means the information is always entirely recoverable.

Extracting Fields from a Heterogenous List

If we have all of the type information for each element that we've inserted into our user list, then we ought to be able to use that to recover specific fields.

Let's imagine that we wanted to extract a list of the users who are identified by name from a heterogenous list of users. How might we approach that? Once again GADTs help make this easy. Let's look at the code:

```
nameUsers :: Heterogenous a -> [User String]
nameUsers EmptyUsers = []
nameUsers (user :++: users) =
  case user of
    UserByName _ _ -> user : nameUsers users
    UserByID _ -> nameUsers users
```

Since the type of Heterogenous a carries all of the type information that we need, we're able to pattern match on each element of the list. The constructor used to create each element also tells us the type of that element, and so we can select all of the values with the type User String.

A GADT-Based Shell Command Wrapper

Being able to determine the type of a value by the constructor used to create it is a powerful technique, but our user example only scratches the surface. Let's return to our ShellCommand example and look at how GADTs can allow us to write an easier to use and more expressive language for writing shell scripts.

Earlier in this chapter, you wrote a small library to help a user write shell scripts in their Haskell applications. In that example, we used a type class called ShellCommand, along with an associated type family to describe a particular command.

This approach had the benefit of extensibility, and we were able to define several different operations that we could run. We could even compose our operations together by defining a Pipe and creating a ShellCommand instance for it. The type class approach also had some drawbacks. The biggest drawback is that each shell command was its own type. Composing commands required creating a new type, and there was nothing to limit a users ability to create an invalid or poorly behaved instance of ShellCommand.

GADTs allow us to implement ShellCommand as a small internal library that gives us many of the same benefits of the type class approach. Let's look at a complete reimplementation of our earlier DSL using GADTs, and then walk through how it works step by step.

```
{-# LANGUAGE TypeFamilies #-}
{-# LANGUAGE GADTs #-}
module GADTShellCmd where
import System.FilePath.Posix ((</>))
import System.Process (readProcess)
import System.IO.Error
```

```
newtype ProgName = ProgName { getProgName :: FilePath }
newtype ProgArgs = ProgArgs { getProgArgs :: [String] }

data ShellCmd a b where
  RunCommand ::
    ProgName -> (a -> ProgArgs) -> (a -> String -> b) -> ShellCmd a b
  Pipe :: ShellCmd a b -> ShellCmd b c -> ShellCmd a c
  XArgs :: ShellCmd a b -> ShellCmd [a] [b]
  MapOut :: (b -> c) -> ShellCmd b c

data GrepMatch = GrepMatch
  { grepMatchingFileName :: FilePath
  , grepMatchingLineNumber :: Int
  , grepMatchingLineContents :: String
  } deriving (Eq, Show)

grep :: String -> ShellCmd FilePath [GrepMatch]
grep matchGlob =
  RunCommand (ProgName "grep") makeArgs parseLines
  where
    makeArgs fileName = ProgArgs $ "-n" : matchGlob : [fileName]
    parseLines fileName = map (parseResponse fileName) . lines
    parseResponse fileName responseLine =
      let (matchNumber, contents) = span (/= ':') responseLine
      in GrepMatch fileName (read matchNumber) contents

listDirectory :: ShellCmd FilePath [FilePath]
listDirectory =
  RunCommand (ProgName "ls") makeArgs parseResponse
  where
    makeArgs filePath = ProgArgs ["-1", filePath]
    parseResponse filePath =
      map (filePath </>) . lines

runShellCmd :: ShellCmd a b -> a -> IO b
runShellCmd cmd input =
  case cmd of
    RunCommand (ProgName exeName) mkArgs parseOut ->
      parseOut input <$> catchIOError processOut (const $ pure "")
      where
        processOut = readProcess exeName (getProgArgs $ mkArgs input) ""
    Pipe inputCmd out -> runShellCmd inputCmd input >>= runShellCmd out
    XArgs inputCmd -> mapM (runShellCmd inputCmd) input
    MapOut mapF -> pure $ mapF input
```

You can start to see the benefits of GADTs more clearly in this example if we look at the way that letting each constructor determine the type of the output allows us to build a DSL that ensures we're composing individual parts of our shell command in a type safe way. For example, the Pipe constructor allows us to create a pipe from two ShellCmd values, but only if the output of the first command matches the input of the second. The result of the Pipe constructor is a new ShellCmd that takes the input needed for the first sub-command, and returns the output of the second sub-command. This is an improvement over our earlier pipe implementation because it allows us to more directly compose individual commands, rather than needing to create an explicit function to map the results of the first command to the second.

The next major difference between our GADT-based approach and our earlier type class approach is that we've added two new constructors, XArgs and MapOut. The XArgs constructor allows us to take a shell command that would run on a single argument, and instead run it on a list of inputs. This is an example of a feature that would have been much harder to implement with our type class based approach. Were we using type classes, we would have needed to add an extra associated type family to handle the different input types of each command, and then we would need to add that type family to each instance we'd defined.

The next constructor, MapOut, is another example of a feature that is much easier for us to add thanks to our use of GADTs. This constructor lets us lift a pure function and treat it as a ShellCmd. This wouldn't have fit well with the runCmd function we defined in our ShellCommand class, since it relies on a polymorphic input type that, like XArgs, would have required an extra type family be added to the class. Worse, MapOut can't provide any useful command name or arguments, and so our application may have encountered a runtime error when it tried to execute an empty command.

Once our ShellCmd GADT is defined, you'll notice that the definitions of grep and listDirectory are largely unchanged. We have a very similar level of expressive power for defining individual commands, while gaining a great deal of composability thanks to our GADT-based types.

The last major difference in this example is the definition of runShellCmd. Instead of calling the runCmd function from a type class, we're pattern matching on each constructor. Take particular note of the way we handle XArgs in this function:

```
runShellCmd :: ShellCmd a b -> a -> IO b
runShellCmd cmd input =
  -- ...
    XArgs inputCmd -> mapM (runShellCmd inputCmd) input
```

What's interesting about this case is that we're calling mapM over input even though the type of runShellCmd doesn't specify that input must be a list. Thanks to GADTs though, we know that XArgs will always result in a ShellCmd that accepts a list and returns a list, so any time we match on the XArgs case we can guarantee that in that particular case, input will be a list.

Type Classes: Functions from Types to Terms

GADTs give us the ability to build up types alongside the values at the term level. In a sense, each GADT constructor is a function from its term level arguments to the type that the constructor returns. Type classes let us go the other direction, taking the type level information that we've built up with GADTs and generating new term level values. In this section, we'll look at how you can use type classes alongside GADTs to get better type safety between different parts of your application.

We'll start by continuing with the ShellCmd type that you built in the last section. Let's imagine that we want to build an application that will let us create a set of pre-defined shell scripts that we've validated and know to be good. We'd like to let our users write safer shell scripts by combining any number of these commands and returning the output of each of them.

The first thing we'll need is a way to define a collection of shell commands. Since each of our shell commands might have different inputs and outputs, our collection of scripts will need to be heterogenous. We'd still like to know what the type of any particular script is, so let's create a new module and use a GADT to define a heterogenous collection of shell script commands. We'll add quite a few extensions in this example, including a new one: ConstraintKinds. You'll learn more about this extension later in the example when we make use of it.

ConstraintKinds

The ConstraintKinds extension has been available since GHC 7.4.1. It's enabled by default in GHC2021 but you'll need to enable it explicitly in Haskell2010. This is a safe extension that shouldn't cause problems with any existing code. You can enable it project wide in your cabal file if you like.

```
{-# LANGUAGE UndecidableInstances #-}
{-# LANGUAGE GADTs #-}
{-# LANGUAGE TypeFamilies #-}
{-# LANGUAGE DataKinds #-}
{-# LANGUAGE AllowAmbiguousTypes #-}
{-# LANGUAGE FunctionalDependencies #-}
{-# LANGUAGE TypeApplications #-}
{-# LANGUAGE RankNTypes #-}
{-# LANGUAGE TypeOperators #-}
{-# LANGUAGE ScopedTypeVariables #-}
```

```
{-# LANGUAGE ConstraintKinds #-}
{-# LANGUAGE FlexibleInstances #-}

module CommandRunner where
import Data.Kind
import GHC.TypeLits
import Data.Proxy
import GADTShellCmd

data CommandSet :: [Symbol] -> [Type] -> Type where
  EmptyCommandSet :: CommandSet '[] '[]
  AddCommand ::
    KnownSymbol name =>
    ShellCmd a b ->
    CommandSet names commands ->
    CommandSet (name:names) (ShellCmd a b : commands)
```

You'll notice in this example that we're using our GADT to track two separate lists. The first list is a list of the human-readable names that we're giving to each of our scripts. When our users want to execute a particular script, they can refer to it by the symbol name we're keeping track of here. The second list is the list of actual shell command types. As in our earlier GADT-based heterogenous list example, this list of types will allow us to get the exact shell command type later, so that we'll know which input and output types to expect for a particular script.

Next, let's create a set of commands that we might want to allow a user to run. This example will use a few hardcoded shell commands, but you can re-use some of the commands you built earlier in this chapter, or pick other commands that work well on your system:

```
commands =
  AddCommand @"ls" listDirectory $
  addLiteral @"free" "free -h" $
  addLiteral @"uptime" "uptime" $
  addLiteral @"uname" "uname -a" $
  addLiteral @"system info" "neofetch" EmptyCommandSet
  where
    addLiteral ::
      forall name {names} {commands}. KnownSymbol name =>
      String ->
      CommandSet names commands ->
      CommandSet (name : names) (ShellCmd () String : commands)
    addLiteral command = AddCommand (literal command)
    literal :: String -> ShellCmd () String
    literal shellCommand =
      RunCommand (ProgName "bash") args outputFunc
      where
        args = const $ ProgArgs ["-c", shellCommand]
        outputFunc = const id
```

You might notice in this example that we haven't added a type annotation. One of the advantages of the style of type level programming we're building out in this section is that it allows us to use type inference to produce lists of commands, and to consume them. Although it's a good practice to add the type annotations when you're finished with development, it's incredibly convenient to be able to allow the compiler to infer the types during the development process when working with type level code like this, since the types tend to get quite verbose. For example, the type of commands if we were to add it would be:

```
commands
  :: CommandSet
       '["ls", "free", "uptime", "uname", "system info"]
       '[ShellCmd FilePath [FilePath], ShellCmd () String,
         ShellCmd () String, ShellCmd () String, ShellCmd () String]
```

Now that we have a way to create a list of commands, we'd like to have a way to run them. Ideally we should be able to look up a command by name, and then run the command by passing it a value of its input type and get whatever type of value that particular command returns. Let's call this function runNamedCommand. How should we write runNamedCommand? Earlier in this chapter on page 598, when we defined a heterogenous list of user types using a GADT, we were able to take advantage of our value constructors to figure out the type of a particular element and return a list of all users identified by name. Now, things are a bit more complicated.

Our earlier nameUsers only took a single argument, the list we wanted to traverse, and it always returned a value of type [User String]. In runNamedCommand we'll need to take a type level parameter with the name of the command we want to run, and a term level parameter whose type will be determined by which command we end up finding. The return type of runNamedCommand will also depend on the particular shell command that we end up extracting from the list. That means the behavior, as well as the input and return types of our function, will depend on the type level name we pass in, plus the type of the command list. When the behavior of a function depends on the types the function was called at, that's our hint that we should start thinking about type classes.

If we make runNamedCommand itself a type class, we'll be limited to only executing the commands directly. Rather than limiting ourselves, let's approach this in two parts. First, we'll add a new type class called CommandByName that will allow us to find a particular command in a CommandSet given the name of a command. Once we have the type class defined, we can use it to write runNamedCommand that will let us execute a command. This will give us the flexibility in the future to do other things, like pipe different commands together, or pretty print a shell script rather than executing the commands.

Let's start by defining CommandByName:

```
class CommandByName
  (name :: Symbol) commands shellIn shellOut |
    commands name -> shellIn shellOut
  where
  lookupProcessByName ::
    proxy name ->
    commands ->
    ShellCmd shellIn shellOut
```

The first thing you'll notice in this example is that we're using a *lot* of type class parameters. You'll also notice that we've brought back the FunctionalDependencies extension, so that we can add a dependency between the command name and set of commands, and the input and output types of the particular command we're retrieving. You might be wondering why we're using functional dependencies instead of an associated type family. There are two important reasons to avoid an associated type family in this example. First, using functional dependencies will simplify type inference and help prevent our type annotations from growing out of control. Type families typically require more verbose type annotations since they need to be applied explicitly, whereas functional dependencies can be inferred. Second, the overlap rules for associated type families can introduce significant challenges when we're trying to carry out computations during type class resolution. Functional dependencies allow us to have types that are dependent on arguments to our type class without having to worry about overlap rules.

Now that we've defined a type class, let's create an instance. We'll start with the easiest case, when the first element of our list of commands matches the command name we're looking for:

```
instance
  CommandByName name (CommandSet (name:names) (ShellCmd a b : types)) a b
  where
  lookupProcessByName _ (AddCommand cmd _) = cmd
```

Although our definition of lookupProcessByName is straightforward, there are a few notable things to take away from this type class instance. First, you'll notice that we're pattern matching on the CommandSet that we're passing in so that we can extract both the current name and shell command. Second, you can see that type classes, like type families, allow us to use the same name to ensure that some types are equal. In this example, we are using name as both the first argument of our type class, and also the head of the list of names in our command set. Similarly, we are pattern matching out the input and output types of our shell command, a and b, and using those as the input and output types for the class instance.

Before we move on, let's take a moment to try out what we have so far in ghci. If we try to run the first command, which is a listDirectory command, and pass in a path, you'll see that everything works exactly as we'd hope:

```
λ runShellCmd (lookupProcessByName (Proxy @"ls") commands) "./"
["./app","./CHANGELOG.md","./dist-newstyle","./src","./examples.cabal"]
```

Similarly, if we try to pass in a command that isn't in our allowed list of commands we'll get an error:

```
λ runShellCmd (lookupProcessByName (Proxy @"erase files") commands) "/"

<interactive>:4:14: error:
  • No instance for (
      CommandByName
        "erase files"
        (CommandSet
           '["ls", "free", "uptime", "uname", "system info"]
           '[ShellCmd FilePath [FilePath], ShellCmd () String,
             ShellCmd () String, ShellCmd () String, ShellCmd () String])
        String
        b0)
      arising from a use of ‘lookupProcessByName’
  • In the first argument of ‘runShellCmd’, namely
      ‘(lookupProcessByName (Proxy @"erase files") commands)’
    In the expression:
      runShellCmd
        (lookupProcessByName (Proxy @"erase files") commands) "/"
    In an equation for ‘it’:
        it
          = runShellCmd
              (lookupProcessByName (Proxy @"erase files") commands) "/"
```

This error is a bit verbose and we'll generate better error messages later on in this section, but we're still successfully using the type system to prevent our user from erasing files.

Unfortunately, if we try to run one of the other commands that we've allowed, like "free" or "system info" you'll get the same error. Our type class is only defined for the case where the command we're looking for is at the head of the list of commands we're checking.

Type class instances, like type families, can be defined recursively. We can use this, along with pattern matching, to implement computations at the type level by traversing data structures like our CommandSet. Let's add a new instance to handle the case where the command we're looking for is in the set of all allowed commands, but it isn't the one at the head of the list:

```
instance CommandByName name (CommandSet names types) a b =>
  CommandByName name (CommandSet (otherName:names) (cmd : types)) a b
  where
  lookupProcessByName nameProxy (AddCommand _ rest) =
    lookupProcessByName nameProxy rest
```

In this example, we're handling the case where the tail of our list of commands has an instance of CommandByName. In that case, we're recursively calling lookupProcessByName with the tail of our list. If a command with a given name exists, it will eventually be at the head of the list as we traverse the list, and that will be the base case of our recursion. The recursive case lets us step through each element of the list, checking the head against the name we're searching for. Unfortunately, we've got a problem. Although our base case instance requires that the name we pass in match the name at the head of the command list, this instance doesn't prohibit the two values from being the same. Once again, we find ourselves dealing with unintended overlap causing a problem. If you load this code up into ghci and try to call lookupProcessByName you can see for yourself that the compiler can't decide which instance to use and will generate an error.

Thankfully, now that we know about type families, we have a way we can work around the overlap and implement our type classes without any overlap. To do that, we need a way to differentiate between cases where the command we're looking for is at the head of the list from the cases where it isn't, and we want it to be unambiguous and without overlap. We'll start by writing a type family to help with this:

```
type family
  HeadMatches (name :: Symbol) (names :: [Symbol]) :: Bool
  where
  HeadMatches name (name:_) = True
  HeadMatches name _ = False
```

This type family will let us check a list of command names to see if the first name is what we're looking for. If it is, the type family will return True and we can proceed with using the first command in our command list. If the type family returns False then we'll know we should proceed with our recursive case. If we want to use this to prevent overlap in our type class instances, we'll need to make it a parameter of the type class. Let's refactor our type class definition and our base case instance to handle this extra parameter:

```
class CommandByName'
  (matches :: Bool) (name :: Symbol) commands shellIn shellOut |
  name commands -> shellIn shellOut
  where
  lookupProcessByName' ::
    proxy1 matches ->
    proxy2 name ->
    commands ->
    ShellCmd shellIn shellOut

instance
  CommandByName'
    True name (CommandSet (name:names) (ShellCmd a b : types)) a b
  where
  lookupProcessByName' _ _ (AddCommand cmd _) = cmd
```

In our refactored class and instance we've added a new parameter, matches, that will tell us if the head of our command list matches the name we're looking for. We've also added an extra proxy argument to pass around this information. You might notice that we've also renamed CommandByName to CommandByName'. Later, as we finish up this example, we'll make CommandByName a helper type class that lets us hide implementation details of our matches argument. Like before, we can load this up into ghci and check to see that it's all working as expected:

```
λ proxyTrue = Proxy @True
λ proxyLs = Proxy @"ls"
λ runShellCmd (lookupProcessByName' proxyTrue proxyLs commands) "./"
["./app","./CHANGELOG.md","./dist-newstyle","./src","./examples.cabal"]
```

Now let's make another attempt at defining our recursive instance, this time using our new boolean parameter to help avoid an ambiguous instance:

```
instance
  (CommandByName'
     (HeadMatches name names)
     name
     (CommandSet names types)
     shellIn
     shellOut
  ) => CommandByName' False name
        (CommandSet (badName : names) (t : types)) shellIn shellOut
  where
  lookupProcessByName' _ nameProxy (AddCommand _ rest) =
    let matchProxy = Proxy @(HeadMatches name names)
    in lookupProcessByName' matchProxy nameProxy rest
```

Just like with our earlier attempt, this instance needs a constraint on the tail of our list to make sure that it contains the name we're looking for. The addition of our new matching parameter adds a bit of difficulty though. There are two possible instances that might be defined for the tail of our list. If the next command in our list is the command that we're looking for, then we need to recursively call the base case. That means we need to pass a proxy True value into lookupProcessByName, and we need to tell the compiler that an instance of our class has to be defined where the match parameter is True. On the other hand, if the next command isn't a match, we need to have an instance defined where the match is False, and we need to pass a proxy False value in our recursive call. In short, if our current command isn't a match, we need to match and make the appropriate recursive call depending on whether the *next* command matches or not.

We're getting this information about which instance to call by using our HeadMatches type family. It works, but it's still quite verbose and it makes our instance hard to read. One way we can make this a little bit easier is to use an *equality constraint*. An equality constraint is a constraint that two type variables must be equal. They can be used as you'd expect, to compare test whether the types for two type variables are equal, but we can also use them as a way of assigning a name to a longer part of a type level expression inside of a constraint. The syntax for an equality constraint is:

```
a ~ b
```

Let's refactor our instance to use an equality constraint so that we can say nextMatches instead of having to repeat our call to HeadMatches:

```
instance
  ( nextMatches ~ HeadMatches name names
  , CommandByName'
      nextMatches name (CommandSet names types) shellIn shellOut
  ) => CommandByName' False name
       (CommandSet (badName : names) (t : types)) shellIn shellOut
  where
  lookupProcessByName' _ nameProxy (AddCommand _ rest) =
    lookupProcessByName' (Proxy @nextMatches) nameProxy rest
```

With our equality constraint, we can refer to nextMatches both inside of our CommandByName' constraint on the tail of our command list, as well as inside of our definition of lookupProcessByName' when we create our proxy value. It only helps a bit, but every little bit helps when we are dealing with the very long constraints and type annotations that come up with type level programming.

Before we move on, let's load up ghci again and test our new instance to see if it works:

```
λ proxyTrue = Proxy @True
λ proxyFalse = Proxy @False
λ proxyLs = Proxy @"ls"
λ proxyFree = Proxy @"free"
λ runShellCmd (lookupProcessByName' proxyTrue proxyLs commands) "./"
["./app","./CHANGELOG.md","./dist-newstyle","./src","./examples.cabal"]

λ runShellCmd (lookupProcessByName' proxyFalse proxyFree commands) ()
  >>= putStrLn
       total    used   free  shared  buff/cache   available
Mem:     31Gi   9.4Gi  1.3Gi   3.3Gi        20Gi        17Gi
Swap:    15Gi   184Mi   15Gi
```

Success! We're now able to call any of the commands in our command list, and get the correct input and output types for them. Now that we've shown that it works, let's clean up the ergonomics and make it nicer to use.

The first major ergonomic problem is that we are requiring that the user know whether a particular command is at the front of the list of commands or not. We can handle this for them automatically by adding a helper type class that will call HeadMatches and pass the information along:

```
class CommandByName (name :: Symbol) commands shellIn shellOut |
  commands name -> shellIn shellOut
  where
  lookupProcessByName ::
    proxy name -> commands -> ShellCmd shellIn shellOut

instance
  (matches ~ HeadMatches name names
  , CommandByName' matches name (CommandSet names types) shellIn shellOut
  ) => CommandByName name (CommandSet names types) shellIn shellOut
  where
  lookupProcessByName _ =
    lookupProcessByName' (Proxy @matches) (Proxy @name)
```

As you can see, our new class only needs a single instance. This instance doesn't do much work on its own, but it will call HeadMatches for us and pass that along, so that we don't have to look ourselves to decide which of the CommandByName' instances we should call. Let's try it out:

```
λ runShellCmd (lookupProcessByName (Proxy @"uptime") commands) ()
  >>= putStrLn
 01:48:58  up 17 days  2:37,  1 user,  load average: 0.19, 0.24, 0.25

λ runShellCmd (lookupProcessByName (Proxy @"delete") commands) "/"
<interactive>:10:14: error:
  • No instance for (
      CommandByName'
        'False "delete" (CommandSet '[] '[]) [Char] b0)
      arising from a use of ‘lookupProcessByName’
```

```
• In the first argument of 'runShellCmd', namely
    '(lookupProcessByName (Proxy @"delete") commands)'
  In the expression:
    runShellCmd
      (lookupProcessByName (Proxy @"delete") commands) "/"
  In an equation for 'it':
    it
      = runShellCmd
          (lookupProcessByName (Proxy @"delete") commands) "/"
```

It works! Our error messages are still not very readable though. Thankfully we can use TypeError with type classes to generate useful error messages, just like we did with type families. However, we can't just add a type error directly inline in our instance. We'll need to write a type family that will generate an error only if the name we're looking for isn't in the list of available commands. Let's start by defining the type family that will generate our error:

```
type family HasMatch'
  (needle :: Symbol) (haystack :: [Symbol]) (ctx :: [Symbol]) :: Constraint
  where
  HasMatch' a '[] ctx = TypeError
    (Text "Missing required command '" :<>:
     Text a :<>:
     Text "' in command list: " :<>:
     ShowType ctx)
  HasMatch' a (a:as) ctx = ()
  HasMatch' a (b:as) ctx = HasMatch' a as ctx

type HasMatch a as = HasMatch' a as as
```

Here we're creating a type family named HasMatch' with three parameters: the symbol we're looking for, a list of symbols we're searching through recursively, and a copy of the original input so that we can generate a more readable error message. We've also created a helper, HasMatch, so that we can have our full list without always needing to pass it in twice.

You'll also notice that the return type of this type family is something we haven't seen before. The Constraint kind is the kind used to represent type class constraints. In earlier versions of GHC you'll need to use the ConstraintKinds extension to enable this. A Constraint can be any single constraint, like Show or Eq, or it can be a tuple of any number of constraints. This means you can programmatically build up constraints with type families. For our example, we're taking advantage of the fact that () is a valid empty constraint, so we can return it if there is a valid match for the command in our list. If there isn't a match, we're generating a TypeError. Thankfully, TypeError is polymorphic, so we can use it in place of a Constraint or any other kind.

Using our error handling is just like using any other constraint. We can add it into our instance definition alongside the other constraints:

```
instance
  (matches ~ HeadMatches name names
  , HasMatch name names
  , CommandByName' matches name (CommandSet names types) shellIn shellOut
  ) => CommandByName name (CommandSet names types) shellIn shellOut
  where
  lookupProcessByName _ =
    lookupProcessByName' (Proxy @matches) (Proxy @name)
```

Now if we try to run a command that hasn't been defined, we'll get a much more readable error:

```
λ runShellCmd (lookupProcessByName (Proxy @"delete") commands) "/"
<interactive>:183:14-32: error:
  • Missing required command 'delete' in command list:
      '["ls", "free", "uptime", "uname", "system info"]
  • In the first argument of ‘runShellCmd’, namely
      ‘(lookupProcessByName (Proxy @"delete") commands)’
    In the expression:
      runShellCmd
        (lookupProcessByName (Proxy @"delete") commands) "/"
    In an equation for ‘it’:
        it
          = runShellCmd
            (lookupProcessByName (Proxy @"delete") commands) "/"
```

Finally, now that we have a CommandByName class and the instances we need to get a particular command, we can get back to writing runNamedCommand. Most of the work for this function will be handled by our type class instances, but there's one extra level of safety we can add if we're using GHC 9.2 or later. Let's look at the definition:

```
runNamedCommand ::
  forall name {commands} {shellIn} {shellOut}.
  ( KnownSymbol name
  , CommandByName name commands shellIn shellOut
  ) => commands -> shellIn -> IO shellOut
runNamedCommand allowedCommands input =
  let process = lookupProcessByName (Proxy @name) allowedCommands
  in runShellCmd process input
```

As you can see, most of the work in this function is done in the call to lookupProcessByName. The type class instance will tell us what the input and output types of our shell command are, and that's defined by the set of commands that we're passing in. To help keep this safe and working as expected, we're using inferred types on page 234 for commands, shellIn, and shellOut. This means the user can't try to work around the type checking that we've added and instead must let the compiler infer these values by working through the type level programming that we've implemented through our CommandByName instance definitions. This is an optional layer of safety, and you can omit the inferred type annotation if you are using an older version of GHC.

Let's load this up into ghci and look at runNamedCommand in action:

```
λ runNamedCommand @"free" commands () >>= putStrLn
         total     used     free   shared  buff/cache   available
Mem:      31Gi    6.8Gi    3.9Gi    3.3Gi        20Gi        20Gi
Swap:     15Gi    184Mi     15Gi

λ runNamedCommand @"ls" commands "./" >>= mapM_ putStrLn
./app
./CHANGELOG.md
./dist-newstyle
./src
./TAGS
./examples.cabal
```

So, what can we do with all of this type level machinery? Outside of ghci this will allow our users to write their own code to make use of the shell scripts that we're telling them that they can use. For example:

```
runScript availableProcesses = do
  runNamedCommand @"ls" availableProcesses "." >>= mapM_ putStrLn
  runNamedCommand @"free" availableProcesses () >>= putStr
  runNamedCommand @"uname" availableProcesses () >>= putStr
```

Thanks to type inference, our users can write scripts like this and the compiler will be flexible, generating type signatures that require the minimum number of commands necessary to fulfill what we're using in our particular script, while permissively allowing as many extra commands as we'd like. This lets us make highly flexible but still type safe APIs available to us, and our users.

Summary

Congratulations! You've made it to the end of this chapter, and the end of *Effective Haskell*. You've learned how to write fast, flexible, type safe code, how to design applications that are easy to refactor, and how to use many of the techniques used in the wild in real Haskell applications. There are many interesting, useful, and sometimes mind boggling clever things to learn in the world of Haskell, but you should close this book knowing that you have all of the tools you need to work with Haskell effectively.

As you move to the exercises at the end of the chapter, and in particular the final capstone exercise, try to take a moment to think through everything that you've learned in this book. Compare the approaches you might have taken early on in the book with the ones you can use now. Think about how many different ways you now have to approach problem solving, with varying degrees of type safety, performance, and maintainability.

Exercises

A Complete Data-Family-Based ShellCommand

Continue with the example code from this chapter and refactor the `ShellCommand` module to use data families. Try to add a few more commands that wrap some of your favorite command line tools.

Better If Expressions

Earlier in the chapter you implemented conditionals inside of type families using `IfThenElse`. Instead of making this a single type family, try to use a mixture of GADTs and type families to explore other ways to encode conditionals that give you more flexibility, or more closely resemble term level conditionals.

Type Level map

Write a type family named `Map` that works like the term level `map` function. It should allow you to apply a function to each element of a type level list. Next, add a new type or type family so that you can add a number to each element of a type level list of naturals, as in this example:

```
λ :kind! Map (Add 5) [0,1,2,3,4]
Map (Add 5) [0,1,2,3,4] :: [Natural]
= '[5, 6, 7, 8, 9]
```

Expanded Shell Commands

Expand the GADT-based shell command DSL to support a new operation, `wc`, that will call the `wc` program to count the number of lines in a file. After you've added that, write a function with the type:

```
countLinesInMatchingFiles :: String -> ShellCmd FilePath [(FilePath, Int)]
```

The function should take a glob that can be passed to `grep`, and it should return a shell command that, given a path to a directory full of files, will output the name of each file that matched with `grep`, along with the number of lines in that file. Be sure to only return one output for each file, even if there are multiple matches within the file.

Classless runScript

Using what you've learned in this chapter, experiment with other ways of defining `CommandSet` and `runScript` so that you don't need to use type classes. What are the trade-offs you need to make?

Capstone Project: Build a Terminal Multiplexer

A terminal multiplexer is an application that lets you run different terminal applications simultaneously. The multiplexer typically gives you tools to switch between different "screens" displaying the output of different applications. They may also allow you to configure a set of applications to open automatically at startup. `screen` and `tmux` are two popular terminal multiplexers that you can look at for inspiration.

Using everything that you've learned in this book, write your own application that integrates a terminal multiplexer capability. For example, you might want to reimplement the `hcat` project that you built in the middle of this book, this time allowing users to open multiple files and switch between them, or even show multiple files side by side. Design your library so that a user writing their own terminal application can easily use your multiplexer to add their own layout and contents.

This is a large project. You will need to use most of what you've learned in this book, and you'll need to learn new libraries and dive into areas we haven't covered in this book, like multi-threaded programming. You can make this project as large or as small as you want. Whatever you decide, have fun with it! Build something for yourself, use it, improve it, and update it with new versions of GHC as they are released. A living project that you can use every day will give you the best possible experience of how to build and maintain effective Haskell code.

Index

SYMBOLS

F

L

N

P

U

Thank you!

We hope you enjoyed this book and that you're already thinking about what you want to learn next. To help make that decision easier, we're offering you this gift.

Head on over to https://pragprog.com right now, and use the coupon code BUYANOTHER2023 to save 30% on your next ebook. Offer is void where prohibited or restricted. This offer does not apply to any edition of the *The Pragmatic Programmer* ebook.

And if you'd like to share your own expertise with the world, why not propose a writing idea to us? After all, many of our best authors started off as our readers, just like you. With a 50% royalty, world-class editorial services, and a name you trust, there's nothing to lose. Visit https://pragprog.com/become-an-author/ today to learn more and to get started.

We thank you for your continued support, and we hope to hear from you again soon!

The Pragmatic Bookshelf

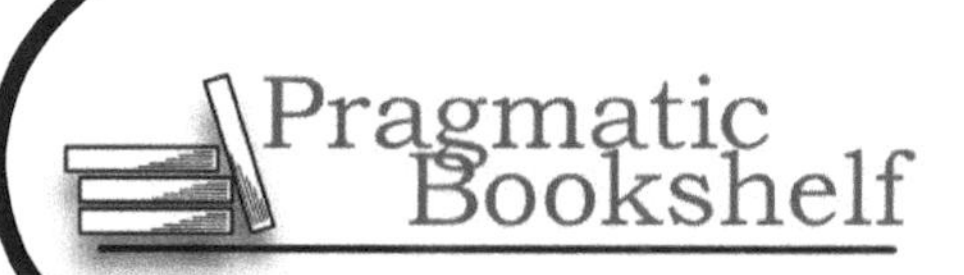

SAVE 30%!
Use coupon code
BUYANOTHER2023

Functional Programming: A PragPub Anthology

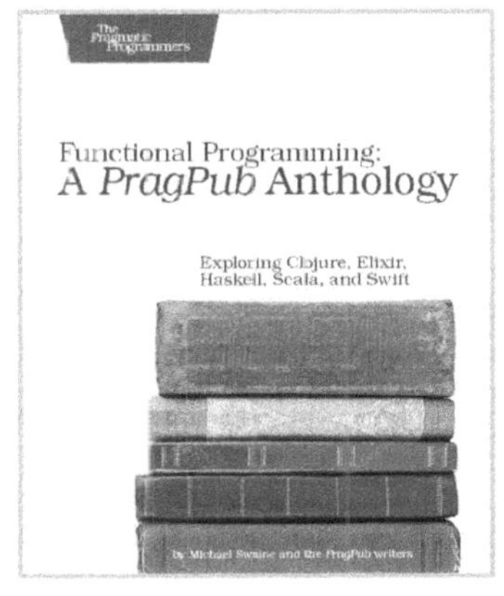

Explore functional programming and discover new ways of thinking about code. You know you need to master functional programming, but learning one functional language is only the start. In this book, through articles drawn from *PragPub* magazine and articles written specifically for this book, you'll explore functional thinking and functional style and idioms across languages. Led by expert guides, you'll discover the distinct strengths and approaches of Clojure, Elixir, Haskell, Scala, and Swift and learn which best suits your needs.

Michael Swaine and the PragPub writers
(282 pages) ISBN: 9781680502336. $47.95
https://pragprog.com/book/ppanth

Seven Languages in Seven Weeks

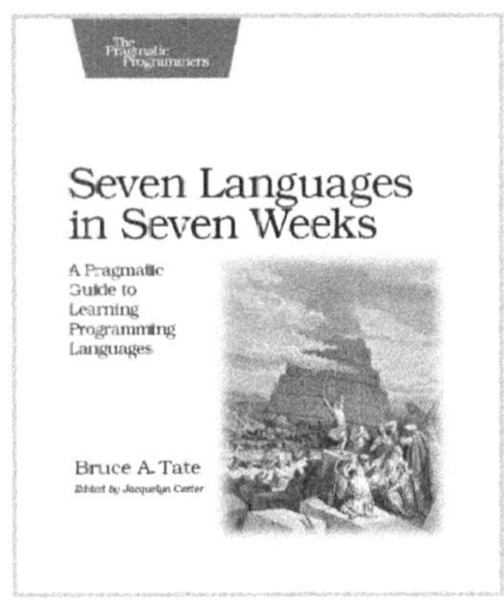

You should learn a programming language every year, as recommended by *The Pragmatic Programmer*. But if one per year is good, how about *Seven Languages in Seven Weeks*? In this book you'll get a hands-on tour of Clojure, Haskell, Io, Prolog, Scala, Erlang, and Ruby. Whether or not your favorite language is on that list, you'll broaden your perspective of programming by examining these languages side-by-side. You'll learn something new from each, and best of all, you'll learn how to learn a language quickly.

Bruce A. Tate
(330 pages) ISBN: 9781934356593. $34.95
https://pragprog.com/book/btlang

Practical A/B Testing

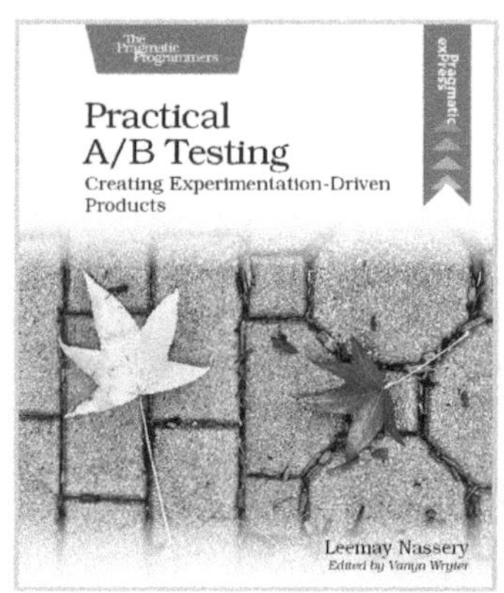

Whether you're a catalyst for organizational change or have the support you need to create an engineering culture that embraces A/B testing, this book will help you do it right. The step-by-step instructions will demystify the entire process, from constructing an A/B test to breaking down the decision factors to build an engineering platform. When you're ready to run the A/B test of your dreams, you'll have the perfect blueprint.

Leemay Nassery
(166 pages) ISBN: 9798888650080. $29.95
https://pragprog.com/book/abtest

Agile Web Development with Rails 7

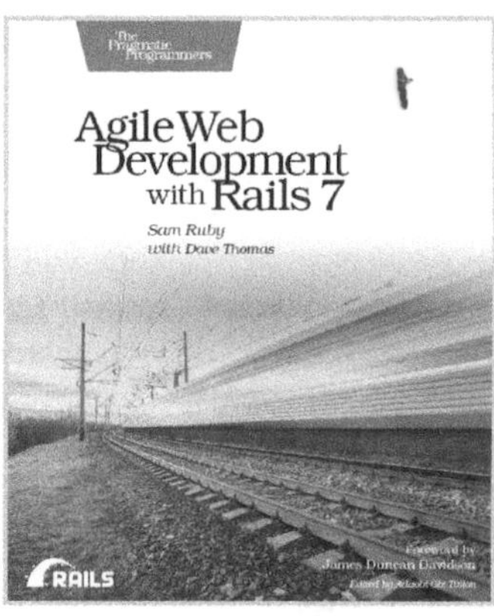

Rails 7 completely redefines what it means to produce fantastic user experiences and provides a way to achieve all the benefits of single-page applications – at a fraction of the complexity. Rails 7 integrates the Hotwire frameworks of Stimulus and Turbo directly as the new defaults, together with that hot newness of import maps. The result is a toolkit so powerful that it allows a single individual to create modern applications upon which they can build a competitive business. The way it used to be.

Sam Ruby
(474 pages) ISBN: 9781680509298. $59.95
https://pragprog.com/book/rails7

Creating Software with Modern Diagramming Techniques

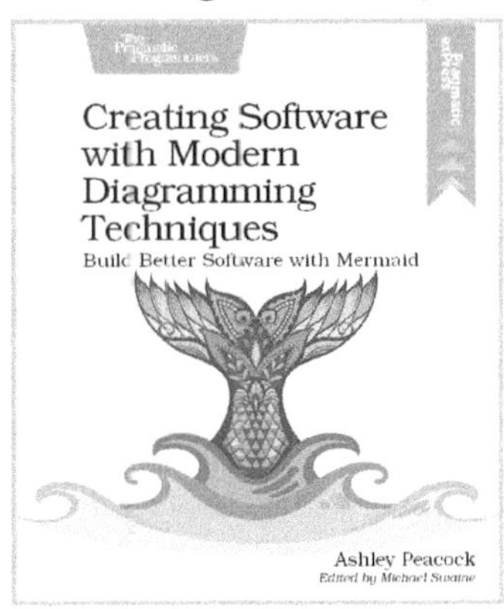

Diagrams communicate relationships more directly and clearly than words ever can. Using only text-based markup, create meaningful and attractive diagrams to document your domain, visualize user flows, reveal system architecture at any desired level, or refactor your code. With the tools and techniques this book will give you, you'll create a wide variety of diagrams in minutes, share them with others, and revise and update them immediately on the basis of feedback. Adding diagrams to your professional vocabulary will enable you to work through your ideas quickly when working on your own code or discussing a proposal with colleagues.

Ashley Peacock
(156 pages) ISBN: 9781680509830. $29.95
https://pragprog.com/book/apdiag

Mockito Made Clear

Mockito is the most popular framework in the Java world for automating unit testing with dependencies. Learn the Mockito API and how and when to use stubs, mocks, and spies. On a deeper level, discover why the framework does what it does and how it can simplify unit testing in Java. Using Mockito, you'll be able to isolate the code you want to test from the behavior or state of external dependencies without coding details of the dependency. You'll gain insights into the Mockito API, save time when unit testing, and have confidence in your Java programs.

Ken Kousen
(87 pages) ISBN: 9781680509670. $14.99
https://pragprog.com/book/mockito

Designing Data Governance from the Ground Up

Businesses own more data than ever before, but it's of no value if you don't know how to use it. Data governance manages the people, processes, and strategy needed for deploying data projects to production. But doing it well is far from easy: Less than one fourth of business leaders say their organizations are data driven. In *Designing Data Governance from the Ground Up*, you'll build a cross-functional strategy to create roadmaps and stewardship for data-focused projects, embed data governance into your engineering practice, and put processes in place to monitor data after deployment.

Lauren Maffeo
(100 pages) ISBN: 9781680509809. $29.95
https://pragprog.com/book/lmmlops

Building Table Views with Phoenix LiveView

Data is at the core of every business, but it is useless if nobody can access and analyze it. Learn how to generate business value by making your data accessible with advanced table UIs. This definitive guide teaches you how to bring your data to the fingertips of nontechnical users with advanced features like pagination, sorting, filtering, and infinity scrolling. Build reactive and reuseable table components by leveraging Phoenix LiveView, schemaless changesets, and Ecto query composition. Table UIs are the bread and butter for every web developer, so it is time to learn how to build them right.

Peter Ullrich
(65 pages) ISBN: 9781680509731. $14.99
https://pragprog.com/book/puphoe

Numerical Brain Teasers

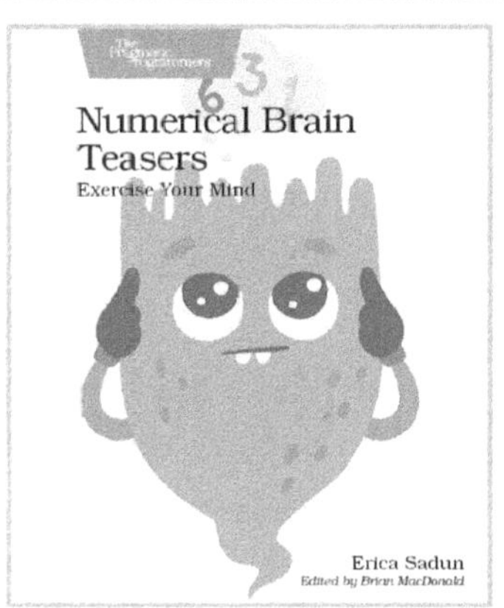

Challenge your brain with math! Using nothing more than basic arithmetic and logic, you'll be thrilled as answers slot into place. Whether purely for fun or to test your knowledge, you'll sharpen your problem-solving skills and flex your mental muscles. All you need is logical thought, a little patience, and a clear mind. There are no gotchas here. These puzzles are the perfect introduction to or refresher for math concepts you may have only just learned or long since forgotten. Get ready to have more fun with numbers than you've ever had before.

Erica Sadun
(186 pages) ISBN: 9781680509748. $18.95
https://pragprog.com/book/esbrain

Exploring Graphs with Elixir

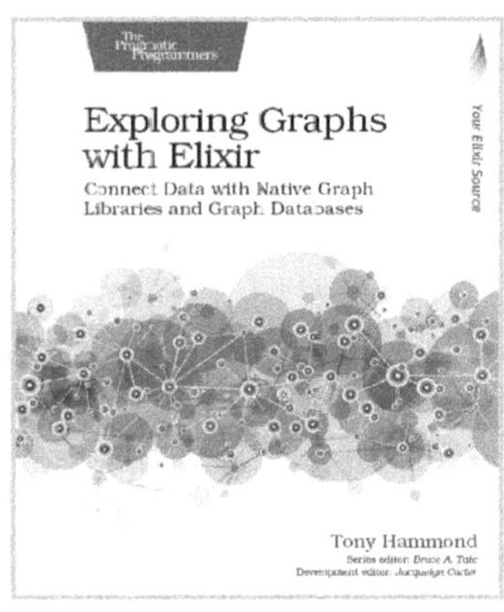

Data is everywhere—it's just not very well connected, which makes it super hard to relate dataset to dataset. Using graphs as the underlying glue, you can readily join data together and create navigation paths across diverse sets of data. Add Elixir, with its awesome power of concurrency, and you'll soon be mastering data networks. Learn how different graph models can be accessed and used from within Elixir and how you can build a robust semantics overlay on top of graph data structures. We'll start from the basics and examine the main graph paradigms. Get ready to embrace the world of connected data!

Tony Hammond
(294 pages) ISBN: 9781680508406. $47.95
https://pragprog.com/book/thgraphs

The Pragmatic Bookshelf

The Pragmatic Bookshelf features books written by professional developers for professional developers. The titles continue the well-known Pragmatic Programmer style and continue to garner awards and rave reviews. As development gets more and more difficult, the Pragmatic Programmers will be there with more titles and products to help you stay on top of your game.

Visit Us Online

This Book's Home Page

https://pragprog.com/book/rshaskell

Source code from this book, errata, and other resources. Come give us feedback, too!

Keep Up-to-Date

https://pragprog.com

Join our announcement mailing list (low volume) or follow us on Twitter @pragprog for new titles, sales, coupons, hot tips, and more.

New and Noteworthy

https://pragprog.com/news

Check out the latest Pragmatic developments, new titles, and other offerings.

Save on the ebook

Save on the ebook versions of this title. Owning the paper version of this book entitles you to purchase the electronic versions at a terrific discount.

PDFs are great for carrying around on your laptop—they are hyperlinked, have color, and are fully searchable. Most titles are also available for the iPhone and iPod touch, Amazon Kindle, and other popular e-book readers.

Send a copy of your receipt to support@pragprog.com and we'll provide you with a discount coupon.

Contact Us

Online Orders:	*https://pragprog.com/catalog*
Customer Service:	*support@pragprog.com*
International Rights:	*translations@pragprog.com*
Academic Use:	*academic@pragprog.com*
Write for Us:	*http://write-for-us.pragprog.com*
Or Call:	+1 800-699-7764

Ingram Content Group UK Ltd.
Milton Keynes UK
UKHW030218200723
425449UK00004B/6